ASPECTS OF ARCHAEOLOGY
AND HISTORY IN SURREY

ASPECTS OF ARCHAEOLOGY AND HISTORY IN SURREY

towards a research framework for the county

EDITED BY

Jonathan Cotton

Glenys Crocker and Audrey Graham

SURREY ARCHAEOLOGICAL SOCIETY

CASTLE ARCH, GUILDFORD

2004

ISBN 0 9541460 3 4

This volume is published with the aid of a grant from English Heritage.

Modern map bases and outlines used in this volume are reproduced from Ordnance Survey mapping with the permission of the Controller of Her Majesty's Stationery Office
© Crown Copyright NC/04/25242

The Council for British Archaeology (CBA) recommended citation styles for current periodicals and monograph series are used in this volume. In addition the abbreviations SyAS and *SyAC* are used for Surrey Archaeological Society and *Surrey Archaeological Collections*.

Front cover: View south across the Weald from Newlands Corner
Back cover: Looking north towards the escarpment of the North Downs near Silent Pool, Albury
Photographs by Giles Pattison

Typesetting and printing by: Unwin Brothers Ltd, Old Woking, Surrey

Contents

Preface

Exactly 21 years ago the Society held a conference on the Archaeology of Surrey which was followed four years later by the publication of *The Archaeology of Surrey to 1540*. The aim then was to fill a major gap, as there had been no survey of Surrey's archaeology since D C Whimster's book, also entitled *The Archaeology of Surrey*, in 1931.

Both are now out of print and, with the volume of new work in all aspects of archaeology amassed over the last two decades, the Society decided to hold a conference in 2001 to review current knowledge of the historic county of Surrey and, importantly, to widen the focus. The Society's stated aims include all matters 'relating to the pre-history and history of the County' and the conference embraced this principle. Whimster regarded the 11th century Guildown Massacres at Guildford as 'a fitting end' to the account of Surrey's archaeology. But archaeology did not stop then – or even at 1540 – and neither do the interests of the Society.

The conference sought to demonstrate that archaeology is not confined to what is left lying buried beneath the soil, but embraces the social and economic context of those remains: the standing buildings, the archaeology of our recent industrial past and not least the defences of the Second World War. All are tools in the understanding of our past and there is a need to recognize the connections between the different disciplines involved.

Since *The Archaeology of Surrey to 1540* was published in 1987, archaeological knowledge has proceeded at a tremendous rate, fuelled by the immense amount of work undertaken by professional units as part of planning procedures introduced in 1990. There has however been little time to synthesize the volume of data becoming available. This publication, as well as being an account of the conference held in 2001, provides an opportunity to pull together the current state of our knowledge in all disciplines and to point the direction of future research.

One of the aspects of this publication that is particularly pleasing is the contribution of amateurs to our current understanding. The Society has always encouraged harmonious relationships between professional and amateur archaeologists, and it is fortunate that a number of professionals give freely of their time to support the Society's activities. Large-scale, developer-funded excavation will remain the province of the professional units – though it is to be hoped with more opportunity for volunteer contribution. Important as they are, these excavations are seldom research led. Essentially, rescue archaeology is dictated by opportunity and funding from sources not necessarily sympathetic to the outcome.

The Society, on the other hand, is well placed to set its own agenda and can sometimes react speedily to threats that have escaped the normal planning controls. A notable example was the Romano-British temple site at Wanborough, which was being immeasurably damaged by irresponsible treasure hunters plundering the site at night. Intervention by the Society in undertaking two rescue excavations led to the site being scheduled; in addition, the experience at Wanborough led to the Society being instrumental in campaigning for a change in treasure trove law. This culminated, after several years of hard work, in the passing of the Treasure Act 1996.

The future for amateur archaeology, in the Society's view, is encouraging. The obligation to pursue research to the best possible standard applies to the professional and amateur alike. Today growing numbers of mature students studying archaeology and history are gaining the knowledge and expertise to undertake further work and exploration, both above and below ground. Without financial constraints, time and enthusiasm as well as local knowledge are on their side.

The more holistic and inclusive approach to archaeology provides a framework within which there is opportunity for all those interested to play a part. The authors of this volume have sought to identify areas for future research and the Society, through its various committees and groups, will encourage and support projects which seek to expand our understanding of the history and prehistory of the historic county. Amateurs continue to have a vital role to play and, as these essays demonstrate, research projects in all disciplines undertaken by non-professionals can inform and contribute to the wider debate.

Audrey Monk
President, Surrey Archaeological Society

November 2003

Foreword

According to the forthright William Cobbett, 'The county of Surrey presents to the eye of the traveller a greater contrast than any other county in England. It has some of the very best and some of the worst lands, not only in England, but in the world.' And Cobbett did not have my view of the ancient county. From an eleventh floor eyrie on Millbank, site of the great prison, and next door to the Tate, I can gaze across what John Evelyn, diarist and gardener, called 'the county of my Birth and my Delight'. The trees, which attracted Evelyn to Surrey, are notable only for their absence. The old county boundary of the Thames is now marked by a cliff of undistinguished offices between Lambeth and Vauxhall Bridges. Only the hanging gardens of the MI6 building punctuate the blandness. In the new generation of glass-fronted apartments the inhabitants, viewing and viewed, probably do not even realize that they are perched over what was once Surrey – the southern district. Perhaps the nearby Oval cricket ground, now grassed within the Great Wen, may remind them. Cobbett was right though about the county of contrasts. Surrey may be small, an eighth the size of my own home county of Yorkshire but, thanks to geology, it is varied.

Surrey is not the most identifiable of counties; lacking any coastline and with few natural boundaries, its shape is not distinctive. And its history is positively confusing. In the *Victoria County History*, the editor H E Malden complained that the county was 'daily encroached upon by the growing cancer of brickwork'. He might equally have bemoaned the tendency of modern government and authorities to mess around with it. In 1965 the Greater London Council snatched the boroughs of Croydon, Kingston, Merton, Richmond and Sutton. In return they gave Surrey Staines and Sunbury. One might think that in a small county, not well endowed with great towns, such poaching would undermine its sense of identity. For the past thousand years Surrey has also had the dubious privilege of living next door to a large, noisy expansionist neighbour. A neighbour which saw Surrey as a suitable site for its overspill, its railway stations, industry and its cemeteries. Yet in spite of this Surrey has fought for and retained its sense of identity. And no one has contributed more – with the possible exception of its cricketers – than the county's historians and archaeologists.

The Surrey Archaeological Society was founded in 1854, the high point of the great Victorian burgeoning of county societies. Unlike Wiltshire, Dorset or Yorkshire, Surrey was not noted for visible prehistoric monuments or spectacular country houses. Yet it is an amazing mosaic of contrasts: remote, yet on London's doorstep; buried in part beneath a tide of brick and concrete and possessing some of southern England's most evocative landscapes. Traditionally home to peasants, industrial workers, immigrants, royalty – and more recently popstars and stockbrokers. You can't get much more varied. This is what makes Surrey so interesting for the archaeologist and historian. It is an ideal place to study change: climatic, economic, political or social.

Historians like W G Hoskins have often bemoaned change; regretted the loss of an idealized golden age. Some archaeologists also talk about their subject in the same way – when beautifully thought-out research excavations could be undertaken at leisure, unpressured by development, the need to stick to budgets or the anxieties of competitive tendering.

Times change for good and bad. When I gave the introductory lecture at the conference in Guildford which initiated this excellent volume the audience was particularly concerned about the implications of the Valletta Convention.

Thanks to the bequest of Donald Margary, the Surrey Archaeological Society has not only had the people and enthusiasm to drive forward archaeological research but also some financial resource. The Society has for over a century and a half been in the forefront of local research. Not surprisingly members of the Society were concerned about publicity which claimed that the Government had signed up to an international treaty which would ban or severely restrict the activities of amateur archaeologists. As the Chief Archaeologist at English Heritage, I was able to assure the audience that there was no intention on the part of the UK Government to put in place a licensing system for archaeological excavations. English Heritage wishes to promote high standards in archaeological fieldwork, whether carried out by professionals or amateurs, but we do not regard another layer of controls, in the form of excavation licences, as the way forward.

The Valletta Convention is one of a series of conventions for the protection of archaeology produced by the Council of Europe over the last 50 years. It is, in fact, an update of the 1969 London Convention. In many cases, the wording has been taken directly from this earlier convention, while in others Valletta has been updated to some extent but without changing the essential meaning of the earlier treaty. The UK ratified the London Convention in 1973 so that it was in force here for nearly 30 years before being replaced by the Valletta Convention.

By ratifying the Valletta Convention the UK Government has undertaken to maintain a legal system for the protection of the archaeological heritage. In my opinion, for anyone who values our historic environment this should be good news.

States joining the Convention agree to promote an integrated policy for the conservation of the archaeological heritage, to arrange for financial support for research, to facilitate the pooling of information, promote public awareness and to improve co-operation between parties signing the Convention. It is for each country to apply the Convention within its own legal system. Despite the concerns expressed at the Guildford Conference, the Convention does not require radical changes to the way in which archaeological sites are protected in this country.

Most concerns relate to Article 3 of the Convention. In fact, this is one of the areas in which the new treaty is based on and expands what was said in the 1969 London Convention. The principal provisions on the control of excavation have actually changed very little from those in the London Convention which, in the past 30 years, have had no adverse affect on the activities of amateur archaeologists. The Government has now said (in a written reply to a Parliamentary question) that 'the Government does not believe that additional legislation, requiring a licensing system, is necessary to fulfil Article 3. Much archaeological work is already controlled through existing mechanisms. There may be scope for developing a voluntary Code of Conduct for those who wish to undertake archaeological work outside the existing systems of control.' By 'existing systems' the statement refers to Scheduled Monument Consent and local planning authority conditions imposed under Planning Policy Guidance note 16 (Archaeology and Planning).

I believe that all responsible archaeologists will support such a move to improve the quality of archaeological work in this country. English Heritage is currently discussing how to develop this policy with the Council for British Archaeology, the Institute of Field Archaeologists, the voluntary sector, and our colleagues in Scotland and Wales at Historic Scotland and Cadw. We intend to promote the role of the responsible amateur in archaeology by providing advice and training, through local societies and also by developing best practice with divers and metal detectorists.

Since 1990 developers have been responsible for mitigating the impact (in the jargon of PPG16) of their developments. This has undoubtedly led to the increasing professionalization of archaeology, the breakdown of old 'territories' and the influx of new organizations – and to some extent the marginalization of organizations such as the county societies.

The response to this lies in part with archaeological societies themselves – and this volume is one such response. We have had a vast increase in data in the past decade. People are desperate – academia, fieldworkers and local communities – to know more about what has been found and what it means. The Society's popular publication *Hidden Depths: An Archaeological Exploration of Surrey's Past*, 2002, told the story to a wide audience. This publication will provide information and ideas for more specialist groups, but it will, I hope, also stimulate future research and future fieldwork, exhibitions and activities in schools.

Archaeology works best when it is embedded in the lives of local communities and tells the story of all our pasts. The Surrey Archaeological Society has been doing this since 1854 and I am sure it will continue to find innovative ways of doing so in the future. If not then we deserve to join the long-suffering on the purgatorial ladder of Chaldon Church.

David Miles
Chief Archaeologist, English Heritage

28 October 2003

Introduction

Seventeen years ago the publication of *The Archaeology of Surrey to 1540* was a landmark in the study of the county. Not since the appearance of D C Whimster's book *The Archaeology of Surrey* over 50 years earlier had a full-length volume devoted to the county's early past been published. In contemplating the arrival of a new millennium it seemed appropriate once again to take stock, initially via a weekend conference held at the University of Surrey on 2 and 3 June 2001.

The essays contained in this volume stem either directly or indirectly from this meeting. The title of the conference, *Archaeology in Surrey 2001: Towards a Research Agenda for the 21st Century*, signalled something of its intent. The word 'towards' was, and remains, the key, for neither the conference nor this volume attempts to set out a research agenda for the county. Each is but a step along the way to a research strategy and, beyond it, to a research framework. However, it is singularly appropriate that this contribution should appear on the occasion of the Society's 150th anniversary.

In the run-up to the original conference the organizers were determined that the meeting should provide a broader and more cross-curricular approach to Surrey's past than had been attempted previously, and this approach has been carried through into the present volume. In part perhaps this reflects the current fashion for general 'inclusiveness'; but in part too a long overdue recognition of the need to accommodate the more recent and often still upstanding past. Accordingly contributions have been drawn from a deliberately wide range of disciplines and backgrounds that include earth scientists, architects and social and industrial historians as well as archaeologists.

At first, the intention was not to attempt a complete chronological overview of the county's past or even necessarily to seek to update *The Archaeology of Surrey to 1540*, but simply to encourage fruitful cross-disciplinary discussion and debate. The conference programme in particular set out to confront barriers rather than erect them and was arranged in such a way as to prompt connections as well as highlight contrasts. Subsequently, in preparing the conference proceedings for publication, it seemed sensible to adopt a more relaxed approach and to round out the coverage by commissioning a number of additional papers. These fell into two categories: chronological contributions, intended to update parts of *Surrey to 1540* and extend its time-span (eg the papers by Cotton, Bird and Crocker); and papers intended to plug some obvious gaps or amplify particular topics (eg those by Branch & Green and Bannister). To this end two maps are provided on the following pages: a simplified geology map, which is also used as a background for data in several of the papers, and a map showing boundaries and locations.

Accommodations had perforce to be made along the way: the untimely passing of Peter Reynolds shortly after the conference robbed not just this volume but the whole of British archaeology of the contribution of a widely respected and witty practitioner. Furthermore, pressure of other work forced the reluctant withdrawal of Phil Jones ('6000 Years of Pottery') and Martin Welch ('Settlement Patterns in Early to Mid Saxon Surrey') from the intended line-up, although John Hines was able to step in for the latter at a late stage in proceedings.

Celebrating the turning of a millennium and indeed of a sesquicentenary offers an obvious opportunity to look back – this after all is the stock-in-trade of archaeologists and historians. Yet it also affords a chance to look forward, in this case to the eventual formulation of an overarching archaeological research framework for the county, and for the wider South East region of which it forms a part. To this end, each of the contributors to this volume was specifically invited to conclude their paper with some ideas which might contribute to this process. This they have all dutifully done and we thank them for it.

Other thanks are due too. First to the large team of people who made the original conference work. These include members of the organizing committee, the staff of the University of Surrey, the Session Chairs, Speakers, Stewards, Exhibitors and the one hundred and sixty or so Delegates, whose close attention never wavered as the lively question sessions demonstrated. Special thanks must, however, be extended to Audrey Monk (then Honorary Secretary of SyAS, now its President) and to John Boult (Lectures and Symposia Committee), whose tireless efforts behind the scenes before, during and after the conference did much to guarantee its success.

As far as this volume is concerned our main thanks are due to the various contributors for delivering to the agreed timetable, to Giles Pattison and David Williams for preparing many of the illustrations, to Giles Pattison also for designing the cover, to Gerry Moss for preparing the index and to English Heritage for providing financial support.

Jonathan Cotton
Glenys Crocker
Audrey Graham

March 2004

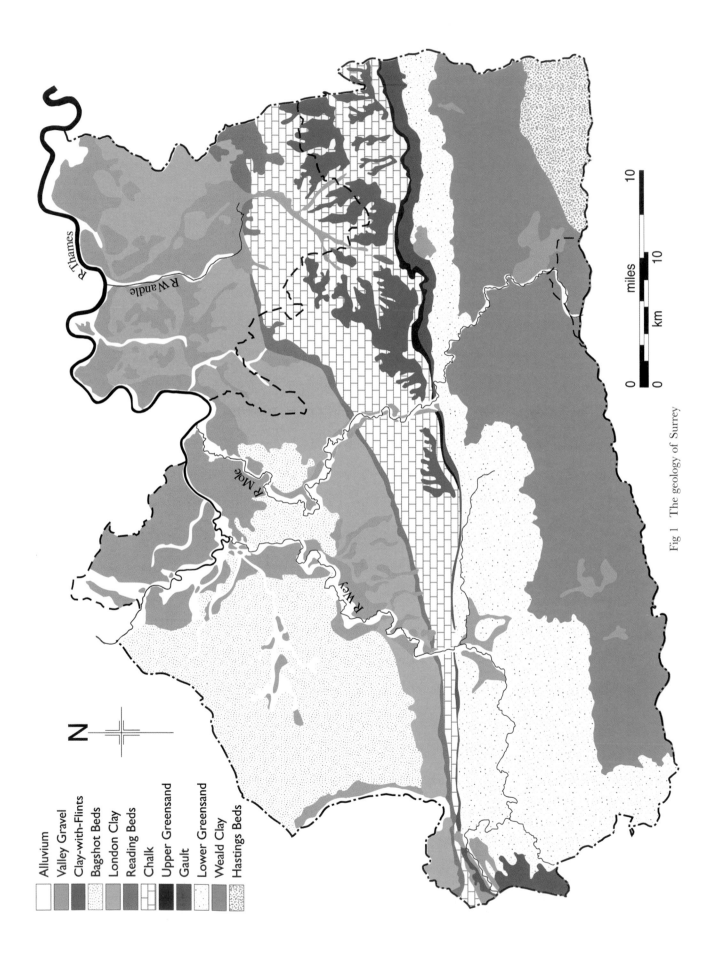

Alluvium
Valley Gravel
Clay-with-Flints
Bagshot Beds
London Clay
Reading Beds
Chalk
Upper Greensand
Gault
Lower Greensand
Weald Clay
Hastings Beds

N

R Thames

R Wandle

R Mole

R Wey

miles

km

10

10

0

0

Fig 1 The geology of Surrey

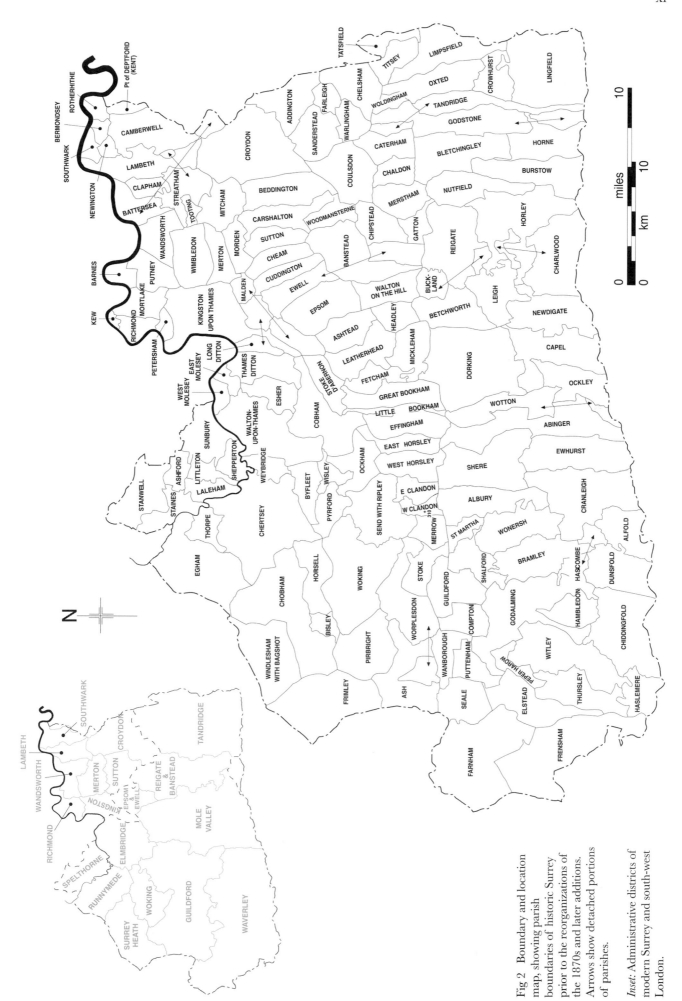

Fig 2 Boundary and location
map, showing parish
boundaries of historic Surrey
prior to the reorganizations of
the 1870s and later additions.
Arrows show detached portions
of parishes.

Inset: Administrative districts of
modern Surrey and south-west
London.

1

Environmental history of Surrey

N P BRANCH and C P GREEN

This chapter provides a review of the environmental history of Surrey from the lower Palaeolithic through to the historic periods, and presents a broad agenda for future palaeoenvironmental (including environmental archaeological) research in the county. The existing data suggest that towards the end of the last glaciation cold climatic conditions existed in Surrey, with vegetation similar to present-day steppe tundra or semi desert environments. The transition to the Holocene was characterized by the colonization of warmth-loving vegetation, and there is unequivocal evidence for human exploitation of natural resources on the flood plain of the middle Thames valley and Lower Greensand. After approximately 5500 years before present, there is some evidence to suggest that clearance of woodland created a mosaic of closed and open forest, temporarily cultivated land, grazing land and meadows. During later periods, the data suggest that agricultural intensification occurred against a background of natural environmental changes resulting in a clear decline in woodland cover and soil degradation in some areas. It is proposed that future palaeoenvironmental investigations should be conducted within a regional research framework, with the focus on understanding the precise effects of natural and cultural processes on the landscape of Surrey.

Introduction

In 1987 Macphail and Scaife, in *The archaeology of Surrey to 1540*, presented a review of the 'geographical and environmental background' of Surrey that highlighted the relative importance of natural and cultural processes in shaping the landscape during the past 14,000 years (since the late Upper Palaeolithic). Since 1987, important new investigations have significantly enhanced our knowledge of the environmental history, with a wide variety of scientific techniques used to reconstruct and explain changes in climate, sea level, vegetation cover, soil properties and landscape morphology (eg fossilized biological remains, geomorphology, sedimentology, pedology and geochronology). This chapter first reviews these data to provide a synthesis of the environmental history, and secondly provides an outline agenda for future palaeoenvironmental research in Surrey. The geology and soils of the county are illustrated in figures 1.1 and 1.2. Note that no attempt has been made to review the present day physiographical characteristics since these were detailed in Macphail & Scaife (1987).

Note: Throughout this chapter, radiocarbon dates are quoted as uncalibrated radiocarbon years before present (before 1950 calendar years AD).

Climatic, pedological and ecological background

Before the start of the present interglacial (Holocene) (*c* 10,000 BP) and following the arrival in Britain of modern humans (*Homo sapiens*) during the last glaciation (Devensian in Britain) (*c*40,000 BP), temperatures were approximately 20°C lower than at the present day and ice sheets covered northern Europe. Between Britain and continental Europe a land bridge, due to a global reduction in sea level by approximately 100m, allowed the migration of plant and animal species into the ice-free tundra environment of south-east England. At approximately 16,000 BP, warmer and more arid conditions resulted in a global retreat of ice sheets and a rise in sea level. Deglaciation in Britain between 13,500 and 10,000 BP oscillated between warm and cold conditions, with profound effects on soils and vegetation. During the Windermere Interstadial, between 13,500 and 11,000 BP, summer and winter temperatures increased to approximately 17°C and 0–1°C (respectively), and soil development (eg raw-humus or rendzina-type; see Catt 1979; Kemp, 1986) provided conditions suitable for a succession of vegetation from open grassland to shrubland and finally birch woodland (table 1.1). A climatic deterioration between 11,000 and 10,000 BP (Loch Lomond Stadial) caused a return to periglacial conditions in southern Britain (eg fossil pingos at Elstead Bog), formation of arctic structure soils, colonization by shrub tundra vegetation, and a reduction in summer and winter temperatures to 10°C and −20°C (respectively). Geomorphic instability during the late-glacial to interglacial transition led to increased river discharge and sedimentation, changes in river morphology, and solifluction in lowland dry valleys.

Climatic amelioration during the early postglacial and the attainment of temperatures similar to those of the present day led by 9000 BP to the development of base-rich brown-earth soils (Catt 1979), a closed vegetation cover (first juniper and willow, followed by birch and pine, and finally hazel, oak, lime, elm and ash), and restoration of landscape stability (table 1.1). On river flood plains, mainly fine-grained sediments

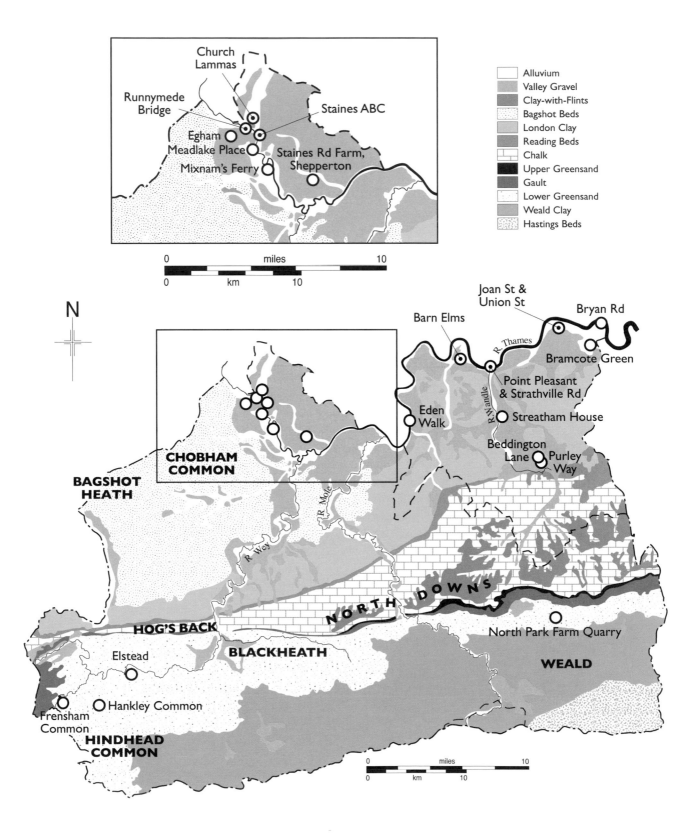

Fig 1.1 Geology of Surrey and location of main sites mentioned in the text

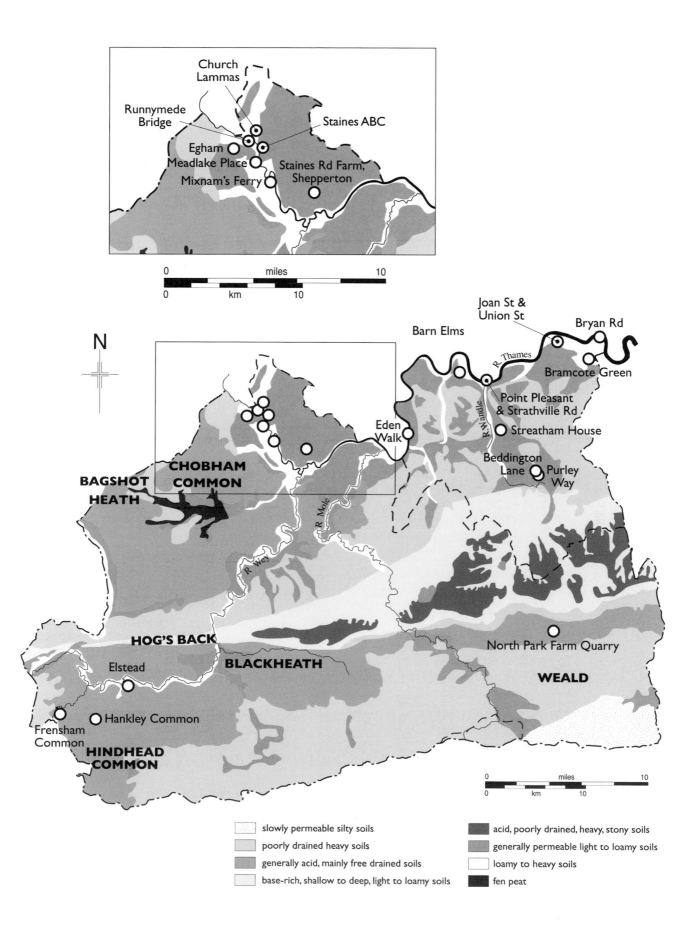

Fig 1.2 Soils of Surrey and location of main sites mentioned in the text

TABLE 1.1   Sequence of pollen zones and approximate ages of zone boundaries for sites in eastern and south-east England (after Bennett 1988, and Branch & Lowe 1994, respectively)

Bennett 1988	eastern England
Betula-Poaceae assemblage	*c* 12,000–9200 BP
Corylus/*Tilia*-*Ulmus* assemblage	*c* 9200–7400 BP
Alnus-*Tilia* assemblage	*c* 7400–6000 BP
Fraxinus assemblage	*c* 6000–4500 BP
Corylus/*Myrica* assemblage	*c* 4500–2000 BP

Branch & Lowe 1994	south-east England
End of the last glacial stage	>10,000 BP
Upper boundary of *Betula*-*Pinus*-*Artemisia* phase	*c* 10,000 BP
Pinus-*Betula*-*Corylus*/*Myrica* phase	*c* 9000–7200 BP
Lower boundary of *Tilia* phase and *Ulmus* decline	*c* 4500 BP *c* 5000 BP
Upper boundary of the *Fraxinus* zone and *Tilia* decline	*c* 3500 BP
Lower boundary of *Salix*-herb assemblage and start of major deforestation	*c* 2000 BP

were deposited or in some cases peat development was initiated. Similar deposits accumulated where lake basins had been created in former periglacial areas, and hydroseral succession led in many cases to the development of fen carr plant communities dominated by alder and willow. Within these early Holocene woodlands, archaeological and palaeoecological data indicate ample resources for human exploitation, including red deer (*Cervus elaphus*), aurochs (*Bos primigenius*), wild boar (*Sus scrofa*), hazelnuts, berries, fruit, fungi and rhizomes (Roberts 1989, 80).

The Climatic Optimum of the Holocene between approximately 8000 and 4500 BP led to an increase in temperatures by 1–2°C, and relatively drier and wetter periods between 8000–6500 and 6500–4500 BP (respectively). After 6500 BP, wetter conditions undoubtedly led to deterioration in soil status, and in lowland areas this was characterized by a continuum from 'argillic brown earth to brown podzolic soil to podzol' (Bell & Walker 1992, 100). During this period, the continuation of global sea-level rise following de-glaciation, and corresponding changes in the vertical displacement of the land, led to inundation of coastal areas, establishment of estuarine conditions in some areas and changes in the configuration of major river systems. According to Devoy (1979), sea level rose in the Thames estuary by approximately 1.3cm yr^{-1} between 8500 and 7000 BP, and 0.5cm yr^{-1} between 6500 and 5000 BP. In many parts of the lower Thames valley, rise in sea

level and changes in river gradient during the Holocene led to the progressive burial of the valley floor by mainly fine-grained estuarine and fluvial sediments (D'Olier 1972; Devoy 1977, 1979). These near-surface sediments comprise 'an interbedded sequence of alluvial sediments, dipping and thickening markedly from west to east, collectively referred to as the Tilbury Alluvium' (Gibbard 1985, 33). Against this background of sea-level rise (table 1.2), five separate phases indicating a reduction or stabilization in sea level ('regression') have also been recorded, resulting in extensive formation of peat and wetland 'carr' woodland. This model of rising and falling (or stable) sea level has been used to explain the origin of numerous sedimentary sequences in the boroughs of Southwark and Lambeth, and is based on height above OD and radiocarbon chronologies (Tyers 1988). However such correlations must be viewed with caution, owing to the influence of local factors other than sea level on sediment accumulation in areas near the head of the estuary and further upstream (Rackham 1994, 195; Haggart 1995).

Following the transition to the Neolithic cultural period (*c* 5500 BP), there was a dramatic, and well-recorded, change in the landscape brought about by the incoming of domesticated plants and animals. Agricultural activities may have been based on a system of shifting cultivation, involving temporary clearance of woodland by burning and felling prior

TABLE 1.2   Age and altitude of Holocene (last 10,000 years) marine sedimentary sequences in the lower Thames estuary (Devoy 1977; 1979)

Phase	Radiocarbon date; metres OD		Radiocarbon date; metres OD
Thames I	8200; -25.5 to -13.2	to	6970; -8 to -12.5
Thames II	6575; -6.8 to -12.3	to	4930; -3 to -6.9
Thames III	3850; -1.9 to -6.7	to	2800; -1 to -2
Thames IV	2600; -0.8 to -1.8	to	?; +0.4 to -0.9
Thames V	~1700; +0.44 to -0.75		

to cultivation, abandonment and finally woodland regeneration. The typical duration of this land-use cycle has been difficult to establish, but estimates vary between 50–100 years (Iversen 1941) and 200–600 years (Smith 1970). The main pollen-stratigraphic indicators of shifting cultivation are cereals, plantains, elm, oak and hazel, which fluctuate in percentage values during the cycle. These changes in vegetation cover undoubtedly led to changes in soil status during the Neolithic and Bronze Age, possibly as a consequence of the progressive reduction in nutrients, and resulted in the formation of acid podzolic soils with more humus (Catt 1979). To what extent these changes were due to human activities is uncertain as there is good evidence for a general deterioration in climate to cooler and wetter conditions between 4500 and 3000 BP, with a reduction in temperature of 1–2°C. These climatic and pedological changes may have led to reduction in woodland cover, in particular of elm, lime and hazel and their replacement by grassland and heathland (table 1.1). Alternatively, there is evidence that the changes in vegetation cover were due to disease and human activity, and two of the most commonly cited factors are the asynchronous declines in elm and lime woodland. Both trees are strongly associated with pastoral economies and the gathering of leaves and lopping of branches for fodder and bedding. In addition, clearance of both trees would have been a prerequisite for cereal cultivation and, in the case of elm woodland, this activity may have accelerated the spread of elm disease.

During the later Holocene, archaeological and palaeoecological data indicate that 'the pace and direction of cultural evolution varied between regions' (Roberts 1989, 122). This resulted in regional variations in the timing of both vegetation change (eg lime woodland decline) and landscape change (eg accelerated erosion on the chalklands of southern England). In addition, patterns of cultural change were superimposed on, and responded to, fluctuations in climate. During the medieval warm period or Little Climatic Optimum (AD900–1300) summer and winter temperatures increased by 1–2°C to 16.5°C and 4°C (respectively). Following this relatively warm period, temperatures declined during the Little Ice Age (AD1300–1850) by 1–3°C below those of the present day, resulting in cooler summers, colder and wetter winters and increased storminess.

Lower and Middle Palaeolithic in Surrey

Lower and Middle Palaeolithic occupation in Surrey is recorded entirely in the form of stone artefacts and the environmental dimension of Palaeolithic archaeology is concerned with the contexts in which these artefacts are found, which is not necessarily a reliable indication of the environment in which they were made and used. The principal occurrences are in the terrace gravels of the river Wey near Farnham (Bury 1935; Oakley 1939) and as surface finds on the North Downs around Banstead, Kingswood and Walton on the Hill (Wymer 1968). The oldest artefacts are in gravels underlying Terrace A of the Wey. These sediments are thought to be the product of the Anglian cold stage (Gibbard 1985), and Wymer (1999) suggests that heavily rolled artefacts from this context may be of pre-Anglian age. Artefacts are also present in the lower terraces of the Wey (Terraces B, C and D), including Levallois material in Terrace C. However, none of this material was recorded in a primary context, and the gravels in which it occurs are all braided river sediments typical of those now generally regarded in southern Britain as having been deposited under periglacial climatic conditions. In Terrace D, from which Bury (1935) and Oakley (1939) record handaxes of 'Mousterian' type, faunal remains are present including mammoth and woolly rhinoceros and organic lenses and peat rafts containing a mollusc fauna and plant remains, all indicative of cold climatic conditions (Roe 1981). A radiocarbon date of 36,000 BP has been obtained from this organic material (Wymer 1999).

Upper Palaeolithic in Surrey (c 40,000–10,000 BP)

There are few detailed records of the environmental history of Surrey during the Upper Palaeolithic (late Devensian Lateglacial period). Records of Lateglacial vegetation succession associated with human activity (eg burning and the exploitation of animals) have been obtained from Church Lammas, Staines (figs 1.1 and 1.2; TQ 027 721; Jackson *et al* 1997, 211) and Staines Road Farm (figs 1.1 and 1.2; TQ 076 683; Bird *et al* 1989, 211), and provide a valuable insight into the environmental context of human activities during this period. The most complete radiocarbon dated palaeoenvironmental records are from Bramcote Green, Bermondsey (figs 1.1 and 1.2; TQ 349 780; -0.80m OD; Branch & Lowe, 1994) and Elstead Bog, between Farnham and Godalming (figs 1.1 and 1.2; SU 899 422; 54m OD; Seagrief & Godwin 1960; Carpenter & Woodcock 1981). They provide an opportunity to reconstruct and compare vegetation succession in the northern and southern parts of Surrey during this period (figs 1.3 and 1.4). Prior to approximately 11,000 BP (Windermere Interstadial) a calcareous lacustrine environment formed at Bramcote Green (table 1.3; fig 1.3) characterized initially by an open treeless landscape with willow and juniper (BEG2a) and then birch woodland (BEG2b and BEGa). Following this period the pollen records from Elstead

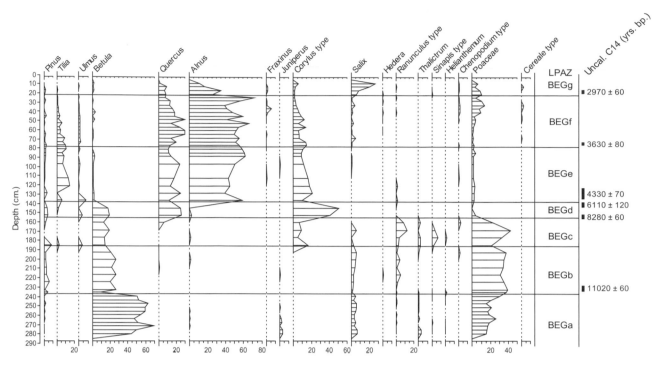

Values expressed as a % of total land pollen

Fig 1.3   Selected taxa pollen diagram from Trench 1, Bramcote Green, London (Branch & Lowe, 1994)

TABLE 1.3   The sedimentary and pollen-stratigraphic sequence at Bramcote Green (Branch & Lowe 1994; Thomas & Rackham 1996)

Metres OD (approx)	Description	Main pollen types/Depth (cm) of local pollen assemblage zones
Trench 1		
-5.00 to -4.45	Dark olive green silt	
-4.45 to -3.18	Dark greyish brown fine calcareous silt with abundant whole shells, discontinuous laminations, some organic and woody inclusions	*Betula, Juniperus,* Poaceae/ BEGa 285–238
-3.18 to -2.38	Very dark brown/grey fine silt, becoming sandy towards base, with occasional organic fragments, some woody matter, occasional shells and rare sub-angular flint clasts	*Betula, Pinus, Artemisia*/BEGb 238–185 *Betula, Corylus, Ranunculus*/BEGc 185–158
-2.38 to -2.18	Black fine silt/clay with woody and fibrous organic matter	*Quercus*/BEGd 158–138
-2.18 to -1.78	Very dark grey/black organic silt/clay	*Alnus, Quercus, Tilia*/BEGe 138–165
-1.78 to -0.80	Black/reddish black peat, moderately humified	*Alnus, Quercus*/BEGf 65–20 *Salix,* herbs/BEGg 20–0
Trench 2		
-3.95 to -3.78	Light olive brown fine calcareous silt, darkening to black fine silt, frequent shell fragments and some faint laminations	*Salix,* herbs/BEG2a 180–168
-3.78 to -3.47	Light olive brown fine calcareous silt, with mottling, patches of laminations, shells and very infrequent organic remains	*Betula, Juniperus,* Poaceae/BEG2b 168–130
-3.47 to -2.78	Very dark brown to grey fine silts/dark yellowish brown sand, with some faint laminations, woody and fibrous organic material, sand and shells	Poaceae, Cyperaceae, herb/BEG2c BEG2c 130–120
-2.78 to -2.25	Yellowish brown sand, flint clasts and woody organic matter	
-2.25 to -2.15	Very dark grey clay, woody and fibrous fine organic matter	*Corylus, Alnus, Tilia*/BEG2d 20–0

Bog, a pingo basin (table 1.4; fig 1.4; EL1 and EL2), and Bramcote Green (BEG2c and BEGb) indicate a vegetation cover consisting of plants commonly associated with cold, harsh environments such as steppe tundra or semi-desert. The presence of short-turf grassland, tall-herb communities (*Helianthemum* (rock rose)), indicator species such as *Plantago lanceolata* (ribwort plantain), *Polygala* (milk-

wort), *Polemonium* (Jacob's ladder) and *Koenigia* (Iceland purslane), and isolated trees and shrubs (*Betula, Betula nana* – dwarf birch and *Pinus*), is compatible with records from other parts of south-east England (Gibbard *et al* 1982; Gibbard & Hall 1982; Kerney *et al* 1982). This period may be equated with the Loch Lomond Stadial between 11,000 and 10,000 BP.

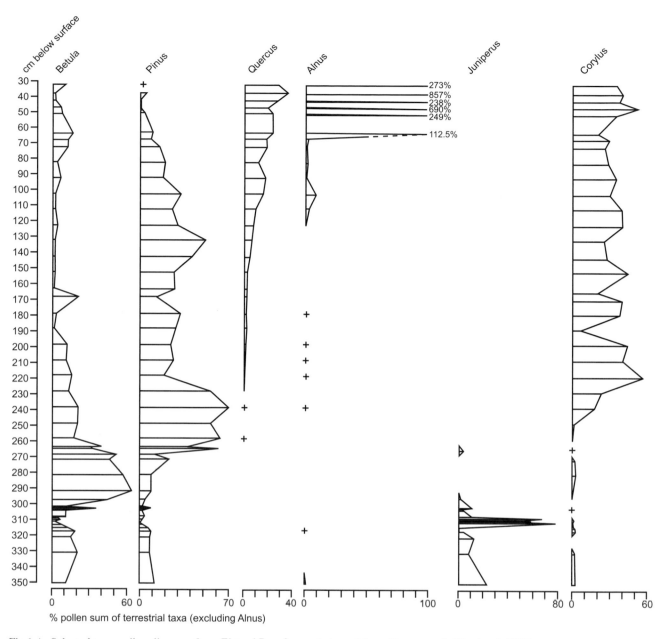

Fig 1.4 Selected taxa pollen diagram from Elstead Bog, Surrey (adapted from Carpenter & Woodcock 1981)

TABLE 1.4 The sedimentary and pollen-stratigraphic sequence at Elstead Bog (Carpenter & Woodcock 1981)

Cm below ground surface	Description	Main pollen types/Depth (cm) of local pollen assemblage zones
295–350	Basal sand and silt	*Juniperus* (juniper), *Empetrum* (crowberry), Ericales (eg heather), Herbs/ EL2 298–318
		Betula, Juniperus, Poaceae, Cyperaceae/EL1 318–350
237–295	Coarse detrital mud with *Pinus* (pine) and *Betula* wood	*Betula, Pinus*/EL3 266–298
200–237	Detrital mud with wood	*Pinus, Betula*/EL4 222–266
163–200	Detrital mud with *Phragmites* (reed-swamp)	*Pinus, Corylus, Ulmus, Quercus*/EL5 146–222
67–163	Detrital mud with Cyperaceae (sedge) and *Betula* (birch) wood	*Pinus, Quercus, Ulmus* (elm), *Corylus* (hazel)/EL6 64–146
0–67	Highly humified detrital mud with wood	*Alnus* (alder), *Quercus* (oak), *Tilia* (lime)/EL7 0–64

Mesolithic in Surrey (*c* 10,000–5500 BP)

Locations of sites are shown in figures 1.1 and 1.2. Radiocarbon-dated palaeoenvironmental records for the Mesolithic period are confined to five key sites:

1 Bramcote Green (Branch & Lowe 1994; Thomas & Rackham 1996).
2 Elstead Bog (Carpenter & Woodcock 1981).
3 Meadlake Place (TQ 020 705; 14m OD; Branch & Green 2001).
4 Staines (TQ 031 715; 16m OD; Branch *et al* 2003a).
5 Runnymede Bridge (TQ 018 719; 16m OD; Needham 1992; Scaife 2000).

Several other sites have also provided important records of either human exploitation of natural resources, such as woodland and hazelnuts, or organic deposits within palaeochannels of Mesolithic age. These include:

a North Park Farm, Bletchingley (TQ 330 520; Branch *et al* 2003b).
b Hankley Common (SU 877 396; Reynier 2002, 226.
c Barn Elms, Richmond, with radiocarbon dates of 10,150 ±100 BP and 7500 ±150 BP.
d Point Pleasant (river Wandle, Wandsworth) with radiocarbon dates of 9410 ±160 BP and 7620 ±80 BP.
e Strathville Road (Wandle valley, Wandsworth) with radiocarbon dates of 9240 ±60 BP and 9270 ±60 BP.
f Streatham House, Merton, with radiocarbon dates of 9423 ±72 BP (Cowie & Eastmond 1997b, 120)

Unfortunately, these sites have so far produced little or no detailed palaeoenvironmental data.

In the middle Thames valley, sites at Staines, Meadlake Place and Runnymede Bridge, are underlain by sediments forming part of the Staines Alluvial Deposits, a stratigraphic unit that can be traced upstream as far as Pangbourne and downstream as

far as the City of Westminster (Gibbard 1985), and almost everywhere overlies the Shepperton Gravel of Late Devensian age. The type-site for the Staines Alluvial Deposits is a palaeochannel fill at Mixnam's Ferry (figs 1.1 and 1.2; TQ 042 685; 14m OD), about 2.9km downstream from Meadlake Place (Gibbard 1985).

The entire sequence at Mixnam's Ferry (table 1.5) is of Holocene age and similar deposits have been described at Penton Hook (TQ 043 692; Cooper 1907, 1922; Howard 1952); Hythe (TQ 032 703; Gibbard 1985); and Bell Weir (TQ 016 721; Kennard & Woodward 1906). At Runnymede Bridge, Needham (1992) described a sequence of cuts and fills, all of which occurred at essentially the same altitude, and which predominantly comprise fossiliferous clayey silts. These sediments incorporate archaeological material of Mesolithic, Neolithic and Bronze Age date. A radiocarbon date from the base of this sediment sequence gives an age of 7790 ±80 BP. The Staines Alluvial Deposits in the Meadlake Place and Staines areas vary considerably in thickness. This is evident in the southern part of the section illustrated by Gibbard (1985, fig 45) based on boreholes along the route of the M25 motorway where it extends along the flood plain between the M3 intersection near Thorpe Green and the river Thames at Runnymede. The Staines Alluvial Deposits reach a maximum thickness of about 3.0m, but may be absent altogether where the underlying Shepperton Gravel comes to the surface. These variations reflect a pattern of channels and intervening bars forming the surface of the Shepperton Gravel. Although the deposits at Staines (table 1.6) are different from those at Mixnam's Ferry, they are also part of the Staines Alluvial Deposits. They overlie the Late Devensian Shepperton Gravel, and their Holocene age is confirmed by three radiocarbon dates located at the base, middle and top of the peat deposit (8960 ±54 BP, 12.05m OD; 8173 ±75 BP, 12.13m OD; 8172 ±46 BP, 12.25m OD). At Staines the sequence of peat overlain by largely un-fossiliferous silty clay suggests a position on the flood plain never affected by flow within, or even near, a river channel, either the river Thames or the river Colne.

TABLE 1.5   The sedimentary sequence at Mixnam's Ferry (Preece & Robinson 1982)

Depth (cm) below ground surface	Description
285–	Orange gravel and sand
275–285	Dark grey organic-rich silts with wood fragments (275–285cm: 8360 ± 100 BP, Q-2042)
265–275	Orange gravel and sand
210–265	Shelly silts and sands, some plant debris
205–210	Gravel
165–205	Shelly sand with several distinct organic seams up to 3cm thick
120–165	Dark grey organic-rich silts with wood fragments, hazel nuts, etc (135–145cm: 665 ± 55 BP, Q-2043)
70–120	Grey, well sorted current-bedded sand
0–70	Brown silty clay, mottled in places

TABLE 1.6 The sedimentary and pollen-stratigraphic sequence at Staines (Branch *et al* 2003)

Metres OD	Description	Main pollen types/Depth (metres OD) of local pollen assemblage zones
11.525–11.625	5Y5/2 olive; sandy, fine to medium gravel of sub-angular flint, becoming more clayey upward; scattered plant debris; acid reaction (calcium carbonate precipitate on clasts); diffuse contact	
11.625–11.695	5Y5/3 olive; fine to medium sand; acid reaction; diffuse contact	
11.695–11.835	5Y5/2 olive grey; predominantly fine sandy gravel of sub-angular flint with some well-rounded quartz, becoming more clayey upward; plant debris throughout; acid reaction; sharp contact	
11.835–11.945	5Y4/2 olive grey; sandy, silty clay with a few flint clasts at 11.915–11.925; structureless; abundant finely divided plant debris; *in-situ* (vertical) roots (1–2mm); numerous worm granules; vivianite; acid reaction in lower part, absent in upper part; diffuse contact	*Pinus*, Cyperaceae, Poaceae Staines 1 11.81–12.05
11.945–11.995	5Y3/2 dark olive grey; slightly sandy silt, passing up into well-humified peat *in-situ* (vertical) roots (1–2mm); no acid reaction; diffuse contact	
11.995–12.205	Peat; sharp contact (8960 ± 54 BP, 12.05m OD) (8173 ± 75 BP, 12.13m OD)	*Salix, Betula, Quercus, Ulmus* Staines 2 12.05–12.21
12.205–12.285	5Y2/1 black passing up to 5Y3/1 very dark grey; silt; structureless; very common finely divided plant debris; *in-situ* (vertical) roots (1–2mm) penetrating downward into peat; no acid reaction; diffuse contact (8172 ± 46 BP; 12.25m OD)	*Tilia, Corylus* Staines 3 12.21–12.28
12.285–12.485	5Y3/1 very dark grey mixed with 5Y3/2 dark olive grey; silt; structureless; no acid reaction; diffuse contact	*Alnus, Salix* Staines 4 12.28–12.38
12.485–12.725	5Y5/1 grey; silt; structureless; near-vertical root channels with iron-stained margins; Mollusca (*Bythinia*); acid reaction; diffuse contact	
12.725–13.315	5Y5/3 olive with patchy Fe staining and black (Mn) speckles; silty clay; structureless; molluscan shell debris, worm granules; acid reaction throughout; diffuse contact	
13.315–13.575	2.5Y4/2 dark greyish brown; stony, silty clay – clasts of weathered sub-angular flint; pottery, tile, brick, mortar	

The peat indicates terrestrial conditions with no input of mineral sediment during its accumulation, and the overlying silty clay suggests deposition from standing or very slow moving flood water. Considering the proximity of the site to both the Thames and the Colne, the lack of evidence for any in- or near-channel activity may seem surprising. However the position of the site between the two rivers is one where the Thames will have tended to divert the main current of the Colne eastward, away from the site, and the Colne will have tended to divert the main current of the Thames southward, away from the site. Thus although the site may have a long history of flooding represented in the thick layer of silty clay alluvium overlying the peat, it has never been occupied by the main channel of either river. The uppermost part of the alluvium seems likely, on the basis of flood plain elevations upstream and downstream from the site, to represent the historic surface of the flood plain prior to urban development.

The sediments recovered from Meadlake Place consist of sandy flint gravel overlain by organic-rich, fine-grained sediments and peat (table 1.7). These deposits are overlain by structureless silty clay in which there is evidence of pedogenic processes, and in which organic (plant) remains are scarce and finely divided. Although the overall geometry of the deposits was not recorded at Meadlake Place, the sediments are likely, by analogy with similar deposits nearby, to represent the fill of abandoned channels, cut into the underlying Shepperton Gravel. It seems probable that during the formation of the channels in which the finer-grained and organic sediments rest, the river was transporting gravel for at least part of the time. Since the radiocarbon dates obtained from the sequence at Meadlake Place indicate deposition in the Mesolithic, it seems likely that the river was reworking the underlying Shepperton Gravel in the early part of the Holocene, and either creating or reshaping a pattern of channels and intervening bars on the valley floor at that time. The radiocarbon date (*c* 9000 BP, 12.43m OD) obtained towards the top of the sequence in one of the channels (column T3) indicates that this channel was already largely filled in the Early Holocene. The later date (*c* 8160 BP, 10m OD) at a lower level in the fill of an adjacent, younger, channel (Borehole 2) may indicate that channels were being actively created and infilled on the valley floor during a period of at least a thousand years in the Early Holocene. Alternatively, both channels were already in existence at the beginning of the Holocene, but differences in the flow of water between channels discouraged fine-grained sedimentation or peat formation in some channels for a longer period in the Holocene. This alternative

TABLE 1.7   The sedimentary and pollen-stratigraphic sequence at Meadlake Place (Branch & Green 2001)

Metres OD	Description	Main pollen types/Depth (metres OD) of local pollen assemblage zones
Borehole 2		
9.00–9.35	5Y3/1 very dark grey; London Clay; numerous pyrite clusters visible under microscope; sharp contact	
9.35–9.74	2.5Y5/6 light olive brown (typical weathered London Clay colour); gravel with clayey matrix in lowermost part, becoming sandier upward and darker in colour (dark grey to black); sharp contact	
9.74–9.81	5Y4/2 olive grey and black organic sand; abundant shell debris; abundant plant debris; wood fragments including bark and root material, seeds, Mollusca including *Bithynia* opercula, fish bones, teeth and scales; sharp contact	
9.81–10.03	Woody peat; scattered shell debris; some mineral material (possibly intrusive); charcoal; insect remains; diffuse contact (10.01–10.03m OD; 8160 ± 50 BP)	
10.03–10.04	Dark grey to black peat; shelly sand; pebble (15mm) present; sharp contact	
10.04–10.06	Peat; diffuse contact	*Pinus, Betula, Quercus, Salix* Meadlake 1 10.10–10.55
10.06–11.07	Irregular alternations of peat and very shelly sand – shell present as debris only; no clear bedding; peat full of twigs and wood fragments; diffuse contact (11.00–11.07m OD; 5860 ± 70 BP)	*Quercus, Ulmus, Alnus, Salix* Meadlake 2 10.55–10.95
11.07–12	Peat; woody debris throughout; peat becoming slightly more humified above 11.75m OD; pockets of sand at 11.24m, 11.32m, 11.43m OD; pebbles at 11.42m and 11.79m OD; scattered mineral grains throughout, becoming less common upward, rare above 11.75m OD; clusters of iron oxide spherules present on woody debris; diffuse contact	Poaceae Meadlake 3 10.95–11.35 *Alnus* Meadlake 4 11.35–11.95
12–12.3	Humified peat – somewhat layered up to 12.15m OD, little layering apparent above 12.15m OD; diffuse contact	Poaceae, *Quercus, Salix* Meadlake 5 11.95–13.00
12.3–12.39	Peat with gradual increase in silt/clay content; discrete lenses of silt from 12.33m OD upward, giving mottled appearance; diffuse contact	
12.39–12.46	5Y5/2 olive grey; silty clay; faint darker mottling; diffuse contact	
12.46–13	5Y4/3 olive with 2.5YR4/8 and 5/8 mottles (red); silty clay; uppermost 15cm penetrated from above by worm holes filled with overlying made-ground material; uppermost 6cm incorporate snail fauna, charcoal, brick, coal	
13–14	Made-ground	
Borehole 3		
11.36–11.4	Dark grey; sandy flint gravel; dark colour associated with organic material; plant debris present as small (<1mm) pieces of recognizable plant tissue	
11.4–11.61	2.5Y4/4 olive brown; sandy flint gravel; recognizable plant debris throughout	
11.61–11.64	5Y4/2 olive grey; sandy clay; plant debris; interrupted by 0.5cm bed of calcareous, medium-fine sand with abundant plant debris; upper surface of sandy clay penetrated from above by vertical piece of wood (?root) that can be traced up from 11.63 to 11.76m OD	
11.64–11.69	Olive brown; coarse sand (cf 11.40–11.61m OD)	
11.69–11.79	5Y5/1 grey; sandy, silty clay; scattered plant debris; penetrated from above by vertical pieces of wood (?root *in situ*); slight acid reaction patchily throughout – one concentration of white sand with strong acid reaction	
11.79–11.9	Transition from silty clay deposition with abundant organic debris to peat with negligible mineral content; horizontal partings indicative of bedding	
11.9–12.37	Peat with negligible mineral content (if any) becoming more woody in uppermost 18cm	
12.37–12.41	Very dark brown to black; well-humified peat with small amount of mineral matter; structureless; sharp contact	
12.41–12.47	10YR4/2 dark greyish brown; peaty clay; finely divided plant material common in the lowermost 2cm, decreasing upward, but some large (15–20mm) fragments present; structureless; diffuse contact	
12.47–12.53	5Y4/2 olive grey and 10YR6/6 brownish yellow patchily mixed; silty clay; organic parting at 12.5m OD; scarce finely divided plant debris; structureless	
12.53–12.57	10YR5/1 grey and 10YR 6/8 brownish yellow patchily mixed; silty clay; very scarce, very small organic particles; structureless	
12.57–12.82	10YR5/1 grey with patches and faint mottles of 7.5YR5/8 strong brown; silty clay; structureless; scarce plant debris, almost all fine but a few larger pieces (2mm); very infrequent granules of flint and quartz in the uppermost 8cm	
12.82–12.99	10YR6/1 light grey with dense mottles of 5YR6/8 brownish yellow; silty clay; structureless; plant debris scarce and small	
12.99–13.35	10YR6/2 light brownish grey with scattered mottles of 5YR5/8 yellowish red; modern roots; structureless; slightly calcareous in the upper part where it interdigitates with made-ground	
13.35–13.95	Made-ground	

TABLE 1.7, *continued*

Metres OD	Description	Main pollen types/Depth (metres OD) of local pollen assemblage zones
Column T2		
12.07–12.27	Peat with gradual increase in silt/clay content; discrete lenses of silt upward, giving mottled appearance; sharp contact	Poaceae, *Quercus, Salix* Meadlake Column T2 1
12.27–12.44	5Y5/2 olive grey; silty clay; faint darker mottling (12.37–12.42m OD; 1920 ± 70 BP)	
Column T3		
12.07–12.16	5Y5/1 grey; sandy, silty clay; scattered plant debris; penetrated from above by vertical pieces of wood (?root *in situ*); slight acid reaction patchily throughout – one concentration of white sand with strong acid reaction; sharp contact	*Pinus*, Cyperaceae, Poaceae Meadlake Column T3 1
12.16–12.43	Peat with gradual increase in silt/clay content; discrete lenses of silt upward, giving mottled appearance; sharp contact	*Salix, Betula, Quercus, Ulmus* Meadlake Column T3 2
12.43–12.49	Wood (8960 ± 130 BP)	
12.49–12.57	5Y5/1 grey; silt; scattered plant debris	

suggestion is supported by a fossil assemblage towards the base of the sequence in Borehole 2 (9.74–10.00m OD) indicating the presence of well-oxygenated, running water and includes numerous fish bones, teeth and scales, and a Molluscan fauna with *Bithynia tentaculata*. The record from Meadlake Place demonstrates the presence of a stable flood plain for much of the Holocene. Peat formation seems to have begun in suitable places on the flood-plain surface at about 9000 BP, and to have continued until *c* 1920 BP (AD 90). The presence of sandy horizons and of freshwater Mollusca within the peat shows that the flood plain remained subject to intermittant flooding during this period, although the influx of mineral material and of shells appears to diminish upward and to

cease altogether in the uppermost 30cm of the peat.

In the lower Thames valley, the palaeoenvironmental record from Bramcote Green indicates the formation of a substantial freshwater lake fringed by *Typha latifolia* (reedmace) and species of Poaceae (grass family). At Elstead Bog, the transition to the early Holocene was also characterized by the formation of an open freshwater lake and finally peat formation.

The palaeoenvironmental data from Staines (fig 1.5), Meadlake Place (fig 1.6), Runnymede and Moor Farm (Staines; TQ 027 725; 15m OD; Keith-Lucas 2000) record the following sequence of vegetation change in the middle Thames valley during the Mesolithic:

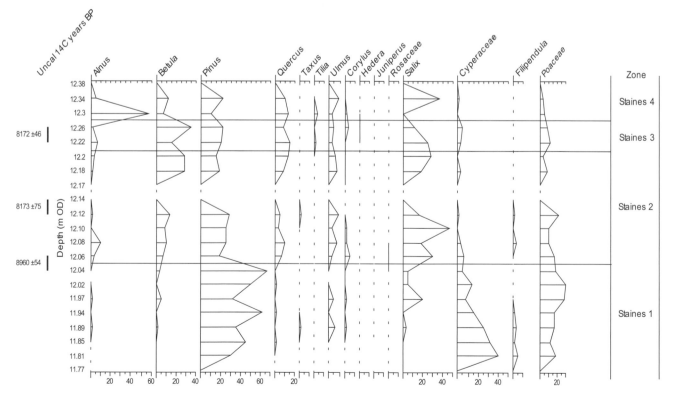

Values expressed as a % of total land pollen

Fig 1.5   Selected taxa pollen diagram from Staines ABC Cinema, Middlesex (Branch *et al* 2003a)

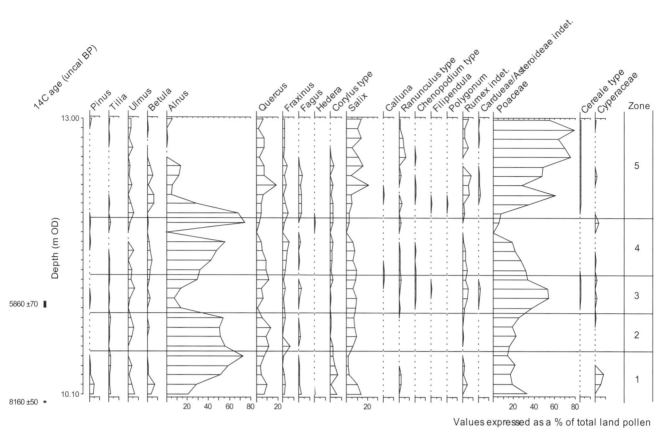

Fig 1.6   Selected taxa pollen diagram from Borehole 2, Meadlake Place, Surrey (Branch *et al* 2001)

a 10,000–9000 BP *Pinus* woodland dominated the surrounding dryland area (eg Staines 1, Meadlake T3 1). Sedge and reed-swamp initially colonized the wetland zones although this was gradually replaced by *Salix* woodland.

b 9000–8000 BP *Quercus*, *Ulmus*, *Betula* and *Corylus* invade the areas occupied by *Pinus* resulting in the formation of mixed deciduous woodland (eg Staines 2 and 3, Meadlake T3 2). The wetland zone was dominated by *Salix* woodland, although there is evidence for isolated trees of *Alnus*.

c 8000–5800 BP *Quercus*, *Ulmus*, *Tilia* and *Corylus* dominated the dryland vegetation cover (eg Staines 4, Meadlake 1 and 2). *Alnus* expanded in the wetland zone resulting in the formation of alder carr woodland.

d 5800–5500 BP Poaceae and a diverse range of herbaceous plant taxa expand during period in which arboreal taxa, such as *Quercus*, *Ulmus* and *Tilia*, indicate a temporary decline (Meadlake 3).

The reduction in arboreal taxa, presence of cereal pollen and microscopic charred particles, and indicators of disturbed ground, such as *Plantago lanceolata*, provides unequivocal evidence for clearance of woodland, probably by burning, and cultivation sometime during the Late Mesolithic–Early Neolithic transition. The temporary decline in *Alnus* woodland and evidence for deposition of mineral-rich sediments at Meadlake Place suggests that the activities of human groups during this period

resulted in erosion and re-deposition of sediments and significant changes in the local hydrological regime. The palaeoenvironmental record from Elstead Bog is broadly similar to that of the middle Thames area, showing succession from aquatic plant communities (eg *Potamogeton* (pondweed)) and shrubland dominated by *Juniperus* (juniper) to mixed woodland with *Betula*, *Pinus*, *Corylus* and finally *Quercus*, *Ulmus* and *Tilia* (EL3–7).

At Bramcote Green, the composition and structure of the Mesolithic vegetation cover was broadly similar to that recorded at Elstead Bog, Meadlake Place, Runnymede Bridge and Staines. However, the sequence differs, with *Pinus* never achieving the dominance it attained in the Early Holocene at the other sites, possibly owing to the development of closed *Betula* woodland. The expansion of *Alnus* between approximately 8200 and 6100 BP is broadly similar to that recorded at Staines and Meadlake Place, although it is highly likely that *Alnus* was already present in both areas at 9000 BP, if not before (eg the presence of alder plant macrofossils at Bramcote Green corresponding to pollen zones BEG2c and BEGb). Finally, the pollen-stratigraphic data from Beddington Lane, Sutton (TQ 290 660) provides further confirmation of the presence of *Pinus*, *Quercus*, *Corylus* and *Alnus* woodland in Surrey during the Mesolithic (Heaton & Hearne 1992).

The record from Meadlake Place provides the only direct palaeoecological evidence for human activity during the Mesolithic period, and suggests that Late Mesolithic human groups were having a significant impact on the local environment during this period. The expansion of *Corylus* throughout Europe during this period has also been equated with exploitation of woodland resources (Smith 1970), and the find of charred hazelnuts at Hankley Common provides some support for this interpretation. However, Huntley & Prentice (1993) present an equally strong case for drier climatic conditions during the early Holocene initiating the expansion of *Corylus*. At Elstead Bog, a distinctive charcoal horizon at 68cm corresponds to a temporary reduction in woodland cover (*Betula*, *Pinus*, *Ulmus* and *Quercus*), and the expansion of heliophilous and fire resistant herbs and shrubs such as *Corylus*, *Artemisia* (mugwort) and *Filipendula* (meadowsweet). Although this may be due to human interference, the absence of any direct evidence for human activity at the site suggests that the vegetation changes are due to a natural event.

Neolithic in Surrey (*c* 5500–3800 BP)

The scarcity of palaeoenvironmental data for the Neolithic in Surrey limits any assessment of the impact of natural environmental change and the activities of human groups on the landscape. The pollen-stratigraphic records from the middle and lower Thames valley indicate that the dryland vegetation cover was dominated by mixed deciduous woodland, especially *Ulmus*, *Tilia* and *Quercus*, and that human interference in natural vegetation succession after 5000 BP resulted in temporary clearance of woodland for cultivation and pastoralism. In wetland areas, several sites indicate that *Alnus* carr woodland dominated the vegetation communities.

In the lower Thames valley, unequivocal evidence for a decline in *Ulmus* woodland has been obtained from:

a Bryan Road (TQ 799 365; Sidell *et al* 1995), radiocarbon dated to 5040 ±70 BP.

b Joan Street (Sidell *et al* 2000), radiocarbon dated after 5000 BP.

c Union Street (Sidell *et al* 2000), radiocarbon dated to *c* 4700 BP.

d Bramcote Green (Branch & Lowe 1994), radiocarbon dated to between 6110 ±120 and 4330 ±70 BP.

At Hampstead Heath, unique evidence for woodland clearance and cultivation prior to the elm decline may suggest that human activity accelerated the spread of elm disease through clearance (Girling & Grieg 1985; Girling 1988). However, compatible evidence from other sites is unfortunately lacking. At Bramcote Green, for example, there is no evidence

for cereal cultivation prior to, during or immediately following the elm decline, which may suggest that it was due to the localized effects of hydrological change (eg fluvial inundation, BEGe; table 1.3) or to activities associated with pastoralism (gathering of fodder and bedding, and the creation of grazing land for animals; see Rasmussen 1989). At Bryan Road and Joan Street, however, there is unequivocal evidence for cereal cultivation following the elm decline. Sidell *et al* (2002) have suggested that these phases of clearance would have 'transformed north Southwark and Lambeth into a relatively open landscape' (*ibid*, 47). However, the pollen-stratigraphic records from all of the sites discussed above indicate that dryland areas continued to be dominated by *Quercus*, *Tilia* and *Corylus* woodland, with *Alnus* forming closed carr woodland on the flood plain and around ponds and small lakes. It is perhaps more appropriate to view the Early to Middle Neolithic landscape of the lower Thames valley around Southwark and Lambeth as being an ever changing mosaic of closed and open woodland, temporarily cultivated land, grazing land and meadows interrupted by tributary rivers and streams, small ponds and lakes. Indeed the evidence for woodland regeneration during the Late Neolithic and Early Bronze Age in some areas (eg Bryan Road) supports this interpretation.

In the middle Thames valley, pollen-stratigraphic records from Meadlake Place and Runnymede Bridge (Needham 1992; Scaife 2000) provide no evidence for a decline in *Ulmus* woodland. In these areas, the complete absence of palaeoecological evidence for Early–Middle Neolithic human activity tends to suggest that interference in woodland succession may have been of low intensity. Other evidence for human activities, including the exploitation of wild plants, comes from Purley Way, Croydon. Located on the flood plain terrace of the Wandle valley, the site provides evidence for a Late Neolithic cooking pit (3860 ±70 BP), a possible remnant of a Late Neolithic ploughsoil and exploitation of wheat, plum, hazelnut and domestic cattle. This range of palaeoenvironmental data is thought to provide evidence for woodland clearance in Croydon from the Late Neolithic (Tucker 1996, 13; see also Potter 1994). At Eden Walk in Kingston, the presence of red deer antler and horn core, and pollen data indicating the presence of *Alnus*, *Corylus*, *Tilia* and *Betula* and a decline of *Ulmus* clearly supports the records from Southwark and Lambeth (Penn *et al* 1984, 216–19). Although archaeological records for the Neolithic period west of Hammersmith (eg Brentford and Stanwell) indicate that the impact of human activities may have been extensive, very little palaeoenvironmental data is available (see O'Connell 1990; Cowie & Eastmond 1997a, b).

Bronze Age in Surrey (c 3800–2800 BP)

In the lower Thames valley, there is good palaeo-environmental evidence for Bronze Age activities associated with, or in close proximity to, several low gravel islands (eg Horsleydown and Bermondsey eyots). Sedimentary successions overlying or adjacent to the islands indicate complex sequences of estuarine, lacustrine and fluvial sediments, and peat deposits. The most extensive peat unit has been correlated with a reduction/stabilization in sea level during the Bronze Age, and this is overlain and underlain by mineral-rich sediments (clay/silt) thought to represent overbank flooding within a tidal environment (Drummond-Murray *et al* 1994; Rackham 1994). At Bramcote Green (BEGf; table 1.3), pollen-stratigraphic records indicate the continued expansion of wetland vegetation dominated by *Alnus* carr woodland, and the presence of *Quercus*, *Corylus* and *Tilia* on nearby dryland during the Late Neolithic and Early Bronze Age. However, between 3600 and 2800 BP the pollen record from Bramcote Green indicates a progressive reduction in woodland. The decline of *Tilia*, followed by *Quercus*, *Corylus* and finally *Alnus* pollen coincides with the continuous presence of cereal pollen indicating a sustained period of cultivation. The diachronous decline in *Tilia* woodland from the Late Neolithic onwards and its direct association with clearance and cultivation are now well established. However, attempts to explain the decline as a consequence of climatic deterioration (Godwin 1956) or paludification (Waller 1994) have found some support. For example, the first lime decline at Union Street (c 4000 BP; Sidell *et al* 2000, 83–6) does not coincide with evidence for cereal cultivation but does occur during a period of peat accumulation. However, by 3000 BP pollen records from Bramcote Green (Branch & Lowe 1994), Union Street, Joan Street and Canada Wharf (Sidell *et al* 2002, 47–50) all indicate a reduction in woodland cover, including lime, with evidence for cereal cultivation. The evidence tends to suggest therefore several phases of clearance and regeneration over a period of approximately 2000 years. Archaeological evidence for Neolithic and Bronze Age plough (ard or nail) cultivation at Phoenix Wharf (dated to 3310 ±40 BP) and Wolseley Street (probably Late Neolithic) has provided important new information on prehistoric farming (Drummond-Murray *et al* 1994) that supports this interpretation.

In the middle Thames valley, evidence for clearance, creation of field systems, cereal production and agricultural intensification during the Late Bronze Age (c 3000 BP) is indicated by the archaeological and palaeoenvironmental evidence from Stanwell (O'Connell 1990). At Eden Walk, Kingston, palaeoenvironmental data indicate utilization of red deer, cattle, pig and sheep/goat (Serjeantson *et al* 1991–92, M73). These records are broadly confirmed by the pollen data from Meadlake Place that indicate, between approximately 5800 and 1900 BP, a reduction in *Quercus* and *Tilia* woodland and evidence for cereal cultivation. Therefore, exploitation of seasonally flooded areas on the margins of the river Thames at Meadlake Place and Runnymede Bridge undoubtedly occurred.

In other parts of Surrey, the evidence is equally compelling. Data from Ockley Bog, Thursley Common (Moore & Wilmott 1976) suggests that accelerated erosion occurred as a response to woodland clearance and may have led to the creation of the mire. According to the authors, two phases of clearance, abandonment and woodland regeneration (*Betula*, *Corylus* and Ericaceae (eg heather)) are recorded. Evidence for cultivation of nutrient-poor, podzolic heathland soils during this period is perhaps surprising, although pollen-stratigraphic data from Ascot supports this interpretation (Bradley & Keith-Lucas 1975). In Carshalton (Middleton Road), Croydon (Purley Way) and Sunbury (Vicarage Road) environmental archaeological data indicate clearance associated with field systems and the formation of grassland (Bird *et al* 1989, 216; Bird *et al* 1996, 201, 224).

Iron Age, Romano-British and later periods in Surrey (c 2800 BP onwards)

In the lower Thames valley, Sidell *et al* (2002) have conducted an exhaustive review of environmental change during the Late Bronze Age and Iron Age. These data suggest that from the Late Bronze Age (c 2900 BP) areas of Southwark and Lambeth on the margins of the river Thames were occasionally being inundated by estuarine mineral-rich sediments eg at Union Street. At Bramcote Green (Branch & Lowe 1994), a reduction in *Alnus* carr woodland from 2970 ±60 BP supports this broad environmental trend with evidence for fluvial inundation and saturation of low-lying soils. Contemporary developments on nearby dry land also indicate a reduction in woodland and the expansion of grassland and cultivation. There is a possibility therefore that extensive deforestation in the lower Thames valley catchment during the Late Bronze Age and Iron Age caused accelerated soil erosion and deposition of suspended sediment on the flood plain. Increased inundation of the flood plain would have resulted in a significant change in the morphology of the river margins and fluvial regime, possibly resulting in reversal downstream of the tidal head. Support for this interpretation may be found in the palaeoenvironmental data from other sites in Southwark and Lambeth, for example Joan Street and Union Street (Sidell *et al* 2000, 83–6). During the Late Iron Age and

Romano-British period archaeological evidence for field boundaries and drainage ditches in Southwark indicates attempts to reclaim low-lying areas, although the presence of fluvial or estuarine sediments overlying these features indicates that rising base levels may have led to their abandonment (Drummond-Murray *et al* 1994, 257). According to Heard (1996, 80) this evidence points to Southwark being part of a managed rural landscape, probably used for market gardening rather than cereal cultivation during the Roman period. However, during the medieval period archaeological evidence suggests that flooding may have led to the land being used for pasture or common land (Drummond-Murray *et al* 1994, 256). In other parts of the borough, there is certainly good evidence for animal exploitation (cattle, sheep and horse) during the Late Iron Age (Heard 1996).

To the south and west of Southwark and Lambeth there is similar Iron Age, Roman and medieval archaeological and palaeoenvironmental evidence for human activities. The evidence indicates farmsteads, ditched field systems, crop husbandry, crop processing (eg emmer wheat), stock breeding (eg cattle, pig, dog, horse) and gardening from East Twickenham, Isleworth, Brentford, Stanwell, Carshalton, Tolworth, Old Malden, Barn Elms and Croydon (eg Beddington sewage works) (O'Connell 1990; Potter 1994; Bird *et al* 1990; 1994; 1996; Cowie & Eastmond, 1997a; Greenwood 1997; Jackson *et al* 1997). However, the timing of woodland clearance and conversion of the landscape into arable or pastureland varies considerably. In Brentford (TQ 184 778), for example, Bishop (2002) records extensive clearance of the landscape during the late Iron Age with archaeological evidence indicating a 'transient community, possibly based around a livestock economy' *(ibid,* 8). During the 1st century AD, the development of a Roman field system for the growing of spelt, barley and possibly oats indicates the use of marginal areas on poorly drained soils for cultivation. It is questionable whether many of these low-lying areas would have been able to sustain arable farming for prolonged periods owing to the poor soils and increasing marshland development for which there is evidence during the late Roman and medieval

periods (eg Kingston – Penn *et al* 1984, 219; Serjeantson *et al* 1991–92, 83–8; Croydon – Potter 1994, 235–6).

In the middle Thames valley, the palaeoenvironmental record from Meadlake Place indicates a transition from peat to structureless silty clay during the Iron Age and Romano-British period (table 1.7). The contact is gradual between 12.30 and 12.39m OD, with the mineral content increasing progressively upward. This silty clay unit resembles closely the silty clays that are widely encountered in midland and southern England forming the upper part of Holocene alluvial sequences. They are generally thought to reflect increased rates of soil erosion associated with intensification of agricultural activity from the Neolithic onward. At Meadlake Place this type of sedimentation does not appear to have become dominant until some time after the first century AD. During this period (Meadlake 5, Meadlake T2) the pollen-stratigraphic record provides evidence for a woodland reduction associated with clearance, probably including burning, and cereal cultivation.

At Frensham Common (SU 843 405), near Farnham, the discovery of a palaeosol associated with a buried artificial terrace by David Graham of the Surrey Archaeological Society allowed the reconstruction of vegetation change and land-use history during the late Iron Age and Roman period in this locality (table 1.8; Branch *et al,* 2002).

The age of the palaeosol was established by the excavation of silver and bronze coins, the majority of which date to the periods AD41–54 and AD138–161 (corresponding to the reigns of the emperors Claudius and Antoninus Pius respectively), although a few coins date to the Iron Age and later Roman period (D Graham, pers comm). Examination of the palaeosol revealed the presence of an acid brown earth overlain by a well-developed podzol. Immediately beneath the buried 'A' horizon, the high-resolution pollen record indicates the presence of open mixed deciduous woodland (*Quercus, Betula* and *Alnus*) with evidence for heathland, grassland and cereal cultivation (fig 1.7).

Within the buried 'A' horizon, three phases of vegetation succession have been identified:

TABLE 1.8 The soil and pollen-stratigraphic sequence at Frensham Common (Branch *et al* 2002)

Depth (cm) below ground surface	Description
0–12	'A' horizon; dark brown/black; 7.5YR 2.5/1; 2.9–46.6% organic matter
12–23.5	'Ae' horizon; brown; 7.5YR 5/6; 1–6.1% organic matter; sharp boundary
23.5–40.2	'Bh' horizon; dark grey; 5YR 4/1; 1.5–3.9% organic matter; charcoal; sharp boundary
40.2–53	'bAh' horizon; black; 7.5YR 2.5/1; maximum 4.7% organic matter; sharp boundary
53–63.5	'B' horizon; reddish brown; 5YR 4/3; 1–2% organic matter; sharp boundary
63.5–75	'C' (?) horizon; brown; 7.5YR 5/6; 1–2% organic matter; diffuse boundary

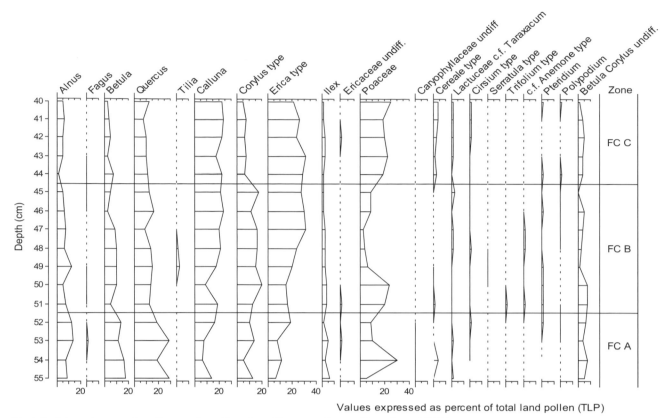

Values expressed as percent of total land pollen (TLP)

Fig 1.7   Selected taxa pollen diagram from Frensham Common, Surrey (Branch *et al* 2002)

a Heathland, shrubland (*Corylus*) and grassland expansion associated with burning of the vegetation cover and cereal cultivation.
b Heathland expansion and a cessation of cereal cultivation.
c Further evidence for cereal cultivation.

These results are entirely consistent with other records from south-east England that suggest that during the Iron Age and Roman period extensive woodland clearance and intensification of arable agriculture led to accelerated erosion and podzolization of soils (see Macphail & Scaife 1987).

An agenda for the future
If the palaeoenvironmental (including environmental archaeological) record in Surrey is to be enhanced, a major priority for the future is the formulation and initiation of a long-term programme of regional research (Environmental Archaeology Sub-Group 2001). This is necessary for two reasons:

• First, the future threat to the cultural and environmental resource from urban and rural development, and possibly environmental change, will lead to a loss of important information concerning the environmental context of human groups living in Surrey since the Palaeolithic. A research strategy will, by formulating thematic programmes of research, as well as highlighting geographical areas for which little or no infor-

mation is available, enable archaeologists, planners and scientists to evaluate the impact of development and environmental change on the resource.

• Secondly, Surrey is a highly important geographical area because of its proximity to one of the world's best known river systems, its close relationship with London and its rich cultural heritage, its biogeographical importance with respect to the migration routes of flora and fauna since the end of the last glaciation, the diversity of geological and geomorphological contexts suitable for human settlement and land-use, and the richness of the cultural resource.

We recognize that, in order to achieve our goal, there is a need to collate and archive all the existing palaeoenvironmental data for the county. Storage and access of data from primary and secondary sources (such as excavation and post-excavation reports, and regional and sub-regional surveys, both published and unpublished) will be achieved using a geographical information system (GIS). The use of a GIS has the following advantages: it provides a digital archive; enables two-dimensional spatial modelling of the data to be carried out at various scales; provides a mechanism for layering of the data (temporal modelling); allows analysis of the data and the formulation of new research questions; provides a platform for future management of the environmental archaeological resource.

The wider implications of this approach will be to create a more integrated approach towards the sharing of information, archived records and medium to long term research plans; to raise the quality of the field and laboratory investigative work undertaken in Surrey, through shared facilities and experiences; to bring the environmental archaeology legacy of Surrey to a wider public forum; and to provide an opportunity to train colleagues in new methods of archiving data, managing the cultural resource and carrying out data analysis.

During compilation of the GIS database, a detailed palaeoenvironmental research agenda for Surrey will be formulated and new research programmes initiated. Access to new sites and the creation of new records will be conducted on a proactive (predictive modelling) and reactive (rescue excavation) basis (Environmental Archaeology Sub-Group 2001).

Based on the information contained in this chapter, two broad research themes can be suggested which require detailed morphological, lithological, biological and dating evidence, and full integration of the scientific and archaeological data:

• Understanding the effects of natural environmental processes (climatic, geomorphological, sedimentological, pedological and hydrological) on the activities of human groups.

• Understanding the effects of human exploitation of organic and inorganic resources on the natural environment (eg accelerated soil erosion and podzolization).

BIBLIOGRAPHY

Bell, M, & Walker, M J C, 1992 *Late Quaternary environmental change*, Longman

Bennett, K D, 1988 Holocene pollen stratigraphy of central East Anglia, England, and comparison of pollen zones across the British Isles, *New Phytologist*, **109**, 237–53

Bird, D G, Crocker, G, & McCracken, J S, 1989 Archaeology in Surrey 1987, *SyAC*, **79**, 179–89

——, 1990 Archaeology in Surrey 1988–89, *SyAC*, **80**, 201–28

Bird, D G, Crocker, G, McCracken, J S, & Saich, D, 1994 Archaeology in Surrey 1991, *SyAC*, **82**, 203–19

Bird, D G, Crocker, G, Maloney, C, & Saich, D, 1996 Archaeology in Surrey 1992–93, *SyAC*, **83**, 187–228

Bird, J, & Bird, D G (eds), 1987 *The archaeology of Surrey to 1540*, SyAS

Bishop, B, 2002 Late prehistoric and Roman Brentford: evolution of an agricultural landscape, *London Archaeol*, **10.1**, 7–12

Bradley, R, & Keith-Lucas, M, 1975 Excavation and pollen analyses on a bell barrow at Ascot, Berkshire, *J Archaeol Sci*, **2**, 95–108

Branch, N P, & Lowe, J J, 1994 Bramcote Green Redevelopment archaeological project 1992/3, Palynology, ArchaeoScape unpublished report

Branch, N P, & Green, C P, 2001 Meadlake Place, Egham, Surrey, palaeoenvironmental analysis, ArchaeoScape unpublished report

Branch, N P, Finch, P, Green, C P, Mansfield, C, & Williams, A N, 2002 Late Holocene environmental history of Frensham Common, Surrey, ArchaeoScape unpublished report

Branch, N P, Cameron, N, Canti, M G, & Green, C P, 2003 Staines ABC Cinema palaeoenvironmental analysis, ArchaeoScape unpublished report

Branch, N P, Green, C P, Kemp, R A, & Swindle, G E, 2003 Environmental archaeological assessment for North Park Farm Quarry, Bletchingley, Surrey (NPF02), ArchaeoScape unpublished report

Bury, H, 1935 The Farnham terraces and their sequence, *Proc Prehist Soc*, **1**, 60–9

Carpenter, C P, & Woodcock, M P, 1981 A detailed investigation of a pingo remnant in western Surrey, *Quaternary Stud*, **1**, 1–26

Catt, J A, 1979 Soils and Quaternary geology in Britain, *J Archaeol Sci*, **30**, 607–42

Cooper, J E, 1907 Holocene Mollusca from Staines, *Proc Malacological Soc London*, **7**, 310–11

——, 1922 Note on a Holocene deposit at Penton Hook, *Proc Malacological Soc London*, **15**, 35–6

Cowie, R, & Eastmond, D, 1997a An archaeological survey of the foreshore in the Borough of Richmond upon Thames, part 1, Time and Tide, *London Archaeol*, **8.4**, 87–94

——, 1997b An archaeological survey of the foreshore in the Borough of Richmond upon Thames, part 2, Down by the riverside, *London Archaeol*, **8.5**, 115–21

D'Olier, B, 1972 Subsidence and sea level rise in the Thames estuary, *Phil Trans Roy Soc London*, **272**, 121–30

Devoy, R J, 1977 Flandrian sea level changes in the Thames estuary and implications for land subsidence in England and Wales, *Nature*, **270**, 712–15

Devoy, R J N, 1979 Flandrian sea level changes and vegetational history of the lower Thames estuary, *Phil Trans Roy Soc London*, **285**, 355–407

Drummond-Murray, J, Saxby, D, & Watson, B, 1994 Recent archaeological work in the Bermondsey district of Southwark, *London Archaeol*, **7.10**, 251–7

Environmental Archaeology Sub-Group, 2001 *Proposal for an environmental archaeology database for Surrey*, Surrey Heritage Strategy Group for Archaeology

Gibbard, P L, 1985 *The Pleistocene history of the Middle Thames Valley*, Cambridge

Gibbard, P L, & Hall, A R, 1982 Late Devensian river deposits in the lower Colne valley, west London, England, *Proc Geologists Assoc*, **93**, 291–300

Gibbard, P L, Coope, G R, Hall, A R, Preece, R C, & Robinson, J E, 1982 Middle Devensian river deposits beneath the 'upper floodplain' terrace of the river Thames at Kempton Park, Sunbury, Surrey, England, *Proc Geologists Assoc*, **93**, 275–90

Girling, M A, 1988 The bark beetle *Scolytus scolytus* (Fabricius) and the possible role of elm disease in the Early Neolithic, in *Archaeology and the flora of the British Isles* (ed M Jones), Oxford Univ Comm Archaeol Monogr, **14**, 34–8

Girling, M A, & Greig, J R A, 1985 A first fossil record for *Scolytus scolytus* (Fabricius) (elm bark beetle): its occurrence in elm decline deposits from London and the implications for Neolithic elm disease, *J Archaeol Sci*, **12**, 347–52

Godwin, H, 1956 *The history of the British flora, a factual basis for phytogeography*, Cambridge

Greenwood, P, 1997 Iron Age London: some thoughts on current knowledge and problems 20 years on, *London Archaeol*, **8.6**, 153–61

Haggart, B A, 1995   A re-examination of some data relating to Holocene sea-level changes in the Thames estuary, in *The Quaternary of the lower reaches of the Thames* (eds D R Bridgland, P Allen & B A Haggart), Durham: Quaternary Research Association, 329–38

Heard, K, 1996   The hinterland of Roman Southwark: part I, *London Archaeol*, **8.3**, 76–81

Heaton, M, & Hearne, C, 1992   Site investigations at Beddington Lane, Sutton, Surrey, *London Archaeol*, **7.1**, 19–23

Howard, M M, 1952   *Planorbis acronicus* Férussac in a Holocene deposit in Surrey, *J Conchology*, **23**, 261–4

Huntley, B, & Prentice, I C, 1993   Holocene vegetation and climates of Europe, in *Global climates since the last glacial maximum* (eds H E Wright jnr, J E Kutzbach, T Webb III, W F Ruddiman, F A Street-Perrott, & P J Bartlein), Minneapolis: University of Minnesota Press, 136–68

Iversen, J, 1941   Landnam I Danmarks Stenalder, *Danm Geol Unders*, **4**, 20–68

Jackson, G, Maloney, C, & Saich, D, 1997   Archaeology in Surrey 1994–5, *SyAC*, **84**, 195–243

Keith-Lucas, M, 2000   Pollen analysis of sediments from Moor Farm, Staines Moor, Surrey, *SyAC*, **87**, 85–93

Kemp, R A, 1986   Pre-Flandrian Quaternary soils and pedogenic processes in Britain, in *Palaeosols, their recognition and interpretation* (ed V P Wright), Blackwell, 242–62

Kennard, A S, & Woodward, B B, 1906   On sections of the Holocene alluvium at Staines and Wargrave, *Proc Geologists Assoc*, **19**, 252–6

Kerney, M P, Gibbard, P L, Hall, A R, & Robinson, J E, 1982   Middle Devensian river deposits beneath the 'upper floodplain' terrace of the River Thames at Isleworth, west London, *Proc Geologists Assoc*, **93**, 385–93

Macphail, R I, & Scaife, R G, 1987   The geographical and environmental background, in Bird & Bird 1987, 31–51

Moore, P D, & Willmott, A, 1976   Prehistoric forest clearance and the development of peatlands in the uplands and lowlands of Britain, in 5th International Peat Congress, Poznan, Poland, 1–15

Needham, S, 1992   Holocene alluviation and interstratified settlement evidence in the Thames valley at Runnymede Bridge, in *Alluvial archaeology in Britain* (eds S Needham & M G Macklin), Oxbow Monogr, **27**, 249–60

Oakley, K P, 1939   Geology and Palaeolithic studies, in *A survey of the prehistory of the Farnham district, Surrey* (eds K P Oakley, W F Rankine & A W G Lowther), SyAS, 3–58

O'Connell, M, 1990   Excavations during 1979–1985 of a multi period site at Stanwell, *SyAC*, **80**, 1–62

Penn, J, Field, D, & Serjeantson, D, 1984   Evidence of Neolithic occupation in Kingston: excavations at Eden Walk, 1965, *SyAC*, **75**, 215–22

Potter, G, 1994   15–17 Brighton Road, Croydon: the investigation of a prehistoric and Roman site, *London Archaeol*, **7.9**, 232–7

Rackham, J, 1994   Prehistory 'in' the lower Thames floodplain, *London Archaeol*, **7.7**, 191–6

Rasmussen, P, 1989   Leaf foddering in the earliest Neolithic agriculture, *Acta Archaeologica*, **60**, 71–86

Reynier, M J, 2002   Kettlebury 103: a Mesolithic 'Horsham' type stone assemblage from Hankley Common, Elstead, *SyAC*, **89**, 211–31

Roberts, N, 1989   *The Holocene: an environmental history*, Blackwell

Roe, D A, 1981   *The Lower and Middle Palaeolithic periods in Britain*, Routledge

Scaife, R G, 2000   Palynology and palaeoenvironment, in *The passage of the Thames, Holocene environment and settlement at Runnymede* (ed S P Needham), 168–87

Seagrief, S C, & Godwin, H, 1960   Pollen diagrams from southern England: Elstead, Surrey, *New Phytologist*, **59**, 84–91

Serjeantson, D, Field, D, Penn, J, & Shipley, M, 1991–92   Excavations at Eden Walk II, Kingston: environmental reconstruction and prehistoric finds (TQ 180 692), *SyAC*, **81**, 71–90

Sidell, J, Scaife, R, Tucker, S, & Wilkinson, K, 1995   Palaeoenvironmental investigations at Bryan Road, Rotherhithe, *London Archaeol*, **7.11**, 279–285

Sidell, J, Wilkinson, K, Scaife, R G, & Cameron, N, 2000   The Holocene evolution of the London Thames, MoLAS Monogr **5**

Sidell, J, Cotton, J, Rayner, L, & Wheeler, L, 2002   The prehistory and topography of Southwark and Lambeth, MoLAS Monogr **14**

Smith, A G, 1970   The influence of Mesolithic and Neolithic man on British vegetation: a discussion, in *Studies in the vegetational history of the British Isles: essays in honour of Harry Godwin* (eds D Walker & R G West, Cambridge), 81–96

Thomas, C, & Rackham, J (eds), 1996   Bramcote Green, Bermondsey: a Bronze Age trackway and palaeo-environmental sequence, *Proc Prehist Soc*, **61**, 221–53

Tucker, S, 1996   Further evidence for prehistoric occupation found on the Purley Way, Croydon, *London Archaeol*, **8.1**, 12–17

Tyers, I G, 1988   The prehistoric peat layers (Tilbury IV), in *Excavation in Southwark 1973–76 and Lambeth 1973–79* (ed P Hinton), London Middlesex Archaeol Soc and SyAS Joint Publ, **3**, 5–12

Waller, M, 1994   Paludification and pollen representation: the influence of wetland size on *Tilia* representation in pollen diagrams, *The Holocene*, **4**, 430–4

Wymer, J J, 1968   *Lower Palaeolithic archaeology in Britain*, John Baker
——, 1999   *The Lower Palaeolithic occupation of Britain*, Wessex Archaeology and English Heritage

N P Branch and C P Green, Royal Holloway University of London, Department of Geography, Centre for Quaternary Research, Egham Hill, Egham, Surrey TW20 0EX

2

Surrey's early past: a survey of recent work

JONATHAN COTTON

An attempt is made to synthesize the results of recent work carried out on the county's prehistory, from the Palaeolithic down to the end of the Bronze Age. (The Iron Age is dealt with separately by Rob Poulton.) The paper proceeds chronologically, rather than thematically or topographically, and is divided into two main sections: a broad-brush commentary, and a detailed Annexe which lists all relevant sites and finds reported within modern administrative Surrey up to the end of 2002. Together, the commentary and Annexe serve to update the Palaeolithic to Bronze Age chapters contained in The archaeology of Surrey to 1540. *A short concluding section outlines some ideas for future work.*

Introduction

The last comprehensive round-up of the county's early past was contained within *The archaeology of Surrey to 1540* which appeared virtually a generation ago (Bird & Bird 1987). Since then, wide-ranging political, practical and philosophical advances have fundamentally altered the ways in which the past is perceived (eg Renfrew & Bahn 1996). Furthermore, as a direct consequence of the implementation of new planning guidance introduced in 1990, larger numbers of archaeological interventions have been undertaken than ever before, and by a wider range of commercial and avocational teams. The distribution of these interventions reflects development pressures in the north and north-west of the modern county in particular, as even the most cursory glance at the annual summary in *Surrey Archaeological Collections* will show. Inevitably, this bias is reflected in the present review (fig 2.1). However, it can be partly offset by the Community Archaeology Project and other local initiatives, and by the increasingly systematic study and publication of stray and metal-detected finds from across the county (eg Williams 1996a; 1999a; 2001) (see Annexe below).

Taken together, this collective endeavour has generated much new evidence for the presence of prehistoric human groups within the Surrey landscape that it is the purpose of this short paper to summarize. While necessarily selective, the approach adopted here is fundamentally chronological, though it stops short of the Iron Age: this is covered separately by Rob Poulton. The paper concludes with a section that offers some suggestions for future work. Furthermore, in order to help free the commentary of overly detailed references an Annexe lists all pre-Iron Age sites and finds reported from the modern administrative county since the appearance of *Surrey to 1540*. The metropolitan area has been excluded from this latter exercise as it has been more or less comprehensively covered in several recent summaries and gazetteers published elsewhere (eg Haynes *et al* 2000; MoLAS 2000; Sidell *et al* 2002). Finally, and crucially,

it must be pointed out that much of the evidence touched on here awaits full analysis and publication.

Early scavengers and hunters: the Lower and Middle Palaeolithic (*c* 500,000–38,000 BC)

Modern political boundaries have little meaning in terms of the prehistoric use of the landscape. This is nowhere more applicable than in the earliest phases, which have to be seen in the context of their Quaternary landforms and environment. The study of the Palaeolithic has enjoyed a renaissance at national level in recent years. This has been brought about by spectacular discoveries such as those at Boxgrove, and by the successful correlation of fluvial sequences with climatically driven phasing reflected in the independently dated marine Oxygen Isotope Stages (OIS) (eg Bridgland 1994). (In this scheme, even numbers indicate cold stages, and odd numbers indicate temperate stages.) At a local level detailed surveys of the artefactual resource have also been completed (Wessex Archaeology 1993; Wymer 1999), and provide a firm benchmark against which future development threats can be assessed.

Within the county two of the previously reported concentrations of Palaeolithic material (Wymer 1987, fig 1.1) have benefited from further work since the publication of *Surrey to 1540*. At Lower Kingswood on the North Downs, fieldwork conducted on a site identified over 30 years ago (Walls & Cotton 1980, Site A) has suggested that the eastern of the two large flint scatters noted previously is actually composed of groups of smaller scatters, each between 5 and 10m in diameter (Harp forthcoming). These scatters have produced small pointed bifaces, together with the thinning flakes and débitage under-represented in the earlier work (Harp 2002a). Similar white-patinated and frost-cracked finds including some twisted forms have also been made on and just off the deposits mapped as Clay-with-Flints at Canons Farm, Burgh Heath (fig 2.2; Harp 2002a) and Tattenham Way a little to the north (Harp 1999b

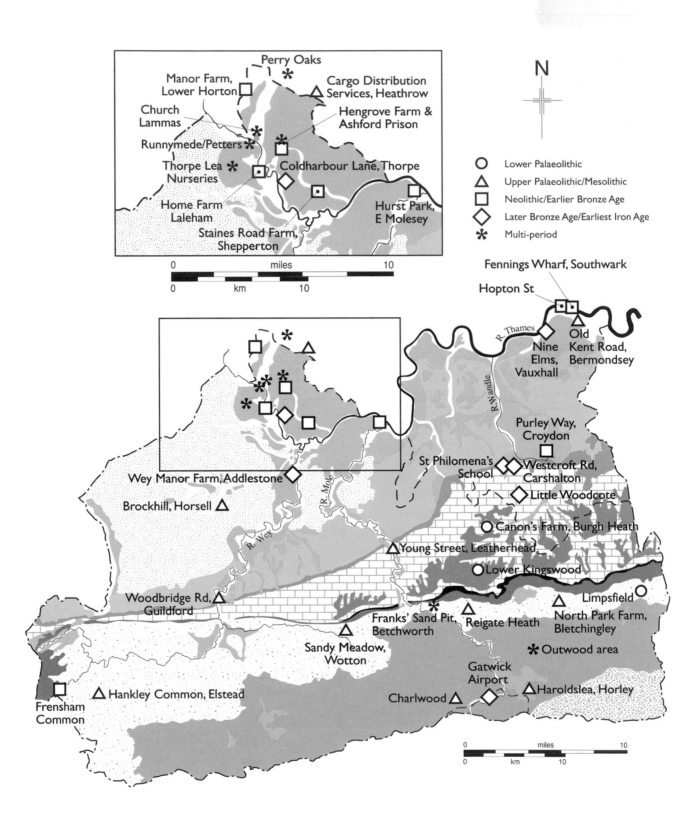

N

Lower Palaeolithic ○
Upper Palaeolithic/Mesolithic △
Neolithic/Earlier Bronze Age □
Later Bronze Age/Earliest Iron Age ◇
Multi-period ✳

Perry Oaks ✳

Manor Farm, Lower Horton □

Cargo Distribution Services, Heathrow △

Church Lammas ✳

Hengrove Farm & Ashford Prison

Runnymede/Petters ✳

Thorpe Lea Nurseries ✳

Coldharbour Lane, Thorpe ◇

Home Farm Laleham

Staines Road Farm, Shepperton

Hurst Park, E Molesey □

0 miles 10
0 km 10

Fennings Wharf, Southwark

Hopton St

R. Thames

Old Kent Road, Bermondsey ◇

Nine Elms, Vauxhall

R. Wandle

Wey Manor Farm, Addlestone ◇

R. Wey

R. Mole

Purley Way, Croydon □

St Philomena's School ◇

Westcroft Rd, Carshalton ◇

Little Woodcote ◇

Canon's Farm, Burgh Heath ○

Brockhill, Horsell △

Young Street, Leatherhead △

Lower Kingswood ○

Limpsfield ○

Woodbridge Rd, Guildford △

Franks' Sand Pit, Betchworth ✳

Reigate Heath △

North Park Farm, Bletchingley △

Sandy Meadow, Wotton △

✳ Outwood area

Gatwick Airport

Frensham Common □

Hankley Common, Elstead △

Charlwood △

Haroldslea, Horley △

0 miles 10
0 km 10

Fig 2.1 Distribution map showing main sites mentioned in the text. For key to geological background see map on page x.

Fig 2.2 Lower Palaeolithic biface from Tangier Wood, Burgh Heath, Banstead, found in the root-plate of a fallen tree. Its fresh condition suggests that it was deeply buried in the Clay-with-Flints deposits and so was protected from the Ice Age climatic extremes to which many of the other North Downs surface finds were subjected. Photograph Peter Harp and the Plateau Group

& pers comm) (see also fig 2.3, no 1), as well as occasional ochreous flakes and bifaces (Harp 2000; 2002a). As at many other high-level surface sites, the dating of this material is problematical (Scott-Jackson 2000, 149–53), though much of it probably belongs within the earlier part of the middle Pleistocene (c OIS 10–9). However, a single white-patinated tortoise core (fig 2.3, no 2) recovered from Mogador a little to the south of the main concentrations at Lower Kingswood hints at a Levallois component which, on current evidence (eg Bridgland 1994, 34), is unlikely to pre-date OIS 8.

The recognition of natural solution hollows on Walton Heath adds a new and potentially significant dimension to this work. Not only could these have provided early hominids with access to ponded water and supplies of flint, but they are also likely to have acted as traps for contemporary environmental and other data. The positions of over 60 hollows have been recorded (Harp 2002a, 23–4 & plate 15), and a 68-point resistivity survey (giving data to a depth of 15.5m) has located others closer to the biface sites identified by Tom Walls and L W Carpenter (Peter Harp & Julie Scott-Jackson, pers comm). These hollows would have occurred over much of the acidic

cover deposits on the North Downs (Sumbler 1996, 154), but now only survive as visible features on ancient common land (eg Banstead and Walton Heaths) and ancient woodland (eg Banstead Wood).

As at Lower Kingswood, a palaeogeographical explanation also offers itself in the context of the prolific biface-dominated sites clustered around the present headwaters of the river Darent at Limpsfield 18km further east (Field *et al* 1999, 26–7). It is possible that these represent repeated visits to topographically advantageous locations on the Lower Greensand on the part of one or more hominid groups. Here again problems surround the dating of surface finds, although the absence of Levallois material suggests that most are likely to fall within the earlier part of the middle Pleistocene. The high number of small twisted ovate forms may help to refine the chronology further, however, for White (1998, 100–1) has argued that such tools represent a purely insular technological phenomenon indicative of Britain's island status during late OIS 11 – early OIS 10. No firm conclusion has been reached regarding the reported presence of *bout coupé* hand-axes in the collection (Roe 1981, 266; Field *et al* 1999, 27–8), although Tyldesley (1987, 72–3) accepted that it might contain a Mousterian component.

Other Quaternary deposits will doubtless repay scrutiny, and the extensive Head deposits (both mapped and unmapped) within the county offer obvious opportunities for such work (eg Cotton 2002). Moreover, concerted fieldwork conducted south of the chalk escarpment on patches of eroded sandstone in the Outwood locality has also located several worn ochreous implements, one of which comprises the butt of an ovate biface (Rapson 2002; Robin Tanner, pers comm). These can be added to the earlier finds of single bifaces made further west at Salfords and Reigate (Wymer 1987, 27; Roger Ellaby, pers comm). Elsewhere, little new fieldwork has been possible at Farnham, while recent evaluations in the Wandsworth locality have failed to shed further light on the implements briefly reported on by G F Lawrence (1890). Finally, sufficient doubt surrounds the bifacially-worked piece from Ripley, originally published as a *bout coupé* (Cotton & Williams 2000), for it to be excluded from consideration here (Roger Jacobi, pers comm).

Anatomically modern hunters: the Upper Palaeolithic and Mesolithic (*c* 38,000–4000 BC)

Anatomically modern humans appear in these islands from around 40,000 years ago, during a phase of quickening climatic change in the mid–late Devensian or last glacial (OIS 3/2). Locally, evidence for the presence of modern humans before the Late Glacial Maximum (*c* 18,000 BP) is sparse. However, a

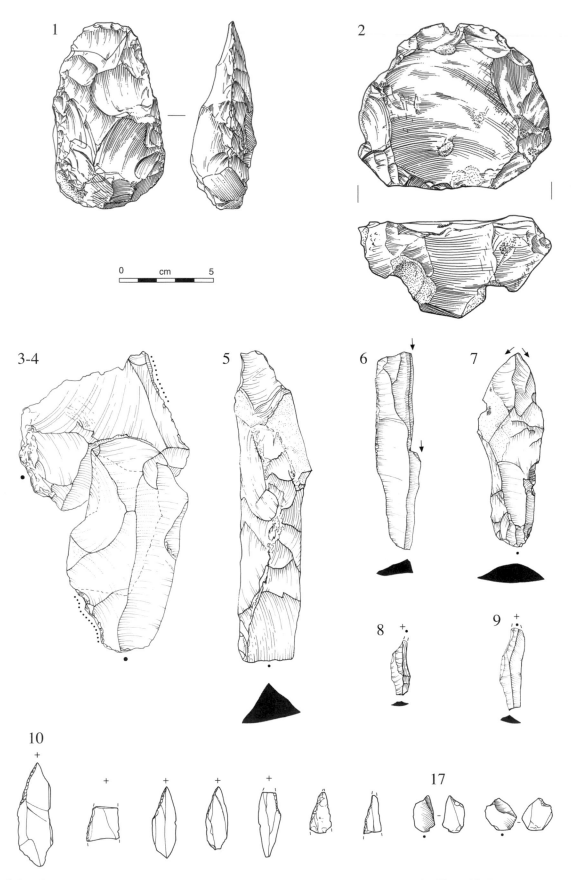

Fig 2.3 Palaeolithic and Mesolithic flintwork, various sites. 1: Lower Palaeolithic biface from the Clay-with-Flints deposits at Sanderstead; 2: Lower Palaeolithic Levallois 'tortoise' core from Walls & Cotton 1980 'Site C', Lower Kingswood; 3–9: Upper Palaeolithic
artefacts from Church Lammas, Staines, including two conjoining 'bruised edge' blades (nos 3 & 4), a crested blade (no 5), burins (nos 6
& 7), and obliquely backed points (nos 8 & 9); 10–18: Early Mesolithic microliths (nos 10–16) and microburins (nos 17 & 18) from
Outwood site 33 (Little Collins Field). All 1:2. Drawings of Church Lammas flints by Giles Pattison; others by the author, courtesy of
Peter Connelly (Sanderstead), Ken Lansdowne (Lower Kingswood) and Robin Tanner (Outwood)

handful of robust white-patinated flint blades from the Cargo Distribution Services site on the southern edge of Heathrow Airport (Lewis forthcoming) now complements the leaf point from Ham (Ellaby 1987, fig 2.3, no 1). The Heathrow pieces can be compared with material recovered from Beedings in Sussex (Jacobi 1986 & pers comm) for which eastern European parallels have been cited. Unlike the Beedings material, however, which was recovered from a number of 'gulls' or 'widened joints' in the surface of the Lower Greensand, the Heathrow assemblage lay on a slight eminence at the edge of the Taplow Gravel overlooking a southward flowing palaeochannel.

Following the Late Glacial Maximum, re-colonization occurred in stages from around 13,000 BP (eg Housley *et al* 1997), as human groups tracked migrating animal herds back into Britain. Two important assemblages of struck flint referable to this Late Glacial period have been located at Brockhill, Horsell, near Woking (Cox 1976; Bonsall 1977; Barton 1992), and at Church Lammas near Staines (Phil Jones, pers comm). Though found in the mid-1920s the Brockhill assemblage has remained unpublished and hence was barely mentioned in *Surrey to 1540* (Ellaby 1987, 53). A preliminary assessment of the material (Barton 1992, 182–3, table 4.29) has since suggested that the assemblage is closely comparable to others recovered from open sites at Hengistbury Head, Dorset, and Titchwell on the north Norfolk coast. The restricted range of retouched tools at Brockhill – straight-backed and shouldered points, end scrapers and burins – probably indicates a short-stay hunting site geared to the processing of large fauna. Comparison with Hengistbury suggests a date sometime around 12,000–11,000 BP, ie during the later part of the Late Glacial interstadial. The presence of a broadly contemporary pen-knife point from nearby Pyrford (Ellaby 1987, fig 2.3, no 2) may be noted here too, though on present evidence this forms part of a separate tool-making tradition.

The new site at Church Lammas, near Staines, has produced a typical 'long blade' flint assemblage incorporating both bruised edge blades (*lames mâchurées*) and retouched pieces including broad blade microliths and burins (fig 2.3, nos 3–9). Although much disturbed, the site also yielded remains of reindeer and horse. 'Long blade' sites occur widely in flood plain or low river valley terrace locations in south-east Britain (eg Barton 1997, 131 & fig 107) and may form a component part of north German Ahrensburgian industries (Barton 1998, 158–9). The closest and best preserved lies 12km further up the Colne valley at Three Ways Wharf, Uxbridge (Lewis 1991). Here, two AMS (Accelerator Mass Spectrometry) radiocarbon dates of 10,270±100 BP (OxA-1788) and 10,010±120 BP

(OxA-1902) on horse molars overlap with dates obtained from the prolific 'long blade' assemblage at Belloy-sur-Somme, France (Barton 1998, 159) – an indication of the close contemporaneity of geographically far-flung sites.

Diagnostic Mesolithic flintwork has been recovered from a range of locations across the county since the publication of *Surrey to 1540*, but undisturbed single-phase sites remain at a premium. Nevertheless, Early Mesolithic sites have been excavated close to the Old Kent Road in Bermondsey (Sidell *et al* 2002) (fig 2.4), on Reigate Heath (Roger Ellaby, pers comm), and Kettlebury (site 103) on Hankley Common, Elstead (Reynier 2002). Late Mesolithic sites have been examined at Woodbridge Road, Guildford (Barry Bishop, Simon Deeves & Peter Moore, pers comm), Haroldslea, Horley (Roger Ellaby, pers comm), and at Charlwood (Ellaby forthcoming). Radiocarbon dates are available for the Hankley Common and Charlwood sites, and these fall within the 8th–7th and 5th millennia cal BC, respectively. Dating for most of the others relies on detailed assessments of microlith typology only (eg Jacobi 1978; Reynier 1998).

Most of these recently excavated sites have produced evidence for single or multiple hearth settings, usually in the form of concentrations of burnt flint and/or charcoal. Carbonized hazelnut shells apart, direct evidence of the subsistence economy remains limited. A single fragment of burnt 'deer-sized' bone (cf roe deer) was recovered from one of two postulated hearth settings at Bermondsey, and a few burnt scraps of roe deer bone from several pits located at Charlwood. This meagre record can now be amplified by the results of use-wear analysis carried out on a sample of the Early Mesolithic flint tools at Bermondsey. Polish identified on a number of the scrapers suggested that they had been used to work dry hide, for example; other pieces had been used to cut meat, plant fibre and, in the case of one burin, antler (Donahue 2002). Furthermore, impact fractures observed on several microliths support their traditional interpretation as projectile points. A cluster of eight Late Mesolithic straight-backed pieces found beneath the earliest Neolithic levels at Runnymede may represent part of a composite side-hafted set (Needham 2000, 71; see also David 1998, fig 26.5).

Topographically, lake sides, valley floors and hill slopes were all favoured localities. A series of sites on the Lower Greensand at North Park Farm, Bletchingley occupied a shallow valley-head depression filled with wind-blown sand (Nick Branch, pers comm). This had sealed various chronologically separate flint-knapping events and small task-specific areas that spanned the period (Hayman *et al* 2003). Moreover, the area within and around the depression was

Fig 2.4   Old Kent Road, Bermondsey: general view of the Early Mesolithic site under excavation. Photograph London Archaeological Archive and Research Centre

taken up by a number of pits similar to those identified at Charlwood. Several discrete clusters apart, no particular pattern could be discerned in their distribution, however. The pit profiles suggest that many had been deliberately dug and speedily backfilled, possibly within the latter part of the Mesolithic. Further pits on other geologies have been reported from Beddington (Bagwell *et al* 2001, 291–2), Woodbridge Road, Guildford (Simon Deeves, pers comm), London Road, Staines (Rob Poulton, pers comm), Netherne on the Hill and Tattenham Way, Banstead. The last two in particular were situated high up on the North Downs and contained flintwork associated with the manufacture, maintenance and use of heavy adzes and axes. An axe roughout was found at Netherne and an adze and five sharpening flakes at Banstead (Harp 1999b). This Late Mesolithic pit-digging tradition represents the earliest evidence for earth-moving on any scale and offers a possible ancestry for certain Neolithic monuments of causewayed enclosure type, though such monuments are locally restricted to the Thames valley (Oswald *et al* 2001, 80, fig 5.1).

Organized fieldwalking and private collecting across the county continues to supplement excavation, and several programmes from the west Surrey greensand have been reported on in final or interim form (eg Bird *et al* 1990, 206). Others are ongoing, as at Wotton (Winser 1987; Richard Jewell, pers comm). Recent work on the Weald Clay at Outwood (eg fig 2.3, nos 10–18) has fully confirmed earlier expectations (eg Ellaby 1987, 58; Cotton & Poulton 1990,

163–5), and demonstrated that human groups were active here throughout the Mesolithic and beyond (Robin Tanner, pers comm). The assessment and publication of the results of these various public and private initiatives remains a pressing priority, likewise their incorporation into the county Sites and Monuments Record. Discussion of other matters such as group size, resource procurement, seasonality of occupation, subsistence strategies, and the organization of butchery and caching practices is still necessarily limited by the nature of the available data. Only the excavation of surface-intact sites with good faunal and environmental data will significantly advance our understanding. Most, like the site(s) located over 50 years ago in the floor of the Mole valley at Young Street, Leatherhead (Carpenter 1952), are likely to lie deeply buried beneath alluvium or colluvium.

Creating new worlds: the Neolithic and earlier Bronze Age (*c* 4000–1500 BC)

The period from around 4000 cal BC witnessed an accelerating transformation of the land through the creation, maintenance and periodic reworking of open space, the latter locally accentuated by the construction of earthen monuments of various forms. Clearance horizons (the so-called 'elm decline') centring on *c* 3900–3500 cal BC have been identified in pollen diagrams along the Thames valley, though the London evidence suggests that such episodes could have been natural in origin and locally asynchronous (Sidell *et al* 2002, 45–7).

Surprisingly, in view of the evidence for monument construction nearby, little sign of early clearance was noted at Moor Farm, Staines Moor (Keith-Lucas 2000). Here and elsewhere along the valley dry-land vegetation cover comprised mixed deciduous woodland, locally dominated by lime (Scaife 2000a) and, as at Runnymede, alder (Scaife 2000b, 184–5). Analysis of species composition within a series of later Neolithic 'drowned forests' in the modern Thames flood plain at Erith in Kent has added important qualifying detail, and has drawn attention to the existence of a mixed alder/yew woodland without modern analogue (Seel 2000, 36; Jane Sidell, pers comm). Data from the remainder of the county is distinctly limited, though the continuing absence of monuments might suggest that clearance and use of the landscape was on a smaller, less invasive, scale. Aside from the Badshot Lea long barrow, there is little obvious evidence for monument construction here much before the early 2nd millennium BC.

A few discrete lithic scatters incorporating leaf arrowheads apart, early Neolithic settlements have largely eluded identification. No new causewayed enclosures have been located within the county since *Surrey to 1540* (Oswald *et al* 2001, 80, fig 5.1), for instance, though a case has recently been made for the re-dating of the large double-ditched enclosure at Mayfield Farm, East Bedfont, just beyond the northern boundary of Spelthorne (John Lewis, pers comm). However, one or more post-and-stake-built 'house' structures surrounded by middens occupied the Thames flood plain at Runnymede (Needham 1992, 251 & pers comm), a kilometre or so south of the Staines causewayed enclosure. A second structure of rectangular form defined by postholes and beam-slots has been claimed at Cranford, on the north side of Heathrow Airport (Nick Elsden, pers comm), while an undated post-and-stake-built rectangular 'long house' or hall has been located at the Woodthorpe Road, Ashford Prison, site near Staines (Tim Carew, pers comm).

These sites skirt the monument-dominated landscapes of the Heathrow terrace where recent work has offered fresh perspectives on the various ways in which land was utilized. It is clear that this flat landscape was laced with subtle complexities that long preceded and were then drawn together by the construction, maintenance and subsequent use of the 4km-long Stanwell cursus with its central raised bank (O'Connell 1990; Barrett *et al* 2000). Dating of the Stanwell structure and of several other smaller cursus and hengiform monuments on the Heathrow terrace has been hampered by the clean state in which they were maintained. This contrasts with the hengiforms on the lower terraces (eg Cotton 2000, 18), of which the ditches contain rich assemblages of finds including human remains, as at Manor Farm,

Horton (Ford & Pine 2003) and Staines Road Farm, Shepperton (Jones 1990). Finds from the former also included plain bowl and Peterborough Ware pottery, struck flint and a series of sewn, birch-bark containers preserved in a locally waterlogged stretch of ditch. Finds from the re-cut ditch of the latter included flint and antler tools, a lump of red ochre and a wolf skull, together with plain bowl and decorated Peterborough Ware pottery. Both sites have also produced radiocarbon dates that centre on the late 4th millennium cal BC.

The two burials from Staines Road Farm – one possibly male and one female (the latter radiocarbon dated to the later 4th millennium cal BC) – offer further insights. Analysis of the stable isotopes in the teeth of the Shepperton female (fig 2.5 a & b) indicates that her place of childhood origin may have lain within one of the UK's lead-zinc orefields, such as the Mendips, Derbyshire or North Pennines (Paul Budd, pers comm). It is possible that she was chosen for burial in this special place precisely because she was an outsider or incomer to the Thames valley. Isotope analyses of several other burials, as at Monkton Up Wimbourn (Green 2000, 79) and later at Amesbury (Fitzpatrick 2003, 151–2) offer some support for this 'incomer' hypothesis. The second Shepperton burial meanwhile had been reduced to a torso through the deliberate removal of the skull and long bones, conceivably for the enactment of ceremonial elsewhere. It is possible that the missing bones were deposited in the river, as was the case with the fragment of a trepanned skull of early 2nd millennium cal BC date recovered from the north bank of the Thames at Chelsea (Fiona Haughey, pers comm). The placing of these burials on the north and north-eastern sides of the Shepperton site was presumably significant too. Similar positions were later chosen for the deposition of human remains in the Early Bronze Age ring ditches at Coldharbour Lane, Thorpe (Robertson 2002) and Fennings Wharf, Southwark (Sidell *et al* 2002, 23–7).

Later Neolithic activity is still principally defined on lithic scatters incorporating various transverse and asymmetric arrowheads, many of which await assessment and publication. These have been reported from a wide range of geologies including the chalk and the Weald Clay (Robin Tanner, pers comm), but – stray finds apart – not the Bagshot Table. No new monuments appear to have been constructed at this time, though existing monuments were re-used, such as the hengiforms at Woodthorpe Road (Ashford Prison), and Staines Road Farm. Truncated soil horizons associated with hearths and cooking or boiling pits have been located at Lower Mill Farm, Stanwell, Staines Road Farm, Shepperton, Purley Way, Croydon and later at Phoenix Wharf, Bermondsey. The Croydon site furnished evidence of charred food remains in the form of wheat, plum and hazelnut. Domestic cattle were also present, and use-wear analysis of a flint knife from a feature dated to the late 3rd millennium cal BC demonstrated that it had been used to cut meat (Tucker 1996, 13).

Further wild food resources have been recovered from small pits containing sherds of Peterborough Ware and Grooved Ware pottery, although these deposits are increasingly viewed as having ritual rather than domestic connotations. The local distri-

Fig 2.5a Staines Road Farm, Shepperton: a female in her thirties lies buried in a crouched position in the ditch of a small hengiform monument. Photograph Surrey County Archaeological Unit

bution of Peterborough Ware, currently dated *c* 3400–2500 cal BC, now also encompasses the Thames flood plain at Southwark/Bermondsey, the eastern headwaters of the Wandle at Beddington and the greensand east of the Mole. Grooved Ware, currently dated *c* 2800–2000 BC, was scarcely represented within the county in 1987, but has since been found in the Bedfont and Stanwell areas (Lorraine Mepham, pers comm; Jones & Ayres forthcoming) and more recently on the greensand at Betchworth and Merstham. The Betchworth assemblage (fig 2.6) was recovered from three pits radiocarbon dated to the early to mid-3rd millennium cal BC (Williams 1998b, 5–6 & pers comm).

The Early Bronze Age is less easy to document, particularly on the higher gravel terraces. However, Beaker and Collared Urn pottery has been recovered from the Thames flood plain and from positions overlooking the headwaters of tributary streams such as the Hogsmill and the Wandle (Howes & Skelton 1992, 15–16 & figs 6 & 7; Orton 1997, 94). (The trepanned skull from Chelsea has been mentioned above.) It is possible that some field systems were established at this period. In the Thames flood plain at Hopton Street, Southwark, for instance, Beaker pottery was associated with a series of ard marks (Ridgeway 1999, 73–4). The evidence from Whitmoor Common (English 2000–1) and Perry Oaks (John Lewis, pers comm) is more circumstantial, though there was clearly some activity on the Heathrow terrace as demonstrated by the burial of a dismembered aurochs with six barbed-and-tanged flint arrowheads at Holloway Lane, Harmondsworth (Cotton 1991, 153–4).

Elsewhere, as at Frensham Common (Graham & Graham 2002), fieldwork has amended and occasionally supplemented the updated list of Surrey barrows published by Grinsell (1987), and provided new insights into constructional techniques and the contemporary setting of individual monuments.

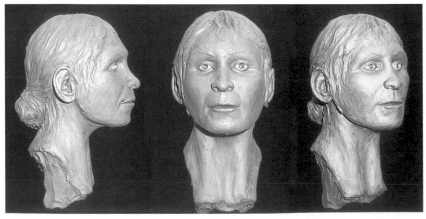

Fig 2.5b Facial reconstruction of the Shepperton woman (fig 2.5a). Study of her bones indicates that she may have been an incomer to the Thames valley and that she may have suffered a nutritional deficiency as a child. The reconstruction, by Caroline Wilkinson, emphasizes her distinctive square jawline. Photograph Museum of London

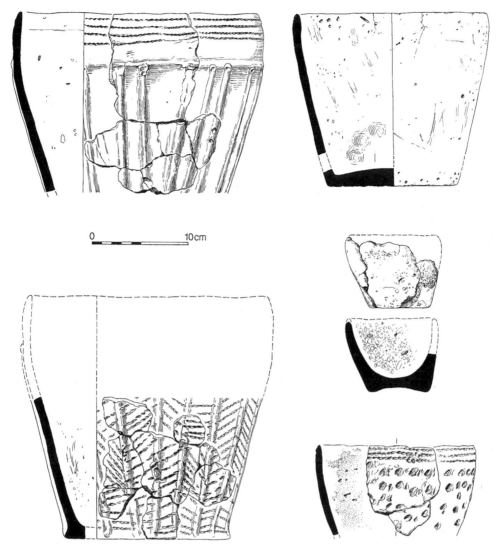

0   10cm

Fig 2.6   Franks' Sandpit, Betchworth: Grooved Ware pottery recovered from a group of three pits.
Scale 1:4. Drawing by David Williams

Only a ploughed-down bell barrow at East Molesey has produced grave goods. Here a double adult cremation (one male, one older female) accompanied by three segmented faience beads had been interred in a Secondary Series Collared Urn (Andrews & Crockett 1996, 61–4). Several small flat axes apart, no Early Bronze Age metalwork has been reported since *Surrey to 1540*. The decorated axe recovered from the Weald Clay at South Nutfield (Cotton & Williams 1997, axe B) can be added to the handful of early metalwork finds from Wealden localities (Needham 1987, 126).

Agricultural intensification:
the later Bronze Age and earliest Iron Age
(*c* 1500–600 BC)

One of the most obvious developments of this period is the proliferation of field systems along the Thames valley and in the valleys of its major tributary streams (eg Yates 1999; 2001). Some may have developed relatively early and those laid out within the Heathrow region took account of the earlier monument-dominated landscape. The setting out and subsequent development of these co-axial field systems suggests changes in the pattern of land tenure that hint in turn at wider social change. Excavations conducted on a heroic scale at Perry Oaks have begun to unravel something of the complexities involved (Barrett *et al* 2001). These have shown that the major north/south divisions pre-date the slighter east/west sub-divisions, and that several of the former were later elaborated into droveways with the addition of a second parallel ditch. Droveways presumably indicate the existence of sizeable flocks and herds (Pryor 1996), as perhaps do deep water-holes – several of which were provided with internal timber revetments and accessed by log ladders (Barrett *et al* 2001, 223–4).

Equivalent evidence on the gravels within the modern county is less extensive, but most of the constituent elements are present. A number of water-holes have furnished useful environmental data documenting the existence of scrub, open grassland and mature hedges. Several Late Bronze Age examples have also preserved otherwise rare wooden objects in their waterlogged fills, such as the maple wood bowl from Wey Manor Farm, Addlestone and a bucket base from Vicarage Road, Sunbury. The existence of these water-holes, often in the corners or at the edges of fields, is circumstantial evidence for the presence of animals, particularly cattle, though further argument is hampered by the continuing absence of good faunal assemblages, Runnymede excepted. Here, pigs were unusually well represented, and their numbers may reflect both the site environment and the special nature of the settlement (Serjeantson 1996, 219–23). The contribution made to the subsistence economy by arable farming is likewise currently difficult to assess. However, well-preserved traces of criss-cross ard marks etched into the sand islands of north Southwark and Bermondsey suggest that it could have been locally extensive, if probably short-lived (Sidell *et al* 2002, 33–8). The burial of placed deposits and acts of feasting that preceded these ploughing episodes (Ridgeway 1999, 73–4; Sidell *et al* 2002, 31) may have been a means of 'claim-staking' or socializing land prior to its formal management. (The dismembered aurochs deposit from the Heathrow gravels at Harmondsworth could be similarly interpreted.) The burial of an oak ard tip at Three Oak Lane hints at a ritual element in the termination of proceedings too (Proctor & Bishop 2002, 8–9).

Elsewhere within the county evidence is again sparse, though opportunities for large-scale excavation seldom present themselves. Elements of field systems have been surveyed in the Mickleham area and, as noted above, on Whitmoor Common, though these have yet to be tested by anything other than trial excavation. Further elements of land management have also been revealed along the foot of the North Downs at Warren Farm, Ewell (Hayman 1995) and around the headwaters of the Wandle at Beddington and Carshalton. Several sites in the latter locality have provided small assemblages of charred plant remains, including emmer, spelt, barley, rye and Celtic bean (Groves & Lovell 2002, 18; Proctor 2002, 93–4). These can be compared with the more extensive assemblages awaiting assessment and publication from Runnymede. Although saddle-querns of Wealden greensand, together with quartzite rubbers and pounders, have been recovered on the Wandle headwater sites (eg Adkins & Needham 1985, 38–9; Proctor 2002, 86–8), they are under-represented in the Thames valley. Moreover, several of those at Runnymede appear to have been used for purposes other than the grinding of grain, for example the preparation of temper for pottery making (Needham 1991, 137).

Enclosed and unenclosed Middle Bronze Age settlements seem to have been single-generation occupancies embedded within field systems. However, their presence usually has to be inferred from the greater quantities and range of 'domestic' debris caught in adjacent features, like the large groups of Deverel-Rimbury pottery recovered from ditches at Thorpe Lea Nurseries and Church Lammas, Staines, for example. Direct traces of house or other structures seldom survive (the 'roundhouse' from Wey Manor Farm, Addlestone is now interpreted as a small ring ditch encircling a cremation burial, for example (Rob Poulton, pers comm). By the Late Bronze Age there is a demonstrable increase in settlement longevity and complexity culminating in the construction of aggrandized enclosures like those on the North Downs at Queen Mary's Hospital, Carshalton and Nore Hill, Chelsham (Needham 1993). It is possible that the occupants of these sites played a pivotal role in the maintenance of long distance exchange networks and in the local movement of commodities such as salt, quern stones and metalwork (eg Yates 1999; 2001). Feasting was another of the principal ways of establishing and enhancing social status, both within the aggrandized enclosures and on lower-lying riverside sites such as Runnymede. Extensive 'midden' deposits of the type found here are increasingly widely recognized (eg Lawson 2000, 264–6). At St Philomena's School, Carshalton, an organic soil rich in finds including pottery, animal bone and metalwork had accumulated over a small circular cairn of river cobbles close to the western headwaters of the Wandle (Jeff Perry, pers comm).

Substantial post-built roundhouses of Late Bronze Age date have proved easier to find than earlier structures, and have been located on a number of the Thames valley sites. Several were furnished with elaborate entrance porches as at Petters Sports Field, Egham (Needham 1990, 115–18 & fig 34) and Home Farm, Laleham (fig 2.7). Novel rectangular structures have also been excavated at Runnymede (Needham 1993, 58–9), while the occasional four-post structure has been identified elsewhere too. Away from the Thames valley few roundhouses have been located; the circular structure defined by a simple ring gully on the edge of the river Mole flood plain at Gatwick Airport is therefore something of a rarity (Wells forthcoming). Though not as standardized as in the Iron Age (Poulton, in this volume), entrance orientation appears to have been carefully chosen. This may reflect adherence to the same set of cosmologies that governed the placement of human remains in the ditches of earlier hengiforms and barrows.

The supernatural was drawn down into other aspects of everyday life as well. This is most obviously demonstrated by the careful placement in and around settlements of cremated and occasionally unburnt human bone and of other special finds such as metalwork, pottery vessels and quern stones (eg Brück 1999). Although no new Middle Bronze Age urn cemeteries have been found within the county

Fig 2.7   Home Farm, Laleham: a Late Bronze Age post-built roundhouse with a substantial porch. Photograph Surrey County Archaeological Unit

since *Surrey to 1540*, un-urned cremation burials have been recorded during large-scale work on the gravels at sites such as Wey Manor Farm, Addlestone, and Home Farm, Laleham. One lay within a small ring-ditch on the former site (Rob Poulton, pers comm). The majority remain undated, though it seems likely that many if not most will fall within the Late Bronze Age, a period hitherto regarded as lacking a normative burial rite (see Brück 1995). Unburnt human bone is scarcer, but comprises several skulls, including one Late Bronze Age example from Runnymede that may have been displayed on a pole. Numbers of skulls were also consigned to the Thames (eg Bradley & Gordon 1988) along with other objects such as metalwork.

That water was an important cosmological referent is suggested by the careful deposition of a wide range of objects, but no metalwork, in the water-holes on inland settlements. Some of these probably represent event-marking offerings that referenced the passage of time and even the distant past. For example, a wooden haft for a socketed bronze axe was placed in a water-hole at Perry Oaks along with a Cornish-type stone axe anything up to two millennia older (Barrett *et al* 2001, 224). Others seem to have been rooted in the promotion of fertility in crops and animals, and productivity in the material world. These included the saddle-querns, briquetage and wild and domesticated animals buried in several pits at Westcroft Road, Carshalton (Proctor 2002), and the saddle-quern and rubber buried right-way-up in a pit at Hengrove Farm, near Staines (Rob Poulton, pers comm). Topographic high points also attracted special deposits. At Betchworth a metalled track skirted a locally elevated

greensand ridge on which a series of deposits had been buried including an in-urned cremation burial and a spiral bronze ring (David Williams, pers comm). These appear to have renewed or endorsed the sanctity of a long-used location: earlier finds included pits containing Grooved Ware (see above), while the same spot was later occupied by a Roman enclosure of curious D-shaped form (Williams 1998b). Bronze Age metalwork from the vicinity of the Farley Heath Roman temple may hint at similar devotional longevity (Rob Poulton, pers comm). Furthermore, other topographic highs including St Ann's Hill, Chertsey (Phil Jones, pers comm), Kingston Hill (Field & Needham 1986) and Priory Park, Reigate (Williams 1994; 1996b) were also used for the deposition of metal finds including tools and occasionally weaponry (see below for finds on the North Downs chalk).

The disposal of bronze metalwork in the river and on land represents the most visible end of a wide spectrum of non-utilitarian behaviour. The steady upsurge of Middle and Late Bronze Age weapon deposition in the Thames has attracted much attention and could in part be explained as a 'coping mechanism' adopted by communities faced with environmental stress in the form of rising river levels. It is possible that this found expression in the enactment of competitive 'potlatch'-type ceremonies and/or funerary rituals (eg Bradley 1990). However see Needham (2001, 275–7) for a critical assessment of recent theoretical developments. Either way, the substantial Middle Bronze Age pile-driven wooden structure close to the contemporary tidal head at Vauxhall (fig 2.8) is likely to have been of special

Fig 2.8   Nine Elms, Vauxhall: the Middle Bronze Age timber 'bridge' or jetty on the Thames foreshore. Photograph Museum of London

relevance. First, it furnishes a fresh perspective on the dynamics of human movement within and across the flood plain, as do the wooden trackways located further downstream (Meddens 1996). Secondly it provides an obvious means by which offerings could have been physically (and perhaps conspicuously) deposited in the waters of the Thames. Satisfyingly, a pair of Middle Bronze Age side-looped spearheads was found pushed, tips down, among the landward piles (Cotton & Wood 1996, 14–16 & fig 7 nos 22 a & b). Furthermore, structures similar to the Vauxhall example have been reported elsewhere, as at Test-wood Lakes, Hampshire, and Shinewater Marsh near Eastbourne, East Sussex. Other recent metal-work finds from Surrey reaches of the river include a fragment of a Middle Bronze Age composite gold ring from Wandsworth (Cotton & Wood 1996, 16 & fig 9, no 23), which fills something of a gap in the distribution of findspots between Sussex and East Anglia. The suggested link between the locally shifting tidal head and the pattern of metal deposition in the river (Needham & Burgess 1980, 452, fig 7) offers a tantalizing avenue of enquiry which may be easier to pursue now that an independent dating framework for Middle and Late Bronze Age metal-work is in place (Needham *et al* 1997).

Away from the Thames new finds of metalwork encompass tools, weaponry and ornaments including the group of three plain Middle Bronze Age armlets of Liss/Bignan type from Cranleigh (Huson 1999), a rare occurrence in the Weald (Needham 1987, 114). Late Bronze Age founder's hoards of Carp's Tongue/Ewart Park type have been recovered from elevated positions on the North Downs along the

Hog's Back (English 2002) and at Little Woodcote, Carshalton (Cotton & Needham 1999), for example, while scatters of often fragmentary metal objects have been located just off the chalk at Bletchingley and Ewell. The Little Woodcote hoard in particular is one of the largest to have been recovered from the county and falls within Needham's (1987, 120) eastern North Downs group. Analysis of its contents has revealed evidence of technological novelty (fig 2.9), while comparison with other caches from the North Downs and beyond hints at the existence of subtle patterns in hoard composition.

Some researchers have interpreted the widespread hoarding or non-recovery of bronze at the end of the Bronze Age as evidence of its obsolescence in the face of new (iron) technology. It remains to be determined whether this is so or whether – as is more likely – it represents a combination of factors: social, spiritual and even climatic, as well as economic and/or tech-nological. What is apparent, however, is that areas of the country such as the Thames valley and the Fenlands undergo a phase of desertion and depopula-tion in the earlier part of the Iron Age compared with the Late Bronze Age (eg Thomas 1999). When activity picks up again in the Middle Iron Age, it does so on a different scale and often in different places, as Rob Poulton's contribution to this volume suggests. Thereafter, it is the adoption (or not) of new Gallic and/or Roman identities by certain individuals in the period leading up to the conquest of AD 43 that is one of the determining characteristics of parts of the South East (eg James 1999, 96–100; Hill 2001). Why the inhabitants of the London region (including Surrey) seemingly chose not to engage in this process

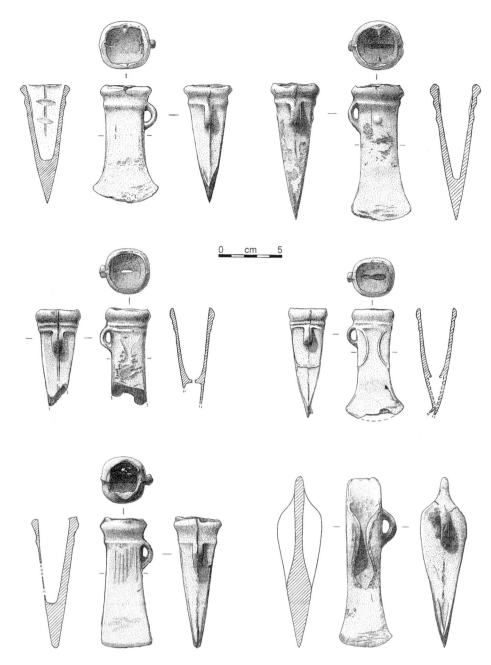

Fig 2.9   Little Woodcote, Carshalton: examples of Late Bronze Age socketed axes and a winged axe from the 129-piece hoard. Several of the axes, like the two wing-decorated forms in the middle row with hollow cavities at the blade-edge, display technological novelty. Scale 1:3. Drawing by David Williams

is an interesting question, and one that may even help to explain the siting of Roman Londinium itself (eg Millett 1990, 89).

Conclusion:
a future for Surrey's early past

Rob Poulton's paper obviates the need for any extended treatment of the centuries leading up to the Roman conquest. However, one or two more general points ought to be drawn together here.

Much new data has been generated since the publication of *Surrey to 1540*, but this inevitably reflects the concentration of development-driven projects conducted in the north of the county. As a result, the archaeology of the Thames gravels is well

represented and increasingly well understood. Large-scale work conducted on a number of sites has revealed elements of a now characteristic sequence of land use involving, in turn, localized hunter-gatherer interventions, wildwood clearance, construction and maintenance of monuments and the adoption, intensification and, ultimately, reorganization of agricultural practices. How applicable this sequence is to other geologies and topographies remains to be seen. Ironically, the Thames inter-tidal zone and the river itself are only just beginning to attract corresponding levels of research inspired by the success of the Thames Archaeological Survey (Milne *et al* 1997; Webber 1999).

Away from the river and the valleys of its tributary streams, the picture is patchier – though not without successes as the fieldwork undertaken around and beyond the Wandle headwaters is demonstrating (eg Groves & Lovell 2002; Proctor 2002; Jeff Perry, pers comm). The greensand, long dominated by lithic scatters, is starting to produce distinctive sites of its own, as at Betchworth, Bletchingley, Merstham and, most recently, Westcott (Rapson 2003), though opportunities for large-scale excavation remain limited. The Weald too is becoming better known (eg Gardiner 1990), and not just as an area likely to furnish evidence of iron working (for which see Hodgkinson in this volume). Recent fieldwork at Outwood, for instance, has demonstrated a considerable and perhaps continuous human presence on the Weald Clay from the early part of the Mesolithic onwards (Robin Tanner, pers comm), though the nature of this presence remains debatable. In certain other Wealden areas, however, the local picture can be brought into sharper focus, as on the edge of the Mole flood plain at Gatwick where a small partially enclosed settlement was engaged in mixed agriculture during the Late Bronze Age (Wells forthcoming). Palaeolithic sites on the deposits mapped as 'Clay-with-Flints' and Late Bronze Age activity in the Croydon zone apart, our understanding of the ways in which the North Downs were used remains surprisingly obscure until later prehistory, when field systems and settlements start to proliferate east of the Mole (eg Batchelor 1990; Hayman 1996; Cotton 2001). Fieldwork conducted by the Community Archaeology Project and the Plateau Group offers hope for the future hereabouts, though so far survey work on the Bagshot Table away to the north-west has tended only to confirm the absence of later prehistoric activity (Rob Poulton, pers comm).

Overall, there is a need for better definition of the topographic and environmental settings of sites, wherever located. Properly integrated multi-disciplinary work of the sort undertaken on the sand islands of Southwark and Bermondsey (Sidell et al 2002; Ridgeway 2003), and on the greensand at Frensham (Graham & Graham 2002) and Bletchingley (Hayman et al 2003) offers a way forward. Site-specific localities that would benefit from new surveys and further problem-oriented fieldwork should be identified, as has been successfully done at Lower Kingswood, for example. A published audit of the county's available aerial photographs is long overdue too, for nothing of the sort has been drawn together since David Longley's survey of the north-west Surrey gravels nearly 30 years ago (Longley 1976). Elsewhere, predictive modelling strategies could be developed and adopted, perhaps along the lines advocated by Bates & Bates (2000). The ultimate goal would be the identification of surface-intact sites where the preservation of good environmental and subsistence data might be anticipated with reasonable confidence. This would allow the development of more sophisticated behavioural explanations, as at Runnymede Bridge, for example (Needham & Spence 1996).

Questions of resource procurement, subsistence strategies/economies and the manipulation of the environment should be more explicitly addressed (as Gamble et al 1999, 5). The assessment and publication of existing botanical and faunal assemblages are central to this undertaking, and should be aided by the impending environmental archaeology project to be hosted by Royal Holloway College (Nick Branch, pers comm). Greater and more imaginative use could also be made of lithic use-wear and lipid analysis to amplify this data, alongside study of stable isotopes and ancient human DNA. Assessment of the many unpublished lithic collections from across the county is another urgent requirement, as is the identification and management of the county's surviving lithic scatters (eg English Heritage 2000). Detailed studies of lithic resource procurement and exploitation would undoubtedly shed new light on social practices, as would, for example, programmes of petrographic analysis of quern stones and pottery. There are enough excavated ceramic assemblages for the county to contribute meaningfully to a dated regional pottery sequence too. Indeed, the development of a sounder chronology is a prerequisite across the board, as is the need to bring various important backlog projects through to publication.

Finally, it is important to assess Surrey's archaeology on its own merits, rather than attempt to fit it into any preconceived system imported from Wessex, London or elsewhere. The regionality of the evidence is its strength and should be appreciated as such (eg Hill 1999). Moreover, while any local research framework ought to take account of national and regional questions, it should not be prescriptive but flexible (and realistic) enough to accommodate serendipity and imaginative local initiatives. It ought also to be kept under regular review. The formulation of an achievable series of research initiatives constitutes a major sesquicentennial challenge for the Surrey Archaeological Society. It is a challenge to which all those committed to studying the county's early past must now rise.

ANNEXE

Prehistoric sites and finds reported from administrative Surrey since 1987

This Gazetteer incorporates sites and finds of Palaeolithic to Bronze Age date reported from modern administrative Surrey since 1987, arranged chronologically in alphabetical order by topographic zone. Sites and finds in metropolitan Surrey are not included as they have been summarized recently elsewhere (eg MoLAS 2000; Haynes *et al* 2000; Sidell *et al* 2002). Numbers in brackets after some entries refer to the SyAS *Bulletin* in which the site or find was first published.

The following abbreviations have been used: LUP = Late Upper Palaeolithic; EMES = Early Mesolithic; LMES = Late Mesolithic; ENEO = Earlier Neolithic; LNEO = Later Neolithic; EBA = Early Bronze Age; MBA = Middle Bronze Age; LBA = Late Bronze Age; EIA = Early Iron Age.

Early scavengers and hunters: the Lower and Middle Palaeolithic

THE FARNHAM AREA

Farnham, Bourne Woods (Terrace 'A'), flake tool (**353**) (Howe *et al* 2002, 269)

Farnham area, bifaces (Fulbrook House Coll, Charterhouse School Museum)

THE NORTH DOWNS PLATEAU AND HIGH LEVEL GRAVELS AND BRICKEARTHS

Banstead, Tattenham Way allotments, twisted biface, biface roughout and débitage (Harp 2000a & pers comm)

Burgh Heath, Canons Farm, pointed and twisted bifaces and débitage (Harp 2002a & pers comm; Howe *et al* 2002, 262–3)

Burgh Heath, Tangier Wood, large pointed biface (Harp 1999a)

Godstone, Church Town, biface (Cotton 2002)

Limpsfield area, pointed and twisted ovate bifaces, flakes/flake tools (Bird *et al* 1989, 182; Bird *et al* 1990, 214; Field *et al* 1999)

Lower Kingswood, Rookery Farm, small pointed bifaces, flakes/flake tools and a Levallois core (Harp 2002a & pers comm; Howe *et al* 2002, 262)

Worms Heath, Chelsham, pointed biface (Field *et al* 1990, 141, fig 8, no 75)

ISOLATED SITES

Outwood area, fragmentary bifaces and flakes (**358**) (Robin Tanner, pers comm)

Anatomically modern hunters: the Upper Palaeolithic and Mesolithic

THE WEALD

Charlwood, LMES site (Ellaby, forthcoming)

Horley, Haroldslea, LMES site (Roger Ellaby, pers comm)

Outwood area, multiple sites of EMES and LMES date (Robin Tanner, pers comm)

THE GREENSAND HILLS

Bletchingley, North Park Farm Quarry, pits and topographic hollow, EMES–LMES date (Rob Poulton, pers comm)

Elstead, Hankley Common, Kettlebury 103, EMES site on Folkestone Beds (**310**) (Jackson *et al* 1997, 216; Reynier 2002)

Reigate Common, EMES site (Roger Ellaby, pers comm)

THE NORTH DOWNS

Banstead, Banstead Heath, flint adze (Harp 2002b; Howe *et al* 2002, 262)

Banstead, Canons Farm, flint adze (Harp 2000b)

Banstead, Preston Hawe, flint adze and other core tools (**224**) (Bird *et al* 1989, 180)

Banstead, Tattenham Way allotments, flint adze, and sharpening flakes in pit (**317**; **319**; **323**; **324**; Peter Harp, pers comm)

Banstead, Tumble Beacon, flint adzes (**314**; **317**; **319**)

Chipstead, Netherne on the hill, pit with struck flint (**337**) (Howe *et al* 2000, 191)

Headley, Headley Heath, flint axe and pick (Harp 2002b; Howe *et al* 2002, 261)

West Humble, Burford Bridge, flint adze (**341**) (Howe *et al* 2001, 345)

THE LONDON CLAY

Ashtead, LUP backed blade (Nicolaysen 1989)

THE BAGSHOT TABLE

Horsell, Brockhill, Parley Bridge, LUP site (**314**) (Cox 1976; Bonsall 1977; Barton 1992; Jackson *et al* 1999, 240)

THE THAMES VALLEY AND ITS TRIBUTARIES

Guildford, Woodbridge Road, LMES site (Peter Moore & Barry Bishop, pers comm)

Staines, Church Lammas, LUP 'long blade' site (**296**) (Jackson *et al* 1997, 211)

Staines, 10–16 London Road, LMES pits (Hayman 2001; Rob Poulton, pers comm)

STRUCK FLINT SCATTERS (MESOLITHIC AND NEOLITHIC INTO BRONZE AGE)

Abinger, Cocks Farm, greensand (Pat Nicolaysen, pers comm)

Abinger/Holmbury transect, greensand, estimated 25,000 struck flints (**230**) (Bird *et al* 1990, 206)

Albury Park, greensand (**275**) (Bird *et al* 1996, 195)

Alfold, Great Wildwood Farm, Weald Clay, four scatters from: Rannett Hill; Waste Water Field; Little Hammer Wood Field; Further Rickett Close (**255**) (Bird *et al* 1991–2, 156–7; Bird *et al* 1994, 211)

Banstead, Banstead Heath, North Downs (Howe *et al* 2001, 346)

Banstead, Canons Farm, North Downs (Harp 2000c)

Banstead, Tattenham Way, North Downs (**317**; **319**; **323**; **324**) (Jackson *et al* 1999, 227; Howe *et al* 2000, 190; Howe *et al* 2002, 262)

Cranleigh, Bridge Farm, Weald Clay, (**335**); other scatters from: Snoxhall; Knowle; Lower Canfold Wood; Vachery High Park; Rydinghurst; Collins Farm; Wales Wood (**245**) (Bird *et al* 1990, 216)

Esso Oil Pipeline, Weald Clay (Cotton & Poulton 1990)

Godalming, Mint Street, greensand (Poulton 1998, 178)

Guildford, Ladymead, Stoke, London Clay (**223**) (Bird *et al* 1989, 180)

Holmbury Hill, greensand (Barfoot & Cotton 1989)

Laleham, Home Farm, Thames gravels (Bird *et al* 1996, 200–1)

Outwood locality, Weald Clay (Robin Tanner, pers comm)

Thursley Common, greensand (Graham *et al* 1999) (**305**)

Walls Collection, scatters from various localities in Ewell, from the North Downs at Walton Heath and Lower Kingswood and from the greensand at Albury, Wotton, Betchworth and Buckland (**278**) (Bird *et al* 1996, 187)

Worms Heath and Slines Oak, Chelsham, North Downs (Field *et al* 1990)

Wotton Estate, greensand (**275**) (Bird *et al* 1996, 195)

Creating new worlds: the Neolithic and Earlier Bronze Age

THE WEALD

Lingfield, ground flint axe (**263**) (Bird *et al* 1994, 210)

South Nutfield, EBA low-flanged bronze axe (Cotton & Williams 1997)

THE GREENSAND HILLS

Abinger, Raikes Farm, flint knife (**357**)

Betchworth, Franks' Sandpit, Peterborough Ware and Grooved Ware pottery, pits and flintwork (**300**; **307**; **324**) (Jackson *et al* 1997, 206 & fig 4)

Betchworth, ENEO leaf shaped arrowhead (Williams 1996a, 167)

Elstead, Bagmoor Common, LNEO oblique flint arrowhead (**339**) (Howe *et al* 2001, 350)

Elstead, Thursley Common, turf-built barrow (**298**) (Jackson *et al* 1997, 217)

Frensham Common, Warren Hill, barrow (Jackson *et al* 1999, 238; Graham & Graham 2002)

Merstham, Battlebridge Lane, Peterborough and Grooved Ware pottery, pits and flintwork (**340**)

Reigate, Park Lane, EBA barbed-and-tanged flint arrowhead (Bird *et al* 1991–2, 150; Williams 1994)

Reigate, Priory Park, EBA barbed-and-tanged flint arrowhead (Williams 1994)

Reigate Heath, further possible barrow(s) (Jackson *et al* 1999, 226)

Witley Common, further possible barrow (Jackson *et al* 1999, 239)

THE NORTH DOWNS

Ashtead, Esso HQ, pottery (? Peterborough Ware) (Bird *et al* 1990, 207; Hayman 1991–2, 9)

Banstead, Tumble Beacon, flints from barrow but no evidence of turf lines (**304**; **320**) (Harp 1999d; Jackson *et al* 1999, 227)

Clandon, blade of ground flint axe (Williams 1996a, 167)

Ewell, Churchyard no 5, ENEO leaf-shaped flint arrowhead (**346**)

Ewell, King William IV public house, beaker (? disturbed burial) (Orton 1997)

Headley, Headley Heath, ENEO leaf-shaped flint arrowhead (Howe *et al* 2002, 261)

Kingswood, stone macehead (Williams 1990)

Lower Kingswood, Rookery Farm, flint arrowheads of LNEO transverse and EBA barbed-and-tanged form (**355**) (Harp 2002c, 30; Howe *et al* 2002, 262)

Lower Kingswood, Sandy Lane, ENEO leaf-shaped flint arrowhead (Harp 2000d)

Mickleham Downs, possible barrow sites (**345**) (Howe *et al* 2000, 189)

Walton Heath, ground axe fragment (Harp 1999c; Jackson *et al* 1999, 226)

Winterfold Heath, EBA flint dagger (**231**) (Bird *et al* 1989, 185; Bird *et al* 1990, 216)

Woldingham, Botley Hill, flaked flint axe (**341**) (Howe *et al* 2001, 349); flint knife (**280**) (Bird *et al* 1996, 203); EBA miniature flat bronze axe (Cotton & Williams 1997)

Woodmansterne area, flint arrowheads of various forms (Harp 2002c; Howe *et al* 2002, 263)

THE LONDON CLAY

Chessington, partially ground flint adze (Field 2000)

THE BAGSHOT TABLE

Chobham, Longcross Estate, ground flint axe (Cotton 1994)

Horsell, Mizen's Farm, gullies and ditches (**321**) (Jackson *et al* 1999, 240)

Lightwater, South Farm, EBA barbed-and-tanged flint arrowhead (**253**) (Bird *et al* 1991–2, 155)

Wisley and Ockham Commons, possible barrow sites (**333**) (Howe *et al* 2000, 188)

THE THAMES VALLEY AND ITS TRIBUTARIES

Ashford, Woodthorpe Road, hengiform monument with Peterborough Ware (Tim Carew pers comm; Howe *et al* 2002, 267 & fig 4)

Chertsey, Crown Hotel, bifacially-worked LNEO oblique arrowhead (Jones 1998, 47)

East Molesey, Hurst Park, EBA ring ditch with cremations in Collared Urn with three segmented faience beads (**292**) (Andrews & Crockett 1996; Jackson *et al* 1997, 197 & fig 1); EBA barbed-and-tanged flint arrowhead (Howe *et al* 2002, 258)

Egham, Thorpe Lea Nurseries, Peterborough Ware sherd and struck flint (Jackson *et al* 1997, 209)

Farnham, The Bourne, EBA plano-convex flint knife (**304**) (Jackson *et al* 1999, 238)

Farnham, Green Lane, EBA flat bronze axe (**225**) (Graham 1989)

Queen Mary Reservoir, south-west, occupation (Bird *et al* 1991–2, 155)

Shepperton, The Margins, animal bone (some worked) and two human skulls from buried river channels (**279**; **282**; **289**) (Bird *et al* 1996, 201; Jackson *et al* 1997, 211)

Shepperton, Sheep Walk, flint axe (Bird *et al* 1990, 211)

Shepperton, Staines Road Farm, ENEO hengiform monument, LNEO water-hole and cooking pit (Bird *et al* 1990, 211 & figs 4 & 5; Jones 1990)

Staines, 42–54 London Road, EBA pit containing a fragment of Collared Urn (**337**) (Howe *et al* 2000, 195)

Staines, Hengrove Farm, isolated feature (Howe *et al* 2000, 195); pit containing a nearly complete Peterborough Ware bowl (Howe *et al* 2002, 267)

Stanwell, Lower Mill Farm, blade of ground axe (**265**) (Bird *et al* 1991–2, 153); midden deposit (**261**) (Bird *et al* 1994, 208)

Stanwell, Park Road, ENEO cursus monument (O'Connell 1990)

Thorpe, Coldharbour Lane, E/MBA ring ditch with inhumations (**355**) (Howe *et al* 2002, 263 & fig 1)

Agricultural intensification: the Later Bronze Age and Earliest Iron Age

THE WEALD

Cranleigh, hoard of three plain MBA bronze armlets (Huson 1999)

THE GREENSAND HILLS

Abinger area, M/LBA pottery scatter (some sherds possibly earlier) (**220**) (Bird *et al* 1989, 180; Keith Winser, pers comm)

Albury, tip of MBA bronze rapier (Williams 1999a, 171)

Albury, Weston Wood, LBA pottery assemblage from settlement (Russell 1989)

Betchworth, fragment of LBA bronze sword blade (Williams 1996a, 167)

Betchworth, Franks' Sandpit, LBA/EIA features including pits and a rutted metalled track (**300**) (Jackson *et al* 1997, 206 & fig 4)

Bletchingley, LBA bronze scrap including fragments of swords and a winged axe (Williams 1996a, 167; 1999a, 171)

Bletchingley, Little Pickle, pottery and LBA bronze metalwork including fragments of winged and socketed axes and ingots (Williams 1998a)

Bletchingley, Place Farm, LBA/EIA pottery (including a virtually complete jar containing burnt flints) and struck flint (Jackson *et al* 1999, 234)

Buckland area, MBA basal-looped bronze spearhead (**290**) (Jackson *et al* 1997, 207; Williams 1999b)

Elstead, Bagmoor Common, fragment of MBA bronze palstave axe (**339**) (Howe *et al* 2001, 350–2)

Peper Harow, MBA bronze palstave axe (**330**) (Howe *et al* 2000, 199; Williams 2001, 309)

Reigate, Priory Park, LBA pottery and bronze metalwork including three socketed axes, a socketed gouge, ingot fragments and a barbed spearhead (**241**) (Bird *et al* 1990, 208; Williams 1994; 1996b; 1999a)

Shamley Green, Alderbrook Main Pipeline, LBA/EIA pottery over a buried soil sealing a row of possible postholes (Jackson *et al* 1999, 240)

THE NORTH DOWNS

Ashtead, Esso HQ, MBA pottery and struck flint (Hayman 1991–2, 9)

Banstead, Perrott's Farm, two LBA socketed bronze axes (Williams 1991–2)

Ewell, Bourne Hall Lake, LBA socketed bronze axe (David Brooks & Jeremy Harte, pers comm)

Ewell, Howell Hill and Seymour's Nursery, LBA metalwork including a vase-headed pin (**300**) (Jackson et al 1999, 220)

Ewell, Warren Farm, MBA side-looped bronze spearhead (David Brooks & Jeremy Harte, pers comm)

Gatton, LBA bronze awl (Williams 1996a, 167)

Godstone, EBA bronze rivet from a halberd or dirk (Williams 2001, 309)

Headley, Cherkley Wood, burnt flint, M/LBA pottery and animal bone (Harp 1999e)

Hog's Back, LBA bronze metalwork hoard (English 2002)

Hooley, fragment of LBA socketed bronze axe (Williams 1996a, 167)

Walton Heath, LBA socketed bronze axe (Harp 1999c; Jackson et al 1999, 226)

THE LONDON CLAY

Ashtead Common area, MBA side-looped bronze spearhead (Cotton 1999)

Epsom, Manor Hospital, shallow pits containing LBA/EIA pottery and struck flint (**310**) (Jackson et al 1999, 219; Saunders 2000)

Guildford, Manor Farm, ditches, LBA pottery and struck flint (**326**; **330**; **331**; **332**) (Howe et al 2000, 186)

THE BAGSHOT TABLE

Worplesdon, Whitmoor Common, field system (**342**) (Jackson et al 1999, 223; English 2000–1)

THE THAMES VALLEY AND ITS TRIBUTARIES

Addlestone, former Marconi Site, LBA/EIA enclosures, pits, water-hole, pottery and loomweights (**358**) (Howe et al 2002, 265)

Addlestone, Wey Manor Farm, MBA barrow with central cremation inside a sinuous enclosure ditch (**326**; **348**) (Howe et al 2000, 192; Howe et al 2001, 346; Rob Poulton, pers comm)

Chertsey, Abbey Meads, human skull on shoreline adjacent to LBA settlement (Bird et al 1989, 181)

Chertsey, St Ann's Hill, LBA/EIA (and later) pottery and features inside the univallate hillfort (Bird et al 1989, 181; Bird et al 1991–2, 153) (For new survey of earthworks see McOmish & Field 1994)

East Molesey, Hurst Park, LBA field system and two settlement areas defined by pits (**292**) (Andrews & Crockett 1996; Jackson et al 1997, 197)

Egham, The Avenue, LBA/IA pottery and other finds in buried river channel (Bird et al 1990, 209–10)

Egham, 64–65 High Street, features containing LBA/EIA pottery (Howe et al 2000, 192)

Egham, Thorpe Lea Nurseries, MBA ditch containing a large assemblage of pottery, together with two small LBA settlement foci defined by pits (Bird et al 1991–2, 153; Bird et al 1996, 199)

Farnham, The Fairfield, EIA bronze brooch of 'leech' form (**299**) (Jackson et al 1999, 238)

Laleham, Home Farm, M/LBA ditches, pits, water-holes, post-built roundhouse, cremations (**262**; **311**; **320**; **321**; **348**) (Bird et al 1994, 208; Jackson et al 1997, 211; Jackson et al 1999, 230; Howe et al 2000, 192–3; Howe et al 2001, 348)

Ripley, Papercourt Farm, Wey gravels, MBA bronze palstave axe (Cotton & Williams 2000)

Staines, Church Lammas, M/LBA enclosure (Bird et al 1991–2, 153; Bird et al 1994, 207 & fig 2)

Staines, Hengrove Farm, M/LBA field system (**337**) and pits (Howe et al 2002, 267)

Staines, Central Trading Estate, LBA ditch system on higher sand islands (Jackson et al 1999, 232)

Staines, 2–8 High Street, LBA activity (Jackson et al 1997, 212)

Staines, Tilly's Lane West, LBA field system and/or flood defences (Howe et al 2001, 347)

Stanwell, Bedfont, Cargo Point, M/LBA ditches (? field system) and pits (**319**; **322**) (Jackson et al 1999, 233)

Stanwell, Park Road, M/LBA field system and water-holes (O'Connell 1990)

Sunbury, Vicarage Road, LBA ditches and water-holes (**278**) (Bird et al 1996, 201 & fig 5; Jackson et al 1999, 231)

Wrecclesham area, eight miniature socketed axes said to have been found (Bird et al 1994, 210)

ACKNOWLEDGEMENTS

Particular thanks are due to a number of people who have freely provided much of the information on which this summary is based. They include:

David Bird, Barry Bishop, Nick Branch, Paul Budd, Tim Carew, Peter Connelly, Simon Deeves, Roger Ellaby, Nick Elsden, Fiona Haughey, Graham Hayman, Peter Harp, Gary Jackson, Roger Jacobi, Richard Jewell, Phil Jones, Ken Lansdowne, John Lewis, Lorraine Mepham, Peter Moore, Jeff Perry, Rob Poulton, Gabby Rapson, Julie Scott-Jackson, Jane Sidell, Robin Tanner, Caroline Wilkinson and David Williams.

Further thanks are due to a number of the above for reading and commenting on the draft manuscript. None of them is complicit in any errors, misrepresentations or misunderstandings that may be contained herein, however; those remain the sole responsibility of the author.

BIBLIOGRAPHY

Please note that where Surrey County Archaeological Unit (SCAU) client reports are referred to they are available either through the Surrey Archaeological Society library at Guildford or through the Sites and Monuments Record (SMR) at County Hall, Kingston.

Adkins, L, & Needham, S, 1985 New research on a Late Bronze Age enclosure at Queen Mary's Hospital, Carshalton, *SyAC*, **76,** 11–50

Andrews, P, & Crockett, A, 1996 *Three excavations along the Thames and its tributaries, 1994*, Wessex Archaeol Rep, **10**

Ashton, N, Healy, F, & Pettitt, P (eds), 1998 *Stone Age archaeology: essays in honour of John Wymer,* Oxford: Oxbow Monogr, **102,** Lithic Stud Soc Occas Pap, **6**

Bagwell, M, Bishop, B, & Gibson, A, 2001 Mesolithic and Late Bronze Age activity at London Road, Beddington, *SyAC,* **88,** 289–307

Barfoot, J, & Cotton, J, 1989 A collection of lithic débitage from the Lower Greensand at Holmbury Hill, *SyAC,* **79,** 147–60

Barrett, J C, Lewis, J S C, & Welsh, K, 2000 Perry Oaks – a history of inhabitation, *London Archaeol,* **9.7,** 195–9

——, 2001 Perry Oaks – a history of inhabitation, part 2, *London Archaeol*, **9.8**, 221–7

Barton, R N E, 1992 Hengistbury Head, Dorset. Volume 2: The Late Upper Palaeolithic and Early Mesolithic sites, Oxford Univ Comm Archaeol Monogr, **34**

——, 1997 *Stone Age Britain*, B T Batsford/English Heritage

——, 1998 Long blade technology and the question of British Late Pleistocene/Early Holocene lithic assemblages, in Ashton *et al* 1998, 158–64

Batchelor, G, 1990 'Friends, Romans, School children!' – archaeology and education in Croydon, *London Archaeol*, **6.8,** 199–205

Bates, M R, & Bates, C R, 2000 Multidisciplinary approaches to the geoarchaeological evaluation of deeply stratified sedimentary sequences: examples from Pleistocene and Holocene deposits in southern England, *J Archaeol Sci*, **27**, 845–58

Bird, D G, Crocker, G, & McCracken, J S, 1989 Archaeology in Surrey 1987, *SyAC*, **79**, 179–89

——, 1990 Archaeology in Surrey 1988–1989, *SyAC*, **80**, 201–27

——, 1991–2 Archaeology in Surrey 1990, *SyAC*, **81**, 147–67

Bird, D G, Crocker, G, McCracken, J S, & Saich, D, 1994 Archaeology in Surrey 1991, *SyAC*, **82**, 203–19

Bird, D G, Crocker, G, Maloney, C, & Saich, D, 1996 Archaeology in Surrey 1992–3, *SyAC*, **83**, 187–228

Bird, J, & Bird, D G (eds), 1987 *The archaeology of Surrey to 1540*, SyAS

Bonsall, C, 1977 Woking: near Parley Bridge, Horsell, *SyAS Bull*, **139**, 4

Bradley, R, 1990 *The passage of arms: an archaeological analysis of prehistoric hoards and votive deposits*, Cambridge

Bradley, R, & Gordon, K, 1988 Human skulls from the river Thames, their dating and significance, *Antiquity*, **62**, 503–9

Bridgland, D R, 1994 Dating of Lower Palaeolithic industries within the framework of the lower Thames terrace sequence, in *Stories in stone* (eds N Ashton & A David), Lithic Stud Soc Occas Pap, **4**, 28–40

Brück, J, 1995 A place for the dead: the role of human remains in Late Bronze Age Britain, *Proc Prehist Soc*, **61**, 245–77

——, 1999 Houses, lifecycles and deposition on Middle Bronze Age settlements in southern England, *Proc Prehist Soc*, **65**, 145–66

Carpenter, L W, 1952 A Mesolithic site near Leatherhead, *Proc Leatherhead Dist Local Hist Soc*, **1.6**, 5–11

Cotton, J, 1991 Prehistory in Greater London, *Current Archaeol*, **124**, 151–4

——, 1994 A Neolithic ground flint axe from the Longcross Estate, near Chobham, Runnymede District, *SyAC*, **82**, 225–6

——, 1999 A Middle Bronze Age side-looped spearhead from Ashtead, *SyAC*, **86**, 199–200

——, 2000 Foragers and farmers: towards the development of a settled landscape in London, *c* 4000–1200 BC, in Haynes *et al* 2000, 9–34

——, 2001 Prehistoric and Roman settlement in Reigate Road, Ewell: fieldwork conducted by Tom K Walls 1945–52, *SyAC*, **88**, 1–42

——, 2002 A Palaeolithic flint biface from Church Town, Godstone, *SyAC*, **89**, 233–6

Cotton, J, & Field, D (eds), forthcoming *Towards a New Stone Age: aspects of the Neolithic in South-East England*, CBA

Cotton, J, & Needham, S, 1999 A Late Bronze Age metalwork hoard from Little Woodcote, *SyAS Bull*, **329**, 4–6

Cotton, J, & Poulton, R, 1990 The Esso pipeline 1981: archaeological observations, *SyAC*, **80**, 161–6

Cotton, J, & Williams, D, 1997 Two Early Bronze Age flat axes from Woldingham and South Nutfield, *SyAC*, **84**, 181–4

——, 2000 A palaeolith and a palstave from the Wey valley near Ripley, *SyAC*, **87**, 179–81

Cotton, J, & Wood, B, 1996 Recent prehistoric finds from the Thames foreshore and beyond in Greater London, *Trans London Middlesex Archaeol Soc*, **47**, 1–33

Cox, N, 1976 Woking: Brockhill, near Parley Bridge, Horsell, *SyAS Bull*, **126**

David, A, 1998 Two assemblages of Later Mesolithic microliths from Seamer Carr, North Yorkshire: fact and fancy, in Ashton *et al* 1998, 196–204

Donahue, R, 2002 Microwear analysis, in Sidell *et al* 2002, 83–4

Ellaby, R, 1987 The Upper Palaeolithic and Mesolithic in Surrey, in Bird & Bird 1987, 53–69

——, forthcoming Food for thought: a late Mesolithic site at Charlwood, Surrey, in Cotton & Field forthcoming

English, J, 2000–1 Whitmoor Common, Worplesdon – a proposed Area of Special Historic Landscape Value, *Surrey Historic Landscape Stud Newsl*, **16**, 6–12

——, 2002 A hoard of Late Bronze Age metalwork from the Hog's Back, near Guildford, *SyAC*, **89**, 249–50

English Heritage, 2000 *Managing lithic scatters: archaeological guidance for planning authorities and developers*

Field, D, 2000 Neolithic flint adze from Chessington, *SyAC*, **87**, 182

——, & Needham, S, 1986 Evidence for Bronze Age settlement on Coombe Warren, Kingston Hill, *SyAC*, **77**, 127–51

Field, D, Nicolaysen, P, & Cotton, J, 1999 The Palaeolithic sites at Limpsfield, Surrey: an analysis of the artefacts collected by A M Bell, *SyAC*, **86**, 1–32

Field, D, Nicolaysen, P, Winser, K, & Ketteringham, L L, 1990 Prehistoric material from sites near Slines Oaks and Worms Heath, Chelsham, *SyAC*, **80**, 133–45

Fitzpatrick, A P, 2003 The Amesbury archer, *Current Archaeol*, **184**, 146–52

Ford, S, & Pine, J, 2003 Neolithic ring ditches and Roman landscape features at Horton (1989–1996), in *Prehistoric, Roman and Saxon sites in eastern Berkshire: excavations 1989–1997* (ed S Preston), Thames Valley Archaeol Serv Monogr, **2**, 12–85

Gardiner, M, 1990 The archaeology of the Weald: a survey and review, *Sussex Archaeol Coll*, **128**, 33–53

Graham, D, 1989 Bronze Age flat axe, Green Lane Farm, Farnham (SU 857 481), *SyAC*, **79**, 216

Graham, D, & Graham, A, 2002 Investigation of a Bronze Age mound on Frensham Common, *SyAC*, **89**, 105–18

Graham, D, Graham, A, & Nicolaysen, P, 1999 Surface collection of worked flints from the Thursley Common area, *SyAC*, **86**, 163–9

Green, M, 2000 *A landscape revealed: 10,000 years on a chalkland farm*, Stroud: Tempus

Grinsell, L V, 1987 Surrey barrows 1934–1986: a reappraisal, *SyAC*, **78**, 1–41

Groves, J, & Lovell, J, 2002 Excavations within and close to the Late Bronze Age enclosure at the former Queen Mary's Hospital, Carshalton, 1999, *London Archaeol*, **10.1**, 13–19

Harp, P, 1999a Palaeolith from Tangier Wood, Burgh Heath, *Plateau Archaeol Grp Bull*, **1**, 2

——, 1999b The Banstead research site, *Plateau Archaeol Grp Bull*, **1**, 3–5

——, P, 1999c Finds from Walton Heath Golf Course, *Plateau Archaeol Grp Bull*, **1**, 6–7

——, 1999d The Tumble Beacon, Banstead – a new survey and superficial excavations, *Plateau Archaeol Grp Bull*, **1**, 8–10

——, 1999e A possible Deverel-Rimbury (Middle Bronze Age) settlement site at Headley, *Plateau Archaeol Grp Bull*, **1**, 11

——, 2000a More palaeoliths from Banstead, *Plateau Archaeol Grp Bull*, **2**, 2

——, 2000b Mesolithic tranchet adze from Canons Farm, Banstead, *Plateau Archaeol Grp Bull*, **2**, 3

——, 2000c Neolithic/Bronze Age lithic scatter at Canons Farm, Banstead, *Plateau Archaeol Grp Bull*, **2**, 3

——, 2000d Neolithic projectile point from Kingswood, *Plateau Archaeol Grp Bull*, **2**, 4

——, 2002a Further work on two Lower Palaeolithic sites on the North Downs in Surrey: Rookery Farm, Lower Kingswood and Canons Farm, Banstead, *Plateau Archaeol Grp Bull*, **3,** 4–24

——, 2002b Five Mesolithic-type bifaces from Banstead and Headley, *Plateau Archaeol Grp Bull*, **3,** 25 & fig facing 24

——, 2002c Neolithic and Bronze Age arrowheads from Banstead, Woodmansterne, Lower Kingswood and Headley, *Plateau Archaeol Grp Bull*, **3,** 29–31

——, forthcoming Report on recent fieldwalking and excavation at a Lower Palaeolithic site at Lower Kingswood, Surrey, with a note on a Levallois flake-core recovered earlier from Kingswood 'Site C', *Plateau Archaeol Grp Bull*

Hayman, G, 1991–2 Further excavations at the former Goblin Works, Ashtead (TQ 182 567), *SyAC*, **81,** 1–18

——, 1995 An archaeological excavation at Warren Farm, Ewell, Surrey, SCAU unpublished client report

——, 1996 Discoveries of Late Iron Age and Roman date at Farleigh Court Golf Course, near Warlingham, *SyAS Bull*, **299,** 5–10

——, 2001 An archaeological excavation on the site of the Old Police Station and 10–16 London Road, Staines, SCAU unpublished client report

——, Marples, N & Branch, N, 2003 An archaeological evaluation of the Mesolithic hollow at North Park Farm near Bletchingley, Surrey TQ 3297 5203 (centred), SCAU unpublished client report

Haynes, I, Sheldon, H, & Hannigan, L (eds), 2000 *London under ground, the archaeology of a city*, Oxbow Books

Hill, J D, 1999 Settlement, landscape and regionality: Norfolk and Suffolk in the pre-Roman Iron Age of Britain and beyond, in *Land of the Iceni: the Iron Age in northern East Anglia* (eds J Davies & T Williamson), Stud East Anglia Hist, **4,** 185–207

——, 2001 Romanisation, gender and class: recent approaches to identity in Britain and their possible consequences, in *Britons and Romans: advancing an archaeological agenda* (eds S James & M Millett), CBA Res Rep, **125,** 12–18

Hodgkinson, J, 2004 Iron production in Surrey, in *Aspects of archaeology and history in Surrey: towards a research framework for the county* (eds J Cotton, G Crocker & A Graham), SyAS, 233–44

Housley, R A, Gamble, C S, Street, M, & Pettitt, P, 1997 Radiocarbon evidence for the Lateglacial human recolonisation of northern Europe, *Proc Prehist Soc*, **63,** 25–54

Howe, T, Jackson, G, & Maloney, C, 2001 Archaeology in Surrey 2000, *SyAC*, **88,** 343–63

——, 2002 Archaeology in Surrey 2001, *SyAC*, **89,** 257–81

Howe, T, Jackson, G, Maloney, C, & Saich, D, 2000 Archaeology in Surrey 1997–9, *SyAC*, **87,** 183–218

Howes, L, & Skelton, A, 1992 Excavations at Carshalton House, 1992, *London Archaeol*, **7.1,** 14–18

Huson, S, 1999 A find of Middle Bronze Age bracelets from Cranleigh, *SyAC*, **86,** 203–5

Jackson, G, Maloney, C, & Saich, D, 1997 Archaeology in Surrey 1994–5, *SyAC*, **84,** 195–243

——, 1999 Archaeology in Surrey 1996–7, *SyAC*, **86,** 217–55

Jacobi, R M, 1978 The Mesolithic of Sussex, in *Archaeology in Sussex to AD 1500* (ed P L Drewett), CBA Res Rep, **29,** 15–22

——, 1986 The contents of Dr Harley's show case, in *The Palaeolithic of Britain and its nearest neighbours: recent trends* (ed N Collcutt), University of Sheffield, 62–8

James, S, 1999 *The Atlantic Celts: ancient people or modern invention?* British Museum Press

Jones, P, 1990 Neolithic field monuments and occupation at Staines Road Farm, Shepperton, *SyAS Bull*, **252**

——, 1998 Excavation at the Crown Hotel, Chertsey, *SyAC*, **85,** 46–60

Jones, P, & Ayres, K, forthcoming A bone 'scoop' and Grooved Ware vessel from a pit in the lower Colne valley, Surrey, in Cotton & Field forthcoming

Keith-Lucas, M, 2000 Pollen analysis of sediments from Moor Farm, Staines Moor, Surrey, *SyAC*, **87,** 85–93

Lawrence, G F, 1890 The prehistoric antiquities of Wandsworth, *J Brit Archaeol Assoc*, **46,** 78

Lawson, A J, 2000 *Potterne 1982–5: animal husbandry in later prehistoric Wiltshire*, Wessex Archaeol Rep, **17**

Lewis, J S C, 1991 A Lateglacial and Early Postglacial site at Three Ways Wharf, Uxbridge, England: interim report, in *Lateglacial settlement in northern Europe: human adaptation and environmental change at the end of the Pleistocene* (eds R N E Barton, A J Roberts, & D A Roe), CBA Res Rep **77,** 246–55

——, in prep An earlier Upper Palaeolithic site at Heathrow, West London

Longley, D, 1976 The archaeological implications of gravel extraction in north-west Surrey, in SyAS Res Vol, **3,** 1–35

McOmish, D & Field, D, 1994 A survey of the earthworks at St Ann's Hill, Chertsey, *SyAC*, **82,** 223–5

Meddens, F, 1996 Sites from the Thames estuary wetlands, England, and their Bronze Age use, *Antiquity*, **70,** 325–34

Millett, M, 1990 *The Romanization of Britain: an essay in archaeological interpretation*, Cambridge

Milne, G, Bates, M, & Webber, M, 1997 Problems, potential and partial solutions: an archaeological study of the tidal Thames, England, *World Archaeol*, **29.1,** 130–46

MoLAS, 2000 *The archaeology of Greater London: an assessment of archaeological evidence for human presence in the area now covered by Greater London*, Museum of London

Needham, S, 1987 The Bronze Age, in Bird & Bird 1987, 97–137

——, 1990 *The Petters Late Bronze Age metalwork: an analytical study of Thames Valley metalworking in its settlement context*, Brit Mus Occas Pap, **70**

——, 1991 *Excavation and salvage at Runnymede Bridge, 1978*, British Museum Press

——, 1992 Holocene alluviation and interstratified settlement evidence in the Thames valley at Runnymede Bridge, in *Alluvial archaeology in Britain* (eds S P Needham & M G Macklin), 249–60

——, 1993 The structure of settlement and ritual in the Late Bronze Age of South-East Britain, in *L'habitat et l'occupation du sol à l'Age du Bronze en Europe* (eds C Mordant & A Richard), Actes du Colloque International de Lons-le-Saunier. Paris: Editions du Comité des Travaux historiques et scientifiques; Documents Préhistoriques, **4,** 49–69

——, 2000 *The passage of the Thames: Holocene environment and settlement at Runnymede, Runnymede Bridge Research Excavations, Vol 1*, British Museum Press

——, 2001 When expediency broaches ritual intention: the flow of metal between systemic and buried domains, *J Royal Anthropol Inst*, **7.2,** 275–98

Needham, S, & Burgess, C B, 1980 The Later Bronze Age in the lower Thames valley: the metalwork evidence, in *Settlement and society in the British Later Bronze Age* (eds J Barrett & R Bradley), BAR Brit Ser, **83,** 437–69

Needham, S P, Ramsey, C B, Coombs, D, Cartwright, C, & Pettitt, P, 1997 An independent chronology for British Bronze Age metalwork: the results of the Oxford Radiocarbon Accelerator Programme, *Archaeol J*, **154,** 55–107

Needham, S, & Spence, T, 1996 *Refuse and disposal at Area 16 East Runnymede, Runnymede Bridge research excavations, Vol 2*, British Museum Press

Nicolaysen, P, 1989 A late Upper Palaeolithic backed blade from Ashtead, *SyAC*, **79,** 215

O'Connell, M, 1990 Excavations during 1979–1985 of a multi-period site at Stanwell, *SyAC*, **80,** 1–62

Orton, C, 1997 Excavations at the King William IV site, Ewell, 1967–77, *SyAC*, **84,** 89–122

Oswald, A, Dyer, C, & Barber, M, 2001 *The creation of monuments: Neolithic causewayed enclosures in the British Isles*, English Heritage

Poulton, R, 1998 Excavation in Mint Street, Godalming, *SyAC*, **85,** 177–86

——, 2004   Iron Age Surrey, in *Aspects of archaeology and history in Surrey: towards a research framework for the county* (eds J Cotton, G Crocker & A Graham), SyAS, 51–64

Proctor, J, 2002   Late Bronze Age/Early Iron Age placed deposits from Westcroft Road, Carshalton: their meaning and interpretation, *SyAC*, **89**, 65–103

Proctor, J, & Bishop, B, 2002   Prehistoric and environmental development on Horsleydown: excavations at 1–2 Three Oak Lane, *SyAC*, **89**, 1–26

Pryor, F M M, 1996   Sheep, stockyards and field systems: Bronze Age livestock populations in the fenlands of eastern England, *Antiquity*, **70**, 313–24

Rapson, G, 2002   Two Lower Palaeolithic bifaces from Outwood, *SyAS Bull*, **359**, 3–4

——, 2003   An Iron Age enclosure at Westcott, *SyAS Bull*, **367**, 4–8

Renfrew, C, & Bahn, P, 1996   *Archaeology: theories, methods and practice*, Thames & Hudson, 2 edn

Reynier, M J, 1998   Early Mesolithic settlement in England and Wales: some preliminary observations, in Ashton *et al* 1998, 174–84

——, 2002   Kettlebury 103: a Mesolithic 'Horsham' type stone assemblage from Hankley Common, Elstead, *SyAC*, **89**, 211–31

Ridgeway, V, 1999   Prehistoric finds at Hopton Street in Southwark, *London Archaeol*, **9.3**, 72–6

——, 2003   Natural environment and human exploitation on the southern shores of Horselydown, *London Archaeol*, **10.4**, 103–11

Robertson, J, 2002   A round barrow discovered at Thorpe, *SyAS Bull*, **355**, 1–3

Roe, D A, 1981   *The Lower and Middle Palaeolithic periods in Britain*, Routledge & Kegan Paul

Russell, M J G, 1989   Excavation of a multi-period site in Weston Wood, Albury: the pottery, *SyAC*, **79**, 3–51

Saunders, M J, 2000   Late Bronze Age/Early Iron Age settlement evidence from Manor Hospital, Epsom, *SyAC*, **87**, 175–78

Scaife, R, 2000a   Holocene vegetation development in London, in J Sidell, K Wilkinson, R Scaife, & N Cameron, *The Holocene evolution of the London Thames: archaeological excavations (1991–1998) for the London Underground Limited Jubilee Line Extension Project*, MoLAS Monogr, **5**, 111–17

——, 2000b   Palynology and palaeoenvironment, in Needham 2000, 168–87

Scott-Jackson, J E, 2000   *Lower and Middle Palaeolithic artefacts from deposits mapped as Clay-with-flints: a new synthesis with significant implications for the earliest occupation of Britain*, Oxbow Books

Seel, S, 2000   The Erith buried forest, in *Coastal environmental change during sea-level highstands: the Thames estuary* (eds J Sidell & A Long), Field Guide, IGCP 437, UK Working Group Meeting, 15–16 December 2000, Environmental Research Centre, University of Durham: Research Publication **4**, 33–9

Serjeantson, D, 1996   The animal bones, in Needham & Spence 1996, 194–223

Sidell, J, Cotton, J, Rayner, L, & Wheeler, L, 2002   *The prehistory and topography of Southwark and Lambeth*, MoLAS Monogr, **14**

Sumbler, M G, 1996   London and the Thames Valley, British Geological Survey, 4 edn

Thomas, R, 1999   Rise and fall: the deposition of Bronze Age weapons in the Thames Valley and the Fenland, in *Experiment and design: archaeological studies in honour of John Coles* (ed A F Harding), Oxbow Books, 116–22

Tucker, S, 1996   Further evidence for prehistoric occupation found on the Purley Way, Croydon, *London Archaeol*, **8.1**, 12–17

Tyldesley, J, 1987   *The* bout coupé *handaxe: a typological problem*, BAR Brit Ser, **170**

Walls, T K, & Cotton, J, 1980   Palaeoliths from the North Downs at Lower Kingswood, *SyAC*, **72**, 15–36

Webber, M, 1999   *The Thames Archaeological Survey 1996–1999*

Wells, N A, forthcoming   Excavations in the North-West Zone Development Area, Gatwick Airport, 2001 by Framework Archaeology, *Sussex Archaeol Coll*

Wessex Archaeology, 1993   *The southern rivers Palaeolithic project: report no 2, 1992–1993. The South West and south of the Thames*, Trust for Wessex Archaeology Limited & English Heritage

White, M J, 1998   Twisted ovate bifaces in the British Lower Palaeolithic, in Ashton *et al* 1998, 98–104

Williams, D, 1990   Two stone hammers from east Surrey, *SyAC*, **80**, 235–6

——, 1994   A Late Bronze Age site in Priory Park, Reigate, *SyAC*, **82**, 197–202

——, 1996a   Some recent finds from east Surrey, *SyAC*, **83**, 165–86

——, 1996b   A Late Bronze Age barbed spearhead and other recent finds from Priory Park, Reigate, *SyAC*, **83**, 234–7

——, 1998a   Two Late Bronze Age axe fragments from Little Pickle, Bletchingley, in R Poulton, *The lost Manor of Hextalls, Little Pickle, Bletchingley*, 195–6

——, 1998b   Franks' Sandpit, Betchworth: a site of special importance?, *SyAS Bull*, **324**, 5–8

——, 1999a   Some recent finds from Surrey, *SyAC*, **86**, 171–97

——, 1999b   A Middle Bronze Age side-looped spearhead from Buckland, *SyAC*, **86**, 201–2

——, 2001   Recent finds from Surrey 1997–9, *SyAC*, **88**, 309–31

Winser, K D, 1987   Prehistoric flint sites at Sandy Meadow, Wotton, *SyAC*, **78**, 184–7

Wymer, J J, 1987   The Palaeolithic period in Surrey, in Bird & Bird 1987, 17–30

——, 1999   *The Lower Palaeolithic occupation of Britain*, Salisbury, Wessex Archaeology & English Heritage

Yates, D, 1999   Bronze Age field systems in the Thames Valley, *Oxford J Archaeol*, **18.2**, 157–70

Yates, D, 2001   Bronze Age agricultural intensification in the Thames valley and estuary, in *Bronze Age landscapes: tradition and transformation* (ed J Brück), Oxbow Books, 65–82

Jonathan Cotton, 58 Grove Lane, Kingston upon Thames KT1 2SR

3

Engraved sequences and the perception of prehistoric country in south-east England

DAVID FIELD

Investigation of the Palaeolithic countryside provides one of the greatest of archaeological challenges and Surrey is ideally positioned to be at the forefront of investigation. However, this essay covers an enormous time-span and attends to aspects of later prehistoric periods as well. Recent work on prehistoric landscapes in central southern England has identified a series of significant chronological 'events' that allows a sequence of land use to be identified. How regional such sequences are remains to be seen, but fragments can be detected across the South and these might provide basic elements on which much of the prehistoric country could be reconstructed. In addition, new approaches in considering the past provide interesting and fresh interpretations of the ancient countryside and allow us to catch a glimpse of how topography may potentially have been perceived at certain times during prehistory. This places greater emphasis on the importance of places and landforms rather than on single sites, but also provides challenges to the traditional interpretations of some monuments.

Introduction

Developer-funded archaeology has added enormous numbers of sites and finds to the inventory during recent decades, providing a wealth of archaeological data for analysis. Unfortunately, synthesis of the material, a now not insignificant task, has not kept pace. This essay does not attempt to remedy the position; however, it approaches the distribution of archaeological features within the countryside in a rather unusual way. It does not aim to be comprehensive: other accounts of prehistory within Surrey and the adjacent counties do that more than adequately, eg essays in this volume, in Bird & Bird 1987, in Museum of London 2000, and in Russell 2002. Neither is its scope site specific. Instead, it considers the whole of the land, treating each part of it as of equal value. It incorporates many new ideas in order to attempt to come to terms with the way in which countryside might have been experienced: it covers an enormous time-scale and consequently there may be unexplained chronological leaps or deviations in the narrative. Inevitably, and of necessity, coverage will be relatively thin and sometimes patchy, an acknowledged problem when trying to cover half a million years of land-use in so few words. There are two main components: an attempt to consider how the prehistoric countryside might have developed, coupled with a consideration of how those present in it might have perceived their contemporary environment.

I have also made an attempt to escape the constraint imposed by the, perhaps overused, term 'landscape', by reverting to other objective terms such as 'land', 'topography', or the 'country' of the title. Use of the word 'landscape' has completely permeated archaeology and the term is used for anything beyond the limits of the site trench. We are not alone in this for it has been used in similar ways in other disciplines too, geography, photography and anthropology, for example, although in the latter case new interpretations are now in vogue. As others have pointed out (eg Hirsch 1995) the very word landscape, or 'landskyp', derives from a Dutch school of painting and art in general has played a considerable role in our romantic view of countryside. The widespread perception of landscape as romantic appears to derive from the Grand Tour. Richard Colt Hoare of Stourhead, Wiltshire, who was ultimately responsible for much of the database for prehistoric Wessex, was enormously influenced by the monuments of Italy and the way they were depicted in paintings by Canaletto and others. Hoare and his contemporaries rearranged huge swathes of land and adorned it with temples, ruins and other features designed to catch the eye and provide pleasing views from a multitude of viewpoints. Implicit in such compositions is the ability to move from one 'view' to another, but for every such constructed harmonious composition, there must be many views in 'natural' country without harmony. The designer/architect has travelled, moved and adjusted to select the aesthetic frame and the selection itself implies movement through various landforms and is something that arrives in a major way with tourism. Tourism allows the land to be appreciated as a 'scape', for beyond the garden, knowledge of wide areas is necessary – we need to know what is beyond the distant ridge, or valley. In the pre-modern agricultural world, however, such travel was the preserve of a few. Most were familiar with the land immediately around them and their knowledge of landforms might be supplemented by an occasional trip beyond the home range. Processes of nomadism or transhumance aside, perception of country during prehistory would be very different from our own.

Surrey landform: looking south across the Weald from Newlands Corner. Photograph by Giles Pattison

In contrast, the land itself can be difficult. It has characteristics of form, texture and colour, of smell, feel and touch that in turn nurture different kinds of flora and fauna. It is not picturesque, but demands sheer hard work. A botanist once pointed out to me the different species that grow on the respective escarpments of the North and South Downs as a result of one receiving more sunlight than the other. Thus the elements are extremely important and even the wind, explained to the medieval peasant only in metaphysical terms, can result in exposure and death where the land provides no natural shelter.

After almost 200 years of 'landscape' archaeology, taking, that is, Richard Colt Hoare's *Ancient Wiltshire*, first published in 1812, as the catalyst, it is perhaps appropriate at the turn of a new millennium to consider new approaches and investigate the impact that factors such as belief, memory and tradition might have had upon the land (Bradley 1998; 2000; 2002; Edmonds 1999). This essay is seeking to stimulate debate, particularly on the manner in which the countryside might be perceived at different points in time during the past, or even about the nature of perception itself. Thus, it is about more than just seeing, or understanding, or experience, but also about repeated tasks, work, received learning through traditions, and the experiences of others (Ingold 2000). At what stage hominid brain capacity became large enough to absorb such concepts is unclear. As one reader wrote: 'Now my two cats are (naturally) very intelligent. They know their territory/landscape, but I don't think that they have any perceptions about it. They do experience and react to their landscape; they know where and when the sun will warm the roof of my neighbour's shed: when it's cold they come in and make a bee-line for the airing cupboard, where they experience its warmth with pleasure.'

Capabilities of vision aside, cats certainly appear to know their own territory, and will fight over it. Though certain features are acknowledged as being present, cat does not recognize the modern boundaries, hedges, or fences as territorial. Instead, it uses boundaries invisible to us. In my own case, the line seems to be half way down our garden and it appears to define a home patch. Cat is not excluded from the area beyond, as there is no rival cat, only foxes, badgers and stoats, but this appears to be a buffer zone or perhaps no-cats-land where dangers might await. Cat often lies alongside this boundary, at a point where stoats and other animals pass by the home range.

The past

In terms of perceptions of land-use, great shifts are required in the economic interpretations placed on the prehistoric countryside as a result of our received cultural preconceptions, for it is unlikely that we will ever understand the pre-Christian, pre-commercial approach to the land if we continue to interpret it by using a 21st century western European template. Recently there has been a widespread recognition of the symbolic, spiritual and metaphysical attributes of certain landforms by non-western societies (eg essays in Carmichael *et al* 1994; Hirsch & O'Hanlon 1995; Bradley 1996; Ashmore & Knapp 1999) and an increased interest in natural landscape features as of archaeological interest (Bradley 2000). New strategies are required to research and investigate these.

To start as close to the beginning as we can get. The chalk cliff at Boxgrove (Roberts & Parfitt 1999) must have provided some comfort to the hominids that preyed upon the animals attracted by the lagoon at its base. While open to the south-westerlies it provided considerable shelter from the biting north winds, the white chalk providing both reflected warmth and light, a natural beacon at once recognized by starlight. Wet or dry, it left a colouring on anyone who ventured close enough to come in contact, a white pigment that would disappear in the calm waters of the lagoon. The same cliff provided nodules of flint that could with care and practice be formed into predetermined shapes for cutting and chopping, and perhaps throwing. At times the beach was a pleasant environment, as it can be now, but it could also be menacing as storms provided uncertainty and encouraged the cliffs to crumble.

Determining how the Palaeolithic topography was utilized some 250,000 or more years ago must be seen as one of the supreme challenges in archaeology. So much has changed. Rivers have moved course dramatically, whole hillsides have shifted so it is no wonder that consideration of the contemporary countryside is rarely attempted. Only occasionally, as at Boxgrove in Sussex, can we manage to catch a glimpse of what may have been going on beyond the immediate site.

Limpsfield on the Surrey and Kent border is one Palaeolithic site where a few clues regarding wider land-use remain. Here, between about 1889 and 1903, A M Bell, a local teacher, assembled a collection of handaxes from the local fields and gravel pits (Field *et al* 1999). His contemporary and fellow collector Benjamin Harrison lived just a little to the east and, at a critical and exciting point in the development of archaeology just 30 years after the publication of Darwin's *Origin of Species*, they engaged in debate over the great antiquity of the human race (Harrison 1928). Bell championed Harrison's finds of 'old olds', struck flakes found in high level deposits evidently earlier than those containing handaxes, though eventually others concluded that the flakes were likely to have been produced by natural forces, and the Eolith debate was over. However, over 500 palaeoliths were recovered from Limpsfield, a well-defined area framed by both the chalk escarpment of the North Downs and by the Lower Greensand escarpment that overlooks the Weald Clay, each separated by little more than 1km of various greensand deposits. The historic village is located on the watershed between two drainage systems, those of the river Mole to the west and the river Darent flowing east, both of which eventually turn north and cut through the chalk massif to disgorge into the Thames. A third drainage system lies in close proximity, that of the Medway which rises in the Weald to the south of the escarpment and flows east before it too turns north to join the Thames. But the finds of handaxes were made in the area to the south-west of the village, for several hundred metres around the present source of the river Darent.

Careful analysis of the artefacts revealed that they came from a number of distinct sites in the vicinity, about twelve in all, scattered around what is now Limpsfield Common. Some were recovered from the surface of fields after deep ploughing, others came from quarrying operations and were recovered *in situ* sometimes from shingle lenses or 'floors' at several metres depth. This indicates the presence of relatively

slow-running water, though it is not clear whether the artefacts ultimately derived from the river or stream bed itself or were washed in from an adjacent bank their condition indicates that they have not moved far. The quarry sections indicate that there were a number of phases of depositional activity, some alluvial as the result of a high-level river flowing along the foot of the Downs, some the result of solifluction. The chalk escarpment here has receded and with it chalk and flint gravels have spread across the area, and these in turn have been caught up by and redeposited by the river. As the river cut down, some of the gravels were left high and dry. While some handaxes were found in these deposits, others were found beneath 'head', an all-encompassing term for unexplained soliflucted gravel; a number were evidently *in situ* just below the topsoil, being brought to the surface by a single episode of deep cultivation. Many frost cracks were present in the artefacts so they appear to have survived at least one glaciation. None of these sites has been archaeologically excavated and for the moment we can only work with the artefacts and reports by geologists of visits to quarries in the vicinity.

So why were so many tools used and discarded at each site? The question was raised but only partially addressed in the original site report (Field *et al* 1999, 26–7) where it was considered that the concentrations of such material represent places in the locale used in ways other than purely kill sites. Wherever a Palaeolithic site containing handaxes presents itself, it is rarely a case of the odd handaxe submerged in great quantities of waste flakes, but of hundreds of handaxes. Sometimes the count runs into thousands (perhaps 1000 at Farnham and about 3000 at Swanscombe – one collector is said to have accumulated some 80,000 from the latter site (Conway *et al* 1996, 7)). In later prehistory, such concentrations of axe types might be interpreted as ritual or ceremonial offerings. Here, at least initially, we might need to think in more practical terms, probably of everyday routine.

At Limpsfield, the greater proportion of the handaxes comprise twisted ovates. Some are so violently twisted that they have C-shaped rather than S-shaped edge profiles. Each piece is extremely neat and must have taken about an hour to make. Flaking technique at least on the twisted ovates is strikingly uniform. It is almost as though the objects were the work of one individual.

In terms of use, the general view is that such handaxes were perhaps all-purpose tools, but had a more precise role in the dismemberment and butchery of animals. If so, each of these areas represents repeatedly visited kill and dismemberment sites. Despite the similarities in manufacturing technique, the possibility that common elements in tool design continued in use for extremely long periods of time cannot be ruled out. We do not know the size of the group involved, and at Limpsfield the tools can represent various scenarios from a group of two or three hundred hominids, each discarding a single tool on the same occasion, to a single discard in each of 100 years or more. To put it another way, if each handaxe represents the tool used to butcher a carcass, each handaxe group represents the killing of a considerable number of animals. Alternatively, there may have been other incentives for repeat visits, spiritual as well as practical. Isaac (1981), for example, describes how a fruit tree might become a favoured stopping place where, after a series of return journeys, evidence of intermittent activity accumulates. However, despite a widely held assumption that these early people were highly mobile and spent their lives endlessly following herds of large animals across open plains, there is an indication that these sites meant something. They provided a reference point or focus of some kind, and in a place of such botanical diversity, where animals were attracted by the foliage, cover, browse and water, it may have been possible to survive on the sheer variety of plant and animal foods available without moving significant distances. Groups here could increase to relativity large sizes and like chimpanzees might form socially complex societies (eg Kohn & Mithen 1999, 523). In such circumstances continued use of similar handaxes might derive from received ideas and traditions of social relevance (eg Gamble 1997, 108; White 1998, 32).

The raw material for tool construction is abundant, and can be found *in situ* in the chalk, now just a few kilometres away but then much closer. However, immediately to hand are the large nodules from the solifluction and river terrace gravels, so there was no need to hoard tools or curate them, at least in a modern sense. It was perfectly feasible to throw them away, and scavenge for flint again the next time a carcass was to be dismembered. To us such behaviour seems to make little sense. Why make new tools on return to the spot when many perfectly good old ones were lying around? Or if made elsewhere, why take another back to the site if it was merely going to be used once and dumped there? In a similar way, it might be considered unlikely that hunters would continue to leave useful tools behind, as they would never know when they might be needed again. To remake identical artefacts and bring them back to the same spot implies an awful forgetfulness – a memory loss not in keeping with the mental agility required to recall the precise method of knapping a handaxe, or of re-finding the same spot left some while, perhaps weeks, earlier. Such discard then might be indicative of regular activity at each spot and it is merely the nature of such activity that remains to be determined. These points have been considered recently by Kohn

& Mithen (1999), who argue persuasively that the role of the manufacture of handaxes, at least symmetrical ones, is to produce an artefact of display in a courtship ritual, handaxes being symbols in a process of sexual selection. This might explain why so many appear in an undamaged condition, but by itself fails to account for the accumulations of great numbers, unless, that is, we are to interpret these accumulations as isolated mating sites or breeding grounds. Clearly such sites and the artefacts found at them played a special role in the lives of these early people.

Identical handaxes left lying around on the surface will have been familiar artefacts with some form of meaning, no matter how little developed memory was. At a complex level they may provide links and associations with the maker, contemporary or ancestral; at a simpler level the mere familiarity of shape would be enough to provide comfort, if not legitimacy. Additionally they would provide a signal to others that this world was occupied. In other words, the country around Limpsfield is likely to have provided all that was needed within quite a small range. The topography itself with its particular type of vegetation would have encouraged certain forms of repeated action. It could be comfortable. It could be home. Like the cat's requirement, there may have been a perceived boundary around the comfort zone.

So what do the artefacts tell us about the country? Kohn & Mithen (1999, 521) indicate that the implications inherent in handaxe manufacture include a good environmental knowledge of, for example, raw material sources and, by default, of other resources in the locality too. How did these early people think of their world? The landforms channel natural movement into the river valley, focusing attention there and encouraging repeated activity in certain localities (Gamble 1996). Thus everything required is contained within an area little more than 5km in width, bounded by the chalk escarpment in the north and the greensand escarpment to the south. In terms of extent, whatever the vegetation, it would be possible to see for a good distance across the Weald from the escarpment edge. Equally the towering chalk escarpment would form a continuous visual backdrop, and experience would provide knowledge that it could be climbed to provide a vantage point from which the valley as a whole could be viewed, or from which other animals, potential hunters or prey, could be observed. It would be implicit that another world lay beyond, perhaps dangerous and unexplored.

All things being equal, we might expect similar numbers of artefacts more or less equally distributed right across the South East. The field walking programmes of the last 40 years have reported few handaxe finds – though surface collection from known sites, eg Limpsfield and Banstead (P Harp, pers comm) continues to produce them. It would appear from this that the apparent clustering of finds does have some validity.

Most handaxes at Limpsfield were left on the surface and sat there through extremes of temperature as the frost cracks on them testify. In the aftermath of the last glaciation, enormous forces influenced the topography and vegetation – solifluction, mudflows, river course changes, dust storms and rising sea levels. As alpine flora gave way, browsing animals will have had an immense impact on the rate and intensity of new growth and the abundance of human population can only have been relative to the abundance of fauna and flora. Many sites, such as springs and streams, provided the same attraction as they had always done, but here the detritus of past activity was visible for all to see.

Perception

Encountering such artefacts, perhaps half a million years later, humans would immediately recognize them as struck implements, though totally alien ones. The surface condition – patina, staining, frost cracks – set them apart. The knapping was of a style not recognized within living memory. Nobody knew why so many almost identical tools had been left lying around the springhead. The nature of the spring itself, which appears quite obvious given a modern knowledge of hydrology, would also be difficult to explain and the reason why the life-giving substance gushed out of the ground at this particular spot could only be explained in metaphysical terms. Were the artefacts that littered the surrounding area perhaps the tools of the gods?

Springs are potentially useful places to explore. For example, the sites at Farnham attracted repeated visits throughout the Mesolithic and Neolithic periods (Rankine 1939, 67–89). Elsewhere in the country such sequences continue intermittently into the Iron Age and Roman period, for example at Bath, Avon (Cunliffe & Davenport 1985, 8–9), Springhead, Kent (Oxford Archaeol Unit 2000, 458–9) or more locally perhaps at Ewell, Titsey and Chiddingfold (Bird 2002), and with the great number of named

Holy Wells (Hope 1893) situated in such places, perhaps even into the Christian period. Standing pools of water, meres, may have similar attributes, some having received deposits of Bronze artefacts (eg Crawford & Wheeler 1921) or garrotted bodies (Green 1986, 128). The Silent Pool at Shere and other similar places in Surrey might be reconsidered in this context. We might think too of the influence of the Thames. Given the spiritual reverence placed on such rivers elsewhere in the world, such as the Ganges, this major artery would almost certainly have been perceived as an important spirit; the deposits of stone axes (Field & Woolley 1984) and bronze artefacts (Needham & Burgess 1980) which have been dredged up might be considered as having symbolic value (eg Bradley 1990), rather than as being lost from boats or during battles, as was often formerly thought (Adkins & Jackson 1978).

Such approaches provide interesting new interpretations of the land and allow us to catch a glimpse of how the topography might have been thought of at certain times during prehistory and as a result greater emphasis might be placed on the importance of locations and landforms rather than on single sites. This also provides a challenge to the traditional interpretations of some monuments. Perceptions of the countryside will of course change through time as well as according to the method of subsistence in operation. Forest dwellers, for example, will have a completely different perception of the world from those who live in open country: their high dark horizon, where few extensive views are possible, may result in additional importance being placed on locations where such views can be obtained (Bloch 1995; Gow 1995). Changes in the dense vegetation itself, the result of long-abandoned clearances, may however signal the former presence of people and signpost areas inhabited by supernatural elements.

Whereas the lithology of the northern part of the Weald mirrors its southern counterpart and the topography of the North and South Downs is almost identical, the distribution of some monuments in the South East, for example round barrows, is variable. Far greater numbers occur along the southern

Surrey wooded landform: early morning view of mature trees near Albury. Photograph by Giles Pattison

formation on both greensand and chalk. An economic interpretation provides an incomplete explanation of this (Field 1998), but in any case of all monuments, those assigned a burial or ritual function such as round barrows might be expected to be constructed to reflect non-economic influence. The accumulation of barrows in what, to us, are often aesthetically pleasing 'planned' cemeteries makes sense only if influenced by some form of spiritual divination of metaphysical forces or geomancy, while the position of many barrows on slopes may have more to do with drainage of such forces than inter-visibility. Equally the metaphysical properties of landforms may help to explain the difference in distribution between those on the North and South Downs. The contrasts of north/south, high/low, dark/light etc being quite obvious fodder for harmonious cosmological schemes. Traditions, myths, legends and belief might easily become established about such places.

In a similar way, the almost consistent orientation of 'Celtic' fields on a north-east/south-west/north-west/south-east axis needs explanation. There appears to be no agricultural reason why this should be and it appears to imply a concern with this alignment, an orientation that first appears to become significant in some barrow cemeteries eg Snail Down, Wiltshire (McOmish et al 2002). The importance of the alignment must lie in its adherence to a framework that must reflect a widely understood system of social values and hint at a perceived cosmos. Original clearance of land for agriculture may itself have been a ritual event. During the Neolithic or Early Bronze Age, clearance involved a process of initiating change if not control over nature, including the removal of natural objects such as trees and boulders. Interference with the natural harmony of the land may have contained a metaphysical dimension (Ingold 2000) which allowed it to be carried out only with due permission and ceremony. Some barrows with a turf core, eg Deerleap Wood (Corcoran 1963), may have resulted from such a process. No formal burial was found in this, or in numbers of other similar mounds, and the purpose of the barrow may have been as much to do with breaking the land as funerary. The presence of turf here, as well as in barrows on the Sussex greensand at, for example, Iping Common, or in nine mounds at West Heath, only two of which contained traces of burial (Drewett et al 1988, 80–4), implies at least a degree of open grazed country around such cemeteries, and it may be that much of the Surrey countryside was more open during the Early Bronze Age than in the historic period. A good sized 'Celtic' field would result from such stacked turves and if not immediately 'managed' even in a pastoral area, natural colonization would rapidly follow, resulting in a natural 'monument' of impene-

trable vegetation. Once established, 'Celtic' fields themselves would become intimately known and while it would be wrong automatically to associate fields with agriculture alone, they may be intrinsically involved with day-to-day existence and favoured or despised according to soils and function and even given field names (Field 2001). They were important places.

Moving through this, at least partly open, land, people may have encountered a four-dimensional topography, the fourth dimension being that of sacred proscription. While the whole land may have been considered sacred in one way or another, even trees and animals possessing spirits, some places may have been more sacred than others. As Jordan (2001), for example, has described for indigenous cultures in Siberia, we might imagine a land for the living, consisting of the usual domestic paraphernalia; a land of the dead that manifests itself in areas where remembered, or half-remembered, dead people have been placed, eg barrow cemeteries, where it may be dangerous or taboo to enter; and a land of the spirits, those places possessing potential interfaces with a supernatural world, such as springs, caves and hill-tops.

Other uncertainties have developed concerning the traditional interpretations of many well-established monuments. Thus interpretations are often economic or military in nature and not necessarily applicable to sites built by prehistoric societies not versed in industrial European, commercial or Christian ideals. This need not stop at the Bronze Age but might extend right through the archaeological record. Just back from the Sudan, Col Lane-Fox described Cissbury, the Caburn and other hillforts in Sussex as prehistoric versions of the defences with which he was so familiar (Lane-Fox 1869). Following his example, the various earthwork camps at, for example, Anstiebury, Holmbury, and Hascombe, were assigned a defensive function even though they often occupy liminal locations. While Hawkes (1971, 6) observed that hillforts were sometimes constructed on former ritual sites and Bradley (1981) too observed the manner in which such sites often located on former sites, in Wessex at least, many forts overlie focal points of the earlier linear ditch system (Hawkes 1939; Bradley et al 1994; McOmish et al 2002). Directly defensive functions are beginning to be questioned and emphasis placed on matters of display (Bowden & McOmish 1987; 1989) or other social factors (Field 2000; Hamilton & Gregory 2000). Underlying linear ditch foci aside, most hillforts were constructed hundreds of years before classical writers could imply a military function and indeed they were already ancient sites when Caesar, Tacitus and others alluded to them. As such the concept of ditch as defensive, or for quarry material, which we accept without question, originally may not have arisen. Elsewhere, digging into the earth is taken to be a disruptive activity that may disturb the balance of nature and may only be carried out with due ceremony. Thus nomads in Mongolia will carefully backfill pits so that the harmony of the land is not affected (Humphrey 1995), for restricting the movement of animals or insects will only invoke appropriate responses, while it is also thought that impeding the free movement of spirits will have similar repercussions. There is adequate evidence of carefully backfilled pits and ditches, with placed deposits during the Neolithic and Bronze Age (eg Thomas 1991, 57–77) at, for example, Carshalton (Proctor 2002). Thus while causewayed ditch systems might allow spirits freedom of access, ditches left open might equally be positioned to entrap supernatural elements and keep them out of certain places (Darling 1998). Thus it is conceivable that the ditches of monuments such as hillforts, as well as more obvious types such as henges and round barrows, may have been originally constructed with more metaphysical aims in mind.

Sequence

Even though there has been increasing acceptance of the need to place archaeological sites within their wider context, archaeology is still seen very much as a site-based discipline. Burial mounds, henges, hillforts and villas are viewed very much as the *raison d'être* of archaeology, and enormous amounts of energy are applied to recording new examples and adding them to the inventory. However, recent work on the archaeological topography of parts of central southern England has identified a series of critical 'events' that allow a broad chronological sequence of land-use changes to be identified (McOmish *et al* 2002). How regional such sequences are remains to be seen, but fragments of the commonly recognized elements of this chronology can be detected across wider areas of the South and, as the geology and available resources are quite similar in all these areas, these might provide basic elements, the building blocks or foundations on which much of the later countryside was constructed. They provide a model that might be tested in different regions.

The key sites here are located on the chalk downs of Wiltshire, on Salisbury Plain and the Marlborough Downs. Here, monuments have been preserved from episodes of historical cultivation by their location on the higher marginal land, at a distance from river lines and historical village centres. Throughout the historic period there was little economic incentive to cultivate these areas and they were therefore given over to stock and became huge sheepwalks, thereby preserving remnants of earlier phases of activity. Not

until the 18th century were inroads made into these areas as agricultural improvers (eg Davis 1811; Young 1813) encouraged new ways of working the land, the change being recorded by travellers like Daniel Defoe (1724–6) and antiquaries like John Merewether (1850) and A C Smith (1884), who lamented the amount of newly cultivated downland.

In these areas a palimpsest of the prehistoric and Romano-British past can be detected as extant earthworks and, where field observation has reported that such remains lie in juxtaposition, they have been investigated, mapped, analysed and interpreted. Consistently a repeated chronological sequence of field monuments has occurred. Extensive co-axial 'Celtic' field systems of the Middle Bronze Age appear later than the construction of round barrows, either respecting or overlying them, but in turn are themselves cut by the equally extensive linear ditch systems of the Late Bronze Age (McOmish *et al* 2002). All three of these elements are sometimes re-used, but particularly the last two. The 'Celtic' fields are invariably re-utilized as fields long after their initial period of use. This applies particularly in the Romano-British period when fields are enlarged and cross-divisions ploughed through. Lynchets take on greater proportions and indeed in some places appear more akin to modern landscape engineering. They are used too as settlement units, as 'green field' sites when Roman villages expand and spill out on to the fields. The Middle Bronze Age 'Celtic' fields thus become the building blocks of the English countryside, the principle being that once something is created it is difficult to eradicate and, on the contrary, far easier to utilize in one way or another. Thus medieval strip lynchets on the chalk rarely represent newly planned strip fields, surveyed and cleared from the waste; for something that provided influence was already there, invariably earlier fields, which were simply adapted to cater for new methods of cultivation.

The linear ditches too became fossilized and re-used, not always as boundaries as originally intended, but as thoroughfares and trackways, and the junctions of these often appear to have influenced the location of subsequent Romano-British settlement. Many ditches subsequently become incorporated as later markers of tithing or parish boundaries, fossilized for history by the Anglo-Saxon charters, or like parts of Bokerley Dyke (RCHME 1990) or Wansdyke (field observation), reconstructed into boundaries with monumental proportions.

While the earliest of monuments, the Neolithic and Early Bronze Age long and round barrows, begin the sequence, the heavy utilization of land around London has ensured that traces of these are now quite rare. Were aerial photographs more numerous (aerial photography is restricted by the air corridors of Heathrow and Gatwick) it may be that greater densities could be recorded. Recent air photography indicates that the density of ring-ditches on Thanet, for example, most of which are interpreted as barrows, approaches that of barrows around Stonehenge. Whether this has something to do with Thanet's liminal, former island, position is not clear. Within Surrey, cemeteries that can be identified tend to cluster in small groups on the dip slopes of the chalk, for example around Leatherhead, and in similar positions on the greensand, eg on Reigate Heath (Grinsell 1987). Distribution thins out to almost insignificant numbers as one travels east, until a slight increase in East Kent can be observed (Field 1998, 310). Distribution throughout the Weald is markedly riverine with clusters on valley slopes appearing at almost regular intervals along the greensand stretch of the rivers Mole, Tillingbourne and Rother (*ibid*). In contrast to the thin scatters on the North Downs and northern greensand, the South Downs and its respective greensand contain enormous numbers; one cemetery, Westmeston, boasts 36 barrows. The reason for this is not clear, but as noted above economic interpretations are not entirely satisfactory and a cosmological explanation might instead be considered.

Where barrows are few and far between, their influence on later land-use may have been negligible, perhaps merely as sight lines when laying out fields, and they may have become incorporated in and obscured by such constructions. Co-axially laid out over hectares, irrespective of the lie of the land, the 'Celtic' fields are the most visible and extensive field monument that can be expected to occur right across the South. These have been recognized on the South Downs since the 1930s, though elsewhere in the region they have been considered quite rare. However, while extant examples might be few, perhaps as a result of intensive pressure on land for cultivation in the London hinterland, developer-funded examination continuously identifies ditches and other features associated with Bronze Age pottery that are assigned an agricultural function. Some 39 examples of such contexts come from the west London gravel terraces alone (Yates 1999; 2001, 68–9), and there are 28 such localities along the Wandle flood plain (*ibid*, 70–1) and even six in Lambeth (*ibid*, 72). Similar evidence for such densities can be paralleled on the Sussex coastal plain and elsewhere (D Yates, pers comm) and might encourage the view that the presence of fields here could match, or surpass, the intensity of field systems present in Wessex. It may be that here too, such fields formed the template on which many later features in the countryside were constructed.

Unfortunately, away from the terraces evidence continues to be less certain. Few extant 'Celtic' field

systems exist, although there is great potential for further discoveries in the wooded areas on the summits of the Downs, especially in those areas devoid of Clay-with-Flints. The evidence was assembled and reviewed by Rosamond Hanworth (1978; 1987, 145), who demonstrated the presence of two chalkland clusters grouped around the Mole gap and around the headwater areas of the river Wandle. The most extensive system appears to be that across Fetcham, Mickleham, Leatherhead and Box Hill Downs (Frere & Hogg 1946, 104–6: Hope-Taylor 1946–7, 60–1; J English, pers comm), situated either side of the river Mole, though whether these are all part of the same system remains to be seen. Occasional Early Iron Age and Romano-British potsherds have been reported from the surface across the area and are perhaps indications of manuring, but in places the system is considerably lyncheted and as a whole is likely to have been laid out much earlier. Another system on Walton Heath was initially thought to be associated with the Roman villa (NMR no TQ 25 SW 3) although excavation provided no support for this (Prest & Parrish 1949, 57–62). A further system was reported at Bletchingley (NMR no TQ 35 SW 22). Aside from locations on the riverside gravels, there is little further evidence of extant fields off the chalk, although cropmarks indicate a potential system at Tilford. One system has been recorded at Whitmoor Common, where fields are laid out on a north-east to south-west axis (English 2001). A nearby round barrow excavated by Pitt Rivers in 1877 produced a Deverel-Rimbury urn (Saunders 1980; Grinsell 1987, 26; illustration in the Pitt Rivers Collection, Salisbury Museum), providing the kind of potential association with the fields that would be comfortable in Wessex.

The North Downs are capped by considerable spreads of Clay-with-Flints. If the pattern of land-use identified in central southern England holds good here, we might expect 'Celtic' field development on the dip slope and along the lips and slopes of valleys, where the Upper Chalk is exposed, while on the interfluves of the higher downland we might instead predict the presence of banjo enclosures and associated features eg at Effingham Common (Gardiner 1921) and perhaps Tadworth (Clark 1977, 189).

Linear earthworks may be more widespread than is initially apparent. If the 'Old Dyke' on Whitmoor Common, which is now more of a hollow way (English 2001) but according to John Aubrey was 'a great old trench' (Fowles 1980, 272–3, 890–1), was originally a ditch as the name suggests (Grymesditch is mentioned in Worplesdon in 1605 – Gover *et al* 1934, 358), it could cut the field system in the same way as the linear ditches in Wessex. Other linear ditches were observed by early antiquaries or mentioned in documents, for example the great ditch crossing the Guildford Road on Albury Down (Fowles 1980, 908), or that mentioned at Mickleham in 1248 (Gover *et al* 1934, 358). Similarly, if the straight parish boundary at Long Ditton is the long ditch referred to in the Saxon place-name (Gover *et al* 1934, 57; Ekwall 1974, 146), it might imply that part at least of the boundary system adopted at that time had its genesis at an earlier date. Others may too, for example the already ancient Fullingadic that extended from south of the Thames at Weybridge, part of which appears to have been observed by John Aubrey (Fowles 1980, 908), or the Rowdyke mentioned in 1445 at Battersea (Gover *et al* 1934, 372). If Bronze Age linear ditches are fossilized in some tithing- or parish-sized allotments based on the Thames, it will be worth searching 19th century tithe or enclosure maps for similar 'ditch' names or investigating the origin of certain significant hedgerows and sunken lanes. At face value, the multiple banks recorded at the foot of the Downs at the unlocated Smytham Bottom (Fowles 1980, 902) are rather different and may be more akin to the kind of multiple ditch systems usually associated with banjo complexes.

Conclusions

This metamorphosis of the archaeological countryside, with its changes of function from one thing to another, finds echoes in the processes taking place at certain individual sites – the stone circles, pit circles, ring-ditches, henges and hengiform monuments – and it has long been observed how monuments often focus around earlier ones (eg Bradley 1981; 1993; 1998; Bradley & Williams 1998). Sites such as Whitesheet Hill, Wiltshire, or Maiden Castle, Dorset, readily spring to mind. The very process of digging the earth is of crucial importance; for example, ditches at causewayed enclosures are repeatedly backfilled and then re-cut, long barrow ditches are extended, and similar processes take place at round barrows, eg Handley 27, Dorset, where the ditch was backfilled and re-cut three times; but we can also see here processes at work that utilize, adapt, complement, and at the same time change, the topography of the wider area.

Of course, it is not clear whether all this is a regional phenomenon, or whether there are implications that are more far-reaching. There may be something that proves to be peculiar to certain geological formations, in this case chalk downland and its surroundings, or that may prove to be a mere component in a wider pattern of land-use. Indeed differences can be observed in the standard sequence in some places. In particular, in some areas that are capped by Clay-with-Flints a countryside of curvilinear enclosure ditches and banjo enclosures, with a corresponding lack of co-axial fields, can instead be identified.

Examples include the extensive sites around Grovely Wood and Savernake Wood in Wiltshire (Corney 1989) and Micheldever Wood, Hampshire (RCHME archive), and considerable areas around Basingstoke, Hampshire, where, judging from the evidence of air photographs, banjos and similar enclosures predominate (NMR). In Wessex such banjo enclosures often occur in pairs and are invariably linked, by complexes of curvilinear banks and ditches, to square enclosures that resemble *viereckshanzen* (Corney 1989). The cambered funnel entrances to extant examples, eg Itchen Wood (RCHME archive), make it unlikely that they were used for stock, as central camber aside, the side ditches of the funnel would lead animals around the perimeter of the enclosure and back down the other side of the funnel instead of into the interior. It is worthy of note that phosphate found at the offset funnelled enclosure at Tadworth indicated that stock were kept outside the enclosure (Clark 1977). Instead, the interior is often raised and an impression is given of a high-status enclosure, an impression invariably enhanced by the later construction of Roman buildings nearby. These sites are often on areas of Clay-with-Flints *sensu-stricto* and, unlike the chalkland sheepwalks, in areas not cultivated in historic times for other reasons (Jones 1960). It is easy to see why forestry later formed a significant component of local economies. All three of the examples given above remain as wooded sites today. Such places may have been particularly unsuitable for Middle Bronze Age and later cultivation and were perhaps utilized as managed woodland or, like parts of Cranborne Chase during the Iron Age, as pasture for horses (Wainwright 1979, 189).

The problem of what lay beyond the Bronze Age field system – whether there were areas of 'common' or open land – has yet to be approached. For the moment, however, these 'events' provide a framework or benchmark against which the presence of other field monuments can be tested and it may be worthwhile teasing out some of the elements that may exist within the South East. The banjo enclosure on Effingham Common (Gardiner 1921) for example, appears to conform to this pattern and it would be interesting to know whether it conforms in other ways and whether a villa, or a *viereckshanze*-like enclosure, lies close by.

The greatest challenge must be in revealing the nature of the Palaeolithic countryside, how early people lived and moved through it. In some cases enough information should be available from quarry sections to start to construct and investigate ancient landforms. Surrey lies in a good position to do this, being geographically bracketed by the Thames, with extensive archaeological work carried out around Swanscombe, on the terraces around Acton and the Wey tributary at Farnham, and with good groupings of palaeoliths in places such as Lower Kingswood (Walls & Cotton 1980) and Limpsfield. Similar clusters occur in Sussex to the south and the potential for linking these sites chronologically and spatially is enormous. The contribution of the Southern Rivers Project (Wymer 1999) in cataloguing the available information has been extremely helpful, but this should not be seen as an end in itself, rather as a catalyst for new work. Both Farnham and Limpsfield would repay investigation of the land-use variety.

In order to test some of these ideas it will be necessary to investigate places rather than sites – landforms, for example springs and prominent hilltops, with or without evidence of monument building – and to work across the artificial constraints of archaeological periods. To what extent are the field boundaries and land divisions that we see today the result of work by the Enclosure Commissioners and what was influenced by former patterns of land-use that had long been engraved on the topography? Rather than treat chronological events as separate episodes there is a need to investigate the whole sequence. It would be of great interest to know if zones of land used as woodland or common during prehistory can be identified today and whether types of use in such zones remains generally constant.

Differences in land-use over time between land types might be investigated. It is an exciting time for 'landscape' archaeology.

ACKNOWLEDGEMENTS

I would like to thank the organizers of the Surrey 2001 Conference for inviting this contribution, in particular Audrey Monk, John Boult and Jon Cotton, but there were others too. My thanks also to Judie English, with whom there was continuous contact, to David Bird, who commented on an earlier draft of this text and suggested some useful and sometimes sweeping changes; to Audrey Monk for her interesting comments and discourse about cats and Giles Pattison for his photographs. I readily acknowledge that I might have broken a few of the rules both with the conference presentation and its written version – both may not have been quite what was expected. The views represented here have largely derived from discussions with colleagues, notably David McOmish, Graham Brown and Peter Topping, during lengthy and intensive periods of field investigation in central southern England and elsewhere, so by default they are partly responsible too. Finally I would like to express my gratitude to Jon Cotton, a colleague of long standing, for his prompting, prodding and above all his cheerful patience in waiting for this article.

BIBLIOGRAPHY

Ashmore, W, Knapp, A, & Bernard, 1999 *Archaeologies of landscape*
Bird, J, & Bird, D G (eds), 1987 *The archaeology of Surrey to 1540*, SyAS
Blair, J, 1991 *Early medieval Surrey: landholding, church and settlement before 1300*, Alan Sutton & SyAS
Bloch, M, 1995 People into places: Zafimaniry concepts of clarity, in Hirsch & O'Hanlon 1995, 63–77
Bowden, M, & McOmish, D, 1987 The required barrier, *Scott Archaeol Rev*, **4**, 2, 76–84
——, 1989 Little boxes: more about hillforts, *Scott Archaeol Rev*, **6**, 12–16
Bradley, R, 1981 From ritual to romance: ceremonial enclosures and hill-forts, in *Hillfort studies* (ed G Guilbert), Leicester Univ Press, 20–7
——, 1990 *The passage of arms*, Cambridge
——, 1993 *Altering the earth*, Soc Antiq Scotl Monogr Ser, **8**
—— (ed), 1996 Sacred geography, *World Archaeol*, **28**, 2
——, 1998 *The significance of monuments*, Routledge
——, 2000 *An archaeology of natural places*, Routledge
——, 2002 *The past in prehistoric societies*, Routledge
Bradley, R, Entwistle, R, & Raymond, F, 1994 *Prehistoric land divisions on Salisbury Plain: the work of the Wessex Linear Ditches Project*, Engl Heritage Monogr, **2**
Bradley, R, & Williams, H, 1998 The past in the past: the reuse of ancient monuments, *World Archaeol*, **30.1**
Carmichael, D L, Hubert, J, Reeves, B, & Schanche, A, 1994 *Sacred sites, sacred places*, Routledge
Clark, A J, 1977 Geophysical and chemical assessment of air photographic sites, in Implications of aerial photography for archaeology (eds J N Hampton & R Palmer), *Archaeol J*, **134**, 187–91

Corcoran, J X W P, 1963 Excavation of the bell barrow in Deerleap Wood, Wotton, *SyAC*, **60**, 1–18
Corney, M, 1989 Multiple ditch systems and Late Iron Age settlement in central Wessex, in *From Cornwall to Caithness: some aspects of British field archaeology* (eds M Bowden, D Mackay & P Topping), BAR Brit Ser, **209**, 111–28
Crawford, O G S, & Wheeler, R E M, 1921 The Llynfawr and other hoards of the Bronze Age, *Archaeologia*, **71**, 133–40
Darling, P, 1998 Aerial archaeology in Africa: the challenge of a continent, *Aerial Archaeol Res Grp Newsl*, **17**, 9–18
Davis, T, 1811 *General view of the agriculture of Wiltshire: drawn up and published by order of the Board of Agriculture and internal improvement*, London
Defoe, D, 1724–6 *A tour through the whole island of Great Britain*, repr 1979 Harmondsworth, Penguin
Drewett, P, Rudling, D, & Gardiner, M, 1988 *The South-east to AD 1000: a regional history*, Longman
Edmonds, M, 1999 *Ancestral geographies of the Neolithic*, Routledge
Ekwall, E, 1974 *The concise Oxford dictionary of English place-names*, 4 edn
English, J, 2001 Whitmoor Common, Worplesdon – a proposed Area of Special Historic Landscape Value, *Surrey Hist Landscape Stud Newsl*, **16**, 6–10
Field, D, 1998 Round barrows and the harmonious landscape: placing of Early Bronze Age burial monuments in south east England, *Oxford J Archaeol*, **17.3**, 309–26
——, 2000 *Midsummer Hill: a survey of the earthworks on Midsummer and Hollybush Hills, Eastnor, Hereford and Worcester*, Engl Heritage Archaeol Investigation Rep Ser A1/16/2000

——, 2001 Place and memory in Bronze Age Wessex, in *Bronze Age landscapes: tradition and transformation* (ed J Brück), Oxford: Oxbow, 57–64

Field, D, Nicolaysen, P, & Cotton, J, 1999 The Palaeolithic sites at Limpsfield, Surrey: an analysis of the artefacts collected by A M Bell, *SyAC*, **86**, 1–32

Field, D, & Woolley, A R, 1984 Neolithic and Bronze Age ground stone implements from Surrey, *SyAC*, **75**, 85–109

Fowles, J (ed), 1980 *John Aubrey's* Monumenta Britannica *annotated by R Legg*, Sherborne: DPC

Frere, S S, & Hogg, A H A, 1946 An Iron Age and Roman site on Mickleham Downs, *SyAC*, **49**, 104–6

Gamble, C, 1996 Hominid behaviour in the Middle Pleistocene: an English perspective, in *The English Palaeolithic reviewed* (eds C S Gamble & A J Lawson), Salisbury, Trust for Wessex Archaeology

——, 1997 Handaxes and Palaeolithic individuals, in *Stone Age archaeology* (eds N Ashton, F Healey & P Pettitt), Oxford: Oxbow Books, 105–9

Gardiner, E, 1921 Effingham: plan of a Surrey earthwork, now destroyed, *SyAC*, **35**, 101

Gover, J E B, Mawer, A, & Stenton, F M, 1934 *The place-names of Surrey*, English Place-Name Soc, **11**

Gow, P, 1995 Land, people, and paper in western Amazonia, in Hirsch & O'Hanlon 1995, 43–62

Green, M, 1986 *The gods of the Celts*, Stroud: Sutton repr 1993

Grinsell, L V, 1987 Surrey barrows 1934–1986: a reappraisal, *SyAC*, **78**, 1–41

Hamilton, S, & Gregory, K, 2000 Updating the Sussex Iron Age, *Sussex Archaeol Collect*, **138**, 57–74

Hanworth, R, 1978 Surrey: the evidence at present, in *Early land allotment in the British Isles* (eds H C Bowen & P J Fowler), BAR Brit Ser, **48**, 61–5

——, 1987 The Iron Age in Surrey, in Bird & Bird 1987, 139–164

Harrison, E R, 1928 *Harrison of Ightham*, Oxford University Press

Hawkes, C F C, 1939 The excavations at Quarley Hill, 1938, *Proc Hampshire Fld Club Archaeol Soc*, **14**, 136–94

——, 1971 Fence, wall, dump, from Troy to Hod, in *The Iron Age and its hillforts* (eds M Jesson & D Hill), Southampton: Millbrook Press

Hirsch, E, & O'Hanlon, M (eds), 1995 *The anthropology of landscape*, Oxford: Clarendon Press

Hope, R C, 1893 *The legendary lore of the holy wells of England*, London: Eliott Stock

Hope-Taylor, B, 1946–7 Celtic agriculture in Surrey, *SyAC*, **50**, 47–72

Humphrey, C, 1995 Chiefly and shamanist landscapes in Mongolia, in Hirsch & O'Hanlon 1995, 135–62

Ingold, T, 2000 *The perception of the environment: essays in livelihood, dwelling and skill*, Routledge

Isaac, G, 1981 Stone Age visiting cards: approaches to the study of early land-use patterns, in *Patterns in the past: studies in honour of David Clarke* (eds I Hodder, G Isaac & M Hammond), Cambridge University Press

Jones, E L, 1960 Eighteenth-century changes in Hampshire chalkland farming, *Agr Hist Rev*, **8**, 5–19

Jordan, P D, 2001 Cultural landscapes in colonial Siberia: Khanty settlements of the sacred, the living and the dead, *Landscapes*, **2.2**, 83–105

Kohn, M, & Mithen, S, 1999 Handaxes: products of sexual selection? *Antiquity*, **73**, 518–26

Lane Fox, A H, 1869 An examination into the character and probable origins of the hillforts of Sussex, *Archaeologia*, **42**, 27–52

McOmish, D, Field, D, & Brown, G, 2002 *The field archaeology of Salisbury Plain Training Area*, English Heritage

Merewether, J, 1850 Diary of the examination of barrows and other earthworks in the neighbourhood of Avebury and Silbury Hill, in *Memoirs illustrative of the history and antiquities of Wiltshire and the City of Salisbury communicated to the Archaeological Institute of Great Britain & Ireland, Salisbury 1849*, London: George Bell, 82–107

Museum of London, 2000 *The archaeology of Greater London: an assessment of archaeological evidence for human presence in the area now covered by Greater London*

Needham, S, & Burgess, C B, 1980 The later Bronze Age in the lower Thames valley: the metalwork evidence, in *Settlement and society in the British later Bronze Age* (eds J Barrett & R Bradley), BAR Brit Ser, **83**, 437–69

Prest, J M, & Parrish, E J, 1949 Investigations on Walton Heath and Banstead Common, *SyAC*, **51**, 57–64

Proctor, J, 2002 Late Bronze Age/Early Iron Age placed deposits from Westcroft Road, Carshalton: their meaning and interpretation, *SyAC*, **89**, 65–103

Rankine, W F, 1939 Mesolithic and Neolithic studies, in K P Oakley, W F Rankine, & A W G Lowther, *A survey of the prehistory of the Farnham district*, SyAS, 61–132

RCHME, 1990 *The archaeology of Bokerley Dyke*, Roy Comm Hist Monuments Engl

Roberts, M, & Parfitt, S A, 1999 *Boxgrove: a Middle Pleistocene hominid site at Eartham Quarry, Boxgrove, West Sussex*, Engl Heritage Archaeol Rep, **17**

Russell, M, 2002 *Prehistoric Sussex*, Gloucester: Tempus

Saunders, P R, 1980 Saxon barrows excavated by General Pitt-Rivers on Merrow Downs, Guildford, *SyAC*, **72**, 69–75

Smith, A C, 1884 *A guide to the British and Roman antiquities of north Wiltshire*, Wiltshire Archaeol Natur Hist Soc

Thomas, J, 1991 *Rethinking the Neolithic*, Cambridge University Press

Wainwright, G J, 1979 *Gussage All Saints: an Iron Age settlement in Dorset*, Dept Environment Archaeol Rep, **10**

Walls, T, & Cotton, J, 1980 Palaeoliths from the North Downs at Lower Kingswood, *SyAC*, **72**, 15–36

White, M J, 1998 On the significance of Acheulian biface variability in southern Britain, *Proc Prehist Soc*, **64**, 15–44

Wymer, J J, 1999 *The Lower Palaeolithic occupation of Britain*, Salisbury, Wessex Archaeology & English Heritage

Yates, D, 1999 Bronze Age field systems in the Thames Valley, *Oxford J Archaeol*, **18.2**, 157–70

——, 2001 Bronze Age agricultural intensification in the Thames valley and estuary, in *Bronze Age landscapes: tradition and transformation* (ed J Brück), Oxford: Oxbow Books, 65–82

Young, A, 1813 *General view of the agriculture of the county of Sussex*, repr 1970, New York: Augustus Kelley

David Field, 2 West Nolands Farm Cottages, Yatesbury, Wiltshire SN11 8YD

4

Iron Age Surrey

ROB POULTON

Since 1984, when Hanworth compiled her survey, a considerable body of excavated evidence for the Iron Age has emerged. This suggests that although fields and farms dominated the landscape of the Thames valley by the Middle Bronze Age, it was only during the Iron Age that they emerged elsewhere in Surrey. River valleys were the core areas for such development, and beyond their confines the resources of much of the county were exploited without the need for permanent settlement.

Introduction

The review of the Iron Age in Surrey prepared in the mid-1980s by Hanworth and published in *The Archaeology of Surrey to 1540* (Bird & Bird 1987) provided a lively and comprehensive summary of knowledge to that time. A rapid expansion in the scale and quantity of archaeological excavation began shortly after her survey was published, was accelerated by the introduction of Planning Policy Guidance note 16 (PPG16) in 1991, and continues to the present day. It is this new fieldwork, especially the larger-scale investigations, which provides the focus for the present paper.

The distribution of the recent work is a reflection of development pressures, the impact of which across the county has been very uneven (eg SCAU 1997; 1998; Poulton 1999a; 2000; SCAU 2001; 2002). The archaeological work has, therefore, occurred almost entirely independently of any research strategy, at least in terms of its initial siting. There have, as a result, been many field interventions of which the results have been wholly or largely negative. These and, paradoxically, the quasi-random approach, are one of the particular strengths of the data that have emerged from the last fifteen years, since they provide, at least partially, a test of the validity of interpreting distribution maps of positive results as a reflection of the nature of Iron Age society.

It is partly for this reason that the present survey reviews the Iron Age in terms of the different scale and character of settlement across the varied physiographic zones (fig 4.1) which make up Surrey (here taken to cover the whole area included within the historic and administrative counties). Part of the reason also is that Hanworth (1987) adopted a thematic approach for her review, and a contrasting method allows a fresh look at the earlier evidence, although the emphasis is on the results of recent archaeological work.

The Annexe includes a full list of Iron Age sites and finds from the administrative county since 1984, and this also provides useful additional references to a number of the sites discussed in the main body of the text.

The Thames valley

It is convenient to treat the Thames and its extensive associated terraces as a unit, although they offer considerable landscape variety, with a wide flood plain dotted with small gravel islands, below the flat brickearth-covered terraces. It is the latter, just outside the modern Surrey boundary, which have seen what may be the most comprehensive examination by excavation of a landscape (some 21ha) in Britain, at the Perry Oaks site, near Heathrow Airport (Barrett *et al* 2000; 2001). This has led to the development of an important interpretative framework for the later prehistoric period, building on a number of recent studies. Merriman (2000, esp 41–3) provides an excellent review of these; see also Yates (2001).

The key development (from the present perspective) at Perry Oaks seems to be the emergence in the Middle Bronze Age of a developed field system, defined by ditches in its early stages, but maintained by hedges through the Iron Age period. Small middle and later Bronze Age settlements are closely associated with the fields, but the Late Bronze Age and Iron Age see an apparent reduction in the quantity of settlement evidence (Barrett *et al* 2001, 223–4).

A similar sequence had earlier been indicated just south of Perry Oaks at Stanwell (O'Connell 1990) through a combination of analysis of aerial photographs and selective excavation. There, scattered evidence for later Bronze Age occupation seemed to be in locations near to the edges of the field system, suggesting that the latter was created first. No evidence was found of Iron Age occupation, although the possibility that such existed within the unexcavated portions of the field cannot be dismissed. This pattern is, however, closely followed at another nearby site, Home Farm Laleham (Hayman 1991b; 1997; 1998a; 2002). An area of about a square kilometre has been examined by a combination of trial trenching, selective excavation and watching brief.

It is clear that a field system and small-scale settlement sites emerged and flourished during the mid–Late Bronze Age, but Iron Age settlement

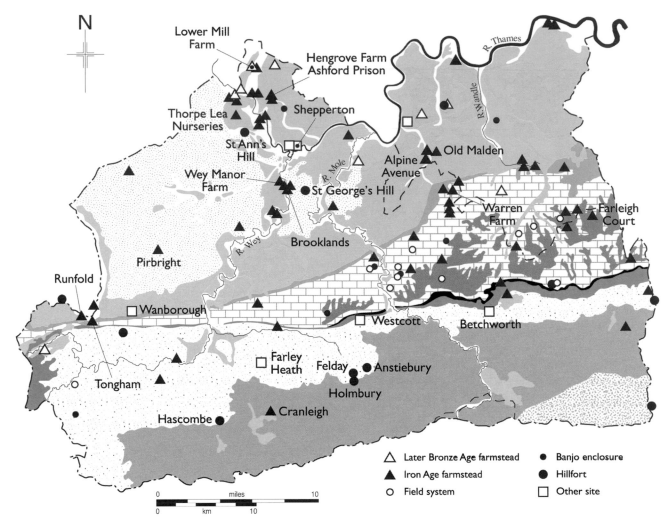

Fig 4.1   The distribution of Iron Age settlement (based on Hanworth 1987, fig 6.1). For key to geological background see map on page x.

evidence (apart, probably, from a single ditch) was conspicuous by its absence. A different pattern is emerging from work (recent and in progress) at contiguous sites at Ashford Prison (by Pre-Construct Archaeology: T Carew, pers comm) (fig 4.2) and at Hengrove Farm, Staines (by SCAU). An extensive area of Bronze Age field systems is apparent, with scattered occupation evidence of similar date, and two distinct areas of Iron Age settlement, only 0.4km apart. In both cases it seems probable that the fields established in the Bronze Age were maintained in use, demarcated by hedgerows adjacent to the silted-up ditches used to create them.

It is generally agreed that the primary purpose of the new field systems was to allow more intensive exploitation of cattle, although arable farming must also have been taking place (Yates 2001, 65–6). At Perry Oaks (Barrett *et al* 2001, 224) evidence has emerged to suggest a loss of fertility, presumably due to over grazing, by the end of the Bronze Age. It would seem that this pattern was widespread across the gravel terraces and that less intense exploitation of the land helped create conditions in which more concentrated settlement foci emerged. It may also be

that these foci tended to be sited on the flood plain, where, presumably, a wider resource base could be exploited. At Ashford Prison, for example, the ten ring gullies (not all of one phase) are close to the river Ash and adjacent to a silted up, but still wet and marshy, palaeochannel. Similarly, part of a mid–Late Iron Age settlement at Laleham lay in the angle between the Thames and one of its tributaries, Sweep's Ditch. It produced evidence for a ring gully and pits and part of an enclosure (Taylor-Wilson 2002).

A further example is the farmstead identified at Lower Mill Farm (Jones & Poulton 1987) within Stanwell parish, but right next to the river Colne. At Thorpe Lea Nurseries, in a low-lying position, two substantial Iron Age enclosures were identified, with occupation beginning in the earlier Iron Age and extending through into the Roman period. The enclosures were associated with field boundaries and trackways, and had been preceded by more scattered mid–Late Bronze Age occupation.

The finds from the settlement sites are, generally, unexceptional in character. In this respect they contrast sharply with the high-quality metalwork which has been recovered from the Thames in this area. Hanworth (1987, 151) noted the fact that metal-work with riverine association in Britain often has funerary associations in central and eastern Europe. The ritual character of such deposition and its frequent (possibly exclusive) connection with death have now become widely accepted (Bradley 1990). Two sites in Surrey provide important confirmatory evidence for this view.

The Chertsey shield, a mid-Iron Age shield made entirely of bronze, generally regarded as 'parade-ground' armour (Stead 1987), has become well known since its discovery in 1985 at Abbey Meads, near Chertsey, but less well appreciated is its findspot, from a buried former channel of the Thames, and the recovery of a series of other arte-facts from nearby in the same channel. These include a Neolithic stone axe and pestle, a Late Bronze Age sword and a complete Late Iron Age or Early Roman beaker (Jones forthcoming, a). There are strong parallels with a site at Shepperton Ranges, where a buried river channel also yielded a rich variety of prestige artefacts of various dates (Poulton & Scott 1992; Poulton forthcoming). These included a Mesolithic antler macehead, a later Bronze Age axe with its haft (Hunt et al 2002, 48) and three Iron Age swords, one with a bronze scabbard mount (fig 4.3), as well as human skulls. Two features deserve partic-ular note. First, the occurrence of artefacts of all periods was confined to a limited area of the river channel, suggesting that a particular spot acquired and retained sanctity over a very long period of time. Secondly, the skulls confirm that for some or all of the

time that sanctity is associated with burial rites. This view is surely strengthened in respect of the Iron Age by the fact that only one definite cremation or inhu-mation burial of the period has yet been identified in the area. The single example is an inhumation, placed in a square pit, of a female in her 40s, found near Shepperton (Howe et al 2000, 192 & fig 3).

It seems reasonable to assume that the deposition of such prestige items was associated with an élite. It is more difficult to be sure what might distinguish the living places of such an élite, although it has been suggested (Barrett et al 2001, 224) that 'as the Late Bronze Age progresses [...] social stratification began to be expressed architecturally. This trend increased during the Iron Age, with rectangular buildings at the centre of settlements, enclosures with complex build-ings, such as Caesar's Camp [Heathrow (Grimes & Close-Brooks 1993)], and hill-forts'.

There is nothing at Thorpe Lea Nurseries (fig 4.4), near to the Abbey Meads site, to place it obviously within this category, although the crucial evidence of building plans did not survive owing to truncation. A more obvious candidate is St Ann's Hill, near Chertsey. A thorough survey (McOmish & Field 1994) has provided detailed confirmation of its univallate defences, and small-scale excavation revealed intensive activity extending through the Iron Age (Jones forthcoming, b).

It is tempting, despite the limited evidence, to try and fit St Ann's into the classic model of the Iron Age hillfort as a central place within a relatively complex settlement hierarchy (cf Hanworth 1987, fig 6.2; Hunt et al 2002, 50). Some further discussion of the

Fig 4.2 Ashford Prison site: a Neolithic ring ditch (centre foreground) remained sufficiently visible to influence the location of the Iron Age roundhouses visible behind it. Photograph by Pre-Construct Archaeology)

function of hillforts is given below but the important issue to consider now is what the nature of the hinterland of the hillfort was. It could, clearly, have encompassed the Thames flood plain and terraces below it, including the settlement at Thorpe Lea Nurseries. These terraces, however, are not very extensive on the Surrey side of the Thames. The feeling is that, as later, the river is likely to have been a border between groups or tribes, although it need not necessarily have been so. On balance, though, it seems probable that a major part of the hinterland of St Ann's would have been the north-west Surrey heathlands of which it is, geologically, a part.

The north-west Surrey heathlands and the Wey valley

Distribution maps of prehistoric discoveries invariably show few within the heathlands (Bird & Bird 1987, *passim*). In the years since the publication of *Surrey to 1540*, there have been very few additional findspots identified. A rapid identification survey of the area by the Surrey County Archaeological Unit (SCAU) concluded that, had prehistoric monuments or settlements of any significant scale existed, they could normally be expected to survive as landscape features, and their paucity demonstrated that the area probably became heathland as early as the Mesolithic, rather than in the Bronze Age as is more commonly assumed (cf Macphail & Scaife 1987, 36; Needham 1987, 130–2). Evaluations and other fieldwork on the heathland proper have also failed to reveal anything of note, although it needs to be remembered that the maintenance of the area as heathland is itself evidence of continuous human interest through culling/grazing/burning (cf Bannister in this volume).

In these circumstances it is probably enlightening to look at the economy of such areas as they emerge into history. When the Domesday survey was undertaken in 1086, settlement outside the river valleys was minimal and this was probably the most lightly settled area, with the lowest proportion of arable, in Surrey. The 'ancient rhythm of seasonal grazing' by large swineherds remained of key importance (Blair 1991, 40–2). It seems reasonable to suppose that the area had a similar economy in the prehistoric period, and that its resources were exploited from permanent settlements in the river valleys associated with it. Iron Age occupation has been identified at Lightwater (G Cole, pers comm) associated with the river. At Pirbright (Hayman forthcoming, a), a mid–Late Iron Age site was identified, near to a small stream, with a ditch re-cut on several occasions on a similar alignment, probably representing part of an enclosure.

The most important Iron Age sites in this area have, however, been identified in the Wey valley, which divides the larger mass of Chobham Heath

from the smaller expanse of Bagshot Beds to its east. The site excavated by Hanworth at Brooklands (fig 4.5) is well known, with its roundhouse associated with specialist areas for iron smelting and smithing (Hanworth & Tomalin 1977). Subsequent discoveries of several sites in the local area with no obvious specialist function suggest that it may have provided a local service, rather than being a component of a regionally important specialization. Two further sites have been excavated within the central area at the Brooklands motor-racing circuit (Hayman 1991a). Both seem to have been farmsteads, with the more interesting of the two including a small circular enclosure (fig 4.6), pits, four-post structures (probably granaries) and other ditches. Some of these seem likely to be field boundaries, but their extent and form is not clear, although an Iron Age origin is apparent.

Nearby, but on the other side of the Wey, at Wey Manor Farm (work in progress, Hayman in prep), a similar pattern is apparent, although here it is clear than an extensive field system developed during the Iron Age. There is scattered evidence of Bronze Age activity (principally in the form of cremation burials), but the Iron Age settlement, including roundhouses and enclosures, is more substantial and seems to be part of a more developed exploitation of the landscape.

The presence of a substantial hillfort at St George's Hill (Poulton & O'Connell 1984) overlooking these sites in the Wey valley invites a comparison with St Ann's Hill. A few finds of earlier and later Iron Age pottery were made around 1910 (Lowther 1949), but extensive investigation in more recent years (eg Stevenson 1999) has failed to identify a single Iron Age find or feature. Settlement within the ramparts must have been confined to a small area, or may never have happened, and the two hillforts would seem to have served very different functions. It is becoming increasingly clear that the uses to which hillforts were put were very diverse, with warfare, perhaps, one of the rarest. St George's hillfort may be best seen as a status symbol, but it may also have been a refuge in times of crisis, or even a periodic meeting place for sacred or profane purposes.

The Weald and the greensand hills

This interpretation of St George's hillfort has some similarities with that advanced for the group of forts in the greensand hills, at the edge of the Weald (Hanworth 1987, 157–61). These hillforts have generally strong defensive positions, occupying promontory sites overlooking the Weald. Noting their apparent isolation from other evidence, Hanworth saw them as central places playing a role in exchange and trade mechanisms, including, for example, quernstones, and (more speculatively) as summer residences for communities centred on the

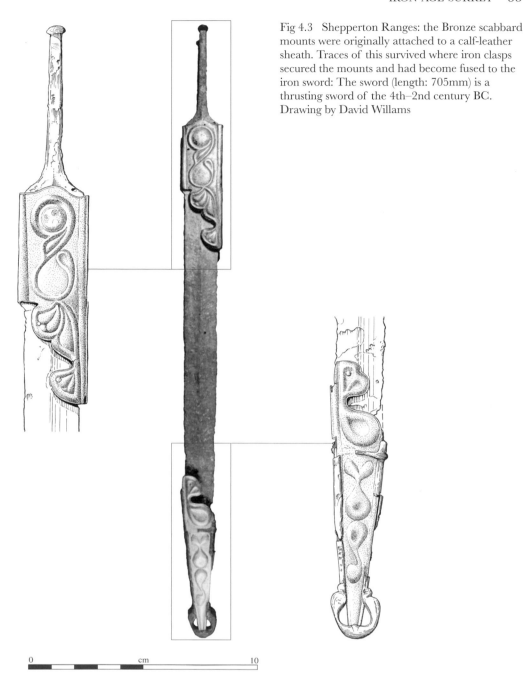

Fig 4.3 Shepperton Ranges: the Bronze scabbard mounts were originally attached to a calf-leather sheath. Traces of this survived where iron clasps secured the mounts and had become fused to the iron sword: The sword (length: 705mm) is a thrusting sword of the 4th–2nd century BC. Drawing by David Willams

North Downs engaged in transhumance of pigs to the summer grazing grounds of the Weald.

An excavation at Anstiebury hillfort (Hayman forthcoming, b) has provided some clarification of these issues. It suggested that occupation of the fort may have been more widespread than Thompson (1979) believed, and that it extended from the Late Bronze Age through to the Late Iron Age, although it is possible that the earliest site activity preceded the creation of the defences. More recently, a regular rectangular enclosure has been identified at Westcott, near Dorking, by aerial photography followed by small-scale excavations (Rapson 2003). It seems to have been constructed around 50 BC and may have effectively replaced the hillfort at Anstiebury (*ibid*, 7). It is, in fact, slightly misleading to include Westcott in this section of the report since it is actually sited on river terrace gravels near the junction of the Gault

clay and Folkestone Beds sand. Several other Iron Age sites have recently been identified near this junction including a D-shaped enclosure, perhaps connected to ritual activity at Betchworth (Williams 1996–7); an enclosed farmstead with a roundhouse at Merstham (Saunders & Weaver 2000); pits and pottery near Gatton (Robertson 1994); and similar evidence from work near Bletchingley (G Hayman, pers comm). The evidence at all these sites is predominantly Late Iron Age, extending into the Roman period. It suggests that by then, if not earlier, the narrower strips of greensand in the central and eastern parts of the county were developing in a different way from the wider expanse in the west.

In contrast, the general lack of positive evidence for Iron Age settlement from trial trench evaluations on either the western greensand or the Weald tends to confirm that the main uses of such areas were for

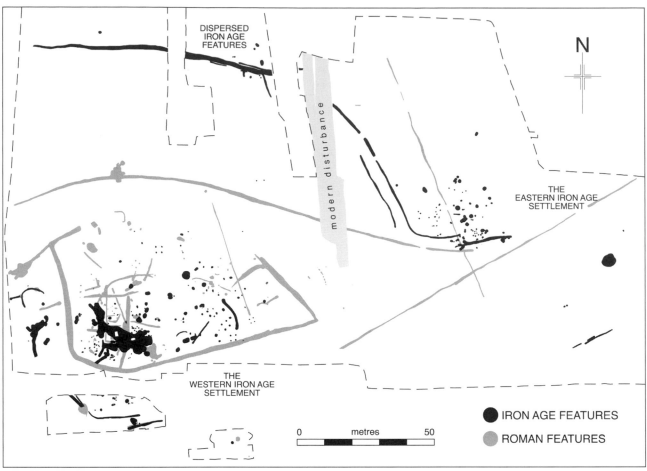

Fig 4.4   Thorpe Lea Nurseries: Iron Age and Roman settlement. Drawing by Giles Pattison

extensive grazing and exploitation of woodland, activities which did not give rise to the type of occupation that leaves much trace for the archaeologist to discover. One of the few new sites to emerge in this area is the promontory enclosure at Felday, near Holmbury St Mary (Field 1989). The evidence suggests that it was built in the Late Iron Age, and it probably performed a similar role to the other hill-forts in this area, perhaps as a replacement for Holmbury hillfort (Thompson 1979). Settlement sites may nevertheless remain to be discovered within this large area, but they will almost certainly be associated with locally favourable topographic conditions. A recent example is the discovery of evidence for Late Iron Age activity, preceding more intensive Roman settlement, on a site near Cranleigh (Dover 2002), within the Weald Clay area, but actually with super-ficial head deposits and on a south-facing slope.

In the Iron Age the Weald Clay was largely occupied by ancient woodland but the widespread discovery of Mesolithic (Ellaby 1987), Neolithic (Cotton & Field 1987) and Bronze Age (Needham 1987) flintwork and other evidence on the greensand indicates that it had been more systematically exploited. It has been suggested (Ellaby 1987, 58) that this had already led to the creation of heathland by about 6000 BC. The overall picture remains unclear,

however, and it may also be that shifting agriculture at later dates, leading to soil exhaustion, helped form heathland, substantial areas of which still survive. A very high proportion of the archaeological evidence has been recovered from fieldwalking, an activity which is relatively unlikely to recover evidence for short-term or low-intensity Iron Age activity, since the debris likely to result from such activities lacks the durable and highly recognizable character of flint-work from earlier periods. It would, therefore, be unwise to assume from negative evidence that there was a complete cessation of such activities.

One other site needs to be mentioned, and gives a rather different perspective. At Farley Heath (Lowther & Goodchild 1942–3) recent excavations (Poulton in prep, a) have confirmed that there was pre-Roman activity at the Roman temple site, perhaps extending as far back as the Neolithic period. It seems all but certain that the Romano-Celtic temple (see also Bird in this volume) was built on the site of an Iron Age sanctuary.

The North Downs and the London Clay
These two topographic zones are very distinct in appearance, but share the characteristic of having produced relatively little new Iron Age information in recent years.

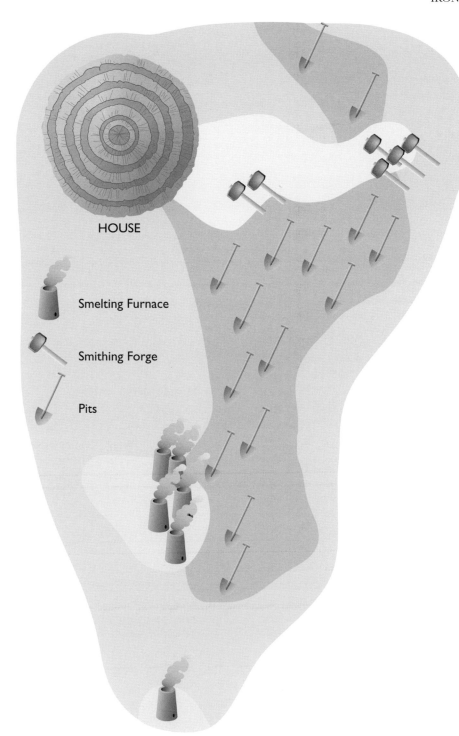

HOUSE

Smelting Furnace

Smithing Forge

Pits

Fig 4.5
Brooklands,
Weybridge:
A diagrammatic
plan of the iron
working site
(based on
Hanworth &
Tomalin 1977,
fig 8). Drawing by
Giles Pattison

The North Downs has previously produced an interesting range of Iron Age evidence, although not really comparable to the South Downs in its intensity, perhaps owing to the extensive tracts of Clay-with-Flints superficial soil cover. The sparsity of evidence between the Mole and the Wey (Hanworth 1987, 142) is also unaltered by recent work. In part this may reflect the limited opportunities which arise in an area largely protected from development by its Green Belt status.

That status is, though, shared by the North Downs east of the Mole, where some new evidence has emerged to join the already more dense distribution. Golf course construction at Farleigh Court (Hayman 1996) did not allow comprehensive investigation of

the scattered evidence (pits and pottery) which was revealed. At Warren Farm, near Ewell (Hayman 1995), rather better evidence for an Iron Age farmstead was uncovered. It is noteworthy that this site lies near the edge of the dip slope, a position it shares with a good proportion of other sites in this zone (Hanworth 1987, fig 6.1). In part this may reflect the practical advantage of being on or near the spring line, but it may also suggest the importance of a position with ready access to the resources of more than one physiographic zone. The earliest unequivocal evidence of how land tenure was organized, that of the estate system of the Saxon period (eg Poulton 1987, 217–8; Blair 1991, 12–34), shows the care that was taken to ensure that each estate shared in the

Fig 4.6   Brooklands, Weybridge: the site lay within the central area of the motor racing circuit. The late Iron Age ring ditch has a concentric palisade trench (foreground). The 23m diameter of the ring ditch suggests it might have contained only a single large roundhouse (truncation had removed the evidence), and it seems likely to have been a high-status residence. Features cutting through the ditch are of Roman date. Photograph by Graham Hayman

varied resources offered by the Surrey landscape. It seems entirely reasonable to suppose that the Iron Age settlement pattern reflects a similar distribution of resources.

The major zone to which these North Downs communities looked was the London Clay, offering opportunities for both the extensive pasture of herds and the exploitation of woodland resources. Neither older nor more recent work has produced evidence to suggest the existence of settled communities within this area. This is equally true of the Bronze Age (Needham 1987, 130) and implies that little clearance of the ancient woodland had occurred. It is true that an enclosed settlement at Old Malden (Hanworth 1987, 142–3, 146) and a recently identified settlement, with evidence for roundhouses and pits, at Alpine Avenue, Tolworth (Hawkins & Leaver 1999) are both on the London Clay (and only 1km apart). They are, however near to the edge of the London Clay, 'close to water courses and outcrops of lighter soil' (Hawkins & Leaver 1999, 149), and thus occupy a key position with ready access to the resources and markets of more than one zone.

Elsewhere, where new work has occurred on the London Clay, positive results have tended to confirm that permanent settlements begin in the Roman period (Bird 1987, 178). At Barnwood, (Poulton 1999b), near Worplesdon, a thorough excavation of nearly 1ha revealed a complex of buildings and other settlement features, beginning in the late 1st century AD, but not a single sherd or artefact to suggest earlier prehistoric activity. The Wanborough temple site (Bird in this volume) is in a class apart, like the Farley Heath site (above), since the pre-Roman activity (if it really happened) must relate to the development of a religious site.

The Blackwater valley

It is arguable that the most important development in Surrey Iron Age studies in the past generation has been the excavation of a series of major sites in the Blackwater valley, in the area around Tongham and Runfold. The amount and intensity of fieldwork, in advance of road building and mineral extraction, is impressive by any standards: around 15km of trial trenches and 8ha of formal excavation.

The sites, owing to a peculiarity of the geology of Surrey, lie in close proximity to almost all the principal physiographic zones that have been mentioned, although the North Downs are only represented by the narrow ridge of the Hog's Back. The Blackwater valley itself forms a broad plain, in this area, rather disproportionate to the small river which flows in close proximity to the main Iron Age settlement sites. The explanation is that the valley was created by the river some 50,000 years ago, prior to the capture of its headwaters by the Wey (Wymer 1987, 17). As a consequence, the reduced water flow means that the valley is not subject to flooding.

Trial trench evaluation of the 13ha of Tongham Nurseries (Bird *et al* 1996, 189, figs 1–3) revealed five concentrations of occupation evidence although the ditches of field boundaries were identified in many of the other trial trenches. Three of these areas produced evidence of typical Iron Age roundhouses, associated with enclosures, set within more extensive field systems. The roundhouses may have all conformed to a standard pattern, although not all elements survived in each case, probably owing to variable truncation by ploughing, although it is also possible that some of the variation is due to different construction techniques. The basic form of each house (assuming they were all of one structural type) consisted of a narrow penannular wall trench of *c* 10–12m diameter. At each end was a substantial posthole, framing the entrance, which faced east to south-east. This last is an almost invariable characteristic of Iron Age houses, and is generally accepted as intended to face the rising sun (eg Hill 1996). A penannular gully running parallel to and about a metre distant from the wall trench was clearly designed to catch water running off the roof of the hut and prevent it from soaking the walls.

The houses were grouped together and set within ditched enclosures. There was clear evidence that houses had both been rebuilt on the same spot and replaced in new locations, implying the existence of such enclosures over a generation or two, or more. The pottery indicates that the earliest occupation began in the early Iron Age, but that Middle-to-Late Iron Age occupation is predominant. Most features produced few finds, hence the contemporaneity of different elements within enclosures is difficult to prove.

The features which were most productive of finds were the water-holes, or wells, identified in three of the enclosures (fig 4.7a). Waterlogged conditions at the bottom of these features led to the preservation of wood, the most important item of which was a log ladder. Finds from the same feature also included complete pots (fig 4.7b) and loomweights. The disposal of items which still had a value and/or function suggests that they were deposited as part of ritual activity – a feature identified as central to the functioning of Iron Age society (eg Hill 1995). It seems probable that this involved (wholly or partially) rites of termination (Merrifield 1987) since some of the material was derived from the dismantling of a building, possibly the one adjacent to the water-hole. This material included cleft oak planks from a timber floor. Dendrochronology has not, as yet, provided an absolute date for any of the features, because the sequence cannot yet be linked to the existing dated sequences, which have a gap in the Iron Age. On the other hand, matching tree ring sequences demonstrated that sites 2 and 4 were in use at the same time.

The water-holes were also the main contributors to a variety of environmental evidence, study of which has shown that the immediate setting of these communities was one of open grassland, with some waste ground, and that they were engaged in both arable and livestock farming with access to extensive mixed woodland nearby.

There are few other clear-cut indications of how these settlements functioned. A number of four-post structures are probably granaries (cf Hanworth 1987, 144–5), but of greatest interest is the open-fronted building identified in site 5. This does not look like a normal dwelling and analysis of a crucible discovered in it suggests that it was a workshop for bronze working. The only other building in this location was of similar type, suggesting an industrial area separate from settlement enclosures.

A second area of intensive Iron Age settlement was identified, only 0.3km from the Tongham Nurseries site, at Farnham Quarry (Runfold Farm: Hayman 2002b). The Iron Age settlement has a similar date range, with an emphasis on the Middle to later Iron Age, to Tongham Nurseries, but seems to show a more complex development sequence than any of the individual sites at Tongham, not least because it continued to develop into the Roman period.

It is, nevertheless, the similarities which are most striking, with some twenty roundhouses associated with ditched enclosures, which contain pits, and other features. What stands out, more clearly even than at Tongham, is the way in which these are set within regular, rectangular fields and trackways defined by ditches (fig 4.8).

There seems little doubt that this regular, organized landscape was created over a short period of time. It is difficult to be precise, but the main development of the enclosed settlements appears to belong to the Middle Iron Age, and this seems most likely to be when the bulk of the fields and trackways were laid out. It would seem reasonable to assume that this represented a more intensive exploitation of the resources of this part of the Blackwater valley than that which preceded it. The exact density of settlement at any one time is, as already discussed, hard to define, but the impression is certainly that it was greater than could readily be supported from the produce of the valley. The excavated evidence hints at the use of mixed woodland resources nearby, and the area, close to a variety of physiographic zones, would have been well placed to exploit a diverse economic base. Beyond this, interpretation has to become increasingly speculative, but should not be avoided. One possibility is that the close proximity of all the settlement sites to the river is significant and that trade, via the Blackwater and possibly the Thames, was important to the prosperity of these communities.

Certainly, there is very little evidence that there was any great density of population in the near vicinity. Very little is known about either Caesar's Camp (Riall 1983), a definite hillfort, or the Soldier's Ring (Graham & Graham 2001), a more dubious example; even if contemporary, their significance is very uncertain as the earlier discussion of hillforts has made clear. The architectural distinction and elevation of a hillfort was not the only way to emphasize status. It has been claimed (Hunt *et al* 2002, 24) that site 4 at Tongham has a plan which strongly suggests that a chief's residence was separated from the rest of the community by a substantial enclosure bank and ditch, although the excavator (G Hayman, pers

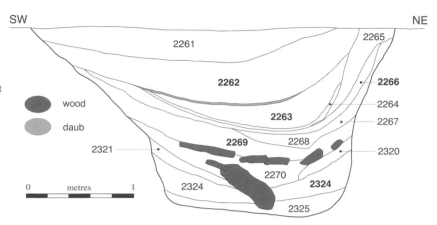

Fig 4.7a Tongham Nurseries: a water-hole revealed a fine collection of Late Iron Age pottery (see fig 4.7b). Bold context numbers indicate those contexts which produced the illustrated pots. Drawing by Giles Pattison

comm) believes that the enclosure could pre-date the more extended settlement. It is worth emphasizing how difficult it is, even on such a thoroughly excavated site, to be sure of which elements are contemporary.

The Iron Age–Roman transition

The South East, including Surrey, was rapidly and largely peacefully brought under Roman control after AD 43. Almost immediately (Bird 1987, 166–8) a new framework of administration was put in place, secured by a network of roads linking major centres. No reputable author has ever suggested that the conquest and its aftermath was accompanied by a major change in population, but a simple reading of the contrasting evidence for the two periods (cf Hanworth 1987 with Bird 1987) would suggest that there was an almost total and immediate economic dislocation.

It is not the least of the successes of recent archaeological fieldwork that it has demonstrated that the truth is far more subtle. In general terms, it should be remembered that archaeological evidence for activity on a site ending at or near the conquest does not in itself imply that the two are linked since it is clear that, looked at in the longer term, settlement shift was a common phenomenon in prehistory. At Tongham Nurseries (fig 4.7) several settlement sites come to an end in the later Iron Age. It is, however, unlikely, given the complete absence of any Roman period artefacts, that this desertion relates to the Roman conquest. The point is emphasized by the clear evidence for continuity of activity at the Farnham Quarry (Runfold Farm) site (fig 4.8). The occupation there ends, however, at around AD 100. A very similar end date is also likely for the Brooklands Central (South) site (fig 4.6), which again demonstrated a clear continuity of occupation from the Iron Age. It may be suggested that this desertion reflects the gradual working through of the effects of the Roman remodelling of the economic system.

Not all sites which exhibit continuity cease to function at the same time. The settlement at Thorpe Lea

Nurseries (fig 4.4) continued into the late 3rd or 4th century AD. It is interesting, however, that field boundaries associated with it were re-modelled, probably in the 2nd century. Elsewhere in the Thames gravels, at Perry Oaks (Barrett *et al* 2001, 227) and Hengrove Farm (G Hayman, pers comm: excavation in progress 2002), for example, there is evidence that the field systems established in the Bronze Age were finally superseded in the Roman period. The effects of the conquest, rapidly obvious in the new roads, towns and villas, were eventually felt in every aspect of society.

Conclusions

It is becoming increasingly apparent that the introduction of domestic animals and cultivated cereals did not transform the hunter-gatherer lifestyle to a sedentary farming existence in such an immediate and dramatic manner as earlier generations supposed. Neither, in turn, should we too readily adopt a new orthodoxy in which the transformation into a settled agricultural landscape of the gravel terraces of the Thames valley in the Middle Bronze Age, which has now been so cogently demonstrated, is regarded as a pattern for the development of the whole region. The evidence presented above makes it clear that semi-nomadic communities continued to be dominant over much of Surrey down to the Late Bronze Age, or even the Middle Iron Age, as in the Blackwater valley.

In some areas this mode of life did not come to an end until well into the Saxon period, in the earlier part of which transhumance is clearly fundamental to a great deal of the economy (Poulton 1987, 215, 218). Viewed from this perspective, there is nothing surprising in the realization that Iron Age settlements were located to allow the exploitation of the diverse resources which Surrey's varied physiographic zones offer. Indeed, the question might reasonably be asked whether the structure of the agricultural estates which emerged in the early Saxon period did not owe much to prehistoric developments, despite the transformation of the macro-economy in the Roman period. In a similar vein, Blair (1991, 22–3) has

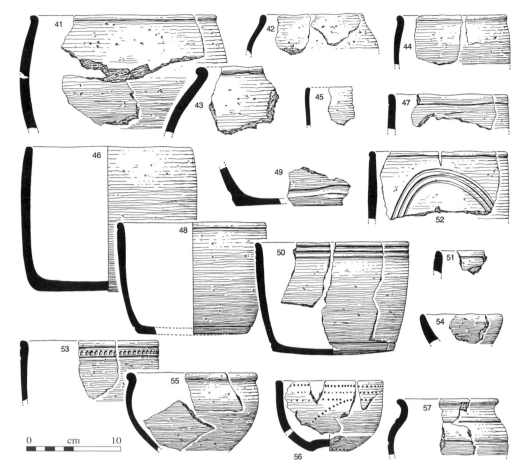

Fig 4.7b Tongham Nurseries: Late Iron Age pottery, including bead-rimmed jars, bowls, and saucepan pots, from the water-hole (fig 4.7a). Pot numbers 41, 43–6, 50, 52, and 56 are warped and may be wasters. The decorated cup with an omphaloid base (56) and the cordon neck jar (57), an antecedent of the early Roman form, are of particular interest. Scale 1:4. Drawing by Phil Jones

wondered how far the territorial geography of early Saxon Surrey derives from that of Iron Age and Roman times.

This, of course, is only one way of looking at the Iron Age evidence and some might argue is a view that, in particular, fails to engage with the people behind the economic developments. Its strength, however, is that it focuses upon what is peculiarly characteristic of Surrey about the evidence. The same evidence undoubtedly has much to contribute to discussion of the structure of society, religion and ritual, and industry, among other topics. Hanworth (1987) addressed some of these but further understanding must await deeper and wider studies than the present essay.

The future

There can be no doubt that the most important advances in our understanding of the Iron Age over the last twenty years have been due to development-led archaeological excavation, and it is certain that this will continue to be the case for some years to come.

The Colne, Thames, and Upper Wey valleys have seen the greatest concentration of work (see also Cotton in this volume). It was such areas that John Barrett was thinking of when in a recent lecture (IFA conference, April 2003) he suggested that further meticulous excavation of individual sites was at risk of accumulating data without necessarily advancing knowledge. The short-term implication, for individual sites, is that effort and resources should be concentrated towards elements which are different from the norm, and into features which will produce the environmental and dating evidence which remains comparatively weak. More generally, there is an urgent need for synthetic studies, at a regional level, of aspects such as Iron Age pottery, or placed deposits, to guide and inform future work.

The remainder of the county has, apart from the Blackwater valley, produced far less new material. In part this may be attributed to less intense development pressures, but it also reflects fundamental differences in archaeological potential between different physiographic zones. This is not to suggest that archaeological evaluation of, for example, developments sited on Weald Clay should be abandoned. It is clear that very localized conditions within such areas can produce an environment much more attractive to settlement, and that these circumstances are not always obvious from surface examination. In addition further negative evidence is still needed to support this hypothesis, while positive evidence is potentially of exceptional importance.

Fig 4.8   Runfold Farm (Farnham Quarry): Iron Age and Roman settlement. Drawing by Giles Pattison

There is, at present, a renewed drive towards the development of research agendas at various levels. Most of those produced in recent years have remained scarcely more than wish lists, with little discernible direct effect on the work carried out. It is probable that this will happen again, unless agendas are explicitly connected to what is practical.

All this presupposes, as Barrett did, that the proper context for archaeological work to be viewed in is that of broad historical themes and enquiry. There is, however, another historical tradition – and one of far greater relevance to the general practice of archaeology – that of local history. Viewed in this way, it is not 'yet another Iron Age roundhouse', but 'Springfield's Iron Age roundhouse', and no more to be regarded as superfluous than one of its 16th century timber-framed buildings. The most important issue from this perspective is one of

accessibility, of how to make archaeological information readily available to the public. Local history has always been well served by record offices (and now excellently in Surrey by the Surrey History Centre) and it is their standard of resource provision and informed advice to which archaeology should aspire.

ACKNOWLEDGEMENTS

I would like to thank all my colleagues at the Surrey County Archaeological Unit, but especially Graham Hayman, who directed many of the excavations referred to and also commented on the text. Tim Carew of Pre-Construct Archaeology kindly provided information on the Ashford Prison site, and Jon Cotton has assisted in a number of ways, not least preparing the Annexe to this chapter. I am very grateful to both of them.

ANNEXE
Reported discoveries of Iron Age date since 1987

This list was prepared by Jon Cotton and is arranged in the same way as the Annexe to his chapter in this volume. The following abbreviations are used: IA: Iron Age; RB: Romano-British; M, L: Middle, Late. Bold numbers in parentheses refer to issue numbers of the Surrey Archaeological Society *Bulletin*.

THE WEALD

Cranleigh, Wyphurst Road, LIA/RB activity (Dover 2002; Poulton, this paper, 56)

Outwood area, LIA/RB iron smelting (Robin Tanner, pers comm)

Oxted, Hurst Green, E/MIA bronze brooch (Williams 1996, 167)

THE GREENSAND HILLS

Anstiebury hillfort, LIA internal features (**247**; **259**) (Bird *et al* 1990, 206; Bird *et al* 1994, 206)

Betchworth, Franks' Sandpit, LIA/RB enclosure with apsidal end (**307**) (Jackson *et al* 1999, 225)

Bletchingley, LIA bronze strap-union (Williams 1999, 172); LIA bronze brooch of Aylesford type and silver unit of Amminus (Williams 2001, 309)

Farley Heath, temple site, IA activity (Jackson *et al* 1997; Poulton, this paper, 56)

Gatton Bottom, Whitehall Farm, IA pits containing traces of iron processing (Jackson *et al* 1997, 209)

Godstone, LIA bronze baldric- or belt-hook (Williams 1999, 171–2)

Holmbury St Mary, Felday, LIA/RB univallate enclosure (Field 1989)

Merstham, Battlebridge Lane, LIA/RB rectilinear enclosure with roundhouse (**340**) (Howe *et al* 2000, 191)

Puttenham, Hillbury Camp, topographic survey (**346**) (Howe *et al* 2001, 350; Howe *et al* 2002, 269 & fig 5)

South Godstone, LIA gold quarter stater of Tasciovanus (Williams 2001, 309)

Westcott, M–LIA rectilinear enclosure with single east-facing entrance (**354**)

THE NORTH DOWNS

Caterham, Gravelly Hill, possible field system close to the War Coppice hillfort (**268**) (Bird *et al* 1996, 202)

Effingham Upper Common, possible banjo enclosure and associated field system (Bird *et al* 1990, 205)

Ewell, The Looe, Reigate Road, M–LIA/RB settlement (Cotton 2001)

Ewell, Warren Farm, M–LIA pits and ditches with quernstones (Jackson *et al* 1997, 199)

Leatherhead, Bockett's Farm, possible field system (**249**; **252**) (Bird *et al* 1991–2, 150)

Mickleham and Leatherhead Downs, field system (**345**)

Shere, Colekitchen Lane, IA sword scabbard mount of cast bronze (**330**) (Howe *et al* 2000, 188)

Warlingham, Farleigh Court, LIA/RB settlement, cremations (**299**) (Jackson *et al* 1997, 214–15)

Woodmansterne, Merrymeet, IA silver coin (Harp 2002; Howe *et al* 2002, 263)

THE BAGSHOT TABLE

Bagshot, 42 London Road, LIA/RB settlement and possibly related iron working (**279**) (Bird *et al* 1996, 201–2)

Pirbright, Manor House, M–LIA ditches and finds of this and earlier date (**300**) (Jackson *et al* 1999, 222)

THE THAMES VALLEY AND ITS TRIBUTARIES

Addlestone, Wey Manor Farm, MIA settlement and field system (**321**; **326**) (Jackson *et al* 1997, 210; Jackson *et al* 1999, 229 & fig 2; 2000)

Ashford, Woodthorpe Road, M–LIA settlement of nine round-houses with 4-post structures (Tim Carew, pers comm; Howe *et al* 2002, 267 & fig 4)

Egham, 64–65 High Street, LIA features including a possible circular stake-built structure (Howe *et al* 2000, 192)

Egham, Thorpe Lea Nurseries, M–LIA/RB enclosures and several settlement foci including field system and trackways (Bird *et al* 1991–2, 153 & figs 5 & 6; Bird *et al* 1996, 199; Jackson *et al* 1997, 209)

Laleham, Fairylands Caravan Park, M–LIA/RB settlement (**315**) (Jackson *et al* 1999, 230 & fig 3; Taylor-Wilson 2002)

Runfold, Farnham Quarry (Runfold Farm), M–LIA/RB settlement with twenty roundhouses, field systems and ditched enclosures containing pits and water-holes (**321**; **348**) (Jackson *et al* 1999, 238 & fig 6; Howe *et al* 2000, 199 & fig 6; Howe *et al* 2001, 350 & fig 5)

Shepperton, Chertsey Road, former Anchor Garage, LIA female inhumation in pit (Howe *et al* 2002, 265 & fig 3)

Shepperton Ranges, three iron swords, one with decorative scabbard fittings, and human skulls recovered from a buried river channel (Bird *et al* 1989, 182; Bird *et al* 1990, 211; Poulton, this paper, 53 & fig 4.3)

Staines, 2–8 High Street, LIA/RB activity (Jackson *et al* 1997, 212)

Staines, Matthew Arnold School, possible banjo enclosure (Howe *et al* 2001, 348)

Stanwell, Lower Mill Farm, MIA roundhouses (Jones & Poulton 1987; Bird *et al* 1989, 182)

Tongham, Grange Road, settlement features (**273**) (Bird *et al* 1996, 189)

Tongham, Tongham Nurseries, five M–LIA settlement areas with roundhouses, pits and water-holes set within field systems (**281**) (Bird *et al* 1996, 189 & figs 1–3)

Weybridge, Brooklands Race Track, two M–LIA settlements, one including a small circular enclosure (?surrounding a roundhouse), pits and 4-post structures (**258**) (Bird *et al* 1991–2, 147 & fig 1)

Wisley, archaeomagnetic dating of hearth to 1st century BC (Bird *et al* 1990, 205)

BIBLIOGRAPHY

Please note that where Surrey County Archaeological Unit (SCAU) client reports are referred to they are available either through the Surrey Archaeological Society library at Guildford or through the Sites and Monuments Record (SMR) at County Hall, Kingston. The volume referred to in the bibliography as SCAU forthcoming has been accepted for publication by Surrey Archaeological Society, but is awaiting (June 2003) completion of revision following referees' and editorial comments.

Bannister, N, 2004 The Surrey Historic Landscape Characterisation Project, in Cotton *et al* 2004, 119–32

Barrett, J C, Lewis, J S C, & Welsh, K, 2000 Perry Oaks – a history of inhabitation, part 1, *London Archaeol*, **9.7**, 195–9

——, 2001 Perry Oaks – a history of inhabitation, part 2, *London Archaeol*, **9.8**, 221–7

Bird, D G, 1987 The Romano-British period in Surrey, in Bird & Bird 1987, 165–96

——, 2004 Roman religious sites in the landscape, in Cotton *et al* 2004, 77–90

Bird, D G, Crocker, G, & McCracken, J S, 1989 Archaeology in Surrey 1987, *SyAC*, **79**, 179–89

——, 1990 Archaeology in Surrey 1988–1989, *SyAC*, **80**, 201–27

——, 1991–2 Archaeology in Surrey 1990, *SyAC*, **81**, 147–67

Bird, D G, Crocker, G, McCracken, J S, & Saich, D, 1994 Archaeology in Surrey 1991, *SyAC*, **82**, 203–29

Bird, D G, Crocker, G, Maloney, C, & Saich, D, 1996 Archaeology in Surrey 1992–3, *SyAC*, **83**, 187–228

Bird, J, & Bird, D G (eds), 1987 *The archaeology of Surrey to 1540*, SyAS

Blair, J, 1991 *Early medieval Surrey: landholding, church and settlement before 1300*

Bradley, R, 1990 *The passage of arms: an archaeological analysis of prehistoric hoards and votive deposits*

Cotton, J, 2001 Prehistoric and Roman settlement in Reigate Road, Ewell: fieldwork conducted by Tom K Walls 1945–52, *SyAC*, **88**, 1–42

——, 2004 Surrey's early past: a survey of recent work, in Cotton *et al* 2004, 19–38

Cotton, J, Crocker, G, & Graham, A (eds), 2004 *Aspects of archaeology and history in Surrey: towards a research framework for the county*, SyAS

Dover, M, 2002 A second archaeological evaluation of the proposed development of land off Wyphurst Road, Cranleigh, Surrey, SCAU unpublished client report

Ellaby, R, 1987 The Upper Palaeolithic and Mesolithic in Surrey, in Bird & Bird 1987, 53–70

Field, D, 1989 Felday, Holmbury St Mary: an earthwork enclosure of the 1st century AD, *SyAC*, **79**, 99–116

Field, D, & Cotton, J, 1987   Neolithic Surrey: a survey of the evidence, in Bird & Bird 1987, 71–96

Graham, D, & Graham, A, 2001   Soldier's Ring, Crooksbury, near Farnham, *SyAS Bull*, **305,** 2

Grimes, W F, & Close-Brooks, 1993   The excavation of Caesar's Camp, Heathrow, Harmondsworth, Middlesex 1944, *Proc Prehist Soc,* **59,** 303–60

Hanworth, R, 1987   The Iron Age in Surrey, in Bird & Bird 1987, 139–64

Hanworth, R, & Tomalin, D J, 1977   *Brooklands, Weybridge: the excavation of an Iron Age and medieval site*, SyAS Res Vol, **4**

Harp, P, 2002   Iron Age and Romano-British finds from Woodmansterne, Walton Heath and Banstead, *Plateau Archaeol Grp Bull,* **3,** 31–3

Hawkins, D, & Leaver, S, 1999   An Iron Age settlement at Alpine Avenue, Tolworth, *SyAC,* **86,** 141–9

Hayman, G, 1991a   Recent excavations at the former Brooklands race-track, *SyAS Bull,* **258**

——, 1991b   Bronze Age settlement evidence at Home Farm, Laleham, *SyAS Bull,* **262**

——, 1995   An archaeological excavation at Warren Farm, Ewell, SCAU unpublished client report

——, 1996   Discoveries of Late Iron Age and Roman date at Farleigh Court Golf course, near Warlingham, *SyAS Bull,* **299,** 5–10

——, 1997   Further archaeological work at Home Farm, Laleham (TQ 059 691), *SyAS Bull,* **311,** 4–5

——, 1998a   Excavations at Home Farm, Laleham in 1997, *SyAS Bull,* **320,** 1–3

——, 1998b   Archaeological excavation of Bronze Age, Iron Age and Roman settlements, enclosures and boundary features at Thorpe Lea Nurseries, Egham, Surrey, SCAU unpublished client report

——, 2002a   Archaeological discoveries, principally of Neolithic and Bronze Age date, within Home Farm, Laleham mineral extraction site 1991–9, SCAU unpublished client report

——, 2002b   Archaeological work at Runfold Farm (Farnham Quarry), SCAU unpublished client report

——, forthcoming (a)   An archaeological excavation at The Manor House, Pirbright, in SCAU forthcoming

——, forthcoming (b)   Archaeological excavations at Anstiebury camp hillfort, Coldharbour, Surrey, in SCAU forthcoming

——, in prep   Archaeological excavations at Wey Manor Farm, Addlestone (TQ 058 634)

Hill, J D, 1995   *Ritual and rubbish in the Iron Age of Wessex*, BAR Brit Ser, **242**

——, 1996   Weaving the strands of a new Iron Age, *Brit Archaeol,* **17,** 8–9

Howe, T, Jackson, G, & Maloney, C, 2001   Archaeology in Surrey 2000, *SyAC,* **88,** 343–63

——, 2002   Archaeology in Surrey 2001, *SyAC,* **89,** 257–81

Howe, T, Jackson, G, Maloney, C, & Saich, D, 2000   Archaeology in Surrey 1997–9, *SyAC,* **87,** 183–218

Hunt, R, Graham, D, Pattison, G, & Poulton, R, 2002   *Hidden Depths: an archaeological exploration of Surrey's past*, SyAS

Jackson, G, Maloney, C, & Saich, D, 1997   Archaeology in Surrey 1994–5, *SyAC,* **84,** 195–243

——, 1999   Archaeology in Surrey 1996–7, *SyAC,* **86,** 217–55

Jones, P, forthcoming (a)   Archaeological fieldwork at Abbey Meads, Chertsey, in SCAU forthcoming

——, forthcoming (b)   Archaeological fieldwork at St Ann's Hill, Chertsey, in SCAU forthcoming

Jones, P, & Poulton, R, 1987   Iron Age hut circles discovered near Lower Mill Farm, Stanwell (TQ 0357 7418), *Trans London Middlesex Archaeol Soc,* **38,** 1–10

Lowther, A W G, 1949   Iron Age pottery from St George's Hill camp, Weybridge, *SyAC,* **51,** 144–7

Lowther, A W G & Goodchild, R G, 1943   Excavations at Farley Heath, Albury, during 1939, *SyAC,* **48,** 31–40

Macphail, R, & Scaife, R 1987   The geographical and environmental background, in Bird & Bird 1987, 31–51

Merrifield, R, 1987   *The archaeology of ritual and magic*

Merriman, N, 2000   Changing approaches to the first millennium BC, in *London underground: the archaeology of a city* (eds I D Haynes, H Sheldon & L Hannigan), 35–51

McOmish, D S, & Field D J, 1994   A survey of the earthworks at St Ann's Hill, Chertsey, *SyAC,* **82,** 223–5

Needham, S, 1987   The Bronze Age, in Bird & Bird 1987, 97–138

O'Connell, M, 1990   Excavations during 1979–1985 of a multi-period site at Stanwell, *SyAC,* **80,** 1–62

Poulton, R, 1987   Saxon Surrey, in Bird & Bird 1987, 197–222

——, 1999a   Fieldwork by the Surrey County Archaeological Unit during 1998, *SyAS Bull,* **328,** 8–14

——, 1999b   The excavation of a Roman settlement site adjacent to Broad Street Common, Worplesdon, Surrey, *SyAS Bull,* **334,** 1–6

——, 2000   Fieldwork by the Surrey County Archaeological Unit during 1999, *SyAS Bull,* **337,** 8–13

——, forthcoming   Excavations at Shepperton Ranges, in SCAU forthcoming

——, in prep   Farley Heath Roman temple

Poulton, R, & O'Connell, M, 1984   St George's Hill fort: excavations in 1981, *SyAC,* **75,** 275–80

Poulton, R, & Scott, E, 1992   The hoarding, deposition and use of pewter in Roman Britain, in *Theoretical Roman archaeology, First Conference Proceedings* (ed E Scott), 115–32

Rapson, G, 2003   An Iron Age enclosure at Westcott: first interim report, *SyAS Bull,* **367,** 4–8

Riall, N, 1983   Excavations at Caesar's Camp, Aldershot, Hampshire, *Proc Hampshire Fld Club Archaeol Soc,* **39,** 47–55

Robertson, J, 1994   An archaeological watching brief on the proposed golf course development at Whitehall Farm, Gattom Bottom, Reigate, SCAU unpublished client report

Saunders, M J, & Weaver, S D G, 2000   Battlebridge Lane, Merstham, a Late Iron Age/Early Roman settlement enclosure, *SyAS Bull,* **340,** 3–5

SCAU, 1997   Fieldwork by the Surrey County Archaeological Unit in 1996, *SyAS Bull,* **314,** 7–13

——, 1998   Fieldwork by the Surrey County Archaeological Unit in 1997, *SyAS Bull,* **321,** 5–11

——, 2001   Fieldwork by the Surrey County Archaeological Unit during 2000, *SyAS Bull,* **349,** 5–7, 10–11

——, 2002   Fieldwork by the Surrey County Archaeological Unit during 2001, *SyAS Bull,* **358,** 7–12

——, forthcoming   Archaeological investigation on a number of sites, principally of prehistoric date, in Surrey, *SyAC*

Stead, I M, 1987   The Chertsey shield, *SyAC,* **78,** 181–3

Stevenson, J, 1999   An archaeological watching brief at St George's Hill, Weybridge, Surrey, SCAU unpublished client report

Taylor-Wilson, R, 2002   Excavation of a multi-period site at Laleham, 1997, *SyAC,* **89,** 137–69

Thompson, F H, 1979   Three Surrey hillforts: excavations at Anstiebury, Holmbury and Hascombe, 1972–77, *Antiq J,* **59,** 245–318

Williams, D, 1996   Some recent finds from east Surrey, *SyAC,* **83,** 165–86

——, 1996–7   Betchworth: excavations at Franks' Sandpit, *SyAS Bull,* **307,** 2–3

——, 1999   Some recent finds from Surrey, *SyAC,* **86,** 171–97

——, 2001   Recent finds from Surrey 1997–9, *SyAC,* **88,** 309–31

Wymer, J J, 1987   The Palaeolithic period in Surrey, in Bird & Bird 1987, 17–30

Yates, D, 2001   Bronze Age agricultural intensification in the Thames valley and estuary, in *Bronze Age landscapes: tradition and transformation* (ed J Brück), 65–82

Rob Poulton, Surrey County Archaeological Unit, Surrey History Centre, 130 Goldsworth Road, Woking, GU21 6ND

5

Surrey in the Roman period: a survey of recent discoveries

DAVID BIRD

This paper aims only to provide a brief update to the survey of the Roman period in Surrey previously published in The Archaeology of Surrey to 1540 *(Bird 1987; for the South East in general see Rudling 1988). The London region part of the relevant area has been covered recently (Bird 1996 & 2000b; Perring & Brigham 2000; Sheldon 2000) and will therefore receive less detailed attention.*

In order to avoid overloading the text with large numbers of references, those that refer to site work have been gathered together at the end, where they are ordered alphabetically by the site name used in the text, grouped where appropriate under a more general heading, for example 'Staines'. The locations of the most important sites are shown on figure 5.1.

Introduction

Although it is under twenty years since the last full survey of Surrey in the Roman period (Bird 1987), there is a great deal of new evidence to be taken into account. There can be no doubt that most of this is the outcome of fieldwork in the last decade, usually because of the increase in development-led archae-ology, as a result of planning policies based on Planning Policy Guidance note PPG16. In conse-quence most of the new work has still to be fully studied and reported. Once this has been done we can expect to know a lot more about Romano-British Surrey, in particular about the countryside, both in terms of how it was ordered and in terms of what was grown or managed and what animals were farmed or hunted. Evidence for these aspects has previously been sadly lacking.

There is still a need for much more fieldwork to put the known sites, in particular the villas, into their setting, and we can also begin to think in terms of studying changes through time, as better-dated sites are becoming available. There are also a growing number of properly reported metal detector finds to be taken into account. These finds add to the picture generally and in some cases point to the existence of previously unlocated sites (Bird, J 1996c; 1999c; 2001). For example cosmetic grinders, previously an unrecorded type in Surrey, are now known from Chipstead (Bird, J 1999a), Beddington, the Mole area and Warlingham (Jackson forthcoming). The last three illustrate well the variety of finds recording: one is from an excavation, one was badly reported in the metal detecting press without proper details; one was reported to and donated to the British Museum. The rare find of a gold bulla (an oval box-like amulet) from Chelsham (Bird 2001, 315, no 39) should also be noted; some years ago Henig could not cite an example from Roman Britain (Henig 1984, 186).

Current evidence still favours a foundation date of *c* AD 50 for London and Southwark, although it has been suggested that there was earlier activity at the latter (Sheldon 2000, 131; Brigham 2001, 8–30; Drummond-Murray & Thompson 2002, 24, 49). Roman settlement at Southwark, however, only makes sense following the creation of the roads which had to be engineered across the marshes in this area, and the only point in doing that was to cross at London because London had been created (Bird, D 1999b). The initial absence of London offers some support to the theory that the Roman forces in AD 43 landed in the Solent area rather than in Kent, and established an early base at Silchester before heading along the river corridor to complete the first campaign (Bird 2000a; see also Frere & Fulford 2001; Bird 2002b; Sauer 2002). In any event the early prominence of Colchester and Silchester implies an early date for the Thames crossing at Staines on the road between them. This would also have required engineering to deal with flood-prone areas. Stane Street is unlikely to have been part of the initial campaigns and before it was built the possibility of a Chichester–Iping–Staines road might be considered (Bird, D 1999b).

It is now thought unlikely that there was an early fort at Staines (Bird 1996, 228, n14) and further consideration of the Westcott cropmark site also makes a military explanation there unlikely. This is in keeping with the rest of south-east England, where it seems that a Roman military presence was not required (apart from the major fortresses) except perhaps following the Boudican revolt. Good evidence for destruction at that time has now been found in Southwark (Sheldon 2000, 132), indicating that Boudica's forces were active south of the Thames, and therefore lending some support to the idea that their next targets would have been the new

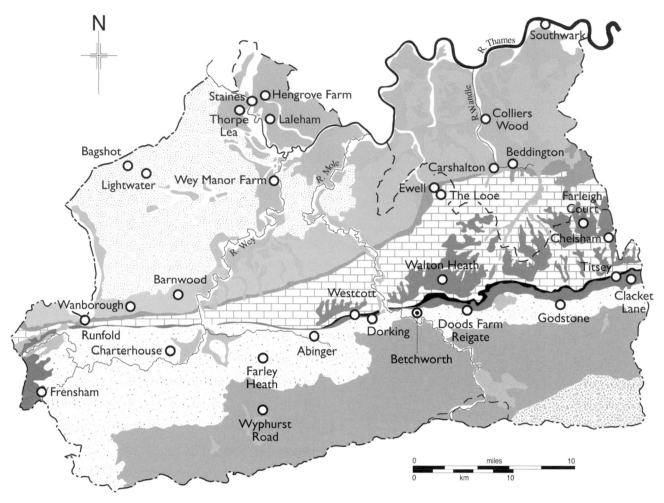

Fig 5.1   Locations of major sites mentioned in the text. For key to geological background see map on page x.

towns to the west (Bird 1987, 192, n9). Surrey probably fell within a general Atrebatic area (the high percentage of Atrebatic coins at Wanborough might be noted: Cheesman 1994, 35–6) and may initially have been administered as part of a client kingdom ruled by Cogidubnus (or Togidubnus) (Henig 2002, 37–62, *passim*), before becoming part of a smaller formalized 'tribal' area of the Atrebates set up when the kingdom was absorbed into the Roman province. The boundary between Atrebates and Cantiaci may, however, have been set somewhere within Surrey. In general there is little to suggest much change at first as a result of the events of AD 43; where there is evidence for the Late Iron Age landscape it seems that this often continued in use into the Roman period (see Poulton in this volume). Indeed available evidence tends to suggest no great landscape change until around AD 200 (see further below).

Communications

There has been little advance in our understanding of communications in Surrey. We still have no good evidence for the use of the rivers for transport (see Bird 1996, 228, nn 12, 13). The known roads have been tested in a number of places; for example: Watling Street in Peckham; the London–Silchester road in Windsor Great Park; Stane Street at Colliers

Wood (where there was apparently more than one track, perhaps because of the river crossing), at Tyrells Wood, in central Dorking (the probable line) and at both North and South Holmwood (Hall 2003); the London–Lewes road at the M25 crossing (Clacket Lane) and further south (Trevereux and Waylands Farm). The linch pin from near Chelsham hints at the kind of traffic using this road (Bird 1997).

The postulated London–Winchester road (Bird 1987, 168) remains unlocated in the county, but the increasing evidence for Romano-British settlement sites around Tongham, Runfold, Wanborough and in the north Guildford area (see below) makes it possible to suggest a route from the Farnham area along north of the Hog's Back, across Broadstreet Common and on to Burpham, where the idea of a Roman-period river crossing has received support (Alexander 1997). It has been suggested that such a road might have acted as a catalyst for opening up the area to settlement (Poulton 1999b), and that it might have continued to Ewell (Orton 1999), but another possibility might be a route following more or less the line of the later London–Portsmouth road, which is carefully laid out to take account of the courses of the Wey, Mole and Thames. If a major Roman road existed on this line, then inns and horse-changing facilities are to be expected at the crossing of the Mole and the Beverley Brook (or perhaps the Hogsmill), and it must be said that at present there is little to suggest that this was the case, although the siting of the Chatley Farm bath-house becomes of interest in this context (Frere 1949).

Larger settlements

There is reasonable evidence for an inner ring of small settlements on the roads radiating out from London, including at Merton and Croydon, where there have been recent finds (Bird 2000b, 156). These probably served the needs of travellers. Settlements at the next journey stage out along the main roads were at Staines and perhaps Dorking; the spread of evidence for occupation at the latter may now indicate more than a farm or villa (see below). Evidence for the settlement at Alfoldean, just south of the county boundary, has recently been reported (Luke & Wells 2000). Development pressures have led to most archaeological work being carried out in Southwark and Staines, with a resulting increase in knowledge, noted briefly below. All the evidence for Ewell has recently been gathered together (Abdy & Bierton 1997), and work for the publication of the excavations at the King William IV site has led to the suggestion that the settlement might have had a religious function, as well as acting as the centre of a woollen industry (Bird 1996, 224; 2000b, 156; 2002b).

Settlement distribution and comparison with the medieval pattern suggests that a roadside settlement similar to Ewell ought to have existed somewhere in south-west Surrey (cf Bird 1996, 227); Orton (1999) has suggested that there may have been something of the sort at the Broadstreet Common site. Recent discoveries at Skerne Road in Kingston may indicate that evidence for a Roman-period settlement north of the present town centre was destroyed by river erosion, thus explaining why residual Roman tile and pottery is found in alluvial deposits there (Duncan Hawkins, pers comm). The inhumation cemetery at Canbury Field nearby (Hinton 1984), if Roman, also suggests a settlement larger than a farm or two. The finds at Godstone might indicate a small roadside settlement, if it is not a religious site (see further below). An interesting question that needs to be addressed is the origin of the population of these small towns or large villages, which apparently had no Iron Age predecessors in this area; does this imply a growth in the population generally or were some of the sites in the countryside abandoned?

Our current understanding of Roman Southwark has recently been summarized by Sheldon (2000; see also Drummond-Murray & Thompson 2002 and Taylor-Wilson 2002). It has become clear that the area was generally low-lying and wet, with a number of islands of slightly higher land. The settlement occupied two of these islands, while others nearby were used for agriculture. Water was managed by channels kept under control by revetments, but if there were ever large wooden waterfront structures along the main course of the Thames, like those in London on the north bank, they will have been destroyed by later river action. There is now good archaeological evidence for clay-and-timber buildings constructed around AD 50 and burnt down at the time of Boudica; rebuilding followed and from the Flavian period the two islands became built up, with buildings possibly occupying more than 12ha. There is no evidence for formal planning; buildings seem to have lined the two main roads and then expanded behind them as required. Excavations currently in progress near Tabard Street have produced evidence for early clay-and-timber buildings on the northern edge of the 'dry land' just to the south of the southernmost island (Gary Brown, pers comm). These were later replaced by a Roman religious site and it may be that settlement as such was moved on to the islands as more space became available through reclamation. There are however indications that there are more later buildings to find; if the settlement did move then these should prove to be burial-related, perhaps like the Great Dover Street cemetery further along Watling Street – cremations have already been found on the site.

Parts of more than twenty stone-founded buildings are known in Southwark, mostly on the 'north island', some with mosaics and tessellated floors. There is also evidence for more than 40 clay-and-timber buildings, more evenly divided between the two islands. One wooden building, dated by dendrochronology to about AD 152, had a remarkably well-preserved floor of oak and is assumed to be part of a warehouse. The stone buildings include the extensive and high-quality complex with baths on the Winchester Palace site. This was started before the mid-2nd century and seems to have had some sort of military connection. An earlier complex at 15–23 Southwark Street began around AD 75 and had a long life; it had tessellated floors and hypocausts and has been interpreted as a mansio. There were no doubt also less official inns and the settlement has produced good evidence for widespread trade, for iron smithing and working of copper alloys, and use of the nearby watery environments. An inscription (fig 5.2) found at the Tabard Street site mentioned above may indicate that Southwark was seen administratively as part of the wider London settlement (Anon 2002), although since the status of London is not fully understood (eg Wilkes 1996) this is not especially helpful.

Most of the archaeological work carried out in Staines is still unpublished, although there is a synthesis based on work up to about 1988 (Burnham &

Fig 5.2   Tabard Street Southwark: inscription to the spirits of the emperors and the god Mars Camulos by Tiberinius Celerianus, *Moritex*. Photograph copyright Pre-Construct Archaeology

Wacher 1990, 306–10), but reports on some of the older excavations are expected soon (Jones & Poulton in prep). The earliest evidence for buildings seems to be for the Neronian/Flavian period, although there are finds of earlier material. Traces of timber buildings have been found on a number of sites, such as Johnson & Clark, 73–75 High Street, Tilly's Lane and 78–88 High Street, although it has been suggested that there were fewer buildings north of the High Street (McKinley forthcoming). The Tilly's Lane site also had a later 2nd century stone-founded building with

red tessellated floors surviving *in situ* (fig 5.3); it probably did not last long as the floors subsided into earlier pits and there may have been a fire. There was evidence for the former existence of a black and white tessellated floor and a hypocaust at Johnson & Clark; at this latter site earlier buildings had been burnt down in the late 1st or early 2nd century. Several sites had evidence for ovens, hearths and wells, and the later dark earth often found in Roman towns – for example at 2–8 and 73–75 High Street. The discovery of a collyrium stamp at this last site should be noted as it implies the presence of a healer probably serving quite a wide area (Jackson 1996, esp 177 and 184).

Evidence for town boundary ditches has been found at a number of sites (eg Clarence Street and Tilly's Lane); they probably served particularly to protect against the flooding for which there is widespread evidence in the later 2nd and 3rd centuries both inside and outside the town. Waterlogged deposits on the western fringes of the town, for example at Clarence Street and in the Riverside Gardens site near the Old Town Hall, have produced evidence for leather working, perhaps associated with previously noted evidence for the butchery of cattle. As well as leather shoes and offcuts, finds included a rare wooden double-sided comb (fig 5.4), a timely reminder of the kind of common item that is usually missing from the archaeological record.

Like Southwark, Staines grew up at a bridging point on a gravel island in a generally wet area. The Courage Brewery site on the next 'island' to the west has produced evidence suggesting Roman buildings, unless it was material taken outside the town to dump.

Fig 5.3   Tilly's Lane, Staines: in the foreground, walls and red tessellated floor of a later 2nd century building; the floors soon subsided into depressions caused by earlier features. The High Street can be seen in the background. Photograph copyright Wessex Archaeology

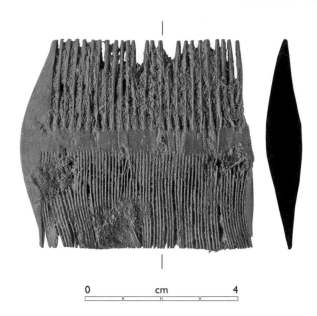

Fig 5.4 Wooden comb from Staines. Photograph copyright Surrey County Archaeological Unit

On more 'islands' to the north, evidence from the Central Trading Estate indicates the existence of fields and enclosures, with some information about the food produced and for the general environment of the town. To east and south, along the London and Kingston Roads, Roman-period burials, both cremations and inhumations, have been found. There is also evidence for occupation in the 4th century, which is unusual in a cemetery area. It may indicate expansion, or possibly implies a radical shift in the settlement pattern, perhaps because of the effects of flooding at the western end of the town.

There has been much less recent archaeological work in Ewell, but the publication of the King William IV site marks an important advance in our knowledge. Recent excavation in Church Field located the course of Stane Street together with evidence suggesting the presence of two buildings including a hypocaust and occupation from the 1st to the 4th centuries. Sites in the High Street, Church Street and West Street have also produced some evidence for buildings, pits and a well and a notable chance find from the churchyard was a probable imported wine strainer with zoomorphic design. In Dorking sites in Church Street, north of the High Street and in the newly created Church Square have produced evidence for buildings, again with 1st to 4th century material.

The countryside

Recent work will provide a great deal more information about the countryside sites when it has been fully studied and the results are available. Some sites have produced evidence for fields and enclosures, especially at Wey Manor Farm, Hengrove Farm, Thorpe Lea Nurseries and around Runfold and Tongham. There is a general impression that field systems continued in use from the Iron Age until they

were replaced by more regular, longer fields at some time around AD 200, perhaps marking a change in land management and ownership also seen elsewhere in the western Empire. Fields close to Southwark and Staines have been noted above and were presumably worked from the towns. A so-called 'corn drier' at Hurst Park, Weybridge, and other possible examples at Farleigh Court and in Ewell (the King William IV site) are noteworthy as they have not been previously recorded in Surrey. Several apparently lower status or 'native' sites have been found, such as at Thorpe Lea, at Brooklands, at Battlebridge Lane, Merstham, and at Farleigh. A fish weir or weirs at Ferry Lane, Shepperton, even if later than Roman, is indicative of exploitation of resources not usually recognized.

More is also known about the villas: newly discovered buildings associated with the known sites at Broadstreet Common (Barnwood School), at Abinger, at Beddington and at Titsey, and new sites at Chelsham and possibly Carshalton and Cranleigh. Conversely, it has been suggested that the Chiddingfold complex of buildings and the postulated villa at Coombe Hill, Kingston, may be religious sites (see Bird in this volume). Work on the distribution of villas by Sheldon and others makes it clear that they favoured certain situations, usually being placed near rivers and at geological boundaries with access to the better soils (Bird 2000b, 157–8). There is, however, a noticeable lack of villas on the main gravel terraces. In general it is becoming apparent that we should be looking for different kinds of landscapes arising from different land-uses based on the varying geological types (Bird 2000b, 164–5). At the moment this can only be speculative, and there is a need for better palaeo environmental evidence from all sites. It is interesting to consider that there were Roman-period attempts to improve some soils: two possible chalk quarries perhaps to provide material for marling have been noted, near Ashtead churchyard and at Clandon (see also Farleigh Court below), and a similar suggestion has been offered to explain the place-name Merrow (Coates 1998).

In the area around Staines, both north and south of the Thames, several sites have produced evidence for occupation and land management in the Roman period, including Vicarage Road, Staines, Hengrove Farm, Staines, Woodthorpe Road, Ashford, Fairylands at Laleham, Lord Knyvett's School at Stanwell, Coldharbour Lane, Thorpe and Thorpe Lea Nurseries. At the last site there was evidence for buildings and occupation for most of the Roman period, following on from the Iron Age. Interestingly, a 60ha site at Home Farm, Laleham, produced very little evidence for Roman-period activity. Other sites on the gravels that did produce such evidence were at Wey Manor Farm and Brooklands, at the second of which two Iron Age sites showed different subsequent occupation patterns; one was apparently abandoned, while the other may have been occupied throughout the Roman period.

The evidence for rural sites in the Kingston area has been summarized by Hawkins (1996); there is now some evidence for use of the London Clay near Old Malden. The corn drier found at Hurst Park near Weybridge had curiously little associated evidence within the area of a large development site. Recently discovered evidence for a stone-founded building, with at least two rooms and a tessellated floor, in Carshalton (West Street) probably indicates a 'new' villa site (fig 5.5), while the surroundings of the long-known Beddington bath-house have been thoroughly explored, producing a separate villa and several associated timber buildings, enclosures, wells, etc. It is to be hoped that this important excavation will soon receive the publication it deserves. Three sites near Croydon, at Lloyd Park, Atwood near Sanderstead, and Farleigh Court, probably represent lower-status settlements, although at the last-named a small square chalk-and-greensand-built structure was found which could possibly be a corn drier, as well as ditches, pits and postholes and a very large pit, presumably a chalk quarry. The use of greensand is of interest as it must have been brought in specially.

Fig 5.5   West Street, Carshalton: foundation wall of a possible Roman villa, looking south-east (the feature in the right foreground is modern). Photograph copyright Jeff Perry, Sutton Archaeological Services

At Chelsham nearby, aerial photography led to the identification of a 'new' villa site, apparently a small winged-corridor building with detached bath-house.

Evidence for lower-status settlements has been found at Battlebridge Lane, Merstham, at Chapel Way, Burgh Heath and at Tattenham Way Allotments, Banstead. Golf course management revealed a few extra finds at the Walton Heath villa site, and more information was located about the building at Headley Court, where there was a small-scale excavation in 1959. As this was a rectangular stone-founded building, it must remain probable that it was a villa. Fieldwork on Mickleham Downs has recently plotted probable Roman-period 'Celtic' fields and relocated a possible contemporary occupation site; further north at Bocketts Farm there is evidence for these earlier squarish fields being replaced by longer ones, and another occupation site. The excavation of a 'native' site at The Looe near Ewell has now been fully published.

The plan of the Ashtead villa has been noted as unique in a recently published study (Smith 1997, 112). Further work at the Chatley Farm bath-house site failed to locate the missing villa. Work in the Woking area has located another three probable lower-status occupation sites, at Wokingpark Farm, at Black Close, Mayford and at Mizens Farm. Sites at South Farm, Lightwater and in Bagshot (42 London Road) may be of higher status, with stone-founded buildings, but discussion must await publication of the evidence. Both sites apparently had extensive building evidence, possibly associated with ironworking.

Several sites east of Farnham around Runfold have produced important evidence for the Roman period landscape, mostly found in large-scale work in advance of mineral extraction. South of the Hog's Back an excavation at Hopeless Moor, near Puttenham, located a possible post-built structure and aerial photography suggests a settlement site of some sort nearby, while another excavation at Charterhouse produced evidence for occupation probably associated with the previously known cremation burials. Attention has been drawn to probably similar sites found in this area by Kerry in the 19th century (Bierton 1990). Several occupation sites have recently been located in the area west and north of Guildford, indicating use of the London Clay here from at least as early as the mid-1st century; they include Manor Farm, Queen Elizabeth Park (Stoughton Barracks) and Northmead School. They may have been linked in some way to the villa on Broadstreet Common, about which more is now known from work at the immediately adjacent Barnwood School site; here there was a post-built structure and then a 'villa' with very substantial stone foundations suggesting an aisled building with internal subdivisions. It is suggested that it had two towers, unusually on one of the shorter sides. The building was demolished in the later 3rd or 4th century. Trial trenches suggested that a bath-house might have been placed nearby.

More has also been learnt about two other previously known villas; at Abinger an extensively disturbed area of Roman buildings may have been where Darwin's famous section (1888, 180–194) was taken, but work also located largely undisturbed rooms, one with a fine late mosaic. This may have been part of the north range of a large villa whose estate perhaps covered a substantial part of the Tillingbourne valley. At Titsey geophysical survey located another villa building parallel to the long-known aisled building; on plan they appear to form two sides of a courtyard but in fact the new building is set much higher on the other side of a stream. These sites and the newly-discovered building at Chelsham are all now scheduled monuments.

Finally, a few sites suggest activity in the Weald. At Trevereux south of Limpsfield, pottery indicates an Iron Age/Romano-British occupation site. Further west, in the Outwood area, the results of fieldwalking suggest more occupation sites. More certainly, a site at Wyphurst Road, Cranleigh has produced evidence suggesting a stone-founded structure, possibly a villa, of considerable interest in view of its location and its proximity to Rapsley.

Trade and industry

Little extra is known about Roman-period trade and industry in Surrey, although full study of all the recent discoveries will make possible much better understanding of trade patterns. There is now extensive evidence for an iron industry in Southwark (Sheldon 2000, 141), as well as other similar activities to be expected in a town. The evidence for a leather industry in Staines is noted above, as is the possibility of a woollen industry based in Ewell. Pottery wasters noted at some of the Runfold sites may indicate that the Alice Holt/Farnham pottery industry spread this far. Initial claims for the discovery of a 'through-draught pottery kiln' at the London Road, Bagshot, site seem later to have been abandoned. Work on the pottery from John Hampton's excavations on Ashtead Common has identified a probable greyware pottery industry at the well-known tileworks (Joanna Bird, pers comm). It has now been established with certainty that there was a tile production site in the Doods Road area of Reigate, producing material for roofs and hypocausts, including relief-patterned box flue tiles. It was probably operating from about AD 140 to 230.

The establishment of London may have had a considerable effect on the surrounding area and it is probable that in due course different places came to specialize in order to supply this major market, as they did in the medieval period (Bird 1996, 223). The pattern of pottery and tile supply may act as markers for the organic materials whose source cannot usually be identified, if the evidence survives at all. Thus in the 3rd and 4th centuries the Alice Holt/Farnham potteries were supplying a high proportion of the coarsewares found in London, and it seems that the Reigate tilery's products have now been identified at over 40 sites in London and even far into Kent, at Canterbury and near Faversham. The distribution of relief-patterned tile including sites in Surrey has recently been studied (Betts et al 1994): it seems likely that the Ashtead tilery should be seen as starting at about AD 120, although secure dating evidence remains elusive. The wide-ranging distribution from tile kilns is well illustrated by the Hartfield kiln, whose products supplied both Beddington and Beddingham (Middleton et al 1992, 52–3). This coincidence of supply and place-names must raise speculation about joint ownership of estates on either side of the Weald, continuing after the Roman period (Copley 1950).

Death and burial and religion

There is still relatively little evidence for Roman-period burials in Surrey, apart from in Southwark, where the evidence for burials has been summarized by Barber & Hall (2000, 103–7). The most impressive recent discoveries have been more than 150 inhumations in America Street near Southwark Bridge and a cemetery alongside Watling Street at 165 Great Dover Street. The latter included a group of well-built tombs and the so-called 'female gladiator' burial (a ritual explanation is more likely). This last was a *bustum* burial, in which a pit dug to aid cremation of the body is then used for the remains and associated offerings. Another *bustum* has been found recently, in Staines (fig 5.6), where the cremations and inhumations on the roads east of the town have already been noted. New finds elsewhere include Iron Age to Roman cremation burials at Farleigh Court and Hurst Park, and one or two other inhumations, including two at Lansdowne Road between Staines and Laleham, and a late burial on the edge of the Croydon Saxon cemetery. A possible inhumation cemetery at Kingston has also been noted above. 'Roman Christian' burials have been claimed in Bagshot, but on currently available information seem unlikely: the so-called graves are irregular and on differing alignments, without any evidence for human burials; the supposed grave goods are said to be in the upper fill and do not seem appropriate to Christian burials; the Christian ring, if with a burial, should have been on a person's hand, and should therefore survive complete and in the lower fill. Nevertheless, the discovery of the jet ring with a rho-cross symbol is of great interest in view of the general lack of Christian material from any part of Surrey (Graham, T 2002).

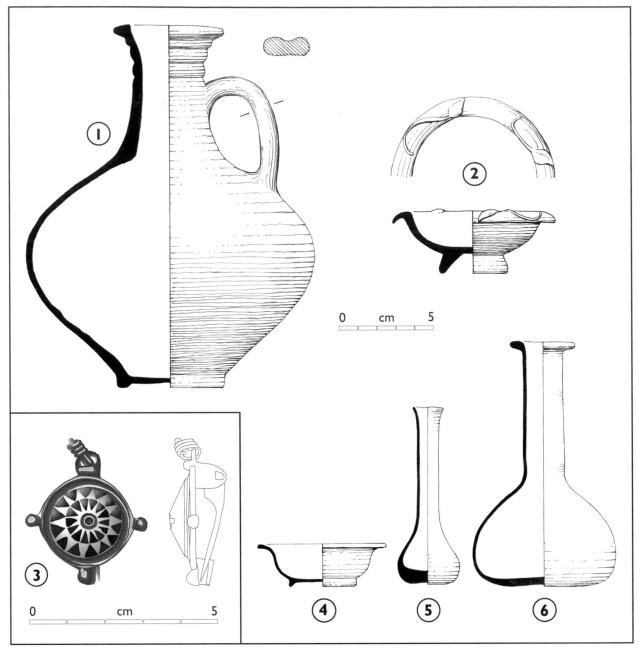

Fig 5.6 Kingston Road, Staines: finds associated with *bustum* burial. 1: Verulamium region single-handled flagon; 2: central Gaulish Samian DR35 dish; 3: one of a pair of enamelled disc brooches, SF1; 4: glass dish, SF59; 5: glass phial, SF61; 6: glass phial, SF60. Drawing copyright Surrey County Archaeological Unit

Most of the new discoveries relevant to religion and ritual are discussed in more detail in another paper in this volume, and it is therefore sufficient to note them here very briefly. The idea of a ritual site in Ewell has been noted above. Further evidence for ritual shafts in the area around the settlement has been recorded at the Seymours Nursery site and at The Looe. Similar deposits have also been noted in a well at Beddington, and in six of the fifteen wells found at a site at Swan Street in Southwark, here probably indicating ritual termination of use. One of these wells contained the skeleton of an adult male as well as a dog skull. Other probable ritual deposits have been noted at a stream crossing in Kingston (Hammerson 1996, 154; Hawkins 1996, 49–50) and in a watery environment at Shepperton Ranges,

where a nest of pewter plates was found (Poulton & Scott 1993).

There has been further work at two of the known temple sites, Farley Heath and Wanborough. Publication of the former will include a full catalogue of all known finds from the site. It would be appropriate to note also the discovery of an aisled shrine building at Beddingham in Sussex (Rudling 1998, 56), as this is reminiscent of the shrine at Rapsley (Hanworth 1968, 17) and both sites have produced fragments of pots decorated with mural crowns (Bird, J 2002). A new religious site has been found at Frensham, marked by many coins and over 65 miniature pots, at least one apparently containing traces of cannabis. Attempts to locate a nearby temple have so far failed. A well-reported scatter of coins and brooches may mark another possible religious site near Godstone, and a poorly recorded group of brooches and other finds from the Hog's Back near Guildford might indicate a further site, or perhaps a cemetery. At Betchworth, excavation has identified a curious late Iron Age/early Roman apsidal-ended enclosure with a ditch cutting off the apse, and associated evidence suggesting a ritual use. A similar use has also been proposed for the Westcott enclosure, where the main use may be in the late Iron Age (Gabby Rapson, pers comm), and for the enclosure at the Matthew Arnold School near Staines (Bird 1987, 189); the latter suggestion should now be withdrawn as the site has been shown to be medieval.

Transition

Perhaps not surprisingly, there is little fresh evidence to throw light on the end of the Roman period. The possible continuity of use of the Croydon Saxon burial ground is undoubtedly of interest, as is the increasing evidence from place-name research that implies a surviving Romano-British population (references in Bird 2000b, 165–6). This remains an area of research greatly in need of fresh information.

Future research

Our knowledge of Surrey in the Roman period remains pitifully small, and it is still the case that significant discoveries can completely revise our understanding and raise new questions. The following brief list is only intended to suggest some of the more important actions required and stimulate debate. Matters relating to religion are included with the relevant paper elsewhere in this volume.

• The transition from Iron Age to Roman is not well understood. Careful analysis of those sites that cover this period is needed.

• There is a need to reassess the information available from material held in museums; eg origins and dating of pottery and tile can provide useful information about sites even when it is unstratified.

• Sources of building stone should be accurately identified and used to target possible quarries for further study.

• Studies of pottery and tile distribution may help in attempting to identify communities such as *civitates* (eg the division between Atrebates and Cantiaci) or the smaller *pagi*.

• The landscape requires much more attention. Most of our information relates to the gravels and the chalk and it is important to try to understand more accurately how the landscape was managed in all areas. This should include changes through time, which at present can be dimly discerned on the gravels; did they occur generally elsewhere?

• Environmental evidence is crucial and should always be a priority.

• Attention should be given to the location of evidence for woodland industry.

• Analysis of existing information should be used to predict villa estates and functions and the link to the 'native' sites. This should then be tested by fieldwork, especially by fieldwalking and geophysics.

• Much better information is needed about non-villa sites and about the settings and surroundings of villas.

• There is a need to discover more burial sites to aid understanding of the population.

• Proper study of the possibility of river transport is required (and other uses of rivers and streams).

• The London–Winchester road and other missing links in the road system should be located.

• Sites relevant to the Roman–Saxon transition should be given high priority.

SITE REFERENCES

Abinger: Dyer 196–7; 1998; Cosh & Neal 1996
America Street, Southwark: Howe *et al* forthcoming
Ashtead churchyard: Bird *et al* 1990, 207
Atwood: Batchelor 1990
Bagshot (42 London Road): Cole 1993–7
Barnwood School: Poulton 1999a
Battlebridge Lane, Merstham: Howe *et al* 2000, 191
Beddington: Adkins *et al* 1987
Betchworth: Williams 1997
Black Close Mayford: Hawkins 1985
Bocketts Farm: Bird *et al* 1992, 150
Brooklands: Hayman 1991
Carshalton (West Street): Howe *et al* forthcoming
Chapel Way, Burgh Heath: Jackson *et al* 1999, 226
Charterhouse: Hall, M 1999
Chatley Farm: Poulton 1986
Chelsham: Hampton 1996; Jackson *et al* 1999, 236

Clacket Lane: Hayman 1997, 10–14
Clandon: Bird *et al* 1994, 205
Coldharbour Lane Thorpe: Howe *et al* 2002, 263
Colliers Wood (Stane Street): Howe *et al* 2000, 206
Croydon Saxon cemetery: McKinley 2003
Doods Road, Reigate: Masefield 1994; Masefield & Williams 2003
Dorking:
    Church Square: Hayman 1998a, esp 91–2
    43/44 Church Street: Ettlinger 1998
    15/16 Church Street: Ettlinger 1998
    29–55 High Street (r/o): Jackson *et al* 1999, 224; Pine 2003
    Stane Street: the probable line: Ettlinger 1998
Ewell:
    Church Field: Orton 2001
    2 Church Street: Bird *et al* 1985, 120
    24/26 High Street: Bird *et al* 1985, 120

46–50 High Street: Jackson *et al* 1997, 198

King William IV: Orton 1997

St Mary's churchyard: Brooks 1996

West Street: Poulton & O'Connell, 1987

Fairylands, Laleham: Jackson *et al* 1999, 230; Taylor-Wilson 2002

Farleigh Court: Hayman 1996

Farley Heath: Bird, J 1996a; Jackson *et al* 1997, 204

Ferry Lane, Shepperton: Bird, D 1999a

Frensham: Graham 1986; 2000; 2001; 2002a; Howe *et al* 2002, 268–9

Godstone: pers comm D Hunt, R Bland, D Williams & J Bird; Bird, J 1996c, 168, no 18; 1999c, 176–8, nos 18, 21, 25, 33; 2001, 310–318, nos 10, 16, 17, 19–24, 26, 28, 33–37, 44, 46, 47, 49, 50, 52

Great Dover Street, Southwark: Mackinder 2000

Headley Court: Corti 1989

Hengrove Farm, Staines: Jackson *et al* 1999, 232; Howe *et al* 2000, 195; Howe *et al* 2002, 267

Hog's Back near Guildford: pers comm David Graham

Home Farm, Laleham: Hayman 1998b

Hopeless Moor: Dyer 1999

Hurst Park: Andrews 1996, 69; 102–3

Lansdowne Road, Staines: pers comm Julian Ayres

Lloyd Park Croydon: Bell 2001, esp 260

The Looe: Cotton 2001

Lord Knyvett's School, Stanwell: Jackson *et al* 1999, 233

Manor Farm, Guildford: Davies & English 1999; English & Davies 2000

Matthew Arnold School: Bird *et al* 1992, 155

Mickleham Downs: Howe *et al* 2002, 261

Mizens Farm, Woking: Jackson *et al* 1999, 240

North Holmwood: Bird *et al* 1986, 219

Northmead School Guildford: Jackson *et al* 1999, 223

Old Malden: Andrews 2001

Outwood: pers comm Roger Ellaby, ex inf Robin Tanner

Peckham (Watling Street): Rogers 1990

Puttenham: pers comm John Hampton

Queen Elizabeth Park (Stoughton Barracks): Howe *et al* 2003

Runfold area: Hayman 1993a; 1993b ; Jackson *et al* 1999, 238; Howe *et al* 2000, 199; Howe *et al* 2001, 350

Seymours Nursery, Ewell: Bird *et al* 1992, 148

South Farm, Lightwater: Cole 1991

Staines:

Central Trading Estate: Jackson *et al* 1999, 232; McKinley forthcoming

Clarence Street/Market Street: Jones 1989a

Courage Brewery: Jones 1987a

2–8 High Street: Richmond *et al* 1997

73–75 High St: Jones 1989c

78–88 High St: Jones 1989b

Johnson & Clark: Jones 1987b

Kingston Road and London Road areas: Jackson *et al* 1997, 212; Jackson *et al* 1999, 232; Poulton 1999a; Howe *et al* 2000, 193–5; Howe *et al* 2001, 347; Howe *et al* 2002, 266

Riverside Gardens: Howe *et al* 2003

Tilly's Lane: Howe *et al* 2000, 193–4; Howe *et al* 2001, 347; McKinley forthcoming

Swan Street, Southwark: Howe *et al* 2000, 208, fig 11, 210

Tattenham Way allotments, Banstead: Howe *et al* 2002, 262

Thorpe Lea Nurseries: Bird *et al* 1992, 153; Bird, J *et al* 1996, 199; Jackson *et al* 1997, 209; Bird 2000b, 160

Titsey: Davies 1997

Trevereux: Jackson *et al* 1997, 215; Jackson *et al* 1999, 237; Howe *et al* 2000, 197

Tyrells Wood: Poulton & O'Connell 1984

Vicarage Road, Staines (to west of town): Jackson *et al* 1999, 231

Walton Heath: Mann & Williams 1995; Clew & Harp 1997

Wanborough: O'Connell 1984; O'Connell & Bird 1994; Bird, J 1996b; Graham 1997; Linford & Linford 1997; Williams 2000; O'Connell 2000; Williams forthcoming

Waylands Farm: Howe *et al* 2001, 349

Westcott: Bird, J 1999b; Rapson 2001; Bird 2002a; Graham 2002b

Wey Manor Farm: Jackson *et al* 1997, 210; Jackson *et al* 1999, 229; Howe *et al* 2000, 192 Windsor Great Park (the London–Silchester road): Bird *et al* 1994, 207

Wokingpark Farm: Hawkins 1984

Woodthorpe Road, Ashford: Howe *et al* 2002, 267

Wyphurst Road, Cranleigh: Howe *et al* 2003

ACKNOWLEDGEMENTS

I am very grateful to the following for assistance in various ways: Joanna Bird, Emily Brants, Jon Cotton, Julie Gardiner, David Graham, Tony Howe, Gary Jackson, Jackie McKinley, Jeff Perry, Rob Poulton and David Williams.

BIBLIOGRAPHY

Abdy, C, & Bierton, G, 1997 A gazetteer of Romano-British archaeological sites in Ewell, *SyAC*, **84**, 123–41

Adkins, L, Adkins, R A, & Perry, J G, 1987 Excavations at Beddington 1984–87: the final interim, *London Archaeol*, **5.13**, 349–52

Alexander, M, 1997 Slyfield Green, Guildford, *SyAS Bull*, **314**, 5–6

Andrews, P, 1996 Hurst Park, East Molesey, Surrey: riverside settlement and burial from the Neolithic to the Early Saxon periods, in P Andrews & A Crockett *Three excavations along the Thames and its tributaries 1994. Neolithic to Saxon settlement and burial in the Thames, Colne and Kennet Valleys*, Wessex Archaeol Rep, **10**, 51–104

——, 2001 Excavation of a multi-period settlement site at the former St John's Vicarage, Old Malden, Kingston upon Thames, *SyAC*, **88**, 161–224

Anon, 2002 Londoners' stone sheds light on city's cosmopolitan ways, *British Archaeol*, **68**, 5

Barber, B, & Hall, J, 2000 Digging up the people of Roman London: interpreting evidence from Roman London's cemeteries, in Haynes *et al* 2000, 102–20

Batchelor, G, 1990 'Friends, Romans, school children!' – archaeology and education in Croydon, *London Archaeol*, **6.8**, 199–205

Bell, C, 2001 Excavation of multi-period sites at Lodge Lane, Addington, Geoffrey Harris House and Lloyd Park, South Croydon, *SyAC*, **88**, 225–65

Betts, I, Black, E W, & Gower, J, 1994 *A corpus of relief-patterned tiles in Roman Britain*, J Roman Pottery Stud, **7**

Bierton, G, 1990 'To the Great Common ... for a little spade exercise', *SyAC*, **80**, 91–103

Bird, D G, 1987 The Romano-British period, in *The archaeology of Surrey to 1540* (eds J Bird & D G Bird), 165–96

——, 1996 The London region in the Roman period, in Bird, J *et al* 1996, 217–32

——, 1999a Possible late Roman or early Saxon fish weirs at Ferry Lane, Shepperton, *SyAC*, **86**, 105–23

——, 1999b Early days at London and Richborough, *London Archaeol*, **8.12**, 331–4

——, 2000a The Claudian invasion campaign reconsidered, *Oxford J Archaeol*, **19.1**, 91–104

——, 2000b The environs of Londinium: roads, roadside settlements and the countryside, in Haynes *et al* 2000, 151–74

——, 2002a The possible 'Roman camp' at Westcott, *SyAS Bull*, **355,** 4

——, 2002b The events of A.D. 43: further reflections, *Britannia*, **33,** 257–63

——, 2002c Roads and temples: Stane Street at Ewell, *London Archaeol*, **10.2,** 41–5

——, 2004 Roman religious sites in the landscape, in *Aspects of archaeology and history in Surrey: towards a research framework for the county* (eds J Cotton, G Crocker & A Graham, SyAS, 77–90

Bird, D G, Crocker, G, & McCracken, J S, 1985 Archaeology in Surrey 1983, *SyAC*, **76,** 119–31

——, 1986 Archaeology in Surrey 1984, *SyAC*, **77,** 217–26

——, 1990 Archaeology in Surrey 1988–1989, *SyAC*, **80,** 201–27

——, 1992 Archaeology in Surrey 1990, *SyAC*, **81,** 147–67

Bird, D G, Crocker, G, McCracken, J S, & Saich, D, 1994 Archaeology in Surrey 1991, *SyAC*, **82,** 203–19

Bird, D G, Crocker, G, Maloney, C, & Saich, D, 1996 Archaeology in Surrey 1992–3, *SyAC*, **83,** 187–228

Bird, J, 1996a A Romano-British priestly head-dress from Farley Heath, *SyAC*, **83,** 81–9

——, 1996b Roman objects from Wanborough: a supplementary note, *SyAC*, **83,** 240–3

——, 1996c Romano-British, in D Williams, Some recent finds from East Surrey, *SyAC*, **83,** 165–86 [167–9]

——, 1997 A Romano-British linch-pin head from Chelsham, *SyAC*, **84,** 187–9

——, 1999a A Romano-British cosmetic mortar from Chipstead, *SyAC*, **86,** 206–7

——, 1999b A Roman cavalry pendant from Westcott, *SyAC*, **86,** 208–9

——, 1999c Romano-British, in D Williams, Some recent finds from Surrey, *SyAC*, **86,** 171–97 [174–8]

——, 2001 Romano-British, in D Williams, Recent finds from Surrey 1997–9, *SyAC*, **88,** 309–31 [310–18]

——, 2002 A group of mural-crowned cult pots from south-east England, in *Céramiques de la Graufesenque et autres productions d'époque romaine: nouvelles recherches. Hommages à Bettina Hoffmann* (eds M Genin & A Vernhet), Archéologie et histoire romaine, **7,** 303–11

Bird, J, Hassall, M, & Sheldon, H (eds), 1996 *Interpreting Roman London: papers in memory of Hugh Chapman*, Oxbow Monogr, **58**

Brigham, T, 2001 Roman London bridge in *London Bridge, 2000 years of a river crossing* (eds B Watson, T Brigham & T Dyson), MoLAS Monogr, **8,** 28–51

Brooks, D, 1996 Archaeological finds during grave digging, *SyAS Bull*, **303,** 6

Burnham, B C, & Wacher, J, 1990 *The 'small towns' of Roman Britain*

Cheesman, C, 1994 The coins, in O'Connell & Bird 1994, 31–92

Clew, J, & Harp, P, 1997 Some recent finds from Walton Heath Roman villa, *SyAS Bull*, **313,** 8

Coates, R, 1998 Merrow and some related Brittonic matters in Surrey, *J Engl Place-name Soc*, **30,** 16–22

Cole, G H, 1991 Excavations at South Farm, Lightwater, Surrey, *SyAS Bull*, **253**

——, 1993–7 Excavations at 42 London Road, Bagshot, Surrey, *SyAS Bull*, **279; 290; 301,** 9–10; **309,** 7–8

Copley, J G, 1950 Stane Street in the Dark Ages, *Sussex Archaeol Collect*, **89,** 98–104

Corti, G, 1989 Headley Court, *SyAS Bull*, **243**

Cosh, S, & Neal, D, S, 1996 [Roman mosaic from Abinger], *SyAS Bull*, **300,** 1

Cotton, J, 2001 Prehistoric and Roman settlement in Reigate Road, Ewell: fieldwork conducted by T K Walls, 1946–52, *SyAC*, **88,** 1–42

Darwin, C, 1888 *The formation of vegetable mould through the action of worms, with observations on their habits*

Davies, E, M, 1997 Fresh findings at Roman Titsey, *SyAS Bull*, **315,** 2–5

Davies, H, & English, J, 1999 Fieldwork at the Royal County Hospital and Surrey Science Research Park Development sites 1980–1998, part 3, *SyAS Bull*, **331,** 6–8

Drummond-Murray, J, & Thompson, P, with Cowan, C, 2002 *Settlement in Roman Southwark. Archaeological excavations (1991–8) for the London Underground Limited Jubilee Line Extension Project*, MoLAS Monogr, **12**

Dyer, S, 1996–7 Cocks Farm, Abinger Hammer: excavations 1996, *SyAS Bull*, **305,** 3; **307,** 8–12

——, 1998 Excavations at Cocks Farm, Abinger in 1997, *SyAS Bull*, **320,** 5–6

——, 1999 Excavations at Hopeless Moor, Seale, *SyAS Bull*, **327,** 5–6

English, J, & Davies, H, 2000 Manor Farm, Guildford, *SyAS Bull*, **337,** 3–5

Ettlinger, V, 1998 Appendix: summary of other work in Dorking, *SyAC*, **85,** 96

Frere, S S, 1949 The excavation of a late Roman bath-house at Chatley Farm, Cobham, SyAC, **50,** 73–98

Frere, S, & Fulford, M, 2001 The Roman invasion of AD 43, *Britannia*, **32,** 45–55

Graham, D, 1986 A note on the recent finds of Bronze Age, Iron Age and Roman material and a site at Frensham manor noted in an air photograph, *SyAC*, **77,** 232–5

——, 1997 Temple site at Wanborough looted again, *SyAS Bull*, **312,** 10–11

——, 2000 A Roman coin deposit on Frensham Common, *SyAS Bull*, **338,** 6–7

——, 2001 Frensham Manor, *SyAS Bull*, **352,** 12–13

——, 2002a Nothing found at Frensham (for a change), *SyAS Bull*, **356,** 13

——, 2002b The Westcott enclosure, *SyAS Bull*, **356,** 4

Graham, T, 2002 A rho-cross engraved on a jet finger-ring from Bagshot, Surrey, *Oxford J Archaeol*, **21.2,** 211–16

Hall, A, 2003 Investigation of Stane Street at South Holmwood, *SyAS Bull*, **370,** 2–3

Hall, M, 1999 Excavation of part of a Roman settlement at Charterhouse, near Godalming, Surrey, 1994, *SyAC*, **86,** 151–61

Hammerson, M J, 1996 Problems of Roman coin interpretation in Greater London, in Bird, J *et al* 1996, 153–64

Hampton, J N, 1996 Chelsham, a 'new' Roman villa, *SyAC*, **83,** 244

Hanworth, R, 1968 The Roman villa at Rapsley, Ewhurst (parish of Cranleigh), *SyAC*, **65,** 1–70

Hayman, G, 1991 Recent excavations at the former Brooklands race-track, *SyAS Bull*, **258**

——, 1993a The excavations of prehistoric, Roman and medieval remains near Runfold, *SyAS Bull*, **272**

——, 1993b The discovery of further prehistoric, Roman and medieval remains near Grange Road, Runfold, *SyAS Bull*, **273**

——, 1996 Discoveries of late Iron Age and Roman date at Farleigh Court Golf Course, near Warlingham, *SyAS Bull*, **299,** 5–10

——, 1997 The excavation of two medieval pottery kiln sites and two sections through the London–Lewes Roman road at Clacket Lane, near Titsey, 1992, *SyAC*, **84,** 1–87

——, 1998a Excavation in St Martin's Walk, Dorking, *SyAC*, **85,** 63–95

——, 1998b Excavations at Home Farm, Laleham in 1997, *SyAS Bull*, **320,** 1–3

Haynes, I, Sheldon, H, & Hannigan, L (eds), 2000 *London under ground: the archaeology of a city*, Oxford: Oxbow Books

Hawkins, D, 1996 Roman Kingston upon Thames, a landscape of rural settlements, *London Archaeol*, **8.2,** 46–50

Hawkins, N, 1984 Excavation of a Romano-British occupation site at Wokingpark Farm, Old Woking (TQ 025 565), *SyAC*, **75,** 161–75

——, 1985 Excavation of a Romano-British and later site at Black Close, Mayford, Woking, *SyAC*, **76,** 69–76

Henig, M, 1984 *Religion in Roman Britain*

——, 2002 *The heirs of King Verica. Culture and politics in Roman Britain*

Hinton, M, 1984 An ancient burial ground in Canbury Field, Kingston upon Thames, *SyAC*, **75,** 285–8

Howe, T, Jackson, G, Maloney, C, & Saich, D, 2000 Archaeology in Surrey 1997–9, *SyAC*, **87,** 183–218

Howe, T, Jackson, G, & Maloney, C, 2001 Archaeology in Surrey 2000, *SyAC*, **88,** 343–63

——, 2002 Archaeology in Surrey 2001, *SyAC*, **89,** 257–81

——, 2003 Archaeology in Surrey 2002, *SyAC*, **90,** 347–71

Jackson, G, Maloney, C, & Saich, D, 1997 Archaeology in Surrey 1994–5, *SyAC*, **84,** 195–243

——, 1999 Archaeology in Surrey 1996–7, *SyAC*, **86,** 217–55

Jackson, R, 1996 A new collyrium-stamp from Staines and some thoughts on eye medicine in Roman London and Britannia, in Bird, J *et al* 1996, 177–87

——, forthcoming *Cosmetic grinders: an illustrated catalogue and discussion of a type unique to Late Iron Age and Roman Britain*, British Museum Occas Pap, **104**

Jones, P, 1987a Courage's Brewery, Staines, *SyAS Bull*, **220**

——, 1987b Johnson and Clark site, Staines, *SyAS Bull*, **221**

——, 1989a Staines, the Mackay Securities site (TQ 0335 7153), *SyAS Bull*, **240**

——, 1989b Staines, 78–88 High Street, *SyAS Bull*, **240**

——, 1989c Staines, 73–75 High Street, *SyAS Bull*, **240**

Jones, P, & Poulton, R, in prep Excavations in the Roman and medieval town of Staines

Linford, P K, & Linford, N T, 1997 Wanborough Roman temple, Green Lane, Wanborough, Guildford, Surrey, report on geophysical survey, 1997, Ancient Monuments Laboratory Report, **100/97,** unpublished

Luke, M, & Wells, J, 2000 New evidence for the origins, development and internal morphology of the Roman roadside settlement at Alfoldean, *Sussex Archaeol Collect*, **138,** 75–101

Mackinder, A, 2000 A Romano-British cemetery on Watling Street. Excavations at 165 Great Dover Street, Southwark, London, MoLAS Archaeol Stud Ser, **4**

Mann, T, & Williams, D, 1995 Recent finds from Walton Heath Roman villa, *SyAS Bull*, **289**

Masefield, R, 1994 New evidence for a Roman tilery at Reigate in Surrey, *SyAS Bull*, **282**

Masefield, R, & Williams, D, 2003 A Roman tilery at Doods Farm, Reigate, *SyAC*, **90,** 247–59

McKinley, J I, 2003 An early Saxon cemetery at Park Lane, Croydon, *SyAC*, **90,** 1–116

——, forthcoming Welcome to Pontibus – gateway to the west, *SyAC*

Middleton, A P, Cowell, M R, & Black, E W, 1992 Romano-British relief-patterned flue tiles. A study of provenance using petrography and neutron activation analysis, in *Sciences de la Terre et céramiques archéologiques. Expérimentations, applications* (ed S Mery), Documents et Travaux Institut Géologique Albert-de-Laparrent (Cergy), **16,** 49–60

O'Connell, M, 1984 Green Lane, Wanborough, 1979 (SU 920 495), *SyAC*, **75,** 185–93

——, 2000 [letter], *SyAS Bull*, **337,** 14–15

O'Connell, M, & Bird, J, 1994 The Roman temple at Wanborough, excavation 1985–1986, *SyAC*, **82,** 1–168

Orton, C, 1997 Excavations at the King William IV site, Ewell, 1967–77, *SyAC*, **84,** 89–122

——, 1999 Roman roads in Ewell and Surrey, *SyAS Bull*, **329,** 3

——, 2001 Archaeology in St Mary's No 5 Churchyard, Ewell, *SyAS Bull*, **346,** 1–3

Perring, D, & Brigham, T, 2000 Londinium and its hinterland: the Roman period, in *The archaeology of Greater London. An assessment of archaeological evidence for human presence in the area now covered by Greater London* (eds K Frederick, P Garwood, P Hinton, M Kendall & E McAdam), 120–70

Poulton, R, 1986 Roman material from Chatley Farm, Cobham, *SyAC*, **77,** 229–31

——, 1999a Excavations at 42–54 London Road, Staines, *SyAS Bull*, **331,** 1–4

——, 1999b The excavation of a Roman settlement site adjacent to Broad Street Common, Worplesdon, Surrey, *SyAS Bull*, **334,** 1–6

——, 2004 Iron Age Surrey, in *Aspects of archaeology and history in Surrey: towards a research framework for the county* (eds J Cotton, G Crocker & A Graham, SyAS, 51–64

Poulton, R, & O'Connell, M G, 1984 Recent discoveries south of Tyrrell's Wood golf course, near Leatherhead, *SyAC*, **75,** 289–92

——, 1987 Excavation of a Romano-British site in West Street, Ewell, *SyAC*, **78,** 119–24

Poulton, R, & Scott, E, 1993 The hoarding, deposition and use of pewter in Roman Britain, in *Theoretical Roman archaeology first conference proceedings* (ed E Scott), 115–32

Rapson, G, 2001 The possible Roman camp at Westcott, *SyAS Bull*, **354,** 3–4

Richmond, A, Lyne, M, & Ennis, T, 1997 Archaeological excavations at 2–8 High Street, Staines, *SyAS Bull*, **309,** 6–7

Rogers, W, 1990 Mesolithic and Neolithic flint tool-manufacturing areas buried beneath Roman Watling Street in Southwark, *London Archaeol*, **6.9,** 227–31

Rudling, D, 1988 A colony of Rome, AD 43–410, in P Drewett, D Rudling & M Gardiner, *The South-east to AD 1000*, 178–245

——, 1998 The development of Roman villas in Sussex, *Sussex Archaeol Collect*, **136,** 41–65

Sauer, E, 2002 The Roman invasion of Britain (AD 43) in imperial perspective: a response to Frere and Fulford, *Oxford J Archaeol*, **21.4,** 333–63

Sheldon, H, 2000 Roman Southwark, in Haynes *et al* 2000, 121–50

Smith, J T, 1997 *Roman villas. A study in social structure*

Taylor-Wilson, R, 2002 *Excavations at Hunt's House, Guy's Hospital, London Borough of Southwark*, Pre-Construct Archaeology Monogr, **1**

Wilkes, J, 1996 The status of Londinium, in Bird, J *et al* 1996, 27–31

Williams, D, 1997 Betchworth: excavations at Franks' Sandpit, *SyAS Bull*, **307,** 2–8

——, 2000 A newly-discovered Roman temple and its environs: excavations at Wanborough in 1999, *SyAS Bull*, **336,** 2–6; [plan] *SyAS Bull*, **337,** 15

——, forthcoming Green Lane, Wanborough: excavations at the Roman religious site, 1999, *SyAC*

Dr D G Bird, Head of Heritage Conservation, Sustainable Development, Surrey County Council, County Hall, Kingston upon Thames KT1 2DY

6

Roman religious sites in the landscape

DAVID BIRD

The discovery of a second temple at Wanborough, together with other recent work at Farley Heath, Betchworth, Godstone and Frensham, has drawn renewed attention to Roman religious sites in Surrey. New interpretations have also suggested that other sites may have had a ritual significance. As a result, we now know of several certain or possible religious sites in the county. This paper aims to review the evidence for these sites and consider their functions in an attempt to understand the way they were placed in the landscape. At the same time consideration is given to the reasons why some sites had temples while others apparently did not.

Introduction

Discussion of Romano-British religion often concentrates on the buildings and associated objects, and there has been much less consideration of the settings of the temples, and the reasons why particular places had temples at all (Derks 1998, 131, but see Wilson 1973 and Blagg 1986). Several sites are now known in Surrey that may have been of religious significance in the Roman period, some of which may have had temples that have not yet been discovered, while others almost certainly did not (fig 6.1). The understanding of these sites requires consideration of other places in southern Britain and further afield; it is valid to use parallels from the western Empire, as it is clear that religious practices and beliefs were generally very similar. In the Roman period local deities were assimilated to the Roman gods, and temples as such were largely a Roman introduction: they were homes for the gods. Nevertheless, although Romano-Celtic temples are often spoken of as though they are all similar across the country, closer examination suggests that their locations vary from area to area and this may indicate that there are locally significant customs, perhaps *civitas*-related.

Pre-Roman religion in Britain seems to have been mostly a matter of worshipping the gods and goddesses of the locality, and for most people this continued in the Roman period. In a sense the whole landscape was sacred. Miranda Green talks of 'the endowment with sanctity of natural features – a river, spring, lake, tree, mountain or simply a particular valley or habitat. The gods were everywhere' (Green 1986, 22; cf Henig 1984, 168). It will, however, be evident that there were sites of special ritual significance in prehistory at least as far back as the Neolithic. We are now used to the idea that some of them were placed with careful consideration of their place in the landscape. In the Roman period most attention centres on temples, and it is more difficult to assess the setting of other sites that may have had religious significance. It is also necessary to try to take account of what the landscape would have been like at the time, but this is also difficult, as we know so little about the landscape of Surrey in the Roman period.

An attempt to explore what evidence we have for the London area suggests that there would have been marked differences across the Surrey landscape then just as there are today (Bird 1996), but at present we can do little more than make informed guesses based on the known sites and the geological background.

The purpose of temples

In the Roman period, religion was practised on a daily basis in the home, and we know of small household shrines from places like Ostia and Herculaneum. By their nature they would be difficult to recognize on British archaeological sites, although a few candidates have been identified in towns (Boon 1983). We quite often have evidence for shrines at villas, for instance Rapsley (Hanworth 1968, 17; cf Bird 1987, 175), and there were of course temples in towns and probably all larger settlements. It is likely that there were also local wayside shrines (Henig 1984, 59); it would be difficult to find archaeological evidence for such things but examples are shown on samian bowls (fig 6.2) (Ludowici & Ricken 1948, Tafn 62, 12; 69, 2; 70, 5; for a reconstruction see Zelle 2000, 65). They may have been quite a regular feature of the landscape, particularly at cross-roads.

If there were household shrines then rural temples must have served a special purpose. If we now have a reasonable idea of their numbers and distribution then they will have been too far apart for everyday use. Indeed where there is evidence of the reasons for offerings, it is clear that circumstances out of the ordinary were involved: stolen property recovered; a journey or business deal successfully accomplished; health restored (a major concern) (Henig 1984, 151). A special trip to the temple might be made on such an occasion, and there is also evidence for annual or more frequent ceremonies; there was in fact a Roman religious calendar with regular festivals, and enough to show that there would have been something similar in native tradition (Henig 1984, 26–32). Animal bones recovered at British temple sites suggest sacrifices at certain times of year (Legge *et al* 2000), and these occasions were probably rather like medieval fairs. Literary evidence from Italy hints at what might

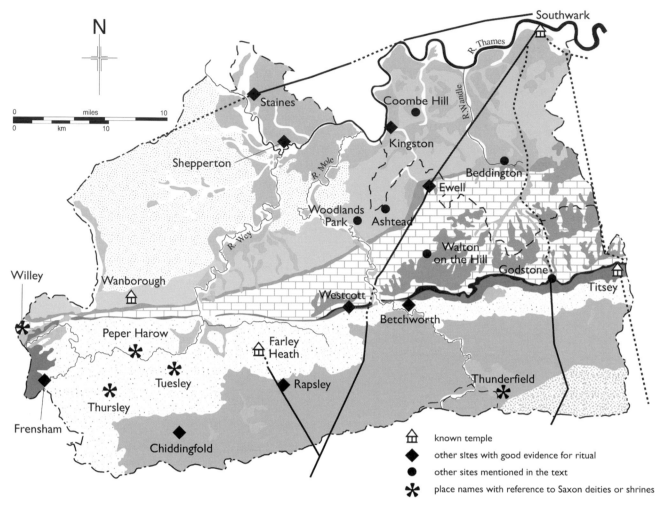

Fig 6.1 Locations of places mentioned in the text. For key to geological background see map on page x.

have been involved, as in this extract from one of Pliny the Younger's letters (see also the extract from letter 4.1, quoted below).

> I am told by the soothsayers that I must rebuild the temple of Ceres which stands on my property; it needs enlarging and improving, for it is certainly very old and too small considering how crowded it is on its special anniversary, when great crowds gather there from the whole district on 13 September and many ceremonies are performed and vows made and discharged. But there is no shelter nearby from rain or sun, so I think it will be an act of generosity and piety alike to build as fine a temple as I can and add porticoes – the temple for the goddess and the porticoes for the public. (Letter 9.39, to Mustius; Radice 1963, 258–9)

It is interesting that Pliny says that vows were made and discharged on such occasions, which may suggest that one could wait for some time to take the appropriate action in fulfilment of a vow. The system of making and paying vows is known throughout the Empire (Henig 1984, 32–3); in Britain it is clearly demonstrated for example by the lead tablets at Uley (Tomlin 1993) and inscriptions with the formula

VSLLM, standing for *votum solvit laetus libens merito*, that is, 'paid his vow joyfully, freely and deservedly' (Hassall 1977, 80). It is likely that at Surrey sites the use of organic materials for the writing of vows means that the evidence is lost. This idea is supported by finds from Wanborough: two 'ox-goads' (Bird 1994, 128) and two recently discovered seal-box lids (Joanna Bird, pers comm). Discoveries at Vindolanda now suggest that the former may actually have been used as pens (Birley 2002, 35), while it has been proposed that seal-boxes at Great Walsingham were used to contain the wax seals of written vows (Bagnall Smith 1999, 50). Finds of seal-box lids are rare in Surrey, so it is interesting that another example is known from a possibly sacred site at Ewell (Orton, 1997, 105). In this area of poor quality building stone there may also have been wooden inscriptions recording the payment of the vows; inscriptions on wood certainly existed, as an official example from Hadrian's Wall makes clear (Collingwood & Wright 1965, 596, no 1935), but of course such survivals are very rare.

It was apparently possible for the vows to be made, and paid, to any deity at many temples, even though there is a tendency among modern writers to claim a particular dedication for each one. Henig (1984, 148)

notes the lack of exclusiveness even at sites apparently closely related to a specific cult. Some vow-makers at the temple 'of Mercury' at Uley had to be reminded that this was the appropriate deity rather than Mars or Silvanus, or referred to him as Mars Mercury (Tomlin 1993, 121–3). Perhaps we should be thinking more in terms of a deity of the locality, who could therefore be worshipped in many different guises, appropriate to different activities and needs. Even some of the exotic Eastern religions are represented by finds at standard Romano-Celtic temples, as at Woodeaton (Henig 1984, 162); a Christian object was dedicated at Uley (Henig 1993, 109).

Pliny's letters also throw light on the role of the local landowner or the community in the construction and upkeep of temples. There are of course no first-hand accounts from Roman Britain but the evidence from Roman Italy is relevant, bearing in mind that the native religious world of this area had a great deal in common with Britain, as the way in which Roman gods were assimilated with British deities demonstrates. These two further extracts are especially interesting:

> Close to my property is the town of Tifernum on Tiber which adopted me as its patron when I was scarcely more than a child [...] The people always celebrate my arrivals, regret my departures, and rejoice in my official titles, and so to express my gratitude [...] I defrayed the cost of building a temple in the town. As this is now completed, it would be sacrilegious to postpone its dedication any longer. So we shall be there for the day of the dedication, which I have decided to celebrate with a public feast, and we may have to stay on for the day following. (Letter 4.1, to Calpurnius Fabatus, Pliny's wife's grandfather; Radice 1963, 109)

> [At the source of the Clitumnus] is a holy temple of great antiquity in which is a standing image of the god Clitumnus himself clad in a magistrate's bordered robe [...] The bridge which spans the stream marks the sacred water off from the the ordinary stream: above the bridge boats only are allowed, while below bathing is also permitted. The people of Hispellum, to whom the deified Emperor Augustus presented the site, maintain a bathing place at the town's expense and also provide an inn. (Letter 8.8, to Voconius Romanus; Radice 1963, 216–7)

These letters draw attention particularly to the role of the 'élite' as sponsors; the temple on the landowner's property, but used by the whole district; a town or community owning a sacred site, providing baths and an inn for worshippers. Woolf (1998, 162) shows that in Roman Gaul the élite in towns were the same people as in the countryside. It was of course expected of them that they would demonstrate their standing in the local community by the building of public monuments (for example Woolf 1998, 1–2; 231). It can readily be argued that in a like manner the known temples in Britain reflect the involvement of local landowners or the Romano-British 'élite'. Henig (1984, 141) points out that 'temples with their cult images and altars, arches, screens and columns, were built or given by officials, merchants and gentry, to enhance their prestige in the community'. According to Tacitus, Agricola encouraged the Britons to build temples, *fora* and noble houses when he was Governor (Woolf 1998, 216–8 with discussion). These temples need not have been classical.

There is a tendency to describe the religion of the Romano-British countryside as 'native' with the implication that it is peasant and local, and that rural temples are different from town temples. In fact the standard 'rural' temple, the Romano-Celtic type, is common in towns, as for example at Silchester (Boon 1974, 152–8). The evidence available from inscriptions and offerings shows that there was no noticeable difference in cult practices between Romano-Celtic temples and more classical types (Henig 1984, 14; cf Cheesman 1994, 33–4). Indeed the architecture of a largely classical temple at Bath can be described as 'idiosyncratic and celticising' (Henig 2002, 48). Although largely restricted to the north-western Empire, Romano-Celtic temples are essentially a

Fig 6.2 Wayside shrines on samian bowls stamped by Cerealis of Rheinzabern. The inscriptions indicate that they were set at two-, three- or four-way junctions. Drawing by Joanna Bird

Roman period phenomenon (Smith 2001, 10; Derks 1998, 183), and what might be called the higher echelons of society, either individually or as a ruling group of an area (*pagus* or *civitas*), must have played a major role in their construction (Derks 1998, 184).

The temples use Romano-British building techniques: they are mostly stone built, or with stone foundations, have tiled roofs, and are in general very reminiscent of villas. We must surely accept that this indicates the involvement of the people who would think in terms of building like this and know where to find the materials and expertise – and the money. There is also a need to take more account of someone owning the land in some way – we have enough evidence from Roman Britain to indicate that land could be owned privately (Bird 1996, 222), and perhaps some was also held in common by a *civitas*. The élite is also likely to have provided the priests for these temples, as can be shown for Gaul (Woolf 1998, 233–4) and Germany (Carroll 2001, 44). The size and embellishment of Christian churches usually reflects the importance of the church and the interest and support of local worthies. It may be that in Roman Britain the sites which have temples are like the bigger churches, ones where someone has taken an interest and put in resources. If this is the case then there will be other Roman-period sacred sites with no obvious marker in the shape of a temple.

Sacred sites without temples

It is clear that temples are associated with sacred sites, that is, they are not themselves essential; this can be demonstrated by the examples of carefully planned regular enclosures which have temples placed off centre, implying the presence of something more important in the middle. The point is very well illustrated by the story of pagans being upset by St Martin cutting down a sacred tree, whereas they had been resigned to the loss of the temple, and the off-centre temple at Drevant in France, whose name apparently comes from *Derventum*, 'the meeting place by the oak tree' (Knight, 1999, 118 and fig 40, 114). In Britain a comparable example would be the temple at Gosbecks (Smith 2001, 229), and the point is also made by the replacement of one temple at Wanborough by another in a nearby but different position (Williams 2000, 437; forthcoming). Roman period temple-less sacred sites can be clearly demonstrated in Gaul (Derks 1998, 132) and in north-west Spain (the most 'Celtic' part of Hispania) (Keay, 161–2). Derks (1998, 200) notes that 'the essence of a Roman sanctuary is not the presence of a temple, but a clearly recognizable enclosure, marking the boundary between the sacred terrain and its profane surroundings'.

There were certainly some local sites regarded as sacred which would not have had temples, represented for example by the pewter plates deposited in a watery environment at Shepperton Ranges in the late Roman period (Poulton & Scott 1993). A similar explanation might account for the discovery of coins and other objects at a stream crossing in Kingston (Hammerson 1996, 154–5; Hawkins 1996, 49–50). Findspots of large numbers of scattered coins or groups of finds such as brooches should be examined more generally to see if they could point to sites of religious significance that never 'grew' temples (cf Derks 1998, 132–3). Sacred sites indicated only by scatters of votive finds could be the explanation for two sites recently found in Surrey, at Frensham and Godstone, both marked out by Roman coins and other objects. At Frensham work led by David Graham has plotted several hundred coins and excavation has produced fragments of sceptre binding (fig 6.3) and a special bronze vessel together with at least 65 miniature pots, some set in pits with burnt material. There can be little doubt that these are evidence for ritual. Tests on one of the first pots to be found has suggested the presence of cannabis (Graham 2000; 2001). At Godstone there are again many coins, but also brooches (fig 6.4) and other

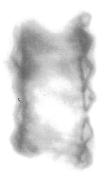

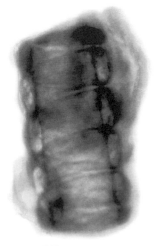

Fig 6.3 Frensham: X-radiographs of fragments of iron sceptre binding. By courtesy of Museum of Farnham, illustration prepared by Brian Wood

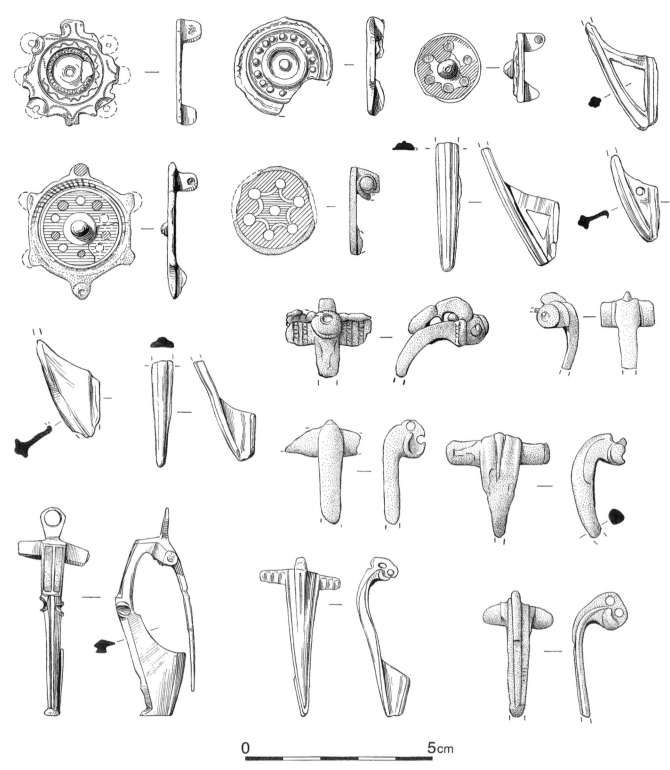

0   5cm

Fig 6.4   Brooches from Godstone; another sixteen brooches have recently been found at this site. Scale 1:1. Drawing by David Williams

objects, found in a carefully recorded metal detector survey by David Hunt (David Hunt and David Williams, pers comm; coins identified by Roger Bland and brooches and other objects by Joanna Bird).

In both cases it may be that there is a temple yet to be found; the distribution of votive offerings at temple sites indicates that they were often placed or later spread outside the temple and may be scattered in a wide area away from it. For example, at Wood-eaton many of the finds were even outside the temenos boundary (Goodchild & Kirk 1955, fig 12,

36) and there is similar evidence at Farley Heath (Poulton in prep); at Uley there were finds from the temple, but many more in the area around it (Wood-ward & Leach 1993, 329–31; cf Smith 2001, 24–6). There are suitable hilltop locations near the object scatters at both Frensham and Godstone, but in neither case is there evidence for a building. The Godstone hilltop is not open to trial work, but an appropriately placed enclosure has been identified on aerial photographs at Frensham. Here, testing has proved negative but there is evidence for nearby buildings (Graham 1986; 2001). It will be of great

interest to see if future work can establish that this is an example of a sacred site without a formal temple building. The site at Muntham Court in Sussex may also fit better in this category; the so-called temple building is hardly convincing, especially as it is on an Iron Age occupation site (Bedwin 1980, 192; Smith 2001, 250).

It is possible that there was such a site at Betchworth, where evidence has been found suggestive of

ritual at a number of periods, dating back to the Neolithic (Williams 1997). In the mid-1st century AD an elongated D-shaped enclosure was laid out, with an extra ditch cutting off the apsidal end (fig 6.5); cut into the outer edge of the main ditch at its western junction with the cross-ditch were a group of five ovens, with a sixth high in the ditch fill. The western side of the main ditch also contained a large amount of pottery, some certainly Roman. Although

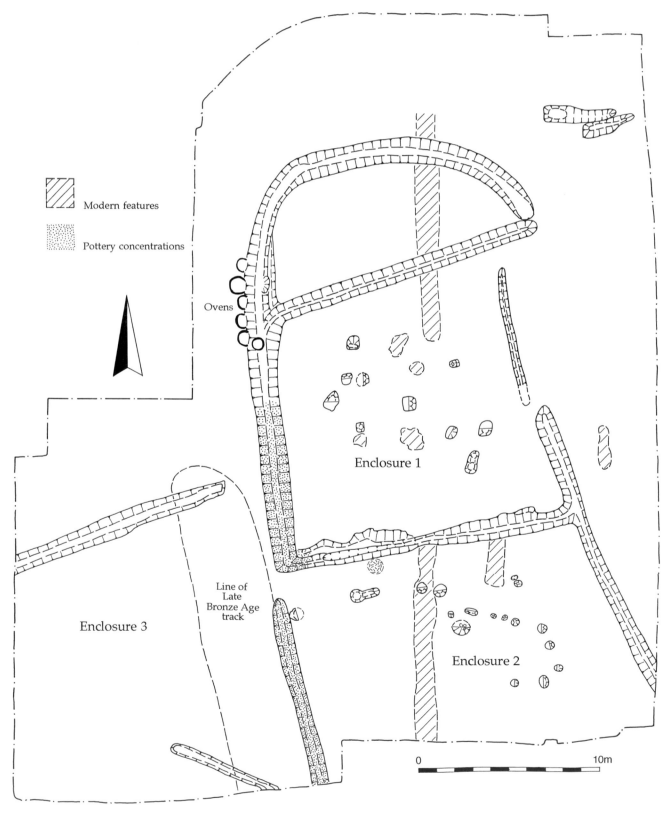

Modern features

Pottery concentrations

Ovens

Enclosure 1

Line of
Late
Bronze Age
track

Enclosure 3

Enclosure 2

0   10m

Fig 6.5 Betchworth: plan of the site in the Roman period. Drawing by David Williams

there were pits and postholes within the enclosure there was nothing that could be interpreted as a building and little room for one, but one pit had a burnt deposit with two animal jaws and there was also cremated animal bone in the western ditch. A ritual explanation is suggested for some of these discoveries and it may well be that it should be extended to the whole site. There is a parallel of a sort at Quinton in Northamptonshire, where a ritual explanation is offered for a similarly shaped and dated, although smaller, enclosure (Friendship-Taylor 1999). In this context it is of interest to note an earlier find from a sandpit some 500–600m to the west of the Betchworth site. This was a pottery sherd with an applied figure of a deity, whose attributes mark him as Jupiter or a native equivalent (Toynbee 1959; Webster 1989, 21); the vessel must have been intended for some ritual use.

Other non-temple sacred sites may be indicated by survivals into the Saxon period. Although there have been some suggestions to the contrary, few would doubt that the late Romano-British countryside remained essentially pagan in outlook. From this it follows that in the sub-Roman period there might have been some continuity of use at the main sacred sites. As already shown, temples as such were not required and so their demolition or collapse need not indicate abandonment of the ritual use of the site. It is interesting that each of the main rural temples in Surrey has produced evidence for some sort of activity even in the medieval period: coins at Wanborough and Farley Heath, pottery at Titsey (Graham 1936, 95; Williams 2000, 437; Williams forthcoming; Rob Poulton, pers comm; cf Poulton in prep). It is now also accepted that we should not think in terms of the British population of Surrey as being totally replaced by 'Anglo-Saxons'; in fact an accommodation of some sort is likely. It must therefore be possible that some of the shrines known to us from Saxon place-names, as at Peper Harow and Willey (if this was *Cusan weoh*) (Gover *et al* 1934, 175; 207), may actually be Romano-British (or even earlier) in origin. A place like Thunderfield ('Thunor's open space': Gover *et al* 1934, 295), deep in the Weald, might have originated as a sacred grove. Its possible later use as a meeting place might reflect earlier activity as suggested below in connection with Wanborough, and the equation of Thunor with a Jupiter-like native god, appropriate to such a setting (Bird 1994, 97), would not be difficult.

It is clearly not easy to assess the setting of religious sites when it cannot even be shown with certainty that they were of religious significance. This is especially the case when the site is actually part of the landscape. If a particular hilltop, or tree or spring is regarded as sacred, then it will have been an impor-tant feature in the landscape but we might now have no way of knowing that this was so (see, for example, recent discussion of the Caburn in Sussex: Drewett & Hamilton 2001). It is also difficult to analyse the landscape effect of features such as ritual shafts. In Surrey these seem only to have been recorded in the Ewell area (Cotton 2001, 36–7), which may hint at some aspect we cannot now comprehend. As Cotton notes, the idea is related to ritual deposits in wells, such as in Staines and Southwark, but in these last two cases we must be dealing with a ritual marking termination of use. This practice has origins stretching well back into prehistory.

The location of temples

When considering Roman religious sites in the landscape, it is usually therefore necessary to concentrate on temples. Clearly some sites were fixed by circumstances, in particular those thought to have healing powers. A medieval example may help to illustrate how this would have happened:

> A few miles from Prato, on a hill above the river Bisenzio, there was a little spring – 'situated in the place called *Il Palco*' – which provides an admirable example of the manner in which legends are created. Apparently its waters had some healing properties and on 8 June 1308 the Council of Prato decided to buy the land around it and to compensate the owner for the damage which his trees and vines had suffered 'from the multitude of persons going to bathe in the spring'. The land was bought for 638 *lire*, 15 *soldi*, and within thirty years a legend had already sprung up, and a little shrine was built. The spring, it was said, possessed healing powers because 'the martyr Proculus, as he was passing through the territory of Prato during his flight from the cruelty of the heathen, by his prayers miraculously produced out of the earth a living spring, which from that day forth has been called the *fontana procula*. And many sick men drink of this water, and are healed of their fever.' (Origo 1963, 245)

In this way some temple sites would effectively choose themselves, particularly at healing springs, but in other cases there might be considerable scope for choosing the exact site. If the temple was set up to the god of the locality or the particular group of people occupying an area (perhaps the same thing), then there might be many suitable locations to choose from. Given that the known temples in Britain reflect the involvement of local landowners or the Romano-British 'upper class', it is possible to think in terms of deliberate attempts to place temples within the landscape or manage their settings, and to see this in the context of the ways in which sacred sites were placed in towns for, as noted above, many of the same people will have been involved. There is good evidence that temples could be established on town sites previously used for some other, non-religious purpose, for example Caerwent (Anon 2001, 237), Verulamium (Henig 1984, 158–9), perhaps the Poultry site in London (Rowsome 2000, 45), Xanten and Cologne (Carroll 2001, 49); note also Pliny's letter 4.1, quoted above. The same may therefore be true for the countryside (cf Derks 1998, 169). There is a tendency to identify any earlier evidence on a Romano-Celtic temple site as evidence for ritual; Smith (2001, 15–16) points to the dangers inherent in this approach, and his summary of the evidence shows the flimsy ground on which some of the so-called Iron Age shrines is based (2001, 167–86). On the other hand a reasonable case can be made for pre-Roman ritual use of some temple sites (for example Farley Heath: Poulton in prep). The question still arises as to why certain sites were chosen for temples in the Roman period.

There can be no doubt that in the Roman world some buildings were sited with special regard to their setting. A splendid example is the Augustan monument at La Turbie, commemorating the conquest of the Alpine areas, magnificently sited overlooking the Riviera coast (Bedon *et al* 1988, 20). Perhaps more thought-provoking is the triumphal arch at Medinaceli in Spain, which was sited impressively at the edge of a steep downward slope (Collins 1998, 183–4), and this, like some temples it seems, was also at a major administrative boundary. These sites are far from Britain, of course, but the same basic planning tradition came to apply throughout the western Empire, as is shown by town plans (Ward Perkins 1974, 31). This approach can be demonstrated in Britain with regard to the placing of temples in the landscape, for instance in the way some temples are sited with respect to roads or high places. Presumably the hilltop temples were intended to be seen for quite some distance, and it has been argued that some of the Somerset hilltop temples were intervisible (Woodward 1992, 24). Being able to see the shrine from a nearby town or other important spot may have been important, and a temple is certainly likely to have been a prominent landmark. It is generally agreed that Romano-Celtic temples would have had towers, with red tile roofs (Wilson 1975, 4–8), so presumably this was something of a statement in the landscape, and they might have been painted white or red, making them even more prominent (see eg Blagg 1986, 19). They also had defined sacred enclosures, which will often have been visible in some way. A concern for the details of the appearance can be demonstrated in Pliny's letter about the old temple of Ceres, already mentioned above. In discussing the porticoes, it goes on:

At the moment I can't think of anything I want from you, unless you will draw me a plan suitable for the position. They cannot be built round the temple, for the site has a river with steep banks on one side and a road on the other. On the far side of the road is a large meadow where they might quite well stand facing the temple; unless you can think of a better solution from your professional experience of overcoming difficulties of terrain. (Letter 9.39, to Mustius; Radice 1963, 258–9)

In general, temples or sacred sites are found at characteristic locations:

- in towns, at town gates and at prominent sites near towns;
- by roads;
- at boundaries;
- on hilltops or prominent locations, including hill-forts;
- at or near earlier monuments such as barrows;
- by water, especially springs;
- associated with trees and groves;
- at or near villas.

Many temple sites fit more than one category. Thus Titsey is on a road, near a spring, set on a locally high spot, possibly at a boundary and not far from a villa.

All towns will have had temples and various finds suggest that there were probably several in Southwark (Haynes 2000, *passim*). The most recent discovery is a small inscription dedicated to the spirits of the Emperors and to Mars Camulos by one Tiberinius Celerianus (Anon 2002; Bird 2004, this volume, fig 5.2), whose choice of a god from his homeland (northern France) probably again demonstrates the eclectic nature of offerings and the option to pay off vows at a local sacred site. Recent large-scale fieldwork at places like Heybridge and Ashford has demonstrated that less formal 'small towns' probably all had temples (Atkinson & Preston 1998, 103; Booth & Lawrence 2000, 480; cf Booth 1998, 12). There can therefore be no doubt that there was a sacred site of some sort within the settlement at Staines; perhaps it was the base of the healer whose presence is demonstrated by a collyrium stamp (Jackson 1996). A ritual use of the King William IV site in Ewell has also been proposed (see further below). Interestingly, at all the sites mentioned (except of course Staines), the location of the temple site is highlighted by its position relative to the road system.

Town temples were presumably used for state or official ceremonies and some may have served specialist groups such as craftsmen. In some cases it may be that town temples also served wider communities, so that the journey for special occasions in this case was into town rather than to a rural location. This may explain the surprising lack of rural temples in central southern England, which contrasts strongly with areas like Surrey and Somerset (Watts & Leach 1996, 9–10). Is this because temples tend to appear in the countryside more often when there are no convenient towns to supply the need? Or perhaps the elite put most of their effort into towns in the more urbanized areas? It may of course be simply that the current picture is false, because the relevant temples await discovery.

Temples at gates were no doubt associated with travel but probably also reflected the sacredness of an important boundary. The new Southwark inscription noted above was found at a site near Tabard Street which has also produced evidence for two possible Romano-Celtic temples placed on the dry land just to the south of the two gravel 'islands' that formed the basis for the main settlement area. It was immediately adjacent to the point where Stane Street and Watling

Street joined before crossing into this area and as such may have been seen as at a gate or boundary as well as marking an important road junction. Temples alongside roads are quite common, as might be expected, but in some cases it is possible that their siting has affected or been affected by the course of the road, as perhaps at Tabard Street. Thus the Titsey temple is right next to the London–Lewes road, but sited at a point where the road changed direction; the effect may have been as though the long straight stretch from the south was heading directly at the temple. The original sacred feature here may well have been the nearby spring that marks the source of the Eden, so the choice of this site on a slight rise (fig 6.6) rather than one a little further north on the top of the scarp slope of the Downs may be significant.

A ritual explanation may also help to explain the unnecessary double bend taken by Stane Street in Ewell, perhaps to go round the King William IV site. A similar effect may be noted at Springhead and

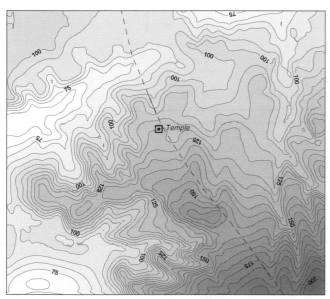

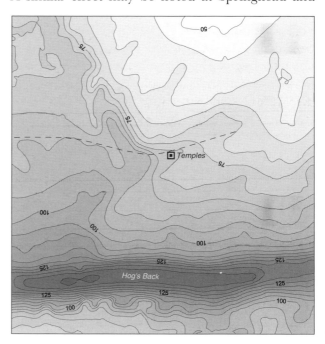

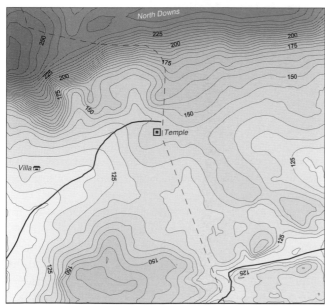

Farley Heath (above left)
A possible route of the Roman road is marked (dashed line).

Wanborough (above)
The route of the postulated Roman road is marked (dashed line).

Titsey (left)
The nearby villa, the line of the London-Lewes Roman road (dashed line), and the stream – the source of which is near the temple – are marked.

0   1km

Fig 6.6 Shaded contour maps showing the settings of the temples at Farley Heath, Wanborough and Titsey, (heights in metres and facing uphill, north at the top). Illustration by David and Audrey Graham. (© Crown Copyright NC/04/25242)

Silchester and in all these cases is likely to be deliberate, to give prominence to the sacred sites (Bird 2002a). This apparently deliberate highlighting of temples is perhaps a good pointer to how other aspects that we cannot now see might have been managed (sacred trees, water, etc). It is often suggested that the Titsey temple was established by the owner of the nearby villa, and it no doubt attracted offerings from passers by. It is difficult to be sure how much archaeological excavation there has been within the *temenos*, and the area around the temple itself was evidently much disturbed in the medieval period, so no meaningful assessment can be made of the quality or quantity of offerings (Graham 1936, *passim*). The presence of 'box-tiles' (Graham 1936, 94) near the temple may imply associated buildings including a bath-house. The temples at Farley Heath and Wanborough may also have been close to roads, as was the site already noted above at Godstone.

Temples at tribal boundaries seem to be common in Gaul (Fauduet 1993, 26–8), but in Britain it would be difficult to be sure because of the lack of certainty about the boundaries. The suggestion has been made for Woodeaton and some others (Henig 1984, 162), and it is possible that Titsey was at the Atrebatic/Cantiaci boundary (Detsicas 1983, 145). This boundary may, however, have been further west. As boundaries are of course linear, they are another example where considerable choice was available as to exact location of a temple. Other temples may be at boundaries we cannot usually hope to recognize, because they are smaller category divisions, like *pagi*. It would be interesting, for example, if Frensham was at a *pagus* boundary, thus prefiguring the later county boundary. It could also be argued that Farley Heath was seen as at the boundary with the Weald (cf Poulton in prep and Derks 1998, 136–7).

A thorough survey of British temples for the English Heritage Monument Protection Programme led to the conclusion that rural temples show a preference for sites which are prominent in the landscape: 'Examples commonly occur on hillsides or ridges of land, from which they could see or be seen; a few lie on the summit of a hill. Some were built in old hillforts and prehistoric earthworks, eg Lydney. The average height of country temples is *c* 120m above sea level.' (Ebbatson 1989, 7) The same phenomenon is noted in Gaul, and it is suggested that the high places are intended to mark the superiority of the gods and emphasize their protective presence. The temples would often have been visible from living or working places (Derks 1998, 137–8).

The location of the Farley Heath temple was presumably chosen for its height, which has interesting implications for the nature of the vegetation at the time. If it was intended to be seen at a distance then the surrounding area must then have been heathland. Like other hilltop sites the temple was not at the highest point, which presumably indicates the direction or directions from which it was intended to be seen. It is at the head of the slope from west, north and east (fig 6.6), which perhaps reinforces the view that it marked the boundary with the Weald beyond. Other hilltop religious sites in Surrey might be at Woodlands Park near Leatherhead (Lowther 1963), where the position implies a temple more than anything else, and perhaps Coombe Hill near Kingston, where again the location does not seem right for a villa and there were apparently many finds of coins (Bird 2000, 167 n4). The Chiddingfold site (see below) is also on a prominent local hill, with wide-ranging views. In all these cases there is of course the danger of a circular argument, and more definite evidence is required to prove that a ritual site existed.

It is sometimes argued that hillfort locations are deliberately chosen for temples (Woodward 1992, 22–6) but this may be chance – the location may be chosen for the high spot regardless of the hillfort. This might be demonstrated by the Henley Wood temple, for example: it is adjacent to but not within the hillfort at Cadbury Congresbury (Watts & Leach 1996, 7–8). Similarly the temple at Maiden Castle is obviously within the hillfort, but the fact that it would have been visible from the town at Dorchester may have been more important. There is no evidence to suggest temples (or indeed sacred sites) at any of the Surrey hillforts. The county also seems to lack clear evidence for ritual associated with earlier monuments like barrows, although the site at Betchworth, discussed above, must have had some sort of marker if, as seems likely, it is a continued use of an earlier sacred place.

It seems clear from both archaeological and written evidence that sacred sites associated with water, especially those at a spring, usually had a reputation for healing (Henig 1984, 155). The resulting pilgrimages ensured that such sites usually gave rise to a larger complex or settlement (Green 2000). Bath is the obvious outstanding British example (and note also the details given above in Pliny's letter about the source of the Clitumnus). Following Clive Orton's recent suggestion (1997, 115–7) that the King William IV site in Ewell had a ritual function, we might one day be able to add this settlement to the list: it is an obvious site for ritual, at the source of the Hogsmill, where offerings have been found (Bird *et al* 1994, 203–4; cf Bird 2002a). Spring-related sacred sites may also have existed at Titsey, as noted above and at Chiddingfold, encouraged by the existence of an abundant spring arising within a few feet of a hilltop (Bird 2002b). Derks points out that water would have been required at all sacred sites, for ritual washing and other purposes, so that the presence of a well or pond should not on its own be regarded as indicating that this was the focus of the site (Derks 1998, 196).

It has already been demonstrated that the positions of some temples or other evidence suggests a sacred tree as the focus of a ritual site. A special tree or grove-related shrine seems most likely at Wanborough in view of the location of the site on the sticky London Clay. Even today this area is well-wooded. The two temples are set on a rise (fig 6.6) but if a hilltop was required then surely the nearby Hog's Back ridge would have been used. It may be that the site was meant to be or at least to feel secret, hidden in woodland. Further work is needed to establish how access was gained to the site; there is some sign of an approach from the east, and there may be a link to a London–Winchester road nearby.

If it were set in a sacred grove, Wanborough would be unusual, as temples within such a setting seem to be uncommon in Britain. A sacred grove or clearing in a wood was a *nemeton*. Clive Cheesman discusses this in the Wanborough site report (1994, 33–4), saying that 'it is this sort of temple which is most readily associated with public activity and business', and noting that such a sanctuary is precisely where we would expect the 'bank' aspect implied by the thousands of coins found at the site (cf Smith 2001, 28;

Knight 1999, 119). He also notes that 'Salway [...] goes on to draw more parallels between the roles of classical and Celtic sanctuaries, based on their operation as a focus of community feeling, and a stage for the enactment of drama'. In this context we might note the results of a geophysical survey carried out by English Heritage (Linford & Linford 1997); this showed a curving feature forming a semi-circle in the area south of the known temples (fig 6.7). Recent excavation has shown that this was a metalled track, but its course is undoubtedly curious and it is possible that it was curving round something that has left no archaeological trace. The shape undoubtedly calls to mind a theatre, which would certainly not be out of place on such a site. It need not have been more than a simple box-frame structure, similar to those discussed by Derks (1998, 192–3); for example the theatre at Möhn in the Eifel is marked by no more than a curving wall (Cüppers 1990, 480).

Villa-related shrines may also have been placed with some regard to their setting. The Rapsley shrine is placed carefully between the buildings (Hanworth 1968, 17). We do not know enough about other Surrey sites to draw conclusions but it might be noted that at Lullingstone in Kent the temple-mausoleum and smaller temple seem to be sited for effect, on the ground above the villa (Meates 1979, 119–127). The temple-mausoleum reminds us

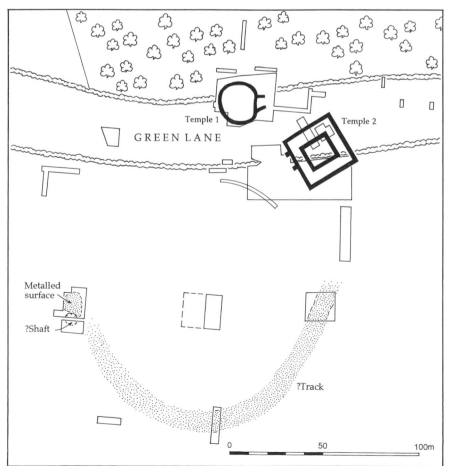

Fig 6.7 Wanborough: plan of the temples and other features. Not all are contemporary. Drawing by David Williams

that there might be sacred landscapes associated with death rituals too, and that cemeteries associated with villas might be some distance away, as at Bancroft near Milton Keynes, where there is a distance of some 200 metres between the villa buildings and the burial ground (Williams & Zeepvat 1994, fig 5 opp 6). In a similar fashion to Lullingstone, this was set higher up the slope and would have been a prominent landmark. It is rare for this relationship to be shown by excavation because of the separation between the sites, but it should be kept in mind. It might explain some of the evidence for extra buildings in the area near the Beddington villa, for example, and indicate the original location of the lead and stone coffins now in the church (Bird 2000, 167 n3). At Keston in Kent the tower tomb is closer to the villa (Philp *et al* 1991, 67, fig 17), but there can be no doubt that such a monument would itself be something of a statement in the landscape, similar to a circular temple. Elaborate roadside cemeteries with mausolea, such as at Great Dover Street in Southwark (Mackinder 2000), also bring a ritual element into everyday surroundings, and must have existed along the roads outside every sizeable settlement. Even much more ordinary burials may often have been placed with care for their setting; there is a marked line of cremations north of Farley Heath (Bird 1987, 179 fig 7.7) which may indicate burial beside a road.

There may therefore have been many sites of ritual significance in Surrey in the Roman period. Some will have been very local, or settlement-specific, others were free-standing and of varying importance. Analysis of the currently known temples in the South East suggests that only a few of the rural temples were well appointed with evidence for extensive offerings (different excavation standards and opportunities of course make it difficult to be certain). These include Weycock Hill, Wanborough, Farley Heath, Hayling Island, Chanctonbury Ring and perhaps Lancing Down and Titsey (summaries and references in Smith 2001, 192–266 *passim*; cf Rudling 2001). At Lancing the possibly associated burials and relatively few known votive finds (Bedwin 1980, 190–1) might perhaps suggest a temple-mausoleum; Titsey has been discussed above. It is noticeable that these sites tend to be placed in such a way that they fill gaps between the larger settlements. This may imply that they served particularly the rural communities, with urban needs provided for by temples in towns, apart from special spring-based healing shrines as at Springhead and perhaps Ewell and Chiddingfold. Alternatively, perhaps they were the most important sacred sites of a large district, a *civitas* or a *pagus*, serving a widespread population with special ceremonies on an occasional basis. It will be apparent, however, that much more evidence is needed before it will be possible properly to understand the way in which these sites functioned and related to one another. Too few sites have been examined to modern standards, and it is probable that many more sites have yet to be located; we should remember that the religious significance of the Wanborough site was unknown until 1985.

Future research
As with the Roman period in general, there is much still to be learned about Roman religious sites in Surrey.

• The possibility of continuity of use of sacred sites from the Iron Age or even earlier needs careful assessment. How might the sites have been marked in earlier periods?
• The origins of material at temple sites should be contrasted to nearby sites of the period to explore the possibility that this would show the catchment area for worshippers.
• Analysis of existing knowledge may allow the location of temple sites in towns and roadside settlements to be identified. Particular attention should be paid to road junctions or changes of course within the settlements.
• Information currently available should be reassessed, especially concentrations of brooches and coins. There may also be new information available as a result of the activities of the Finds Liaison Officer appointed under the Portable Antiquities Scheme.
• Detailed study of potential non-temple sites is needed in an attempt to confirm that they did not have temples; if this is thought to be the case, how might the site have been marked?
• The setting of temples should receive careful analysis, including views to and from the site.
• Environmental evidence is crucial and should always be a priority. It is possible that offerings at some sites were largely of organic material which would otherwise be difficult to recognize.
• Attention is needed to the means of access to the Wanborough and Chiddingfold sites.
• The possibility of continuity of use into the Saxon period should be explored.

ACKNOWLEDGEMENTS

I am particularly grateful to Joanna Bird for advice and encouragement; Jon Cotton, David and Audrey Graham, Sarah Hemley, Martin Henig, Alex Main, Rob Poulton, David Rudling, Alex Smith, David Williams and the staff of neighbouring Sites and Monuments Records (Kent, West Sussex, Hampshire and Greater London) are also thanked for their assistance in various ways.

BIBLIOGRAPHY

Anon [R Brewer & P Guest], 2001   Caerwent: Venta Silurum, *Current Archaeol*, **15.6,** 232–40

Anon, 2002   Londoners' stone sheds light on city's cosmopolitan ways, *Brit Archaeol*, **68,** 5

Atkinson, M, & Preston, S J, 1998   The Late Iron Age and Roman settlement at Elms Farm, Heybridge, Essex, excavations 1993–5: an interim report, *Britannia*, **29,** 85–110

Bagnall Smith, J, 1999   Votive objects and objects of votive significance from Great Walsingham, *Britannia*, **30,** 21–56

Bedon, R, Chevallier, R, & Pinon, P, 1988   *Architecture et urbanisme en Gaule Romaine. Tome 1. L'architecture et la ville (52 av. JC–486 ap. JC)*, Paris

Bedwin, O, 1980   Excavations at Chanctonbury Ring, Wiston, West Sussex 1997, *Britannia*, **11,** 173–222

Bird, D G, 1987   The Romano-British period in Surrey, in *The archaeology of Surrey to 1540* (eds J Bird & D G Bird), 165–96

——, 1996   The London region in the Roman period, in J Bird *et al* 1996, 217–32

——, 2000   The environs of Londinium: roads, roadside settlements and the countryside, in Haynes *et al* 2000, 151–74

——, 2002a   Roads and temples: Stane Street at Ewell, *London Archaeol*, **10.2,** 41–5

——, 2002b   Chiddingfold Roman villa: a suggested reinterpretation, *SyAC*, **89,** 245–8

——, 2004   Surrey in the Roman period: a survey of recent discoveries, in *Aspects of archaeology and history in Surrey: towards a research framework for the county* (eds J Cotton, G Crocker & A Graham), SyAS, 65–76

Bird, D G, Crocker, G, McCracken, J S, & Saich, D, 1994   Archaeology in Surrey 1991, *SyAC*, **82,** 203–19

Bird, J, 1994   Other finds excluding pottery, in O'Connell & Bird 1994, 93–132

Bird, J, Hassall, M, & Sheldon, H (eds), 1996   *Interpreting Roman London. Papers in memory of Hugh Chapman*

Birley, A, 2002   *Garrison life at Vindolanda. A band of brothers*

Blagg, T, 1986   Roman religious sites in the British landscape, *Landscape Hist*, **8,** 16–25

Boon, G C, 1974   *Silchester: the Roman town of Calleva*

——, 1983   Some Romano-British domestic shrines and their inhabitants, in *Rome and her northern provinces* (eds B Hartley & J Wacher), 33–55

Booth, P, 1998   The regional archaeological setting of the Roman roadside settlement at Wilcote – a summary, in A R Hands, *The Romano-British roadside settlement at Wilcote, Oxfordshire. II. Excavations 1993–96*, BAR Brit Ser, **265,** 8–20

Booth, P & Lawrence, S, 2000   Ashford. Westhawk Farm, *Current Archaeol*, **14.12,** 478–81

Carroll, M, 2001   *Romans, Celts and Germans. The German provinces of Rome*

Cheesman, C, 1994   The coins, in O'Connell & Bird 1994, 31–92

Collingwood, R G, & Wright, R P, 1965   *The Roman inscriptions of Britain. I. Inscriptions on stone*

Collins, R, 1998   *Spain. An Oxford archaeological guide*

Cotton, J, 2001   Prehistoric and Roman settlement in Reigate Road, Ewell: fieldwork conducted by Tom K Walls 1945–52, *SyAC*, **88,** 1–42

Cüppers, H (ed), 1990   *Die Römer in Rheinland-Pfalz*

Derks, T, 1998   *Gods, temples and ritual practices. The transformation of religious ideas and values in Roman Gaul*

Detsicas, A, 1983   *The Cantiaci*

Drewett, P, & Hamilton, S, 2001   Caburn. Sacred mount or classic hillfort, *Current Archaeol*, **15.6,** 256–62

Ebbatson, L, 1989   *Monuments Protection Programme. Single monument description. Romano-Celtic temples,* English Heritage

Fauduet, I, 1993   *Les temples de tradition celtique en Gaule Romaine*

Friendship-Taylor, R M, 1999   *Iron Age and Roman Quinton. The evidence for the ritual use of the site (Site 'E' 1978–1981)*

Goodchild, R, & Kirk, J R, 1955   The Romano-Celtic temple at Woodeaton, *Oxoniensia*, **19** [1954], 15–37

Gover, J E B, Mawer, A, & Stenton, F M, 1934   *The place-names of Surrey*, English Place-Name Society, **11**

Green, M, 1986   *The gods of the Celts*

Green, M A, 2000   On the road, *Brit Archaeol*, **52,** 14–17

Graham, D, 1986   A note on the recent finds of Bronze Age, Iron Age and Roman material and a site at Frensham Manor noted in an aerial photograph, *SyAC*, **77,** 232–5

——, 2000   A Roman coin deposit on Frensham Common, *SyAS Bull*, **338,** 6–7

——, 2001   Frensham Manor, *SyAS Bull*, **352,** 12–13

Graham, J G, 1936   A Romano-Celtic temple at Titsey, and the Roman road, *SyAC*, **44,** 84–101

Hammerson, M J, 1996   Problems of Roman coin interpretation in Greater London, in J Bird *et al* 1996, 153–64

Hanworth, R, 1968   The Roman villa at Rapsley, Ewhurst (parish of Cranleigh), *SyAC*, **65,** 1–70

Hassall, M W C, 1977   Altars, curses and other epigraphic evidence, in *Temples, churches and religion: recent research in Roman Britain* (ed W Rodwell), BAR Brit Ser, **77,** 79–89

Hawkins, D, 1996   Roman Kingston upon Thames, a landscape of rural settlements, *London Archaeol*, **8.2,** 46–50

Haynes, I 2000   Religion in Roman London, in Haynes *et al* 2000, 85–101

Haynes, I, Sheldon, H, & Hannigan, L (eds), 2000   *London under ground. The archaeology of a city*

Henig, M, 1984   *Religion in Roman Britain*

——, 2002   *The heirs of King Verica. Culture and politics in Roman Britain*

Henig, M [with contributions from M Hassall & J Bayley], 1993   Votive objects: images and inscriptions, in Woodward and Leach 1993, 89–112

Jackson, R, 1996   A new collyrium-stamp from Staines and some thoughts on eye medicine in Roman London and Britannia, in J Bird *et al* 1996, 177–87

Keay, S J, 1988   *Roman Spain*

Knight, J K, 1999   *The end of antiquity. Archaeology, society and religion AD 235–700*

Legge, A, Williams, J, & Williams, P, 2000   Lamb to the slaughter: sacrifice at two Roman temples in southern England, in *Animal bones, human societies* (ed P Rowley-Conwy), 152–7

Linford, P K, & Linford, N T, 1997   Wanborough Roman temple, Green Lane, Wanborough, Guildford, Surrey, report on geophysical survey, 1997, Ancient Monuments Laboratory Report, **100/97,** unpublished

Lowther, A W G, 1963   An enamelled bronze roundel of the Romano-British period, *Proc Leatherhead Dist Local Hist Soc*, **2.3,** 69–72

Ludowici, W, & Ricken, H (eds), 1948   *Katalog VI meiner Ausgrabungen in Rheinzabern 1901–1914. Die Bilderschüsseln der römischen Töpfer von Rheinzabern: Tafelband*, Speier

Mackinder, A, 2000   *A Romano-British cemetery on Watling Street. Excavations at 165 Great Dover Street, Southwark, London*, Museum London Archaeol Service Archaeol Stud Ser, **4**

Meates, G W, 1979   *The Roman villa at Lullingstone, Kent. Vol I: the site*, Monogr ser Kent Archaeol Soc, **1**

O'Connell, M, & Bird, J, 1994   The Roman temple at Wanborough, excavation 1985–1986, *SyAC*, **82,** 1–168

Orton, C, 1997   Excavations at the King William IV site, Ewell, 1976–77, *SyAC*, **84,** 89–122

Origo, I, 1963   *The merchant of Prato Francesco di Marco Datini*

Philp, B, Parfitt, K, Willson, J, Dutto, M, & Williams, W, 1991   *The Roman villa site at Keston, Kent. First report (excavations 1968–1978)*

Poulton, R, in prep   Farley Heath Roman temple

Poulton, R, & Scott, E, 1993   The hoarding, deposition and use of pewter in Roman Britain, in *Theoretical Roman archaeology first conference proceedings* (ed E Scott), 115–32

Radice, B, 1963   *The letters of the Younger Pliny*

Rowsome, P, 2000   *Heart of the city. Roman, medieval and modern London revealed by archaeology at 1 Poultry*

Rudling, D, 2001   Chanctonbury Ring revisited. The excavations of 1988–91, *Sussex Archaeol Collect*, **139,** 75– 121

Smith, A, 2001   *The differential use of constructed sacred space in southern Britain, from the Late Iron Age to the 4th century AD*, BAR Brit Ser, **318**

Tomlin, R S O, 1993   The inscribed lead tablets: an interim report, in Woodward & Leach 1993, 113–30

Toynbee, J M C, 1959   A Romano-British pottery-sherd with applied decoration from Betchworth, *SyAC*, **56,** 160–1

Ward-Perkins, J B, 1974   *Cities of ancient Greece and Italy. Planning in classical antiquity*

Watts, L, & Leach, P, 1996   *Henley Wood, temples and cemetery. Excavations 1962–69 by the late Ernest Greenfield and others*, CBA Res Rep, **99**

Webster, G, 1989   Deities and religious scenes on Romano-British pottery, *J Roman Pottery Stud*, **2,** 1–28

Williams, D, 1997   Betchworth: excavations at Franks' sandpit, *SyAS Bull*, **307,** 2–8

———, 2000   Wanborough Roman temple, *Current Archaeol*, **14.11,** 434–7

———, forthcoming Green Lane, Wanborough: excavations at the Roman religious site, 1999, *SyAC*

Williams, R J, & Zeepvat, R J, 1994   *Bancroft: a Late Bronze Age / Iron Age settlement, Roman villa and temple-mausoleum. I: excavations and buildings materials*, Buckinghamshire Archaeol Soc Monogr, **7**

Wilson, D R, 1973   Temples in Britain: a topographical survey, *Caesarodunum*, **8,** 24–44

———, 1975   Romano-Celtic temple architecture, *J Brit Archaeol Assoc*, 3 ser, **38,** 3–27

Woolf, G, 1998   *Becoming Roman. The origins of provincial civilization in Gaul*

Woodward, A, 1992   *Shrines and sacrifice*

———, & Leach, P, 1993   *The Uley shrines. Excavation of a ritual complex on West Hill, Uley, Gloucestershire: 1977–9*, Engl Heritage Archaeol Rep, **17**

Zelle, M, 2000   *Götter und kulte*, Führer und schriften des Archäologischen Parks Xanten, **21,** Köln

Dr D G Bird, Head of Heritage Conservation, Sustainable Development, Surrey County Council, County Hall, Kingston upon Thames KT1 2DY

7

Sūþre-gē – the foundations of Surrey

JOHN HINES

The county name of Surrey has an Anglo-Saxon root, meaning 'southern district'. This has been taken to mean that Surrey originated as a subordinate attachment to some other area, such as Middlesex. A review of the Anglo-Saxon archaeology of Surrey, however, shows that the early sites here were at the core of the distribution of prestigious artefact-types of the 5th and 6th centuries. The location of the sites at Croydon, Mitcham and Ewell implies a successful take-over of the Late-Roman infrastructure of London's southern hinterland. Even up to the end of furnished burial in the second half of the 7th century, when historical sources show that Surrey had fallen successively under the rule of Kentish, West Saxon and Mercian kings, the archaeological record reveals a strikingly diversified but geographically coherent community. Surrey may be a good example of a type of smaller political entity that could flourish in the earliest Anglo-Saxon period, but did not expand and could only be swallowed up in the consolidation of the major kingdoms.

The 'southern district'

There is a specific and significant sense in which the very idea of 'Surrey' can only trace its origins to the Anglo-Saxon period. In the 5th century AD nearly four centuries of Roman rule over a large part of the island of Britain came to an end, to be followed by a period of dramatic and extensive change. This saw the introduction to Britain, starting in the south and east, of material culture, Germanic language, and notions of inherited identity previously found in northerly parts of the Continent – in particular from northern Germany and southern Scandinavia. It was precisely these changes that laid the foundations of England and Englishness.

The name of what is now the county of Surrey is thoroughly Germanic in its origins. Its original form can be reconstructed with complete confidence as early Old English *Sūþræ-gē*, meaning 'southern district' (þ and ð were used in Old English to spell the sounds we spell *th* in Modern English). The element *gē* is a neuter noun rare in Old English, but familiar from modern German, Dutch and Frisian as *Gau, ga* and *goo* (Gover *et al* 1934, 1–2; Gelling 1978, 123). The final *-æ* of the neuter nominative singular ending of the adjective meaning 'southern' became *-e* as a normal sound-shift of Old English. Old English and Latin spellings of the name of the area often in fact have the vowel *-i-* here, eg *Suþrige, Sudrica*, a form that represents the raising of the point of pronunciation of the vowel *-e-* under the influence of the following sound, the palatalized or 'softened' *g-* of *gē* (Hogg 1992, §§6.41–2). This variant is recorded as early as the 8th century, and is of some importance as it implies that the name was by then no longer analysed and treated as a descriptive phrase but rather perceived as a single word, the proper name of the area. In practice, most of the earliest records of the name present it in a derived, plural form, representing 'the people of Surrey'. Hence in the 13th century copy of a Latin charter dated to AD 672–4 it appears in the phrase *prouinci[a] Surrianorum* (Birch 1885, no 34; Sawyer 1968, no 1165),

while 8th century copies of Bede's *Historia Ecclesiastica Gentis Anglorum*, completed in the 730s, refer to the *regio Sudergeona* or *Suðrigeona* (Bede, *HE*, iv.6).

A good deal can be inferred from the early references to Surrey in precisely such ways, but that process inevitably also defines a series of finer, supplementary questions concerning the foundation of Surrey. Just when and why, in the period between the early to mid-5th and mid- to later 7th century, did the term come into use? What exactly did it refer to, in terms of the geographical extent of the district (*gē*), and what form and level of social organization was there within that area itself? Most specialists have been content to interpret the relative geographical term (*Sūþræ*) as a sign of subordinacy: most probably to a Middle Saxon territory (Middlesex) which was of importance to ambitious Mercian kings in the second half of the 7th century (Cameron 1961, 54; Poulton 1987, 214 and note 44; Bailey 1989; Blair 1989; Dumville 1989); Morris (1973; 322–3 and 587–8), thought that it must imply the sometime existence of a complementary Norrey (a form that is reconstructed rather than historically recorded). Just as the area of Surrey seems to lie somewhat indeterminately in between the *civitates* of Cantium, the Atrebates and the Regni in the late Iron Age and Roman period (Bird 1987, esp fig 7.1), it is treated as a left-over area, finally defined, named and organized only to tidy up the administration of a much larger territory centred elsewhere and to the north. This partly reflects and partly reinforces an underlying view that the origins of Anglo-Saxon Surrey are not a matter of any great historical consequence. That, however, is somewhat at odds with the archaeological evidence for the early Anglo-Saxon period in Surrey. A consideration of the full range of evidence from this, Surrey's 'protohistoric' period, introduces us to an area and a case-study of special interest in the quest for a better general understanding of the transition between Roman Britain and Anglo-Saxon England.

The archaeological evidence

In other parts of England a comparison of 5th to 7th century archaeological evidence with the political geography of the following phase of Mercian over-lordship has shown that, rather than radically redrawing the map of England, the process of establishing that large-scale political order could include the appropriation of substantial and viable territorial units and social networks that already existed (Hines 1999a). This is essentially what we can also claim for Surrey. From early in the Anglo-Saxon period, certainly no later than the second half of the 5th century, there are sites within the historical county that have a special place in the national Anglo-Saxon archaeological record. Absolutely nothing comparable has been found within a corresponding distance and area north of the Thames from London at this time. On the gravels along the Thames itself, on both sides of the river, a number of recent finds have provided us with important insights into settlement sites with characteristically Anglo-Saxon artefact and structural types from no later than the 6th century and quite possibly the second half of the 5th century onwards (fig 7.1). Within the area of our particular interest, a band of these now runs from Shepperton downriver to the Covent Garden area just outside the Roman city of London to the west (eg Canham 1979; Andrews & Crockett 1996; *Current Archaeology*, Special London Issue, July 1998; Cowie & Harding 2000, 178–81). West of Surrey, early Anglo-Saxon finds are very few indeed in a large area bounded by the Wey and the Kennet to the east and west, and the Thames and the Itchen valleys to the north and south. To the south of Surrey, the great Wealden forest separated the southern coastal lands of the *Meonware* in Hampshire and the South Saxons of Sussex from the Thames basin. To the east, meanwhile, it has long been recognized that early Anglo-Saxon Kent east of

the Medway shows a markedly different archaeological profile from those parts of the historic county west of the Medway, and that in western Kent the earliest sites show much greater affinities with their contemporary counterparts in Surrey (Hawkes 1982; Blair 1991, 6–9). While in comparison with the quantitative wealth of eastern Kent, the material record from the early Anglo-Saxon period in the area between the Medway and the Wey appears restrained, perhaps controlled, we can still identify significant patterns in the material cultural remains within this whole territory, a notional 'Greater Surrey'.

A group of items of metalwork that is crucial not only to an understanding but also to an evaluation of the Surrey/west Kent area in this early period does, however, occur in significant forms both west and east of the Medway. This is the corpus of what is known as quoit-brooch-style metalwork. This is metalwork drawing on a technical repertoire of decoration rooted in late Roman skills and practices. It is found in Anglo-Saxon contexts from the mid-5th century onwards, subsequently also appearing on the far side of the English Channel (Inker 2000; Suzuki 2000; Ager 2001). While the exact history of this style remains a matter for debate – a debate that is often keen, not least because of the crucial historical implications of different interpretations of these early instances of late Roman influence on Anglo-Saxon culture – both technically and typologically, the earliest instances of this style group are probably, as Peter Inker stresses, the quoit-brooch-style fixed-plate buckles, these being the closest relatives to the artefact types on which the style's Roman-period sources are most widely found. The findspots of the relevant quoit-brooch-style buckles are Mitcham in Surrey, Orpington in the Cray Valley (West Kent), Bishopstone (East Sussex), and Mucking overlooking

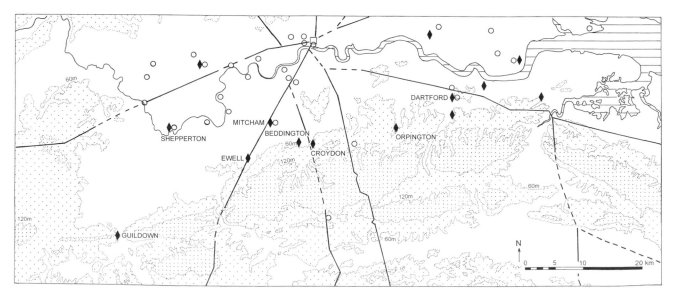

Fig 7.1 Surrey, West Kent and adjacent areas: Anglo-Saxon settlement sites (circles) and Migration-period burial sites (lozenges). The solid lines indicate the alignments of Roman roads. (© Crown Copyright NC/04/25242)

the Thames Estuary in Essex (Evison 1968; on the Mitcham and Orpington cemeteries see Bidder & Morris 1959; Tester 1968; 1969). Croydon, meanwhile, produced a quoit-brooch-style strap distributor from a belt (Griffith 1897; Shaw 1970). West of the Medway and south of the Weald, however, occurrences of the style are predominantly in the form of brooches and other dress accessories, which we may argue represent a secondary phase of application of the style.

This allows us to be confident that the Anglo-Saxon burial sites at Mitcham, Croydon and Orpington originated around the third quarter of the 5th century and that those buried there were provided with some of the earliest products in a new, technically proficient and elegant style of metalwork emerging from a Roman-influenced milieu in south-eastern England. A range of other finds at these sites is consistent with such early starting dates – for instance a Saxon applied brooch and pedestalled bowl at Mitcham (Welch 1975), an early form of francisca (throwing axe) of Frankish character at Croydon (Griffith 1897, figure on p 20, lower; Siegmund 1998, 106–7 (FBA-1.1); Nieveler & Siegmund 1999) and a variety of early brooch types, predominantly Saxon, at Orpington (Dickinson 1979; Hines 1999b, 24). Mitcham and Croydon are located on major Roman roads running southwards from Londinium; early predecessors of the modern A20 and A21 passing Orpington have been suspected but remain unproven. The three sites are approximately 14, 15 and 20km from London Bridge respectively (fig 7.1). Croydon and Mitcham are both by the river Wandle and Croydon and Orpington both on the northern dip slope of the North Downs. It is impossible too to overlook the probable importance of all three of these locations in the late-Roman infrastructure of the territory south of Londinium. Relatively little is known about the precise character of Croydon and Mitcham as Roman-period sites, and speculation about their status in terms of the modern classification of Roman settlement sites is not particularly helpful. However, whether as a 'village' or even a 'small town' – like that of which rather more is known at Ewell, almost exactly the same distance out of London along Stane Street as Orpington – in these locations they are intrinsically likely to have fulfilled a common function in this hinterland as posting stations, or *mutationes* (Bird 1987, 168–9; Perring & Brigham 2000, 150–7). Close to Croydon is the Roman villa site of Beddington, and the Orpington cemetery is immediately adjacent to the Roman villa of Fordcroft (Bird 1987, 171–8; Philp & Keller 1995).

We can consequently regard these sites as having been located upon nodes within and indeed serving the communications networks south of Londinium.

As long as the latter flourished, the city must have placed considerable demands on these nearby areas and upon such sites within them. It is interesting to note that Nicholas Brooks and James Graham-Campbell, discussing a Viking-period coin hoard from Croydon, explain its presence there by attributing precisely the same function to the area during the late 9th century Viking occupation of London (Brooks & Graham-Campbell 1986). It is perfectly plausible that such sites could have continued to function as focal sites in the exploitation and redistribution of produce from the local area even if the network they originally belonged to had lost its heart or head at a now-defunct city of London. Such de-urbanization is indeed widely and authoritatively argued to have been characteristic of the functioning structure of late Roman Britain as a whole (Reece 1980; Esmonde Cleary 1989, 131–61; cf Dark 1994, 12–19).

Beyond this, the quality of retrieval and recording of finds from the sites means that it is not, unfortunately, possible to say much about the Anglo-Saxon communities at Mitcham and Croydon. Both cemeteries were probably in use for between 150 and 200 years. That at Mitcham contained at least 238 burials. If we assume a mean life expectancy of 25 for this period, it would appear, therefore, to represent a small burying community with an average of only some 25–30 adults living at any one time. Various excavation campaigns at Orpington have so far produced just over 80 graves from a period of use of about a century. Both Croydon and Mitcham, however, are impressively furnished with weapon graves, especially in terms of swords of which thirteen are recorded from Mitcham and about six from Croydon (including the limited excavations conducted in 1999: McKinley 2003). The size of the visible burying community implies that these were the burial places of a special group in this area, not of the total population linked to these foci. That group was clearly associated with power and authority, although we should be cautious about identifying these burials as those of members of the regional social élite themselves. What they unquestionably represent is social and territorial dominance at key nodes within the area. This dominance was established early in the Anglo-Saxon period, and lasted there to the eve of the historical period.

From such significant 5th century beginnings, it is remarkable how limited is the increase in the number and the expansion of the distribution of known Anglo-Saxon burial sites in Surrey from the following century. This is not least the case when we compare the situation here with the virtually unrestrained increase in the number of sites over much of the rest of southern and eastern England (Hines 1990). Within the distinctive phase of Anglo-Saxon material practices we can call the Migration period, which came to an end around the 560s, the only further securely dated examples of Anglo-Saxon burial sites coming into use in Surrey are at Beddington, Ewell and Guildown (fig 7.1; Lowther 1931; 1935; Poulton 1987, 197–200). There is a string of more doubtful cases, from which very little evidence has been preserved and which therefore are uncertainly datable (Morris 1959; Meaney 1964, 237–45), together with the uncontextualized evidence of metal-detector finds of artefacts definitely of this date from a few further locations (Welch 1996). Among the sites that were certainly cemeteries, only the finds attributed to Watersmeet at Fetcham look at all capable of representing a further burial site in use by the mid-6th century, as these include a number of Type-H spearheads with concave-sided blades and a shield boss of Dickinson & Härke's group 3 that could well be of this date (Smith 1907; Cotton 1933; Swanton 1974; Dickinson & Härke 1991; Härke 1992, 94–6). In western Kent, meanwhile, a group of important sites of the same date emerges in the Darent valley with burials near Dartford and at Horton Kirby (alias Riseley), together with a cremation cemetery at Northfleet, and a few more stray finds such as a button brooch from East Malling (Cumberland 1938; Wilson 1957; Walsh 1981; Kelly 1989, 312; Batchelor 1990; Tyler 1992).

Once again, Beddington and Ewell had been prominent sites in the map of Roman Surrey, as the locations of a villa and a small town respectively. Darenth too is the site of a Roman villa (Philp 1973, 119–54). The expansion of Anglo-Saxon burial sites in this area is thus not only remarkably limited, but also reveals all the more clearly the dominance of the northern dip slope of the Downs, which includes agriculturally the most attractive light soils in a narrow strip overlying the Reading Beds, as the basis for the settlements of communities demonstrating their presence by adhering to the conventional Anglo-Saxon furnished burial rite. No contemporary evidence of places of occupation has yet been found in these areas, although such settlements have been found on the riverine gravels (fig 7.1). Regrettably we have far too little information to be confident how to interpret the possible hoard of at least ten early 6th century Byzantine gold coins (tremisses) of Justin I apparently found in the river bed at Kingston upon Thames (Rigold 1975, nos 3–12). Their deposition here very probably represents significant activity along the river in this period, but does not allow us to infer the presence of any specific type of site there.

It is, however, not only in terms of access to and control over the most advantageous land locally, but also in terms of long-distance connections and influence, that the few and small communities represented by the furnished burials seem to have been at the heart of a widespread and important social network. While it is in this area that we may find our first small cluster of manifestations of the quoit-brooch style in the 5th century, from the very early 6th century we can trace even more certain and considerably more expansive influences emanating from here through an ostentatious type of woman's brooch, the great square-headed brooch. At the head of the genealogy of a distinctively Saxon group of these brooches, Group I, stand brooches from Dartford and Mitcham (fig 7.2A–B; Hines 1997, 17–32, pls 1–9), in effect as a pair of prototypes of which the descendants in subsequent generations of brooch design spread out over an area from Sussex to the Upper Thames and Warwickshire Avon valley, and eventually as far north as to Rutland and the Peterborough area in the East Midlands (figs 7.2C and fig 7.3). The Dartford and Mitcham brooches also represent particularly clearly the direct Scandinavian influences that underlay the adoption of this brooch type in England around the beginning of the 6th century. We can be less certain about the status and relationships of another great square-headed brooch fragment from grave 116 at Mitcham (fig 7.2D), but there is enough there to suggest very strongly that this may equally be the earliest specimen yet found of Group VII (Hines 1997, 67–76, pls 23–9). Group VII is itself an early descendant of Group I, and has much the same overall distribution in southern England.

Over most of southern and eastern England where the introduction of Anglo-Saxon material culture during the Migration period is marked by conspicuously furnished burial rites, both inhumation and cremation, the known number of burials and burial sites diminishes markedly from the late 6th century and through the 7th, in the 'Final Phase' (Leeds 1936, 96–114; Boddington 1990; Geake 1997). In a few areas, such as East Kent, however, there is quantitatively little difference between the two phases, while in a number of locations around the country the inverse is the case, with an increase in burial finds from the later phase. Examples include areas on or just beyond the boundary of visible Anglo-Saxon culture prior to this date, eg in Somerset and Dorset, the Derbyshire Peak District, and Northumberland and south-eastern Scotland, and also some 'enclaves' within the anglicized Lowland Zone, including Hertfordshire north of London and Surrey to the south (eg Ozanne 1963; Kennett 1972; 1973; Rahtz et al 2000, 96–8). The substantial increase in the number, area and diversity of burial sites in the Final Phase in Surrey and West Kent is represented by sites at Merrow just east of the Wey at Guildford (Saunders 1980); Hawk's Hill near Fetcham as well as further burials from Watersmeet in what may be one extended cemetery; the Goblin Works cemetery, Ashtead (Poulton 1989); Headley Drive, Tadworth

Fig 7.2 Great square-headed brooches. A: Dartford (Group I). B: Mitcham, grave 225 (Group I). C: Guildown, grave 116 (Group I).
D: Mitcham, grave 116 (Group VII). Scale 1:1. Copyright (A) The British Museum, (B) Museum of London, (C, D) the author

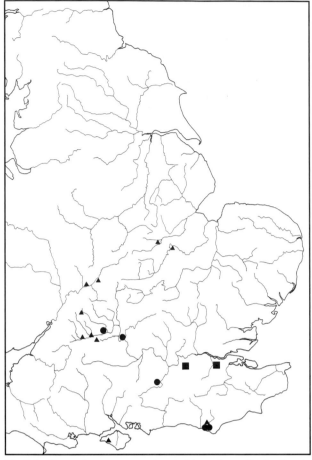

Fig 7.3 Group I great square-headed brooches, distribution in three stages of development. Squares: first stage; circles: second stage; triangles: third stage. It should be noted that another early Group I great square-headed brooch is from the cemetery at Alveston Manor, by Stratford-on-Avon, Warwickshire. However it is unclear whether this brooch should be assigned to the first or the second stage (Hines 1997, 27).

(Harp & Hines 2003); Quelland, East Ewell; Gally Hills, Banstead (Barfoot & Price Williams 1976); and Farthing Down, Coulsdon (Flower 1874; Hope-Taylor 1950). In Kent west of the Medway there is a barrow cemetery in Greenwich Park, a series of further sites in and around the Darent valley at Farningham, Polhill (Philp 1973, 164–214) and Wrotham, as well as further burials at Horton Kirby, and several sites close to the Medway itself, eg at Cliffe-at-Hoo, Holborough (Evison 1957), Snodland, Strood and within what is now Rochester itself. While burial continues in this period at Croydon and Mitcham, there is, curiously, no evidence for the continuing use of the Migration-period burial sites at Guildown, Ewell, Beddington and Orpington.

Despite the local shifts and apparently regular relocations of burial sites around the late 6th to early 7th centuries that we can thus make out (cf Hyslop 1963), in the area that was to become the county of Surrey, the dominant topographical zone for furnished burial – Mitcham on the Wandle apart – continued to be the strip of land along the dip slope of the Downs eastwards from the crossing of the Wey at Guildford (fig 7.4). Other finds show activity in different zones leaving other types of archaeological deposit. Only at Shepperton and Hanwell north of the river, and, through very recent finds, Mitcham, are any of the known settlement remains of this general period sufficiently close to known furnished burials that the two may be directly associated. In the 7th century we have coin finds showing activity at Brockham, where the Mole crosses the greensand belt south of the North Downs scarp, and a particularly important hoard from Crondall (Hampshire), just 5km north-west of Farnham, which included two coins of the same type as that found at Brockham, one possibly even die-linked to it (Sutherland 1948; Rigold 1975, no 56). Furnished burial thus continues to be curiously restricted to a specific and dominant zone in a variegated landscape. While the changes that take place as we enter the Final Phase are undoubtedly striking, there is no reason to see them in any terms other than evolutionary ones: as a consis-

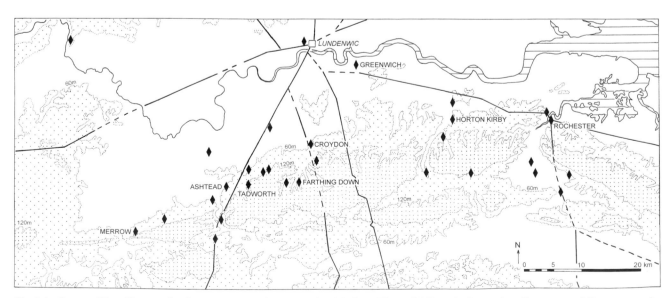

Fig 7.4 Surrey, West Kent and adjacent areas: 7th century burial sites. The solid lines indicate the alignments of Roman roads. (© Crown Copyright NC/04/25242)

tent development from what had gone before. It is possible that there were substantial changes of personnel in the commanding positions of society in the region south of London at this date, but the pattern of territorial exploitation there remained essentially the same. If the embryonic region of Surrey was taken over, that would appear to have been as an effectively organized and functioning entity.

Within the wider range of sites to examine from this period, however, we can now observe more diversity and even a hierarchy between burial sites. Most impressive to us now, and presumably intended to be equally so then, are the barrow burials with specially crafted and precious, prestigious grave goods (cf Struth & Eagles 1999). The most striking examples are Farthing Down and Gally Hills, within a distance of 6km of one another up on the Downs and 7–8km south-south-east of the Croydon and Mitcham cemeteries respectively. The one excavated barrow at Gally Hills revealed a weapon grave furnished also with a hanging bowl. The sugar-loaf-type shield boss from this grave is closely paralleled nearby at Quelland, East Ewell, and at Farthing Down (cf Evison 1963). Weaponry dominates the finds recovered from Farthing Down, including one sword, although well-furnished female burial here is also represented by an example containing a gold composite disc pendant, six small monochrome beads and a disc-headed pin. Given the almost uniformly haphazard retrieval of material and its consequently highly fragmentary character, it is difficult to be confident that the Gally Hills and Farthing Down barrows represent a distinctly more richly furnished stratum than, say, Quelland or the Merrow barrows; but we are certainly here looking at a deliberately richer range of material deposits than those from the more populous cemeteries with no recorded barrows at Fetcham and Ashtead. Meanwhile the prevalence of weaponry among the diagnostic artefacts from these sites and thus a military emphasis is quite striking – all the more so if we can attribute the vaguely dated, presumed Anglo-Saxon burial sites at Carshalton, Cheam, Coulsdon, Cuddington, Dorking, Mickleham and Ripley (Morris 1959; Meaney 1964, 237–46), all tentatively identified from the finding of one or more Anglo-Saxon spearheads, to the same period as the attested majority of Anglo-Saxon graves in the county. A corresponding situation is encountered in Hertfordshire and south Bedfordshire.

The newly published cemetery at Headley Drive, Tadworth, with more than 40 adequately investigated graves and not a single item of weaponry, is thus a conspicuous exception (Harp & Hines 2003). Yet this cemetery is well-ordered, and the sparse grave goods it yielded include a rare and quite fine double-tongued buckle, and an imported, wheel-thrown pot, so that on the internal evidence of the cemetery we have no good reason to regard the community burying there as a generally deprived and low-status one. It seems more appropriate to consider what sort of systematic differentiation of cemetery types within this region might have provided a distinct place for a site such as Headley Drive. With the proviso, of course, that some of this site remains unexcavated, we need to consider why weapon burial may have been neither needed nor appropriate here, without simply invoking subordinancy in social status. Among the other very poorly recorded burial sites from Surrey, that at Sanderstead – just a little further from Farthing Down than Headley Drive from Gally Hills – where a dozen graves produced one small pot, a tooth pendant, and two knives, looks the most credible equivalent.

The progressive introduction of Anglo-Saxon culture into Britain in the 5th and 6th centuries is revealed to us primarily by material remains: by archaeology. In the 7th century written records – history – gradually take over the narrative. The proper way to work towards an answer to the questions just formulated is to integrate these two forms of evidence, and to compare the inferences that may be drawn from those with what has more wisely been suggested concerning general processes and conditions of change in the earliest centuries of Anglo-Saxon England. Although we have had a series of fine and authoritative surveys of early Anglo-Saxon Surrey, both archaeological (Morris 1959; Poulton 1987) and historical (Blair 1989), these have all shown considerable diffidence about the importance to be afforded to the evidence for the foundations of Surrey, either in the national perspective or in terms of its significance to the key themes identified in the historical record generally. This has now to be challenged.

Despite the early, powerful, and significantly located introduction of Anglo-Saxon groups at Mitcham, Croydon and Orpington, the archaeologically visible Saxonization of the area south of the Thames was limited. As we have seen, compared with most of the rest of southern and eastern England the Migration-period burial sites are unusually few. Interestingly this is no longer the case in respect of settlement sites with characteristic Anglo-Saxon structural types (sunken huts) and pottery forms, where again the known examples are consistently confined to certain topographical zones. As Poulton recognized (1987, 216), the whole scenario, synchronic and diachronic, lends itself to the idea that an extant sub-Roman social and economic infrastructure in the territory was taken over as a going concern rather than the area being an abandoned landscape which saw just a few pockets of 5th and 6th century occupation. Surviving British Celtic place-names such as *Leatherhead* (Coates 1980), English place-names incorporating Latin elements apparently locally adopted as loanwords (eg *Croydon*: Gelling 1978, 66, 75–6, 81–2), and ethnically specific place-names (*Walton*: Cameron 1961, 42–3), lend support to the general view of interaction and gradual transition between one period and population and its successor. In contrast to what can be argued for the same period in Sussex, however (Welch 1971), the overall impression here is of the early Saxon settlers merely taking what they found and acting as if free to do just what suited themselves best, not of a surviving sub-Roman system governing or even dictating the shape of the nascent Surrey. The Roman villas in the west of Sussex were rooted in a rich agricultural area, whereas the villas of Surrey depended considerably more on production and trade of an industrial character. Like the Alice Holt potteries west of Farnham, these must simply have failed as the Roman period came to an end (Bird 1987, esp 178–87).

The strength and importance of the Saxons of Surrey and west Kent at the very beginning of the Anglo-Saxon period are reflected not so much in the volume or density of their furnished burial sites but rather in their evident influence within a network of contacts and exchange over a large area of Saxon southern England. While the archaeological picture changes quite substantially during the later 6th and early 7th centuries, one may reasonably suggest that this should be perceived in terms of continuity and evolution rather than a dramatic interruption, restructuring and redirection of social development in Surrey. Hierarchy both within and between communities seems to become deeper, or at least more regularly marked. Such changes were indeed taking place throughout Anglo-Saxon England at this time, and their outcomes were more substantial and consequential outside of the London area. In the great kingdoms of Wessex, Mercia and Northumbria in particular, they led to a new scale of political ambition and expansion. A clear economic manifestation of such pressures was the establishment – in some cases re-establishment – of urban ports, at *Hamwic* (Southampton), Ipswich, York and, of particular relevance to Surrey, London. In the religious-ideological sphere, the conversion of England to Christianity is an entirely comprehensible concomitant to these developments.

The historical questions

Documentary sources give us no precise information about the political and religious history of Anglo-Saxon Surrey before the mid-660s, a date undoubtedly close to that of the latest furnished burials in Surrey. These records evidently reveal only the end points of a series of processes, the earlier mass of which can only be conjectured. The characterization of Surrey from the later 5th to mid-7th century offered above on the basis of the archaeological evidence implies that there was a well-ordered and influential community here across this period. We are not in a position to pre-suppose how this community and territory would have been governed – in other words we may not specifically postulate an early and historically unrecorded kingdom of (or in) Surrey. What we can do, however, is to dispute the pejorative conclusions too readily drawn from the negative evidence of the silence of our early sources, which, in the form of charters, Bede's *Historia Ecclesiastica*, and the Anglo-Saxon Chronicle, resolutely provide us with an external, Mercian, West Saxon and sometimes Kentish view of the area: that (as its name is supposed to imply) Surrey was always marginal and subordinate to places where all the important developments were taking place and all the important things were happening. It is, for instance, inappropriate to read the Chronicle entry for 568, reporting that the West Saxon king Ceawlin (with Cutha) then drove Ethelberht back into Kent, as evidence that there was nothing of note or name between Wessex and Kent in southern England at that time (cf Blair 1991, 6). We can accept the part-contemporaneity of these two powerful kings and thus the plausibility of their fighting a battle in southern England, albeit not as early as in AD 568; but there is no doubt whatsoever that the West Saxon Chronicle's account of the creation of the West Saxon kingdom suppresses a good deal about constituent groups and territories melded into that polity (Yorke 1989). Whatever it may have been known as and however it may have been constituted, there is no historical reason to object to the archaeologically derived view of a significant entity of 'proto-Surrey' in the 5th to 7th centuries.

When *Sūþre-gē* does appear in history, however, it is under external control. Around the mid-660s Eorcenwald, subsequently bishop of London, founded the monastery of Chertsey with the permission and support of King Egbert of Kent (664–72). However the charter of 672–4 that records this fact while endowing the monastery with more land was issued by Frithuwold, ruling Surrey as a sub-king of King Wulfhere of Mercia. In the 680s Caedwalla, king of Wessex, granted land at and around Farnham for another monastery (Birch 1885, no 72). By this time, as the charter of Frithuwold explicitly notes, the port of London had been re-established. From this period onwards until the irruption of the Vikings in the second half of the 9th century, London and Middlesex, and indeed Essex and East Anglia much of the time, were firmly under Mercian control. Not only in the case of London, however, but also now in respect of Surrey, we can argue that the Mercian royal power annexed territory and sites that were already well established. Anglo-Saxon Surrey came into being through the survival and maintenance of at least elements of the structure of the southern hinterland of Roman Londinium. Developments in Surrey and west Kent – more, so far as we can tell, than anything that happened in Middlesex and Essex – thus seem to have played a key role in maintaining the life and influence of the London area. It is as reasonable as anything else, although also as unprovable, to hypothesize that the concept of *Sūpre-gē* emerged as the designation for the southern half of the large area around the practically empty hub of London on either side of the Thames (Bird *et al* 1975, 141). And there is no reason at all why this should not have taken place around the same time as three or four districts of the early Kentish kingdom west of the Medway were defined as *gē* units, centred upon Eastry, Sturry, Lyminge and probably Wester too (Brooks 1989, 68–71). The absence of any known 'northern district' as its counterpart can reflect the simple fact that only on the southern side did an efficiently organized community establish itself.

But even the archaeological evidence sheds only uncertain light upon how that southern district was organized within itself. Historians such as the late Eric John have found it difficult enough to draw a clear and coherent picture of the tenurial, territorial and social arrangements underlying the period of our earliest reliable Anglo-Saxon charters of the later 7th and 8th centuries, let alone to extrapolate back from those to the state of affairs in the earliest centuries of Anglo-Saxon England (John 1960; 1966). John Blair (1989; 1991) has more recently worked within the framework of such historical studies in endeavouring to make a realistic reconstruction of the earliest elements out of which Surrey was formed. He has demonstrated the practical logic of a pattern of four major blocks of territory subdividing the county of Surrey. Of most direct relevance to the early Anglo-Saxon period are two oblong blocks in the east of the county which he associated with historically identifiable centres at Croydon and Leatherhead respectively, both the locations of later minster churches (Blair 1991, esp 12–24); these two areas contain nearly all of our known 5th to 7th century Anglo-Saxon sites. The two blocks run south from the Thames into the Weald, and thus form the final pair in the north-west of a larger series of such units comprising also the 'lathes' of Kent and the 'rapes' of Sussex. Blair was willing to consider these territories as possible ' "primary" provincial units', and gives a number of reasons for regarding them as old enough to precede the historical horizon of the charters.

It is understandable that when a historian finds it possible to divide early territories into coherent constituent elements it is tempting also to believe that one is stripping away historical accretions and uncovering chronologically earlier strata. This is, however, a perspective that tends to atomize historical reconstructions of very early Anglo-Saxon society (Bassett 1989; cf Scull 1993), and which I would argue sits uneasily with the archaeological evidence. Indeed, purely as a matter of historical reconstruction, it is far from problem-free. This is not the place for an extensive critique of that model, but in brief one may note how, for instance, Eric John's reasoned case for the creation and introduction of individual landholding rights in the 8th century struggles with the problem of determining what arrangements these practices superseded. Even the dimly attested phenomenon of an earlier *folcland* and its communal rights is subject from the earliest available evidence to the political control of kings who could apportion access to and even give such rights away. Rather than revealing the growth of kingship over polities that gradually merged and swelled in size, kingship appears to have been primary in the historical record, and the elements we can observe which are manifestly innovations are the definition of identities and roles at intermediary levels in the social hierarchy.

Certainly, when we attempt to find any counterparts to Blair's suggested pattern in the early archaeological evidence, the greatest difficulty lies in identifying anything that convincingly represents important boundaries between primary units rather than a network of relationships between and across them. It is, as Blair notes, interesting to observe that a particular cluster of rich 7th century weapon graves and barrows (few of which, however, have been proved to house Anglo-Saxon burials) lies around the boundary between these two territories in the Ewell Downs/Gally Hills area. There are, however, several more barrows along the Downs of quite unknown character and date, while for the Farthing Down barrows to the east, the ad hoc hypothesis of 'a lost lathe boundary destroyed by the creation of the Croydon estate' has to be mooted. The common grave goods of these sites and their probably narrow date range hardly lend themselves to a hypothetical sequence of development of this kind. Meanwhile the Croydon and Mitcham cemeteries lie within a single unit, not, complementarily, one in each, and, contrary to what Blair tentatively suggests, there is little evidence overall in the form of later parochial land interests to suggest early formal territorial links between the clayey, low-lying plain of the Eocene Basin where Mitcham is situated on the river Wandle and the Downs themselves and the Weald – none at all in the specific case of Mitcham. Finally, the great square-headed brooch evidence points to a concrete association between Dartford and Mitcham, in the early 6th century, reminding us of the vital importance of looking beyond the historical county in seeking to form an image of this early phase.

As yet we cannot identify the individuals in the richest barrow and weapon graves of 7th century Surrey, nor properly explain the motivations for making these burials. We do not know whether those buried there were genuinely local men and women, from families seeking to assert their superiority over lower ranks in the area, or seeking to put on a show of strength against their neighbours, or even to defy the expansive forces of the Kentish, West Saxon or Mercian kings. These might be the burials of the henchmen of those kings, either outsiders or still from local stock. In the period of considerable historical change we know of, it is unlikely that we shall ever be able to date these burials quite precisely enough to be confident of the exact circumstances of their formation, while the symbolism of their contents gives us insufficient clues in this respect. What we may, however, confidently assert is that the archaeological background out of which they emerge is at least as useful in enabling us to talk about what they represent as the still highly fragmentary historical framework into which they may eventually be fitted.

Archaeology has its own innate tendencies, of course. By looking at sites collectively, and comparing their material features, it is predisposed to focus upon relationships between them – although these may as well be contrastive as matters of similarity: usually, indeed, we can expect a combination of the two. By comparing across time the archaeology of the 5th and 6th centuries in Surrey and its neighbouring areas with that of the 7th century, we can nonetheless be particularly confident that we can observe significantly changing patterns of relationship. In the earlier phase, the pattern is wide-reaching and expansive: not just because the sites are few and far between, and we have to look over considerable distances to reach their nearest comparable neighbours, but also as positively expressed by the artefactual evidence of the quoit-brooch style and the Group I great square-headed brooches. The increase in the number and density of burial sites in the 7th

century with what, it has been suggested here, is a strikingly differentiated local system, appears, by contrast, to throw much greater emphasis on local relationships, and on marking the central zones of the extended resource areas, or 'territories' as Blair suggests we may see them. Here there does indeed seem to be a shift to a system in which status and security are defined far more by one's local, land-based, social position, rather than by an extensive network of social connections. It is suggested here that to try to interpret specific archaeological sites in terms of the precisely conceptualized social and economic systems postulated by historians, such as the multiple estate, is to ask too much of that evidence. That there is a general agreement between the trends separately indicated by the two disciplinary perspectives seems undeniable, however, and to be a positive observation that should be welcomed.

A study of the very origins of Surrey at the beginning of the Anglo-Saxon period can only ever be an attempt to read or reconstruct a story from an extremely fragmented script. It is proposed here that the archaeological and the historical evidence do harmonize, and, most encouragingly, do not have to be made to do so by forcibly reading one in the light of the other. By allowing the early archaeological finds their full autonomous value, we can postulate a transitional period from Roman Britain to Anglo-Saxon England in which the earliest 'men of the southern district' occupied a distinctly secure and influential position. It is conceivable that their exceptionally early establishment here subsequently served to lock them into a way of life that did not develop dynamically as Anglo-Saxon society and culture did elsewhere in England, and so led to the gradual diminution in significance of this area, and eventually its political subordination. There is a great deal in this picture that can only be tentatively suggested; much that is far from certain. Yet these very uncertainties show how vital it is for the archaeology of this period to be valued and cared for, so that the clumsy neglect so many of Surrey's early Anglo-Saxon burial sites have suffered – even a recently discovered site such as Headley Drive – will itself become a thing of the past.

BIBLIOGRAPHY

Ager, B, 2001   Review of Suzuki 2000 (qv), *Medieval Archaeol*, **45**, 387–9
Andrews, P, & Crockett, A, 1996   *Three excavations along the Thames and its tributaries, 1994*, Wessex Archaeol Rep, **10**
Bailey, K, 1989   The Middle Saxons, in Bassett (ed) 1989, 108–22
Barfoot, J F, & Price Williams, D, 1976   The Saxon barrow at Gally Hills, Banstead Down, Surrey, SyAS Res Vol, **3**, 59–76

Bassett, S, 1989   In search of the origins of Anglo-Saxon kingdoms, in Bassett (ed) 1989, 3–27
—— (ed), 1989   *The origins of Anglo-Saxon kingdoms*
Batchelor, D, 1990   Darenth Park Anglo-Saxon cemetery, Dartford, *Archaeol Cantiana*, **108**, 35–72
Bede, *Historia ecclesiastica gentis Anglorum* (eds B Colgrave & R A B Mynors), Oxford, 1969
Bidder, H F, & Morris, J, 1959   The Anglo-Saxon cemetery at Mitcham, *SyAC*, **59**, 51–131

Birch, W de G, 1885   *Cartularium Saxonicum: a collection of charters relating to Anglo-Saxon history. Vol I: AD 430–839*

Bird, D G, 1987   The Romano-British period in Surrey, in Bird & Bird 1987, 165–96

Bird, D G, Crocker, A G, Douglas, R I, Haber, L F, Sturley D M, & Sykens, R, 1975   The archaeology and history of Surrey, in *The Surrey countryside: the interplay of land and people* (ed J E Salmon), 133–76

Bird, J, & Bird, D G (eds), 1987   *The archaeology of Surrey to 1540*, SyAS

Blair, J, 1989   Frithuwold's kingdom and the origins of Surrey, in Bassett (ed) 1989, 97–107

——, 1991   *Early medieval Surrey: landholding, church and settlement before 1300*

Boddington, A, 1990   Models of burial, settlement and worship: the final phase reviewed, in *Anglo-Saxon cemeteries: a reappraisal* (ed E Southworth), 177–99

Brooks, N, 1989   The creation and early structure of the kingdom of Kent, in Bassett (ed) 1989, 55–74

Brooks, N, & Graham-Campbell, J, 1986   Reflections on the Viking-age silver hoard from Croydon, Surrey, in *Anglo-Saxon monetary history: essays in memory of Michael Dolley* (ed M Blackburn), 91–110

Cameron, K, 1961   *English place-names*

Canham, R, 1979   Excavations at Shepperton Green 1967 and 1973, *Trans London Middlesex Archaeol Soc*, **30**, 97–124

Coates, R, 1980   Methodological reflexions on Leatherhead, *J English Place-Name Soc*, **12**, 70–4

Cotton, J R, 1933   Saxon discoveries at Fetcham, *Antiq J*, **13**, 48–51

Cowie, R, 2000   Saxon settlement and economy from the Dark Ages to Doomsday, in MoLAS 2000, 171–206

Cumberland, A, 1938   Saxon cemetery, 'Riseley', Horton Kirby: excavated 1937–1938, *Trans Dartford District Antiq Soc*, **8**, 14–30

Dark, K R, 1994   *From civitas to kingdom: British political continuity 300–800*

Dickinson, T M, 1979   On the origin and chronology of the Anglo-Saxon disc brooch, *Anglo-Saxon Stud Archaeol Hist*, **1**, 39–80

Dickinson, T M, & Härke, H, 1991   Early Anglo-Saxon shields, *Archaeologia*, **110**, 21–3

Dumville, D N, 1989   Essex, Middle Anglia and the expansion of Mercia in the south-east Midlands, in Bassett (ed) 1989, 123–40

Esmonde Cleary, S, 1989   *The ending of Roman Britain*

Evison, V I, 1957   An Anglo-Saxon cemetery at Holborough, Kent, *Archaeol Cantiana*, **70**, 84–141

——, 1963   Sugar-loaf shield bosses, *Antiq J*, **43**, 38–96

——, 1968   Quoit brooch style buckles, *Antiq J*, **48**, 231–46

Flower, J W, 1874   Notices of an Anglo-Saxon cemetery at Farthing Down, Coulsdon, Surrey, *SyAC*, **6**, 109–17

Geake, H, 1997   *The use of grave-goods in conversion-period England*, BAR Brit Ser, **261**

Gelling, M, 1978   *Signposts to the past*

Gover, J E B, Mawer, A, & Stenton, F M, 1931   *The place-names of Surrey*, English Place-Name Soc, **11**

Griffith, F L, 1897   On some Roman and Saxon remains found at Croydon in 1893–94, *SyAC*, **13**, 18–25

Härke, H, 1992   *Angelsächsische Waffengräber*, Köln

Harp, P & Hines, J, 2003   An Anglo-Saxon cemetery at Headley Drive, Banstead, *SyAC*, **90**, 117–45

Hawkes, S C, 1982   Anglo-Saxon Kent c 425–725, in *Archaeology in Kent to AD 1500* (ed P E Leach), CBA Res Rep, **48**, 64–78

Hines, J, 1990   Philology, archaeology and the *adventus Saxonum vel Anglorum*, in *Britain 400–600: language and history* (eds A Bammesberger & A Wollmann), 17–36

——, 1997   *A new corpus of Anglo-Saxon great square-headed brooches*

——, 1999a   The Anglo-Saxon archaeology of the Cambridge region and the Middle Anglian kingdom, in *The making of kingdoms* (eds D Griffith & T M Dickinson), Anglo-Saxon Stud Archaeol Hist, **10**, 135–49

——, 1999b   Angelsächsische Chronologie: Probleme und Aussichten, in *Völker an Nord- und Ostsee und die Franken* (eds U von Freeden, U Koch, & A Wieczorek), 19–31

Hogg, R M, 1992   *A grammar of Old English. Vol 1: Phonology*

Hope-Taylor, B, 1950   Excavation on Farthing Down, Coulsdon, Surrey, *Archaeol News Letter*, **2.10**, 170

Hyslop, M, 1963   Two Anglo-Saxon cemeteries at Chamberlain's Barn, Leighton Buzzard, Bedfordshire, *Archaeol J*, **120**, 161–200

Inker, P, 2000   Technology as active material culture: the quoit-brooch style, *Medieval Archaeol*, **44**, 25–52

John, E, 1960   *Land tenure in early England: a discussion of some problems*

——, 1966   Folkland reconsidered, in *Orbis Britanniae and other studies* (ed E John), 64–127

Kelly, D B, 1989   Archaeological notes from Maidstone Museum, 297–320 in Researches and discoveries in Kent, *Archaeol Cantiana*, **105**, 287–320

Kennett, D H, 1972   Seventh century finds from Astwick, *Bedfordshire Archaeol J*, **7**, 45–51

——, 1973   Seventh century cemeteries in the Ouse valley, *Bedfordshire Archaeol J*, **8**, 99–108

Leeds, E T, 1936   *Early Anglo-Saxon art and archaeology*

Lowther, A W G, 1931   The Saxon cemetery at Guildown, Guildford, Surrey, *SyAC*, **39**, 1–50

——, 1935   Excavations at Ewell in 1934: the Saxon cemetery and Stane Street, *SyAC*, **43**, 16–35

McKinley, J I, 2003   The early Saxon cemetery at Park Lane, Croydon, *SyAC*, **90**, 1–116

Meaney, A L S, 1964   *A gazetteer of early Anglo-Saxon burial sites*

Morris, J, 1959   Anglo-Saxon Surrey, *SyAC*, **56**, 132–58

——, 1973   *The age of Arthur*

MoLAS, 2000   *The archaeology of Greater London*

Nieveler, E, & Siegmund, F, 1999   The Merovingian chronology of the lower Rhine area: results and problems, in *The pace of change: studies in early-medieval chronology* (eds J Hines, K Høilund Nielsen & F Siegmund), 3–22

Ozanne, A 1963   The Peak dwellers, *Medieval Archaeol*, **6–7**, 15–52

Perring, D, 2000   Londinium and its hinterland: the Roman period, in MoLAS 2000, 119–70

Philp, B, 1973   *Excavations in west Kent 1960–1970*

Philp, B, & Keller, P, 1995   *The Roman site at Fordcroft, Orpington*, Kent Special Subject Ser, **8**

Poulton, R, 1987   Saxon Surrey, in Bird & Bird 1987, 197–222

——, 1989   Rescue excavations on an early Saxon cemetery site and a later (probably late Saxon) execution site at the former Goblin Works, Ashtead, near Leatherhead, *SyAC*, **79**, 67–97 and microfiche

Rahtz, P, Hurst, S, & Wright, S M, 2000   *Cannington cemetery*

Reece, R, 1980   Town and country: the end of Roman Britain, *World Archaeol*, **12**, 77–92

Rigold, S E, 1975   The Sutton Hoo coins in the light of the contemporary background of coinage in England, in R L S Bruce-Mitford, *The Sutton Hoo ship-burial. Volume I: Excavations, background, the ship, dating and inventory*, 653–77

Saunders, P R, 1980   Saxon barrows excavated by General Pitt-Rivers on Merrow Downs, Guildford, *SyAC*, **72**, 69–75

Sawyer, P H, 1968   *Anglo-Saxon charters: an annotated list and bibliography*, Roy Hist Soc Guides Handbooks, **8**

Scull, C, 1993   Archaeology, early Anglo-Saxon society and the origins of Anglo-Saxon kingdoms, *Anglo-Saxon Stud Archaeol Hist*, **6**, 65–82

Shaw, M E, 1970   A re-assessment of the material from the pagan-Saxon cemeteries in Croydon, *Proc Croydon Natur Hist Sci Soc*, **14**, 95–113

Siegmund, F, 1998   *Merowingerzeit am Niederrhein*

Smith, R A, 1907   Recent and former discoveries at Hawks-hill, *SyAC*, **20**, 119–28

Struth, P, & Eagles, B, 1999   An Anglo-Saxon barrow cemetery in Greenwich Park, in *Patterns of the past: essays in landscape archaeology for Christopher Taylor* (eds P Pattison, D Field & S Ainsworth), 37–52

Sutherland, C H V, 1948   *Anglo-Saxon gold coinage in light of the Crondall hoard*

Suzuki, S, 2000   *The quoit brooch style and Anglo-Saxon settlement*

Swanton, M, 1974   *A corpus of pagan Anglo-Saxon spear types*, BAR Brit Ser, **7**

Tester, P J, 1968   An Anglo-Saxon cemetery at Orpington: first interim report, *Archaeol Cantiana*, **83,** 125–50

——, 1969   Excavations at Fordcroft, Orpington: concluding report, *Archaeol Cantiana*, **84,** 39–79

Tyler, S 1992   Anglo-Saxon settlement in the Darent valley and environs, *Archaeol Cantiana*, **110,** 71–81

Walsh, R, 1981   Recent investigations at the Anglo-Saxon cemetery, Darenth Park Hospital, Dartford, *Archaeol Cantiana*, **96,** 305–20

Welch, M G, 1971   Late Romans and Saxons in Sussex, *Britannia*, **2,** 232–7

——, 1975   Mitcham grave 205 and the chronology of applied brooches with floriate cross decoration, *Antiq J*, **55,** 86–95

——, 1992   *Anglo-Saxon England*

——, 1996   Early Saxon, 169–70 in D Williams, Some recent finds from East Surrey, *SyAC*, **86,** 165–86

Wilson, D M, 1957   An Anglo-Saxon grave near Dartford, Kent, *Archaeol Cantiana*, **70,** 187–91

Yorke, B, 1989   The Jutes of Hampshire and Wight and the origins of Wessex, in Bassett (ed) 1989, 84–96

John Hines, School of History and Archaeology, Cardiff University CF10 3XU

8

Medieval settlement in the Blackheath Hundred

JUDIE ENGLISH and DENNIS TURNER

The Blackheath Hundred stretches from the North Downs into the Weald, encompassing a range of soil types and, therefore, natural resources. Development of the late Anglo-Saxon and medieval settlement pattern is largely governed by this factor and clear variations between the different parts of the Hundred can be seen in the distribution of selected place-name elements and in the ecclesiastical and tenurial divisions.

'Another desire is for far more detailed regional studies. Although it has always been axiomatic that landscape history is based on the results of such studies, the inevitable drive for generalization and synthesis has meant that local and regional differences have often been smoothed over or ignored. Yet, no matter how awkward the results of such studies may be to the theories of the generalists, they remain fundamental to landscape history.' (Taylor 2000, 161)

Introduction

This paper is intended to respond to Chris Taylor's plea and to argue that the chronology and economic basis of late Saxon and medieval settlement varied on a very local scale within a single territorial unit, the Blackheath Hundred (fig 8.1).

The economy of rural Anglo-Saxon England was agricultural. The basic unit of land, the hide, was a unit of assessment and not a fixed area, but the manner in which hides were grouped together to form estates has exercised many minds. Attempts to see regularity have often revolved around an 80-hide round number assessment for units such as hundreds (for groupings of 160 or 80 *sulungs* in Kent, see Jolliffe 1933, 44–8 etc), or multiples of 5 hides for estates (eg Round 1908, 276). Although such work has tended to result in circular arguments, the Surrey Domesday does hint at an early and stable basic unit of 20 hides and a number of territorial units consist of divisions or multiples of this unit. The Blackheath Hundred, coincidentally or not, is an 80-hide unit that appears to have been divided at an unknown, but pre-Conquest, date into two portions, each of 40 hides. These may be named for convenience the Bramley (or western) and Gomshall (or eastern) half. The western half comprised the multiple estate (Blair 1991, 25–6) of Bramley and at Domesday supported double the population of the Gomshall half, despite the similarity in both area and geldable assessment.

The grouping of pre-existing small units into large estates may have been taking place from the 7th century and the concept of the multiple or multi-*vill* estate has many adherents. The model originates in Welsh law books from the medieval period thought to

be based on older texts (Vinogradoff & Morgan 1914, v) and the concept was later specifically related to the lathes of Kent and the rapes of Sussex (Jolliffe 1933, *passim*). Part of Jolliffe's view was that the multi-*vill* estate reflected the situation in some past golden age when the Jutes imported into south-east England a life which could be 'lived without servitude, without debasing inequality, and yet preserve a fabric of order, adequately protected justice, and continuity' (Jolliffe 1933, 119). More recently the view has been taken that rather than being Jutish imports, multi-*vill* estates represent a survival of an earlier 'Celtic' tradition and its adoption by the incoming Germanic peoples (eg Jones 1976). An alternative view relates

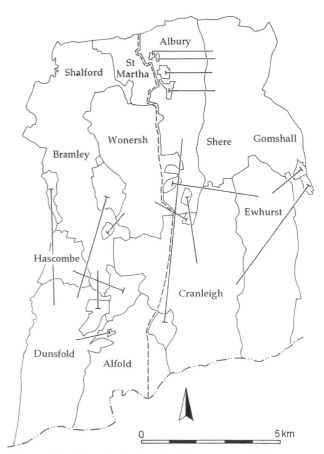

Fig 8.1 The Blackheath Hundred showing late 19th century parochial boundaries and the eastern boundary of the putative Bramley estate. Dashed line represents approximate position of boundary between Bramley and Gomshall halves.

territorial development to changes within society and sees multiple estates as a response to the need for large production units to support royal *vills* with, perhaps, an associated minster (Gelling 1976, 829–33; Hooke 1998, 52). Whatever their origins, the individual units within these estates are considered to have taken on specialized functions and to have been answerable to an administrative centre. Certainly place-names and

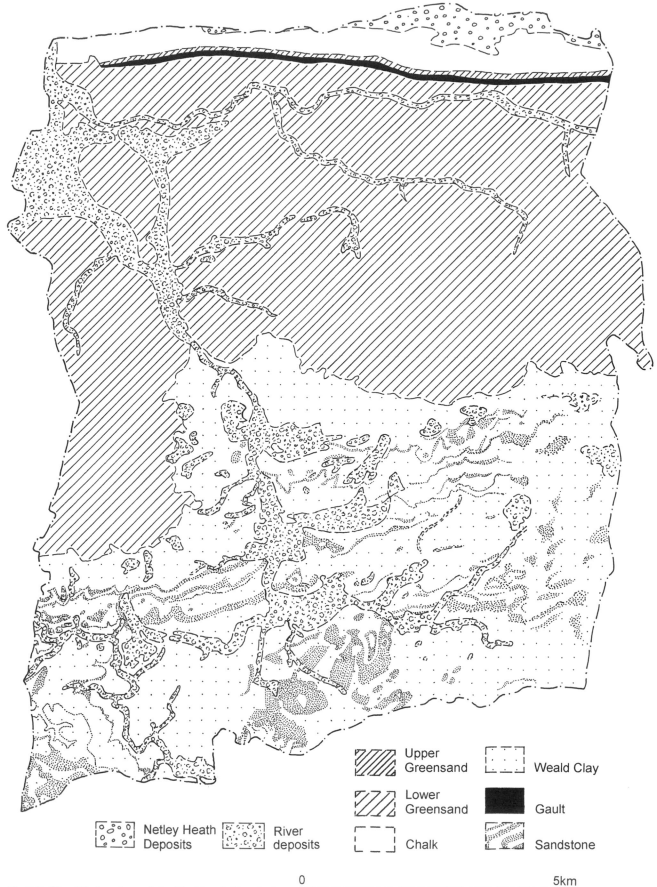

Upper Greensand

Weald Clay

Lower Greensand

Gault

Netley Heath Deposits

River deposits

Chalk

Sandstone

0   5km

Fig 8.2 Simplified geology of the Blackheath Hundred

other evidence can be used to define holdings which appear to have a particular place within a mixed farming economy. In many cases it is difficult to know whether this situation derives from the organized specialization implied by the multiple estate model or from more independent selection of areas best suited to a particular type of resource utilization. However, the ecclesiastical and tenurial relationships within the western half of the Blackheath Hundred encourage the belief that the Bramley of 1086 represented a phase in a fast fragmenting multiple estate.

The Domesday entry for Bramley in Surrey describes a holding of 40 hides with a population of 147 heads of household, including *servii* as head of household, and three churches, placing it as the third most populous estate in the county after Guildford and Kingston. Bramley is now a village which did not become a parish until 1844 – clearly the Domesday assessors recorded a large estate which stretched into the Weald probably encompassing the settlement areas of Bramley, Wonersh, Hascombe, Dunsfold, Alfold and parts of Cranleigh and Shalford (fig 8.1). The three churches assessed under Bramley in 1086 have been identified as Shalford, the mother church of the estate, Wonersh, and the Wealden church at Hascombe (Blair 1991, 119).

The two halves of the Blackheath Hundred present contrasting geology and topography and also different ownership in the 11th century – Bramley passed from secular to ecclesiastical control while Gomshall was primarily under royal control. In 1086, the Bramley half supported double the population of the Gomshall half and it has been suggested (Blair 1991, 53) that the earlier development of Bramley resulted from entrepreneurial ownership. However, it is the contention of the authors that the wider range of available resources, easier communications and the presence of the late Saxon *burh* of Guildford (Hill 2000, 177–8) may have been the cause of the preferential exploitation of this area of the Weald.

Geology and topography

The geology and topography of the Blackheath Hundred and its immediate surroundings are shown in simplified form in figures 8.2 and 8.3. The western half of the Hundred is dominated by the Bramley Wey (also known as Cranleigh Waters) and its alluvia, gravel terraces and head deposits which lie between the greensand (Hythe Beds) ridge which bears Hascombe hillfort at its southernmost point and the dry, infertile plateau of Farley Heath and Blackheath. There are areas of head and gravel to both east and west of the river, some are associated with present day tributaries and some with streams diverted when the Dunsfold Arun captured the headwaters of the Bramley Wey (Gallois 1965, 77). The northern end of the valley contained the Peasmarsh, an extensive area

of wet land enclosed and drained during the early 19th century in response to the raised food prices occasioned by the Napoleonic Wars (Gorton 1996). South of the line of the Lower Greensand escarpment these outcrops and deposits of sandstone, limestone, head and gravel account for some 30% of the land. In modern agricultural terms only 3.1% of the present administrative county comprises grades 1 or 2 land but several patches of grade 2 exist in this valley, the southern end of which is marked by the sandstone and limestone ridge forming the watershed between the rivers Wey and Arun (and the county boundary between Surrey and Sussex). The eastern half of the Hundred forms a more typical section through Wealden geology with, from north to south, the chalk of the North Downs, the Gault clay and Lower Greensand of the Tillingbourne valley and the arid, acid sands of the Lower Greensand ridge with its steep scarp overlooking the Weald Clay. This simple pattern is, however, complicated in the south of the Hundred by the faults and folding of the Walliswood anticline, the Oakwood Hill syncline, the Alfold anticline and the Plaistow syncline, allowing exposure of sandstone and limestone strata contained within the clay (Gallois 1965, 54).

Communications

Communications within the eastern half of the Blackheath Hundred are dominated by a series of north–south tracks running from the Tillingbourne

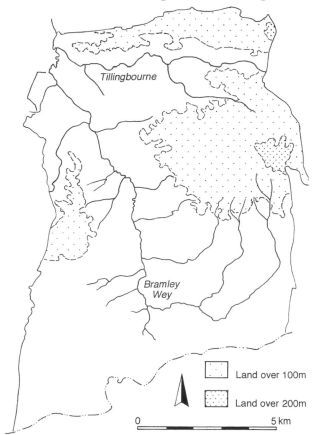

Fig 8.3 Simplified topography of the Blackheath Hundred. (© Crown Copyright NC/04/25242)

valley which have cut deep holloways over the green-sand ridge and stretch into the Weald, in some cases as far south as the Surrey/Sussex boundary. Such tracks, common in all counties bounding the Weald, originated as drove-ways linking parent holdings with their Wealden outliers and form the basis of the present road system. Other tracks lead north from the villages in the Tillingbourne valley to provide access to grazing on the North Downs and the villages themselves are linked by a route along the valley. Some short-distance east–west links of uncertain antiquity take advantage of the higher ground south of the valley while the medieval and later drove-way from Guildford to Dorking is still a prominent feature along the crest of the Downs. There is no evidence that this was ever part of a long-distance route (Turner 1980).

The northern end of the Bramley half of Black-heath Hundred, arguably the first to come under Anglo-Saxon influence with its proximity to the 5th/6th century cemetery at Guildown, (Lowther 1931), is dominated by the junctions of the Wey with its tributaries the Bramley Wey and the Tilling-bourne. The resultant wet area of the Peasmarsh must have impeded traffic between the Bramley estate and Guildford, its closest market at least from the early 10th century. The modern road crosses the Tillingbourne near the mother church of the estate at a point where the original crossing gave its name to the village of Shalford. After crossing the Tilling-bourne, the early road passed to the east of the Peasmarsh, keeping to the better-drained sandy soils of the present Shalford Common until it reached Wonersh. One branch then continued south to Cran-leigh, Ewhurst and Alfold while the other turned west to cross the Bramley Wey and pass through the settle-ment of Bramley before climbing the greensand ridge which bounds the west of the valley to reach Hascombe and Dunsfold.

While routes in use during the medieval period and probably earlier can be located, communication was difficult and resulted in delayed and inhibited devel-opment. Some produce, in the form of stock, could be walked to market but heavy goods – grain, timber, iron or brick and tile for example – could not be reli-ably and cheaply transported to non-local end-users for considerable periods of the year.

The evidence of place-names (fig 8.4)

Place-name derivations used in this section are taken from Gover *et al* (1934).

ERSC – STUBBLE OR PLOUGHED LAND

Of nineteen examples of the place-name element -*ersc* occurring in Surrey before 1450, fifteen are in the Blackheath Hundred and of these twelve are found in the valley of the Bramley Wey. *Ersc* is considered to indicate areas particularly suitable for arable farming

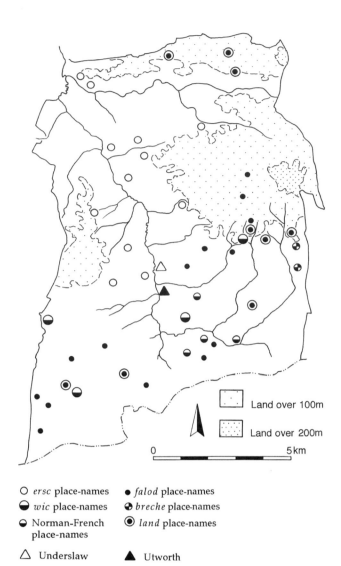

○ *ersc* place-names   ● *falod* place-names

◑ *wic* place-names   ◕ *breche* place-names

◒ Norman-French place-names   ◉ *land* place-names

△ Underslaw   ▲ Utworth

Fig 8.4 Location of place-names in Old English, Norman French and Middle English indicative of land use. (© Crown Copyright NC/04/25242)

and Brandon (1978, 148) suggested that use of this element may have denoted an early phase of shifting agriculture. More recently this and other clusters of this element have been identified, all in areas not totally suited to arable farming, and a meaning has been suggested of 'occasional ploughland amid woodland, pasture, marsh or moorland and repre-senting early attempts to cultivate later-settled areas of England' (Gelling & Cole 2000, 268). Use of this place-name element to indicate early land use in Surrey is problematic since the term survived in local dialect as *errish*, *arish*, *ersh* or *arsh* until recently. Indeed, one of the present authors (JE) met an elderly farmer in Ewhurst in the 1980s who could define an *arish* as a field, or often only part of a field, where it was possible to grow oats or rye instead of the all-perva-sive wheat. Late usage accounts for the many fields called Ryarsh or Oatersh and this discussion is limited to those names which occurred before 1450 and became attached to a habitation site.

Arguably the word relates to relatively light soils, usually in clay areas. Within Blackheath Hundred (fig 8.4) seven *ersc* names are situated on Hythe Beds bounding the northern and western sides of the Bramley Wey valley, three are on gravel terraces overlying Weald Clay, two are on Atherfield Clay and two are on small sandstone outcrops surrounded by Weald Clay. The exact site of one is lost. The four other Surrey locations are all on small areas of gravel surrounded by Weald Clay. While this concentration within the western half of the Blackheath Hundred emphasizes its relative suitability for arable farming when compared with the remainder of the Weald, it is the exceptional nature of small areas of lighter soils that appears to be indicated – the word does not occur on the large areas of light soil provided by either chalk Downs or the greensand.

North of the North Downs the estates of settlements on the spring line are spaced at narrow intervals, as are those in the Tillingbourne valley. Both held land from the crest of the Downs, those to the north out on to London Clay and those in the Tillingbourne valley on to Weald Clay. These settlements had ample arable land on the gentle dip slope of the Downs and the lack of any need to utilize small areas of suitable land set within the London Clay probably accounts for the lack of place-names containing the element *ersc* in this area.

The prefixes of the *-ersc* place-names do not conform to any pattern: six examples are duplexed with personal names, four describe the location as close to a stream (Rydinghurst), a meadow (Medersh), or a particular species of tree (Mapledrakes and Purnish (pear)). Two define crops grown as flax and rye, plants requiring relatively well-drained soil, and others describe the fields as, for example, 'spotted' or 'crooked'. The change in place-name element from *-ersc* to *-hurst* in Rydinghurst indicates the possible loss of further examples of the use of this element.

LAND AND *BRAEC* – OTHER ELEMENTS DENOTING ARABLE LAND

The word *land* as part of the name of a habitation site occurs nine times in the Blackheath Hundred and in no case is the settlement located in an area well suited to arable cultivation. In three cases the name is attached to an isolated farm situated high on the scarp slope of the North Downs. One became the name of a hamlet, Pitland, which developed in a steep-sided, east-facing valley in an elevated position on the Hythe Beds of the Lower Greensand where the soil is an acid, infertile sand. The remaining five examples are all found on Weald Clay in areas particularly distant from recognized foci of medieval settlement.

Only two examples of the word *braec* – meaning newly broken land – have been found and both appear to be in the ME form of *breche*. They are located in Ewhurst parish, an area generally thought to be of late settlement (Balchin *et al*, forthcoming).

FALOD – AN ENCLOSURE FOR ANIMALS

This place-name element clusters within a limited area of south-west Surrey and north-west Sussex and the Blackheath Hundred is within the former concentration. No names containing *falod* occur in the Bramley Wey valley; they are found predominantly in the Weald Clay area in the southern part of the Hundred (thirteen out of fifteen). Even so, some effort was made to avoid the worst of the clay and eleven out of the thirteen are situated on small outcrops of better-drained land, on sandstone, limestone, head, gravel or alluvium. This careful selection of sites is typical of Wealden settlement and has long been recognized (Marshall 1817, 367). Of the two found on Hythe Beds one, Winterfold, was relatively close to its parent settlement, Shere, and unusually appears to have been in a place used for winter grazing (fig 8.4).

WIC – A SPECIALIZED SETTLEMENT

The place-name element *-wic* is unusual in that it appears to have more than one meaning. When used as a suffix, it may have implied specialized settlement, the full meaning depending on the context. In the context of rural settlement, it appears to denote some kind of special farm.

Of the 26 names found in Surrey, sixteen are situated in the Weald and of these four are in the Blackheath Hundred (fig 8.4). None are found in the valley of the Bramley Wey but with the exception of Howicks in Dunsfold none are on the heaviest of the Weald Clay. Markwick (Merkewyke in 1282) is on well-drained land on the greensand ridge bounding the west side of the Bramley Wey valley and may have been thought special from its position on a boundary: that between Hascombe and Dunsfold. Wickhurst is also situated on the scarp slope of the Lower Greensand and Rutwick (now lost) was on an outcrop of sandstone.

ELEMENTS DESCRIBING USE OF WOODLAND RESOURCES

Like most areas of the Weald the Blackheath Hundred abounds in place-names denoting either the presence or clearance of woodland. Some, for example OE *graf* meaning a coppice (as in Grafham) and *holt* (a single-species wood), indicate managed woodland, although it is unlikely that much if any woodland remained unmanaged by the medieval period. A few specific examples of use of timber resources survive in place-names. Ridgebridge in Wonersh is first mentioned as *la Risbrigge*, the first element of which derives from OE *hris* meaning 'brushwood'. The area is one of wet land on either side of the Bramley Wey and the name indicates that the road crossing this marsh was carried on a causeway of brushwood. Emply Barn has the early form *Ymphagh* and denotes an enclosure made of *imps* or young saplings, presumably a hedged enclosure and, from its position on the greensand ridge to the west of the Bramley Wey, one made either to hold stock or possibly to enclose land held in severalty in an area of common grazing. Plonks Farm may have been built entirely of planks, instead of the more common timbered framework, or may possibly have been a supplier of prepared timber planks (A Reynolds, pers comm).

PLACE-NAMES OF NORMAN-FRENCH DERIVATION

Three place-names in the Blackheath Hundred are derived from Norman-French and all relate to cattle raising. The capital messuage for the manor of Shere Vachery (post-1309), *la Vacherie* (first recorded in 1245) is situated adjoining the Surrey/Sussex border and denotes a dairy farm. The other two, Butcherhouse and Boverishe (now called Wyphurst, SHC: RB591) indicate butchery and are located in the south of the Hundred on Weald Clay.

PLACE-NAMES CONTAINING OTHER SIGNIFICANT ELEMENTS

Underslaw – Thondurslaghus

The present Underslaw Farm is situated close to the southern end of the Bramley estate. The late first mention of this name, in 1419 (Penshurst 1925 (derived Gover *et al* 1934)), precludes any real discussion of its origins but the possibility exists that it derives from the element *hlaw* and the name of the god Thor (English 1988).

Utworth

Place-names containing the element -*worth* are rare in the Weald of Surrey. It has been suggested (English 2002) that this element distinguished early enclosures held in severalty (ie by an individual tenant) from land otherwise held in common, and that these may have been for arable use within areas generally used for grazing stock. Edgeworth, in Horley, is close to Thunderfield Common, deep in the Weald Clay. This is usually thought to be the *thunres felda* where Alfred had a *ham*, and also the *thunresfelda* where the *witan* met in the 930s but there is no certainty in this identification (Turner 1997): the name suggests an area of early religious significance. The position of Utworth, also on Weald Clay but at the southern end of the Bramley estate, may add weight to the designation of this latter area as one of early Wealden settlement.

Identification of early grazing areas and permanent settlements

Use of Wealden woodland for transhumance grazing has been extensively discussed (eg Witney 1976). However, in the absence of surviving documentary evidence contemporary with the use of the Wealden area of the Blackheath Hundred for transhumance, any identification of early grazing areas must rely either on the use of later documents or on evidence in the field. The former approach has recently been used by Ellaby (2000) to identify the precise location of the demesne lands of Reigate Priory in Horley parish, recognizing that, with their original ownership by manors north of the Weald, they provide an insight into a local complex of pre-Conquest distant pastures. While these are commonly described as swine pastures, the point has been made that, given the difficulty of driving pigs over long distances, these areas may originally have been used for summer pasturing of cattle (Turner 1997). The alternative technique of attempting to recognize the boundaries of early enclosures where they have survived into the modern landscape is described here using two examples within the Blackheath Hundred.

WILDWOOD, ALFOLD

La Wyldewode is first mentioned obliquely in an Alfold deed of 1294/5 transcribed by Giuseppi (1903, 222). In 1313 *le Wylwode* was held by John d'Abernon as a detached Wealden portion of Albury Manor and a survey of that manor in 1327 included 40 acres of oak wood not for pasture valued at 5 shillings and no more because of the shade of the trees (*XL acr boscis querci ni cujus pastura val p vs et non plus pro umbra arborum*), which probably refers to Wildwood (SHC: 1322/4/56). The contrast recognized here seems to be between wood pasture and woodland where only sparse grazing, or possibly pannage, was available. Buildings are first mentioned in 1391 when Elizabeth Grey, lady of Stoke d'Abernon, granted the soil and wood of Wildwood except for the moat, grange and manorial rights (Manning & Bray 1809, 71; Redstone 1911, 78).

The moated site in Wildwood Copse lay within a detached portion of Albury parish until rationalization of the boundaries in the late 19th century. The exact status of Wildwood in the medieval period is uncertain: between 1498 and 1558 several holdings in Alfold which later paid suit at Wildwood are mentioned in the court rolls of Albury Manor (SHC: 1322/1/1–25) suggesting that Wildwood was not then a separate manor despite the mention of manorial rights in 1391 (Redstone 1911, 78 n11). A court book for Wildwood Manor (known to be in private ownership *c*1995 but now said to be lost) intermittently details courts baron and views of frankpledge between 1632/3 and 1901. Most of the holdings paying suit to Wildwood Manor lay outside, and to the south of, the Albury parochial detachment and an attempt to reconstruct the outline of the 17th

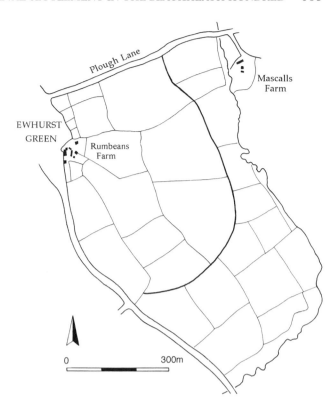

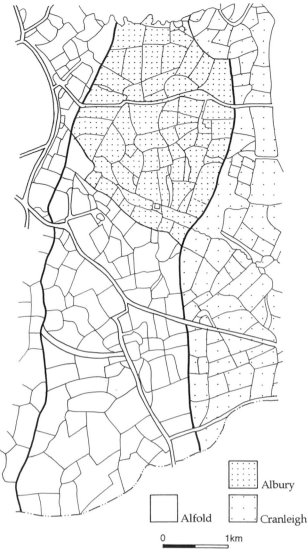

Fig 8.6 Arc-shaped boundary associated with Rumbeams Farm, reconstructed from the Ewhurst tithe map and award (after English, 1997).

Fig 8.5 Putative outline of an early grazing area associated with the extra-Wealden settlement of Albury, and later with the sub-infeudated manor of Wildwood, reconstructed from the relevant mid-19th century tithe maps and awards.

century manor from later sources is shown in figure 8.5. They can be seen to form a compact block of land stretching to the Surrey/Sussex boundary, the eastern and western boundaries of which are continuous with the respective boundaries of the detached portion of Albury parish. This may, in turn, have been the demesne of Wildwood Manor. It seems likely that these continuous boundaries, which enclose an area about 4.5 x 1.5km, represent the outline of the original grazing area.

RUMBEAMS, EWHURST

This example of a possible early Wealden holding has already been published (English 1997). In summary, a 60-acre holding adjacent to an area of common, Ewhurst Green, was until recently surrounded by an arc-shaped bank and ditch notably at odds with the usual pattern of polygonal shapes (fig 8.6). Field boundaries on either side of this arc abut and therefore post-date it. A holding of this form would seem either to have been imposed upon an existing land-

scape of fields or to have pre-dated the development of the surrounding field system. In the absence of any evidence for a park or similar feature the former explanation seems unlikely and, particularly since the area enclosed appears to be the size of a virgate locally, it is tempting to see Rumbeams as an area specifically allocated, and demarcated from otherwise unenclosed land. The inference from this is that the demarcated land was held in severalty.

The smoothly arcing hedge-line implies a much more organized approach to Wealden clearance than the generally accepted piecemeal assarting and presages a high degree of landscape clearance before the hedge was set out.

The administrative mechanisms underlying the granting of Wealden land may have been variable but in some cases at least hidated units were involved. One such may have been Yard Farm, situated 1km north-east of Rumbeams, which in 1314 was named *de Virga*, derived from the OE *gierd, gyrd* meaning a measure of land (Gover *et al* 1934, 241); others are suggested by the not uncommon Hyde Farm. While land clearance may have proceeded gradually, delineation of the holding boundaries may have been a priority or even a requirement.

The outline of other similarly shaped holdings may well have survived to be recorded on early maps and, although an origin in parks and other enclosures needs to be eliminated and supporting evidence found in each case, this may represent one way of identifying early settlements in a particular area.

Ecclesiastical, administrative and tenurial history

The early ecclesiastical history of the Blackheath Hundred is relatively well understood and the outlines of its parochial structure are shown in figure 8.7.

Shalford, the mother church, is situated at the older-settled, northern end of the estate. Of the other two churches assessed with the Bramley estate in 1086, Wonersh retains signs that it once contained late 11th century fabric (Johnston 1911, 125b) and an extant print of the church at Hascombe which was demolished in about 1860 shows what appears to have been a pre-Conquest architectural style (Blair 1991, 116, fig 29a). The present Bramley church dates from the 12th century and originated as a chapelry of Shalford (as did Wonersh) and a set of depositions dating to the late 16th century record the resentment of the people of Bramley at having to pay burial rites to Shalford, despite Bramley being the larger settlement (SHC: LM454). Bramley did not become an independent parish until 1844 (Redstone 1911, 80a, 86b) although Wonersh had done so by 1291. Some link between Shalford and Dunsfold may be suggested by the gift of the advowsons of both churches by Edward I to the hospital of St Mary at Spital without Bishopgate in 1304 (Redstone 1911, 111b, 96b). The church assessed under Shalford *vill* in 1086 appears to have been that at its Wealden outlier, Alfold: when first mentioned in the 13th century it was appurtenant to [East] Shalford Manor (Blair

1991, 122). The antiquity of the hill top site of St Martha's Chapel is uncertain. No church is recorded under Chilworth in 1086 but lack of a mention in Domesday cannot be taken as definitive. The present church fabric is essentially 19th century, replacing an early 12th century structure, but the discovery of a 6th century urn close to the church (Anon 1916), the prominence of the hilltop site and its unusual dedication have led to the suggestion that the location may have been of significance during the early Saxon period (Morris 1959). Churches at Albury and Shere are recorded in 1086 and the former retains a late Saxon building.

Cranleigh church, not mentioned in 1086, originated as a daughter church of Shere (Redstone 1911, 91–2). Although the earliest structural evidence is thought to date to about 1170, excavations on the island of the moat that was later to enclose the Rectory produced pre-moat pottery of the early 11th century (English 2001). The capital messuage of Vachery, the southern portion of Shere manor, is a moated site some 2km south-east of Cranleigh. The present settlement of Cranleigh may have originated as two separate hamlets of farms placed around areas of common, one in each half of the Blackheath Hundred. Cranleigh Common would have been within the Bramley estate while the church, sited on the northern edge of an area of common later called Luck's Green, and within the southern portion of Shere manor, seems to have been placed to serve the populations of both hamlets, as was common practice in the Weald. Cranleigh glebe abutted upon the eastern boundary of the Bramley estate, which was probably represented by the later manorial and property boundary, the Spital Ditch (SHC: G46/6/15–18; G96/4/1). Ownership of both Shere and Gomshall by members of the royal family before the Conquest may suggest that the division between them had only recently taken place. Unusually, for a royal manor, Gomshall was not provided with a church and that of Ewhurst, its southern, Wealden, portion, was another daughter church to Shere, albeit a most impressive one. Despite having a smaller population and value in 1086, Shere, owned by Queen Edith before the Conquest, appears to have been the senior holding and its church, provided with a large glebe, would have served the entire estate prior to its division into Shere and Gomshall and both holdings after that event.

Of the eleven medieval churches in the Blackheath Hundred, seven are in the Bramley half of the hundred and only four in the Gomshall half; of those mentioned in 1086 the figures are four and two respectively. However, this continuing imbalance is not reflected in the population trends between the 1086 Domesday survey and the 1332 lay subsidy returns (SRS 1932, 22–31). Neither of these sources

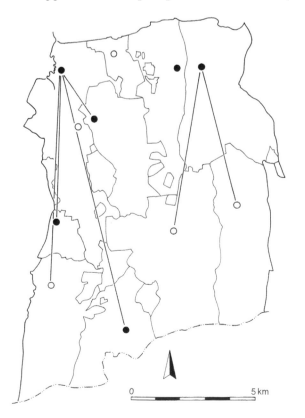

● Churches mentioned 1086   O Churches not mentioned in 1086

Fig 8.7 Ecclesiastical organization in the Blackheath Hundred.

can easily be used to give an absolute measure of the contemporary population or wealth, but comparative statistics between different areas can be gauged (Darby *et al* 1979; Williams 1982, *passim*). The figures resulting from such a comparison for the taxation areas of the Blackheath Hundred are shown in table 8.1.

The population figures in this table show a faster relative growth for the taxation areas of Albury, Shere and Gomshall, in the eastern portion of the Hundred, than for the western half. Although it is possible that the named settlements were expanding at different rates it is more likely that the portions of the Weald Clay which were to become the parishes of Cranleigh and Ewhurst were being extensively settled for the first time. The relative taxable value for Shere and Gomshall is only slightly higher than for the other *villata* despite the higher rate of population expansion, again emphasizing the low returns resulting from attempts to exploit the heavy clay. This suggestion of a number of poor farmers in the eastern half of the Hundred indicates a need to treat these figures with some circumspection. The 1332 population figures are counts of heads of household above a taxation threshold and a difference in the proportion between those above and below the threshold will thus distort the ratio. Tax avoidance also leads to unquantifiable errors.

By the 14th century, the present Wealden churches were all in existence and had been assessed individually in the taxation levied by Pope Nicholas in 1291, but the settlements to which they were attached to do not appear in the lay subsidy returns of 1332. Of those listed in the returns, about 25% have a given name attached by the preposition *de* or *atte* to their place of habitation. Where those place-names can be identified with modern names, the positions of the settlements have been mapped (fig 8.8). The relationship between the parent holdings and their Wealden subordinates in the eastern part of the Hundred is clear, as is the position of Cranleigh parish astride the boundary between the two halves. The inclusion within Bramley of holdings in Shalford, Wonersh, Dunsfold and Hascombe reflects the size of the Bramley estate. The Shalford holdings appear to have some similarity with the strip distribution that

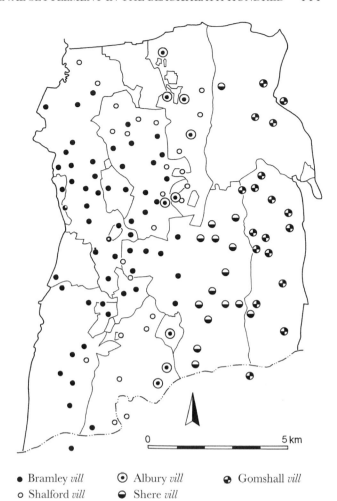

● Bramley *vill*   ⊙ Albury *vill*   ◑ Gomshall *vill*
○ Shalford *vill*   ◗ Shere *vill*

Fig 8.8 Relationship between place-names mentioned in the lay subsidy returns of 1332 and ecclesiastical parishes derived from relevant tithe maps.

was common further east and, since in 1086 and later Shalford was clearly part of the Bramley estate, it is possible that this distribution reflects an earlier arrangement that was overridden by an expansion of that estate. The number of holdings south of the southern boundary of the Hundred is an indication of the instability of the county boundary between Surrey and Sussex in this area.

Manors do not always respect hundredal boundaries. Most notable among these anomalies are those which affect the eastern boundary of the Hundred since this is postulated by Blair (1991, fig 4) as representing a primary boundary between the Godalming and Leatherhead territorial units. At least two tenurial links cross that boundary. First, the manor of

TABLE 8.1 Relative changes in population and value parameters for medieval taxation areas in the Blackheath Hundred.

Area	Population			Value		
	1086	1332	1332/1086	1086	1332	1332/1086
Bramley	155	282	1.82	£63.85	£18.83	0.29
Shalford	50	92	1.84	£20.00	£6.63	0.33
Albury	20	54	2.70	£9.00	£2.95	0.33
Shere	31	78	2.52	£15.00	£5.33	0.36
Gomshall	44	118	2.68	£20.00	£8.00	0.40

Sutton, now in Shere, was in Wotton Hundred in 1086 and was owned there by Bishop Odo of Bayeux, holder of the Bramley estate. During the medieval period, Sutton (in Shere and Abinger) was called Holdhurst at Downe and was associated with Hold-hurst, a Wealden holding in the western portion of Cranleigh parish and an outlying portion of the manor of Shere (Redstone 1911, 116a). Secondly, post-medieval court rolls (in private ownership and now apparently lost) for the manor of Wildwood, sub-infeudated by Albury and forming a detached portion of that parish in the Weald between Alfold and Cranleigh parishes (fig 8.1), owed suit of court to the Sheriff's 'toon' at Wotton (WM Court Book). Other holdings which fail to respect the hundredal boundary involve the northern part, where the Clere portion of the divided Bramley estate included the tithing of West Clandon, north of the North Downs in Woking Hundred, and the western part, where the Fay portion included the tithings of Puttenham and Catteshall in Godalming Hundred. This division into Fay and Clere, which will be further discussed later in this paper, took place in 1241. The instability of the southern boundary has already been noted. It is not certain that any of these breaches in the integrity of the hundredal boundary date from a sufficiently early period to challenge the division of Surrey into primary regions based on the hundredal structure as suggested by Blair (1991, 12–24). However, as the link between Holdhurst at Downe in Wotton Hundred and Holdhurst in Cranleigh in Blackheath pre-dates the Domesday survey, an automatic acceptance of the details of his boundaries is premature.

There are considerable differences in manorial arrangements between the two halves of the Black-heath Hundred. In the eastern half, the older manors were located in the Tillingbourne valley. If, as seems likely, this half was once a single holding, the division between Shere and Gomshall would have occurred before 1086. Both these manors originally stretched south towards the Surrey/Sussex boundary and both were later sub-divided, Shere as a split inheritance into Shere Eboracum and Shere Vachery and Gomshall by grants of Henry I into moieties that eventually became known as Gomshall Netley and Gomshall Towerhill (Redstone 1911, 115). With the

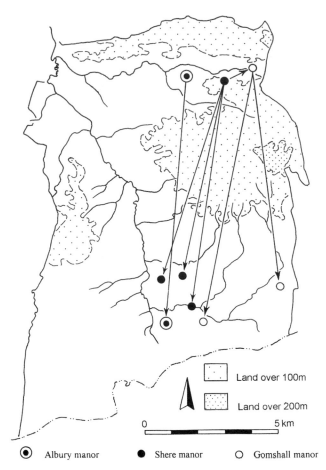

Fig 8.9 Manorial fragmentation in the eastern portion of Blackheath Hundred predating 1303. (© Crown Copyright NC/04/25242)

exception of Holdhurst, the southern, Wealden, members became detached, often as sub-infeudated manors at various times between the 12th and early 14th centuries; the information available from Manning & Bray (1804, 499, 501, 537; 1809, 71) is summarized in table 8.2 and figure 8.9. In the following two tables italic print indicates holdings situated primarily on Weald Clay.

All these manors and sub-manors and their holdings formed compact areas of land and no attempt appears to have been made to ensure that each contained a range of soil types and hence a varied resource base. The Wealden manors had little but cold, heavy Weald Clay to farm while the manors of the Tillingbourne valley lost their Wealden prod-ucts, a situation which led to the development of

TABLE 8.2 Manorial fragmentation in the eastern half of Blackheath Hundred pre-dating 1303. *Italic* indicates holdings situated primarily on Weald Clay.

Parent manor	Sub-division	Date
	Division into Shere & Gomshall	pre-1086
Shere	*Holdhurst* detached	pre-1086
Gomshall	Divided into Gomshall Netley, Gomshall Towerhill and *Somersbury*	c 1170
Gomshall	*Pollingfold* detached	c 1280
Albury	*Wildwood* detached (but see text)	1291
Shere	Divided into Shere Eboracum & Shere Vachery	1297
Shere	*Knowle/Knoll* detached	pre-1303

plantations on the North Downs in Albury by the late 15th century (SHC: 1322/1/2).

In contrast, the break-up of the western half of the Hundred resulted in such a complex jigsaw of inter-mixed manors that by the 17th century it had become impossible to decide to which of several manors many small areas of common land belonged (see for example SHC: G24/7/1). Such was the uncertainty that in 1847 the lords of the manors of East Bramley and Wintershall took the pragmatic decision to utilize the newly built turnpike road, which passed through a number of the disputed areas, as the boundary between their relative jurisdictions (SHC: 3243/12/13). The fragmentation of the manors of Shalford and Bramley is indicated in table 8.3 and figure 8.9.

Within Bramley manor further divisions into tithings are evidenced from the court records. The Fay portions comprised five tithings, of which one, Catteshall, lay to the west of the Wey (ie in Godalming Hundred). The Clere portion comprised nine tithings. In addition, Wintershall manor (alienated from Bramley by 1227) was itself divided into three tithings. The other manors detached before 1241 may also have comprised similar divisions (SHC: 892/5/2; SHC: 212/15/1; SHC: 892/5/1. However Blair (1991, 26, 184 n 92) counts only twelve tithings, ie those contained within the Fay and Clere portions.

The exact areas encompassed by these manors are difficult to define since the core Bramley manors were further divided in the post-medieval period and then recombined in 1809 and much of the medieval integrity (and supporting documentary evidence) has been lost. An attempt to reconstruct the medieval manors from the available court rolls and rentals is shown in figure 8.10. It is clear from this exercise that, unlike the eastern half of the Blackheath Hundred, the Bramley estate was not divided into compact manors but that each manor held land dispersed throughout the area. The most common manifestation of this is that all the manors held some land in the clay of the Weald, holdings which may have originated as grazing areas. However, several manors held detached areas in the Bramley Wey valley favourable for arable use and some also held detached areas of downland suitable for grazing sheep.

Only one document survives which gives complete details of the formation of a new manor through this fragmentation process and that is the grant dated to the early 13th century by which Brother Simon, prior of Bysshemead (possibly Bushmead, Bedfordshire) granted to William de Wintershall 29 men, their families and successors, and their lands and tenements, rights and services, to form the manor of Bramley Wintershall alias Selhurst (SHC: Zg36). The details of this land, mainly freehold and, as far as can be deduced, its location, are given in table 8.4 and figure 8.11. These identifications have been confirmed from later, more detailed, descriptions in the court rolls for Wintershall manor of 1319–95 (SHC: G47/1–6). These court rolls enable a further number of holdings of Wintershall to be identified which may have originated in sub-divisions of the original holdings. These are also shown in figure 8.11.

The capital messuage of Wintershall manor was set on a gentle south-east facing slope on the greensand above one of the small streams feeding into the Bramley Wey. The manor encompassed much of the ridge bounding the western side of the main valley. The soil is an acid sand that supports grass suitable for grazing sheep but, except in small areas in valleys, deteriorates rapidly if ploughed. A number of holdings – Slades, Thorncombe and Brookwell, for example – are situated in these valleys but others – viz Carringham, Cowgate and Jerseys – are on high

TABLE 8.3 Manorial fragmentation in the western half of Blackheath Hundred. *Italic* indicates holdings situated primarily on Weald Clay.

Parent manor	Subdivision	Date
Shalford [East]	*Markwick* detached	*c* 1200
Shalford [East]	*Monktonhook* detached	*c* 1200
Shalford [East]	Divided into Shalford Bradeston and Shalford Clifford	1297
Shalford Bradeston	*Rickhurst* detached	1413
Shalford Bradeston	Losterford detached	pre-1547
Bramley	Chilworth detached	pre-1086
Bramley	*Thorncombe* detached	pre-1205
Bramley	*Wintershall* detached	pre-1227
Bramley	*Burningfold* detached	pre-1233
Bramley	*Utworth* detached	pre-1234
Bramley	Unstead detached	pre-1256
Bramley	Haldish detached	pre-1304
Bramley	Divided into Clere and Fay moieties	1241
Fay moiety	Divided into Appesley and Pope moieties	1485
Clere moiety	Divided into East Bramley (Tangley), West Bramley and an un-named third estate	1656
Utworth	*Rydinghurst* detached	pre-1331

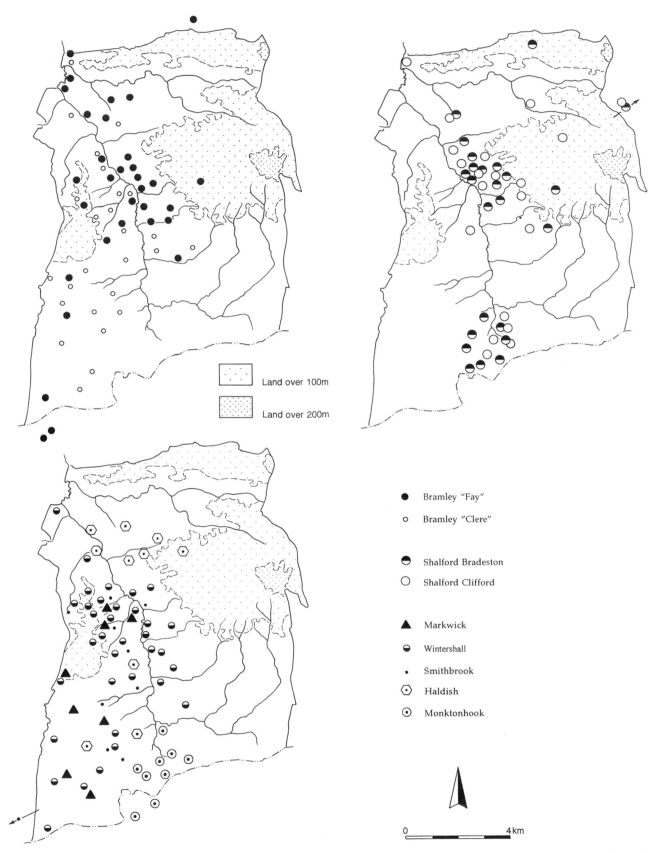

Fig 8.10 Manorial holdings in the western portion of the Blackheath Hundred based on evidence from court rolls and rentals. (© Crown Copyright NC/04/25242)

ground and were probably used for stock raising. The name Emply, also situated on the greensand ridge, suggests that some at least of this ground was still wooded. Areas of good arable land in the Bramley Wey valley were included in the holdings Wipley, Elmbridge, Birtley, Garston and Rydinghurst – the

last mentioned containing the element *ersc*. Close to the river, water-meadows would be available at Risbridge, Run, Brigham and, in the Wey valley, at Unstead. Access to resources on Weald Clay were available at Howicks, Rams, Oakhurst, Burningfold and Hall Place. The holdings selected when this

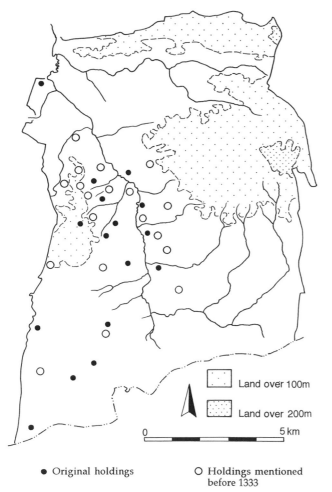

● Original holdings   ○ Holdings mentioned
                                       before 1333

Fig 8.11 Holdings of Bramley Wintershall als Selhurst manor (based on SHC: Zg36). (© Crown Copyright NC/04/25242)

manor was created, with a core area around the capital messuage and a patchwork of detached farms with access to a range of resources, produced an economically viable entity and suggests a deliberate policy behind the break-up of the former multiple estate.

Discussion

The lack of either pre-Conquest documentary survival or any relevant archaeological data[2] renders impossible a consideration of the early administrative history of the Blackheath Hundred or even the location of any early settlement sites. While the hundredal system in evidence in the Domesday survey of 1086 can be used to reconstruct hypothetical earlier primary territories (Blair 1991, 12–24), there are suggestions that these hundreds replaced still earlier units. An argument based on the topography of the area south of the North Downs, and following the model proposed by Klingelhofer (1992) for Hampshire, might see the Godalming primary unit, after the excision of the Farnham estate, as two valley estates based on the Wey and the Bramley Wey, and a further similar unit to the east with an estate based on Dorking and the valley of the Mole.

The Hundred meeting place for the Blackheath Hundred is assumed to have been somewhere on the high, exposed sandy area of Blackheath. Rosemary Hill has been suggested as a location (Knox 1963) and, while the attempt to derive the name from the roast meat consumed at Hundred meetings seems fanciful, a small hill on high open land would conform with the type of site for open-air meetings elsewhere (Meaney 1997). The parishes of St Martha's, Shalford, Wonersh and Albury converge on Rosemary Hill, placing it on the boundary between the western and eastern halves of the Hundred and a number of tracks also meet there. In 1377, however, a meeting of the Blackheath Hundred took place at Perrybridge, a point on the extreme western boundary of the Hundred where the road from Shalford crosses the Wey. This has been dismissed as aberrant since the meeting discussed a specific dispute relating to a bridge over the Wey (Knox 1963) but the route links the major settlements of Godalming and Blackheath Hundreds and may preserve some memory of a period when the two were linked administratively – fords and bridges have been seen as primary locations for hundred meeting places (Meaney 1997).

TABLE 8.4 Men and land granted in the creation of Bramley Wintershall manor before 1227.

Name given	Present name	Name given	Present name
Andrew de Tunhamsted	Unstead	Robert Glede	Slade's Farm
Richard fabr'	Smithbrook	Robert de Ochurst	Ockhurst
William prepositum		William de la Brok	Brookwell
John de Howyk	Howicks	Richard de Fraxino	Elmbridge Farm
Ailwin of Bramley		Geoffrey de la Legh	Lea Farm
Henry de Howyk		Howicks	Henry de la Lythe
Henry de Boueton		Robert de Ram	Ramsnest
Gilbert Glede	Slade's Farm	William Russel	
William Luffe		John de la Fuchte	Furtherfits
Richard Coleman		William de Sudhescoumbe	
William le Hevenere		Norman de Keringham	Carringham
John de Godebrug		Gilbert de Risbrugh	Risbridge Farm
Nicholas de Bernolegh		Richard de Keringham	Carringham
William de Vippelee	Wipley	Richard Hupehill of Bramley	Hullbrook
John Franceys	Francis Ride		

Place-names give clear evidence of differential development within the Blackheath Hundred although the suggestion of early settlement in the western half when compared with the Weald in general rests with the highly speculative pagan place-name of Underslaw and the occurrence of a -*worth* name, Utworth, both close to the southern extreme of the Bramley Wey valley. Later however, there is clear evidence from place-names indicative of types of land use of the importance of the differences in geology and therefore soil type within the Hundred. An early emphasis on labour-intensive, arable farming with permanent settlements on suitable land in the Bramley Wey valley and stock raising, initially on a transhumance basis, in the remainder of the Hundred, was the probable genesis of the higher population in the western half of the Hundred noted in 1086.

Although some settlement almost certainly occurred earlier, possibly in the 9th or 10th century, the transfer of status from the defensive *burh* at Eashing to the commercial centre of Guildford (Hill 2000) provided impetus in the form of a population centre and market for the development of its hinterland, including the Bramley Wey valley. Linked to this is the holding by both Shalford and Bramley of properties in Guildford in 1086 (Darby & Campbell 1962, 398).

The ecclesiastical arrangements noted in the Domesday survey indicate the presence of a multiple estate but the specialization suggested by place-name evidence relates land use to soil type rather than to anything centrally imposed, although these two explanations are not mutually exclusive. The Bramley estate comprised at least seventeen tithings which may represent internal divisions pre-dating the formation of the estate and a similar situation in the Mole valley south of Dorking in Surrey has been claimed (Blair 1991, 26). The archiepiscopal estate of South Malling in Sussex provides a possible parallel (Jones 1976). There the estate stretched from Lewes on the coast north through the Weald towards the Sussex/Surrey boundary. It contained two groups, each of six *borghs*, one group within and one without the wood. Within each *borgh* were a number of hamlets and isolated holdings, all of which owed complex and well-defined services to the archbishop's court at South Malling.

The question arises as to why Bramley, not a parish until 1844, was named as the estate *caput* in the Domesday survey and as a parent manor thereafter. The mother church was almost certainly on the site of the present Shalford church, at the northern extremity of the estate, the closest point to the mercantile centre of Guildford and close to an important fording point over the Tillingbourne: this latter point is of particular relevance since the place-name Shalford contains the potentially early topographical element *ford*. However, the later manorial *caput* of Shalford manor was probably the moated site at East Shalford (TQ 0145 4740) and it is this area, bordering on the north side of Shalford Common and close to another fording point on the Tillingbourne which may represent the centre of the Domesday estate. The fair and market granted by John to the rector of Shalford took place within the church and churchyard of the present village but, immediately it grew too large for that location and spread beyond the churchyard wall, it came into the fee of Bramley (Redstone 1911, 110). South of the present churchyard is an open triangular area which seems to have been the site of the market from which coloured Wealden glass was bought for the windows of Farnham Castle in 1224 (Brooks 1985, 7). This area now forms the historic core of Shalford village and the long street of Bramley with its 12th century chapel lies some 3km to the south. This may represent a deliberate spatial separation between the ecclesiastical power of an important mother church and the secular centre owned before the Conquest by Alnoth *cild* (Aethelnoth of Canterbury, a major Kentish *thegn* and among William's leading hostages in 1067) and later by Odo of Bayeux.

While the *falods* of the Blackheath Hundred were used for grazing, this does not seem to have involved the long distance transhumance associated with the Weald of Kent and East Surrey (cf Turner in prep). Although, long after Domesday, the villages of the Tillingbourne valley and the Bramley estate held land as far south as the Surrey/Sussex boundary – land for the Wealden triad of uses: grazing, timber and iron – the distances involved were relatively short and the grazing areas probably never far removed from the dispersed farmsteads. That some of this area was still being used for stock raising after the Conquest is indicated by the occasional occurrence of relevant place-names in Norman-French.

The word 'land' now has a very general meaning but during the medieval period and later, in the Latin form *terra* it usually referred to arable land. Gelling has suggested that the meaning could be further narrowed to 'ground newly broken-in for arable farming' and, more recently, to 'one of the terms employed to denote new settlements of the 7th to 12th centuries, established is areas colonised or reclaimed in response to an increasing need for arable' (Gelling & Cole 2000, 279). *Breche*, derived from ME rather than OE, is also associated with new arable land and both elements occur in the eastern half of the Blackheath Hundred emphasizing again the later development of that portion (neither element appears in the western half).

Fragmentation of the larger estates had started before 1086 and continued through the medieval period and later. Most of the divisions that are documented occurred when manors were split between heirs but the creation of Bramley Wintershall can be seen as a grant of men, their families and their freehold land to a local landowner. In the eastern half of the Hundred the divisions resulted in compact manors but in the western half a different pattern emerged. A clear factor in this latter area was the continuing concern to ensure that all manors had a wide range of types of land. This resulted in a patchwork of holdings within the Bramley Wey valley and the area of the Weald to the south. The reason for this contrast between the two halves of the Hundred is uncertain but the division of the Bramley estate appears to have been a more controlled exercise over several centuries. Ownership by the de Fay family from 1156 until after 1241, and the division of the estate at that date between two de Fay sisters, may provide some context.

In summary, the underlying geology played a fundamental role in the division of the Blackheath Hundred into four areas settled at successive periods and, initially at least, with different types of land utilization. The first of these is the Upper Greensand, Gault Clay and Lower Greensand of the Tillingbourne valley, an area of eventually nucleated settlements and open field systems with land stretching from the top of the North Downs, across the valley and into the Weald; the second is the geologically intermixed valley of the Bramley Wey, location of the late Saxon multiple estate and confused manorial geography; the third the Weald Clay in the southern portion of the Hundred, where the present dispersed settlement pattern developed from a stock-based, transhumance economy; and, last, the high escarpment of the Lower Greensand (which reaches 294m at Leith Hill outside the Blackheath Hundred). These hills are capped by beds of rock resistant to erosion: chert bands protect the Hythe Beds at Leith, Coneyhurst and Hascombe Hills, while ironstone (carstone) masses cap the Folkestone Beds on Albury, Farley and Black-heaths. These areas of rapidly draining, acid, sandy podzols – the 'rascally heaths' of Cobbett – remain only sparsely populated.

These differences indicate the risks inherent in regional or supra-regional studies in terms of rendering particular geological areas as homogeneous entities. The area provides one example of the skill with which late Saxon and early medieval people identified, selected and utilized resources on a very local basis with concomitant differences in both the chronology and economic basis of development.

Towards a research agenda

We return to the quotation with which we headed this paper. The thesis advanced can only be tested by continuing study within the Blackheath Hundred and by similar exercises in other hundreds to provide comparisons. As with other work proposed by Turner in this volume, such projects would benefit from a careful reappraisal of the Surrey Domesday entries on the lines of that undertaken for Wiltshire and Essex by McDonald & Snooks (1986). On the topographical front, one or two topic-based enquires demand attention. For example, the superficial variations across the county in field systems thrown up by recent work by Nicola Bannister (Bannister & Wills 2001; Bannister in this volume) need to be explored to illuminate their historical basis. Many aspects of this, such as holdings of the Rumbeams type described in the foregoing and the 'ladder' fields recognized in the Nutfield– Tandridge area, should be susceptible to archaeological as well as documentary and topographical investigation.

ACKNOWLEDGEMENTS

JE wishes to thank Chris Budgen and Roger Ellaby for helpful discussions over many years and Dr Andrew Reynolds (formerly of King Alfred's College, Winchester, now of the Institute of Archaeology, University College, London) for advice and encouragement. DJT would like to thank too many people for a list to be practicable but particular gratitude is due to Dr John Blair. The authors would also like to thank David Williams for drawing the maps.

NOTES

1 A decade or so ago occasional citations of 'Turner & Blair, forthcoming' appeared, mostly made by the two authors but also by colleagues who had seen one or other of various drafts that were prepared. The paper (working title 'Churches and manors in the Blackheath Hundred') was never brought to fruition as both authors became absorbed by different problems. Some of the content appeared in John Blair's *Early*

Medieval Surrey (1991); much of the remainder is treated in the current paper. All citations of 'Turner & Blair forthcoming' should be treated with caution.

2 The Surrey Sites and Monuments Record surprisingly contains no entries for the Blackheath Hundred dated between the 4th and 13th centuries, other than churches.

BIBLIOGRAPHY

Manuscript sources

SHC: Surrey History Centre, Woking
  212/15/1 Court rolls, 1485
  892/5/2 Court rolls
  892/5/1 Bramley: view of frankpledge and court baron 5 Sept 1570
  1322/1/1–25 Manor of Albury court rolls and court book
  1322/1/2 Manor of Albury court rolls
  1322/4/56 Extract from deed, 1327
  3243/12/13 Agreement to partition waste, 1847
  G24/7/1 Letter, 1507
  G46/6/15–18 Deeds
  G47/1–6 Court rolls of the manor of Selhurst alias Wintershall
  G96/4/1 Mortgage, 1650
  LM454 Loseley manuscripts, depositions, 16th century
  RB591 Uncatalogued collection of deeds
  Zg36 Court rolls and rentals of the manor of Wintershall in Bramley, 1330–1676
WM Court Book: Wildwood Manor 17th century Court Book in private ownership

Published sources

Anon, 1916   Additions to the Museum: Saxon pot, *SyAC*, **29**, 152–3

Balchin, J, *et al*, forthcoming   *Ewhurst*, SyAS Villages Project

Bannister, N R, 2004   The Surrey Historic Landscape Characterisation Project, in *Aspects of archaeology and history in Surrey: towards a research framework for the county* (eds J Cotton, G Crocker & A Graham), SyAS, 119–32

Bannister, N R, & Wills, P M, 2001   *Surrey Historic Landscape Characterisation*, 2 vols, Surrey County Council limited distribution

Blair, W J, 1991   *Early medieval Surrey; landholding, church and settlement before 1300*, Alan Sutton & SyAS

Brandon, P, 1978   The South Saxon *Andredesweald*, in *The south Saxons* (ed P Brandon), Phillimore, 138–59

Brooks, P D, 1985   *Farnham Castle: the forgotten years*, Farnham & District Museum Society

Darby, H C, & Campbell, E M J, 1962   *The Domesday geography of south-east England*, Cambridge University Press

Darby, H C, Glasscock, R E, Sheil, J, & Versey, G R, 1979   The changing geographical distribution of wealth in England 1086–1334–1535, *J Hist Geog*, **5**, 247–62

Ellaby, R, 2000   The Horley demesne of Reigate Priory, *SyAC*, **87**, 147–55

English, J, 1988   Underslaw, Cranleigh (TQ 046 390) – a possible 'pagan' religious place-name, *SyAS Bull*, **233**

——, 1997   A possible early Wealden settlement type, *Medieval Settlement Res Grp Ann Rep*, **12**, Hartlepool

——, 2001   *Place-names and the resource base – a study of late Saxon settlement on clay-based soils in south-east England*, University of Southampton unpublished MA dissertation

——, 2002   Worths in a landscape context, *Landscape Hist*, **24**, 45–51

Gallois, R W, 1965   *British Regional Geology: the Wealden District*, HMSO

Gelling, M, 1976   *The place-names of Berkshire*, **3**, English Place-name Soc, **51**

Gelling, M, & Cole, A, 2000   *The landscape of placenames*, Shaun Tyas, Stamford

Giuseppi, M S, 1903   Deeds in the society's library, *SyAC*, **18**, 222–5

Gorton, P, 1996   The enclosure of the Pease Marsh, *Surrey Hist Landscape Stud Newsl*, **9**, 9–12

Gover, J E B, Mawer, A, & Stenton, F M, 1934   *The place-names of Surrey*, English Place-name Soc, **11**

Hill, D, 2000   Athelstan's urban reforms, *Anglo-Saxon Stud Archaeol Hist*, **11**, 173–85

Hooke, D, 1998   *The landscape of Anglo-Saxon England*, Leicester University Press

Johnston, P M, 1911   [Descriptions of churches in Blackheath hundred] in *VCH*, **3**, *passim*

Jolliffe, J E A, 1933   *Pre-feudal England: the Jutes*, Oxford University Press

Jones, G R J, 1976   Multiple estates and early settlement, in *Medieval settlement* (ed P H Sawyer), 11–40

Klingelhofer, E, 1992   *Manor, vill and hundred: the development of rural institutions in early medieval Hampshire*, Pontifical Inst Medieval Stud Studies and Texts, **112**, Toronto

Knox, C, 1963   The meeting place of the Hundred of Blackheath, *SyAC*, **60**, 86–7

Lowther, A W G, 1931   The Saxon cemetery at Guildown, Guildford, Surrey, *SyAC*, **39**, 1–50

McDonald, J, & Snooks, G D, 1986   *Domesday economy*, Oxford

Manning, O, & Bray, W, 1804–14   *The history and antiquities of the county of Surrey*, 3 vols

Marshall, W, 1817   *The review and abstract of the county reports to the Board of Agriculture from the several Agricultural Departments of England*

Meaney, A L, 1997   Hundred meeting places in the Cambridge region, in *Names, places and people: an onomastic miscellany for John McNeal Dodgson* (eds A Rumble & A D Mills), Paul Watkins, Stamford, 195–240

Morris, J, 1959   Anglo-Saxon Surrey, *SyAC*, **56**, 132–58

Penshurst 1925   *Report on MSS preserved at Penshurst Place*, **1**, Historic Manuscripts Commission

Redstone, C J, 1911   [Manorial and advowson histories for Blackheath Hundred] in *VCH*, **3**, *passim*

Round, H L, 1908   Domesday Surrey, in *VCH*, **1**, 275–93

SRS, 1932   Surrey taxation returns, Surrey Record Soc, **11**

Taylor, C C, 2000   The plus fours in the wardrobe: a personal view of landscape history, in *Landscape: the richest historical record* (ed D Hooke), Soc Landscape Stud suppl ser, **1**, 157–162

Turner, D J, 1980   The North Downs trackway, *SyAC*, **72**, 1–13

——, 1997   Thunderfield, Surrey – central place or shieling, *Medieval Settlement Res Grp Ann Rep*, **12**, 8–10

——, 2004   Manors and other settlements, in *Aspects of archaeology and history in Surrey: towards a research framework for the county* (eds J Cotton, G Crocker & A Graham), SyAS, 133–46

——, in prep   Surrey: east versus west (working title)

VCH: *The Victoria history of the county of Surrey* (ed H E Malden), 1902–12, 4 vols

Vinogradoff, P, & Morgan, F W (eds), 1914   *Survey of the Honour of Denbigh*

Williams, M, 1982   Marshland and waste, in *The English medieval landscape* (ed L Cantor), 126–39

Witney, K P, 1976   *The Jutish forest: a study of the Weald of Kent from 450 to 1380 AD*

Judie English, MIBiol, MA, 2 Rowland Road, Cranleigh GU6 8SW

Dennis Turner, BSc, FSA, 21 Evesham Road, Reigate RH2 9DL

9

The Surrey Historic Landscape Characterisation Project

NICOLA R BANNISTER

with maps and tables prepared by PATRICK M WILLS

The Surrey Historic Landscape Characterisation Project forms part of English Heritage's national programme of 'historic landscape characterisation' undertaken by local government. It covered the modern administrative county of Surrey. The project is concerned with understanding how the landscape has developed through human intervention and interaction with the physical environment over time. Areas of the landscape are categorized into different historic landscape types according to defined attributes. The Surrey project followed a similar methodology to that undertaken in Hampshire and Kent with the results plotted on to a GIS-based digital system held by Surrey County Council. The results of the mapping revealed that Surrey is essentially a rural landscape with fields making up 36.5% of the county, while commons, heaths etc contribute 7%. Woodland cover was calculated at 13%, significantly lower than the figure of 23% quoted by Surrey County Council (SCC 1997). This difference reflects the method of grouping the character types with some heath woods sub-types being included in the heathland character type. Settlement covers 23% with industry another 4%. Many parts of the county, especially in the south (Weald) and across the Downs dip slope, retain historic landscape character types pre-dating 1811 and often with medieval origins. The resulting database provides a broad-brush base-line for understanding Surrey's historic landscape and is an aid in conservation management, development control, research and education. The aim is for the Historic Landscape Character Map and database to be available to the public via the internet as well as through more conventional sources such as libraries and schools.

Introduction

There has been increasing interest by archaeologists, historical geographers and, more recently, historical ecologists in the historic landscape, pioneered by the now classic work *The making of the English landscape* by W G Hoskins (1955). The work of C C Taylor in the 1970s and Oliver Rackham in the 1980s drew attention to the way the countryside has developed through time and the components (including living ones) that make up particular types of landscapes (Taylor 1975; 1979; Rackham 1976; 1986).

Increased knowledge and understanding of the historic landscape has resulted in appreciation of the need to afford it better protection in order to manage landscape change in a far more sympathetic way and with regard to what has gone before. In response to this greater knowledge, the government in its white paper *Our common inheritance* (DoE 1990) asked English Heritage (EH) to produce a register of historic landscapes of national importance. The outcome of several studies commissioned by English Heritage was the decision that all the country's landscape is historic because humans have changed and modified nearly all the British countryside to some degree. Some landscapes contain features and remains of human activities stretching back thousands of years, such as heathlands and downlands, while others represent a particular activity which has taken place over a short period, for example some formal designed landscapes.

Thus the emphasis was placed on the understanding and identification of the historic character of the whole of the country's landscape, and to this end English Heritage's national programme of historic landscape characterization was born in 1992. It was also a means by which the aims of Planning Policy Guidance note 15 (PPG15), with regard to the all-pervasive quality of the historic environment (Sections 1.3, 2.26), could be addressed. Historic landscape characterization also fitted with the Countryside Commission's 'Character Map of England' and English Nature's 'Natural Areas Map'. A detailed account of the historic landscape characterization programme to 1994 is given by Fairclough, Lambrick and McNab (1999), with a review of the current position presented by Fairclough, Lambrick and Hopkins, who state (2002, 69):

> Historic landscape characterisation is concerned with recognising the many ways in which the present countryside reflects how people have exploited and changed their physical environment, and adapted to it through time. It considers this with respect to different social, economic, technological and cultural aspects of life, and the varied underlying influences of geography, history and tradition.

Initially there were several independent pilot historic landscape characterization projects running concurrently, developing their own approaches and methodologies, for example at Durham, Oxford and Avon (Fairclough *et al* 1999, 38–47). However, a historic landscape character assessment of Bodmin Moor in Cornwall was developed to cover the whole of that county (Herring 1998). It is from the Cornwall project that the most widely accepted historic landscape characterization method was formulated, and subsequent counties then modified it to fit their local context. So far a third of England has been completed with another six counties in progress and six more that were planned to commence in 2002/3 (Fairclough *et al* 2002, 71).

The concept that the whole of the rural landscape is historic was being widely accepted (*ibid*, 69–70), but the idea of some landscapes being of greater historical and archaeological importance than others was taken on board in some counties, and Surrey implemented a programme of identifying within the county Areas of Historic Landscape Value (AHLV; now called Areas of Special Historic Landscape Value: ASHLV). This process proceeded until 2001 without the benefit of a county-wide assessment of the historic landscape of Surrey. One of the objectives of the Surrey Historic Landscape Characterisation Project was to provide the base-line information for identifying systematically across the county future candidates for ASHLVs and areas where resources regarding future research could be targeted.

Methodology

In April 2000 Surrey County Council, together with its partner organizations English Heritage and the Countryside Agency, commissioned the author to undertake a historic landscape characterization of the administrative county of Surrey following the methodology already adopted for its neighbours, Hampshire and Kent (Lambrick & Bramhill 1999; Bramhill & Munby 2001). The administrative county was selected on practical grounds and also on the basis that those parts of the historic county that fell within the London boroughs are essentially suburban in character and will be the subject of a later historic landscape characterization project. The characterization was achieved by producing a digital map using key archive material, existing detailed historic landscape surveys and assessments combined with the author's knowledge of the county drawn from extensive fieldwork. The Countryside Agency was involved because of the value the characterization project would have for the Surrey Hills Area of Outstanding Natural Beauty (AONB) and in particular in the drafting of the new management plan (in progress). The objective for using the same method as that for Hampshire and Kent (with local modifications) was to ensure continuity across the South East, thus facilitating a regional historic landscape assessment in the future.

In essence the objective of historic landscape characterization is to assign units of the landscape (usually fields or groups of fields as defined on the OS 1:2500 map) to a historic landscape character type (HLT) identified by pre-defined attributes. These attributes take account of the process by which that particular piece of landscape has come about, its physical appearance and the time period over which the process has taken place (time-depth). The HLT is a description of what a particular piece of landscape looks like today and takes account of current land use characteristics. The morphological, spatial, functional and chronological attributes of the HLTs have to be easily recognizable and definable, with the number of types being large enough to capture the diversity of the historic character but not too large to become unwieldy, resulting in a loss of patterning. Thus for Surrey a total of 99 historic landscape sub-types (HLsT) were identified which could be grouped into fourteen major historic landscape types (HLT). The full list of HLsTs (with their geographical information system (GIS) code), is given in an Appendix and on the key to the Historic Landscape Character Map (fig 9.1). The full list of HLTs with their attribute descriptions is presented in volume 2 of the *Surrey Historic Landscape Characterisation Report* (Bannister & Wills 2001). For each of the HLsTs there is a written description and historical rationale, together with a description of identifying characteristics. Predominant locations of the types together with variations, typical associations with other HLsTs and other similar types are also given. For each HLsT key indicative sources used to identify the type are also listed (see discussion below). One example of a HLsT is 101: Small irregular assarts intermixed with woodlands (fig 9.2).

The plotting of the information in digital format using one of a number of GIS programmes enables detailed analyses to be produced of the database, highlighting trends and patterns in the distribution of HLTs. It also allows cross-referencing with other databases, for example the county's Sites and Monuments Record (SMR), or with development control constraints. For Surrey the historic landscape characterization was mapped directly on to the GIS at 1:25,000 and 1:10,000 from the archive sources without an intermediate paper stage. This differed from previous computerized assessments which had undertaken mapping on paper bases prior to digitizing. It was agreed that mapping direct on to computer made the optimum use of limited resources, especially as the archive material was always kept to hand for cross-reference. However, since the completion by the author of a contribution to a review of the historic landscape characterization methodology, on behalf of Somerset County Council for English Heritage (Aldred 2002), it has been concluded that, for technical reasons, a paper map stage might have been beneficial. By viewing at 1:25,000 scale much larger areas of the county than can be seen on a screen, it may have been possible to achieve greater clarity by drawing out some of the more ephemeral trends with regard to field patterns.

The Surrey Historic Landscape Characterisation project was divided into seven clearly defined tasks, the completion of each leading on to the next.

- Collection of data, drawing on published and unpublished sources.
- Identification and documentation of attributes and drawing up lists of historic landscape character types (HLT) and sub-types (HLsT).
- Characterization of key pilot areas, namely eight 5km grid squares, as examples of the varied geological and landscape areas across the county.
- Characterization of the whole of the county, digitized on to GIS.
- Description and analysis of the historic element of the Surrey Landscape Character Areas.
- Production of report with accompanying maps.
- Production of recommendations with reference to the Surrey Hills AONB.

The objective of the pilot mapping stage was to test the list of HLsTs with the mapping process, together with detailed cross-referencing with archive sources and with the digitized 1999 county aerial photographs. The pilot exercise was also a means by which the author could become familiar with the GIS programme Microsoft 'WINGS'. Technical support was provided by the GIS team in the Environment Section of Surrey County Council led by Patrick Wills. The list of HLsTs was revised in the light of the pilot mapping with, for example, the sub-division of golf courses based on their landscape origin. Back-up copies of the database were regularly sent to Surrey County Council. The author kept a daily diary charting the mapping progress across the county, from west to east and north to south, in one seamless process. Each identified historic landscape unit was defined by a polygon and assigned a HLsT together with other information such as confidence levels, archive sources, and previous character types (where known).

The amount of information available for the project was considerable and, given the time-scale and resources, the number of archive sources used had to be restricted yet provide the maximum amount of information in a readily accessible format. Essentially historic landscape characterization is a mapping exercise and to provide the element of time-depth, key archive maps were the main sources consulted. They provided snapshots of landscape change from the late 18th century to the mid-19th

century and included John Rocque's Survey of the County of Surrey (published 1768, surveyed 1762); the Ordnance Surveyors' draft drawings for the 1-inch 1st edition (1797–1801); the OS 1-inch 1st edition (1811); the OS 6-inch 1st edition (c 1870s); OS 1-inch 1940–5 and the current OS 1:25,000 Explorer Series. The tithe maps and enclosure maps were only consulted for the pilot survey, when it was found that extracting information from them was time-consuming. However it would be possible in the future to add this information in the form of overlays to the data set. In addition to the maps, the other extremely useful source was aerial photographs, namely the RAF mosaic (1946–9) and the most recent full county flight in digital format (1999). The latter aerial photographs were so clear and detailed that they replaced the need for cross checking on the ground. However for future more detailed assessments, ground checking will probably need to take place. Of limited use were other data sets, for example English Nature's Ancient Woodland Inventory and Phase I Habitat Maps. As part of the background research to the drawing up of the list of HLsTs, the numerous detailed historic landscape surveys which have been completed for either candidate ASHLVs or for National Trust properties were also consulted. These tended to be areas concentrated on either the North Downs or the Wealden greensand.

Results

The results of the Project were presented in a two-volume report together with the completed database in digital format (Bannister & Wills 2001). Copies of the report were distributed to the partner organizations with a copy also going to the Surrey Archaeological Society library. The 'WINGS' GIS programme enables any number of analyses to be undertaken of the data set, in the form of overlays together with computed summary tables and charts. However, the analysis of the database took two main directions. First a comparison with the county's landscape character areas as identified in *The future of Surrey's landscape and woodlands* (SCC 1997), together with the historic character of the Surrey Hills AONB area. Secondly the identification of historic landscape character areas, based on defined patterns in the distribution and patterning of HLsTs across the county. In addition the distribution of woodland in relation to settlement and parish boundaries was examined together with the time-depth characteristics across the county.

The Historic Landscape Characterisation Project supports the commonly held view that Surrey is one of the most wooded counties in England (13%). This figure is significantly lower than that usually quoted (eg SCC 1997) and reflects the grouping of the

Fig 9.1 The Surrey Historic Landscape Character Map

Facing page: Key and diagram showing the proportions of all landscape types

Settlement related

Scattered settlement with paddocks pre-1811 ext
Scattered settlement with paddocks (post-1811 & pre-1840 extent)
Common edge/roadside waste settlement pre-1811 extent
Common edge/roadside waste settlement (post 1811 & pre-1840 extent)
Post 1811 & pre-1940 settlement (small scale)
Village or hamlet (pre-1811 extent)
Town pre-1811 extent
Caravan sites
Large cemeteries (i.e. not adjacent to churches)
Hospital complexes (i.e. not within settlements)
Regular settlements with paddocks post-1840
Common edge and roadside waste settlement post-1840
Post-1811 & pre-1940 settlement – large estates
Post-1811 & pre-1940 settlement – med. estates
Post-1940 luxury estates
Post-1940 small to medium estates

Parkland and designed landscape

Pre-1811 parkland
19th century and later parkland and large designed gardens
Deer parks
Arboreta
Smaller designed gardens

Recreation

Racecourses
Motor racing tracks and vehicle testing areas
Golf courses – heathland origin
Golf courses – parkland origin
Golf courses – downland origin
Golf courses – farmland origin
Major sports fields and complexes
Marinas
Studs and horse paddocks

Extractive industry

Active and disused chalk quarries
Active and disused gravel workings
Active and disused clay pits
Active and disused sandpits

Other industry

Industrial complexes and factories
Modern large scale industry
Reservoirs and water treatment
Sewage works/water treatment

Communication facilities

Railway station and sidings complexes
Airfields
Motorway service areas
Motorway junctions

Military and defence

Prehistoric (hillforts & other defensive encl)
Medieval (mottes and baileys; ring works)
19th century forts
20th century

Field patterns

Small irregular asserts intermixed with woodland
Medium irreg. asserts & copses with wavy bdys.
Large irreg. asserts with wavy or mixed bdys.
Regular asserts with straight boundaries
Enclosed strips and furlongs
Medium to large regular fields with wavy bdys. (late medieval to 17th/18th century enclosure)
Small irreg. rectilinear fields with straight bdys.
Small rectilinear fields with wavy boundaries
Regular "ladder" fields
Small regular fields (parliamentary encl. type)
Medium regular fields (parliamentary encl. type)
Large regular fields (parliamentary encl. type)
Variable size, regular fields (parliamentary encl.)
"Prairie" fields (large enclosures with extensive boundary loss)
Fields bounded by roads, tracks and paths
Previously hops/orchard
Parkland conversion to arable
Fields, formerly ponds now dried up

Commons

Common heathland
Common downland
Other commons and greens
Wooded over commons

Horticulture

Orchards
Nurseries with glass houses
Nurseries without glass houses

Woodland

Assarted pre-1811 woodland
Replanted assarted pre-1811 woodland
Other pre-1811 woodland
Replanted other pre-1811 woodland
19th century plantations (general)
Pre-1811 gills (scarp & steep valley-side wood)
Post-1811 gills
Pre-1811 heathland/common land encl. wood
Pre-1811 heathland/common land regenerated woodland (unenclosed; not plantation)
19th century heathland plantations
Pre-1811 wood pasture
19th century or later wood pasture
Alder Carr (wet woods next to rivers & wetlands)
Worked coppice
Regenerated secondary woodland on farmland

Heathland

Unenclosed heathland and scrub
Enclosed heathland and scrub
Purlieus and other enclosed heathland pastures

Downland

Chalk grassland
Chalk grassland and scrub

Valley floor and water management

Miscellaneous valley floor fields and pastures
Valley floor woodlands
Marsh and rough grazing
Water meadows or common meadows
Unimproved hay meadows or pasture and common meadows
Watercress beds
Pre-1811 fishponds, hatchery complexes, 'natural' ponds and lakes
Post-1811 ditto
Watermills, mill ponds, hammer ponds and leats

All Landscape Types

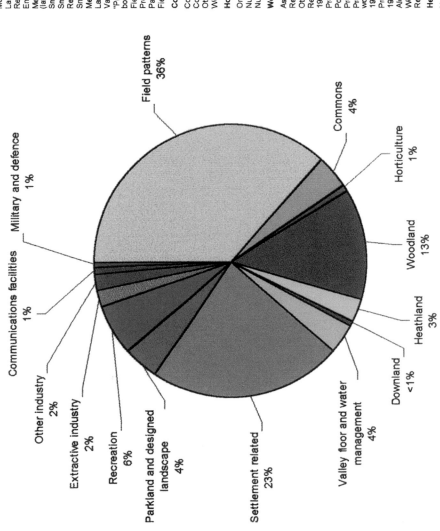

Field patterns 36%

Commons 4%

Horticulture 1%

Woodland 13%

Heathland 3%

Downland <1%

Valley floor and water management 4%

Settlement related 23%

Parkland and designed landscape 4%

Recreation 6%

Extractive industry 2%

Other industry 2%

Communications facilities 1%

Military and defence 1%

ENGLISH HERITAGE

SURREY
COUNTY COUNCIL

The Countryside Agency

Fig 9.2 An example of an historic landscape sub-type (HLsT). Small irregular assarts intermixed with woodland in the south of Abinger parish (HLsT 101): Renfold (TQ 126 383).

Editors' note: This map has been reproduced from the original project report (Bannister & Wills 2001).

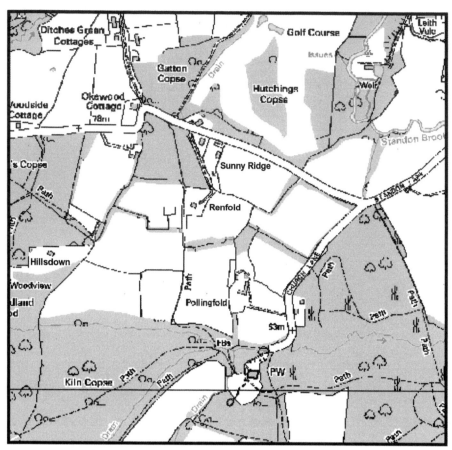

Description and historical rationale

Assarting, or the clearance of woodland to create fields, produced the dominant field patterns in the Weald. These field systems were created by the piecemeal clearance of the original woodland cover. This probably took place in the early medieval period.

Identifying characteristics

The fields are small, between one and five acres, though there may be larger ones created by some boundary removal. The boundaries are wavy and formed of shaws, or narrow strips of woodland or mature hedgerows, traditionally managed by coppicing. Mature oaks often dominate the boundaries and these, combined with the mix of small woods or coppices, create a landscape which appears densely wooded. The general topography tends to be undulating, with valleys, streams and small hilltops.

Predominant locations and variations

The Low Weald and along the Sussex border. Field boundary removal has made some fields appear larger. Isolated patches occur elsewhere in the county where larger areas of woodland have been encroached upon.

Typical associations with other types

This type is strongly associated with ancient woodland and wooded gills and also with some secondary woodland where fields have been abandoned.

Similar types and distinguishing criteria

Medium assarts but defined by their size.

Key indicative sources

OS 6-inch 1 edn
RAF OS Mosaic Aerial Photographs
1999 aerial photographs
OS 1:25,000 Explorer

HLsTs. For example some types of woodland, such as 'wooded over commons' (HLsT 204) and heathland and chalk and scrub (HLsTs 501, 502, 602), were not included in the woodland type category for the historic landscape characterization. In addition some smaller parcels of woodland especially in the Weald were characterized with fields, for example small irregular assarts (HLsT 101). Despite the perception of the county being a dormitory suburb of London, it is essentially a rural landscape (over 65% is not developed or built over). Table 9.1 presents the summary of this initial analysis. The full Historic Landscape Character Map is present in figure 9.1.

Immediately, at this scale, the underlying structure of landscape as defined by its geology is reflected in the pattern of its historic landscape sub-types. The east-west spine of the North Downs escarpment and to a lesser degree the Greensand Hills can clearly be seen, divided by the Holmesdale and the Tillingbourne valley. The wooded nature of the Weald is very distinctive, as is the distribution of the tracts of heathland in the west of the county. The spring lines along the chalk and greensand define the lines of older settlement, while in the north and north-west are areas of greatest landscape change with high concentrations of extractive industry and suburban development.

Fields dominate the landscape at 36.5% (table 9.1), but further analysis of the HLsTs shows that it is the prairie field sub-type which covers the great-

TABLE 9.1 Summary of the Historic Landscape Character Types by area.

Historic Landscape Character Type	Area in ha	Area by Historic Landscape Character Type (%)
1 Field Patterns	61243.2	36.59
2 Commons	6539.8	3.91
3 Horticulture	1690.5	1.01
4 Woodland	21896.5	13.08
5 Heathland	4568.7	2.73
6 Downland	805.6	0.48
7 Valley Floor and water management	6191.9	3.70
8 Settlement related	38343.7	22.91
9 Parkland and designed landscape	7145.6	4.27
10 Recreation	10258.1	6.13
11 Extractive industry	2935.4	1.75
12 Other industry	3682.8	2.20
13 Communications facilities	939.1	0.56
14 Military & defence	1158.2	0.69
Totals	167399.1	100.00

est area, at 7.5% (HLsT 114). These are large enclosures where there has been extensive boundary loss since the 1870s. The figure provides graphic evidence of the erosion of historic field patterns across the county but most frequently on the chalk and also in the Weald. The wooded origins of Surrey are reflected in 6.43% of fields being characterized by large irregular assarts with wavy or mixed boundaries (HLsT 103). Medium regular fields with straight boundaries of the parliamentary enclosure type (HLsT 111) cover 3.72% of the county, reflecting the amount of formal enclosure of either open fields or of commons, downlands and heaths.

The great influx of people in the late 19th and early 20th century settling in suburban estates is shown by the relatively high percentage of post-1811 and pre-1940 medium estates (HLsT 814; 6.43%), with post-1940 small to medium estates (HLsT 816) covering 4.49% of the county. (A full breakdown of the percentage coverage of each HLsT is given in tables 2a and 2b in Appendix II of Bannister & Wills 2001).

SURREY'S LANDSCAPE CHARACTER AREAS
The pattern of distribution of HLsTs for each of the landscape character areas identified in the county's landscape assessment was examined and compared with the descriptions given in *The future of Surrey's landscape and woodlands* (SCC 1997). It was found that the historic landscape assessment supported the county landscape assessment and provided the detailed mapping required to justify the visual descriptions. For example, the Ockham and Clandon County Landscape Character Area is described as being open but with small pockets of woodland. Designed landscapes form an important part of the local character (SCC 1997), while the historic landscape characterization analysis supports

this with the identification of landscape dominated by regular parliamentary and prairie-type fields interspersed with small copses and woods. Parkland forms 6% of this character area. In comparison the Wooded Weald is described as low-lying, undulating, small-scale, intimate farmed landscape enclosed by woodland, hedges and shaws, with distinctive villages centred on greens and commons (SCC 1997, 2.71). The historic landscape characterization reveals that it is dominated by assarted fields (35%), ancient woodland (8%) and gills (narrow wooded valleys, 3%). Older settlement is scattered across the character area in the form of small villages and farms.

SURREY HILLS AONB
The Surrey Hills Area of Outstanding Natural Beauty was one of the first landscapes to be so designated in 1958, its designation being due to the very diverse nature of its landscape (Surrey Hills JAC 2000). This diversity is clearly revealed in its historic landscape character (fig 9.3). Over 38% of the AONB is covered by fields (compared with 25% for the county as a whole) with woodland covering 24% (compared with 13% for the county). Over 20% of the Surrey Hills is covered by heaths, commons, downs and heath woodland. This is owing to the fact that much of the AONB covers what were formerly manorial 'wastes' and grazing commons on relatively unproductive soils. These belonged to the parishes and manors which have settlements either in the Holmesdale and the Tillingbourne valley or on the dip slope of the North Downs, where the soils are more productive and conducive to cultivation. The 'wastes' were subject to specific forms of management and manorial rights regarding what could be grazed and when, and what resources could be exploited. It is the lack of intensive landscape change and in particular cultivation in the past

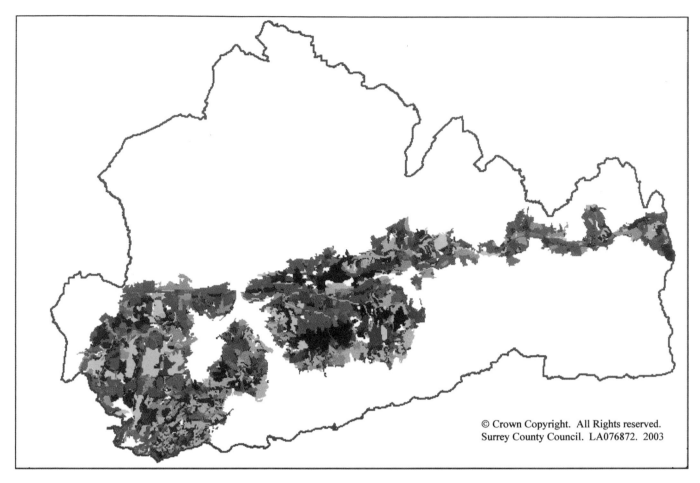

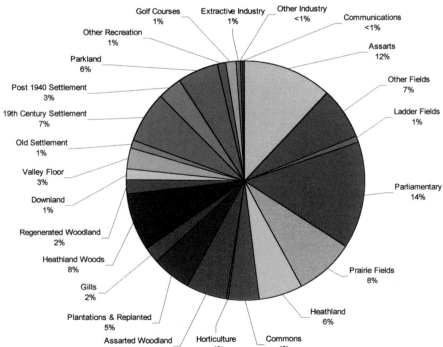

Golf Courses 1%
Extractive Industry 1%
Other Industry <1%
Communications <1%
Other Recreation 1%
Assarts 12%
Parkland 6%
Other Fields 7%
Post 1940 Settlement 3%
Ladder Fields 1%
19th Century Settlement 7%
Old Settlement 1%
Valley Floor 3%
Parliamentary 14%
Downland 1%
Regenerated Woodland 2%
Heathland Woods 8%
Gills 2%
Prairie Fields 8%
Plantations & Replanted 5%
Heathland 6%
Assarted Woodland 6%
Horticulture <1%
Commons 4%

Fig 9.3 Historic Landscape Character of the Surrey Hills Area of Outstanding Natural Beauty

which has preserved the unique landscape so highly valued in the Surrey Hills today. Development covers only 11% of the AONB area dominated by 19th century settlement (7%), while older pre-1811 settlement makes up only 1% and post-1940 development 3%. The high figure for the 19th century reflects the expansion in settlement with the coming of the railways and the development of the 'Surrey style' in vernacular architecture, with detached 'cottages' set within their own grounds commanding positions with extensive views or in picturesque settings. This pattern is frequent in the Greensand Hills with detached properties overlooking the Weald from the greensand escarpment. The western part of the AONB is dominated by heaths and commons around Hindhead and Thursley, while to the southwest the dramatic hilly landscape gives way to a more gentle countryside of woods, gills and small fields on the edge of the Weald. Of the 38% of fields, assarts contribute 12% while parliamentary fields cover 14%. The latter are dominant on the North Downs dip slope where enclosure either by private agreement or by act of parliament took place both of open downland and commons, and of medieval open fields associated with villages such as Bookham, Horsley and Effingham.

Surrey Hills is the most wooded of the AONBs but this is probably a 19th and 20th century phenomenon as heathland woods make up 8% of the total (24%). With the decline in grazing management on the heaths and commons, secondary woodland has developed. This, combined with the development of conifer plantations (5%), has significantly reduced the areas of open heaths and downs.

HISTORIC LANDSCAPE CHARACTER AREAS

An attempt was made to identify Historic Landscape Character Areas based on distinct visual patterns in the distribution of the HLsTs. These are areas of more or less coherently dominant historic landscape sub-types and their associations with other sub-types. As the historic character of the landscape is led by settlement, these areas are defined by the settlement pattern in relationship with other sub-types. The distribution of these areas as identified by the HLTs is shown in figure 9.4. Dispersed lowland woodland settlements characterize the Weald while ancient scarp-foot settlements lie in the east of the county in the Holmesdale. The river corridors form another area of nucleated and river-orientated settlement.

HISTORIC LANDSCAPE CHARACTER OF WOODLAND

More detailed interrogation of the database provides interesting overlays which can form the starting point for research projects, for example the distribution of woodland in relation to parish boundaries shown in figure 9.5. (The recent civil parish boundaries were used in this instance; there are plans for developing an overlay of historic ecclesiastical parish boundaries which will give a much clearer picture of historical relationships). It was found that generally across the county the distribution of ancient woodland was concentrated around the edges of the parishes with the centres of older settlement towards the middle. However in the Weald, woodland occurs throughout the parishes, reflecting both the later piecemeal clearance of the woodland in Saxon and medieval periods, and the predominance of woods occupying small steeply sloping stream valleys – gills. This supports observations made by Rackham for East Anglia (1981, 113) and by Aston (1985, 11, 104). The pattern is reinforced by the cessation in grazing and livestock management on many heaths and commons which were

also located on the margins of manors and parishes. Such commons as at Holmbury and along the Greensand Hills have become forest through secondary development of woods or planting with conifers.

TIME-DEPTH OF SURREY'S LANDSCAPE

The historic landscape characterization can be used to 'pull apart' the present historic landscape character along defined time periods. Describing these as 'windows' in the landscape, it is possible to obtain a feel for the antiquity of different parts of the county (Lambrick & Bramhill 2000). Essentially the Surrey landscape is generally post-medieval in character but there are areas especially in the Weald which are dominated by HLsTs that have origins in the medieval period. The approximate cut-off divisions are based on the OS 1-inch 1st edition of pre- and post-1811. Areas which are dominated by HLsTs pre-dating 1811 are indicative of antiquity where landscape change has been relatively slow and where there is likely to be extant evidence of prehistoric activity, for example in the west of the county in the heathlands and on the Greensand Hills (fig 9.6).

The north of the county shows the greatest evidence of landscape change and thus is historically a relatively modern landscape dominated by industry and 20th century development. And yet from an archaeological perspective it is a landscape rich in prehistoric remains, with the Thames gravel preserving flints and occupation evidence of some of the earliest human occupation in the county (Ellaby, 1987).

The development of the Historic Landscape Characterisation Project

A part of the Surrey project was to explore proposals for using the database especially as a tool in the conservation and management of Surrey's landscape. This included looking at ways of disseminating the information, both through the planning and development control process and also to the wider audience. As a means of furthering the project, a technical seminar was held shortly after the completion of the final report. Professionals and members of the public with an interest in the history and archaeology of Surrey were invited to a presentation of the Characterisation where the Historic Landscape Character Map was displayed. There then followed a series of discussions whereby people were grouped according to their interests. For example planners, local researchers, and members from non-governmental organizations were asked specific questions about how they would like to access the database, for example what they would use it for and whether they could contribute to any up-dating programme. The

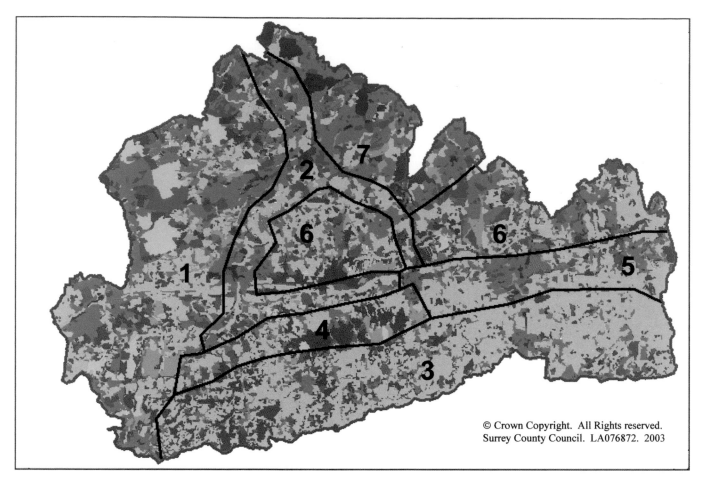

Fig 9.4   Map of the Historic Landscape Character Areas of Surrey

1 Dispersed lowland heathland-edge settlement
2 Nucleated and river-orientated settlement
3 Dispersed lowland woodland settlements
4 Dispersed upland heathland-edge settlement

5 Ancient scarp-foot settlement
6 Dispersed upland settlement
7 Ancient nucleated settlements

results of the seminar were collated and used in the preparation of a draft strategy for the future development of the Characterisation Project (Bannister 2001).

Two issues arose from this seminar. First the desire by development control officers to have a value placed on the HLsTs. Secondly, the need for the database not only to be accessible through the internet but also in more conventional forms, especially as paper maps. It also became apparent that some people had difficulties grasping the concept of historic landscape character being based on visual attributes, with little or no reference to below-ground archaeological features or land use activities which survive only in documentary evidence.

The first stage in the dissemination of the Characterisation Project is the production of a leaflet by Surrey County Council in collaboration with the Surrey Hills AONB, to be widely distributed throughout the county. This leaflet explains historic landscape character, the character map, and ways of accessing it, as well as ways of getting involved with aspects of either management or research into local landscapes. In addition a web

page and interactive CD are being produced of the database for dissemination to the public. Meanwhile this is available for consultation at County Hall. A steering group has been set up to take the project forward by looking at various options.

A second piece of work arising from the characterization has been the identification of future candidate Areas of Special Historic Landscape Value (Bannister 2002). Over 40 new candidate areas have been listed which reflect Surrey's varied industrial and agricultural past, together with smaller designed landscapes. Emphasis has also been placed on field patterns, for example areas of north–south co-axial systems which tend to lie on the northern edge of the Weald and also in the Tillingbourne valley and the Holmesdale. This list has been presented to the Historic Countryside Group of Surrey's Countryside Strategy for consideration.

Research directions arising from the Characterisation Project

The Historic Landscape Characterisation Project now provides a base-line from which more detailed landscape research projects can be taken forward.

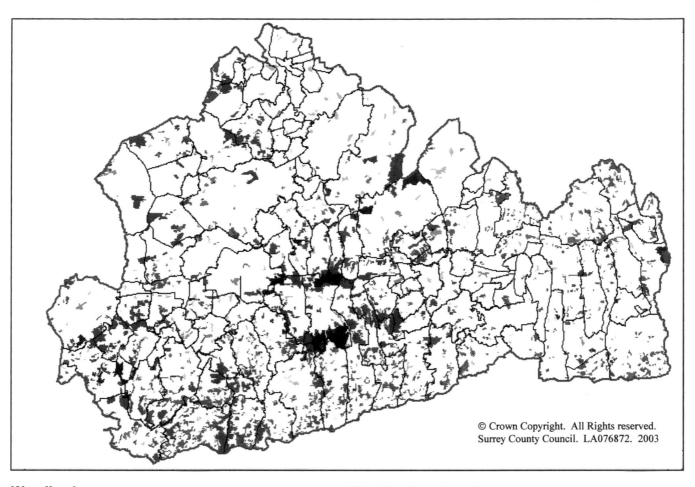

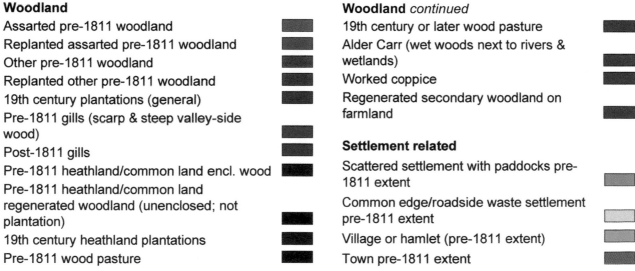

Woodland

Assarted pre-1811 woodland

Replanted assarted pre-1811 woodland

Other pre-1811 woodland

Replanted other pre-1811 woodland

19th century plantations (general)

Pre-1811 gills (scarp & steep valley-side wood)

Post-1811 gills

Pre-1811 heathland/common land encl. wood

Pre-1811 heathland/common land regenerated woodland (unenclosed; not plantation)

19th century heathland plantations

Pre-1811 wood pasture

Woodland *continued*

19th century or later wood pasture

Alder Carr (wet woods next to rivers & wetlands)

Worked coppice

Regenerated secondary woodland on farmland

Settlement related

Scattered settlement with paddocks pre-1811 extent

Common edge/roadside waste settlement pre-1811 extent

Village or hamlet (pre-1811 extent)

Town pre-1811 extent

Fig 9.5   The distribution of woodland in Surrey

There are also opportunities to integrate this project with research work being undertaken in the county, for example on the history of manorial settlements, especially villages (see Turner in this volume).

Further research is needed to integrate the historic character map with information from the tithe maps such as place and field names and the development of ecclesiastical parish boundaries.

The Characterisation Project highlighted areas where further academic research is needed in understanding how Surrey's landscape has evolved. Key to this is the movement of stock from the north to the south of the county during seasonal tranhumance that took place in the early medieval period and may even have origins in prehistoric times. This north–south movement has left highly visible features in the landscape, in the form of lanes, paths, administrative boundaries, and possibly co-axial field patterns. Associated with this movement is the very frequent occurrence of small commons and greens strung out along apparent droving routes. A greater understanding of the origins and development of these elements in the wider development of parishes and settlements is needed.

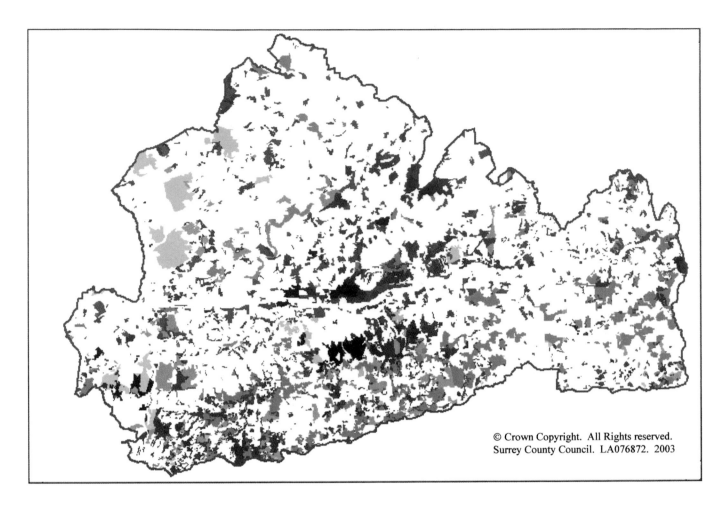

© Crown Copyright. All Rights reserved.
Surrey County Council. LA076872. 2003

Field patterns
Small irregular assarts intermixed with woodland
Medium irreg. assarts & copses with wavy bdys.
Large irreg. assarts with wavy or mixed bdys.

Commons
Common heathland
Common downland
Other commons and greens
Wooded over commons

Woodland
Assarted pre-1811 woodland
Replanted assarted pre-1811 woodland
Other pre-1811 woodland
Replanted other pre-1811 woodland
19th century plantations (general)
Pre-1811 gills (scarp & steep valley-side wood)
Post-1811 gills
Pre-1811 heathland/common land encl. wood
Pre-1811 heathland/common land regenerated woodland
(unenclosed; not plantation)
19th century heathland plantations
Pre-1811 wood pasture

Heathland
Unenclosed heathland and scrub

Enclosed heathland and scrub
Purlieus and other enclosed heathland pastures

Downland
Chalk grassland
Chalk grassland and scrub

Valley floor and water management
Water meadows or common meadows
Pre-1811 fishponds, hatchery complexes, 'natural'
ponds and lakes

Settlement related
Village or hamlet (pre-1811 extent)
Town pre-1811 extent

Parkland and designed landscape
Pre-1811 parkland
19th century and later parkland and large
Deer parks

Military and defence
Prehistoric (hillforts & other defensive encl)
Medieval (mottes and baileys; ring works)

Fig 9.6 Time-depth of Surrey's landscape – distribution of pre-1811 historic character sub-types

Further research into the origins of field patterns and systems, together with the boundaries that define them, is considered fairly urgent in the light of changes to the management of hedges and shaws resulting from the cessation of cutting or coppicing. Field boundaries are one of the most prominent features identifying landscape character. Understanding the origins of field boundaries and the antiquity of field systems will help in directing resources to those which are most vulnerable.

Conclusions

In conclusion, the Surrey Historic Landscape Characterisation Project marks a major development in the understanding of the Surrey landscape. It provides a systematic broad-brush statement of the historic character of the county and areas of local distinctiveness. The database, while of interest in its own right, also provides the springboard for future research, especially at the local level.

APPENDIX
Summary list of historic landscape character types

Code	Type
1	**Field pattern/systems**
101	Small irregular assarts intermixed with woodland
102	Medium irregular assarts and copses with wavy boundaries
103	Large irregular assarts with wavy or mixed boundaries
104	Regular assarts with straight boundaries
105	Enclosed strips and furlongs
106	Medium to large regular fields with wavy boundaries (late medieval–17th/18th century enclosure)
107	Small irregular rectilinear fields with straight boundaries
108	Small rectilinear fields with wavy boundaries
109	Regular ladder fields (long wavy boundaries sub-divided by straight cross divisions
110	Small regular fields with straight boundaries (parliamentary enclosure type)
111	Medium regular fields with straight boundaries (parliamentary enclosure type)
112	Large regular fields with straight boundaries (parliamentary enclosure type)
113	Variable size, semi-regular fields with straight boundaries (parliamentary enclosure type)
114	'Prairie' fields (large enclosures with extensive boundary loss)
115	Fields bounded by roads, tracks and paths
116	Previously hops and orchards
117	Parkland and conversion to arable
118	Fields, formerly ponds now dried up
2	**Commons**
201	Common heathland
202	Common downland
203	Other commons and greens
204	Wooded-over commons
3	**Horticulture**
301	Orchards
302	Nurseries with glasshouses
303	Nurseries without glasshouses
4	**Woodland**
401	Assarted pre-1811 woodland
402	Replanted assarted pre-1811 woodland
403	Other pre-1811 woodland
404	Replanted other pre-1811 woodland
405	19th century plantations (general)
406	Pre-1811 gills (scarp and steep valley sided woodland)
407	Post-1811 gills
408	Pre-1811 heathland/common land enclosed woodland
409	Pre-1811 heathland/common land regenerated woodland (unenclosed not plantation)

Code	Type
410	19th century or later wood pasture
411	Pre-1811 wood pasture
412	19th century or later wood pasture
413	Alder carr
414	Worked coppice
415	Regenerated secondary woodland on farmland – not plantations
5	**Heathland**
501	Unenclosed heathland and scrub
502	Enclosed heathland and scrub
503	Purlieus and other enclosed heathland pasture (not in Surrey)
6	**Downland**
601	Chalk grassland
602	Chalk grassland and scrub
7	**Valley floor and water management**
701	Miscellaneous valley floor fields and pastures
702	Valley floor woodlands
703	Marsh and rough grazing
704	Water meadows or common meadows
705	Unimproved hay meadows or pasture/common meadows
706	Watercress beds
707	Pre-1811 fishponds, natural ponds and lakes
708	Post-1811 fishponds, natural ponds and lakes
709	Water mills, mill ponds, hammer ponds and leats
8	**Settlement related**
801	Scattered settlement with paddocks (pre-1811 extent)
802	Scattered settlement with paddocks (post-1811 and pre-1940)
803	Common edge/roadside waste settlement (pre-1811 extent)
804	Common edge/roadside waste settlement (post-1811 and pre-1940 extent)
805	Post-1811 and pre-1940 small scale settlement
806	Village or hamlet (pre-1811 extent)
807	Town (pre-1811 extent)
808	Caravan sites
809	Large cemeteries (ie not adjacent to churches)
810	Hospital complexes (ie not within settlements)
811	Regular settlement with paddocks (post-1940 extent)
812	Common edge/roadside waste (post-1940 extent)
813	Large-scale estates (post-1811 and pre-1940 extent)
814	Medium estates (post-1811 and pre-1940 extent)
815	Luxury estates (post-1940 extent)
816	Small to medium estates (post-1940 extent)

Code	Type
9	**Parkland and designed landscapes**
901	Pre-1822 parkland
902	19th century and later parkland plus larger designed gardens
902	Deer parks
903	Arboreta
904	Smaller designed gardens

Code	Type
10	**Recreation**
101	Racecourses
102	Motor racing tracks and vehicle testing areas
103	Golf courses – heathland origin
104	Golf courses – parkland origin
105	Golf courses – downland origin
1006	Golf courses – farmland origin
1007	Major sports centres and complexes
1008	Marinas
1009	Studs and equestrian centres

Code	Type
11	**Extractive industry**
1101	Active and disused chalk quarries
1102	Active and disused gravel workings
1103	Active and disused clay pits
1104	Active and disused sandpits

Code	Type
12	**Other industry**
1201	Industrial complexes and factories
1202	Modern large scale industry
1203	Reservoirs and water pumping
1204	Sewage and water treatment

Code	Type
13	**Communication facilities**
1301	Railway stations and sidings
1302	Airfields
1303	Motorway service areas
1304	Motorway junctions

Code	Type
14	**Military and defence**
1401	Prehistoric hillforts and other defensive enclosures
1402	Medieval fortifications (motte and baileys, ringworks)
1403	19th century forts
1404	20th century military

ACKNOWLEDGEMENTS

The author would like to thank Dr David Bird (Surrey County Council) and Graham Fairclough (English Heritage) for their assistance and guidance during the Surrey Historic Landscape Characterisation Project and also Dr Bird for his comments on this paper.

Considerable appreciation is extended to Patrick Wills for his patience and forebearance in teaching the author the intricacies of 'WINGS' GIS and for his continued support with requests for further analyses of the Characterisation Map.

BIBLIOGRAPHY

Abbreviations: EH: English Heritage; SCC: Surrey County Council

Aldred, O, 2002   *Historic landscape characterisation method review: taking stock of the method*, EH

Aston, M, 1985   *Interpreting the landscape*

Bannister, N R, 2001   *Surrey Historic Landscape Characterisation Project: strategy for implementing the map and database*, for SCC

——, 2002   *Areas of Special Historic Landscape Value: review of the ASHLV designation process*, Surrey Historic Countryside Group of Surrey Countryside Strategy & SyAS

Bannister, N R, & Wills, P M, 2001   Surrey Historic Landscape Characterisation, vols 1 & 2, SCC, EH & the Countryside Agency

Bramhill, P, & Munby, J, 2001   *Kent historic landscape characterisation report*, Oxford Archaeol Unit for Kent County Council & EH

DoE: Department of Environment, 1990   *Our common inheritance*, White Paper HMSO

Ellaby, R, 1987   The Upper Palaeolithic and Mesolithic in Surrey, in *The archaeology of Surrey to 1540* (eds J Bird & D G Bird), SyAS, 53–69

Fairclough, G, Lambrick, G, & McNab, A, 1999   *Yesterday's world, tomorrow's landscape*, EH Landscape Project 1992–94

Fairclough, G, Lambrick, G, & Hopkins, D, 2002   Historic landscape characterisation in England and a Hampshire case study, in *Europe's cultural landscape: archaeologists and the management of change* (eds G Fairclough & S Rippon), EH & Council of Europe

Herring, P, 1998   *Cornwall's historic Landscape – presenting a method of historic landscape character assessment*, Cornwall Archaeological Unit & EH, Cornwall County Council

Hoskins, W G, 1955   *The making of the English landscape*

Lambrick, G, & Bramhill, P, 2000   *Hampshire historic landscape characterisation report*, 2 vols, Oxford Archaeological Unit for Hampshire County Council & EH

Rackham, O, 1976   *Trees and woodlands in the British landscape*

——, 1986   *The history of the countryside*

SCC, 1997   *The future of Surrey's landscape and woodlands*

Surrey Hills JAC, 2000   *Surrey Hills AONB management strategy*

Taylor, C C, 1975   *Fields in the English landscape*

——, 1979   *Roads and tracks of Britain*

Turner, D, 2004   Manors and other settlements, in *Aspects of archaeology and history in Surrey: towards a research framework for the county* (eds J Cotton, G Crocker & A Graham, SyAS, 133–46

Nicola R Bannister, PhD, AIFA, Consultant Landscape Archaeologist, Ashenden Farm, Bell Lane, Biddenden, Ashford, Kent TN27 8LD

10

Manors and other settlements

DENNIS TURNER

The argument that village creation can frequently be tied to lordship is rehearsed and the point made that the discoveries of archaeologists can illuminate current views of village creation and development. A case has previously been made for a wave of reorganization and plantation in Surrey in the 12th and 13th centuries, accompanied by a growth of regulated open-field agriculture. This move can be linked to the growing power of feudal landlords. The consequent network of rural manors comprised seigneurial estates with a wide range of size, wealth and status but several manorial lords played a leading part in village creation. However, not all estates became manors in the strictest sense and not every manorial lord encouraged village formation. Not all the nucleated villages visible in Surrey's landscape by the 19th century appear to have originated in this way. Since manors varied greatly in size and might be held by persons of vastly differing status and show great tenurial variation, it is not surprising that manor houses also varied greatly in size and function but their study is essential if we are to understand the variations between the manors themselves. Although few buildings in the Surrey countryside survive from the plantation period, a study of later medieval buildings can sometimes shed light on village morphology and the process of village creation. It can also reveal a considerable disparity between such elements as the size and wealth of an estate on the one hand and the social use to which its capital messuage was being put on the other. Topographical, architectural and archaeological evidence can illuminate earlier movements and suggest questions for a research agenda.

Introduction

By the time written records appear in any quantity, there are no firmly fixed relationships between farm, hamlet, village, tithing, parish, manor and even hundred: many of these may be territorially identical to one or more of the others. Even when they appear, the written records never give the complete picture. The explanation of rural development has therefore to be sought not only in the limited documentary record but also in all other available sources, such as the landscape itself, the buildings it contains and archaeological sites, all of which bear the unconscious record of the past.

The origin and development of Surrey's villages are currently being explored through the Surrey Archaeological Society's Village Studies Project and aspects of this were discussed at a conference held by the society in November 2000. At that conference, the chronology of some Surrey village types was discussed and a case made by the writer for a wave of reordering and plantation in the 12th and 13th centuries (Turner 2001). This suggestion was based on morphological and documentary grounds but the dating is supported by archaeological evidence. The present paper attempts to pursue the concept of and motivation for village creation; discusses some of the background to the movement towards settlement nucleation and its continuing development; and proposes topics to be taken into a research agenda for the county. The locations of Surrey villages mentioned in the text are shown in figure 10.1.

The possibility of a wave of nucleation in the 12th and 13th centuries must not be taken to suggest either that all Surrey villages became nucleated at this date or that all nucleated Surrey villages are the result of

deliberate creation or reordering. Substantial pagan cemeteries at, for example, Mitcham and Croydon strongly suggest that a settlement large enough to be thought of as a village may have existed at both of these locations before the conversion to Christianity: at Mitcham there are topographical hints for early Saxon development, and similar suggestions are found elsewhere. Comparisons with neighbouring counties – especially Hampshire – suggest that some medieval villages in Surrey may be the result of migration from failed locations but it will clearly be difficult to locate archaeological traces of 5th or 6th century settlement in such a highly occupied county as Surrey.

By the end of the Middle Ages, a number of nucleated Surrey villages were in existence that show traces neither of deliberate planning nor of reordering (Charlwood is a good example: Shelley 2003), and the date at which they became nucleated cannot be hazarded without much further study.

Lordship and village nucleation

Surviving documentary evidence does not become substantial until the later Middle Ages and is inevitably rarely relevant to the question of village nucleation: the medieval village has itself left us virtually no records. The institutions that did produce records – the manor, the Church, and central government – naturally only reveal the village through the eyes of the landlords, the higher clergy and royal officials. A generation ago, scholars could still find this only a minor problem and some believed that the records of the manor reflected the life of the village (eg Raftis 1965) but, subsequently, there have been few prepared to follow that line: indeed, Professor

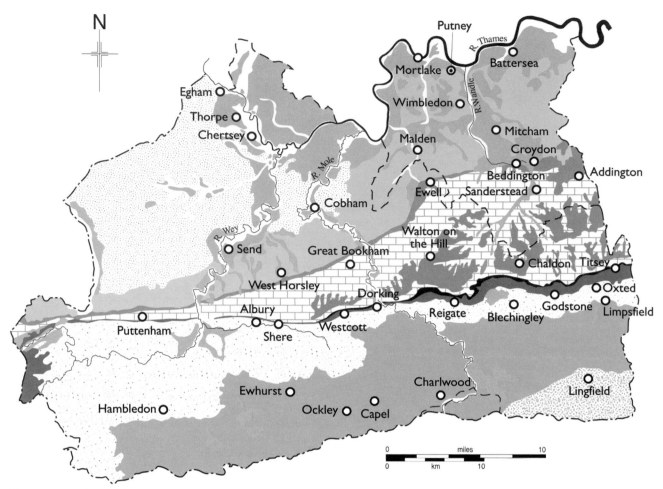

Fig 10.1 Locations of Surrey villages mentioned in the text. For key to geological background see map on page x.

Dyer (1985, 27) called it wishful thinking. The documents have, therefore, to be supplemented by inference and by topographical evidence while the resources of archaeology must be more fully employed.

Although the seeds of much present thinking can actually be seen in century-old writings by Andrews (1892), Maitland (1897) and Vinogradoff (1905), current ideas of village creation owe much to the inspiration of such historical geographers as Peter Sawyer, Della Hook, Chris Dyer, Brian Roberts and Stuart Wrathmell, most of whom sat at the feet of Joan Thirsk.[1] As a result of their work, it is considered today that much village nucleation occurred later than had previously been believed and that it arose as one of several solutions available to meet problems of increasing scarcity. Some of the scholars involved have suggested that the scarcities in question were of arable land and of farm produce in the face of rising population. For a full discussion of possible influences in the East Midlands, the most studied area to date, see Lewis *et al* (1997, esp ch 7).

Population estimates for the Middle Ages are inevitably uncertain and tend to have risen over the years. McKisack (1959, 312–13) estimated England in 1086 was home to between one and a quarter and one and a half million people (cf Poole 1955, 36) and that numbers rose to between two and a half and four

millions just before the plague. It seems generally agreed today among historical demographers that these figures are on the low side: there may have been closer to two million people in England at Domesday and between four and seven million on the eve of the Black Death. Initially this growth created prosperity. Indeed, the most important characteristic of the English economy during the 12th and early 13th centuries was its growth. It has been argued, for example, that the increasing agricultural surpluses and taxes, as well as better central organization by the crown, indirectly financed the building of new stone castles (Hughes 1989, 29). All over southern Britain, the growing wealth also encouraged the creation of new towns (Beresford 1967).

On this basis, we can doubt whether the drive by the agricultural sector to feed increasing population would have caused significant land hunger until some time in the 13th century. The drive to nucleation seems to have begun well before this date and it would seem, therefore, that the need to solve problems of land hunger may not have featured as the prime motivation. A stronger impulse may have been the desire or need to improve returns.

Many recent historians have been concerned to 'strip away the layers of myth and sentiment that have formed around the pre-industrial village' (Dyer 1985, 27) but Dyer warned that the revisionism might have gone too far and was particularly critical of Campbell (1981) who had seen the landlord rather than the village community as the motive force behind the creation of field systems (cf Dyer 1988). Nevertheless, much writing since then (including some by Dyer himself) seems to point to village nucleation and the creation of organized field systems as two sides of the same coin and to imply, if not actually demand, the active role of the lord in many, possibly in most, cases. Where a degree of regularity is involved (Turner 2001, *passim*), the operation of the land surveyor and the guiding hand of the lord are likely to be present. By the end of the period of nucleation, the nascent profession of land management was beginning to acquire its textbooks (Oschinsky 1971).

Nucleation is related to the integration of land use and settlement and it is no coincidence that the development of regular forms of open field systems often accompanied the creation of a nucleated village: this conjunction is at least inferentially linked to lordship and power. Evidence from central England, where the question has been more intensively studied than elsewhere, has provided dates ranging from the 9th to the 12th century. Recent work in the East Midlands has shown the 10th and 11th centuries to be the most likely period for village formation and agrarian reorganization in that part of the country (Saunders 1990; Lewis *et al* 1997). Similar conclusions have been provided for Somerset by the well-known Shapwick study (Somerset VBRG 1996; Aston & Gerrard 1999).

Thus the current wisdom (eg Roberts & Wrathmell 1998, 2000) has it that, whatever the causes, in the Central Belt – a broad band of 'champion' countryside running roughly from Dorset and Somerset to County Durham – the classic medieval landscape of nucleated villages and well-regulated open fields was not established until several centuries after the first waves of pagan English settlement – waves that were once thought to have brought the nucleated village and regulated fields into England. The view is further widely held today that this landscape was produced as part of a series of manorial changes which had a wide date range and which obliterated earlier landscapes. It is argued that the regular open fields and nucleated villages that dominated Midland England during the Middle Ages were formed at different times in different places between about AD 800 and 1150.

Some holders of this view consider that the landscape of the Central Belt is quite distinct from woodland countryside where irregular open fields, or even enclosed landscapes, were associated with dispersed settlement. This latter combination – termed by Oliver Rackham (1986), developing an idea offered a century ago by Maitland (1897, essay 3, part 1), as 'ancient countryside' – lasted well into the Middle Ages and sometimes into modern times. Much of Surrey falls into this classification. It is believed that, while the layout of regular open fields and the imposition of settlement nucleation varied in time from place to place, it usually occurred for similar reasons and in a similar way. Where nucleation is itself irregular or organic and not accompanied by anything resembling regular open fields – as at Charlwood in the Weald – factors other than lordship may have been at work and the tenantry may have chosen to nucleate for reasons we cannot hope to understand.

The feudal construction of space

The best archaeological evidence for the reordering of the landscape into nucleated villages and systematized open fields has come from Raunds in Northamptonshire (Cadman 1983; Cadman & Foard 1984; Foard & Pearson 1985; Dix 1987; Saunders 1990; final report in prep). Saunders (1990, 187ff) has used the evidence from Raunds to explore the feudal construction of space at the level of lord/peasant relations in the 9th and 10th centuries and concluded that it emphasized the importance of lordship. The study of lordship is not currently fashionable in local history but is, perhaps, overdue for revival. The usually ill-documented and frequently confusing and irrational-seeming problems of rural lordship in relation to the peasantry are rarely given the attention they deserve (cf Turner 2003).

The feudal mode of production had its material basis in agrarian societies in which the overwhelming majority of the population were engaged in the cultivation of the land, primarily for subsistence but also in order to produce a surplus. This surplus provided rent – service, produce or cash rent – rent that was essential for the system to function. Critically, it is the extraction of this surplus by direct and individual methods that distinguishes feudalism from other agrarian-based models of production (Hindess & Hirst 1975, 183–93).

The feudal framework was thus tied to the land, to space. The historical geographer Robert Dodgshon (1987, 186) encapsulated the argument when he wrote that 'under feudalism, spatial order became socially regulated. Far from being an unintended side effect, this structuring of relations in space [is] part of the very essence of feudalism.'

Once the feudal lord obtained judicial rights to collect the food-rents that may previously have been rendered to the king (Jolliffe 1954, ch 1 etc), his economic power over the peasants became important. The lord was able to invest his resources into rearranging the relationship between himself and his peasantry in his favour (Sawyer 1979). He was able to improve productivity and increase rent by encouraging regulated open-field agriculture based on nucleated villages and, according to the currently favoured model, many lords chose to do so.

Dodgshon again (1987, 192), seemingly with a backward glance at a long-lost 'era of the folk' (Jolliffe 1954, ch. 1):

> For the peasantry, feudal space *became* [my emphasis] bounded space. It was no longer a world of boundless or unlimited opportunities to be colonized when the need arose. For each and all, it was a world delimited by the land assessment imposed on the settlement. In effect, the landscape became divided into a chequerboard on which occupation was legitimised in some spaces but not others.

The evidence available for Surrey field systems is ambiguous (Gray 1915, 356–69; Bailey & Galbraith 1973). Open-field systems in the county seem rather poorly organized and not confined to manors with strong control. Even villages that provide strong suggestions of planned reordering in their morphology do not have strong evidence of highly regulated or regular fields, eg Great Bookham (Parton 1967; Currie 2000, 59–61), Ewell[2] (Bailey & Galbraith 1973, 77–9) and Putney (*ibid* 80–3). A number of villages show clear evidence of reordering or migration consequent on emparkment but, generally, this is post-medieval – for example Titsey and Albury – and not relevant to the creation of villages in medieval times. Earlier emparkment creations – Beddington, West Horsley – are inevitably only dimly visible, if at all, in the documents but may be susceptible to topographical analysis or careful and systematic archaeological research.

The formation of villages

We may expect to find that many if not most lordly village formations were too early to be within the reach of documentary research. The lordly formations of market towns, to which reference has already been made, are well known and attested (Beresford 1967) and seem to be even more strongly related to the lord's desire to maximize income. Some of the earliest of these are at the very limits of documentary inference – Reigate and Blechingley are familiar Surrey examples; the slender documentation for the former has, however, received strong archaeological support (Williams 1983; in prep). Some other Surrey settlements (eg Dorking) included in the society's *Historic towns* volume (O'Connell 1977) seem only doubtfully to have justified the appellation in medieval times and their origins still await adequate study. In the elucidation of the formation of both towns and villages, topographical implications have to be exploited to the full and the assistance of archaeology invoked wherever possible.

One group of Surrey villages that is undoubtedly linked by a strong common lordship and appears to show some of the consequences, are those found on the Chertsey Abbey estates. Excavations have hinted that Chertsey itself became established as a small town in the early 12th century (Poulton 1998b) and John Blair (1991, 58) has pointed out that many villages on the abbey lands from Egham to Great Bookham have sufficient regularity in their plot layouts to imply an act of deliberate planning of the kind usually associated with plantation or reordering. Blair favoured a 14th century date for this process and saw the hand of the energetic and reforming Abbot Rutherwyke at work. Archaeological work in Egham has, however, suggested that the settlement there (two rows of house plots with back lanes) was laid out in the 12th century (Ford 1998; Jackson *et al* 1999, 230) and the present author has argued that the reordering of Chertsey Abbey villages as a whole may be more reasonably dated to the 12th or 13th century than the 14th (Turner 2001, 12).

Recent reappraisal of the documentary and topographical evidence at Cobham, another Chertsey holding, suggests that the core of the settlement at Church Cobham was laid out as a single row in the mid-12th century (Taylor & Turner 2003). The church was built or rebuilt at the same date. The house plots were relatively short: it is possible that the village had a specialist function connected with the river (fig 10.2). The abbot received an arguably contemporary grant of a market at Cobham during the reign of Stephen: it seems likely that this market was at Street Cobham where a characteristic triangular space exists at the heart of the settlement, but there is no suggestion there of any formal house-plot development. The market does not feature in later records and may have been short lived.

Midway between the apparently planned Chertsey Abbey nucleations of Egham and Chertsey itself lies the small village of Thorpe. Recent research by Jill Williams and the Egham-by-Runnymede History Society as part of the Village Studies Project has shown little trace of medieval nucleation at Thorpe: the pattern there appears to have been a polyfocal one of five or more small hamlets (Williams 2002).

The archbishop of Canterbury's village of Mortlake seems in late medieval times to have been similar in topography and layout to Church Cobham: a single-row settlement backed on to the Thames and faced its open fields. A series of excavations here in advance of redevelopment has shown that the medieval archaeology has been greatly truncated by 17th century and later industrial developments and the regularity or otherwise of plot layouts has been obscured. However, clear evidence of early Saxon occupation has been exposed (Gostick *et al* 1997, 53; Gostick & Maloney 1998, 95; Jackson *et al* 1999, 245–6; Howe *et al* 2001, 356; 2002, 275; Darton forthcoming).

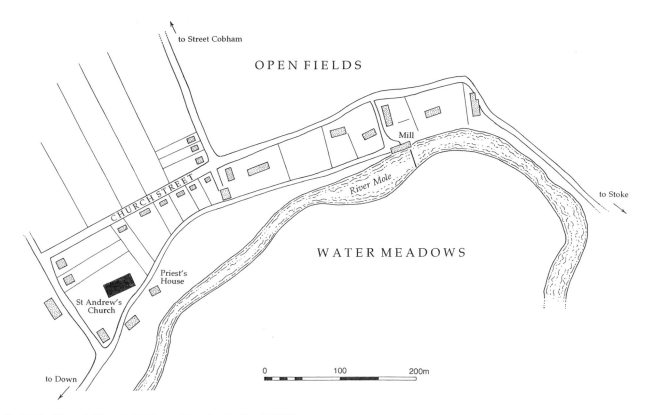

Fig 10.2 Plan of Church Cobham. Drawing by David Williams

One Surrey village whose formation was on the very cusp of documentary inference is that of Shere, recently studied by the Shere, Gomshall and Peaslake Local History Society (Shere 2001; Turner 2001, 11). Few of the buildings in the core of Shere can be dated earlier than the second half of the 15th century and the available documents identify few properties as early as this. Archaeological sampling has produced a surprising lack of medieval pottery sherds – or even of early post-medieval sherds (Shere 2001, vii). But there are strong indications that the buildings and the archaeological samples do not give the full picture.

The manor of Shere Vachery received a market grant in 1309 and this can probably be equated with a market-place immediately west of the much older church. There is the well-known account of early 14th century William the carpenter and his saintly daughter. Personal names that occur in the late 14th century poll tax returns are found attached to property in the village centuries later (Noyes 2001). Without this extra evidence, it might be thought that Shere did not develop into a village before the 15th century but, with it, there can be confidence that there was a village here before the oldest surviving house. Further analysis suggested an early 14th century plantation but with little, if any, contemporary planning.

As can be seen from Shere, not every powerful manorial lord established a village at the earliest possible moment. And not every powerful manorial lord established a village with open fields organized on the Midland pattern.

Room for research

It has already been noted that the best archaeological evidence for the reorganization of the landscape into nucleated villages and systematized open fields has come from Raunds in Northamptonshire. Earlier work at Catholme, Staffordshire, (Losco-Bradley & Wheeler 1984) and earlier still at Maxey, Northamptonshire, (Addeyman 1964) had uncovered evidence for dispersed and fluid settlements which Taylor (1983, 107–24) interpreted as being left behind by the introduction of more stable nucleated villages associated with the ordering of the landscape for open-field farming. The work at Raunds seemed to provide solid confirmation of Taylor's hypothesis.

The Medieval Settlement Research Group has set up the Whittlewood project to follow up the results from Raunds (Dyer 1999; 2001; Page & Jones 2001). Whittlewood is on the edge of Northamptonshire and it has been critically pointed out (Oosthuizen & James 1999, 17–18) that most of the detailed fieldwork on which the current model is based has already been carried out in Northamptonshire (Hall 1995) and that fieldwork further away might show that the model is not sustainable over a wider area. However, Raunds is only a firm sample of one and the other Northamptonshire evidence is somewhat circumstantial and it makes statistical sense to seek a second sample from the same broad area before branching out. At the time of writing (March 2003) the five-year Whittlewood project is just over halfway through and results are promising.

A separate research programme has been initiated by Oosthuizen and James covering four parishes in south-west Cambridgeshire in an attempt to clarify some of the issues. Even though south-west Cambridgeshire is hardly outside the Central Belt, the work immediately challenged the proposition that a clear distinction can be made between open field and woodland landscape (Oosthuizen & James 1999; Oosthuizen & Hesse 2001). This is a finding that most students of the problem in Surrey will certainly find comfortable, possibly even comforting.

It is clear that research is needed further away from the Central Belt if the current paradigm is to be properly tested. Surrey could be an admirable location for such research. The county has a varied landscape and a curious mixture of medieval agricultural traditions that has only been partially studied (eg Gray 1915, 356–69; Parton 1967; Bailey & Galbraith 1973). Both nucleated and dispersed settlements developed within relatively short distances of each other. However, much of the archaeological and topographical evidence retained in what is left of the historic villages and countryside of Surrey is under a severe threat of destruction and the time left for research must be limited.

The research might best be approached via a pilot project across three or four contiguous parishes, as is being done at Whittlewood. The main aims and objectives would be, first, to assess the surviving archaeological and historical resources in order to identify areas of particular interest or potential for more intensive investigation and, secondly, to reconstruct the landscape of the project area during the later Middle Ages, as a necessary precursor to the more difficult task of reconstructing the landscape of the earlier medieval and Roman periods.

Early cartographic evidence would be especially useful and the selection of areas within the county might be influenced by the availability of this. Information from the early maps would need to be transferred to a Geographical Information System (GIS) dedicated to (or available for) the project. Archaeological data, obtained partly from existing sources (such as the county Sites and Monuments Record (SMR) and aerial photographs) and partly from the project's own fieldwork, would be added to the GIS. In addition, paper archives of previous archaeological research would need to be transcribed into the GIS. Following the county council's Historic Landscape Characterisation Project (Bannister & Wills 2001; Bannister in this volume) an appropriate GIS base is in place for the administrative county.

The role of buildings studies
Some may question whether the study of buildings has much to say about the origin of the villages in

which they stand: there will always be an expectation that the village is older than the oldest surviving building other than the church and, occasionally, the manor house. However, such studies are currently being given greater precision by the application of dendrochronology and they can greatly refine our understanding of the morphology of the village. As a result, morphological analysis supported by buildings studies can contribute substantially to our investigation of village origins (Shere 2001; Turner 2001; Williams 2002; Abdy in prep).

The study of village buildings can illuminate the physical, social and institutional growth of a village – and set new problems. Internal survey has shown that there are some buildings that were more than just domestic in their initial state, although in few cases is this obvious from their external appearance. In Blechingley, no 1 The Cobbles is a modest medieval building facing the market place and studies have shown this to have been originally not a house but an institutional building of some kind (Gray 1991, 14; 2002, 77). Blechingley had borough status and a possibly institutional building there presents no surprise. But Brook House at Oxted, a seemingly similar structure, is not in a market-place and not even quite in the heart of the village; it is thus harder to explain (Gray 2002, 83; Hughes in this volume). Shere has three buildings, not all of them medieval and none of them in the market-place, which may present similar problems. The attrition rate of similar buildings within village envelopes may have been much higher than that of domestic buildings and the rarity of current survivals may be misleading. The distance from the church of all the examples mentioned would seem to militate against their being 'church houses' (cf Chatwin 1996, 94–7; Wild 2001).

The reverse of this particular coin may be the apparent under-representation of evidence within our surviving medieval village buildings for specialist activities and trades found in the documentary record. Inns, alehouses, tanneries, cloth-working, butchery, and a host of other trades occur frequently in documents but are rarely identified in the surviving medieval buildings (Hughes in this volume). This is clearly an area requiring more research.

Village buildings of possibly administrative function can be paralleled at seigneurial centres, both within and outside villages. The one-time aisled court house or steward's residence at Limpsfield, shown in figure 10.3, is one of the oldest surviving secular structures in the county (Mason 1966; 1969, ch 9; Gray 2002, 81) but has nothing about it to indicate its more than domestic role. There is a late medieval, first-floor courtroom annexed to Send Court farmhouse (Gray 2002, 47) in the church-manor farm hamlet. These buildings clearly had a more than domestic role within their community but less easily understood are houses like White Hart House in Ewhurst (not really a village until the late 19th century). This timber-framed, medieval building has no known seigneurial role but appears of higher status than other contemporary houses in the vicinity. The upper chamber in one of the two cross wings is itself of higher status than the rest of the building and was apparently provided with a separate entry (Hughes & Higgins 2001; Gray 2002, 90). Its original function remains problematic.

The study of medieval seigneurial and similar buildings in relation to their estates illuminates questions of lordship but equally provides problems (cf Meirion-Jones & Jones 1993; Meirion-Jones *et al* 2002). In the Surrey context, there are a number of particularly puzzling manor houses for which Walton on the Hill and Chaldon can stand as exemplars.

The stone-built manor house at Walton, rare for Surrey, survives in part within the largely late 19th century Walton Manor. The writers of the *VCH Surrey* confidently dated the medieval structure to *c* 1340 but an examination of the published manorial history shows this to be a time of tenancy by a minor under-wardship. This might seem a most unpropitious circumstance for the construction of a major building but the wardship was in the hands of the earl of Surrey. On the other hand, either the dating or the published manorial history could be mistaken.

Timber-framed Chaldon Court (fig 10.4) shows a considerable disparity between such elements as the modest size and wealth of the estate on the one hand and the social uses for which its capital messuage appears to have been designed on the other. Of Chaldon Court, the late Peter Gray wrote (2002, 9):

Chaldon Court is still quite a large house but in fact represents a three-bay solar block with two further face wings: of the presumed original hall and service end nothing now remains. A solar complex of this size must relate to a house of considerable importance. Nothing similar is known elsewhere in the county.

Gray ascribed Chaldon Court to *c* 1330 but other specialists have suggested a slightly later date in the same century (Rod Wild, pers comm). The estate to which it was attached was a small one and lacked a village to provide support (Turner in prep). The family to which it belonged were not members of the nobility and are not known to have held a position at court but they were landowners in Sussex. Their ancestor had come to England with the Conqueror (presumably from Couvert, near Bayeux) and held four hides and one virgate (of Bramber and Arundel respectively) in Sullington by 1086. By the early 13th century, Bartholemew de Covert was known as 'of Chaldon'. Later in the century, the major part of the family's Sullington sub-infeudation was rated at two knights' fees while land held at Broadbridge Heath large enough to contain a park appears to have been part of this estate. Various other interests in land are visible in the records but cannot be evaluated (Annabelle Hughes, pers comm).

Fig 10.3   Old Court Cottage, Limpsfield. Drawing by J Raymer

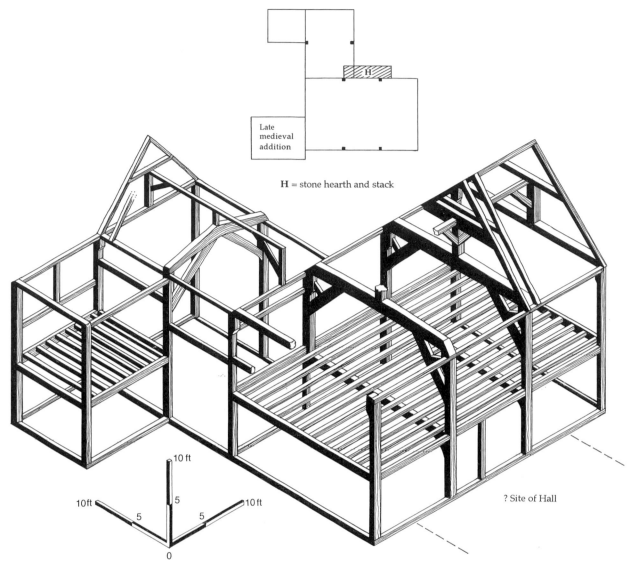

H = stone hearth and stack

Fig 10.4   Reconstruction of Chaldon Court. Drawing by David Williams (after Peter Gray)

Studies of standing seigneurial buildings can illuminate earlier movements and suggest questions for a local research agenda. The local research agenda, in turn, will undoubtedly have to pay attention to early peasant buildings and this will be an increasingly pure archaeological matter.

The role of archaeology

Archaeology is too often seen as concerned only with buried evidence. It should, of course, just as frequently be seen as concerned with the surface and with the upstanding. Building studies, particularly vernacular building studies, more often than not employ principles (eg typology and sequence) and thought processes that are central to an archaeological approach. Landscape archaeology is an increasingly appreciated discipline (eg Lewis *et al* 1997; Aston & Gerrard 1999; Taylor 2002). The boundaries are blurred and incapable of definition.

Surviving structures at the seigneurial centre, for example, can be studied archaeologically by the building specialists while the 'dirt' archaeologist can search for traces of the lost elements in the complex

and for evidence of predecessors. Former manorial sites without standing buildings or ruins are very much the preserve of the 'dirt' archaeologist who can sometimes achieve spectacular results as, for example, at Hextalls, Blechingley (fig 10.5; Poulton 1998c) and the landscape archaeologist can provide additional context.

Much attention, both nationally and locally, has been devoted to seigneurial and similar settlements but there are still unanswered questions. There are many problems, for example, concerning the status and nature of individual moated sites and about the class as a whole (Aberg 1978; Lewis *et al* 1997, 133–40). There is an uncounted number of half-recognized and possibly manorial earthworks such as Castle Bank at Westcott (Rapson 2002; 2003) and Castle Hill south of Godstone (*VCH*, **4**, 284, 380; O'Connell & Poulton 1983), to name only two of the more obvious – these earthworks remain largely unstudied and are often dubiously classified. There are also numerous seigneurial or similar sites and countless peasant sites to which we cannot give grid references. Fieldwork is capable of revealing hitherto

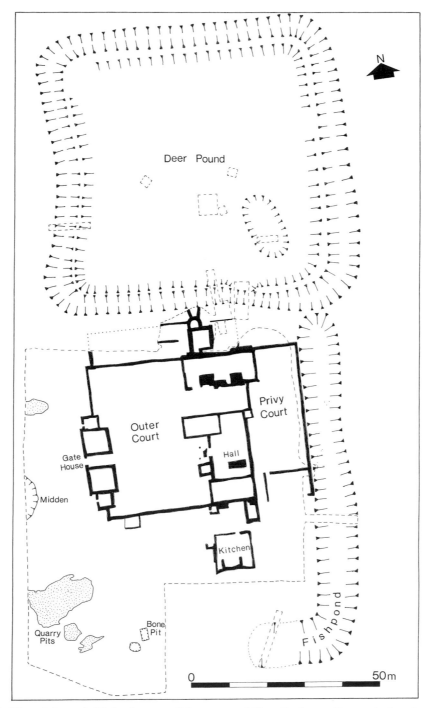

Fig 10.5   Plan of the early Tudor features of the manor of Hextalls. Surrey County Archaeological Unit

unknown sites such as the group of house platforms south-west of Lingfield recently discovered by members of the RH7 Local History Group. Such sites urgently need identification and require examination in any future study of manors and other settlements or of village origins.

Many of the seigneurial or similar sites that can be identified appear isolated in their medieval context, but the appearance may be deceptive – in heavily farmed, overbuilt and infilled Surrey the attrition of minor buildings and other medieval landscape features has inevitably been extremely high and is likely to remain so. However, it should not be forgotten that a manorial centre which lacks a village or part of a village to service it presents a set of chal-

lenging problems that complements those discussed in this essay.

Both seigneurial and peasant sites (taking the terms at their broadest) relate to field systems and boundaries – parochial, manorial and lesser boundaries – which can sometimes be traced on the map or examined on the ground and in the record room to allow the landscape as a whole to be reconstructed at different dates (cf English & Turner in this volume).

In many cases, a study of the documents, buildings and landscape morphology can lead us to construct historical hypotheses, even with regard to such abstract aspects as motivation. Hypotheses regarding sequence can often be readily tested, usually by 'dirt' archaeologists (cf Aston & Gerrard 1999). Those

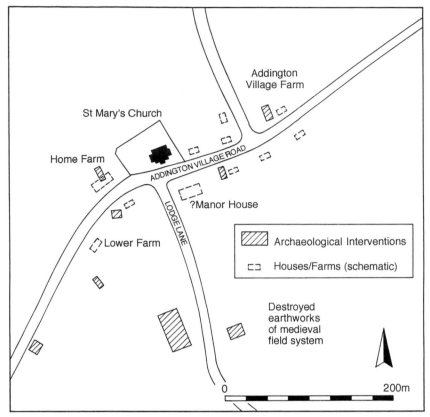

Fig 10.6   Plan of Addington village showing the location of excavations (Thornhill 1975; Thornhill & Savage 1979; Thornhill 1985; Bell 2001; Maloney & Holroyd, 2001). Drawing by David Williams

recently formulated for Shere, Thorpe and Cobham are cases in point. The testing of morphological and chronological hypotheses should have a place in the county's archaeological research agenda. But archaeology can also be used more actively to illuminate questions of lordship and motivation.

Nationally, the archaeological evidence concerning lordship-driven reordering is as yet slight: it has, after all, only been sought in a handful of places. At Raunds, one of the few places where such a search has been made, evidence was found. The archaeological research showed that the landscape of Raunds had been reordered and provided a date for the reorganization in the late 9th or early 10th century. Furthermore, it confirmed that some of the morphological characteristics still visible today were set out during this reorganization.

Whether the lord of the manor encouraged nucleation at an early stage, or left it until later, will remain a difficult question to answer in most cases and it is likely to take a research-based approach to illuminate the problem, as at Raunds. There has been little archaeological work within Surrey village envelopes – work undertaken in administrative Surrey before 1998 has been summarized by Poulton (1998a, 242) – and results have generally been disappointing. Nevertheless, the archaeology, although not research-based, has supported the view that the initial development of many Surrey villages occurred in the 12th or 13th centuries.

Archaeology can also support the view that not all villages were nucleated that early. At Addington (fig 10.6), within the historic county but now in London, the village appears to have been a 'two-row' one lying along the road from Sanderstead to West Wickham and in the late 19th century it was reported (Walford 1884, 130) that 'this place was formerly of much greater extent than at present, and it is related that timbers and other materials of ruined buildings have sometimes been turned up here by the plough'.

A brief view of the ground shows that a number of archaeological opportunities have been missed here as elsewhere, but nevertheless several attempts have been made to recover archaeological evidence – first by local archaeologists (Thornhill 1975; 1985; Thornhill & Savage 1979; Tucker 1992; 1995; Bell 2001, 225–47) and later under the rules of Planning Policy Guidance note 16 (PPG16). As a result a picture has been produced of a settlement that was little more than a church-farm hamlet (possibly with a manor house nearby), retaining this form well into post-medieval times. The most recent excavation in advance of development, an evaluation at Addington Village Farm (fig 10.6; TQ 372 640), produced more secure evidence of medieval occupation – pits and postholes were found above the natural gravel: those that were datable were of 11th to 13th century date (Saunders 2000). However, the claim that they 'suggest that the medieval village may have extended further east than was previously thought' (Maloney &

Holroyd 2001, 73) can be questioned. Unfortunately, the evaluation was not followed up and no further excavation of the development site was undertaken.

Many Surrey villages have, of course, been completely overbuilt and excavations at Battersea (Blackmore & Cowie 2001; Cooke 2001) clearly demonstrate how slender may be the surviving evidence. Work at Mortlake and Egham, already mentioned, Old Malden (Andrews *et al* 2001) and elsewhere has shown that valuable results can be achieved even where circumstances are less than favourable.

The conclusion is that no opportunity should be missed for examination within and around the village envelope. The kind of field techniques necessary to extract the maximum information has been developed at a number of deserted medieval village excavations (eg Austin 1989) and applied successfully in living villages (eg Shapwick and Raunds). Unfortunately, the degree of overbuilding and infilling that has occurred in most Surrey villages will mean surviving medieval features or strata are likely to be rare but even the smallest-scale developer-funded archaeological work may be able to supplement historical and morphological studies.

Evaluation procedures are usually severely limited horizontally and the methodology restricted to the removal mechanically of modern made ground 'until horizons deemed to be of importance' are reached (Tucker 1995, 7). The limitations of such techniques may militate against the discovery of the more fugitive evidence for earlier occupation that could survive on village sites. Few arguments can be based on the absence of evidence from such evaluations. The 'curators' supervising the practitioners of competitive development-based archaeology often seem to feel themselves constrained by the 'small print' of PPG16 against taking note of either the problems or of the opportunities. At the time of writing (March 2003), the combination of PPG15 and PPG16 into PPS15 is in progress and it is possible that this will weaken the hands of 'curators' still further.

If the best is to be obtained from such evaluations within village envelopes or near manorial sites, it is important that the planning administrators and specialists and the field archaeologists concerned consult or inform any groups or individuals undertaking local research. Unfortunately, there have been many cases where this has not occurred, representing at least the possibility of lost opportunities. A minor example from Wimbledon is illustrative and perhaps not untypical. Research into the history of Wimbledon (Milward & Maidment [2000]) had shown that, while the present village centre could be traced back to the 16th century, no evidence was forthcoming concerning the earlier location of the village. There is a suspicion that settlement closer to

the church and manor house may have been forced to migrate when the Elizabethan Wimbledon House was being built. A recent small-scale evaluation behind 25A Wimbledon High Street produced a pit containing a medieval sherd while two other medieval sherds were found nearby (GLAAS 2002, 30). This is far from conclusive but there was no sign in the evaluation brief that attention was paid to the particular local historical problem and there was no attempt to pursue matters further. We are left with no more than the faintest ambiguous hint.

Even if techniques were refined and co-operation improved, in most cases such developer-based excavations would still be too arbitrary to be a substitute for properly conducted research. A properly designed research project is well overdue. Although many Surrey villages have been hopelessly overbuilt, there are a dozen or more from Limpsfield to Thorpe to Puttenham where work on the scale undertaken at Raunds or even Shapwick could still be carried out and a project on these lines is much to be desired. A series of projects centred on villages with different characteristics (including different historic field patterns) would be even more valuable and could form a viable alternative to the wider landscape project proposed earlier in this paper. The archaeological evidence may not survive but it will certainly not be found unless it is looked for. The rate of house-building and other development in Surrey villages is so high that if an opportunity is not taken soon, it will probably be too late – it is already the eleventh hour.

Current work under the society's Village Studies Project should help to identify suitable candidates for such archaeological research. For example, some 'street' (two-row) villages (or two-row elements of villages) may be organic rather than planned developments – Puttenham, Capel, Ockley, Hambledon, for example – and this hypothesis may be susceptible to painstaking archaeological testing. Where migration seems to be involved (Ockley, Oxted, West Horsley) archaeology may be able to demonstrate the date of migration, as has been shown in East Anglia (Wade-Martins 1980).

Towards a research agenda

It is possible to outline some points for a research agenda.

First, there are undoubtedly a number of villages in Surrey where there is still an opportunity to seek archaeological evidence for their origins and this search must be closely coupled to consideration of morphology, adjacent historic field patterns and lordship. The author has elaborated this point elsewhere (Turner 2001).

The search needs to be project based, not just opportunistic, but the advantages of multi-parish projects outlined in the foregoing should not prevent the pursuit of viable single-parish or village projects. As Francis Pryor (2001, 218), president of the CBA, said in relation to the prehistoric period: 'Sometimes our obsession with conservation is merely conserving our state of ignorance. We need new knowledge if we are properly to understand what it is that we are attempting to protect for posterity.'

Secondly, we need to study the failure to create villages as well as actual creations themselves. A number of Surrey parishes (Ewhurst, Merton) lacked a nucleated village right down to the 19th century (Turner 2001, 4). A study of this will probably require a serious examination of lordship within the county – not just the social aspects of lordship, but the economic aspects as well.[3] Such a project might need, as its foundation, a careful reappraisal of the Surrey Domesday entries on the lines of that undertaken for Wiltshire and Essex by McDonald & Snooks (1986). It will also require the examination of isolated seigneurial and peasant sites.

Thirdly, we must recognize that the work of vernacular building specialists is not only refining our understanding of the chronology and social gradations of our later medieval houses; it is also uncovering a whole range of structures that we can distinguish but, as yet, hardly interpret. These occur in villages and outside and their relation to the manorial hierarchy is unknown. Some resources need to be devoted to continuing this work – particularly in the areas of dating and interpretation. And this, again, will involve consideration of status as well as of function. As the earliest houses of every status level and the later houses of the humbler levels only survive as below-ground archaeological remains, the bridge will be made to more conventional archaeologists.

Lastly, for now, seigneurial centres, villages and other settlements need to be set in their landscape. We must not stop at the edge of the village envelope or even at the outer edge of its fields. We need to study the relationships between nucleated and dispersed settlements, the tenurial patterns, and the landscape.

NOTES

1 For an excellent summary of the discussions from the time of Andrews, Maitland, *et al*, to that of Latham & Finburg, see Klingelhöfer 1992, 1–15.
2 The regularity of the house plots around the crossroads in the centre of Ewell may be an illusion – cf Shearman 1955, maps page 106.
3 This paper has concentrated on questions of lordship, village creation and agricultural organization but it may be as well to point out that lordship frequently had a considerable effect on many other aspects of landscape and economic history that have not been fully examined. Elsewhere in this volume Dr Hughes briefly mentions the possibility of links between lordship and variations in vernacular building techniques. The exploitation of mineral resources is another area that may have been affected by lordship. There are many more examples.

BIBLIOGRAPHY

Abbreviations: DBRG: Domestic Buildings Research Group (Surrey); MoLAS: Museum of London Archaeology Service; TVAS: Thames Valley Archaeological Services

Abdy, C, in prep   *Ewell: the development of a Surrey village that became a town*, SyAS
Aberg, A (ed), 1978   *Medieval moated sites*, CBA Res Rep, **17**
Addeyman, P, 1964   A Dark Age settlement at Maxey, Northants, *Medieval Archaeol*, **8**, 20–73
Andrews, C, 1892   *The old English manor*, Baltimore
Andrews, P, 2001   Excavation of a multi-period settlement site at the former St John's Vicarage, Old Malden, Kingston upon Thames, *SyAC*, **88**, 161–224
Aston, M A, & Gerrard, C, 1999   'Unique, traditional and charming', the Shapwick project, Somerset, *Antiq J*, **79**, 1–58
Austin, D, 1989   *The deserted medieval village of Thrislington, County Durham: excavations 1973–74*, Soc Medieval Archaeol Monogr, **12**
Bailey, K A, & Galbraith, I G, 1973   Field systems in Surrey: an introductory survey, *SyAC*, **69**, 73–87
Bannister, N R, 2004   The Surrey Historic Landscape Characterisation Project, in Cotton *et al* 2004, 119–32
——, & Wills, P M, 2001   Surrey Historic Landscape Characterisation, 2 vols, Surrey County Council, limited distribution
Bell, C, 2001   Excavation of multi-period sites at Lodge Lane, Addington, Geoffrey Harris House and Lloyd Park, South Croydon, *SyAC*, **88**, 225–65

Beresford, M W, 1967   *New towns of the Middle Ages*
Blackmore, L, & Cowie, R, 2001   Saxon and medieval Battersea, excavations at Althorpe Grove, 1975–8, *SyAC*, **88**, 67–92
Blair, W J, 1991   *Early medieval Surrey: landholding, church and settlement before 1300*, Alan Sutton & SyAS
Cadman, G, 1983   Raunds 1977–83: an excavation summary, *Medieval Archaeol*, **27**, 107–22
Cadman, G, & Foard, G, 1984   Raunds, manorial and village origins, in *Studies in late Anglo-Saxon settlement* (ed M Faull), 81–100, Oxford Committee for Archaeology
Campbell, B M S, 1981   The regional uniqueness of English field systems? Some evidence from eastern Norfolk, *Econ Hist Rev*, 2 ser, **29**, 16–28
Chatwin, D, 1996   *The development of timber-framed buildings in the Sussex Weald*, Rudgwick
Cooke, N, 2001   Excavations at Battersea Flour Mills, 1996–7: the medieval and post-medieval manor houses and later Thames-side industrial sites, *SyAC*, **88**, 93–131
Cotton, J, Crocker, G, & Graham, A (eds), 2004   *Aspects of archaeology and history in Surrey: towards a research framework for the county*, SyAS
Currie, C K, 2000   Polesden Lacey and Ranmore Common estates: an archaeological and historical survey, *SyAC*, **87**, 49–84
Darton, L, forthcoming   Medieval and post-medieval riverside buildings at Mortlake, *SyAC*
Dix, B (ed), 1987   The Raunds area project: second interim report, *Northamptonshire Archaeol*, **21**, 3–29
Dodgshon, R, 1987   *The European past: social evolution and spatial order*

Dyer, C C, 1985   Power and conflict in the medieval English village, in *Medieval villages* (ed D Hook), Oxford Univ Comm Archaeol Monogr, **5,** 27–32

——, 1988   Documentary evidence: problems and enquiries, in *The countryside of medieval England* (eds G Astill & A Grant), Oxford, 12–35

——, 1999   The MSRG Whittlewood project, *Medieval Settlement Res Grp Ann Rep,* **14,** 16–17

——, 2001   The Whittlewood project, *Soc Landscape Stud Newsl,* Spring/Summer 2001, 7–8

English, J, & Turner, D, 2004   Medieval settlement in the Blackheath Hundred, in Cotton *et al* 2004, 103–18

Foard, G, & Pearson, T, 1985   The Raunds area project: first interim report, *Northamptonshire Archaeol,* **20,** 3–21

Ford, S, 1998   Excavations [at] 81–84 High Street, Egham, Surrey, TVAS unpublished client report

GLAAS, 2002   Greater London Archaeological Archive Service, Quarterly Review, Nov 2001 to Feb 2002

Gostick, T, Greenwood, P, & Maloney, C, 1997   London fieldwork and publications roundup 1996, *London Archaeol,* **8,** Supplement 2

Gostick, T, & Maloney, C, 1998   London fieldwork and publications roundup 1997, *London Archaeol,* **8,** Supplement 3

Gray, H L, 1915   *English field systems*

Gray, P J, 1991   *Blechingley village and parish*

——, 2002   *Surrey medieval buildings: an analysis and inventory,* DBRG

Hall, D, 1995   *The open fields of Northamptonshire*

Hindess, B, & Hirst, P, 1975   *Pre-capitalist modes of production*

Howe, T, Jackson, G, & Maloney, C, 2001   Archaeology in Surrey 2000, *SyAC,* **88,** 343–63

——, 2002   Archaeology in Surrey 2001, *SyAC,* **89,** 257–81

Hughes, A, 2004   Vernacular architecture, in Cotton *et al* 2004, 147–54

Hughes, A, & Higgins, M, 2001   White Hart House, Ewhurst, *DBRG News,* **87,** 5–9

Hughes, M, 1989   Hampshire castles and the landscape, 1066–1216, *Landscape Hist,* **11,** 27–60

Jackson, G, Maloney, C, & Saich, D, 1999   Archaeology in Surrey 1996–7, *SyAC,* **86,** 217–55

Jolliffe, J E A, 1954   *The constitutional history of medieval England,* 3 edn

Klingelhöfer, E, 1992   *Manor, vill and hundred,* Pontifical Inst Medieval Stud: Studies and Texts, **112**

Lewis, C, Mitchell-Fox, P, & Dyer, C, 1997   *Village, hamlet and field: changing medieval settlement in central England*

Losco-Bradley, S, & Wheeler, H M, 1984   Anglo-Saxon settlement in the Trent valley, in *Studies in late Anglo-Saxon settlement,* ed M Faull, Oxford Committee for Archaeology, 101–14

McDonald, J, & Snooks, G D, 1986   *Domesday economy*

McKisack, M, 1959   *The fourteenth century*

Maitland, F W, 1897   *Domesday Book and beyond: three essays in the early history of England*

Maloney, C, & Holroyd, I, 2001   London fieldwork and publication roundup 2000, *London Archaeol,* **9,** Supplement 3

Mason, R T, 1966   Old Court Cottage, Limpsfield, *SyAC,* **63,** 130–7

——, 1969   *Framed buildings of the Weald,* 2 edn, Horsham

Meirion-Jones, G, & Jones, M (eds), 1993   *Manorial domestic buildings in England and northern France,* Soc Antiq London Occas Pap, **15**

Meirion-Jones, G, Impey, E, & Jones, M (eds), 2002   *The seigneurial residence in Western Europe AD* c *800–1600,* BAR Int Ser, **1088**

Milward, R, & Maidment, C, [2000]   *Wimbledon, a Surrey village in maps,* Wimbledon

Noyes, A, 2001   The poll tax of 1380 for Shere and Gomshall, *Surrey Hist,* **6.3,** 130–43

O'Connell, M, 1977   *Historic towns in Surrey,* SyAS Res Vol, **5**

O'Connell, M, & Poulton, R, 1983   An excavation at Castle Hill, Godstone, *SyAC,* **74,** 213–15

Oosthuizen, S, & Hesse, M, 2001   The SW Cambridgeshire project: summary report 1999–2000, in *Medieval Settlement Res Grp Ann Rep,* **15,** 19–20

Oosthuizen, S, & James, N, 1999   The south-west Cambridgeshire project: interim report, in *Medieval Settlement Res Grp Ann Rep,* **14,** 17–25

Oschinsky, D, 1971   *Walter of Henley and other treatises on estate management and accounting*

Page, M, & Jones, R, 2001   The Whittlewood project: interim report 2000–1, in *Medieval Settlement Res Grp Ann Rep,* **15,** 10–18

Parton, A G, 1967   A note on the open-fields of Fetcham and Great Bookham, *Proc Leatherhead Dist Local Hist Soc,* **3.1,** 25–6

Poole, A L, 1955   *Domesday Book to Magna Carta,* 2 edn

Poulton, R, 1998a   Historic towns in Surrey: some general considerations, *SyAC,* **85,** 239–42

——, 1998b   Excavations at 14–16 London Street, Chertsey, *SyAC,* **85,** 6–45

——, 1998c   *The lost manor of Hextalls,* Surrey County Archaeological Unit

Pryor, F, 2001   [Review of Whittle *et al* 1999, The Harmony of Symbols], *Antiquity,* **75.287,** 218–19

Rackham, O, 1986   *History of the countryside*

Raftis, J A, 1965   Social structures in five east Midland villages, *Econ Hist Rev,* 2 ser, **18,** 17–29

Rapson, G, 2002   A suggested location of Black Hawes 'Castle' at Westcott, *SyAS Bull,* **357,** 11–12

——, 2003   Castles at Westcott – some corrections, *SyAS Bull,* **367,** 13

Roberts, B, 1985   Village patterns and forms: some models for discussion, in *Medieval villages* (ed D Hooke), Oxford Univ Comm Archaeol Monogr, **5,** 7–26

——, 2000   *An atlas of rural settlement in England,* English Heritage

Roberts, B, & Wrathmell, S, 1998   Dispersed settlement in England: a national view, in *The archaeology of the landscape* (eds P Everson & T Williamson), 95–116

Saunders, M J, 2000   Addington village farm, Addington village road, TVAS unpublished client report

Saunders, T, 1990   The feudal construction of space: power and domination in the nucleated village, in *The social archaeology of houses* (ed R Samson), 181–96

Sawyer, P, 1979   Medieval English settlement: new interpretations, in *English medieval settlements* (ed P Sawyer), 1–8

Shearman, P, 1955   Ewell in 1577, *SyAC,* **54,** 102–7

Shelley, J, 2003   *History in maps: Charlwood, a parish on the Weald Clay* (privately printed)

Shere 2001: Shere, Gomshall and Peaslake Local History Society, 2001   *Shere, a Surrey village in maps: a record of its growth and development,* SyAS

Somerset VBRG, 1996   *The vernacular buildings of Shapwick*

Stewart, S, 2000   What happened at Shere, *Southern Hist,* **22,** 1–20

Taylor, C C, 1983   *Village and farmstead, a history of rural settlement*

——, 2002   People and places: local history and landscape history, *Local Historian,* **32.4,** 234–49

Taylor, D C, & Turner, D J, 2003   The origins of Cobham village, *SyAS Bull,* **366,** 2–7

Thornhill, L, 1975   Report on fieldwork in Addington, Surrey, 1970–72, *Proc Croydon Natur Hist Sci Soc,* **14.4,** 501–21

——, 1985   *Coombe, Shirley and Addington,* Living History Local Guide no 2

Thornhill, L, & Savage, R W, 1979   Excavations at Addington, Surrey, 1973–7, *Proc Croydon Natur Hist Sci Soc,* **16.7,** 232–69

Tucker, S, 1992   The Shell Addington site, MoLAS unpublished client report

——, 1995   Home Farm, Addington Palace Golf Club, MoLAS unpublished client report

Turner, D J, 2001   The origin and development of Surrey villages, *SyAS Bull,* **347**

——, 2003   The manor and the feudal construction of space, *Surrey Hist,* **6.5,** 293–303

——, in prep   Chaldon, Chaldon Court and Tollsworth Manor

VCH: Victoria history of the county of Surrey (ed H E Malden), 1902–12, 4 vols

Vinogradoff, P, 1905   *The growth of the manor*

Wade-Martins, P, 1980   *Village sites in Launditch Hundred,* E Anglian Archaeol Rep, **10**

Walford, E, 1884   *Village London,* vol 2

Wild, R, 2001   An extraordinary 'church house', *DBRG News,* Oct 2001, 8–11

Williams, D W, 1983   16 Bell Street, Reigate: excavation of a medieval and post-medieval site, 1974–6, *SyAC,* **74,** 47–89

——, in prep   Bell Street, Reigate: excavations in 1988–99

Williams, J, 2002   *Thorpe: a Surrey village in maps: a record of its growth and development,* SyAS

Dennis Turner, BSc, FSA, 21 Evesham Road, Reigate RH2 9DL

11

Vernacular architecture

ANNABELLE F HUGHES

This paper attempts to summarize the way in which the study and interpretation of traditional buildings has developed from the work of pioneers such as Eric Mercer and R T Mason. It examines and contrasts approaches by the two main research groups working in the region and considers the problems of establishing a terminology that is both user-friendly and technically acceptable. The accumulation of data has necessitated analytical approaches, best exemplified by the work of Peter Gray who, before his untimely death, was able to produce the text now available as Surrey medieval buildings: an analysis and inventory. *Issues that he raised are presented in this paper and two of his distribution maps are included. Finally, examples are given from the Sussex Weald and the work of members of local buildings research groups to illustrate the importance of an integrated approach to the environmental and historical background within which traditional buildings were constructed and developed.*

Introduction

Everyone lives in a house, or part of one, and most people have some experience of buying, selling or renting property and making changes, large and small, so that it suits their particular requirements. It follows that one of the easiest ways to help the general public to relate to historical change is by showing them how buildings have changed and asking them why. Although it has been suggested that the term 'vernacular architecture' should be replaced by 'traditional buildings', the first phrase has been in use for long enough for most people to know what it implies.

The serious study of vernacular architecture owes its beginnings to a number of pioneering individuals such as Maurice Barley, Eric Mercer, Stuart Rigold and R T Mason. Their followers were drawn from amateurs and professionals in a wide range of disciplines, and no qualification was required other than a great deal of enthusiasm and commitment. In this lay both strength and weakness. The strength of being without received or entrenched opinions, the weakness of having little by way of terms of reference, agreed terminology, or an established framework upon which to hang the information which accumulated.

Two strands emerged – recording and interpretation – and in this region two groups evolved, each with a different emphasis but with some common membership.

Looking at buildings from Kent to Hampshire, the Wealden Buildings Study Group has concentrated on trying to understand the ways in which buildings were originally intended to be used, how they have developed over time, and the reasons behind their siting and form. The Domestic Buildings Research Group (DBRG) has concentrated on recording historical buildings, principally in Surrey, and has amassed an impressive collection of records.

As increasing numbers of houses were studied, the need arose to develop a technical vocabulary and some categories for different types. The Council for British Archaeology (CBA) has produced the most recent glossary of terms, in an attempt to standardize across the country, but regional variations (and their groups) are resistant to absolute uniformity.[1] However, the terms medieval and post-medieval are familiar to historians, who have taken the accession of Henry VII or the dissolution of the monasteries as the change-over point, although this matter also is open to debate. For students of buildings, medieval has become shorthand for anything built within the period when the open hall[2] was the norm, and post-medieval for types succeeding these, which were fully floored from the start and had some kind of smoke control. As increasing numbers of houses have been examined, it has become clear that not all buildings fall neatly into these two groups. We have now arrived at a point when many constructions throughout the 16th century are described as transitional, illustrating changes and development in both construction and plan. As studies progress, it has also become apparent that there are differences in both styles and pace of change within regions and counties.

So where do we start and stop? In the Weald we are concerned mainly with timber-framed buildings and the survival rates of early examples means it is unlikely that we will find anything earlier than the second decade of the 13th century, although it has been possible to make comparisons with, and draw conclusions from, the roof constructions over earlier solid-wall buildings. With some notable exceptions, framing as a constructional approach generally began to descend the social scale towards the end of the 17th century, although local forms of traditional building persisted until the canals and railways spread materials – and styles – nationwide. And although the original building material may have been timber, the older the building or the more changes it has undergone, the greater the variety of materials that can be involved, so we have needed to become familiar with the characteristics of brick and stone.

The increased amount of data collected has brought its own problems, for the more examples we have found, the more we have to qualify and modify our conclusions. We have a mental picture of the norm, but increasingly we are having to decide what to do with the oddballs – and whether they really are oddballs at all.

Papers in a recent publication by the CBA have explored the existing and future patterns of understanding, recording and conserving vernacular buildings.[3] While this is not the place to précis or comment on the opinions expressed, some points are worth reiterating in the context of this paper. The contributors come from a variety of backgrounds – university teaching, historic building consultancy, archaeological units, English Heritage – but there is general recognition of the continuing value of the amateur in the field, the original implication of the word not being second-rate, but doing something simply for the love of it. It is even pointed out that the amateur is often able to record and carry out research on vernacular buildings outside the constraints of planning briefs, project time and restricted funding that are experienced by professionals. Also, the amateur can often gain access to buildings where anything that smacks of officialdom is unwelcome.

The work of amateur groups in recording and trying to understand vernacular buildings can and should be harnessed to lead towards a wider understanding of historical context, regional patterns and differences. It was with this in mind that, as soon as Peter Gray knew that his time was limited, he set about a project that he had been considering for some time – the construction of a database of the medieval buildings of Surrey, using the records and experience of the two groups mentioned, in such a way that it would be easier to make useful analyses. Even before this was finalized, he was able to tell me that a large proportion of the estimated medieval buildings in Surrey had been surveyed, there were few moulded dais beams, end jetties were not common, and there were 28 Wealdens[4] with an interesting pattern of distribution. Two of the maps from Gray's analysis[5] have been used to illustrate points in this paper. This work has been the stimulus to the DBRG to pioneer and test a method of recording that could make it easier to enter information directly on to a database, and to codify the existing records. A cottage at Salfords provided a good example of how the dating evidence of a lease in 1629, referring to a house 'recently erected', correlated with details recorded using this new approach.[6]

Categories of medieval buildings

From Peter Gray's work it now transpires that of 856 buildings with medieval characteristics identified in Surrey, surveys are available for 712, which is probably over 80% of those extant. This has to be qualified by the observation that the area north of the North Downs lacks data from a significant number of buildings. In comparison, the publication of *An Historical Atlas for Sussex* in 1999 made it possible to get some idea of the state of surveys in that county, and it highlighted the areas where little work has been done, such as the extreme west of the county and patches of mid-Sussex.[7] Of buildings surveyed in Sussex, excluding the Rape of Hastings, which has been the subject of exhaustive study by David and Barbara Martin,[8] 355 proved to be medieval, including 194 in twelve Wealden parishes. Of these 46 have sans-purlin roofs (17 being aisled), 246 are crown-posted, 31 have side-purlins and 40 are Wealdens (the count has since gone up by two). However, these figures alone are only a limited outcome of more thorough identification and recording.

Gray's draft analysis includes nine categories for open-hall houses:
1 The double-ended hall.
2 The single-ended hall (2 bays).
3 The single-ended hall (1 bay).
4 The simple 2-bay building.
5 The house with a 3-bay hall.
6 The hall with an open service bay.
7 The hall with aisles.
8 The hall with fine cross-wings.
9 Wealdens and jettied single-range houses.

This is not the place to discuss each of the categories, but serves to illustrate the complexities that are introduced the more houses are recorded. As increasing numbers of buildings are identified, we have been able to move from the norm of two- or three-unit buildings towards recognizing new categories – the house built in instalments, detached kitchens, smoke-bay houses, buildings that seem to have special functions – and we have begun to identify particular groups of buildings that need more in-depth study.

Early surviving buildings have always exercised a fascination, and nearly 30 years ago R T Mason noted eight features he called 'archaic', and maintained that where two or more were observed in a building 'it could probably be assigned to the turn of the 13th century, if not earlier.'[9] This contention is still largely valid today, although we have also begun to identify features which help us to assign buildings to the 14th century with more confidence.

Among the other features we have begun to recognize which seem to be characteristic of early houses are the low-floored end and end aisles. The original flooring of an end bay can be so noticeably low, that the ground floor space was virtually no more than an undercroft, although in most cases later modification has all but obscured the evidence. Often it can be shown that at the same time, the other end beyond the hall was unfloored, and this was almost certainly the case when there is, or was, an end aisle.

On the basis of these agreed early features, 28 houses in Surrey have been identified as 'early'. Among these, Highland Cottage, Coldharbour (Capel), shown in figure 11.1, Tigbourne and Sister Cottage (Witley), Greens Farm (Newdigate), Long Vere House (Hascombe), and the Blue Anchor Inn (Godstone) have evidence for low-floored ends.[10] The recognition of these early variations is leading to fresh considerations as to the uses of the bays which flanked the hall.

Two other significant houses in this group have to be Burstow Lodge (Burstow), with a wealth of moulded timbers, and Chaldon Court (Chaldon), where in spite of the fact that the hall does not survive, there is still a substantial house comprised of three ranges that once formed the high end.

Another newly recognized category is the house with detached kitchen or service block. Because these features have usually become absorbed into the main house, or converted into separate dwellings, it is only with the improved experience of those who study and record buildings that their significance has been recognized. Since they are usually of two or three bays, the implication has been that at least one bay was unfloored to contain a cooking hearth, but this was not always so, and their exact use is still not clear – it may even have varied from house to house. To date, thirteen possible examples have been identified in Surrey, but much remains to be learned about them.

Here an example from Capel serves to underline the need to combine documentary research and an understanding of buildings. Aldhurst Farm (figs 11.2, 11.3) is made up of three significant timber-framed ranges: a rather crude three-bay crown-posted building, heavily sooted, and a four-bay house with a smoke-bay, which are linked by a single bay that appears to be contemporary with the latter. As there was a crown-posted barn (now removed) it seemed reasonable to suppose that the first range represented the earliest surviving dwelling, although there were some reservations. However, a transcript of the Dorking Court Rolls contains an entry dated 1529, when Robert Yong was allowed to move a kitchen to Aldhurst from another tenement called Tepehams.[11] Interpreting the crown-posted building as a kitchen makes far more sense, although it raises the question as to whether either of the other ranges could have been there in 1529.

Jetties in the countryside do appear to have been used as an aesthetic rather than as a functional detail, as the extra accommodation achieved was hardly significant, and a face jetty could make framing the roof more complicated. The Wealden with a single roof is the most effective design visually with the least structural complications. Although the style appears to have originated in the Weald, where the greatest concentrations are found, it spread throughout the country and was adapted for different requirements. The database has revealed a concentration of the type in the southern half of the county, with significant clusters to the east (fig 11.4).

Fig 11.1 Highland Cottage, Coldharbour, Capel, photographed c 1930. This is a good illustration of how the outward appearance of an old building can be very deceptive. It gives no clue to the 'notable early features' noted by Peter Gray of a fine open truss and evidence for a low-floored end. Dorking Museum: SC5/197

Fig 11.2 Aldhurst Farm from the rear. This shows the smoke-bay range to the left, the end elevation of the detached kitchen from Tepehams on the right, and the central linking bay. Reproduced by permission of Surrey History Service: Surrey Photographic Record 2873. Copyright of Surrey History Service

Fig 11.3 Aldhurst Farm looking towards the detached kitchen range (centre) with end elevation of crown-posted barn on left (since removed). Courtesy of the Frith Collection (53534, 1905) and Mary Day

Transitional houses

Only in recent years have we begun to recognize the need for a whole new classification for those buildings that form a bridge between the medieval and post-medieval periods. These transitional houses demonstrate a number of features, such as a variety of techniques to control and confine smoke, flooring inserted in stages to increase floor space, change in the ways in which houses were planned, rooms used and their occupants moved around them, and combinations of both medieval and post-medieval elements, which could sometimes be explained by the conservatism of builders or owners.

An example of the latter is the way in which the medieval plan of service, cross-passage, heated hall and solar or parlour persisted, even when the smoke from the open fire was being confined by a stone wall around the fire at ground-floor level, surmounted by a timber-framed flue. Sometimes the fire was contained against the line of the cross-passage, or

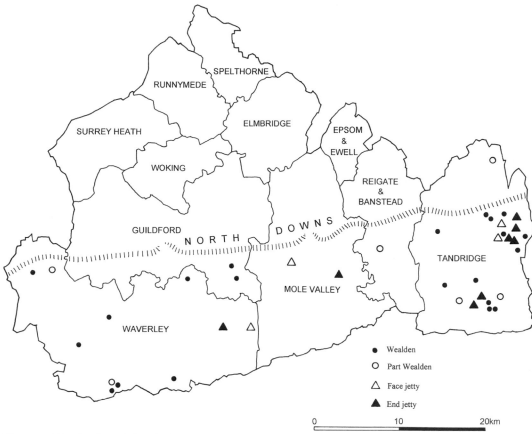

Fig 11.4 Distribution of face-jetties, end-jetties and Wealdens, after Gray 2002, fig 9, by permission of the Domestic Buildings Research Group (Surrey)

even against the front or rear wall of the hall, and experience is showing that these arrangements could be either the result of an adaptation of an earlier type, or of an innovative new build. In either case, these are evidence of a significant period of experimentation with new ideas which is reflected in the variations to be found in the 16th century.

Specialist buildings

Both form and position have forced us to reinterpret a number of buildings as non-domestic, even if these are sometimes in settlements we would now hesitate to term urban or industrial. Work remains to be done on collecting and comparing data about such buildings, and exploring associated documentary records for possible clues to their use. There are two examples in Old Oxted, which were recognized by Peter Gray – Brook House and the Old Bell – both of them crown-posted. Brook House was jettied on both sides, suggesting it may have stood on an island site, is unusually narrow, and may even have had some kind of original chimney stack. The Old Bell (fig 11.5) had three jettied bays with an open bay at one end, which provides evidence for some kind of rear access and for the more significant rooms being on the first floor. Although at the time Gray thought it unlikely that it had been an inn originally, and it was almost certainly not a house, new research into inns, taverns and alehouses would support the theory that it had been a

tavern, since taverns usually contained public rooms of some kind at first floor, and often ground-floor shops.[12]

Just a few miles away, in Westerham, a similar building has been identified, facing the Green. With four crown-posted bays, fully floored and jettied along the street elevation, but with no indication of how it might have been heated, its plan and position strongly suggest a commercial function.

Discussion: approaches for the future

Increased recording throughout the Weald from Kent to Hampshire has begun to demonstrate a pattern of changing ratios from east to west between open halls with crown-posts and those with side-purlins, the latter being more predominant in Hampshire. How far Surrey fits into this pattern, if it does, is a question open to closer examination (see Peter Gray's distribution map reproduced as figure 11.6). It was in Surrey that the smoke-bay house was first identified by Joan Harding, and a significant number of examples have been recorded. It remains to be explored whether this type is especially characteristic of the county's development, and if so, exactly what it is telling us. Is it a product of the pattern of settlement that was prevalent, or of the soil types and landscape, or a combination of both? This leads on to the need to consider how buildings vary across the county, and if so, why.

Fig 11.5 The Old Bell Inn, Godstone, showing the jettying of its long elevation. The open-hall bay was at the left end, down the hill. Drawing by R W Oram from *Oxted explored*, by A Wells and K Percy, 1975, courtesy of Tandridge District Council

Because the study of buildings has brought together people from different fields of expertise and interest, a variety of resources are being employed. Dendrochronology, which is the technique of dating buildings by comparison of growth rings in timber, thus arriving at a felling date, is being developed and refined, although it is clear that even this will not supply all the answers we would like. For various technical reasons it has proved difficult to obtain such dates for buildings in this region, but recently some have been arrived at for buildings in East Grinstead, Rudgwick and Charlwood, which have useful implications. Documentary material from parish, property and probate records, manorial and ecclesiastical courts, maps and surveys, are all helping to supply evidence for building and change. Two

examples from my own area of Sussex will have to suffice.

A barn at Eastlands, in Cowfold, was reported to be 'interesting'. Apart from a few visible curved braces, the first impression was not promising as most of the building was covered with corrugated iron sheeting, but once through the doors I realized it was no ordinary barn. Clearly it had been built as a four-bay open-hall house with a crown-posted roof, to which a bay had been added in the 17th century after it had been downgraded to a barn, when a new farmhouse had been built. Fortunately it came within the outlier of a manor, Stretham, in Henfield, belonging to the bishops of Chichester, for which a number of records survive, and these provided unusually detailed documentary evidence.[13] A custumal of 1373 recorded a copyhold with house and yardland, and the tenant's name made it possible to trace it through 200 years. In 1583 the tenant of this copyhold applied for a licence to demolish and rebuild the 'mansion dwelling house', and a survey of 1647 listed a messuage, house, granary and other outbuildings with 60 acres. One unsatisfactory photograph and the ground plan on maps is all that has survived of the replacement house, which was demolished in the 1960s, unrecorded. The early house remained in use as a barn, and has now been restored to residential use. The combination of constructional and documentary evidence from this example has provided additional points of reference for future assessments and comparisons.

Not far away, visible from a new by-pass around Billingshurst, is a house that has the proportions,

Fig 11.6 Distribution of crown post and clasped purlin and windbraced roofs, after Gray 2002, fig 11, by permission of the Domestic Buildings Research Group (Surrey)

some joisting and the remains of trusses all supporting the theory that it is a medieval house updated with a chimney-stack in the 17th century. However, an initial reading of written sources suggested there was no building on this site, then known as Hilland, until the second quarter of the 17th century, although parish records indicated tenants from at least the 1530s, which was supported by the constructional evidence. Further documentary evidence was contained in depositions before a church court in 1633, arising from a dispute over the assignment of church seats, and aiming to establish the continuity of a building belonging to the tenancy. Unfortunately, although two of the witness statements may have been sufficient for that particular purpose, they contained puzzling ambiguities. They agreed about alterations made in about 1612, but they also raised the possibility that the building had actually been moved within the holding. This sounds a note of caution when using documentary sources, with or without a building, for even when both are available, it is not always possible to be certain about what has taken place.

It has become ever clearer that structural investigation must go hand-in-hand with an appreciation of landscape and an understanding of the historical setting. Not only do we have to be aware of the underlying geology and topography of a given area, but also of the changes that have happened over time. As some of the buildings were erected four or five hundred years ago, a great deal may have happened to the landscape around them – some of it natural, some man-made. In their turn, these changes may have influenced modifications made to the buildings. We need also to appreciate the economic background to the original build and how that may have changed, and to investigate the patterns of administration – of manors, hundreds, parishes – and the documents these generated.

Members of buildings groups are finding themselves increasingly drawn into studies of parishes which involve building surveys. Diana Chatwin has produced books focused on the parishes of Rudgwick and Slinfold.[14] Jean Shelley has co-ordinated field days which have contributed to booklets on the buildings of Horley and Ardingly.[15] Peter Gray's work is well known to many in Surrey and beyond. All three are, or have been, members of both the groups

mentioned above. There are continuing studies of the parishes of the Arun valley, near Amberley, which focus on or include the buildings. All the framed buildings of Northchapel were recorded when a new history of the parish was produced to mark the millennium, and as a follow-up to this, came the opportunity to study the seven historical houses which make up the neighbouring hamlet of Hillgrove.

Hillgrove is at the northernmost point of Lurgashall parish, where it abuts Northchapel, originally a chapelry to Petworth, and is close to the Surrey border. Its heart is ten acres of common land belonging to the Petworth estate, which research discovered was bordered by outliers of three other manors. Historically it drew in owners or tenants from both Hampshire and Surrey, for example from Alton and Haslemere. It became clear that the building development of the hamlet was directly related to the ownership and pattern of land tenure. Because of the position of the hamlet, the residents did not necessarily use their parish church but the one that was nearest, so it was necessary to examine the records of both Lurgashall and Northchapel. Likewise administrative and family issues had even more inter-parish connections than usual.

Two medieval houses survived, one each on two of the outliers adjoining the common land. In the context of the area, the constructional type suggested that these dated from the end of the medieval period, but because of the position of the hamlet they might be reflecting influence from the western tradition, and be proportionally earlier. Three houses were transitional or post-medieval, and illustrated both fragmentation of early holdings and encroachment on to common land. Of the remaining two, one was an 18th century update, the other a complete 18th century new build, and both could be linked to different members of the same family.

Both this work and studies in the Arun valley, bringing together landscape, history of settlement, buildings and documents, are showing how an understanding of buildings, their use and development can contribute to unravelling the interdependence and relationship between apparently separate communities. This must sign-post the way ahead for those who are passionate about buildings, and those who would use their specialist knowledge.

NOTES

1 Alcock, N W, Barley, M W, Dixon, P W, & Meeson, R A, *Recording timber-framed buildings: an illustrated glossary*, revised edn, CBA, 1996.
2 A unit of the house without a first floor and heated with an open hearth.
3 Pearson, S, & Meeson, R A, *Vernacular buildings in a changing world*, CBA Res Rep **126**, CBA, 2001.

4 Type of medieval open-hall house, where a single span roof over front jettied end bays make the central open-hall bay or bays appear recessed. One of the best-known examples is Bayleaf, at the Weald and Downland Open Air Museum at Singleton.
5 Gray, P, *Surrey medieval buildings: an analysis and inventory*, DBRG, 2001.

6   The Little, Staplehurst. Information provided by R Wild.

7   Leslie, K, & Short, B, *An historical atlas of Sussex*, Phillimore, 1999.

8   Martin, D, & Martin, B, Hastings Area Archaeological Papers for and on behalf of the Rape of Hastings Architectural Survey, 1974–.

9   Mason, R T, *Framed buildings of England*, Coach Publishing, Horsham, 1974.

10 Houses with similar evidence in Rudgwick, north Sussex, have been dated by dendrochronology to between 1369 and 1379.

11 Surrey History Centre: C21/10/2/118 (transcription of Arundel Castle Archives: M793). Information from Vivien Ettlinger provided by Mary Day.

12 Pennington, J, *The inns and taverns of western Sussex, 1550–1700: a regional study of their architectural and social history*, PhD thesis, University of Southampton (Chichester), 2003.

13 Records held by West Sussex Record Office, Chichester.

14 For example Chatwin, D, *The development of timber-framed buildings in the Sussex Weald: the architectural heritage of the parish of Rudgwick*, Rudgwick Preservation Society, 1996.

15 For example Shelley, J, *Maps and houses of Horley from Tudor times until the railway came*, Horley Local History Society, 1997.

Dr Annabelle F Hughes, Research Consultant on Historical Buildings, 32 Hillside, Horsham, West Sussex RH12 2NG

12

The impact of royal landholdings on the county of Surrey 1509–1649

SIMON THURLEY

This paper starts by describing the increasing intensity of royal interest in Surrey and its formalization in the reign of Henry VIII. It argues that Surrey became the most popular county for the Tudor and early Stuart monarchs. It goes on to outline the ways in which royal interests may have affected the economy and social structure of the county. It is then asked whether a significant personal presence by the Tudor and early Stuart monarchs was an advantage or a disadvantage to the inhabitants of Surrey. The paper concludes that although it is too early to say whether there was a long-term impact on the development of the county, intensive royal interest between 1509 and 1649 is certainly a factor that should be considered in devising a research framework.

An Elizabethan complaint

The mid-Elizabethan inhabitants of Surrey believed that their county was disadvantaged because of the weight of crown interest in it. They claimed that despite it being one of the 'least and most barren' of English counties 'it is the most charged of anie, by reason that her majesty lieth in or about the shire continuallie, and thereby [it] is chardged with contynualle removes and caridge of coles, wood and other provision to the court [...] also by my Lord Treasurer for the reparacions of her Majesty's houss'.[1] Surrey is, of course, an artificial construct and using a county boundary to explain the history or archaeology of a region is a blunt tool.[2] Nevertheless, as it is an ancient administrative unit there is value in looking at the Elizabethan claim that the crown imposed a particularly heavy burden on the county. Therefore this paper sets out to provide an introduction to some of the principal impacts of the crown that might be considered as important in explaining the history and archaeology of Surrey.

The Elizabethans were right that Surrey was small. It is in fact the eighth smallest county in England and one of the most compact, being 40 miles wide and 30 deep. In the Middle Ages it was so remote that there was no town with more than 2000 inhabitants and not a single large parish church.[3] During the 15th century, owing to the fact that nowhere in the county is further than 50 miles from Westminster, it became the backyard of the metropolis. It was its proximity to London and the nature of its landscape (which made it excellent hunting country) that meant that by the death of Henry VIII there were no less than eleven royal houses in Surrey. Only Middlesex, with fourteen, had more, and this total included the metropolitan houses such as Whitehall and St James's. Surrey was thus home to more royal domestic country residences than any other county.[4] They included some ancient royal seats such as Byfleet and Guildford as well as houses acquired during Henry's reign such as Beddington and Oatlands; they even included his only completely new house, Nonsuch. Of the eleven, three were really important residences – Richmond, Oatlands and Nonsuch. These were principal houses of Henry VIII and even more frequently used by Elizabeth. Immediately on the borders of Surrey were two other major seats whose impact on the county was as great as any house in it, that is to say Windsor Castle and Hampton Court. There was also a cluster of smaller houses over the river in Middlesex including Syon and Hanworth.

In all, Henry and his court paid 289 visits to these Surrey-based houses totalling 2880 days, that is to say 25% of his reign.[5] Because Elizabeth I made much greater use of Richmond and Nonsuch the proportion of the total number of visits she made to this group of houses was 42% and as we shall see when her visits to courtier houses are added the percentage is even higher.[6] The Stuarts were no less enthusiastic occupants of their Surrey properties. James I spent about a third of his time in Surrey and the neighbouring houses of Hampton Court and Windsor. Both Anne of Denmark and Henrietta Maria were granted Oatlands as their principal country seat and their independent progresses took them via other Surrey houses to Weybridge throughout the early 17th century.

The growth of crown interest in Surrey

Therefore royal houses in Surrey and its immediate hinterland were a very significant centre of residence during the 16th and 17th centuries. Historians have generally concentrated on interpreting royal houses architecturally or as expressions of dynastic power and have usually failed to consider the significance of their locality. The Tudor and Stuart age was one in which social structure was based on land. Not only was rank most frequently expressed in terms of landed wealth but royal control was exercised through what can loosely be termed land patronage. In other words by granting land and the offices linked to land the crown could fulfil both the economic and social aspirations of the nobility. The crown itself, at the pinnacle of the social order, was England's greatest landowner.[7] Recent years have seen a number of excellent studies on the crown lands and although there is still much to be learned, scholars have recognized that, although the crown lands were important economically, providing 34% of Elizabeth's revenue and a smaller 14% of Charles I's, their real importance was in their social, recreational and political potential.[8]

There had, of course, always been royal houses in Surrey but Henry VII's construction of Richmond Palace at the turn of the 15th century triggered a chain of events that would see the county dominated by royal palaces (fig 12.1). In order to be close to Richmond, Giles, Lord Daubeney, Henry VII's Lord Chamberlain, began to develop a house at Hampton Court, one that was subsequently massively expanded by Cardinal Wolsey and finally appropriated by Henry VIII. Henry completed Hampton Court in 1538 and instructed his Hampton Court team to design him a new house, Nonsuch in Ewell, and rebuild another, older house, Oatlands, in Weybridge. At this point he passed an act of parliament creating a new hunting ground near Hampton Court called Hampton Court chase and an honor centred on the house.[9] In 1540 another act of parliament added Nonsuch and other lands to the honor.

The creation of the honor

Essentially an honor was a group of manors or landholdings held by one lord with a capital seat as its administrative centre.[10] In the 1520s there was a discernible change in royal land policy which saw the king group many of his disparate landholdings into compact territorial and administrative units as honors.[11] The first two were at New Hall and Hunsdon. Both these houses were potential principal seats. In 1516 Henry VIII bought New Hall in Essex and renamed it Beaulieu. Between its acquisition and its completion in about 1522 £17,000 was spent on transforming the house into a substantial royal manor. Henry decided to create an honor centred on it and an act of parliament was passed to do this in 1523.[12] Hunsdon House, in Hertfordshire, was bought in 1525. This was another major property, probably one of the most important courtier houses built in the 15th century. Henry spent just under £3000 on Hunsdon in about ten years enlarging and improving it. In 1531 an honor was created here too, focused on the royal manor house.[13]

This is, perhaps, what might be expected. Any great courtier or magnate was eager to set his house in a matrix of lands to give it status. At the duke of

Buckingham's house of Thornbury, just outside Bristol, successive dukes had aggrandized their landholdings. The third duke embarked on a major emparkment, in 1508.[14] Charles Brandon, duke of Suffolk, the first of Henry VIII's parvenu dukes, had the same aim but approached the problem from the opposite direction. He decided to build his great country house Westhorpe near Stowmarket in the centre of his existing great estates and the honor of Eye.[15] So before the great royal building works of the 1530s began Henry, almost certainly on the advice of Thomas Wolsey, erected honors as part of the necessary process of making Hunsdon and New Hall major royal seats.

In 1538 Henry could rightly be proud of Hampton Court. It was his greatest single building to date, a house acquired by him and developed to his precise specifications, a house furnished to a higher standard than any other apart from Whitehall. But what of its surroundings? Hampton Court had two large deer parks, but this was merely part of the immediate estate. So an act of parliament was passed in 1539 that stated 'because the saide manour of Hampton Courte ys thus [...] decored and environed with thinges of highe and princely comodities' an honor would be created centred on it.[16] The king went on to acquire tens of thousands of acres in Surrey and Middlesex to set Hampton Court in the centre of a massive landholding; however the honor was to have a special feature – Hampton Court chase created by the same act of parliament.

The creation of the chase

A chase was a private forest.[17] A royal forest was a geographically precisely defined game reserve protected by forest law enforced by royal bailiffs. Forest law took precedence over common law and partly excluded it; its aim, in the words of the act that created Hampton Court chase, was 'for thencrease of Venery and Fowle of Warren'. The land within a royal forest did not have to belong to the crown although some or much of it might; the important point for whoever owned land in it was that there were restrictions on its use. Like a modern National Park, the environment and the balance of nature was protected, and any changes in land use, such as tree felling, ploughing or new grazing were only permitted with special permission.

It was in August or early September 1537, with works at Hampton Court rapidly approaching a conclusion, that Henry VIII ordered the start of work on fencing (or paling) the new chase. It was a gigantic undertaking that involved enclosing four whole parishes, East and West Molesey, Walton-on-Thames and Weybridge and parts of Esher and Cobham. In 1537–8 £1473 was spent on fencing, ditching and hedging the boundaries of this new ground which was

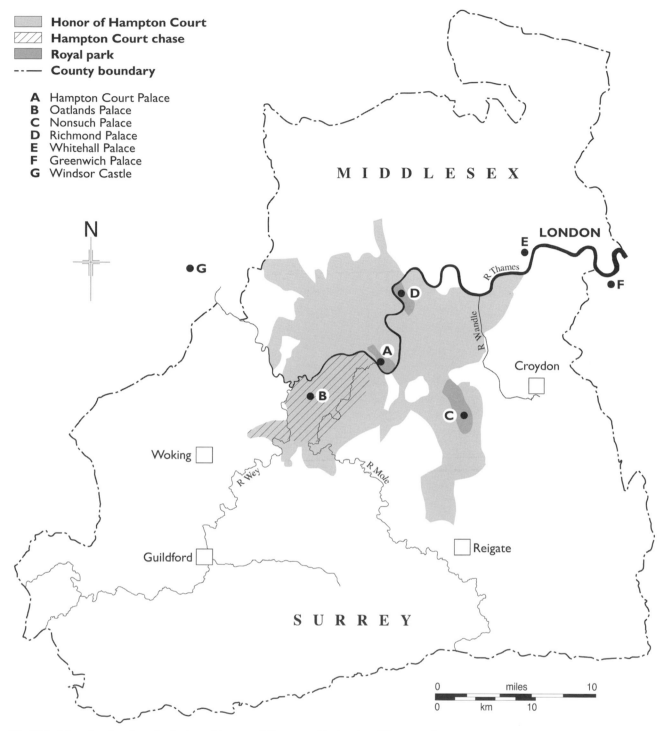

Fig 12.1   Map showing the principal royal houses of Surrey and its borders, Hampton Court chase and the honor of Hampton Court

completely encircled by the time parliament next met in April 1539 and gave the land the status of a chase.[18] Although Hampton Court chase was a forest in its legal sense, forests were not fenced and the deer stayed in the forest through habit rather than confinement. Thus, in being fenced, Hampton Court chase was technically not a forest but an enormous 10,000-acre park under forest law. Within it, owners were entitled to fence their own land to protect it from the deer, but were forced to accept forest law outside it.[19]

There is no doubt of the motivation to create the chase. Henry was a fanatical and bloodthirsty huntsman and this required careful husbandry and

land management to keep herd sizes up. After the creation of the chase the king settled into a round of hunting trips in Surrey using Hampton Court more than ever before. The reason for creating the chase can thus be explained but its precise boundaries (fig.12.1) require more explanation. At first sight it would have made more sense to develop the chase south-east of Hampton Court towards Nonsuch, on the building of which so much money and care was being lavished. Yet it was extended westwards for two reasons. The practical reason was that the western boundaries of the chase could largely be defined by rivers, reducing the quantity of expensive fencing required. But there was another far more important reason: the chase as defined linked Hampton Court and a much more significant house than Nonsuch – Windsor Castle.

Windsor forest was one of the five great forests listed in Domesday book and had, in the time of Henry II, included parts of Buckinghamshire, Middlesex, Berkshire and most of Surrey. Windsor Forest extended, in Henry VIII's time, as far east as the river Wey and thus joined Hampton Court chase at Weybridge and Byfleet. Therefore by creating the chase, Henry was not merely creating a vast park for Hampton Court; he was in fact enabling hunting to continue uninterrupted south of the Thames from Hampton Court to Windsor.

How the honor was created

Henry VIII created Hampton Court honor and chase through a commission that studied and surveyed lands in Surrey and Middlesex, and made recommendations for purchase. Sadly we have no detailed documentation to record the progress of the work.[20] Yet we do have information regarding the purchase of the site of Nonsuch. A detailed 25-page survey of the manor of Cuddington exists, covering all the manorial lands, woods, arable lands, tenants, leases and common land.[21] Each item is carefully measured and valued. James I followed an identical procedure in 1605 when he decided to extend the size of Nonsuch Park. Commissioners were appointed and they made enquiries into the ownership of lands and their value. This done, a note was prepared of the lands that the commissioners recommended to acquire with an acreage and list of owners.[22] None of the Henrician or Jacobean survey maps survive for the Hampton Court honor but one relating to Charles I's plans to expand Richmond Park does (fig 12.2). Drawn by the land surveyor Nicholas Lane, the map was used by Charles's 1634 Commission to determine the boundaries of the park and the ownership of the land.[23] This survey must be very similar to those Henry VIII commissioned to assemble the honor of Hampton Court in the 1530s.

However, many of the lands that were acquired for Henry VIII's honor were not purchased. The majority were acquired either by exchange, attainder or as a result of the dissolution of the monasteries. Land exchanges were crucial and had formed the basis of the earlier honors at New Hall and Hunsdon. They were cost effective for the king who had a massive and diverse landholding across England and Wales. Exchanges allowed remote and isolated crown lands to be swapped for lands closer to hand to form part of the honor. These swaps were usually highly advantageous for the king. For instance large tracts of the honor came from the archbishop of Canterbury, Thomas Cranmer, by exchange. The archbishops of Canterbury had long been the principal landowners in Kent but had increasingly built up estates around London reflecting their move to become the leader of the national church in the nation's capital. The manors of Wimbledon and East Cheam, Ewell and Morden came to the king this way.[24] Another very large land exchange was effected with Merton Priory in 1536 (in other words before it was dissolved). By this the king gained East Molesey in exchange for the church of Ellastone in Staffordshire.[25]

A rather less happy means of aggrandizing the honor was through the lands of attainted subjects. Both Thomas Cromwell and Sir Nicolas Carew unwittingly contributed significant landholdings in this way.[26] Carew's former lands included Beddington, Walton on the Hill, Sutton and Coulsdon.[27] The dissolution of the monasteries likewise brought lands from reluctant former owners to the honor. Merton Priory contributed the most land but Westminster Abbey contributed Toddington and Wandsworth among six other manors, Barking Abbey contributed Weston and St Mary Spital and Sandon.[28] Oatlands, so important to Henry's scheme, was acquired in perhaps the most underhand way of all. In 1534 when William Reed, the owner of the manor, died his son and heir, John, was a minor who was put under the guardianship of Thomas Cromwell. This made it a fairly straightforward transaction for John and his guardian to exchange the property very much in the king's favour.[29]

Thomas Cromwell was almost certainly the mastermind behind the creation of the honor. It was he who, in 1530–2 organized the acquisition of the lands for Whitehall Palace and surviving correspondence concerning the land transactions bears his name.[30] Given the extent of the honor (fig 12.1) and the fact that we have some transaction records, it should in theory be possible to recreate it on a map. Unfortunately this is not as easy as it seems. Sixteenth century parish boundaries are often difficult to determine and manorial boundaries even harder. In addition many parishes comprised more than one manor. So it would be almost impossible to draw the map of the honor of Hampton Court in 1547. What we can do is identify the parishes in which the major landholdings were royal[31] and doing this produces a startling result. Vast swathes of Surrey and Middlesex were owned by the crown, and almost all the principal manors were royal.

The social impact of the honor

These Surrey lands fell into two classes. The lands that were let as part of the crown estate yielding an income for the crown and those that were non-economic holdings used for sport.[32] There was a double cost to the crown for these latter holdings – the opportunity cost of not using the land for agriculture and the considerable maintenance and staffing costs. The crown hunting lands were therefore a direct contributor to the local economy and not a drain. The lands that were let were a crucial part of the structure of society and politics. As already indicated the crown estate was not merely a source of income and *in extremis* capital, it was one of the key tools of patronage. Grants of land or leases on favourable terms were one of the principal means in which past services to the monarchy could be rewarded and future services anticipated. A lease of crown land on favourable terms provided a more secure income for a royal official than a salary or fees. Over a long period land was considerably more valuable than a pension.[33] Thus the extensive crown lands of Surrey were frequently let by the crown to royal officials and courtiers colouring the social mix of the county land-holders. This in turn attracted more royal attention. Many of the places where Queen Elizabeth stayed were royal lands on lease occupied by leading royal servants or courtiers. West Horsley, for instance, was a crown lease occupied by Lord Clinton, Elizabeth's Lord Admiral. The queen visited him there four times, once for a week. Nearby was East Horsley the home of Sir Thomas Cornwallis, comptroller of the household. While Henry VIII stayed in royal houses 80% of the time Queen Elizabeth on progress liked to stay 80% of the time in courtier houses. As Harrison neatly put it she made 'everie noble mans house [...] hir palace'.[34] The queen stayed in at least 33 private Surrey mansions during her reign making, in all, some 227 visits to the county. Twelve of her 23 summer progresses were conducted largely or wholly in the county too. The queen spent fewer than half that number of days in Middlesex, the next most popular county, and Kent and Essex were only visited on 79 and 86 trips respectively.[35]

Under Elizabeth sales of crown lands became an important source of revenue. In the first decade of the reign they grossed a modest £76,648, but during the period immediately following the Spanish Armada in 1588–92 sales totalled over £120,000 a year and, although the rate of sale slowed towards the end of the reign, it has been calculated that £817,350 worth of land was sold during her reign. Yet certain types of land were not sold: the large manors, the ancient holdings such as Cornwall and Lancaster, strategic defensive sites and crucially land close to the queen's houses. For this reason despite the dispersal of many of the Henrican lands Surrey maintained its particular heavily royal character.[36]

The impact of royal lands: recreation

Surrey was thus a major centre of royal property owning, of royal recreation and home to a large part of the cream of Tudor society. The impact of this on the county now needs to be considered. First in terms of royal recreation, Hampton Court Chase and the royal forests: we have seen that the hunting grounds provided employment and required consumables as well as providing sinecures for local landowners. Yet for the majority of the population they were very unpopular. Embodied in a plea to the Privy Council from the start of Edward VI's reign the petition of the inhabitants of the parishes in the Hampton Court chase survives 'by reason of the making of the late Chase of Hampton Court forsomyche as their commons, medowes, and pastures be taken in, and that all the same parisshes are overlade with the deere nowe increasing daly uppon them, very many house-holdes of the same parisshes be lett fall down, the familes decayed, and the Kinges liege people miche diminished; the cuntre therabout in maner made desolate, over and besides that that the Kinges Majeste loseth [...] hys yearly revenues and rentes, to a great summe'.[37] Because of this and the fact that the fence needed expensive repairs it was dechased the same year Henry VIII died. This was not, however, the end of the matter. The rights of the crown over the former chase and the forest of Windsor were asserted well into the 17th century. James I commissioned John Norden to make a survey of the honor and forest of Windsor in 1607 because 'the true limites and boundes beinge also nere worne out of knowledge. And will shortlie be worne out of mind without means of reformation'. Norden's map, for which James I paid £200, is a key document in illustrating the importance laid on crown hunting rights in the early Stuart period (fig 12.3).[38] It led to subsequent royal actions such as James removing local swine that disturbed his progress riding through what was described as 'the district of his forest'.[39] The question of the Surrey boundary of the forest was reopened in an enquiry at Bagshot in 1632 at which the Attorney General claimed that the whole Surrey Baliwick, that is to say the whole county west of the Wey and north of the Hog's Back were part of the forest.[40] In doing so he found old residents of Surrey to swear that this was the case in Queen Elizabeth's time. The court accepted this and the area was re-affirmed as being forest and not merely in its purlieu.[41] The matter was reopened by the Long Parliament that appointed a Commission to look at royal forests in Surrey under the act 'for enquiring into the boundaries of all forests'.[42] They met at Guildford in 1642 and unsurprisingly found that the royal claims for the forest of Windsor were void and the only forest they recognized was Guildford Park; on the basis of this the whole of Surrey was deafforested, including any parts of the honor of Hampton Court that had residual forest rights.[43]

The loss of the forest and chase did not, in any sense, mean that the hunting grounds of the monarchy in the vicinity were reduced. John Speed's

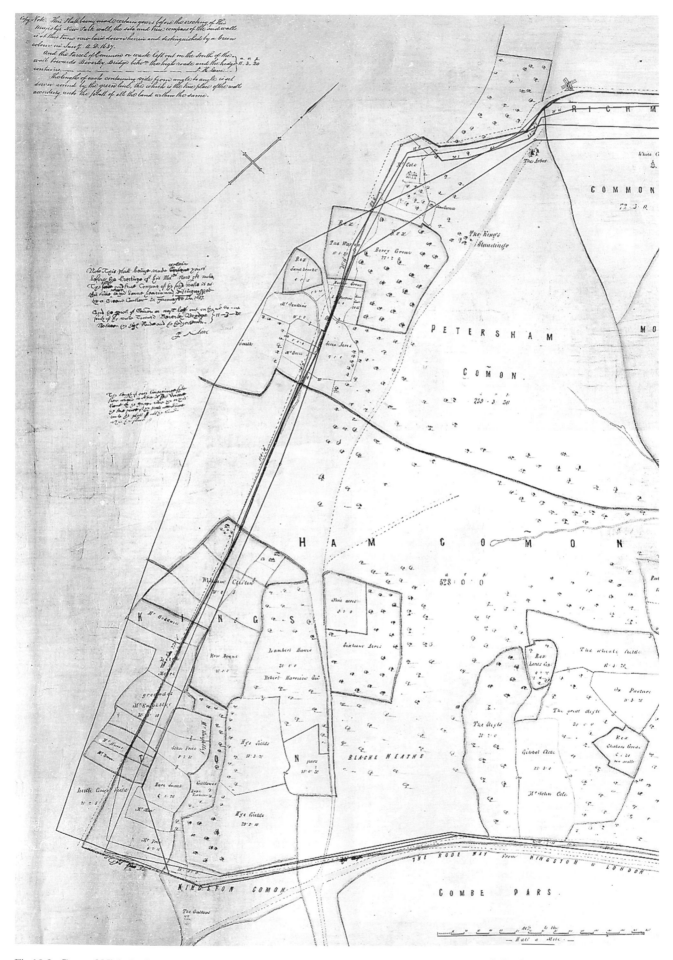

Fig 12.2   Copy of Nicholas Lane's 1634 survey of lands adjacent to Richmond Park. Various proposals for the new park's boundaries are drawn in by his commissioners as are existing crown lands marked REX. The map shows that most of the rest of the land was either common land or in private ownership. The map is reproduced in two overlapping parts with the north-eastern portion on the opposite page.

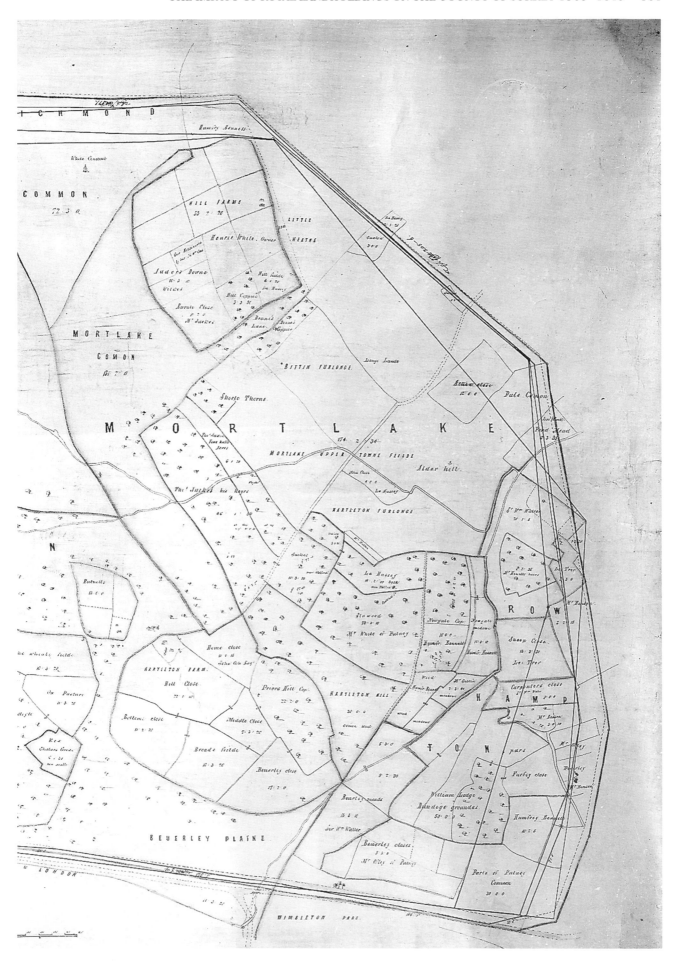

Fig 12.2 *continued*   North-eastern portion of the copy of Nicholas Lane's 1634 survey of lands adjacent to Richmond Park. The south-western portion is shown on the opposite page. The National Archives Image Library MR 1/295

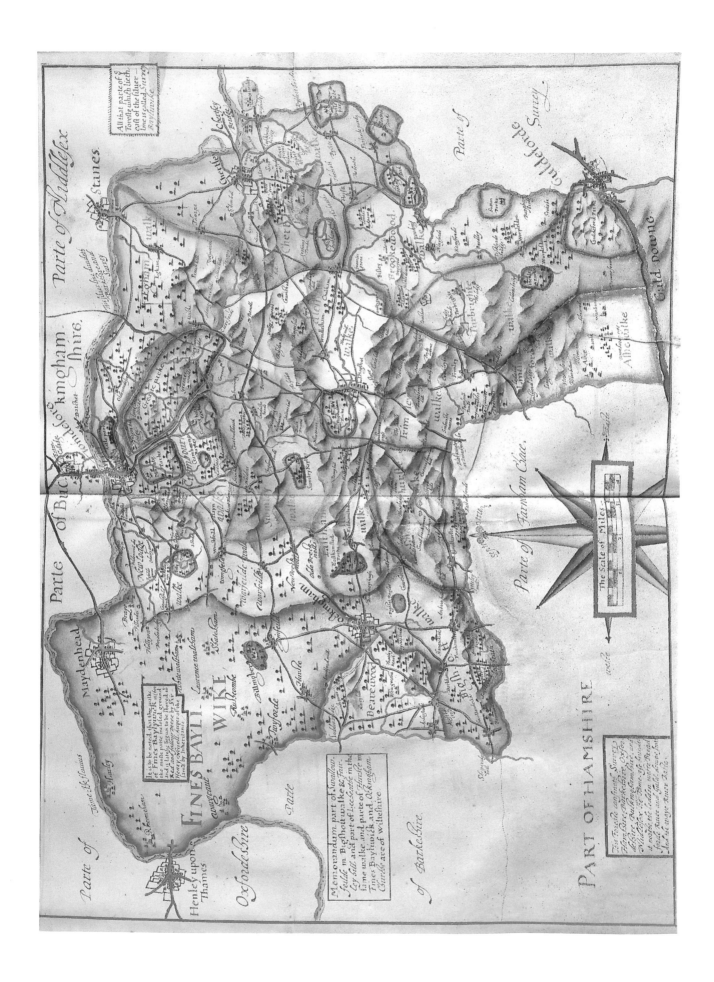

map, drawn up between 1596 and 1610 and published in 1612, makes this point clearly (fig 12.4). Thus although the chase had gone the honor still contained considerable facilities for hunting and at least four major royal houses. As late as the reign of George I the royal family, attended by sometimes as many as 150 riders, would charge through the Surrey countryside in pursuit of deer, causing destruction and chaos as they went. The influence of the park-lands of Surrey should not be ignored.

The impact of royal lands: the court

The royal court was peripatetic, it moved around its houses in the Thames valley never staying for more than six weeks at any house and usually for much shorter times than that. In the winter, spring and autumn the court was at its largest, numbering about 800 people. In the summer much of the household returned to their country seats and the court went on progress. So as the court moved between Hampton Court, Nonsuch, Oatlands and Richmond, over land largely owned by the crown and stopping in the royal parks to hunt, it had a considerable impact on the local inhabitants.

CART TAKING

Law obliged local justices of the peace to supply a certain number of horses and carts that could be used by the court as it moved from palace to palace. Additionally an act for 'the increase of horses' compelled private owners of parks of more than a mile in circumference to keep brood mares in them. Speed's map (fig 12.4) shows 36 such parks in Surrey alone. The county assessment laid down that when the court left Richmond the people of Surrey were obliged to provide 80 carriages, when it left Oatlands 100 and for Nonsuch 110. The carts were paid for by the household but at a lesser rate, only 2d a mile rather than the market rate of 10d or 12d. Carts had to be supplied when demanded, even in the middle of harvest. Carts were also needed by the various household offices for transporting food and supplies and by the Office of Works for building materials. These were requisitioned sepa-rately by each department, some like the woodyard and coal house requiring sometimes hundreds of carts. Carters were obliged to travel as far as 25 miles at the request of a royal cart-taker. Cart taking was a source of major grievance in Surrey as the royal family travelled there every year. This received recognition in a small number of towns next to major royal houses. For instance in 1604 Windsor was relieved of all cart taking as the town only had three carriages and Weybridge, which only

had one cart, was given exemption from carrying victuals. Yet such exemptions were rare and cart taking remained an issue until it was abolished in 1688.[44]

PURVEYANCE

Perhaps the most contentious royal prerogative that affected the people of Surrey was that of purveyance. This was an ancient right that allowed the monarch to purchase food and supplies at a rate cheaper than the market rate for the goods. Therefore the royal purveyors would travel, for example, to Guildford market and buy food for cash at the discounted 'king's price'. This was modified during Elizabeth's reign to a practice known as compounding. This essentially meant that a local tax known as the composition was levied and with it the compounders (a group of local JPs) would buy a specified list of goods at the market price and sell them to the house-hold at the king's price. This resulted in each county compounding with the household, in other words agreeing a level of payment for supplies. In 1578 Surrey had to provide finance for 60 geese, 190 capons, 130 coarse hens, 350 coarse pullets, 1300 coarse chickens and 600 lambs. They also had to finance fuel for cooking and this totalled 400 loads of coal, 300 loads of logs and 900 loads of kindling. In one sense, by compounding Surrey limited the impact of a continual royal presence in the county as the inhabitants now knew their yearly obligation. It also spread the burden of the royal household more equally across England, and was thus popular in Surrey. However supplies for the queen's own table were exempt and her privy bakehouse and kitchen could buy at the queen's rate in local markets. More-over the crown reserved a right to purvey additional supplies while the court was on progress. Surrey was thus at a considerable disadvantage, having compounded and still having to sell at a discount for the queen's table and for progress.[45] Just as towns close to major houses might obtain an exemption from cart taking so, on occasion, an exemption from purveyance could be granted. Queen Elizabeth, for instance, exempted a group of bailiwicks in Surrey in compensation for losses suffered by the local people from grazing royal deer.[46] Such privileges were, however, rare.

The case of Kingston market might suggest that purveyance was perhaps not so devastating as was made out. In about 1540 Leland in his *Itinerary* described Kingston as the best market town in Surrey and in receipt of great privileges from the crown.[47] These privileges were a source of envy among the surrounding towns, particularly its right to a market.

Opposite: Fig 12.3 John Norden's 'Description of the Honor of Windsor', 1607 for which he was paid £200. The Royal Collection 1142252 © HM Queen Elizabeth II

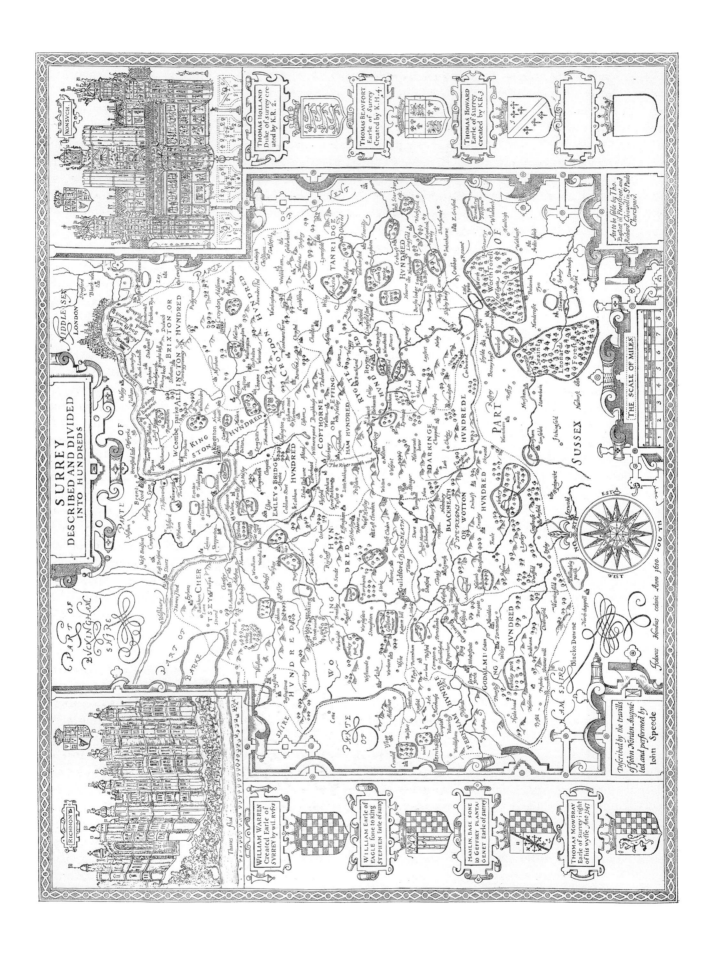

This was described by Camden in his *Britannia* of 1607 as 'considerable'.[48] In 1618 Hounslow attempted to get permission for a market on Saturdays and the aldermen of Kingston moved to prevent it. Similarly in 1624 when Hampton attempted to hold a market Kingston opposed it. Kingston's charter was re-granted in 1628 and established the town's right to hold the only market within seven miles. The vexed question of Hounslow's claim to a market arose again in 1653 and was again seen off. At the Restoration Kingston successfully re-secured its charter for a Wednesday market. The reason that the corporation of Kingston fought so long and hard for its market was largely because it supplied Hampton Court with so much. All the straw and hay for the horses and stables came from Kingston, as well as meat, vegetables, eggs and beer. After 1660 the value of this was much increased as all purveyance was abolished, but even under the compounding system Kingston profited enormously from the proximity of so many royal houses.[49]

IMPRESSMENT

Finally there was the matter of impressment, another unpopular royal prerogative. Since the 13th century the officers of the King's works had enjoyed sweeping powers over those in the building trade. The purveyors of works could, under royal commission, impress men, materials and carts, arrest those who deserted, gaol those who misbehaved and recover materials that had been purloined. During Henry VIII's building works of the 1530s thousands of craftsmen were impressed. In 1532, 900 at Whitehall alone. Hampton Court was built using impressed labour largely from Surrey but some from as far afield as Norfolk. The problem with impressment was not that the craftsmen were not paid (they received compensation for working away from home) rather that their removal from the county prevented private work from progressing. At the same time the county was scoured for materials, for good brickearth, for lime, for timber and other building materials. When a major royal building project was in hand a private owner suffered a chronic shortage of craftsmen and often materials too. For instance, during the major royal works of the 1530s and 40s the building industry in Surrey must have been boosted for tradesmen but highly constricted for patrons.[50]

The impact of royal lands: the benefits
While impressment and requisitioning of materials was a problem for some it was also a great benefit for the economies of the towns of Surrey. For instance the growth of Reigate must have owed much to the stone

quarries so essential to the construction of the royal houses.[51] Almost as important to Kingston as its market was the local building industry. Building materials were key to Kingston's economy as they were to a wide band of villages and hamlets along the Thames. At Kingston brick and tile was made throughout the 16th century and men and materials made trips throughout the day to the adjacent royal palaces.[52]

Other benefits accrued to local towns. It has recently been estimated that household expenditure in progress time increased by about £1000, much of which went into the locality. The market and the inns of Kingston were virtually an outpost of Hampton Court continually used by everyone from the most important ambassador to the children of the chapel. Indeed inns and taverns throughout Surrey were rarely empty and when the court was near could charge a hefty premium to the royal harbingers who attempted to find beds for courtiers. Even when the court was just passing through towns and villages would have the chance to sell refreshment to hundreds of members of the royal household. A town like Guildford, a royal centre and a staging post to Portsmouth, benefited enormously from the frequent passage of the court.

On a wider scale too the passage of the court brought benefits to Surrey. In the 1550s a number of well-travelled aristocrats and diplomats began to import a new type of passenger road vehicle from Germany and the Low Countries. The coach, although not used at Queen Elizabeth's coronation, soon found a patron in the queen and the first royal model was delivered in 1564. This was the start of a royal revolution in transport that had an enormous impact on the royal houses, their locality and the whole of the south-east of England. First Elizabeth, and then the Stuart monarchs, gradually moved away from the use of Thames barges and horses towards coach travel, although on ceremonial occasions the river was still used.[53] The church bells of towns and villages were rung each time the monarch passed through. From 1570 the Kingston churchwardens' accounts show that Queen Elizabeth increasingly moved by road. In 1571 the bells were rung eight times, but on only one of these occasions was it the royal barge that carried the queen. Carriages required a much higher standard of road maintenance than previously. Under an act of parliament of 1555 this work fell to local inhabitants. In 1598, for instance, the chamberlain of Kingston paid 21d to mend the road to smooth the elderly queen's passage from Sir Thomas Cecil's house at Wimbledon to Nonsuch.[54] An act of parliament passed in 1606 stated in its preamble that as the road

Opposite: Fig 12.4 Speed's Map of Surrey, 1612 is unique among the county maps in his atlas in showing vignettes of two royal palaces rather than views of towns. Surrey, for Speed, was a royal county. © Museum of London

between Kingston and Nonsuch was the 'waye the chief parte of the cariages to his majesties houses of nonsuche richmond oatlands and hampton Courte of necessity passeth as also great store of ship tymber and other provisions for his majesties houses at london' the burden for the repair rested on the locality.[55] Local justices were appointed to levy tax and organize overseers to maintain the road for the king's use. In this way the key royal routes around Middlesex and Surrey were more developed and better maintained than anywhere else in the country.

Finally it must be noted that although Surrey had cause to be considered as a special case other counties suffered at royal hands too. Kent, for instance had few royal houses, but military installations imposed an equivalently large burden. The people of Kent had to watch the coastal beacons and coastal landing points, feed stationed troops, supply the navy, supply labour for the storehouses at Chatham, Deptford, Woolwich and Rochester, provide carriage for visiting dignitaries and for military and building materials while also servicing four royal palaces (Greenwich, Eltham, Dartford and Canterbury).[56]

Conclusions and possible future directions for research

In conclusion, there was clearly intense royal activity in Surrey in the 16th and early 17th centuries. Eleven Royal palaces and their parks were regularly used for a hundred years. Surrounding them vast parts of the county were royal property, much of it let out to rich and influential courtiers, the rest maintained as hunting park. Special rights of access and passage were reserved to the monarch. Roads had to be specially maintained, food was requisitioned at preferential prices, horses and carts were commandeered, masons, bricklayers, plumbers, tilers and carpenters were ordered to work on royal building projects. It was all this activity that caused the inhabitants of mid-Elizabethan Surrey to complain about the effect of the continual presence of the court on their doorstep. Yet the intensity of royal activity certainly had a beneficial economic effect too, particularly in the development of prosperous towns and good transport infrastructure.

This paper has focused on my own area of interest, that is to say the mechanisms of court life and their physical impact. How significant these impacts were in the development of the county I am unable to say, but the identification of the issue raises a number of questions. It would be good to know, for instance, how strong the case is for the positive economic influence of the court in the development of key towns in Surrey. Did the growth of Surrey building industries, stimulated by crown programmes, have a significant impact on the wealth of towns too? Conversely was the pattern of non-royal building affected by the intensive development of royal houses in the 1530s and 40s? How much did the development of the road network south of the Thames owe to royal usage as opposed to the development of roads in parts seldom used by the court? Can the relatively intense settlement by courtiers and the economic activity triggered by their estates be said to characterize Surrey in any way? For instance did the number of hunting parks impact on the county's topographical or economic development? These questions and others may help to advance our understanding of the archaeology of Surrey.

NOTES

Abbreviations
PRO: The National Archives, Kew, Public Record Office
SHC: Surrey History Centre, Woking

1 *VCH*, **1**, 367–8.
2 I mean historic Surrey that included, before 1888, all London south of the Thames.
3 Nairn *et al* 1982, 17; Clark & Thompson 1934, 99.
4 The Surrey houses are Bagshot, Beddington, Byfleet, Chobham, Guildford, Mortlake, Nonsuch, Oatlands, Richmond, West Horsley and Woking (known in the 16th century as Oking). Other counties: Kent 8; Berkshire, 4; Oxfordshire, 4; Essex 3; Bedfordshire, 2; Buckinghamshire, 2; Northamptonshire, 2; Sussex, 2; Northumberland, Wiltshire and Worcestershire 1. See Colvin 1982.
5 Thurley 1988, fig 123.
6 Chambers 1923, Appendix A.
7 Wyndham 1980, 18–19.
8 Wolffe 1970 & 1971; Hoyle 1992; Madge 1968.
9 *Statutes of the Realm*, **3**, 721–4. It is not clear why the king needed an act of parliament to create an honor. Perhaps statute was used to give the process greater weight and dignity.
10 For honors see Maddox 1736, 2, 5, 7–9, 261, 262.

11 Miller 1986, 218–9, 229, 248–9.
12 'Forasmuch as the Kyng our Soveign Lord hath lately caused a Palesse Roiall to be byelded and edified at his manour of Newhall in his countie of Essex at his great costes and charges to the which place his Highness hath great pleasure to resorte for the helth comforte and preservacion of his moost roiall person' he intends to annex certain lands which came into his hands from the attainder of the Duke of Buckingham 'and to make his said manour and Palais of Newhall' and the lands annexed to it 'to be an Honour Royal' and he intends that it should be 'hensforth nambed accepted and takyn the kynges Honour of Beaulieu'. *Statutes of the Realm*, **3**, 245 (14 & 15 Henry VIII c.18).
13 The wording is precisely the same as that for New Hall, excepting the part about changing the name of the house. *Statutes of the Realm*, **3**, 410–11 (23 Henry VIII c.30).
14 Rawlcliffe 1978, ch 3.
15 Gunn & Lindley 1988, 273–4.
16 *Statutes of the Realm*, **3**, 721–4 (31 Henry VIII c.5).
17 Madge 1968, 26–7.
18 *Statutes of the Realm*, **3**, 721–4 (31 Henry VIII c.5). Accounts for erecting the chase are in SHC: LM 717, 718, 720, 721, 722. Also see Walker 1965, 83–7.

19 For forests and forest law see Rackham 1986, 130–9. A list of the woodland enclosed in the chase is in SHC: LM 723.

20 A list of lands purchased among the augmentation accounts is in PRO: E323/1 Part 1 (m.11). A summary of lands in the honor and wages and perquisites of the High Steward is in SHC: LM710.

21 Dent 1962, 35.

22 Titford 1967, 78–9.

23 Cloake 1995, **1**, 197–206.

24 Letters and Papers XIII (I) pp 569, 571; *Statutes of the Realm*, **3**, 585.

25 Letters and Papers X no 243 (26); Letters and Papers XV no 498; Letters and Papers XIII (i) no 779.

26 Letters and Papers XIV (I) P.29 no 71; Letters and Papers XV, no 498 (36) (p 214)

27 Letters and Papers XV No 498 (36) (p 214).

28 Letters and Papers XV no 498 (36) (p 214).

29 Colvin 1982, 205–6.

30 For instance see Cromwell's letter to the Prior of Merton Priory, Letters and Papers, VIII no 345 (p 139).

31 Ash Lees (*VCH*, **3**, 473); Balham (*VCH*, **4**, 98); Banstead (*VCH*, **3**, 255); Battersea (*VCH*, **4**, 11, 112); Beddington (*VCH*, **4**, 170–2); Brooklands (*VCH*, **3**, 476); Byfleet (*VCH*, **3**,.401); East and West Cheam (*VCH*, **4**, 196); Cuddington (*VCH*, **3**, 267) ; Ewell (*VCH*, **3**, 279); Imworth (*VCH*, **3**, 465); Kingston (*VCH*, **3**, 495); Kingswood (*VCH*, **3**, 281); East and West Molesey (*VCH*, **3**, 453); Mortlake (*VCH*, **4**, 70); Oatlands (*VCH*, **3**, 476); Talworth (*VCH*, **3**, 521); Wandsworth (*VCH*, **4**, 112–3); Walton-on-the-Hill (*VCH*, **3**, 317); Walton Leigh (*VCH*, **3**, 471); Walton-on-Thames (*VCH*, **3**, 468); Weston (Thames Ditton) (*VCH*, **3**, 464); Weybridge (*VCH*, **3**, 476); Wimbledon (*VCH*, **4**, 122).

32 It is worth noting that the crown estates were not homogenous. They were managed by different arms of the state, most by the Exchequer, some by the duchy of Lancaster and then the lands of the royal family, including the duchy of Cornwall and the queen's lands, by their own officers.

33 Wyndham 1980, 21–2.

34 Furnivall 1877, 270.

35 On twelve years her progresses were mainly or completely in Surrey, on eleven in Hertfordshire and Middlesex. Next came Bedfordshire, Berkshire and Essex with eight years and then Kent with three. The houses in Surrey stayed in by Elizabeth I were: Bagshot, Barn Elms, Beddington, Byfleet, Chessington, Chertsey, Chobham, Clandon, Croydon, Egham, Farnham, Guildford Manor, Ham House, Horsley, Katherine Hall, Lambeth, Leatherhead, Loseley, Merton Abbey, Mitcham, Mortlake, Nonsuch, Putney, Pyrford, Seale, Stoke d'Abernon, Streatham, Sutton Place, Tooting, Thorpe, West Molesey, Wimbledon, Woking. Source: Chambers 1923, app A; Cole 1999, 24–5, app 2.

36 Madge 1968, 40–2; Hoyle 1992, 12, 17.

37 Acts of the Privy Council, n.s. **2** (1547–1550), 190–2.

38 The survey exists in two versions. The King's presentation copy, British Library, Harleian MS 3749, and another for the Prince of Wales now in the Royal Library. Tighe & Davis 1863, **2**, 1, 27–30; Lawrence 1985, 54–6.

39 *VCH*, **1**, 403.

40 *Cal SPD*, Sept 19 1632.

41 Purlieu, in other words land that had once been part of the forest but that still, in some respects, remained subject to forest law.

42 *Statutes of the Realm*, 16 Chas I c.16.

43 British Library: Harleian MS 546.

44 Woodworth 1945, 71–4; PRO: LS 13/168 ff 86v, 124v.

45 Woodworth 1945; Aylmer 1957–8.

46 *Cal SPD*, Jas I (1603–10), **17**, nos 58–9; Cole 1999, 49–50.

47 Toulmin Smith 1964, **4**, 86.

48 Copley 1977, 13.

49 Woodworth 1945, *passim;* Roots 1797, 215.

50 Colvin 1975, 5, 18, 61, 113; Airs 1995, 74–5, 201; Salzman 1952, 37–8.

51 Tatton-Brown 2001.

52 Musty 1990, 411–15.

53 Mumby forthcoming. I am most grateful to Mr Mumby for allowing me to see his draft manuscript.

54 Kingston Borough Archives KG2/3 (1567–1681), p 18; KD5/1/1 (1567–1637) p 195, see also pp 185, 196.

55 *Statutes of the Realm*, **4(ii)**, 1094–5. Two earlier Elizabethan acts had required the JPs of Surrey to repair their roads, but in order to preserve the smooth transport of minerals and aggregates: *Statutes of the Realm*, **4(i)**, 726–7; **4(ii)**, 919–2.

56 *Cal SPD*, Elizabeth I (1591–4), **245**, no 69.

BIBLIOGRAPHY

Airs, M, 1995 *The Tudor and Jacobean country house: a building history*

Aylmer, G E, 1957–8 The last years of purveyance 1610–1660, *Econ Hist Rev*, 2 ser, **10**, 81–93

Cal SPD: Calendar of State Papers Domestic 1547–1964, Record Commission, 94 vols, 1856–1964

Cantor, L M & Hatherly, J 1979 The medieval parks of England, *Geography*, **64**, 70–83

Chambers, E K, 1923 *The Elizabethan stage*, 4 vols

Clark, G, & Thompson W H, 1934 *The Surrey landscape*

Cloake, J, 1995 & 1996 *Palaces and parks of Richmond and Kew*, 2 vols

Cole, M H, 1999 *The portable queen. Elizabeth I and the politics of ceremony*, Massachusetts

Colvin, H M (ed), 1975 *The history of the king's works*, vol **3**, 1485–1660 (part 1)

——, 1982 *The history of the king's works*, vol **4**, 1485–1660 (part 2)

Copley, G J, 1977 *Camden's Britannia, Surrey and Sussex*

Dent, J, 1962 *The quest for Nonsuch*

Furnivall, F J (ed), 1877 *Harrison's Description of England in Shakespeare's youth*, London, New Shakespeare Society, 6 ser pt 1

Gentles, I, 1973 The sales of crown lands during the English Revolution, *Engl Hist Rev*, 2 ser, **26**, 614–35

Gunn, S J & Lindley, P G, 1988 Charles Brandon's Westhorpe: an Early Tudor courtyard house in Suffolk, *Archaeol J*, **145**, 272–89

Hammersely, G, 1957 The crown woods and their exploitation in the sixteenth and seventeenth centuries, *Bull Inst Hist Res*, **30**, 136–61

——, 1960 The revival of forest laws under Charles I, *History*, **45.154**, 85–102

Hoyle, R W (ed), 1992 *The estates of the English crown 1558–1640*, Cambridge

Lambert, H, 1933 Some account of the Surrey manors held by Merton College and Corpus Christi College, Oxford, in the seventeenth century, *SyAC*, **41**, 34–9

Lawrence, H, 1985 John Norden and his colleagues: surveyors of crown lands, *Cartographic J*, **22**, 54–6

Letters and papers foreign and domestic of the reign of Henry VIII (eds J S Brewer & R H Brodie), 21 vols, London, 1861–3

Madge, S J, 1968 *The Doomsday of crown lands*

Maddox, Thomas, 1736 *Baronia Anglica*, London

Miller, H, 1986 *Henry VIII and the English nobility*, Oxford

Mumby, J, forthcoming Medieval carriages and the origins of the coach: the archaeology of the European transport revolution, *Antiq J*

Musty, J, 1990   Brick kilns and brick and tile suppliers to Hampton Court Palace, *Archaeol J*, **147,** 411–19

Nairn, I, Pevsner, N, & Cherry, B, 1982   *The buildings of England, Surrey*

Outhwaite, R B, 1967   The price of crown land at the turn of the sixteenth century, *Engl Hist Rev*, 2 ser, **20,** 229–40

Rackham, O, 1986   *The history of the English countryside*

Rawlcliffe, C, 1978   *The Staffords, earls of Stafford and dukes of Buckingham 1394–1521*, Cambridge

Richardson, W C, 1952   *Tudor chamber administration 1485–1547*, Louisiana

——, 1961   *History of the Court of Augmentations 1536–1554*, Louisiana

Roots, G (trans), 1797   *Charters of the town of Kingston upon Thames*, London

Salzman, L F, 1952   *Building in England down to 1540*, Oxford

Speed, John   *The counties of Britain*, with an introduction by Nigel Nicholson and county commentaries by Alisdair Hawkyard, The British Library, 1995

Statutes of the Realm, Record Commission, London, 1810–28

Tatton-Brown, T, 2001   The quarrying and distribution of Reigate stone in the Middle Ages, *Medieval Archaeol*, **45,** 189–201

Thurley, S, 1998   *English royal palaces 1450–1550*, unpublished PhD thesis, Courtauld Institute of Art

Tighe, R R, & Davis, J E, 1863   *Annals of Windsor being the history of the castle and town*, 2 vols

Titford, C F, 1967   The Great Park of Nonsuch, *SyAC*, **64,** 78–9

Toulmin Smith, L, 1964   *Leland's itinerary in England and Wales*, 4 vols, Fontwell

VCH: Victoria history of the county of Surrey (ed H E Malden), 4 vols, 1902–12

Walker, T E C, 1965   The Chase of Hampton Court, *SyAC*, **62,** 83–7

——, 1961   Cobham: manorial history, *SyAC*, **58,** 47–78

Wolffe, B P, 1970   *The crown lands 1461–1536. An aspect of Yorkist and early Tudor government*

——, 1971   *The royal demesne in English history. The crown estate in the governance of the realm from the Conquest to 1509*

Woodworth, A, 1945   Purveyance for the royal household in the reign of Queen Elizabeth, *Trans American Philosophical Soc*, new ser, 25.1

Wyndham, K S H, 1980   Crown land and royal patronage in mid-sixteenth century England, *J Brit Stud*, **19.2,** 18–34

Dr Simon Thurley, English Heritage, 23 Savile Row, London W1S 2ET

13

Kingston – Saxon royal estate centre to post-medieval market town: the contribution of archaeology to understanding towns in Surrey

PHIL ANDREWS

Excavations and documentary studies over the past 30 years have considerably enhanced our knowledge of the origins and development of Kingston, though many gaps remain to be filled. The increase in archaeological work in the town since 1990 has been particularly dramatic, fuelled by developer funding resulting from changes in planning policy. In other Surrey towns, even Guildford, investigations have generally been more sporadic and of insufficient size to provide such a comprehensive database of information. Completion and assessment of the Extensive Urban Surveys currently being undertaken for these towns will result in a better understanding of the archaeological resource and enable a more informed targeting of sites to be made when these become available for excavation. This should provide more information about all aspects of the towns, their relationships to one another, to London, and to their hinterlands. Here there is a need to place archaeology within a broader framework of academic enquiry. As the amount of information from archaeological investigations, building recording and documentary work by various organizations and individuals rapidly increases, the challenge will be to synthesize and publish this information in appropriate ways without compromising the academic integrity of the work.

Introduction

'The potential of towns for dramatically increasing knowledge concerning the growth of pan-European economies and societies at a formative period in western culture must not be underestimated' (Ayres 1997, 64).

In *The Archaeology of Surrey to 1540* (Bird & Bird 1987, 223–61) Dennis Turner wrote: 'Some urban investigations have been among the great successes of the archaeology of the Middle Ages but medieval archaeology in Surrey towns has been modest.' However, he went on to say that 'Kingston provides the clearest archaeological view of a Surrey town' and that work in towns such as Kingston and Reigate is particularly important to redress the balance of work in larger more successful towns elsewhere. Since that was written there has been an upsurge in archaeological investigations throughout the county, the vast majority of these funded by developers as a result of the introduction of Planning Policy Guidance note 16 (PPG 16). A variety of desktop studies, evaluations and excavations have been undertaken in all Surrey's towns, and some of the resulting information from this and earlier work is now beginning to appear in print. Several investigations in Reigate and Guildford have been published and a recent volume of *Surrey Archaeological Collections* (*SyAC* 1998) was devoted to work in four other towns: Chertsey, Dorking, Farnham and Godalming. Kingston, however, now a London borough and no longer within Surrey, was not considered in that volume (Poulton 1998) nor in *Historic Towns in Surrey* (O'Connell 1977).

Apart from the possible exception of Southwark, Kingston is the most extensively excavated town in the historic county of Surrey. Archaeological and documentary work over the past three decades has continued to add to our knowledge of its development, particularly in the Saxon and medieval periods. Many people have taken an active interest in the history and archaeology of Kingston, and among these the late Joan Wakeford should be singled out for her perceptive essays (Wakeford 1990) which provide much food for thought. The many articles and books published by June Sampson (eg Sampson 1997) and, more recently, Shaan Butters (1995) have also done much to draw attention to the town and the impact of modern development on historic Kingston. (In what follows, references to the extensive documentary evidence that exists for Kingston are largely based on the Charter Quay report by Wessex Archaeology (2003), where full bibliographic details can be found). In the 1960s and 1970s the Kingston upon Thames Archaeological Society (KuTAS) focused attention on the archaeology of the town and initiated modern excavation work which has been regularly undertaken by various organizations ever since. The excavations carried out at Charter Quay in 1988–90 and 1998–9 in advance of new development have been the most extensive ever undertaken in the town. They have brought to light a continuous sequence of urban development, commercial growth and land reclamation that began in the early 12th century and in many ways reflects the wider history of Kingston upon Thames. The influence of topography on the town's development is now better understood, especially with respect to the gravel islands which provided foci for settlement and the surrounding watercourses.

Topography

The pattern and history of the river channels and gravel 'islands' in and around Kingston is complex (Penn & Rolls 1981; Hawkins 1998) and will undoubtedly be further clarified by future work. The Hogsmill river appears now to flow around the southern edge of the 'central island' with other, smaller gravel 'islands' further to the south. Earlier archaeological work, particularly at Eden Street and Eden Walk (Penn *et al* 1984), indicates the former presence of a channel (the so-called 'east arm' of the Hogsmill) which appears to have flowed northwards, bounding the east side of the 'central island'. This probably joined another channel, the so-called 'Latchmere/Downhall channel', comprising the Latchmere stream (an existing watercourse) and the Downhall ditch (a watercourse known from documentary evidence) which together ran east to west to join the Thames and formed the northern boundary to the 'central island' as shown in figure 13.1 (Hawkins 1998, 271). Both the east arm of the Hogsmill and the Downhall channel remained active into the medieval period, although subject to progressive silting, rubbish disposal and eventual culverting.

There is evidence from archaeological, documentary and photographic sources of flooding in Kingston in the medieval and post-medieval periods, particularly around the High Street area, and the course and confines of the Thames and Hogsmill were not stabilized until the end of the 19th century. The Hogsmill has been canalized close to where it joins the Thames, and now flows in a deep concrete-lined channel to the west of the Clattern Bridge. The sequence of flooding and reclamation forms the basis for much of the settlement history of Kingston up to the end of the medieval period, particularly in the areas of the town bordering the Thames.

Prehistoric and Roman (fig 13.1)

A few flint tools of late Upper Palaeolithic and Mesolithic date have been recovered in Kingston town centre, but the earliest evidence for settlement is in the Neolithic period. The most important site yet discovered is at Eden Walk where both Early and Late Neolithic pottery, worked flint, worked antler and animal bone were recovered from a former river channel, part of the east arm of the Hogsmill (Penn *et al* 1984). Whether this represents temporary occupation in the channel itself or debris deposited from an

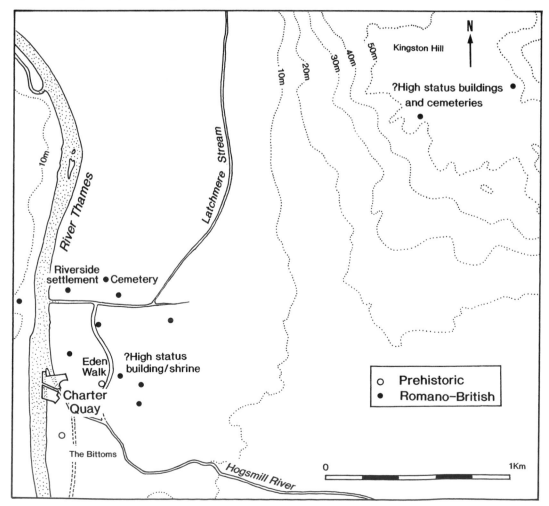

Fig 13.1 Prehistoric and Roman sites (after Hawkins 1996, fig 1) (© Crown Copyright NC/04/25242)

adjacent site is unclear. This part of the former channel also contained some brushwood, perhaps a platform or trackway of Middle Bronze Age date, overlain by a spread of burnt flint. Again, it is uncertain what this represents, but it may have been localized consolidation on the edge of the channel for seasonal use. A variety of Neolithic, Early and Middle Bronze Age finds, including stone and flint axes and collared urns, found during quarrying at Kingston Hill may represent intermittent prehistoric activity (Field & Needham 1986, 148). Other (Late) Bronze Age features and finds have been found during excavations at East Lane, South Lane and the Bittoms (Hawkins *et al* 2002); these sites may all represent part of a single, dispersed Late Bronze Age settlement on the southern gravel 'island'. A relatively dense scatter of pottery of Late Bronze Age/Early Iron Age date has also been found a short distance to the east at Orchard Road (Jackson *et al* 1997, 222), perhaps part of another settlement. A site at Kingston Hill to the north-east, largely destroyed by quarrying in the 19th century, may have been a Late Bronze Age defended settlement enclosed by a ditch, and the considerable quantity of metalwork recovered suggests that bronze working may have been carried out there (Field & Needham 1986). More recent work in the vicinity has recorded occasional Late Bronze Age features and some pottery perhaps representing part of this settlement (Bird *et al* 1989, 185; Bird *et al* 1996, 210). In addition to these discoveries, the Thames at Kingston has produced a number of Neolithic axes and a large assemblage of Bronze Age weaponry, some probably deliberately deposited as votive offerings (eg Needham 1987, 135).

Few Iron Age finds have been recovered from Kingston and there is no evidence for substantial Romano-British occupation in the area. However, evidence is accumulating which indicates the existence of a Romano-British rural settlement north of the 'central island' (Hawkins 1996). Excavations in 2002 exposed the possible remains of a post-built building and two pits containing Roman building material including fragments of box-flue tiles (Duncan Hawkins, pers comm), lying to the south-west of a cemetery recorded during brickearth digging in the early 19th century (Hinton 1984). Investigations on the west bank of the Thames, in Hampton Wick, have also revealed evidence for settlement, and together these sites may indicate the location of a fording or crossing point foreshadowing the construction of Kingston Bridge some 1000 years later.

Antiquarian discoveries suggest that there were Roman buildings, some possibly of high status, and (cremation) burials perhaps representing more than one settlement (?country estates) on a relatively flat area on the western slope of Kingston Hill (Hawkins 1996, 47–8). However, there have been no modern discoveries that might substantiate this and provide further information on the earlier findings. This is not the case at Eden Street where a small Roman altar was reportedly found in the 19th century, although its provenance is far from secure and it may have been brought to Kingston from elsewhere at this time. More recently, however, coins, jewellery, rolled lead strips (possibly curses) along with stone, tile and painted plaster suggesting an important building, perhaps a shrine, were recovered from part of the east arm of the Hogsmill close to the supposed findspot of the altar (Hawkins 1996, 47–8).

Saxon (fig 13.2)

Recent excavations at South Lane indicate that there was Early–Mid Saxon settlement, probably a farmstead, on the gravel 'island' to the south of the Hogsmill (Hawkins *et al* 2002), and Early Saxon occupation is also attested on higher ground to the north-east (Bird *et al* 1990, 218); Hawkins 1998, 275–6). However, during the 8th or 9th century the focus of settlement shifted to the central Kingston 'island'. There is a late tradition in Kingston that the 'town' was refounded in the Late Saxon period and had previously been called *Moreford* (marshy ford), a recollection perhaps of the earlier Roman settlement which lay a short distance downstream around the putative crossing point (Hawkins 1998, 273). It has been suggested that the lost royal estate centre of *Freoricsburna* can be identified with Kingston, but this remains an unproven hypothesis (Blair 1991, 20) and is now considered unlikely.

Documentary evidence suggests that in the 9th and 10th centuries, Kingston was not a village or a town but rather a royal estate centre. The first reference to Kingston by that name (*Cyninges Tun* or *Cingestune*) is in an agreement between King Ecgbert and King Athelwulf and Coelnoth, archbishop of Canterbury, at a council held there on 20 November 838. The venue was clearly of sufficient prominence to host this important diplomatic conference, a key moment in the establishment of the Wessex monarchy. Its location on the shore of the Thames was probably regarded as a frontier zone between the power centres of the kings and the archbishops.

At least two and possibly as many as seven Late Saxon kings are known to have been crowned at Kingston during the 10th century, the earliest in 901 and the latest in 979, and a number of royal charters are recorded as having been witnessed there. While Kingston was not a major power centre it may have seemed the natural choice in the early 10th century as a central point of the realm which comprised Wessex, Kent, Mercia and East Anglia. The location was probably determined by the original reason for

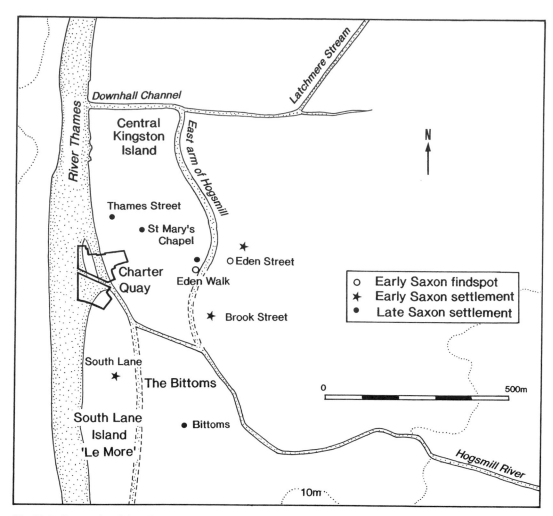

Fig 13.2   Saxon sites (after Hawkins 1998, fig 1) (© Crown Copyright NC/04/25242)

Kingston's national role as the regular and agreed meeting place of the kings of Wessex and the archbishops of Canterbury who played a key role in the coronation process. Its position near the tidal limit of the Thames may also have been of significance for a dynasty which claimed to be kings of the sea. However, there is no reason to assume the presence of a large number of buildings or extensive settlement – Anglo-Saxon kings were peripatetic and most of the retinue probably lived in tents.

The location of the royal estate centre, likely to comprise a timber hall, church and ancillary buildings, is unknown. However, it most probably lay in the area now occupied by the parish church of All Saints and the associated churchyard that is today somewhat smaller in extent than in medieval times. Further support for this suggestion comes from the fact that this is the site of the former chapel dedicated to St Mary the Virgin – perhaps a powerful Late Saxon minster church in origin (Blair 1991) and possibly part of the royal complex. This chapel lay on the south side of the parish church and survived until 1730, when it collapsed during the digging of graves inside the chapel. It had been preserved as the traditional place of coronation of the first kings of England, although excavations in the 1920s (Finny

1927) and engravings of the building suggest that it was Romanesque in style and of 11th rather than 10th century date. Furthermore, a 10th or 11th century re-used cross fragment (Tweddle *et al* 1995, 146) has been recovered from the existing 13th century and later church fabric. However, the chapel may have replaced an earlier, timber church or chapel, and it has recently been suggested that the site of the Late Saxon minster may lie beneath All Saints Church, itself replacing or incorporating a substantial late 12th century church (Hawkins 2003). Hawkins further suggests that St Mary's Chapel may have been a (smaller) replacement of the destroyed or demolished Late Saxon minster church and that this chapel was retained when the 12th century (and later) parish church of All Saints (formerly All Hallows) was constructed.

From the 9th century onwards a small settlement probably grew up around the royal complex and ditches of 9th–10th century date, which perhaps served both for drainage and as plot boundaries, have been found at Thames Street and at Eden Walk. A small number of pits and some pottery have also been found to the south around the Bittoms (Bird *et al* 1991–2, 158) and to the east in the vicinity of Tiffin School (Jackson *et al* 1997, 223; Howe *et al* 2001, 353), indicating further settlement away from the central 'island'. However, evidence for Late Saxon structures remains elusive and our archaeological knowledge of Kingston in this crucial period remains frustratingly slight.

In the Domesday survey in 1086, Kingston was the largest settlement in the Kingston Hundred, an administrative unit extending approximately from Kew in the north to Hook in the south, and from Malden in the east to East Molesey in the west. Within this, the extensive royal estate of Kingston had a population of more than 100 families operating 30 ploughs on the arable land, as well as meadow and woodland, fisheries and five mills. It is clear from the size of the estate that its central settlement, described as a *vill*, had kept its earlier status. However, it is likely that this settlement continued to comprise a small village focused around the church and former estate centre. Again, we have very little archaeological evidence from this period although two ditches of possible Saxo-Norman date were found during recent investigations at Cromwell Road (Howe *et al* 2001, 353) and London Road (Duncan Hawkins, pers comm) respectively, in the vicinity of what later became the main route out of the town to the east.

Medieval: 12th–13th century (fig 13.3)
During the 12th century the settlement grew in size, and its urban status was recognized by King John's grant of a charter in 1200, allowing the freemen of Kingston to pay him a fixed annual sum in return for becoming lords of the manor. By this time Kingston was one of the wealthiest towns in Surrey and some-times paid more in taxes than Guildford, and occasionally more than Southwark. The 12th and 13th centuries saw rapid urban growth throughout the country, mainly as a result of the great increase in trade. The main impetus for the development of Kingston, however, was probably the building, around 1170, of a wooden bridge across the Thames, the first bridge upstream from London and a short distance downstream from the position of the present bridge opened in 1828. Excavations have shown that Kingston Bridge in its earliest form dated to *c* 1170 (Potter 1988, 140), while the Clattern Bridge across the Hogsmill also contains elements which date to the late 12th century. Barre Bridge to the north, which crossed the Downhall channel, and Stone Bridge to the east across the east arm of the Hogsmill are also likely to have been built around this time. The cons-truction of these bridges, together with the establishment of the Market Place, can be seen as a deliberate act of town planning when Kingston was laid out on the central 'island' in the late 12th century. Although the area south of the church may have been used for buying and selling goods and produce from the Late Saxon period, the excavations at Charter

Quay have confirmed that the present Market Place, granted a charter in 1208, was not in existence until the mid-12th century. Many other planned towns established at this time, for example Reigate, also had market places at the core of the settlement, although towns in Surrey lack the regular street layouts seen elsewhere.

Kingston had no formal defences, such as a ditch and bank or circuit wall, although the surrounding watercourses, which effectively marked its bound-aries, may have provided some protection. There is a reference to a castle being captured at Kingston during the Barons' Wars in 1263–5 (*VCH*, **1**, 345), but no trace of it survives above ground and the form and precise location remain to be demonstrated archaeo-logically. It may have been built in the mid-13th century to guard the river crossing and a location to the east of Eden Street has been suggested, although map evidence provides no clues in this respect.

The eastern edge of the Thames in the 12th century lay some 50m to the east of its present line, and a small gravel bank split the mouth of the Hogsmill (Lurteborne) into two channels (of which only the southern, now canalized, survives). The northern channel (unknown before the Charter Quay excavations) was *c* 20m wide and ran north-north-west across the northern part of the site, probably joining the Thames south of the present-day Bishops Place House. The presence of this former channel of the Hogsmill had a major effect on the medieval topography of the town in the adjacent area, influencing the layout of streets and alleys, the shape of the Market Place, and the boundaries and extent of adjoining properties to the west. Further-more, it is clear that this channel marked the western edge of the gravel 'island' on which the 'central core' of Kingston is built, and also broadly defined the limit of building in this direction until at least the 17th century when more extensive development of the reclaimed land began.

The excavations at Charter Quay revealed evidence for continuous medieval occupation, inter-spersed with episodes of flooding and land reclamation, dating from the early 12th century onwards. The earliest phase of land reclamation can be assigned to the early 13th century and began along the east side of the former channel of the Hogsmill. Reclamation may have had the dual purpose of extending westwards the properties alongside the market, as well raising the level of the land to alleviate the problem of flooding which would have been a constant threat. This threat was perhaps increased after the construction of Kingston Bridge in the late 12th century which may have slowed the flow of the Thames upstream causing an increase in silting, particularly around the mouth of the Hogsmill. Flooding is recorded at regular intervals in Kingston

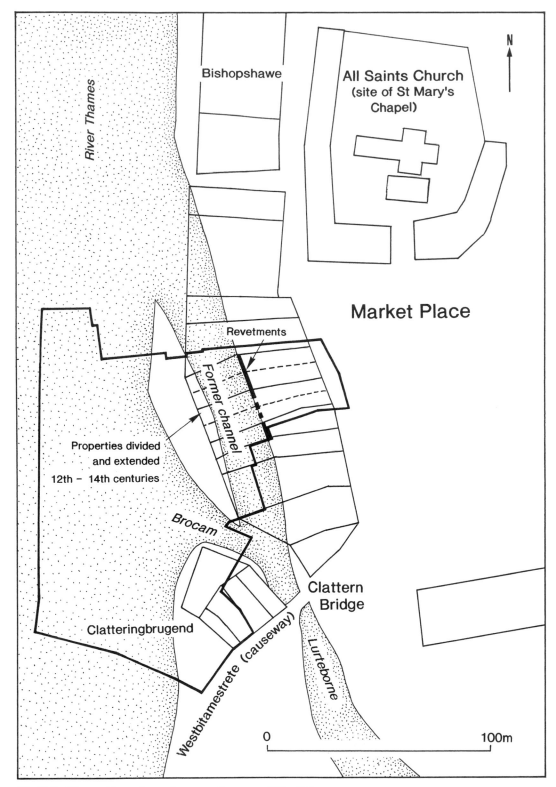

Fig 13.3 Charter Quay site and surrounding area: 12th–13th century

during the second half of the 13th century – in the 1250s, the 1260s and the 1280s. In this and later periods revetments may also have served as riverside wharves, but this was probably not the primary function of those in the former Hogsmill channel in the early 13th century.

Documentary sources indicate that the town did not originally extend to the south of the Hogsmill, and in 1253 the boundary of the borough was considered to be where the Creek (Hogsmill) lay at the south end of the market towards Guildford. The tenants of

Merton Priory's manor of Canbury refused to perform watch duties south of the Hogsmill as this was seen as beyond the limit of the town. However, a small suburb of houses and yards was established there by the 1290s, and archaeological evidence indicates activity there a least a century earlier. The pattern of property divisions south of the Hogsmill suggests that this was a piecemeal process of settlement, advancing from the south end of Clattern Bridge by a series of small-scale reclamations from the Thames and Hogsmill shores. The suburb was known as *Clateringbrugende* in the 1290s, and by 1314 the roadway was called *Westbitamestrete* (later West-by-Thames Street, and now High Street). Other suburban development probably took place in the vicinity of London Road, the principal route out of town to the east, and pits of mid/late 13th–14th century date found recently in this area may reflect this expansion (Howe *et al* 2001, 353).

Many of the town's earliest medieval buildings would have been constructed around the market, with the frontage at Charter Quay being fully occupied by houses (possibly with street-level shops and workshops) by 1200. The land behind, initially open to the Thames, is likely to have been used as wharfage. Later cellars along the market frontage had removed all traces of earlier, timber buildings in this area. However, it appears that the earliest structure in one of the three 12th century properties identified on the frontage had been dismantled and several substantial timbers re-used as part of an early 13th century revetment on the edge of the river channel at the rear of the property. One of the timbers from this revetment contained sufficient rings to allow dendrochronological dating and this indicated a felling date of *c* 1120, indicating a probable construction date for the building around the end of the first quarter of the 12th century. This would mean that it was probably in use for around 75 years before being dismantled and re-used, perhaps coinciding with a more general phase of property division and rebuilding as the prosperity of the town increased.

Building timbers have been found re-used in revetments elsewhere along the Thames in Kingston (Potter 1988, 144–5), but have invariably comprised smaller elements such as the vertical studs which formed the infill of the timber-framing: these were generally re-used as posts. The structural remains from Charter Quay are unique in that not only are they earlier than those so far recorded on other sites in Kingston (which are generally of 14th century date), but they are altogether more substantial and include an almost complete wall plate. In fact, comparatively little survives of any timber buildings of 12th century date from anywhere else in the country, and so the Charter Quay discovery is of particular importance in terms of the information it provides on vernacular architecture of this period.

Little can be gleaned about the function or internal layout of the early, 12th–13th century buildings, but it is likely that they may have been used as shops or workshops as well as domestic accommodation. They were set within what were originally relatively large plots or properties which were wide enough to allow the buildings to be built parallel to the street frontage. On the market frontage at Charter Quay the three original plots appear, from later evidence, to have

been approximately 10–12m wide (?two poles) – the suggested length of building based on the re-used wall plate in the later revetment. The properties to the south of the Hogsmill, on the High Street frontage, may have been slightly narrower, perhaps 10m wide.

Documentary evidence indicates that trades and occupations known to have been represented on the west side of the Market Place included fishmongers; Kingston was famous for its salmon, and eels were also caught in large numbers. There were also some occupational surnames in this area, which must have become formalized in the 13th century. They included *le Coliere* (charcoal supplier), *le poter* (potter) and *le Orfevre* (silversmith/goldsmith). Trades and occupations to the south of the Hogsmill included a chandler and butchers. The riverside site on the south side of the mouth of the Hogsmill is first known to have been occupied by Symon le Merchaunt, a 13th century occupational surname which suggests that the plot was used for trade.

Kingston was a major pottery production centre from at least as early as the mid-13th century. Prior to the beginnings of the well-documented Surrey whiteware industry at this time, the local pottery industries of Kingston and the surrounding region are less well understood. The major traditions have been defined (eg Vince & Jenner 1991) and include Early Surrey sandy wares, shelly wares and flint-tempered wares, all with origins in the 11th or 12th centuries; source areas for each have been postulated, although actual production sites are as yet elusive. However, recent excavations have recovered a large number of pottery wasters (but no kilns), provisionally interpreted as South Hertfordshire Grey ware and dated to the early 12th–late 13th century (Howe *et al* 2001, 353).

The origins and development of the Surrey whiteware industry, and in particular that of Kingston-type ware, have already been thoroughly explored (Pearce & Vince 1988; Miller & Stephenson 1999), and are merely summarized here. On the basis of existing evidence from both Kingston and various sites in London, the manufacture of Kingston-type ware, the earliest of the Surrey whiteware industries as currently defined, seems not to have begun before the early 13th century. It was not until the middle of the 13th century that Kingston-type wares appeared in London, and in Kingston itself earlier excavations have produced some evidence of a pre-whiteware phase in which London-type Rouen style jugs were used, a type introduced at the end of the 12th century.

Several pottery kilns have been found in Kingston, around Eden Street, Union Street and more recently along London Road which lay on the eastern outskirts of the town – tanning also took place in this area. Wasters associated with all these kilns are exclusively of 14th century date, and it seems that earlier kilns in the town remain to be discovered. Documentary sources refer to the supply of 3300 'pitchers' from Kingston to the royal court between 1264 and 1266, and the repertoire of the late 13th century potters of the town can be reconstructed from the range of Kingston-type wares excavated from London (Pearce & Vince 1988, figs 39–42).

Wherever the earliest whiteware kilns were established, it is apparent that their location in Kingston itself was anomalous, for the simple reason that there is no local source of white-firing clay here – the nearest known outcrops of iron-free clay from the Reading Beds are several miles away. The largest market for Kingston-type wares was always London, and the discovery of a dump of whiteware wasters at Bankside in Southwark, in a fabric identical to the Kingston wasters, tends to support the conclusion that the Kingston industry was founded by potters from London, moving closer to the source of the white-firing clay. Why they chose Kingston is uncertain, but may not be unconnected with the expansion of the town following the construction of the bridge across the Thames in *c* 1170, and the establishment of the market in 1208. The proximity of the river (for the transport of both raw clay and finished goods) and access to large supplies of timber for fuel were probably also important factors.

The original potters may have come from London, but the Kingston- and London-type industries soon diverged, and Kingston became the centre for the production of a range of highly decorated jugs, with vibrant polychrome motifs, stamped bosses and anthropomorphic forms, produced alongside plainer utilitarian jars, bowls and pipkins. The *floruit* of the industry was in the second half of the 13th and first half of the 14th century, after which Kingston wares declined in popularity in London in the face of competition from rival whiteware industries at Cheam (some six miles away) and on the Surrey/Hampshire border.

As well as the local whitewares, Kingston, as a major market, might have been expected to act as the redistribution centre for a number of other wares. While Kingston products were supplying London, London-type wares travelled in the opposite direction. Products of the various 13th/14th century greyware industries located around London in Hertfordshire, Berkshire and Surrey are also represented in the town, but imported Continental wares are extremely rare.

Medieval: 14th–15th century (fig 13.4)

The 14th and 15th centuries witnessed continued expansion of Kingston as the prosperity of the town increased, and market rights were established by the Borough Charter of 1441. At Charter Quay this development was represented by a phase of 'industrial' activity assigned to the 14th century, and by the construction of timber buildings on stone and tile foundations which extended over a far more extensive area than before. The yard areas behind these buildings were progressively built up with ancillary buildings such as workshops, stores and stables. Land reclamation and the expansion of properties to the west continued throughout this period, and the construction of timber revetments, some of the later ones incorporating re-used boat timbers, began on the Thames waterfront, probably in the 14th century.

To the north of the Hogsmill, all trace of the late medieval buildings on the market frontage had been destroyed by later cellars, but documentary evidence provides some indication of the nature of these buildings, with evidence for jettied upper storeys and shops at ground-floor level. Part of the west side of the Market Place was known as le Hyerowe, presumably because of the height of its terrace of buildings. This development is likely to have involved some encroachment on to the west side of the Market Place, and may be reflected in the rental of 1417 which records several sets of posts in the street, probably supporting jettied upper stories. The earliest cellar remains surviving on the market frontage have been assigned to the 16th century, but it is possible that some replaced earlier, medieval cellars or undercrofts. An undercroft, well-known in the 19th century but rediscovered in 1986, was excavated at the Horsefair site immediately to the north of Kingston Bridge, but it appears that Kingston as a local market centre did not possess the wealth of medieval undercrofts which survive in regional centres such as Guildford.

It is clear that there were sub-divisions of the properties on the west side of the Market Place during this period. Evidence for this appears in town rentals of quit-rents compiled in 1383, 1417 and 1427, and at least one of the properties on the market frontage at Charter Quay may have been divided at this time. In this area, the pattern of property boundaries exhibits a characteristic curvilinear 'bridgehead' form that would have provided maximum access to both the market and the waterfront. Small changes in alignment of these boundaries, some of which still survive today or are recorded on 19th and 20th century maps, reflect the periodic advances of the properties across the reclaimed ground. Several alleyways providing access between the Market Place and waterfront can also be seen to have become permanently established at this time. The sub-divisions, from wider to narrower properties, resulted in new buildings being constructed at 90° rather than parallel to the street frontage, a common development in medieval towns at this time as the pressure on land increased, particularly in areas such as market places.

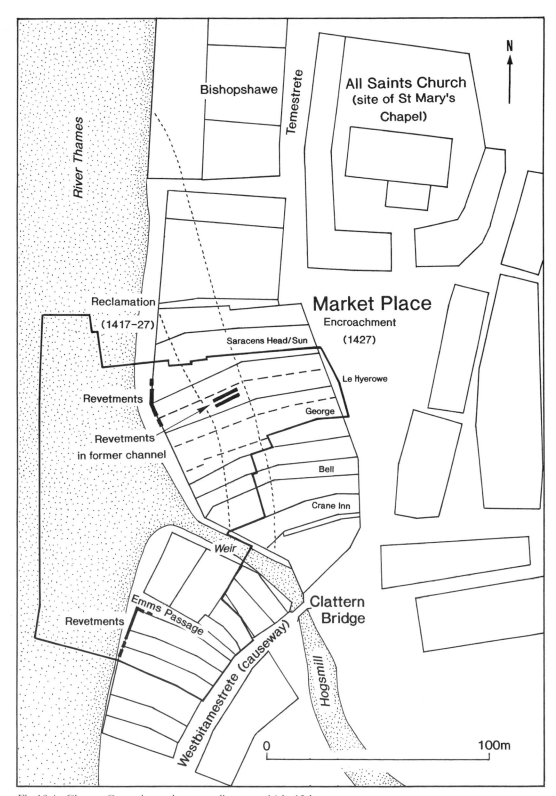

Fig 13.4   Charter Quay site and surrounding area: 14th–15th century

The southern suburb now stretched further to the south of the Hogsmill along both sides of Westbita-mestrete (High Street), and Emms Passage probably became formalized as an alleyway at this time, linking the waterfront and the High Street. Two properties were identified on the street frontage north of Emms Passage, but it appears that the division of what had previously been a single property may not have taken place until around the end of the 14th century. The late 12th/13th century timber building which had previously occupied this property apparently fell into

disuse, may have been dismantled and was not replaced. Instead, the area was given over to some form of industrial activity. What this activity was is uncertain, but the whole of the frontage was occupied by a series of pitched-tile hearths dated archaeomagnetically to the last quarter of the 14th century. Pottery production can be ruled out, but the concentration of hearths in this area may reflect the location of a 'dirty' industry on the edge of the town. Baking is a possibility, although documentary study has failed to determine the names of the occupiers of the properties on the street frontage. Trades represented along the High Street are known to have included iron smithing and possibly gold working, but there is no evidence that these particular hearths were associated with metalworking.

It is clear that not all the buildings to the south of the Hogsmill were timber structures. In the 19th century some early capitals and pier bases were found on land formerly called *La Ryole*, in the Bittoms area; a fragment is now displayed outside Kingston Library. A date of *c* 1300 has been suggested for these and their presence clearly indicates a stone building (perhaps an undercroft) of some importance and architectural merit – possibly that of a London wine merchant. It may be no coincidence that there was a substantial house in Vintry Ward (the district of wine importers) in the City of London also called *la Ryole*, and perhaps this merchant also had a house in Kingston. Some Bordeaux wine may have brought by boat directly to Kingston where it could have been transferred to smaller boats for distribution inland. Kingston lay near the tidal limit of the Thames and the low clearance of the old bridge would have prevented larger vessels from sailing further upstream. It is known that other important City merchants held property in Kingston and these included the Lovekyns who were involved in some of the town's inns and wine shops. These merchants were presumably attracted by its location which provided both an important local market and a transhipment point.

Around the end of the 14th or the beginning of the 15th century the properties at Charter Quay were divided, new buildings were constructed and there was a change in use of the area. This may have resulted from a change in ownership. The London Charterhouse, founded in 1370, acquired the considerable Kingston property of John Wenge as part of its initial endowment and the Priory continued to purchase property in Kingston in the 15th century. Several inns on the west side of the Market Place were probably first established in the 15th century, their rear yards stretching westward to the Thames. They included the Saracen's Head (later the Sun) at the north end of site, which was established at least a generation before 1417, and the George further to the south which was part of the Charterhouse estate, developed out of Wenge's tenements.

Reclamation of the former Hogsmill channel continued throughout the 14th century, interspersed with periods of flooding, and as earlier was carried out within individual properties. However, this phase of reclamation progressed from north to south, rather than east to west, within the central part of the area excavated. At least three revetments of 14th century date were recorded in the same property which had earlier been extended to the west by revetments dating to the early 13th century. The later 14th century revetments present a slightly ambiguous picture in terms of their interpretation. Certainly, the early 13th century ones represent reclamation and may also have served as wharves on the edge of the channel. However, as the channel silted up, access to the Thames would have become more difficult and the importance of the waterfront may, as a result, have temporarily declined in this area during the later 14th century. The later revetments are more likely, therefore, to have been built for reclamation, stabilization and flood control rather than as wharves. The reason for them being built across rather than along the line of the channel can probably be explained by the changing nature of the channel. During the 14th century it became shallower largely as a result of silting, and building revetments across it would have served finally to block the channel and provide a 'bridge' across to the low island or 'ait' at the mouth of the Hogsmill which itself could then be reclaimed. Once this 'bridge' was established then further reclamation of the channel took place, proceeding to the north and south in adjacent properties, eventually as far as the edge of the Thames and the Hogsmill respectively. A 15th century documentary reference may be relevant to this phase of reclamation for it records 'a way for water to go backwards' at the George Inn. This probably refers to the remains of the former Hogsmill channel, now blocked, at the rear of the property in which water could have flowed southwards (ie 'backwards') into the Hogsmill, but no longer northwards into the Thames. Another reference indicates that between the rentals of 1417 and 1427, Richard Est added a purpresture at the Thames end of his property, which lay to the north of Charter Quay. This may refer to a further phase of reclamation, at the north end of the channel, and suggests that by this time it had been effectively closed off.

As properties were extended to the west there were also attempts to manage the shores of the Thames and the Hogsmill by a system of revetments, in order to limit the effect of flooding. Close to the Thames, there were several irregular lines of posts which probably represented evidence for reclamation and flood control in the 14th century. There were no horizontal timbers between these posts, and perhaps originally they merely consisted of a series of closely but irregularly spaced 'piles' along the river's edge. These were succeeded in the late 15th or early 16th century by revetments incorporating re-used boat timbers. These revetments comprised small sections of clinker-built boats similar to the earlier 14th century examples in the channel but these were held in place by a series of elm posts rather than re-used building timbers. The use of elm roundwood was a characteristic feature of the late 15th/early 16th century revetments in this area and probably reflects an increasing shortage of suitable oak timber.

Elsewhere, the earliest Thames-side revetments so far discovered in Kingston were found in the immediate vicinity of old Kingston Bridge during excavations there in the late 1980s (Potter 1988). A sequence of at least six revetments either side of the old bridge were recorded, together spanning some 200 years from the early 13th century to the later 14th century, with the last going out of use early in the 15th century. These revetments exhibited a variety of

construction techniques, some being apparently purpose built and containing sawn planks, others containing re-used boat and building timbers.

Post-medieval (fig 13.5)

Kingston continued to expand in the 16th and 17th centuries, and at the hearth tax assessment of 1664–6 the town consisted of 455 households, representing a population in excess of 2000. By comparison, London had a population of *c* 100,000, and Kingston's relatively small size must in part be a reflection of the

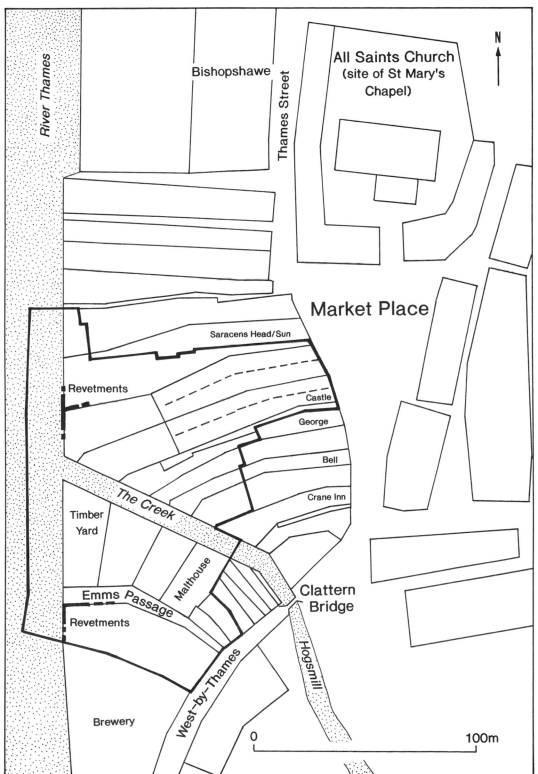

Fig 13.5   Charter Quay site and surrounding area: 16th–17th century

proximity of the capital. During this period Kingston became established as an important centre for boat building, tanning, milling, brewing and river barge traffic, and by 1580 various other trades were organized into guilds (woollen drapers, mercers, butchers and shoemakers). Kingston was a flourishing market town, aided by a charter granted by Charles I in 1628 forbidding the holding of any other market within a 7-mile radius. This charter heavily emphasizes Kingston's role as a port, and the town continued to serve as an inland port throughout the 17th century, daily transporting goods to London which by the end of the century was the largest city in Europe. Its boats at this time included pinnaces, which were capable of going to sea, and presumably could sail upstream as far as Kingston Bridge. Goods being transported upstream would have been unloaded at this point and transferred to smaller barges, to carts for transport overland, or were sold in the market. A recent study of Kingston trade tokens (Everson 2001) indicates how much trade in Surrey went by river, with only Guildford and Croydon of the large centres not being on the Thames. Of the 55 towns and smaller settlements recorded as issuing tokens in the middle of the 17th century, Kingston (21 issues) lies fourth behind Southwark (400+), Rotherhithe (54) and Guildford (22), emphasizing the importance of London within the region.

The presence of a royal residence on the other side of the river Thames at Hampton Court appears not to have had an extensive or permanent effect on Kingston's development, even after the royal family began to make more frequent use of the palace in the 17th century. However, many courtiers stayed in the town, with the Crane Inn on the west side of the Market Place being the principal lodging house. Inns were an important feature of the Market Place throughout this period and several had a continuous life from the medieval period. Kingston remained virtually free of the plague which swept England in the 1570s, largely because it banned all people coming from infected areas and established what was in effect an isolation hospital outside the town. However, the town succumbed in 1625 and 1636, and precautions were taken to prevent the disease spreading to Hampton Court. The town certainly transported goods to the palace up the river, although traffic was suspended for a time during the outbreak of plague and in 1625 there were virtually no boats travelling downstream to London. Notwithstanding these interruptions, the volume of trade was the pretext for the grant of a second market day in the week in 1662.

At the beginning of the 16th century houses in Kingston were generally small, some with tiled roofs but the majority thatched. The houses were mostly built of timber on stone footings, with wattle-and-daub infill, and it was forbidden to burn furze bavins in the town for fear of a general conflagration. There is evidence, however, for a phase of rebuilding that began around the middle of the 16th century and continued into the 17th century, with some of the later buildings being constructed at least partly of brick with timber framing above and tiled roofs. This was part of a widespread phase of urban rebuilding that took place throughout much of the country at this time. The results can be seen in the buildings of other towns in Surrey, for example Guildford, particularly along the High Street. Unlike Guildford, however, Kingston has few obvious survivals of buildings of this period. Nevertheless, elements of these may survive even in the most unpromising of circumstances. At Charter Quay parts of the cellar and roof structure of a 17th century range were recorded within a 19th–20th century department store (Hides) which had been formed from several earlier, largely 19th century, buildings and given a new façade. Also present, although not in its original location, was an elaborately carved mid-17th century staircase.

The properties to the north of the Hogsmill at Charter Quay retained their medieval boundaries until the 19th century. However, there were further sub-divisions of other properties along the Market Place and Thames Street frontage in the 17th century, and there was continued encroachment on to the Market Place itself. As further land reclamation at the confluence of the Thames and Hogsmill took place there was also lateral division of the tails of the properties behind the street frontage to form new tenements, accessed through lanes and alleyways from the Market Place. What had been open areas became more intensively built-up, and although yards and alleyways were retained they often became hemmed in and encroached upon by new buildings. The digging of new wells and cesspits in the remaining open areas may reflect an attempt to improve sanitation following outbreaks of the plague in 1625 and 1636.

The former Hogsmill channel was finally infilled at the beginning of this period, and there is a mid-16th century documentary reference which almost certainly relates to its closure where it joined the Thames. In 1563 John Jenyns was leased a piece of land at the Thames-side end of Bishop's Hall Lane with 50 feet (15.24m) of a drainage channel called the Creek – the same name was also given to the lower part of the Hogsmill below Clattern Bridge from the 16th century. He was required to fill and level this drainage channel while maintaining a watercourse for water to drain from Thames Street into the river. There were continuing efforts made to manage the rivers and defend against floods. Reclamation proceeded, particularly to the north of the confluence of the Thames and Hogsmill, and reclaimed land along the Thames shore in this area was consolidated by extensive dumping of soil and rubbish, which raised the ground level by up to a metre in places.

Seventeenth century Kingston is known to have contained maltings and brewhouses, slaughterhouses and tan-yards, forges, timber-yards and a brickyard. Especially represented in the area to the south of the Hogsmill were the carpenters, joiners and wood merchants who operated the timber yards. Numerous other crafts and small-scale industries are recorded in documentary sources, and presumably many of these activities were reflected in the town's waterborne trade. However, there are few archaeological finds which might reflect the function of Kingston as an inland port at this time, and no indications of specialized vessel forms in the post-medieval pottery assemblage which might be related to specific craft or industrial functions.

Kingston was well within the catchment area for provisioning London with wood and charcoal via the Thames (Galloway et al 1996), and most woodlands around the town were probably dedicated to this lucrative fuel trade. During the medieval period the supply of livestock would have been mainly from the local area, but by the post-medieval period trade was extensive and far-reaching. It is possible that some of the cattle bone deposits at Charter Quay came from animals brought to Kingston's livestock market, slaughtered there and sent to London as processed meat. Dumps of horse bone have also been found on several sites including Eden Walk and Charter Quay where there is evidence of both skinning and disarticulation, with at least some meat removal. Horse remains from most medieval and post-medieval sites are consistently of older or diseased animals presumably at the end of their useful lives, and the animals at Charter Quay are no exception. Tanning and related industries were often situated next to rivers for easy access to water and this part of the town, close to the Horsefair, may have become a specialist area for these activities from the 16th century onwards, perhaps replacing that in Eden Walk. The Bishops Hall property to the north had become a tanner's yard by 1631 and subsequently developed into Kingston's largest and most important tannery which continued to operate on the same site until its closure in 1963 (fig 13.6).

This brings us up to the more recent, relatively well-documented history of Kingston, but even here archaeology can provide unexpected and important new information. For example, recent excavations of the Quaker burial ground in London Road 'provided a rare opportunity to investigate an early Quaker community through analysis of their burial practices and physical remains' (Bashford & Pollard 1998, 154).

Discussion and thoughts for the future

The history of Kingston is not exceptional, apart perhaps from its role during the Late Saxon period, and were it not for this it would be like many medieval and post-medieval towns further afield which functioned as local market centres. In Surrey, however, the small size of most of the other towns – partly a reflection of the proximity of London – and Kingston's location at a major crossing point on the Thames, meant that it assumed a relatively greater importance in the county, and at times paid more tax than Guildford.

Prehistoric and Roman discoveries will undoubtedly increase with further work, but these are likely to refine rather than substantially change our knowledge of Kingston's topography and early settlement history. However, any opportunities further to investigate and understand the important Neolithic (and Bronze Age) remains in the east arm of the Hogsmill should prove worthwhile, as should a programme of environmental sampling of channel deposits here and elsewhere. As part of this investigation of channel deposits one should include the interpretation of data from boreholes and test-pits routinely undertaken prior to new development, for this can provide much useful information on the Holocene geology without recourse to more extensive (and expensive) excavation.

The pattern of Early and Mid-Saxon occupation in the area is now becoming clearer, with evidence for settlement shift(s) between the 6th and 9th centuries, a recurrent trend elsewhere in the country. However, further investigations would be useful to provide more information on the nature and extent of these successive settlements. The Late Saxon period in archaeological if not documentary terms remains shadowy. All Saints Church, the churchyard and immediate surrounding area are likely to contain evidence for the royal complex, but opportunities to undertake investigations are likely to be few and restricted in area. However, any works in and around the church itself, such as new heating ducts, drains and flooring, may provide important information on the structural sequence of this, if not the layout and nature of the other buildings in this complex.

Recent work appears to demonstrate conclusively that Kingston's Market Place and street layout were a medieval development and that the town did not originate as a Late Saxon burh. However, there are hints of a (?early) rectilinear layout in the street pattern either side of Bridge Street to the east of the old bridge (fig 13.6), and perhaps the Horsefair was the site of an early market. Much of this street pattern has been obliterated by major retail developments over the last three decades and only a small area in the north-west corner, to the north of Bridge Street, survives unaltered. Further excavation would, therefore, be

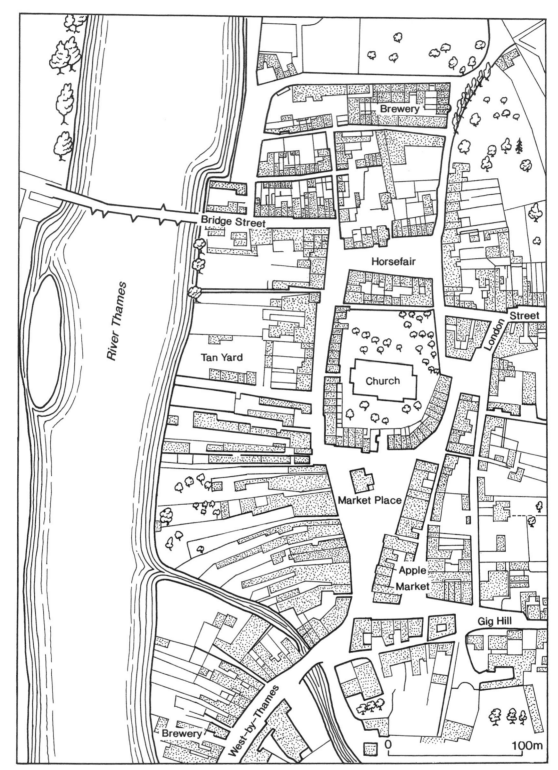

Fig 13.6 Extract (redrawn) from Thomas Horner's map of Kingston in 1813

desirable in this area and also to the east and west of the church where pockets of archaeological deposits may survive and reveal more of the Late Saxon settlement. A single ditch recorded at Thames Street during limited investigations many years ago remains our only archaeological evidence for this settlement, and the results from the extensive excavations at the Horsefair site in the mid-1980s remain unpublished. A case might be made for some further analysis of the records and, particularly, the pottery from this site in order to clarify, in the first instance, whether or not there is any evidence for Late Saxon occupation in this area.

The medieval and post-medieval sequence in Kingston is becoming increasingly better understood through a combination of excavation and study of documentary evidence. The large-scale excavations at Charter Quay, and to a lesser extent the Horsefair, along with numerous smaller investigations, have gone a considerable way to 'filling out' the picture of urban development in the town. Like many smaller towns of similar size, the depth of archaeological deposits is, for the most part, relatively shallow and has in some cases, particularly along street frontages, been entirely truncated by later cellars. However, on larger sites at least some of these important sequences are likely to survive, and it is these sites which help provide a framework into which the results from the smaller excavations and watching briefs can be fitted. The larger sites can also provide the opportunity to undertake more meaningful investigation of finds and environmental analysis, as well as complementary documentary work (Wessex Archaeology 2003). While this may not be successful at linking occupiers or trades to particular properties, it can provide very useful information on, for example, the layout and development of properties, the economic character of an area and changes in this over time. In Kingston we can now see more detail of the commercial nature of the waterfront and market areas in the medieval period, with a mixture of trades represented, while the main 'industrial' area – principally engaged in potting and leatherworking – lay on the eastern and south-eastern periphery of the town. A subtle change is apparent in the post-medieval period, with the market becoming the location for several important inns and the town, particularly the waterfront area, becoming well-known for its maltings, breweries, tanneries and timber-yards.

In Surrey, only Southwark and Guildford could really be considered as regional centres in the medieval period, despite Kingston sometimes paying more in taxes, and excavation has confirmed Kingston's status as a local market and redistribution centre. It had tradesmen and craftsmen who provided goods and services for the surrounding villages, and to some extent London itself, but it lacked the long-distance trading contacts which characterized the regional centres. Also missing are the religious houses and other institutions which were to be found, for example, in Guildford. The archaeological potential of Guildford has yet to be realized for, although there have been numerous excavations undertaken in the town in recent years, almost all have been small-scale in nature and often in the rear parts of properties which have yielded little structural evidence. This, of course, reflects the lack of large-scale redevelopment within the historic core of the town, in contrast to Kingston where there have been several major developments over the past fifteen years and a number of other sites are currently proposed for development. This lack of recent, large-scale redevelopment is also a general feature of the centres of other Surrey towns and is the main reason why we have relatively little archaeological evidence for their origins and development.

John Schofield (1994, 195) identified three stages in the archaeological investigation of towns: data collection, construction of typologies, and the study of the archaeological evidence of specific activities and of groups which functioned within towns. In some larger towns the wealth of available data may be overwhelming, resulting in problems of access, interpretation and synthesis, whereas for smaller towns the quantity of data is usually very much smaller. The completion of Urban Archaeological Databases (UADs) for larger towns and Extensive Urban Surveys (EUSs) for smaller towns are of great importance for assessing the available resources and targeting future data collection. The EUSs currently being compiled by the Surrey County Archaeological Unit (SCAU) will be of particular help in these respects and will provide a framework for urban study on which detailed archaeological investigations can be based to address specific, often basic, questions of settlement morphology and chronology. It is certain that much remains to be done to realize the urban potential of archaeological deposits, standing buildings, artefacts and ecofacts, and towns will remain a priority area for future research.

Towns are complex entities which have a rich material culture. They contain a great store of medieval deposits, buildings, churches, defences, evidence for commercial and industrial activity, documentary sources, artefacts and ecofacts. Towns develop and change through time, undergoing changes which may be reflected differently in the archaeological and documentary evidence – evidence which may not be in agreement in showing, for example, the extent of late medieval urban decline. Here there is a need to place archaeology within a broader framework of academic enquiry. Further evidence must also be sought for proto-urban origins, the role of the church in urban development and topography, the nature and extent of commercial and industrial activity, the distribution and survival of buildings, and the links between towns and, especially, between town and hinterland (Carver 1987). On a more specific note, environmental sampling in towns in Surrey has been very limited and any opportunity should be taken to sample contexts which reflect events (eg fires or floods), industrial processes, and any deposits which may reflect the relationship with the hinterland. Waterlogged deposits are likely to offer the greatest potential in this respect and are particularly important.

Urban archaeology is, almost without exception, likely to remain developer-led for the foreseeable future, but this should be seen in a positive rather than negative light, for it provides an excellent opportunity to add to the archaeological database. This is particularly so in towns such as Kingston which, prior to PPG 16, usually drew only sporadic and limited funding because 'they rarely offer the spectacular opportunity for excavation provided in the more important towns by urban development' (Turner 1987, 250). Today, there is also more of an onus to publish or make available the results of investigations, as this is another requirement of PPG 16, something which all too often was not achieved in the past, particularly in the case of many urban excavations. The challenge today is for curators who prepare specifications and monitor archaeological work to set and maintain standards, as work in Kingston, for example, may be undertaken by at least half a dozen different organizations, not all of whom may be familiar with the area. There is also the difficulty of developing some mechanism for synthesizing the vast amounts of data which are now accumulating in the so-called 'grey literature', such as summary and archive reports. Contract archaeology allows little scope for research except on the largest and most prestigious projects, for example Charter Quay (Wessex Archaeology 2003), and there is an increasing danger of generating too much dispersed and indigestible data.

However, this surely must be an improvement on the lack of information which was a concern so often voiced in the past, even as recently as 1987 for the Anglo-Saxon and medieval periods in Surrey. The computerization of Sites and Monuments Records and the development of geographical information systems will undoubtedly make such syntheses easier, although it is not always clear who will be in the best position, or have the time, to undertake them. Up to now Surrey has been fortunate in having people willing to organize conferences and undertake the publication of archaeological syntheses, most notably the 1987 volume (Bird & Bird 1987) and now this volume; it is to be hoped that there will be worthy successors to these in the next 50 years.

ACKNOWLEDGEMENTS

Thanks go first and foremost to Duncan Hawkins who has had a long association with Kingston and more recently the Charter Quay project. His papers on Roman and Saxon Kingston, borrowed from extensively above, represent important syntheses of disparate evidence and provide a framework for future research. I am also indebted to Dr Christopher Phillpotts whose documentary research undertaken as part of the Charter Quay project foreshadowed many of the discoveries and added much to the 'dry bones' of the walls, floors and revetments revealed in the excavations.

Archaeological work continues apace and I would like to thank the individuals and organizations whose information I have drawn upon, usually by way of the useful summaries published in *Surrey Archaeological Collections, London Archaeologist* and the archaeological reports of the South West London Archaeological Liaison Committee. For historical information the published work of Joan Wakeford, June Sampson and Shaan Butters has been of considerable assistance.

My own involvement in Kingston and the surrounding area is relatively recent and I am grateful to Ken Whittaker (formerly English Heritage's archaeological advisor for South London) and colleagues at Wessex Archaeology, including Jonathan Nowell and Lorraine Mepham who themselves have associations with Kingston, for the benefit of their knowledge. The illustrations were prepared for this paper by Brenda Craddock and are based on drawings produced by Duncan Hawkins, Dr Christopher Phillpotts and Karen Nichols.

Finally I would like to thank Martin O'Connell, Dennis Turner and Rob Poulton whose publications in the 1970s, 1980s and 1990s respectively have continued to focus interest on increasing our understanding of the development of Surrey's towns.

BIBLIOGRAPHY

For full details of documentary sources for Kingston see Wessex Archaeology 2003.

Ayres, B, 1997 Anglo-Saxon, medieval and post-medieval (urban), in *Research and archaeology: a framework for the eastern counties 1. Resource assessment* (ed J Glazebrook), E Anglian Archaeol Occ Pap, **3,** 59–66
Bashford, L & Pollard, A, 1998 'In the burying place' – the excavation of a Quaker burial ground, in *Grave concerns: death and burial in England 1700 – 1850* (ed M Cox), CBA Res Rep, **113,** 154–66
Bird, D G, Crocker, G, & McCracken, J S, 1989 Archaeology in Surrey 1987, *SyAC,* **79,** 179–89
——, 1990 Archaeology in Surrey 1988–1989, *SyAC,* **80,** 201–27
——, 1991–2 Archaeology in Surrey 1990, *SyAC,* **81,** 147–67
Bird, D G, Crocker, G, Maloney, C, & Saich, D, 1996 Archaeology in Surrey 1992–3, *SyAC,* **83,** 187–228
Bird, J, & Bird D G (eds), 1987 *The archaeology of Surrey to 1540,* SyAS

Blair, J, 1991 *Early medieval Surrey: landholding, church and settlement before 1300*
Butters, S, 1995 *The book of Kingston*
Carver, M, 1987 *Underneath English towns*
Everson, T, 2001 Kingston trading tokens and their issuers, *SyAC,* **88,** 43–66
Field, D, & Needham, S P, 1986 Evidence for Bronze Age settlement on Coombe Warren, Kingston Hill, *SyAC,* **77,** 127–51
Finny, W E St L, 1927 The Saxon church at Kingston, *SyAC,* **37.2,** 211–19
Galloway, J A, Keene, D, & Murphy, M, 1996 Fuelling the City: the production of firewood and the distribution in London's region, 1290–1400, *Econ Hist Rev,* **69.3,** 447–72
Hawkins, D, 1996 Roman Kingston upon Thames: a landscape of rural settlements, *London Archaeol,* **8.2,** 46–50
——, 1998 Anglo-Saxon Kingston: a shifting pattern of settlement, *London Archaeol,* **8.10,** 271–8

——, 2003   From Norman estate centre to Angevin town':
Kingston upon Thames urban origins, *London Archaeol,*
10.4, 95–101

Hawkins, D, Kain, A, & Wooldridge, K, 2002   Archaeological
investigations at East Lane and South Lane, Kingston upon
Thames 1996–8, *SyAC,* **89,** 185–210

Hinton, M, 1984   Ancient burial ground in Canbury Field,
Kingston upon Thames, *SyAC,* **75,** 285–7

Howe, T, Jackson, G, & Maloney, C, 2001   Archaeology in
Surrey 2000, *SyAC,* **88,** 343–363

Jackson, G, Maloney, C, & Saich, D, 1997   Archaeology in
Surrey 1994–5, *SyAC,* **84,** 195–243

Miller, P, & Stephenson, 1999   *A 14th century pottery site in Kingston
upon Thames, Surrey,* MoLAS Archaeol Stud Ser, **1**

Needham, S P, 1987   The Bronze Age, in Bird & Bird 1987,
97–137

O'Connell, M, 1977   *Historic towns in Surrey,* SyAS Res Vol, **5**

Pearce, J, & Vince A, 1988   *A dated type series of London medieval
pottery, part 4: Surrey whitewares,* London Middlesex Archaeol
Soc Spec Pap, **10**

Penn, J S, & Rolls, J D, 1981   Problems in the quaternary development of the Thames Valley around Kingston, 'A framework for archaeology', *Trans London Middlesex Archaeol Soc,*
32, 1–11

Penn, J S, Field, D, & Serjeantson, D, 1984   Evidence of
Neolithic occupation in Kingston: excavations at Eden
Walk, 1965, *SyAC,* **75,** 207–24

Potter, G, 1988   The medieval bridge and waterfront at
Kingston upon Thames, in *Waterfront archaeology* (eds G L
Good, R H Jones, & M W Ponsford), CBA Res Rep, **74,**
140–52

Poulton, R, 1998   Historic towns in Surrey – some general considerations, *SyAC,* **85,** 239–42

Sampson, J, 1997   *Kingston past*

Schofield, J, 1994   Medieval and later towns, in *Building on the
past* (ed B Vyner), 195–214

SyAC, 1998   *Archaeological investigations of historic Surrey towns:
Chertsey, Dorking, Farnham and Godalming, SyAC,* **85**

Turner, D J, 1987   Archaeology of Surrey, 1066–1540, in Bird
& Bird 1987, 223–61

Tweddle, D, Biddle, M, & Kyølbe Biddle, B, 1995   *Corpus of
Anglo-Saxon stone sculpture, vol 4 South-East England,* British
Academy

VCH: The Victoria history of the county of Surrey (ed H E Malden),
1902–12, 4 vols

Vince, A, & Jenner, A, 1991   *Aspects of Saxon and Norman London:
finds and environmental evidence,* London Middlesex Archaeol
Soc Spec Pap, **12**

Wakeford, J, 1990   *Kingston's past rediscovered*

Wessex Archaeology, 2003   *Charter Quay, the spirit of change: the
archaeology of Kingston's riverside*

Phil Andrews, Wessex Archaeology, Portway House, Old Sarum Park, Salisbury, Wiltshire SP4 6EB

14

What did London do for us? London and towns in its region, 1450–1700

JOHN SCHOFIELD

This paper outlines a model or set of questions for one aspect of the archaeology and history of towns in Surrey in the period 1450–1700: the increasing influence of London, and how archaeologists may chart this. The paper starts by avoiding the traditional division between the medieval and post-medieval periods, and argues that many of the effects of London's needs and its resulting influences were already at work in the 14th and 15th centuries. After 1450, these influences increased. They can be divided into the needs of London for food, fuel and other necessaries, which would increasingly determine the character of the surrounding countryside and the small towns; the way that architecture, pottery and other cultural items and ideas spread from the capital into the region via the towns; and the degree to which the towns themselves, by specializing in providing a narrow set of services or products to London, actually prospered in the 15th to 17th centuries. There were also serious changes to towns everywhere at this time, such as the Dissolution and Reformation, and some aspects of urban culture are shared by all towns. Surrey products such as Border Ware pottery were marketed, presumably through London, throughout the region and beyond to the New World. Despite some appearance of local resistance, however, the period as a whole sees the gradual domination of London in the towns around in many aspects of life, and archaeology can illuminate this process and tension.

Introduction

In this paper, I would like to outline a single theme or question: how London's influence and needs changed the region around it, and especially the towns, during the period 1450 to 1700. Some illustrations will be taken from Surrey, but others come from other parts of the region and beyond. The study of medieval and post-medieval urban archaeology in Surrey can only profit when the county is seen as one part of London's immediate hinterland, and the common patterns to be observed may be illustrated just as well or better in other counties around the capital.

My first suggestion is that to discuss the archaeology of these centuries, we must remove, or at least temporarily forget, the traditional division between the medieval and post-medieval periods; a division put variously between 1485 and 1540. This imprecision says something about the usefulness of the boundary. There were political changes to be sure, from invasion in 1485 to the greatest transfer of land within the country since the Norman Conquest, at the Dissolution in the 1530s. But archaeology measures best the changes which happen more slowly, over the longer term. To understand the towns and countryside around London in 1600 or even 1700, we have to delve back into the medieval period, sometimes back to 1200. I will use the terms medieval and post-medieval for convenience, but ignore the division between them.

The London region in the medieval period

Archaeologically, the London region is difficult to define. Indeed, it is best to think of London as in many different regions, depending on the question. By the close of the 13th century London appears regularly to have drawn on an area of over 4000 square miles to obtain its annual grain requirement. Normally it satisfied its requirements from within a 60 to 90 mile radius. A certain emphasis on the growing of oats in the region may have been related to London's need for fodder for all its horses. Low-value grain crops such as oats and rye were grown close to the city, with wheat further out – its higher price made transport worthwhile (Campbell *et al* 1993). The perishable products of market gardening and dairying assumed importance on manors within a few miles of the city, as did firewood and charcoal sales on manors close to London or those with easy access by water. A recent suggestion is that it is now possible, from the amount of archaeological work undertaken in the London area, to chart and model London's changing ecological footprint: the impact of its demands upon the surrounding landscape, both in terms of agrarian production and 'the ways in which ecosystems changed and developed in response to urbanisation' (Roseff & Perring 2002, 124).

From the 13th century, the market towns and villages of the region and of the upper Thames valley were part of a system which supplied London with corn, fuel and other basics (Keene 1989; Galloway & Murphy 1991; Galloway *et al* 1996). London's river trade influenced the growth of towns along the Thames such as Henley (the trans-shipment point for grain for London, mentioned in 1179) and Maidenhead (1202). Through Ware on the river Lea, London drew supplies from the East Midlands. Maidstone and Faversham also flourished around 1300, from the grain trade. Archaeologists should also be studying the supply of London with building materials – stone and brick – and glass. In this, in addition to looking at the sources such as quarries (Tatton-Brown 2001), we should also be looking at the way in which small towns such as Reigate and Maidstone organized the supply of building materials, both to their localities and to the capital. The stone industries of these two towns were particularly long-lived: large quantities of stone from Reigate and probably from Maidstone ('Kentish') were used by Wren in building St Paul's between 1675 and 1710.

Kingston supplied London with livestock, fish, wood (for both firewood and construction) and pottery by the 13th century. There were numerous Kingston merchants in the capital. In 1270, for instance, Peter de Kyngeston, vintner, held a stone house near Billingsgate which was excavated on the New Fresh Wharf site in Lower Thames Street in 1974. In the case of pots, it may be that an industry which seems originally to have been set up in the capital to make a product imitating an import from overseas subsequently migrated to a cheaper site of production outside the capital (Keene 1995, 233; Walker 2000, 117–18). Another town which probably profited from its London connections was Thaxted in northern Essex, famous for its knives (Andrews 1989). As towns grew in London's orbit, so they often specialized in a craft or form of commerce.

Being on a major road also helped the small towns generally, as in the case of Enfield and Tottenham to the north of London, with their large late medieval churches. The widespread problems for towns throughout England in the second half of the 15th century do not seem to be shared by many small towns in the immediate environs of London, which profited in supplying the capital. This was especially true for those on river routes, such as Enfield, Henley and Faversham.

Nationally the roadside inn for travellers was essentially a new form of building in the 17th century, though there were medieval precedents (Barley 1985, 590, 682–5). One sign of the capital's influence would be groups of inns at stopping places along the main routes to London, often in places which were a typical day's journey apart. A broadsheet of about 1600 bore a chart of such mileages from London in all directions: the main routes across Surrey were from London to Southampton via Wandsworth, Kingston, Coveham (Cobham), Ripley, Guildford and Farnham; and to Exeter, via Staines, Bagshot, Hartleyrow (? Hartley Wintney) and Basingstoke (Orlin 2000, frontispiece). Guildford was already known as full of inns by the time of William Camden in 1607. Groups of inns at such places (as at Croydon, which had many coaching inns on the main London

road) merit more study. One would suppose that inns were firstly metropolitan in their form, since the small town or village in which they were being erected probably had nothing like them before, and secondly metropolitan in their details and decoration, particularly mouldings of windows, doors and gateways (this can still be seen in Guildford High Street). Galleries and suites of rooms for travellers were probably medieval developments. Many London inns are known in their 18th century forms (fig 14.1), though they are largely unstudied. There were many inns in Southwark and, as argued in the 14th century (Johnson 1969, 40), Surrey extended right up to the south end of London Bridge .

The example of Croydon is instructive. By the 15th century there was an Old Croydon around the archbishop's palace, and development to the east around the main road to London; this shifting of the centre of gravity was confirmed finally by the formation of the London to Brighton road through Croydon in the 18th century. In this case a small town moved its centre to be on a communication route with the capital (Drewett 1974, 2–4).

One influence from the capital outwards may have been via ownership of land and buildings by Londoners, and in consequence higher land values. From the 13th century Londoners can be found as owners of land both in the countryside and in the towns. By 1300 London merchants held manors at such places as Crayford, Erith, Gravesend and Walthamstow (Williams 1970, 56, 59, 231–7). Retirement into the countryside continued to be popular in the 15th century; rich Londoners bought lands in all the surrounding counties, including Surrey (Thrupp 1948). In Hertfordshire, land values already reflected distance from the capital as early as 1270; throughout the remainder of the Middle Ages, a line drawn between Sawbridgeworth in the east and Langley in the south-west would divide the county into two almost separate regions. This can apparently be followed in the vernacular architecture, settlement patterns and manorial customs (Munby 1977, 35–41). The southern of these two areas presumably reflected London fashions and innovations more.

But what were the material consequences which might be observed by archaeologists? There seems to be no distinctive timber-framing style for buildings in the (inner) London region (Bond 1998), though close-studding from about 1440 is probably a London fashion, and arch-bracing (in which diagonal braces stretch from a vertical up to a horizontal member) is found on 15th century buildings in south-west Essex and thought to be the result of London influence (Stenning et al 1996). What little is known of the styles of timber framing present in the medieval and Tudor City of London does not throw much light on this question (Schofield 1995).

Artefacts or features recorded by archaeologists within medieval buildings, whether houses or churches, could have originated in London itself or be a product of somewhere in the region but distributed through the capital. For many luxuries both in life and in death, prominent people throughout the south-east of England looked to London, as exemplified by church monuments and brasses (Blair 1991; Badham & Norris 1999). In contrast some household items made in the London area, quite possibly originally for the London market, found their way into other parts of the region, and this may have been through London itself. The distribution of Penn floor tiles, made in Buckinghamshire but found throughout Essex and Kent, suggests that some regional entrepreneurs were based in London in the 1380s (Schofield 1995, 112; Keen 2002, 229). On Essex sites such as Maldon Friary, small amounts of Kingston-type ware are found (Walker 1999, 94), and Cheam and Coarse Border Wares in Colchester (Walker 2000, 118).

One consequence of highlighting the access which smaller towns had to London, by road or river, is to expect that foreign imports would come to them more easily from the metropolis along those routes and would be found in modern excavations on medieval urban sites. It is therefore to be noted that, at present, there is a 'near-total absence of imported pottery' from urban excavations at least in west and central Surrey (Jones 1998b, 236). This does not accord with our model, unless we wish to propose that in this earlier, medieval (pre-1500) part of the period, most of Surrey was comparatively immune to the capital's influence or was a backwater, or both.

Several of the features of London's post-medieval dominance of the towns of the region were therefore present in the medieval period. From the London point of view, the towns, like the agricultural areas, functioned to furnish the capital with all kinds of provisions. This led to specialization in many towns, and the greater definition and use of road and river routes, with accompanying infrastructures, particularly inns. The capital sent down these routes all kinds of new ideas, particularly fashions in architecture and artefacts. There was also a move towards standardization of certain artefacts, in that the London guilds tried to extend their powers of search to the rest of the country, ostensibly to maintain standards. The outer districts, but perhaps the towns more than the countryside, absorbed goods which came via the capital: both from other parts of England and Britain, and from overseas.

Towns in the period 1450–1600

After 1450, London sucked in people and resources on a scale not seen before. Though the actual figures are sometimes disputed, we can suggest that from *c* 1520 to *c* 1700, the population of the central conurbation increased more than tenfold. The spectacular periods of growth were the second half of the 16th

Fig 14.1 The yard of the Bell Inn, Aldersgate, drawn by T H Shepherd in 1857. Though this is a central London example, it shows the variety of building components to be sought when looking for inns at smaller towns: galleries, a variety of window forms, and a mixture of brick and timber walls. Guildhall Library (79)

century and again in the first half of the 17th century; by 1600 the population of the conurbation may have reached 200,000, and by the early 1670s it was between 475,000 and 550,000 (Harding 1990). The consequences of the periods of rapid growth on the capital itself, for instance a doubling in population and therefore presumably of the built-up area, both within the first half of the 17th century, have not yet been studied in detail by archaeologists. Between 1600 and 1700, London's share of the national population of England rose from 5% to almost 12%. Because London's growth after 1600 was faster than that of the nation at large, it exerted a progressive damping effect on the natural surplus created outside London. In 1550–74 London accounted for 5% of the nation's burials, but by 1724–49 this figure was over 17%. Areas close to London suffered sharp falls in their levels of population between 1670 and 1720 (Smith 1990).

London and all surrounding towns also shared certain upheavals and changes which are national in scope. The dissolution of the monasteries in the 1530s and 1540s had a direct and enduring effect on the topography and archaeology of towns. Whole areas of each town, previously private precincts, were thrown open and claimed for secular use; new streets, new neighbourhoods, new ghettos of immigrants quickly appeared. In London, and probably elsewhere, the former precincts were quickly colonized by new communities of immigrants from the countryside and from abroad. There had no doubt always been a large number of urban poor and homeless, and probably shanty towns on the edges of urban settlements; but the 16th century is when urban authorities thought the problems of vagrancy and public order were both new and related problems.

With clear destruction levels and new buildings, some (but not many) with distinctive industrial overtones, the Dissolution is a clear archaeological objective. The material survives to be recorded in Surrey towns, on a large scale as at Blackfriars, Guildford (Poulton & Woods 1984) or on a small scale as seen when scrutinizing individual walls of apparent medieval character in Chertsey (Jones 1998a). The Reformation is far less studied and yet potentially equally rewarding. The archaeology of churches at this time is hardly developed, partly because churches have mostly been in constant use since the 16th century, and have changed their interiors many times since then. Later, the archaeology of the nonconformist movement is also worth archaeological study: there were early Quaker meeting-houses in Dorking (about 1702), Esher (1793), Godalming (1701) and Reigate (1688) (Butler 1999; Stell 2002, 315–28). It would be interesting to enquire whether religious dissent was particularly an urban phenomenon. In 1811 Lysons claimed that the first meeting

of the Presbyterians in the country was held at Wandsworth in 1572 (Lysons 1811, **1**, 383).

Town leaders espoused classicism in their public buildings and in the more substantial decorative components of their own houses, and this was for a reason. Advanced Protestant reformers deliberately created complete innovations in architecture such as Somerset House in the Strand (1547–52) to mark a complete break with the past (Wells-Cole 1997, 12–14). Similarly, as the Reformation had stripped away urban ceremony, ritual and forms of social organization orchestrated by the Church, towns themselves were trying to find a new symbolic vocabulary. Town halls and market halls were built in large numbers, or embellished with classical detail such as a civic porch added to a medieval building (eg King's Lynn); but sometimes, as at Staines, deliberately plain (fig 14.2). By the middle of the 17th century, civic buildings had a common architecture which was the focal point and 'front door' of the town itself, and sometimes proclaimed it so (fig 14.3).

A fourth aspect which merits urban archaeological research is the post-Reformation town house. Before 1550, the leaders of small town and county society no doubt had large and distinctive houses, but our knowledge of them is not great. After this date, in contrast, some of their mansions survive, perhaps only one or two in a town (like Tonbridge), occasionally more (as in Chester or York), or in records (in London and Southwark). In the larger centres such as London, we might use these houses as the starting-point of a study of bourgeois culture, specifically post-Reformation and increasingly nationwide in character (in that one town began to look like another, and the habits of their citizens likewise). During the 17th century there was a remarkable urban culture in Holland, which comprised buildings, artefacts and attitudes; there should be the same in Britain. London, with its immediate hinterland, would be the place to start, but the point here is that by 1600 we may perceive that richer townspeople everywhere were becoming more self-conscious, more desirous of joining a national club than of continuing to be embedded in their localities.

Surrey towns in the London orbit, 1450–1600

By 1450, the demands of London were beginning to shape the countryside and the small towns. By 1600, the nearer parts of Surrey, Hertfordshire, Essex and Kent probably shared with Middlesex a concentration of market gardening – growing fruit and vegetables for the capital's tables. This area also concentrated on producing butter, eggs and milk, pork and bacon (Fisher 1935, repr 1990, 70–1). After 1640, vegetable gardens began to occupy the former common fields of Croydon (Thick 1985, 507).

Fig 14.2 The Market House at Staines, drawn by John Oldfield about 1820. This simple building seems to be of 17th-century date. There presumably was an external stair to the door to the council chamber on the first floor, which for some reason is not shown. Guildhall Library (32496)

Outside the central zone, London's demands on more distant sources of supply for food were more selective, as we have already seen in the medieval period: now grain, malt, and cattle came from more or less specific counties or regions. As before, towns such as Kingston, Reigate and Croydon specialized or grew as regional centres. The consequent intensification of agriculture in south-east England may have pushed major industrial areas away from the capital. It is noticeable, stated Fisher (1971, 196), that in the 16th and early 17th centuries there were considerable textile industries in Surrey and Kent and a flourishing iron industry in the Weald; but by 1700 the textile industries had almost disappeared and the Wealden iron industry was languishing. A contributory factor was that London, from 1550,

Fig 14.3 The Market House at Kingston, drawn by Nathaniel Whittock in 1829. With the exception of the statue of Queen Anne of 1706 by Francis Bird, who also carved the west pediment at St Paul's. The degree to which the style of both buildings was metropolitan has yet to be researched in detail. Guildhall Library (28974)

rapidly increased its use of sea coal from Newcastle; this freed the land in the environs of the capital of the necessity to produce wood fuel, and thus it could now turn even more to food production (Keene 2000, 68). In the middle of the 17th century new crops were introduced: beans, peas, lettuce, asparagus, clover, artichokes. All these changes might be charted by archaeological work.

It was not good news for all towns. Some markets were in decline in the 16th century, such as Bletchingley, Haslemere and Leatherhead; at Staines, it seems that by 1593 the church stood in an area of dereliction, about a quarter of a mile from the rest of the town (*VCH Middlesex*, **3**, 16). Other towns in contrast prospered or improved, for instance Godalming, Chertsey and Dorking; the small amount of excavated evidence, such as a house site in Godalming (Poulton 1998), might be placed in this context. Chertsey profited from being on the river (should we think of it as a small port?), and Dorking was a regional market for poultry. Being a staging post on the road to London was good for small towns, as noted above, and this was the case in many other parts of England, for instance Towcester, Market Harborough, Stamford and Grantham to the north, or Thetford in Norfolk. It might be suggested that the fortunes of towns in the South East at this period were linked in large measure to their relations with London.

One dimension worth further exploration is the relation between a small town and large rural industries. The countryside on the Surrey-Hampshire border, around Farnborough and Hawley, was the site of a flourishing pottery industry in the 16th and 17th centuries, producing what is now called Border Ware (Pearce 1992; 1999). Border Wares are found in Surrey towns (Fryer & Selley 1997; Jones 1998a & b), throughout the London area and south-east England; and much further afield, such as in the American colonies until the 1620s. At Jamestown in Virginia, they are one of the most common kinds of everyday household wares. Perhaps the London-based Virginia Company had something to do with this, supplying the early colonists with pots until their own pottery production could begin. This Surrey-Hampshire industry must have been working through London networks. Similarly, the links through the small towns with the two Wealden industries, iron and glass-making, could be further elucidated. Both must have looked to London for their markets. The Wealden glass industry had medieval precedents in Surrey, and started up again in the late 16th century; the 'lack of reliable archaeological evidence' from the Weald is seen to be a stumbling-block for research, and future investigation is rated as a high priority (Crossley 1990, 226–32).

Traditionally, the late 16th century also sees the rise of the gentry. Who were these people? There had always been, since at least 1300, a metropolitan feel about the style of some rural mansions, and this became more intense in the late 16th century. The Elizabethan country house, joyously quirky and seemingly independent in its architectural flamboyance, probably reflected in part the civility of the urban and especially London mansion. Provincial builders like the Smythsons came to the capital to absorb new architectural ideas (Girouard 1983). We need studies in all the Home Counties of the houses and rural estates of individuals who made fortunes out of provisioning towns, which is one of the main characteristics of the gentry. Smith (1992) on Hertfordshire is a start. But we should not particularly look for the large Elizabethan mansion. To quote A G Dickens in his study of the English Reformation, 'nothing can be more misleading to students of Tudor and Stuart England than a visit to Burghley House, to Montacute, to Audley End, to Hardwick Hall' because 'these superb piles did not belong to gentlemen of anything resembling average resources' (Dickens 1989, 189). Archaeological study of the gentry and their estates in Surrey, and especially their use of the towns, seems to be lacking.

The themes which might be explored in Surrey for the period 1450 to 1600, therefore, are the specializations of small towns, the fortunes of towns on roads (and rivers) which led to London, towns and rural industries like Border Ware pottery, and the use of towns by the gentry class.

Reflections of the metropolis, 1600–1700

By the early 17th century, it has been suggested, all the land including the towns around London for a distance of 15 to 20 miles was essentially part of the capital so far as goods, trade and prices were concerned (Chalklin 2000, 56). The landscape was a rather surreal mixture of rural and urban elements (fig 14.4). A ring of market towns between 20 and 40 miles from London served as collecting points for London dealers; one of the largest was Farnham (Dyer 2000, 437). For some foodstuffs, the regulations in London were shared with the surrounding towns: in 1632 it was argued that the assize of bread should be regulated by the price of wheat in Uxbridge, Brentford, Kingston, Hampstead, Watford, St Albans, Hertford, Croydon and Dartford (Fisher 1935, 65). By the early 18th century the costs and prices on a typical Surrey farm were higher than in most other parts of the country, because of the strength of metropolitan demand (Bowden 1985, 85). This was probably the case decades earlier.

Four matters may be worth investigation: London tastes in (secular) architecture and building construction, including gardens; consumer goods and the

Fig 14.4 Wandsworth from the east, about 1750, by an anonymous observer. The church tower of about 1630 survives. Around it in this picture are fields and a windmill, but also small urban terraces deposited in the fields, the first hints of what was to follow. Guildhall Library (22190)

role of London in their spreading; the archaeological consequences of trading with London; and London culture and the emergence of polite society by 1700.

In Surrey, there is more surviving evidence of the 17th century London architectural style called Artisan Mannerism than in any other county. It is 'at its best quite up to the best of the Court style' and 17th century houses and their interiors mark 'the first point at which Surrey makes a contribution to the history of English architecture as a whole' (Nairn & Pevsner 1971, 43, 44). The prime example of this is Kew Palace, built for a merchant in 1631. This house is a City product, a town house in the countryside. The slightly later panelled room from Poyle Park, Tongham, nearly as far west as you can go in Surrey, now stands in the Museum of London, with a ceiling from a separate London house, as a model metropolitan interior. Later still in the century, there are urban terraces in rural but polite enclaves, such as Old Palace Terrace, of 1692, at Richmond Green (fig 14.5); the modern village of upper class residences is not a new idea. From this date, between 1690 and 1730, there survives a remarkable number of prestigious houses built in north Surrey, which represents another wave of London influence (Nairn & Pevsner 1971, 49). A villa like Eagle House, Mitcham (1705), is thought to be a direct transplant from central London, though in truth we have not yet provided the models in the centre of the metropolis (I am sure they will be found). But certainly the compact 18th century villa had arrived in Surrey, and within the first decade of the century.

Related to this was the passion for gardens and parks. The formal garden and fashions for a managed landscape spread from London throughout the South East during the 17th century, with one epicentre being the Thames-side villas and palaces at Twickenham, Hampton Court, Richmond and Kew (Brandon & Short 1990, 238–47); a notable example is the garden laid out at Moor Park near Farnham by Sir William Temple after 1686, with its Dutch affinities (Hunt & de Jong 1988, 245–7). In his *Tour through the whole island of Great Britain* in 1738, Defoe wrote that 'the ten miles from Guildford to Leatherhead make one continuous line of gentlemen's houses [...] their parks and gardens almost touching each other'.

At the level of ordinary buildings, we still need to chart how features of construction – the use of timber, brick and stone – changed during the 17th century. There is no comprehensive summary of this matter for any part of the London area, except for the work of Smith (1992) on Hertfordshire. In the Rape of Hastings in Sussex, study has shown that there are clear changes in the way both rural and urban houses were built (Martin & Martin 1987). From the late 16th century wall braces were no longer set to be visible, but were made to be covered, and crown-post roofs were no longer built, giving way to side-purlin or clasped-purlin roofs; ovolo mouldings appeared in window frames. From about 1650 close-studding went out of favour, and straight (as opposed to curved) raking struts were widely used in frames. After about 1680 first-floor crossbeams were lodged into bressumers rather than jointed into principal posts, timber window casements were now fitted with

Fig 14.5   Old Palace Terrace, Richmond Green. By the 1690s, terraces of houses in central London style were spreading into north Surrey. Photograph John Schofield

iron window frames, and Flemish bond appeared in brickwork. All these changes might be sought in Surrey buildings of the period, and the evidence from central London (in chance finds of dendro-dated pieces of carpentry, or from engravings) should also be fitted into this picture to see if, as might be expected, some of these changes began in the capital (straight raking struts, for instance, are shown in engravings of buildings which probably dated from the 1640s). Eight of the nine Surrey towns studied by O'Connell in 1977 had secular buildings dating to before 1550 on their streets (Bletchingley, Dorking, Farnham, Godalming, Guildford, Haslemere, Leatherhead and Reigate); all nine, including Chertsey this time, had (and hopefully still have) buildings dating to between 1550 and 1700. I have the impression that only a small amount of recording work has been undertaken on standing buildings in Surrey towns, for instance in Kingston (Nelson 1981), as opposed to work in the medieval and post-medieval countryside round about (eg Harding 1976; Gray 1980; 2002).

One strong element in traditional historical and archaeological thinking about the 17th century is that the Great Fire of London in 1666 had effects, not only on the capital, but on future designs of streets, buildings and services in other towns. A large area of the City of London was indeed destroyed in the Great Fire, and the area rebuilt in brick. The catastrophe was noted in towns in England and abroad, and the reconstruction of London in brick was imitated when fire struck elsewhere, such as at Warwick and Northampton. City of London parishes made collections for the relief of people affected by the fire in Northampton, even while their own city was rebuilding. But the Great Fire has had a distorting effect on scholarship; we know far more about the new brick houses than their more numerous contemporaries, the timber-framed buildings. The Fire, destructive though it was, devastated only about one-third of the conurbation of London then standing. Within the area of the Fire a new city of brick and occasionally stone arose; but around it, a larger area remained timber framed for generations to come. Much has been made of the apparent newness of these houses and the related phenomenon of residential squares (McKellar 1999). The latter had begun in the 1640s at Covent Garden and Lincoln's Inn Fields, west of the City and outside the area of the Fire, and there were more on the outskirts of the City, on both the east and west sides, in the 1680s. But were the houses, sometimes in rows, really new and thus a modernizing phenomenon? Probably not. The plan types of houses after the Fire had all existed before the Fire. The arrangement of rooms inside them had not changed; neither had their shape, except for some regulation of height. They were probably more sanitary, and now lasted longer. But in many ways, they were only the Tudor houses reclothed in brick. Shops were still shops, and for several decades after 1666 they were allowed to have projecting signs outside just as they had before the Fire. The great majority of buildings after the Fire had the same functions as before.

Did the history of ordinary houses in Surrey towns reflect these metropolitan changes? We need a study of houses in Surrey towns from the medieval period to the 18th century, as Smith has produced for Hertfordshire, so that we can see when brick buildings undoubtedly influenced by post-Fire London regulations and practice appeared in the smaller towns, as in Hertford by about 1670 (Smith 1992, 164–5). Further, the spread of brick buildings may reflect local wealth and industry as much as metropolitan taste, as shown by the present fabric of Farnham, which in the 18th century grew prosperous from local production of hops. The town is said to have had a 'hop period' (O'Connell 1977, 21–2).

People in towns around London also participated in London's new and fashionable consumer patterns which would leave artefacts in the ground. Joan Thirsk has argued that there was a deliberate government policy to encourage the native manufacture of consumer goods from 1540 onwards (Thirsk 1978). The capital led England in smoking tobacco and consuming sugar from about 1600, and tea was imported in great quantities after about 1680. There were new eating habits, cooking techniques, new drinks and domestic decorations; there were new industries concerned with 'import substitution' such as glass-making and metalworking, or luxuries such as joined furniture, coaches, clocks and books. China (pottery) was virtually unknown in 1675, but a normal part of the household in London and the area around by 1715 (Weatherill 1996; Boulton 2000, 324–6). By 1650, coal had replaced wood as the main domestic fuel (or at least, the adoption of coal in the extensive and increasing new suburbs was creating alarming air pollution). From the second decade of the 17th century there were several flourishing industries in Southwark, notably brewing and the making of new styles in pottery, especially tin glazed (delftware) (Edwards 1974).

Archaeologically, pottery is at present one of the few indicators of change and influence. Apart from pottery, the archaeological material culture of town and country throughout Britain was fairly uniform. Local manufacture of objects in most materials cannot be differentiated from imports, from other regions or from abroad. Pottery, however, included distinctive foreign wares. A good example is provided by the excavation of a site in Moulsham Street, Chelmsford, the periods running from about 1400 to about 1800 (Cunningham & Drury 1985). Here copper-alloy, iron, bone, stone and glass objects and debris are described, but the parallels are local or at best regional. This may be because objects in these materials cannot at present be sourced as to whether they are local or foreign in origin; this may change as archaeological science develops in the future. For the present, as shown on the Chelmsford site, pottery is far more significant, with Metropolitan Slipware perhaps from Harlow, salt-glazed stoneware and slipware from Staffordshire, redware from the Low Countries, slipwares and stonewares from Germany, maiolica from the Southern Netherlands, and fragments of pots from Italy and Spain. We can cite a Surrey parallel: a small site in Croydon, excavated in 1968–70, found sherds of early 17th century Frechen stoneware from Germany in the remains of a small building with cob walls, at the rear of a property facing the medieval church (Drewett 1974, 5, 14). Thus the small towns probably exhibited this juxtaposition of foreign material in humble settings.

There are links between the rise in consumer spending and my third strand, London's provision of foreign goods. In the 16th century, trade for England generally and London in particular was predomi-

nantly export led; but in the 17th century, it became increasingly import led. There was a greater appetite for imports, for instance of the new commodities sugar and tobacco. The increased emphasis on imports led to greater prominence for the London merchants who handled the traffic and made lots of money from it (Fisher 1971, 188–90). Many of the imported commodities came from the new colonies, especially after the acquisition of Barbados in 1627 and the invasion of Jamaica in 1655, both by the English. By 1700, money made in colonial trade must have been diffusing through London into the surrounding area, and there must be an archaeology of colonial trade to be developed for the capital and the smaller towns.

The trade in imports was an important contributory factor in the emergence of polite society, which took its lead in everything from London. This may have begun earlier in the 17th century, but can certainly be observed from the 1670s. Traditional culture focused inwards on local customs and practices, whereas its polite counterpart looked outwards towards London and beyond to the Continent (Borsay 1989). London was both the actual and cultural gateway to the rest of Europe.

To a large extent the new forms of socializing and culture filled the vacuum left by the Reformation. As Collinson has written with only slight intended exaggeration, 'in 1740 there would be assembly rooms, coffee shops, theatres, the first public libraries, musical events, all the necessities of a polite and cultivated existence. In 1600 there was only religion' (Collinson 1988, 49). This is an interesting idea to examine archaeologically: there should be more evidence of secular and civic 'culture' in the strata of the 17th century.

A peculiar example of metropolitan culture was the spa, and Epsom was one of the first. Tree-lined walks had been laid out in London since 1616, but the first public walk in England to be called a parade was in Epsom, to be later followed by Bath (Girouard 1990, 147). But Epsom was only filled with tourists in the summer; in winter it hibernated, largely deserted. But like other resorts it pioneered new building and landscape forms such as the assembly room by about 1710, bowling greens by 1711, and circular tracks for coaches, just like in Hyde Park (Borsay 1989, 141–2, 158, 174, 180). Its popularity also had an effect on nearby Ewell, which changed from being an important village to little more than the last port of call on the way from London to Epsom (Titford 1973). Thus pressures from the capital were transmitted through small towns to the villages and countryside.

I do not mean to suggest that small towns in London's orbit had no other function than to reflect the capital. Equally important, probably, to people in the towns was the growth of provision of services to the surrounding countryside. By 1700, the spread of retail shops in small towns had generally eclipsed the former predominance of markets and fairs. At this time, over half the urban population of England lived in small towns of fewer than 5000 inhabitants which deserve study on their own terms. Further, the great majority of gentry could not afford many visits to London, and opted instead for longer stays in county towns or resorts (Clark 1984, 22–3). So there may be aspects of the larger towns in Surrey, especially Guildford, which rivalled the capital with their own forms of civilized culture. Many small towns had cultural roles in the 17th and 18th centuries (Reed 1995). Thus we should not rush to judgement and claim that all improvements were the result of contact with London; some may have been due to local initiative.

In 1673 Surrey had seven market towns which gives an average of 108 square miles per town; in national terms, a slightly larger average area for each town than Westmorland or Herefordshire, and way behind neighbouring counties Essex (21 markets, average 73 square miles per town) and Kent (31 markets, 53 square miles per town) (Dyer 2000, 430). So it seems that in the 1670s Surrey was less urbanized, in terms of frequency of towns, than Essex or Kent.

Conclusions and suggestions for future work

It is fair to suggest that by 1700 the traditional, semi-autonomous world of the country town every-where in England was beginning to be superseded by the dominance of London in many affairs. The objective here has been to suggest how archaeological work might elucidate the process. This has been a series of outline questions, not a summary of recent work, and I would hope that archaeologists in Surrey towns take up these questions.

Three overall suggestions are made. First, we should see the period 1450 to 1700 as one continuous phase, with the Reformation and Dissolution as the main turning points in every town's history. Secondly, what is at present only partially known, and should be susceptible to archaeological investigation, is how London fed and clothed itself, especially in the period of its exceptional growth in the 16th and early 17th centuries. And thirdly, London's relationship to the towns around it was probably always selective, and thus a local speciality would give the small town strength.

The period up to 1700 is one of declining, if spirited, small town independence, in Surrey and other counties around London. Thereafter, to play with the question in the title of this paper, London really did do for you. But perhaps it was not all bad; in 1600 the journey from Farnham to London, on foot or by cart, was in six stages (marked by towns or villages) which may have taken between four and six days, whereas now, by train on a good day, it takes about one hour.

ACKNOWLEDGEMENTS
I am grateful to Geoff Egan and Jacqueline Pearce for comments incorporated into this text.

BIBLIOGRAPHY

Andrews, D, 1989 A late medieval cutlery manufacturing site at Weaverhead Lane, Thaxted, *Essex Archaeol Hist*, **20,** 110–19
Badham, S, & Norris, M, 1999 *Early incised slabs and brasses from the London marblers*
Barley, M W, 1985 Rural building in England, in Thirsk 1985, 590–685
Blair, J, 1991 Purbeck marble, in Blair & Ramsay 1991, 41–56
Blair, J, & Ramsay, N (eds), 1991 *English medieval industries*
Bond, R, 1998 Timber-framed building in the London region, in Stenning & Andrews 1998, 16–21
Borsay, P, 1989 *The English urban renaissance: culture and society in the provincial town, 1660–1770*
Boulton, J, 2000 London 1540–1700, in Clark 2000, 315–46
Bowden, P J, 1985 Agricultural prices, wages, farm profits and rents, in Thirsk 1985, 1–118
Brandon, P, & Short, B, 1990 *The South-East from AD 1000*
Brooks, H, 2000 Excavations at 79 Hythe Hill, Colchester 1994–5, *Essex Archaeol Hist*, **31,** 112–24
Butler, D M, 1999 *The Quaker meeting houses of Britain*
Campbell, B M S, Galloway, J A, Keene, D, & Murphy, M, 1993 *A medieval capital and its grain supply: agrarian production and distribution in the London region c 1300*, Hist Geog Res Ser, **30,** The Queen's Univ Belfast & Univ London
Chalklin, C W, 2000 South-East, in Clark 2000, 49–66
Clark, P (ed), 1984 *The transformation of English provincial towns*
—— (ed), 1995 *Small towns in early modern Europe*
—— (ed), 2000 *The Cambridge urban history of Britain, II: 1540–1840*
Collinson, P, 1988 *The birthpangs of Protestant England: religious and cultural change in the sixteenth and seventeenth centuries*
Corfield, P J, & Harte, N B (eds), 1990 *London and the English economy 1500–1700*
Crossley, D, 1990 *Post-medieval archaeology in Britain*
Cunningham, C M, & Drury, P J, 1985 *Post-medieval sites and their pottery: Moulsham Street, Chelmsford*, CBA Res Rep, **54**
Dickens, A G, 1989 *The English Reformation*, 2 edn
Dodgshon, R A, & Butlin, R A (eds), 1990 *An historical geography of England and Wales*, 2 edn
Drewett, P, 1974 *Excavations in Old Town Croydon, 1968/70: a Middle Saxon to post-medieval occupation sequence*, SyAS Res Vol, **1**
Duvosquel, J-M, & Thoen, E (eds), 1995 *Peasants and townsmen in medieval Europe*, Ghent
Dyer, A, 2000 Small market towns 1540–1700, in Clark 2000, 425–50
Edwards, R, 1974 London potters circa 1570–1710, *J Ceram Hist*, **6**
Egan, G, & Michael, R L (eds), 1999 *Old and New Worlds*
Fisher, F J, 1935 The development of the London food market, 1540–1640, *Econ Hist*, **5,** 46–64, repr in Corfield & Harte 1990, 61–79

——, 1971   London as an engine of economic growth, in *Britain and the Netherlands IV: Metropolis, dominion and province* (eds J S Bromley & E K Kossmann), 3–16, repr in Corfield & Harte 1990, 185–98

Fryer, K, & Selley, A, 1997   Excavations of a pit at 16 Tunsgate, Guildford, Surrey, *Post-Medieval Archaeol*, **31**, 139–230

Galloway, J A, & Murphy, M, 1991   Feeding the city: medieval London and its agrarian hinterland, *London J*, **16**, 3–14

Galloway, J A, Keene, D, & Murphy, M, 1996   Fuelling the City: production and distribution of firewood and fuel in London's region, 1290–1400, *Econ Hist Rev*, **49**, 447–72

Girouard, M, 1983   *Robert Smythson and the Elizabethan country house*

Gray, P, 1980   *Nutfield and Burstow: the history of the landscape and buildings*, Joint Parish Councils Conservation Committee, Tandridge Council Offices, Caterham

——, 2002   *Surrey medieval buildings: an analysis and inventory*, Domestic Buildings Research Group (Surrey)

Harding, J M, 1976   *Four centuries of Charlwood houses, medieval to 1840*, The Charlwood Society

Harding, V, 1990   The population of early modern London: a review of the published evidence, *London J*, **15**, 111–28

Hunt, J D, & de Jong, E (eds), 1988   The Anglo-Dutch garden in the Age of William and Mary, *J Garden Hist*, **8.2–3** (special double issue)

Isserlin, R M J, 1999   The Carmelite Friary at Maldon: excavations 1990–1, *Essex Archaeol Hist*, **30**, 44–143

Johnson, D J, 1969   *Southwark and the City*

Jones, P, 1998a   Excavation at the Crown Hotel, Chertsey, *SyAC*, **85**, 46–60

——, 1998b Towards a type series of medieval pottery in Surrey, *SyAC*, **85**, 211–38

Keen, L, 2002   Windsor Castle and the Penn tile industry, in Keen & Scarff 2002, 219–37

Keen, L, & Scarff, E (eds), 2002   *Windsor: medieval archaeology, art and architecture of the Thames Valley*, Brit Archaeol Ass Conf Trans, **25**

Keene, D, 1989   Medieval London and its region, *London J*, **14**, 99–111

——, 1995   Small towns and the metropolis: the experience of medieval England, in Duvosquel & Thoen 1995, 223–38

——, 2000   Material London in time and space, in Orlin 2000, 55–74

Lysons, D, 1811   *The environs of London, 1: County of Surrey*, 2 edn

Martin, D, & Martin, B, 1987   *A selection of dated houses in eastern Sussex 1400–1750*, Historic buildings in eastern Sussex, **4**, Rape of Hastings Architectural Survey

McKellar, E, 1999   *The birth of modern London*

Munby, L M, 1977   *The Hertfordshire landscape*

Nairn, I, & Pevsner, N, 1971   *Surrey*, Buildings of England series, 2 edn, rev B Cherry

Nelson, S, 1981   Post-medieval archaeology in Kingston, in Woodriff 1981, 52–61

Newman, J, 1980   *West Kent and the Weald*, Buildings of England series, corrected 2 edn

O'Connell, M, 1977   *Historic towns in Surrey*, SyAS Res Vol, **5**

Orlin, L C (ed), 2000   *Material London, c 1600*

Pearce, J, 1992   *Post-medieval pottery in London, 1500–1700, 1: Border Wares*,

——, 1999   The pottery industry of the Surrey/Hampshire borders in the 16th and 17th centuries, in Egan & Michael 1999, 246–63

Perring, D, 2002   *Town and country in England: frameworks for archaeological research*, CBA Res Rep, **134**

Poulton, R, 1998   Excavation at 5–7 Holloway Hill, Godalming, *SyAC*, **85**, 162–76

——, & Woods, H, 1984   Excavations on the site of the Dominican Friary at Guildford in 1974 and 1978, SyAS Res Vol, **9**

Reed, M, 1995   The cultural role of small towns in England 1600–1800, in Clark 1995, 121–47

Roseff, R, & Perring, D, 2002   Towns and the environment, in Perring 2002, 116–26

Schofield, J, 1995   *Medieval London houses*, New Haven and London

Smith, J T, 1992   *English houses 1200–1800: the Hertfordshire evidence*, Royal Commission on the Historical Monuments of England

Smith, R M, 1990   Geographical aspects of population change in England 1500–1730, in Dodgshon & Butlin 1990, 151–80

Stell, C, 2002   *Nonconformist chapels and meeting-houses in eastern England*

Stenning, D F, & Andrews, D D (eds), 1998   *Regional variation in timber-framed buildings in England and Wales down to 1540*, Essex County Council

Stenning, D F, Richards, P M, & Ryan, P M, 1996   Orsett, Old Hall Farm, *Essex Archaeol Hist*, **27**, 277–88

Tatton-Brown, T, 2001   The quarrying and distribution of Reigate stone in the Middle Ages, *Medieval Archaeol*, **45**, 189–201

Thick, M, 1985   Market gardening in England and Wales, in Thirsk 1985, 503–32

Thirsk, J, 1978   *Economic policy and projects: the development of a consumer society in early modern England*

——(ed), 1985   *The agrarian history of England and Wales, Vol 5 part 2: 1640–1750, agrarian change*

Thrupp, S, 1948   *The merchant class of medieval London*

Titford, C F, 1973   Medieval Ewell and Cuddington, *SyAC*, **59**, 27–35

VCH Middlesex: Victoria history of the county of Middlesex, Vol 3 (ed S Reynolds), 1962

Walker, H, 1999   Medieval and later pottery, in Isserlin 1999, 93–116

——, 2000   A summary of the medieval and post-medieval pottery, in Brooks 2000, 116–19

Weatherill, L, 1996   *Consumer behaviour and material culture in Britain 1660–1760*, 2 edn

Wells-Cole, A, 1997   *Art and decoration in Elizabethan and Jacobean England*

Williams, G, 1970   *From commune to capital*

Woodriff, B (ed), 1981   *The archaeology of Kingston upon Thames*, Kingston Polytechnic for Kingston upon Thames Archaeological Society

John Schofield, Department of Early London History and Collections, Museum of London, London EC2Y 5HN

15

The archaeology of industrialization: towards a research agenda

MARILYN PALMER

This paper is a contribution towards the process of constructing an archaeological research framework for south-east England and is intended to encourage the production of an archaeology of industrialization, rather than an industrial archaeology, of the county of Surrey. It is argued that, if we are to understand the effects of industrialization in the last two centuries on both the landscape and the lives of those who made up the workforce, then we need to study not just the evidence for past technological activity but also that of the society in which they lived. The material evidence for this encompasses the changes in agriculture, rural and urban settlement patterns, social and religious institutions etc which went hand in hand with the actual processes of industrialization. Like all archaeologists, the student of this period cannot be an expert in all fields and needs to call upon the services of others where necessary. However, two broad areas of research are suggested. The first of these is landscapes of industry, including those of transport, extractive industry, woodlands, towns and parks and gardens. The second is landscapes of social memory, utilizing the physical remains of the industrial period to understand more of the motivation and activities of those responsible for its creation, including settlements, leisure and entertainment, institutions, religious buildings and the ritual of death and burial. The paper is not confined to Surrey but attempts to create a broad context for further research into the archaeology of the industrial period.

Introduction

The purpose of archaeology is to ascertain changes in the human condition through the analysis of the material record. The industrial period, from *c*1750 onwards, offers unparalleled opportunities to do just that, because of the wealth of artefacts, standing structures and alterations to the landscape which survive. But, if we accept that what we are referring to is a period archaeology with as much coherence as 'Roman' or 'post-medieval' archaeology, we also have to accept that we must include the material evidence for the whole range of human experience which occurred in this period, not just that which has technological relevance. This material evidence encompasses the changes in agriculture, rural and urban settlement patterns, social and religious institutions etc which went hand in hand with the actual processes of industrialization.

It has often been argued that there is adequate documentary evidence for the industrial period without resorting to the material evidence. The process of industrialization has been seen as the province of the economic historian, who was protected from the realities of its human outcomes by the nature of the archive material. The social historian did become immersed in the conflicts generated by the changing relationships between employers and employees, but since most of the latter were illiterate, the written sources are not first-hand accounts in most instances and can only indicate what it was assumed they felt. Documentary sources certainly inform us about the innovators and inventors that characterize the period: what they do not illuminate are the nameless and the faceless who made up the workforce, nor the effect of the process of industrialization on patterns of agriculture, settlements and the landscape. This is why archaeology, in its now accepted broad sense as a discipline that embraces the study of standing structures and landscapes and not just the excavation of sites, is so important to the understanding of the process of industrialization.

However, in order to do this, industrial archaeologists have to modify their preoccupation with identifying, classifying and describing industrial monuments and to consider these in their temporal, spatial and cultural contexts. It is, of course, undoubtedly true that industrial archaeology arose out of a need to record and preserve the relics of the industrial past at a time when they were fast disappearing without record (Rix 1955; Hudson 1963; Buchanan 1972). To this end, many volunteer industrial archaeologists have produced numerous gazetteers of industrial sites: the Association for Industrial Archaeology (AIA), for example, has certainly done this since 1980 by producing gazetteers of industrial sites for the region in which its annual conference is held (Alderton 1980). In Surrey, the Surrey Industrial History Group (SIHG) produced such a gazetteer in 1990 when the annual conference was held in Guildford (Crocker 1990) but has also, to its great credit, probably produced more published regional gazetteers of sites than any other county, with Derbyshire following close behind. This process has been necessary: industrial sites have not been regularly included on most Sites and Monuments Records (SMRs), and so have not until recently been considered in the development control process, resulting in drastic loss of structures and landscapes. The AIA's *Index Record of Industrial Sites* (Trueman 1995) project and other local initiatives have moved some way towards remedying this situation and ensuring that the material evidence of the recent past is taken into account in local structure plans. Inevitably, this has been more effective in some counties than others, depending on the interests of the individuals involved in the planning process. Essex, for example, has made extensive use of Planning Policy Guidance notes PPG15 and 16 in identifying and recording the recent archaeological and architectural heritage (Gould 2001) and Manchester is well on its way to achieving similar objectives (McNeil & George 1997; Nevell & Walker 1999; McNeil & Nevell 2000; McNeil & George 2002). So, although it certainly cannot be categorically stated that the need to identify industrial sites is past, we do need to move on and consider these sites in a wider context. The industrial aspect of English Heritage's Monuments Protection Programme (MPP) has encouraged this process although it is not yet complete. In 2000, the initial Step 1 reports, which provide an overview of an industry with the emphasis firmly on the material remains, had been produced for 33 industries or groups of industries. These reports have been circulated to SMRs and specialist bodies, and are hugely important in giving a national context to particular landscapes or structures in a way that has not been possible before (Cranstone 1995; Stocker 1995; English Heritage 2000a). The Step 3 reports, providing a systematic site-by-site national evaluation, have had more limited circulation and need much wider dissemination if they are to achieve their full value, a point currently being discussed by English Heritage's Industrial Archaeology Advisory Panel. These are likely to be supplemented with *State of the Historic Environment Reports* (SHIERs), position papers on various industries, building on the methodology developed for MPP but incorporating the results of list review programmes where these have taken place.

The industrial MPP has therefore initiated the process of the contextual understanding of a wide range of industries. However, English Heritage's encouragement of the formulation of regional research frameworks in archaeology should eventually have an even more far-reaching effect on the future development of the archaeology of industrialization than the industrial MPP. The fragmentation of archaeological understanding resulting from developer-funded work under the auspices of PPG15 and 16 led English Heritage to try to take steps to ensure that appropriate research values underpin all archaeological activity. This is the main purpose of the regional research frameworks,

although their formulation varies from region to region. Generally, a series of seminars has been held on each period of archaeology to consider the nature of the archaeological resource and decide on a research agenda: Cadw, the Institute of Field Archaeologists (IFA) and the Council for British Archaeology (CBA) are encouraging a similar pattern for Wales (Geary 2002). Although for the industrial period, common themes emerge such as transport, extractive industries etc, each region is able to identify its own key industries: in the East Midlands, the textile industries and outworking are important themes, while military installations, the development of the farmstead and planned industrial settlements have been selected as important themes in East Anglia (Brown & Glazebrook 2000). This paper is a contribution towards the process of constructing an archaeological research framework for south-east England and is intended to encourage others to work towards the production of an archaeology of industrialization, rather than an industrial archaeology, of the county of Surrey.

It is, of course, difficult to define either the beginning or the end of the period of industrialization. English Heritage has argued that 'it is the classic constituents of the Industrial Revolution – capital investment, organized labour, technological development and the factory scale of production which characterize the field of industrial archaeology' (English Heritage 1995, 1). This would postulate a beginning in the middle of the 18th century, but it is often difficult to explain the development of an industry without going back further than this, as is shown very clearly in both Jeremy Hodgkinson's article on 'Iron production in Surrey' and in Glenys Crocker's 'Surrey's industrial past: a review', both in this volume. Equally, some industries such as framework knitting, which was largely based in the East Midlands but also important in Godalming in Surrey (Crocker 1991), remained outside factory production until late in the 19th century and are characterized not so much by technological development as by the lack of capital investment and the determination of the workforce to remain outside the factory environment, although it cannot be argued that the independent artisan survived in many places. Generally, however, *c* 1750 is a convenient date to begin the industrial period. Its end is even more difficult to define. Some would argue that it extends to the present day but others, this author included, would draw the period to a close sometime in the mid-to-late 20th century, accepting that we are perhaps now in a post-industrial period with a completely different range of attitudes and expectations.

But we cannot leave it at that. Because industrial archaeologists are more concerned with standing buildings and structures than archaeologists of other periods, we cannot remain outside the current debates on the nature of the historic environment and its place in society, a debate fostered by the two recent documents, *Power of Place* (English Heritage 2000b) and *The historic environment: a force for our future* (DCMS 2001*)*. Many of us may prefer to research past industries, but their material remains form part of the contemporary historic environment and we are inevitably drawn into discussions on the significance and economic value of our cherished sites. We therefore have to make judgements on the adaptive re-use of former industrial buildings, for example, the splendid Coxes Lock mill on the Wey Navigation (fig 15.1). Another pressing problem is that of the regeneration of derelict industrial sites: how far can, or should, their past significance be taken into account in the modern environment? To quote DCMS, the Government 'wants to see more regeneration projects, large and small, going forward on the basis of a clear understanding of the existing historic environment, how this has developed over time and how it can be used creatively to meet contemporary needs' (DCMS 2001, 45). The key word in this statement is 'understanding': there is a clear need for the results of the research we carry out on the archaeology of industrialization. Our understanding of the industrial past is not an ivory tower exercise: it has contemporary relevance and so it is even more important that we establish a clear research framework for the industrial period.

This paper is not intended to be an archaeology of industrialization in Surrey, which is much more fully covered by Crocker and Hodgkinson in this volume. The author hopes that the comparison of aspects of Surrey's industrial past with areas of the country more familiar to her may raise various questions which prompt those who carry out research in Surrey to think perhaps more broadly about their research areas. Superficially, Surrey appears to be one of the least industrialized of the counties of England, at least in terms of the definition of industrial archaeology cited above (English Heritage 1995, 1). It does not, for example, have vast areas of mining activity or large numbers of redundant textile mills as elsewhere in the country. The nature of its industrial past is far more subtle, but perhaps can be teased out by adopting broad headings for areas of research. The author would like to suggest two of these here, landscapes of industry and landscapes of social memory, which might help to give a topographical and social dimension to the physical remains of past industrial activity.

Landscapes of industry
Landscape is often taken to mean natural scenery to which the onlooker reacts aesthetically and is therefore devoid of human interference. But to the historian and the archaeologist, landscape is the physical manifestation of changes wrought by man in both space and time. In some areas, it is possible to talk about 'industrial landscapes' ie those in which the practice of industry appears to be the dominant factor

Fig 15.1   Coxes Lock Mill on the Wey Navigation. A mill was first built on the site by the ironmaster Alexander Raby *c* 1776. It became a corn mill and silk mill in the 1830s and a new corn mill was built in 1901. This operated until 1983, milling grain brought by barge on the Navigation. The complex has been converted to residential apartments. Photograph Marilyn Palmer

in their creation and in their 'human' role. One can thus talk about the mining landscapes of south-west England, the Black Country or south Wales; the textile landscapes of the Pennine districts of Lancashire and Yorkshire and the colliery landscapes of north-east England. In Surrey – as in many other southern and eastern counties of England – industry is perhaps more of an element in the development of the landscape than the chief factor responsible for its present form. Yet individual sites in a landscape do become industrial landscapes when we move beyond them to consider the human manipulation of space for economic ends. Indeed, the harnessing of power sources, particularly water power, has a regional impact which goes beyond an individual site: transport networks link individual centres of production to national or international markets; industrial settlements often exhibit evidence of the means of control and surveillance practised by employers to exploit their workforce. Industrial landscapes are a physical record of the way in which people carried out various kinds of industrial activity in the past. They therefore include buildings, not as discrete entities in themselves but in their relationship to one another and to their topographical setting. Different industrial processes are represented by often distinctive buildings which the industrial archaeologist must learn to recognize. These may survive intact or as ruins: the landscapes may also include earthwork remains or buried structures, particularly those associated with extractive industries. One of the major reasons for studying industrial landscapes is to transform such a collection of individual sites and structures into a coherent whole with meaning in both technological and cultural terms (Everson 1995). Technologically, the important elements are the linkages between the various field monuments: these may be physical in the form of watercourses supplying power or transport networks, or functional in the way in which structures were placed to facilitate the processing or manufacturing process. Culturally, these inter-relationships can reveal systems of industrial organization and social relationships, particularly those between the employer and his workforce. The task of the industrial archaeologist is to analyse the industrial landscape in terms of both the spatial and sequential relationships of structures and features to illuminate the process of industrialization.

LINEAR LANDSCAPES

One of the most important features of Surrey is the use made of water power for various purposes – milling, paper making, the manufacture of gunpowder, for example. Even small rivers were tortured into submission by the construction of ponds and leats to maximise their potential. The study of the industry created by the use of a particular river demonstrates the spatial and sequential relationships referred to above. The type of wheel may differ depending on its position on the river profile: quite often, mills in the upper reaches of a river have overshot or breast wheels, to be replaced by undershot wheels in the more sluggish lower reaches (Palmer & Neaverson 1998, 26). Alan Crocker (2001) has shown how in the course of the 19th century many wheels were replaced by turbines, enabling the use of water power to continue as an economic form of power. The use of good water-power sites changed over time: the Wandle began with corn mills at the time of Domesday; many were converted to fulling mills, grinding logwood for dyeing, gunpowder manufacture and textile printing and dyeing until in 1805 it was said to be the hardest worked river in the world (Twilley & Wilks 1974). The Tillingbourne, a more rural stream, nevertheless supported a number of paper mills and the nationally important gunpowder works at Chilworth (Crocker, G & A 2000). It is important to look at the rivers themselves and their contribution to industrialization rather than just looking at individual mills, attractive though they might be.

A similar approach can be taken in the case of artificial waterways. Although the more profitable canals were built in the north of England, Surrey can boast one of the most fascinating of all, London's 'lost route to the sea', the barge route which connected the Thames with Portsmouth via the Wey Navigation, the Wey and Arun Junction Canal, the Arun Navigations and the Portsmouth and Arundel Canal (Vine 1986). As a through route it had a very short life but, since part of it is in the care of the National Trust and the Wey and Arun Canal Trust is pursuing its ambitious Wey-South project, considerable survey and restoration work has been carried out on various sections in recent years. What is perhaps needed is further research into the effect the whole navigation system had on the landscape through which it passed – is there material evidence of any trade or industry it stimulated, such as stone or clay quarries, corn mills or warehouses? Is there evidence for the growth of settlements, perhaps where the waterway was crossed by a turnpike road? The surviving treadwheel crane in Guildford (fig 15.2) is important evidence for trading activities: do documents or engravings provide evidence of similar monuments which once existed? A good model for the study of a waterway as a linear landscape is Stephen Hughes' far-ranging *The archaeology of the Montgomeryshire Canal*, with its studies of bridges, limekilns, warehouses and vernacular housing (Hughes 1981).

Similar questions can be asked about the railway network, particularly as the earliest public railway not owned by a canal company was built in Surrey. The Surrey Iron Railway opened from Wandsworth to Croydon in 1803, to be followed by the Croydon,

Fig 15.2 Treadwheel crane on the Wey Navigation at Guildford. One of the few treadwheel-operated cranes surviving in Britain, now located on the redeveloped riverside, close to its original site on Guildford Wharf. Probably dating from the late 17th century, it was restored by Guildford Borough Council for the National Trust in 1971. Similar cranes used to exist at Stonebridge Wharf, Shalford, and Godalming. Guildford Museum (G9431A)

Merstham and Godstone Railway in 1805, although it never actually reached Godstone. Seen as the first stage in a possible route to Portsmouth, its main use was in fact industrial, the transport of stone and lime to London. The relationship of settlements in relation to transport routes can also be asked about 19th and 20th century locomotive railways, which converged on London and led to the growth of commuter towns and villages.

WOODLAND LANDSCAPES

David Crossley has emphasized the important economic role of woodland in the post-medieval period (Crossley 1994). The woodlands of Surrey, although not so extensive as the neighbouring Wealden county of Sussex, have nevertheless been an important industrial resource for centuries, but the industries carried on in them, such as iron (fig 15.3), glass production and gunpowder manufacture, have been studied individually rather than related to each other and to their woodland environment.

The woodlands were the source of charcoal, the most important fuel for industry until the 17th century. Gunpowder, which made use of charcoal as a raw material rather than a source of fuel, has been extensively studied by Glenys and Alan Crocker (1990 and this volume). The siting of mills such as Chilworth was, of course, related more to water power than to charcoal production since special kinds of charcoal were needed for good quality gunpowder. Jeremy Hodgkinson's paper in this volume on the iron industry in Surrey indicates the importance of woodland areas for the exploitation of iron from the Roman period onwards, but says little about the ways in which

the woodlands must have been managed for the production of charcoal for both bloomeries and water-powered blast furnaces. Glass production was established in the woodlands of the Surrey-Sussex border in the 13th century and extended once French immigrants improved the design of furnaces in the mid-16th century (Crossley 1990, 226–42). Several furnaces have been excavated and David Crossley re-examined the evidence for the MPP reports (Crossley 1993; 1996), re-emphasizing the need to study the relationship between furnace sites and coppice woodland. A survey relevant to this theme was carried out in the north of England by the Royal Commission on the Historical Monuments of England (RCHME) just before its amalgamation with English Heritage and published as *Furness Iron* (Bowden 2000). Southern Cumbria boasts some spectacular remains of blast furnaces, such as Duddon Furnace, but these too had been considered as isolated monuments rather than as part of a complex of woodland industries. RCHME surveyed the trackways leading from charcoal platforms in the woodlands and identified bloomery sites, potash kilns, charcoal burners' huts and bark peelers' huts, demonstrating the inter-relationships between these different industries. Although Surrey woodland remains nowhere near as intact as that of Cumbria, a similar study of a discrete area of Surrey woodland – even vanished woodland – making use of documentary and place-name evidence as well as archaeological remains, might equally reveal this relationship and indicate the long-standing industrial importance of these woodlands. Such a study should be high on the research agenda for archaeology in Surrey.

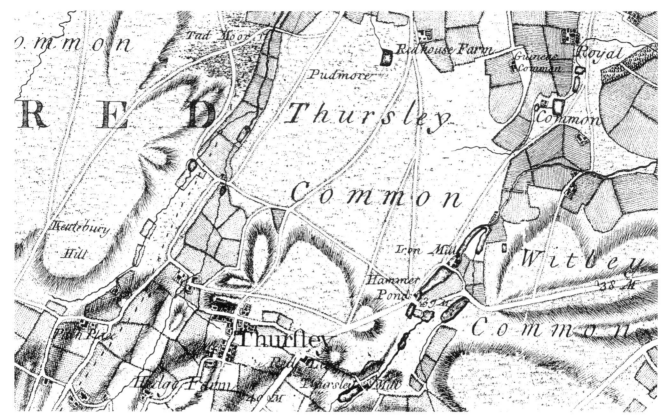

Fig 15.3 Thursley iron mills shown on Rocque's map of Surrey, 1768, scale of 1 inch to 1 mile. 'Hammer Pond' probably corresponds to Upper Hammer, 'Iron Mill' to Lower Hammer and the pond south of the road on a stream to the east to Coldharbour Hammer (Cleere & Crossley 1995, 359–60). The forges were associated with Witley Park furnace *c* 3km south-south-east. Courtesy of Surrey Archaeological Society

DESIGNED LANDSCAPES

Designed landscapes have become increasingly important as indicators of social and cultural evolution and have consumed considerable quantities of land in a region. Surrey is no exception to this, as city gentlemen and industrialists built themselves country retreats within reasonable commuter distance of London. It would be interesting to know how much these took up common land, as happened so frequently in East Anglia. How often were villages moved to improve the views of the country house owner, as in the case of Weston Street, to which the villagers of Albury were moved in the mid-19th century and which then took the name of Albury from the now-demolished village in Albury Park (Crocker, G & A 2000, 124). How far are boundaries, gates and gate houses indications of the social control exercised by the landowner in keeping the public at a distance? All these are legitimate archaeological questions which can be asked of landscapes formed within the industrial period. Equally, country estates are frequently repositories of monuments to technology, especially in the means used to create the landscapes: the 30ft (9m) water-wheel made by Bramah and Sons in Painshill Park, to operate a pump delivering water to an ornamental lake, is a spectacular example of this (fig 15.4). The National Trust is in the process of cataloguing industrial artefacts on its own properties, both inside and outside the house, but the study of country house technology in Surrey would advance our understanding of this little-known area of industrialization.

LANDSCAPES OF EXTRACTIVE INDUSTRY

Fortunately for those who live there, the landscape of Surrey has never been blighted by the huge excavations created by open-cast mining elsewhere in Britain or Europe. The evidence for extractive industries in Surrey is largely underground and hidden from public view – except where sudden subsidence occurs. The Upper Greensand between Reigate and Merstham provided useful resources of building stone, while there are several underground caverns in the Guildford area where chalk was mined, as it was also between Reigate and Dorking. Much of the hard, calcareous stone derived from the Upper Greensand was used for prestigious buildings in London from the 14th century but a useful research area would be the relationship between local building materials and social status: for example, even where good local stone was available in the late 18th or early 19th centuries, was brick considered a more fashionable building material? Hearthstone, used for whitening steps, was extensively mined throughout much of the region in the 19th century, but how much research has been carried out on the nature of underground workings and their relationship to surface remains? The extensive chalk deposits in Surrey have led to the

Fig 15.4   Water-wheel in Painshill Park. This 9m-diameter wheel was made by Bramah and Son in the 1830s to pump water to an ornamental lake and was restored in 1988. Technology played an essential role in many designed landscapes of the 18th and 19th centuries. Photograph by Jack Chinn, courtesy of Painshill Park Trust

erection of numerous banks of limekilns, such as those at Brockham (Sowan 2000a) and Betchworth (fig 15.5; Sowan 2000b). Another item on any research agenda for the industrial period ought to be a consideration of the typology of these structures and an investigation into whether the nature of chalk demanded different types of kilns from those more commonly associated with limestone and how far this is reflected in their construction. The close connection between these commercial kilns and transport has already been noted (Tarplee 1995, 6–7). The Wealden clays yielded good quality brickearth, and numbers of kilns from different periods have been recorded and, in some cases, excavated and consolidated. Again, however, it would be worth analysing the spatial distribution of these kilns in relation to available transport as well as constructing a typology of these structures with reference to the local geology. The variations in the latter also means that there can be few places better than Surrey (and the other Wealden counties) where the relationship between vernacular architecture and resources of building materials can be studied.

URBAN LANDSCAPES

Although most of us resent new building work taking place in historic towns, urban centres have always been dynamic environments which have continually been refurbished, re-shaped and renewed. The urban fabric is probably more rapidly responsive to social change than the countryside, as those in charge of the administration of towns have usually been able to finance and organize change to a far greater extent than is possible on the wider canvas of the countryside. So, understanding the historic environment of towns is vital to understanding the development of human society. Urban regeneration must be based on knowledge and understanding of the past, a theme emphasized in both *Power of Place* and *A Force for our Future*. Such understanding will bring with it a sense of identity and a sense of place, both of which have been shown in recent surveys to be important in people's consciousness. Urban landscapes must therefore have an important role in a future archaeological research agenda.

What themes will contribute to a greater understanding of the role played by towns in the industrial period? First the relationship between towns and their hinterland, between towns and the countryside. Now that towns seem to concentrate more and more on retail and leisure activities rather than industrial pursuits, it is easy to forget that towns were also seen as places where the products of the countryside were processed for sale. We need to know more about industries such as urban grain-milling, tanning and textile production. Guildford and Godalming, for example, had all these – Gomshall tannery, the remains of the medieval woollen industry and several grain mills. Secondly, towns were also centres of retail trade. Many of the towns of Surrey were founded as market towns, and sites of markets often survive as open spaces – we tend to forget the importance of spaces as well as buildings when studying the topography of towns. It would be useful to ask how far the original sites of markets changed as towns expanded and whether separate markets came to exist for different types of goods, as in Guildford. How far were market sites given permanence by the provision of a market building, often one combining other civic functions as in Kingston. Archaeologists of industrialization perhaps pay too much attention to production of goods at the expense of consumption, and further studies of the physical evidence for retail trade would enhance our understanding of the distribution of goods.

Thirdly, as population grew in the post-medieval period, what evidence is there that thought was given to the positioning of public buildings as a means of expressing social control? In the USA, Paul Shackel, Mark Leone and others have looked at the deliberate planning of Annapolis in Maryland to reflect the

Fig 15.5   Betchworth limekilns. These kilns form part of the industrial landscape of the chalkpits and limeworks on the North Downs. The Betchworth site was worked from 1865 to 1934 by the Dorking Greystone Lime Company and these rare Dietzsch kilns were added in the 1890s to convert chalk into quicklime. The 1924 hydrator for converting the quicklime to slaked lime, seen to the right of the kilns, went out of use in 1956 and has since been demolished. Photograph by Paul Sowan

relationship between church and state – the systematic uses of streets, for example, with important buildings closing off the vistas within the built environment (Shackel *et al* 1998). The more organic growth of towns in Britain makes the study of the symbolism of public buildings more difficult, but there are examples of such deliberate planning, as in London and Edinburgh. Is it possible to determine the motivation for the placing of town halls or new churches within the confines of Surrey towns? Were the towns zoned in any way to separate classes of people, or different trades, such as separate tanners' quarters, for example? Can archaeological evidence help us to understand how order was imposed on very large numbers of people living in close proximity? How, too, did the urban population cope with everyday living? What evidence survives for water supply and sewerage systems? Attention is carefully drawn to individual examples of public utilities in all the SIHG *Guides*, but they do need to be seen in the context of the burgeoning 19th century town.

Finally, of course, we need to look at the built fabric of towns. There are many studies of vernacular buildings or public buildings within towns, but what about the housing of the workforce? Is there evidence for housing on previously empty plots such as urban gardens which could imply considerable population growth? The distribution of assemblages of excavated artefacts, too, would provide clues to both the zoning of the inhabitants in towns as well as to changes in consumption. Surrey has no industrial towns on the scale of, say, Sheffield or Manchester, but it did not entirely escape 19th century slum housing – all towns housed workers as well as artisans in all periods. Interesting results are beginning to appear from the urban work carried out by contract archaeologists in response to PPG15 and 16, such as a recent study of a slum area of Sheffield (Belford 2001). There are, then, many themes that we ought to consider in studying urban landscapes which would enhance our understanding of the role played by towns in the industrial period.

LANDSCAPES OF WAR
Man's attempt to defend himself against his fellow man has always been of concern to archaeologists, and this is as true for the 19th and 20th centuries as it was for the Roman or medieval periods. The study of how defence structures have changed in response both to developments in technology, such as the long-range rifled guns which could fire horizontally over longer distance, and the direction of threat, with defence against aerial attack taking precedence over defences against land invasion, is a very necessary one. Since, however, a paper by Chris Shepheard and Alan Crocker is included elsewhere in this volume, the question will not be further pursued here.

Landscapes of social memory
Archaeologists of any period need to 'read' the society behind the physical remains of the past and to accept that material culture is not a passive reflection

of society but an active element in its creation. This applies to the material culture of the working past as much as it does to that of the prehistoric past, and industrial archaeologists should be even more successful at deducing the actions and purposes of the individuals responsible for that material culture since they have a much wider range of data with which to work. The second broad heading of this paper is consequently entitled 'landscapes of social memory' and indicates how we might try to utilize the physical remains of the industrial period to understand more of the motivation of those responsible for its creation.

MANUFACTURING INDUSTRIES, EMPLOYERS AND THE WORKFORCE

As suggested earlier, documentary sources provide some evidence for the lives of those who built and those who worked in mills and factories, but a study of the buildings and related settlements can add much to our understanding. For example, the early textile colonies of the late 18th century in Derbyshire, Cheshire and Scotland or colliery settlements such as Elsecar in South Yorkshire reveal the paternalism of the entrepreneurs who provided the housing for their mill- or mine-based workforce, but they also reveal a pattern of social control which the occupiers had to accept if they wished to retain their homes. Owners' houses adjacent to their works, perhaps best seen in the textile industries of the west of England, are also an example of implicit social control. The continuation of outwork beyond the introduction of the factory can also indicate resistance by the workforce to factory discipline and was common in the textile industries of the north and west of England (Timmins 1977; 2000), south-west England (Palmer & Neaverson 2003), the boot and shoe industry of Northamptonshire (Menuge 2001) and the small metal industries of the West Midlands (Cattell et al 2002). There is perhaps some evidence of worker resistance in Surrey, for example in the Godalming hosiery industry, although the factory system was introduced there quite early (Crocker, G 1991). Employer-provided housing often accompanied the development of 20th century industry, for example, in the production by Crittalls of metal windows in Essex (Crosby 1998). Dennis Bros of Guildford certainly built housing for their workforce in the early 20th century, but it would be interesting to know how far their example was followed by other employers in the car and aircraft industries. How far, too, were manufacturers responsible for commissioning the design of their own premises, perhaps trying to establish their social status by architectural pretension (Jones 1985)? The form taken by the many trading estates which developed is also a potential subject for study (see Stratton &

Trinder 2000). Study of 20th century industrial archaeology in Surrey should be an important element of a research agenda, since its closeness to London resulted in considerable development in this period.

SETTLEMENTS

The process of industrialization undoubtedly changed the nature and spatial composition of settlements, although this perhaps had less of an impact in Surrey than in the more industrialized Midlands and North. The attitudes of landowners considerably influenced this: in the East Midlands, for example, the pattern of 'closed' and 'open' villages (ie those either dominated or free from the influence of a particular landowner) has had an important effect on the development of industry, particularly outworking in the textile, boot and shoe and small metal industries. The methodology developed by Mike Nevell and John Walker for examining the relationship between the development of industry and the patterns of landholding exercised by lords, tenants and freeholders may well be applicable to areas of Surrey, especially water-powered industry of different types (Nevell & Walker 1999). Equally important in Surrey is the influence of London and of transport networks on the changing pattern of settlement.

BUILDINGS OF SOCIAL CONTROL: WORKHOUSES, HOSPITALS, PRISONS

The burgeoning population of the late 18th and early 19th centuries created a need for more centralized systems of dealing with health, poverty and crime. The building of hospitals, workhouses and prisons is equally an aspect of the archaeology of the industrial period and continues the themes of paternalism and social control discussed earlier. RCHME (shortly before its amalgamation with English Heritage) produced excellent surveys of hospitals, prisons and workhouses, and these provide good starting points for an investigation of the location and role of these social institutions (Richardson 1998; Brodie et al 1999; Morrison 1999). Six workhouses in Surrey were built in the period immediately after the 1834 Poor Law Amendment Act, with others following before 1880. The comparatively small number probably reflects the fact that Surrey was not so subject to cyclical unemployment as the more industrialized regions further north. Some of the first of the new workhouses were built in Kent, following the courtyard plans of Sir Francis Head, as did the now demolished ones in Surrey in Reigate, Hambledon and Farnham, while that at Chertsey was built to the hexagonal plan devised by Samuel Kempthorne (Morrison 1999, 60). The layout of these buildings, where males, females and children were segregated not only into different dormitories but also different exercise areas, exemplify social control at its most extreme, and need to be related to the changes in both agricultural and industrial employment (or unemployment) which brought them into being. Prisons are obviously buildings designed with social control in mind but, even more than the workhouses, as buildings of surveillance. Hospitals, particularly those designed as asylums like the Surrey County Asylum (later Springfield Hospital) in Wandsworth, the Epsom cluster (fig 15.6) and Brookwood Hospital, were equally concerned with surveillance, but also included provision for therapy, such as the farm at Brookwood. All three classes of building demonstrate how aspects of the built environment were structured to promote desired patterns of human behaviour and to achieve social control of certain classes of people during the industrial period.

RELIGIOUS BUILDINGS AND THEIR COMMUNITIES, INCLUDING CEMETERIES

Death and burial is a major theme in the archaeology of all periods, but has rarely played a role in the archaeology of industrialization. Yet it is integral to the study of social memory as shown through the material culture of the period. In the East Midlands, both nonconformity as shown through its chapels and the foundation of Roman Catholic churches following toleration in 1829 made a substantial impact on industrialized villages: how far did this happen in the far less industrialized county of Surrey? Study of the decoration of headstones can reveal changing attitudes to death, a subject of increasing importance to historical archaeologists since the pioneering work of James Deetz in the USA (Deetz 1977; see also Tarlow 1999). There are many references in the Surrey gazetteers to the use of cast-iron grave-markers (fig 15.7); is this use related to social class in any way? As population grew, how were the dead accommodated? What effect did this have on the shape of villages as churchyards became full and cemeteries were located around the perimeters of settlements?

Of particular importance to Surrey, of course, is the construction of Brookwood cemetery to bury the dead who could not be accommodated in London. In 1852 the London Necropolis and National Mausoleum Company purchased the whole of Woking Common for this purpose, eventually creating what is certainly the largest cemetery in Britain, if not in Western Europe. Archaeologists are traditionally interested in past ritual significance, and they could not have a clearer example of this than Brookwood's specially constructed railway line from the so-called Necropolis Junction on the London and South-Western Railway, with its branches into the two sections reserved respectively for Anglicans and all other denominations, each with its own station (Wakeford 1987). This massive cemetery was followed by the construction in 1879 of Britain's first crematorium (fig 15.8), but as the Home Office would not legalize cremation, it was not used until 1885 and then only sporadically until the 20th century. Surrey therefore played a seminal role in the development of 20th century burial practices.

Fig 15.6 The Manor Hospital, Epsom. Opened in 1899, this was the first of the cluster of five hospitals for the mentally ill built by London County Council on the Horton Estate. It was used as a war hospital in the First World War. Bourne Hall Museum (OP 846)

Fig 15.7   One of the many cast-iron grave markers made by the Guildford firm of Filmer and Mason. This example is at Pyrford and contrasts with the marble gravestones behind it. Tony Yoward Collection

LEISURE AND ENTERTAINMENT

Mass entertainment in the Roman period created great monuments in the forms of theatres and hippodromes. It was not until the 19th or even early 20th centuries that anything on a similar scale was constructed for the purposes of entertainment. Racecourses and football grounds therefore merit some attention and study of their structures can also reveal substantial changes in their form as, for example, public health and safety considerations became important. Most football grounds have been reconstructed since the Taylor Report, replacing the terraces with covered stands (Smith 2001). Epsom racecourse, in fact, dates back to the 17th century, with covered stands built in the 19th century which have undergone considerable refurbishment and renewal (fig 15.9); it would be interesting to know what changes of form have taken place to cope with 20th century crowds and to accommodate modern media equipment. Cinemas became popular in the early 20th century and the Odeon chain, for example, developed its own style of architecture (Richardson & Upson 2001) but many have been adapted for other purposes as television enabled people to see films without having to leave home. Finally, Brooklands was the world's first purpose-built banked race track, dating from 1907 and involving vast earthworks, as well as diverting the river Wey in three places. The track was also used for early aeroplane trials, and eventually Vickers Armstrong began aircraft production near the site, purchasing it in 1946, after which racing ceased. A question that could be asked when looking at provision for mass entertainment in Surrey is the effect of proximity to London: does this appear to have helped or hindered local provision? And does the type of entertainment provided in Surrey differ from that, say, in the industrial towns of the north? What does this suggest about the social composition of the population of Surrey?

Fig 15.8   Britain's first crematorium, constructed in 1879 at Brookwood cemetery in Woking. Since the Home Office refused to legalize cremation, it was not used until 1885 and then only sporadically until the 20th century. Surrey Industrial History Group Collection

Asking questions about the social meaning of sites and structures surviving from the recent past is an important but often neglected aspect of industrial archaeology.

Conclusion

There are many more areas of the archaeology of the industrial period that could be included in a research agenda. Of particular concern is the lack of actual excavation of sites of the industrial period in England compared with Australia and the USA, which means that we have never been able to study changes in consumption from the material evidence, another major theme in all other periods of archaeology. It also means that we lack basic reference collections of artefacts from the period such as ceramics, glass bottles and metal objects: the only class of objects for which we have an adequate reference collection is the clay tobacco pipe. This may well change in the future as more multi-period excavations are carried out by contract unit staff ahead of development. The task of these archaeologists is to evaluate the archaeological potential of a site prior to re-development and as these are not officially research excavations, there is no longer the tendency to strip off the top layers in quest of the medieval or Roman layers beneath, as was the case until the last decade or so. Industrial archaeology has already benefited substantially from contract archaeology but the results tend to be published as part of the 'grey literature', not often reaching the public domain, although the past editors of *Industrial Archaeology Review* were active in soliciting the results of such contract work for publication. Some of the results of such excavations are listed annually in the CBA's *British and Irish Archaeological*

Bibliography and are available on websites such as that maintained by the Archaeology Data Service (ADS), but much more could be done to prevent this considerable archaeological archive remaining largely in oblivion.

The archaeology of the industrial period, then, must be a broad-ranging study encompassing the material evidence of all aspects of human activity in the last two centuries or so. No single person can be equally familiar with all aspects so, like the archaeologists of any other period, we have to resort to specialists when dealing with buildings or artefacts beyond our range of experience. The term 'industrial monument' should perhaps be abandoned, except perhaps for statutory purposes, and sites and structures of the industrial period seen in their temporal, spatial and cultural contexts. Finally, the landscapes, artefacts and buildings of this period should, like those of any other archaeological period, be thought of as material evidence for the past human condition and not only as indicators of technological processes. As David Smith said right back in 1965:

> Industrial archaeology is ultimately concerned with people rather than things: factories, workshops, houses and machines are of interest only as products of human ingenuity, enterprise, compassion or greed – as physical expressions of human behaviour. From whatever standpoint the subject is approached, man is the basic object of our curiosity (Smith 1965, 191).

It is hoped that this brief paper will help point the way to a broad-ranging research framework for the archaeology of the industrial period in Surrey.

Fig 15.9 Epsom racecourse, Derby Day, *c* 1910, showing the 1830 grandstand. The variety of headgear indicates the differing social status of those who enjoyed a day at the races. Bourne Hall Museum (OP 1117)

ACKNOWLEDGEMENTS

The author is grateful to the Surrey Industrial History Group for the production of a series of useful gazetteers on Surrey's industrial past, and particularly to Glenys Crocker for her comments on a draft of this paper and for the further information she supplied. Chris Shepheard, Paul Sowan, Tony Yoward, the Painshill Park Trust and Bourne Hall and Guildford Museums are thanked for providing illustrations.

BIBLIOGRAPHY

Alderton, D, 1980 *Industrial archaeology in and around Norfolk*, AIA

Belford, P, 2001 Work, space and power in an English industrial slum: 'the Crofts', Sheffield, 1750–1850, in *The archaeology of urban landscapes: explorations in slumland* (eds A Mayne & T Murray), Cambridge University Press, 106–17

Bowden, M (ed), 2000 *Furness iron: the physical remains of the iron industry and related woodland industries of Furness and Southern Cumbria*, English Heritage

Brodie, A, Croom, J, & Davies, J, 1999 *Behind bars: the hidden architecture of England's prisons*, Swindon, English Heritage at NMRC

Brown, N, & Glazebrook, J, 2000 *Research and archaeology: a framework for the eastern counties. 2: Research agenda and strategy*, E Anglian Archaeol Occ Pap, **8**

Buchanan, R A, 1972 *Industrial archaeology in Britain*, Pelican

Cattell, J, Ely, S, & Jones, B, 2002 *The Birmingham jewellery quarter: an architectural survey of the manufactories*, English Heritage

Cleere, H, & Crossley, D, 1995 The iron industry of the Weald, 2 edn, Leicester University Press

Cotton, J, Crocker, G, & Graham, A (eds), 2004 *Aspects of archaeology and history in Surrey: towards a research framework for the county*, SyAS

Cranstone, D, 1995 Steps 2 and 3 in the Monuments Protection Programme: a consultant's view, in Palmer & Neaverson 1995, 115–17

Crocker, A, 2001 Water turbines in Surrey, *SyAC*, **88**, 133–60

Crocker, G (ed), 1990 *A guide to the industrial archaeology of Surrey*, AIA

Crocker, G, 1991 The Godalming knitting industry and its workplaces, *Ind Archaeol Rev*, **14.1**, 33–54

——, 2004 Surrey's industrial past: a review, in Cotton *et al* 2004, 213–32

Crocker, G, & Crocker, A, 1990 Gunpowder mills of Surrey, *Surrey Hist*, **4.3**, 134–58

——, 2000 *Damnable inventions: Chilworth gunpowder and the paper mills of the Tillingbourne*, SIHG

Crosby, T, 1998 The Silver End model village for Crittall Manufacturing Co Ltd, *Ind Archaeol Rev*, **20**, 69–82

Crossley, D, 1990 Post-medieval archaeology in Britain, Leicester University Press

——, D, 1993 *MPP: The glass industry step 1 report*, report for Engl Heritage

——, 1994 Early industrial landscapes, in *Building on the past* (ed D Vyner), Royal Archaeological Institute, 244–63

——, 1996 MPP: the glass industry, introduction to Step 3 site assessments, report for Engl Heritage

DCMS: Department of Culture, Media and Sport, 2001 *The historic environment: a force for our future*

Deetz, J, 1977 *In small things forgotten*, rev edn 1996, New York: Doubleday

English Heritage, 1995 *Industrial archaeology: a policy statement*

——, 2000a *MPP 2000: a review of the Monuments Protection Programme*

——, 2000b *Power of place; the future of the historic environment*

Everson, P, 1995 The survey of complex industrial landscapes, in Palmer & Neaverson 1995, 21–8

Geary, K, 2002 A research agenda for Wales – progress report, *CBA Wales Newsl*, **23**, 5–6

Gould, S, 2001 The identification, recording and management of the more recent archaeological and archaeological heritage of Essex, *Ind Archaeol Rev*, **23.1**, 11–24

Hodgkinson, J, 2004 Iron production in Surrey, in Cotton *et al* 2004, 233–44

Hudson, K, 1963 *Industrial archaeology: an introduction*, John Baker

Hughes, S, 1981 *The archaeology of the Montgomeryshire Canal*, Aberystwyth, Royal Commission on the Ancient & Historic Monuments of Wales

Jones, E, 1985 *Industrial architecture in Britain*, Batsford

McNeil, R, & George, A D (eds), 1997 *The heritage atlas 3: Warehouse album*, Univ Manchester Field Archaeology Centre

——, 2002 *The heritage atlas 4: Manchester – archetype city of the industrial revolution; a proposed world heritage site*, Univ Manchester Field Archaeology Centre

McNeil, R, & Nevell, M, 2000 *A guide to the industrial archaeology of Greater Manchester*, AIA

Menuge, A, 2001 Technology and tradition: the English Heritage survey of the Northamptonshire boot and shoe industry, in *TICCIH2000: From industrial revolution to consumer revolution* (eds M Palmer & P Neaverson), AIA, 101–10

Morrison, K, 1999 *The workhouse: a study of poor law buildings in England*, Swindon: English Heritage at NMRC

Nevell, M, & Walker, J, 1999 *Tameside in transition: the archaeology of the industrial revolution in two north-west lordships, 1642–1870*, Tameside Metropolitan Borough Council

Palmer, M, & Neaverson, P A (eds), 1995 *Managing the industrial heritage*, Leicester: School of Archaeological Studies

——, 1998 *Industrial archaeology: principles and practice*, Routledge

——, 2003 Handloom weaving in Wiltshire and Gloucestershire in the 19th century: the building evidence, *Post-Medieval Archaeol*, **37.1**, 126–58

Richardson, H (ed), 1998 *English hospitals 1660–1948: a survey of their architecture and design*, Royal Commission on the Historic Monuments of England

Richardson, S, & Upson, A, 2001 The Embassy Cinema, Braintree, *Ind Archaeol Rev*, **22.1**, 25–36

Rix, M, 1955 Industrial archaeology, *Amateur Historian*, **2.8**, 225–9

Shackel, P A, Mullins, P R, & Warner, M S (eds), 1998 *Annapolis pasts: historical archaeology in Annapolis, Maryland*, Knoxville: Univ Tennessee Press

Shepheard, C, & Crocker, A, Second World War defences in Surrey, in Cotton *et al* 2004, 245–54

Smith, D, 1965 *The industrial archaeology of the East Midlands*, Newton Abbot: David & Charles

Smith, J, 2001 An introduction to the archaeology and conservation of football stadia, *Ind Archaeol Rev*, **22.1**, 55–66

Sowan, P W, 2000a Brockham lime works kilns (TQ 197 509): interim report, *SIHG Newsl*, **113**, 9–13

——, 2000b A newly-discovered lime kiln type at Betchworth lime works (TQ 207 512), *SyAS Bull*, **343**, 4–6

Stocker, D, 1995 Industrial archaeology and the Monuments Protection Programme in England, in Palmer & Neaverson 1995, 105–10

Stratton, M, & Trinder, B, 2000 *Twentieth century industrial archaeology*, Spon

Tarlow, S, 1999 Wormie clay and blessed sleep: death and disgust in later historic Britain, in *The familiar past?* (eds S Tarlow & S West), Routledge, 183–98

Tarplee, P, 1995 *A guide to the industrial history of Mole Valley District*, SIHG

Timmins, J G, 1977 *Handloom weavers' cottages in central Lancashire*, Lancaster, Centre for North West Regional Studies

Timmins, G, 2000 Housing quality in rural textile colonies, *c* 1800–*c* 1850: the Ashworth settlements revisited, *Ind Archaeol Rev*, **22.1,** 21–3

Trueman, M, 1995 The Association for Industrial Archaeology's IRIS initiative, in Palmer & Neaverson 1995, 29–34

Twilley, R, & Wilks, M (eds), 1974 *The river Wandle, a guide and handbook*, Sutton Libraries

Vine, P A L, 1986 *London's lost route to the sea*, 4 edn, Newton Abbot: David & Charles

Wakeford, I, 1987 *Woking 150: the history of Woking and its railway*, Mayford & Woking District History Society

Marilyn Palmer, Professor of Industrial Archaeology, School of Archaeology and Ancient History, University of Leicester LE1 7RH

16

Surrey's industrial past: a review

GLENYS CROCKER

This paper provides a summary review of work carried out on the history and archaeology of medieval and later industry in Surrey. It deals principally with manufacturing and extractive industries, motive power, transport and utilities. Agriculture is touched upon only incidentally. Emphasis is on the modern administrative county but examples from metropolitan Surrey are included as appropriate. The paper attempts to identify gaps in present knowledge and suggest directions for future research.

Introduction

Surrey is fortunate in its *Victoria County History*. Published in 1902–12, it contains a substantial account of the manufacturing and extractive industries of the historic county contributed by Montague S Giuseppi, one time Secretary of the Surrey Archaeological Society (*VCH*, **2**, 243–424). This still provides a starting point for inquiry in many fields. A few specialized works followed but it was in the 1970s, with growing interest in industrial archaeology, that publications on the subject began to proliferate. The British Association's Surrey conference volume discusses past and contemporary industry (Salmon 1975, 161–4, 177–99) and the first gazetteer of industrial sites appeared two years later (Payne 1977). The Surrey Industrial History Group (SIHG) then compiled gazetteers for the modern county (Crocker, G 1990) and for each of its eleven administrative districts. These are (with abbreviations used for locations in the text): Elmbridge (El; Baker 1989; Tarplee 1998), Epsom & Ewell (EE; Wakefield 1997), Guildford (Gu; Haveron 1993), Mole Valley (MV; Tarplee 1995), Reigate & Banstead (RB; Stidder 1979; 1996), Runnymede (Ru; Mills 1991), Surrey Heath (SH; Mills 1995), Spelthorne (Sp; Mills 1993), Tandridge (Ta; Tadd 1994), Waverley (Wa; Haveron 1985; Crocker 2003), and Woking (Wk; Wakeford 1995). These districts, together with London boroughs (LB) formerly in Surrey, are shown on the location map in the Introduction to this volume.

Medieval industries

Corn milling for local communities represents the first use of water power. The Domesday survey recorded 118 mills, plus five parts of mills, in the historic county of Surrey. All were water-powered corn mills as windmills did not appear in England until the late 12th century. The location of early mill sites known from documentary evidence and their correlation with later rebuilds and features in the landscape is a matter for continuing investigation, which has been discussed and speculated upon by many authors. Published work includes county-wide surveys and gazetteers (Hillier 1951; Reid 1987;

1989; Stidder 1990; Blythman 1996), studies of mills in particular areas such as Wandsworth (Gerhold & Ensing 1999), the lower Wey and Mole (Greenwood 1980) and the estates of the bishops of Winchester in the Farnham area (Brooks & Graham 1983). There are unpublished works on mills on the Wandle (Wilks MS) and Surrey volumes on watermills and windmills in the Simmons manuscript collection (Simmons 1940s). The standard work on Surrey windmills (Farries & Mason 1966) notes that one of the earliest known windmills in England is recorded at Warlingham (Ta) at the close of the 12th century. The distribution of known wind and watermill sites is shown in figure 16.1.

Commercially significant industries in medieval Surrey were the manufacture of woollen textiles, pottery, Wealden iron and glass and the quarrying of Reigate building stone. The early iron industry is discussed by Jeremy Hodgkinson in this volume and is mentioned only briefly here.

THE WOOLLEN INDUSTRY

An early cloth-manufacturing region extended from Sussex across south-west Surrey and Hampshire to Berkshire, Wiltshire and Dorset (Kerridge 1985, 15). Research on the woollen industry in southern England has tended to concentrate on counties farther west where it achieved greater prominence and survived longer and the industry in Surrey has received relatively little further attention since the publication of Giuseppi's account in 1905 (*VCH*, **2**, 342–9). There is evidence for the export of Guildford cloth in the late 14th century (Origo 1957, 72–3) and records show that in the 16th century products of the district were made chiefly for export (*VCH*, **2**, 343). Dyeing was carried out by clothiers and some specialist dyers (*ibid*, 346–7, 363–4). Woad was prominent among the dyes used and was mainly imported but some was cultivated in the Godalming area in the 1580s (SHC:LM1966/2–4).

The woollen industry was the next after corn milling to use water power. Mechanized fulling mills, for the controlled shrinking and thickening of the

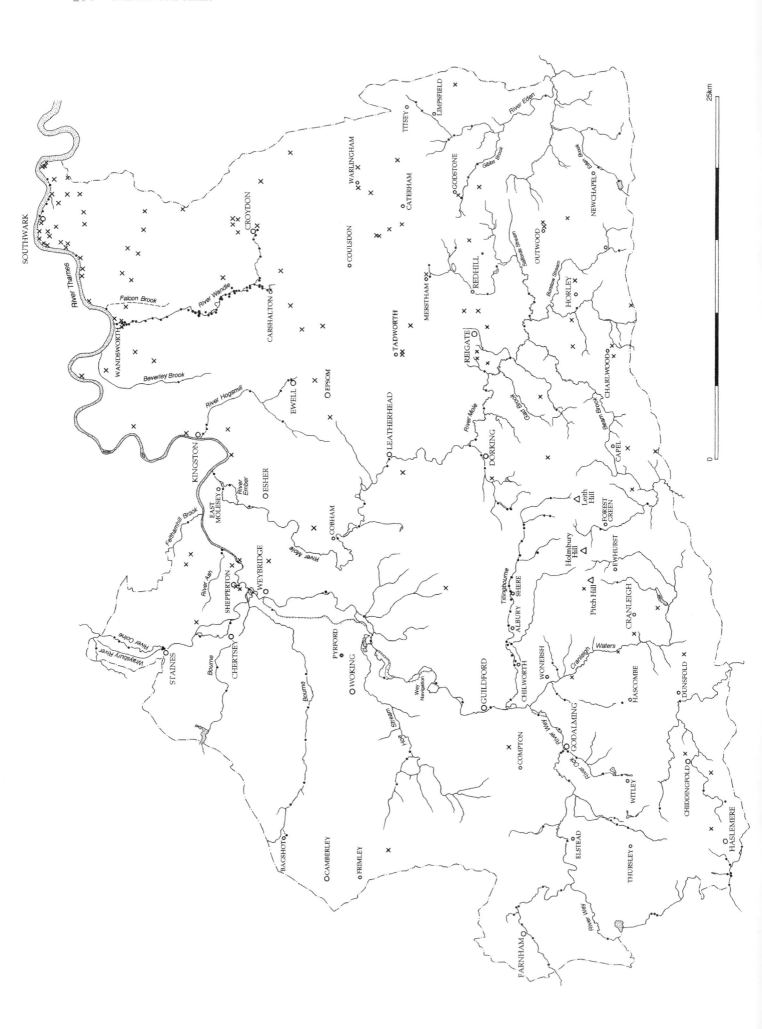

SOUTHWARK

River Thames

Falcon Brook

River Wandle

WANDSWORTH

Beverley Brook

River Hogsmill

EWELL

EPSOM

KINGSTON

River Ember

EAST MOLESEY

ESHER

Felthammill Brook

River Ash

River Colne

Wraysbury River

STAINES

SHEPPERTON

WEYBRIDGE

River Mole

COBHAM

CHERTSEY

Bourne

Bourne

Bourne

PYRFORD

WOKING

BAGSHOT

CAMBERLEY

FRIMLEY

CARSHALTON

CROYDON

COULSDON

WARLINGHAM

CATERHAM

TADWORTH

LEATHERHEAD

Hoe Stream

GUILDFORD

COMPTON

FARNHAM

TITSEY

LIMPSFIELD

GODSTONE

Gibbs Brook

River Eden

MERSTHAM

REDHILL

Salfords Stream

OUTWOOD

Burstow Stream

HORLEY

Eden Brook

NEWCHAPEL

CHARLWOOD

Bean Brook

CAPEL

Gad Brook

REIGATE

River Mole

DORKING

Leith Hill

FOREST GREEN

Holmbury Hill

EWHURST

Tillingbourne

SHERE

ALBURY

Pitch Hill

CRANLEIGH

Cranleigh Waters

CHILWORTH

WONERSH

River Wey

GODALMING

HASCOMBE

DUNSFOLD

WITLEY

CHIDDINGFOLD

HASLEMERE

ELSTEAD

THURSLEY

River Wey

River Wey

Wey Navigation

25km

0

woven cloth, were widely adopted in England in the 13th century as shown by Carus-Wilson (1941), whose conclusions regarding their economic significance is however disputed (Holt 1988, 145–58). Many have been noted especially at mill sites in south-west Surrey and also in the east of the county and on the Wandle but a systematic search is needed to establish a pattern of distribution.

The use of fuller's earth in south-west Surrey and its sources are matters for investigation. Deposits in east Surrey around Nutfield (Robertson 1986, 178–90) are often mentioned in the context of the county's woollen industry, for example by Giuseppi (*VCH*, **2**, 342) although he states elsewhere (*ibid*, 280) that there is no definite evidence that they were worked at an early date. Transport costs would have been high and alternative detergents may have been used, for example lye from plant ashes and stale urine (Patterson 1956, 215). Chemical analysis of fuller's earth found in late 12th to early 13th century hearths at Swan Lane, City of London, suggested that it could have come from east Surrey (Robertson 1986, 97; Egan 1991, 12–14, 18n7). There were deposits in Hampshire (Robertson 1986, 216–18) close to the Surrey textile area, and in Kent (*ibid*, 171–7) where coastal transport was convenient. Fuller's earth occurs in a Winchester fuller's inventory of 1433 (*ibid*, 101n) and reached Alton in Hampshire from Southampton (Platt & Coleman-Smith 1975, **2**, 18).

The decline of the woollen industry was recognized as early as 1621, in Guildford Corporation's proposals for making the river Wey navigable (Nash 1969, 34). There was a general shift in demand from heavy woollen textiles to the lighter mixed fabrics known as the 'new draperies' which had been taken up by merchants in the 16th century (Coleman 1969; Kerridge 1972, 27–30). The local circumstances by which the decline was accelerated in the 1630s, through the fortunes of an individual merchant, Samuel Vassall, are related by Crowe (1973).

WEALDEN GLASS

A forest glass industry was established in several parishes around Chiddingfold (Wa) and the Surrey-Sussex border in the first half of the 13th century and 45 of some 80 known glasshouses in Britain in the period 1250–1600 were in this region. Improved technology was brought by Jean Carré of Antwerp and a community of French workmen in the 1560s.

Further technological advance came with the successful use of coal as fuel in glass furnaces in Southwark in 1611 and Lambeth in 1613. A monopoly of coal-fired glass acquired in 1615 by Sir Robert Mansell was enforced and the forest industry ended by 1620 (Crossley 1994, 68).

The first detailed account of the Wealden industry and its surviving traces was published by Kenyon (1967). The early 14th century site at Blunden's Wood, Hambledon, and the mid-16th century furnaces at Knightons, Alfold, both pre-dating the immigrant phase, were excavated by Wood (1965; 1982). A reassessment of the archaeological evidence of the industry was begun by Crossley in 1991 and continued under one of the English Heritage Monuments Protection Programmes referred to by Marilyn Palmer in this volume. All previously recorded sites were visited and their condition assessed and a research agenda was proposed. This emphasized (a) laboratory examination of material from past work, including establishing the source of clays for crucibles, (b) more field walking to locate further sites and relocate those not recently confirmed, and (c) study of the relationship between furnace sites and coppice woodland (Crossley 1994).

POTTERY

The medieval pottery industry and its continuation into the post-medieval period, is a large subject which can be touched upon only briefly here.

The whiteware industry of north and west Surrey and the Surrey-Hampshire border was a major supplier to the London market from the mid-13th to the 16th century (Pearce & Vince 1988, 6). The first comprehensive study of this industry was made by Holling (1971; 1977). Pearce & Vince (1988) have since published a dated type-series of medieval Surrey whiteware found in the City of London which comes from the industries at Kingston upon Thames (see Andrews in this volume), Cheam (LB Sutton) and in the Surrey-Hampshire border region. Kiln sites of this period have been reported at Kingston (Hinton 1980; Nelson 1981; Miller & Stephenson 1999) and at Cheam (Marshall 1924; 1941; Orton 1979; 1982). Pearce (1992) has continued the study of the whiteware industry into the 16th and 17th centuries when production sites are known at Farnborough Hill and Cove in east Hampshire (Haslam 1975), Hawley, Ash (Holling 1969), and possibly Pirbright.

Opposite: Fig 16.1 Distribution of known water-powered sites and windmills in Surrey. Windmills are more numerous in the eastern part of the county, reflecting the landscape, and near London reflecting the demand for power. Particular concentrations of watermills are seen on the Wandle and Tillingbourne and a number of tide mills operated along the Thames. Note that the definition of a water-mill site is imprecise since many mills were composite and in multiple use. The map is a compilation for all periods from that of the Domesday survey onwards, and is based on information from many sources, in particular Blythman 1996; Brandon 1984; Brayley 1848, 35; Cleere & Crossley 1995; Crocker, A 1989–90, 1992, 1994; Crocker, G & A 1990; Farries & Mason 1966; Hillier 1951; Reid 1987, 1989; Stidder 1990; Wilks MS.

The industry of the Limpsfield area, which produced coarseware from the mid-13th to the mid-14th century, is discussed by Prendergast (1973; 1974). The excavation of kiln sites at Limpsfield Chart is reported by Ketteringham (1989) and at Clacket Lane, near Titsey, by Hayman (1997). A production site of coarseware at Earlswood, near Redhill, included a 14th century kiln (Turner 1974) and the occurrence of white slip on jugs from this site raised the issue of the transport of materials (*ibid*, 50). From the point of view of industrial history, more work is needed on such matters as sources of materials, transport, production sites and methods, and on the producers themselves. In his important study of the pottery from Clacket Lane, Jones (1997, 76) notes the advantages of opening up large areas around kilns for showing relationships between kiln, workshop and waster heap. He also calls for more work on production sites on both sides of the Surrey-Kent border and for local historians to continue their search for references to the industry in documentary sources.

Medieval kilns for roof tiles have been excavated at Borelli Yard in Farnham (Riall 2003), Guildford Castle (Poulton forthcoming), and in Farnham Park (Riall 1997) and a kiln for the production of the important pictorial Chertsey Abbey floor tiles has been discovered in excavations at the Abbey (Poulton 1988, 39–40, 81).

REIGATE STONE
Building stone was extracted from underground workings in the Upper Greensand of east Surrey, between Brockham (MV) and Godstone (Ta), from pre-Conquest times to the 19th century (Sowan 1975). An example from the extensive Chaldon-Merstham complex is illustrated in figure 16.2. The Domesday survey records two stone quarries at Limpsfield (Ta) (*VCH*, **1**, 311). Reigate stone was used in some of the earliest Saxon churches and prestige buildings in the London area but its susceptibility to erosion was recognized in the mid-15th century (Tatton-Brown 2001, 198) and from then to the 17th century it was used mainly for internal work. It continued to be used locally as building stone into the 19th century. It had later uses also as 'firestone' for refractory purposes and 'hearthstone' for whitening stone floors and doorsteps (see section on stone quarrying below).

A research project was set up in 1998 by the Historic Royal Palaces Agency to study the stone and the quarries in order to establish procedures for the conservation of buildings and locate suitable stone for repairs. Sowan observes that Reigate stone is a unique type which is not sandstone, limestone or calcareous sandstone so that established methods are not always appropriate for its conservation; also the quarrymen's skill in distinguishing good from inferior stone has been lost (Sowan 2000a).

Documentary evidence indicates that stone was transported to London and stored in Battersea on a site called 'Bridges' on which the archbishop of York's mansion was built in the late 15th century (Tatton-Brown, 2000; 2001, 193–5). Evaluation excavations were carried out in 1996 and 1998 to establish the extent of York House and ancillary buildings prior to development (Hawkins 2000a). No traces of Reigate stone were found but the inferred location of 'Bridges' is under the late 19th/early 20th century Price's candle factory building which was not affected by the development (Hawkins 2000b).

Post-medieval and later developments

Post-medieval industry was advanced by the enterprise of 'projectors' and the granting of letters patent and by the acquisition of expertise from the Continent and the formation of chartered companies (Donald 1961; Thirsk 1978). Most of the new industries which were established in Surrey in Tudor and Stuart times continued into the period of accelerated growth and innovation of the industrial revolution and some survived into the 20th century. An overview of manufacturing industry in the mid-19th century, with some quantitative data, is given by Brayley (1848).

MILLS AND MOTIVE POWER
After its application to corn milling and fulling, water power was used in bloomery iron furnaces in England from the 14th century (Crossley 1990, 154) and from the 16th century onwards was applied to a growing number of industrial processes. Some new industries occupied the sites of fulling mills which closed as the woollen industry declined but many new water-powered sites were brought into use. The Tillingbourne and the Wandle had particularly intensive use (fig 16.1). Brandon (1984, 75) comments that of 21 water-powered sites identified on the Tillingbourne nine were in use before 1500 as corn or fulling mills and the rest were established in the Tudor and Stuart period. The Wandle had at least 24 corn mills by 1610, when a proposal to abstract water for London was successfully opposed (Giuseppi 1908), and Wilks has gathered information on 49 mill sites, many in multiple use, which were eventually developed on this river for a wide range of industries (Twilley & Wilks 1974; Wilks MS). Tide mills were used along the Thames and these require further research and analysis (fig 16.1; [Plunkett 1999]).

The establishment of a new mill site might involve construction works to provide a head of water or increase an existing one or to form a reservoir. The topography of water supply to mills, as outlined by Crossley (1990, 140–4), and its links with other

Fig 16.2   Quarry Field building stone quarry, Merstham, showing part of the Chaldon-Merstham complex of drift mines in the Upper Greensand of east Surrey. The tunnels appear to be medieval in origin but were reopened by 1807 and extended below the water table by the civil engineering partnership of Joliffe and Banks. The drainage adit no longer functions, hence the flood water as photographed in January 2001. The floor–ceiling height is generally *c* 1.5m. These early 19th century workings show characteristic pillar-and-stall features, with stalls or tunnels at right angles to the joint system. The pillar wall shows pick marks indicating up-dip working and distinct beds of stone, some more suitable for building than others. Spoil was backfilled underground. The notice was placed by the Wealden Cave and Mine Society to provide information on safety procedures and cave rescue during a detailed survey of the workings, of which some 17km were recorded. Photograph by Paul Sowan

aspects of water management, for example in agriculture and transport, requires more understanding. The projects of Sir Richard Weston on the Wey near Guildford in the 1620s are of national significance, involving early experiments with new crops and land improvements by irrigation which were linked to plans for making the river navigable (Hartlib 1650; McDonald 1908, 68–78; Nash 1969; Mayford History Society 1979); the Wey Navigation, eventually authorized in 1651, was one of the earliest in Britain (Vine 1996). John Evelyn (1675, [7]) alludes to the irrigation of land in the Tillingbourne valley, where his forebears were engaged in industry, and water management there has been discussed by Brandon (1984) and by G & A Crocker (2000, 10–12, 16–17). Other examples include works on the Mole at Cobham (Crocker, A 2000, 25–6, 27), its bifurcation the Ember at Thames Ditton (Greenwood 1980, 9), and on the Wandle (Montague 1992; 1999; Gerhold 2002). The bays and hammer ponds of the Wealden iron industry, in which a steady source of power was needed to keep furnaces in blast for extended periods, are an important category in the remit of the Wealden Iron Research Group (Cleere & Crossley 1995). Some new mill sites were situated on the artificial cuts of waterways, where a head of water would coincide with a lock. Four such sites are recorded on

the Wey and Godalming navigations (Stidder 1990, 88; Crocker 1992, 215–6; 1994, 4–6; Barker 2000).

Many mill sites were occupied by several industries in succession, and sometimes in parallel, adopting new sources of motive power and new technologies, and eventually changing from manufacturing to modern business use. There is scope for detailed documentary research such as that by Greta Turner (2003 and forthcoming) on the parish of Shottermill, Haslemere, and on Catteshall Mill, Godalming (Crocker, A & G 1981). Standing buildings and evidence of power installations were recorded at Catteshall but little evidence of past usage now survives at large manufacturing sites since they have been cleared for redevelopment.

Watermills which remained relatively small have however survived in many cases, occasionally intact but more often adapted for commercial or residential use. Surviving structures mostly date from the 18th century or later. The county-wide surveys of watermills noted above give varying amounts of historical detail and physical description. Detailed recording of structures has been undertaken at Paddington Mill, Abinger (MV), on the Tillingbourne (Crocker 1999), and unpublished surveys of High Mill, Farnham, Shalford (Gu) and Wonersh (Wa) mills are held by SIHG.

The industrial revolution is generally associated with the adoption of steam power and mineral fuel. Water and wind power remained important however. For example, the generator for Godalming's pioneering electricity supply in 1881 was powered by a water-wheel (Gravett 1981/2, 103–5). The problems for small businesses investing in steam power are illustrated by entries for 1851–3 in the diaries of James Simmons, papermaker of Haslemere (Crocker & Kane 1990, 113, 119–22, 126, 130–2). Eminent engineers, notably John Smeaton, increased the power and efficiency of the traditional prime movers in the late 18th century. A catalogue of Smeaton's drawings held by the Royal Society includes designs for water-wheels and other machinery in Surrey mills engaged in corn, bark and oil milling and the manufacture of paper, gunpowder and iron hoops (Dickinson & Gomme 1950, 10–11, 16, 18–19, 27, 30–1, 33).

Windmill design was improved from the 18th century onwards, for example in Smeaton's design (undated) for a 'china mill' at Nine Elms, Vauxhall (Dickinson & Gomme 1950, 5). Rocque's map of Surrey (1765) marks eighteen windmills and Farries & Mason (1966, 15) estimate there were nearer 25 by that date. They list 85 windmills known to have stood in the historic county since 1800, of which eleven plus six mill bases survived in 1964 (*ibid*, 241). Distribution was weighted towards the east of the county including the London area where many windmills were sited along the Thames (*ibid*, 14, 16/17), as shown in figure 16.1. Standing structures of windmills were also recorded by Simmons (1940s) and a survey was carried out in 1970–4 by Smith (1976).

There is doubt about the date of 1665, accepted by Farries & Mason (1966, 165), for Outwood (Ta) postmill, from which it is claimed the miller, Thomas Budgen, watched the Great Fire of London in 1666. Mills specialists consider that there is no firm evidence for this date and that the present structure is more typical of 18th century work. Their view is however based on an instinctive feeling derived from experience rather than on evidence which would justify publication (Stephen Buckland *et al*, pers comm).

Gregory (2002) has shown that, while steam became the dominant power source, the windmill played a significant part in the industrial revolution since it was sometimes the most economic way of obtaining more power, particularly for family-sized businesses. Many corn millers owned both wind and watermills, on the same site in the case of 'Brazil Mill' at Wandsworth. Gregory discusses industrial windmills, as distinct from those used for corn milling or pumping. His list (*ibid* 2002, 28–30) covers eighteen industrial uses and for the whole of England contains entries for 79 mills operating in the 18th century and 88 in the 19th. It includes sawmills at Horsell (Wo) and Lambeth (LB) and six other windmills in metropolitan Surrey for uses including paper making and the crushing of oil seeds, gypsum and bone manure.

Perrett (1979; 1980) discussed the early employment and manufacture of steam engines in London and noted those which survived in 1978. The early reciprocating engines were used for pumping and ten were in use in 1775 by water supply companies in London, including engines at Lambeth and London Bridge. Rotative engines were available from 1782 and were used in the late 18th century for rolling iron at a forge in Rotherhithe and at several locations in Southwark: a brewery, a dye-crushing works and the huge Albion corn mill (at the south end of Blackfriars Bridge) which had two steam engines each driving ten pairs of millstones, and a third planned, when it burned down in 1791.

Before the rotative steam engine became available to drive machinery, reciprocating engines were used to pump water back up for re-use in water-wheels. Such a water-returning engine was proposed by Boulton and Watt, and probably installed, at gunpowder mills at Worcester Park on the Hogsmill in 1778 (Crocker 1996, 17–19).

Data on the size and structure of water-wheels and on the use of steam engines in manufacturing is scattered in such sources as trade directories, sale particulars of properties, newspaper reports and legal documents. For example Esher (El) paper mill, which was built in 1847 but closed after a fire in 1853, had three steam engines (*The Times*, 26 Dec) in addition to water-wheels (**PRO**: J90/1206) and a fatal accident at Merstham (RB) stone quarries in 1811 involved a steam-powered winding engine (Sowan 1985/6, 88). Both the gunpowder and paper mills at Chilworth (Gu) installed steam engines in the 1860s (Crocker, G & A 2000, 86–7, 90, 94). Oil and gas engines were also used and some factories made their own gas, for example Catteshall paper mill, Godalming, in the 1890s (Crocker, A & G 1981, 20). A systematic collection of data has been made in the case of water turbines (Crocker 2001), which provided a more efficient form of water power from the mid-19th century onwards. Two peaks in usage are indicated: one between 1880 and 1910, to obtain more power, and a larger one in the 1920s and 1930s when many turbines were installed for generating electricity at mill sites and for operating pumps at waterworks and hydraulic power sites.

TRANSPORT: ROADS, WATERWAYS AND RAILWAYS

Manning & Bray (1804–14, **3**, xxxii–lx) list Acts of Parliament relating to Surrey and give details of the county's bridges, roads and navigable canals. A summary account of roads, waterways, railways and aviation services has been compiled by SIHG (Crocker 1999a, 73–94) and selected features on transport routes are noted in SIHG District *Guides*.

Little detailed historical research has been carried out on particular road routes, apart from a study of the Bramley and Rudgwick turnpike trust of 1818, which incidentally corrects a popular misunderstanding of the date of the obelisk in Cranleigh (Wa) (Budgen 1991–2). The development of roads in the Weald, including routes radiating out from London and crossing Surrey, is discussed by Fuller (1953). An important subject for a research agenda is a consideration of transport routes for heavy freight, in particular products of the Wealden iron industry and of east Surrey's stone quarries bound for London and the transport of building materials within the county.

Historical accounts of the Wey and Godalming Navigations, authorized respectively in 1651 and 1760, and of the Wey & Arun Junction Canal, authorized in 1813, are provided by Vine (1996). A survey of the Wey and Godalming Navigations has been carried out for the National Trust for management purposes (Currie 1996). Fairclough (1999, 62–9) discusses records of boat building and voyages on the Thames and Wey for the transport of gunpowder by the shipping entrepreneur and philanthropist Thomas Coram in 1723. Vine (1968) gives an historical account of the Basingstoke Canal, authorized in 1778, which enters the Wey Navigation at New Haw. Historical guides to the Grand Surrey and Croydon canals, now in south London, have been published by Living History (1986).

The first railways in Surrey were horse-drawn plateways which pre-date the railway era proper. The Surrey Iron Railway (SIR) from Wandsworth to Croydon, the first public railway, opened in 1803 and in that year the Croydon, Merstham and Godstone Railway (CM&GR) was authorized. It opened from Croydon to Merstham in 1805, effectively as an extension to the SIR, but was never completed to Godstone and was used to transport products of the Merstham stone quarries and limeworks. It was bought out by the London & Brighton Railway in 1838. Archaeological and historical research on the CM&GR has been reported by Osborne (1982), Sowan (1982) and Burgess (1983; 1987) and the route is described by Bayliss (1981).

A history of the Southern Railway (Dendy Marshall 1936) was published by the company. Among the many more recent works on railway history, the Surrey Record Society's edition of the Minutes of the Board of Directors of the Reading, Guildford and Reigate Railway Company (RG&R), broke new ground in the Society's publishing programme (Course 1987). The minutes cover the period 1845–52 when the RG&R existed as an independent company. Jackson (1999) gives an account of the development and modernization of the county's rail network and discusses its influence on settlement patterns and the lives of communities and its relationship with industry. This deals with private railway sidings and private industrial rail systems; freight for public utility undertakings such as gasworks and pumping stations and for major institutions, such as the vast mental hospitals in the Epsom area, and internal rail layouts for various industries. The largest group is extractive industries and there are also examples in a corn mill and in timber, linoleum, chemical and motor vehicle works.

The value of geological and water supply records in understanding 19th century civil engineering methods has been demonstrated in relation to the construction of railway tunnels by Sowan (1979; 1984a; 2000b).

UTILITIES

An historical account of water, sewerage, gas and electricity supplies and communications services is provided by SIHG (Crocker 1999a, 103–24) and the Group's district *Guides* include sites relating to utilities. Of particular significance are those for Elmbridge (Tarplee 1998) and Spelthorne (Mills 1993) which feature the extensive reservoirs constructed for London's water supply. Croydon holds an important place in the history of town water supply and drainage (Lancaster 2000). An English Heritage Monuments Protection Programme on water and sewage industries assessed ten sites in Surrey, all in the north of the county, of which eight were rated of national importance, in particular Surbiton waterworks (Trueman 2000, 43). Rivers, hydrogeology and water undertakings are also discussed by Fish *et al* (1975) in the British Association's volume on Surrey. Godalming had the first public electricity supply in Britain and very early street lighting which was celebrated in its centenary year of 1981 (Gravett 1981/2; Haveron 1981). In the field of communications, the county has surviving structures of the early 19th century Admiralty semaphore system (Wilson 1976, 33–63; Holmes 1983).

Surrey industries: the 17th to 19th centuries
Industries which have received particular attention in recent decades are Wealden iron (see Hodgkinson in this volume), the extractive industries and the manufacture of gunpowder, paper and certain textiles.

EXTRACTIVE INDUSTRIES
Stone quarrying, chalk extraction and lime burning, clay industries and the extraction of fuller's earth, sand and gravel have a long history in the county but developed on an industrial scale in the 19th century (Crocker 1999a, 4–22). Sowan (2000c) draws attention to valuable research resources, in particular non-statutory lists compiled in 1858.

Stone quarrying

It has been noted that the underground building-stone quarries in the Upper Greensand of east Surrey (fig 16.2) were reworked in the 19th century for the softer hearthstone, for whitening stone floors, doorsteps and hearths. This fashion continued into the 20th century and the last hearthstone mine, at Colley Hill, Reigate, which had been developed solely for the purpose, closed in the 1960s.

An account of the firestone and hearthstone mines by Sowan (1975) deals with the mines, geological and economic factors, working methods and uses of the stone and contains a summary gazetteer of sites. A more recent account (Sowan 1991) follows extensive surveying and photographic recording of the Chaldon-Merstham complex of underground workings. Funding is being sought to extend the Reigate Stone Project to include medieval and post-medieval underground quarrying and the distribution, use, performance and conservation of Reigate stone, to carry out conventional excavations at selected quarry entrances, extend and crystallize the research carried out from 1967 onwards and publish the completed surveys of underground workings (Paul Sowan, pers comm).

The firestone quarries at Merstham were, together with the limeworks, served by the CM&GR. Osborne (1982) describes the structure of the CM&GR plateway and of plateways in the quarries themselves, mainly at Merstham and Godstone, and provides a schedule and analysis of known extant plates.

In west Surrey a stone strongly resembling Reigate stone was used in and around Farnham but little is known about the quarrying of this material (Paul Sowan, pers comm). Surrey's second most important building stone quarries are those of the distinctive Bargate stone in the Godalming area. There is scope for research further to that by Withers (1969) and Janaway (1993) and the listing of numerous workings in a survey of heritage features in Waverley (Waverley Borough Council 1986). The largest site, at Ockford Hill, was served by a private siding 1km south of Godalming station but this closed in 1935 and quarrying ceased shortly afterwards (Jackson 1999, 204).

Chalk and lime

Underground chalk quarries at Guildford were described by Lee & Russell (1924) and Williamson (1930). The quarrying of chalk for building stone at Guildford and at Westhumble near Dorking, where the site warrants archaeological study, is discussed by Sowan (1976; 1984b).

Limeburning has long been practised for soil improvment and building mortar and demand for both increased rapidly from the 18th century onwards. Deneholes and chalk wells, now generally interpreted as medieval and post-medieval agricul-

tural chalk mines (Le Gear 1978), are found in northeast Surrey. Chalkpits occur throughout the length of the North Downs but extraction and limeburning developed on an industrial scale in east Surrey with the coming of rail transport. The promoters of the CM&GR, Joliffe & Banks, established limeworks at Merstham in 1805 (Gravett & Wood 1967; Sowan 1982). These closed in 1956 and the site was lost to landfill waste disposal from 1961 and the building of the M23 motorway in 1983. An early 19th century limeworks at Dorking, which had a high reputation for greystone building lime which hardened under water, was never rail-linked and never a limited company. It continued into the 20th century but was lost to landfill in the 1950s and 1960s.

Other major sites which developed around the 1860s have also been affected by landfill and site clearance involving the loss of hydrator plant, aerial ropeways and other features. However they retain 19th century kiln structures which are of major technological significance, in particular patent 'Brockham' kilns and, in the case of Betchworth (MV), Dietzsch and Smidth kilns which show technology transfer, having been developed on the Continent for cement, and a 20th century separate-feed kiln (Sowan 2000d, 5). Recording was carried out by Subterranea Britannica and others in the 1990s at Oxted (Ta), Brockham and Betchworth. An English Heritage Monuments Protection Programme (Richardson & Trueman 1997) assessed these limeworks as sites of national importance. The kilns at Brockham are scheduled monuments and are being conserved in association with wildlife interests. Progress has been reported by Sowan (2000d; 2000e).

Chalkpit railway systems are discussed by Jackson (1999, 196–200) and Townsend (1980). The Narrow Gauge Railway Society established a museum on the Brockham site in 1962 (Down & Smith 1977; Smith 1979), from which material was transferred to the Chalk Pits Museum, Amberley, Sussex, founded in 1979. Records of the Merstham Limeworks and of the Dorking Greystone Lime Company of Betchworth are held by the Surrey History Centre (Gravett & Wood 1967, 142–7; Sowan 2002).

Fuller's earth

The history of fuller's earth extraction in Surrey is discussed by J Greenwood (1982) and Robertson's comprehensive and literary account of the substance from the ancient world onwards includes a section on Surrey (Robertson 1986, 178–90).

It has been noted in connection with the textile industry that there is a lack of definite evidence for the working of the east Surrey deposits at an early date, before Aubrey (1718–19, **4**, 214, 237) reported the prices fetched by Nutfield fuller's earth in the late 17th century.

Large-scale extraction began with William Grece near the end of the 18th century and developed rapidly with the coming of the railway. The CM&GR may have been a factor but a major expansion was begun by James Cawley at Nutfield in the 1840s. In 1890 the Surrey and Somerset businesses amalgamated into the Fuller's Earth Union, which merged with Laport Industries in 1954.

Tadd (1994, 24–5, 28; in Crocker 1999a, 15–18) discusses modern uses of fuller's earth and the related material bentonite, describes working methods, notes physical features of the industry remaining in 1994 and reports the announced closure of the last Surrey pit in 1996. Since then all workings have been landfilled or reclaimed and process buildings demolished.

Clay, sand and gravel
Brickworks and sand and gravel extraction are discussed in the context of industrial railways by Jackson (1999, 200–4, 208–9). Brickmaking has been widespread in the past (Crocker 1999a, 20–2) and most of the SIHG district *Guides* record selected sites, in particular those for Mole Valley (Tarplee 1995, 3–11) and Tandridge (Tadd 1994, 35–7). Very large modern brickworks and a hand-made tileworks are operating in the south of the county, on Weald Clay, in the 21st century. The subject warrants a systematic study, perhaps following the example of Beswick's history and gazetteer of the industry in Sussex (1993; 2001). Gower (1998) discusses the long history of brickmaking at Streatham (LB Lambeth) where the industry reached its peak in the 16th century.

Gravel extraction in north-west Surrey was discussed as a contemporary issue in the British Association's conference volume in 1975, when there were nearly 40 active pits in the Thames basin gravel field, about half of them in Surrey (Hollinghurst *et al* 1975, 195–8). Farther south, around Farnham, gravel pits were largely worked out in the 19th and early 20th centuries. Sand has been extracted from the Lower Greensand along the length of the county and latterly in areas east of Farnham and west of Reigate (Crocker 1999a, 6, 14–15). Silver sand for glass making was obtained from underground workings which have been found to be very extensive beneath Reigate where at least six distinct mine systems are known, some of which warrant archaeological study (Sowan 1980; Brown *et al* 1985–6; Arup 1991.)

Pottery
The manufacture of tin-glazed earthenware (known as delftware) and stoneware, based on imported prototypes, became established in Southwark and Lambeth in the post-medieval period (Edwards 1974) and there is also evidence of red ware production in Lambeth and Rotherhithe (*ibid*, 4; TBAOG 1964, 9). Delftware production declined in the late 18th century with the development of hard-fired cream and white wares and the domestic market came to be dominated by the pottery industry of the Midlands. Stoneware manufacture continued to expand in the London area however, particularly in the 19th century with the development of public sanitation and civil engineering works. Contemporary descriptions of the manufacture of tin-glazed earthenware at Lambeth and stoneware pottery at Fulham in the late 17th century are reported by Weatherill & Edwards (1971) and the Doulton stoneware works at Lambeth at the beginning of the 20th century are described in some detail by Giuseppi in his historical and contemporary account of Surrey potteries (*VCH*, **2**, 281–95).

Several kiln sites in south London have been excavated since the late 1960s (eg Bloice 1971; Dawson 1976; Edwards, R 1981–2; Killock *et al* 2003). The development of kiln types has been discussed, in particular the use in London in the 17th and 18th centuries of rectangular, single-flue, sub-surface kilns of Continental type and the later use of multi-flue round surface kilns of native tradition (Dawson 1981) and it is noted that there are still technical issues to be resolved (Graham Dawson, pers comm).

Farther from the metropolitan area Giuseppi comments, in particular, on potteries at Ewell, Cheam and Epsom and notably at Farnham where, at Wrecclesham, a 19th–20th century country pottery drew upon the local post-medieval tradition under the influence of the Arts and Crafts movement. With its rare surviving example of a circular twin-flued updraught kiln, this pottery was recorded in the 1990s (Menuge 1999) and is being restored and maintained as workshop units by the Farnham (Building Preservation) Trust. Giuseppi notes that country potteries producing the commoner sorts of earthenware were numerous and cites examples at Charlwood, Cranleigh, Crowhurst, Dorking, Godstone, Kingston, Leatherhead and Redhill which were active at the beginning of the 20th century (*VCH*, **2**, 295). A gazetteer of sites of country potteries in Surrey was compiled by Felix Holling (Brears 1971, 212–16). Ashtead Potters Ltd was formed in 1922 to train ex-servicemen. Its art deco products are collected and workers' housing survives (Hallam 1990; Tarplee 1995, 46–7).

GUNPOWDER
Giuseppi's 1905 account of the gunpowder industry (*VCH*, **2**, 306–29) dealt in detail with the 16th and 17th centuries, when Surrey powdermakers played a major role nationally, and more briefly with the period after 1700. Research has made considerable progress since the 1980s.

Sixteen manufacturing sites have been identified in the county (Crocker, G & A 1990). Water power was first used in the industry by the 1540s at tide mills on the Thames at Rotherhithe. The Evelyn family, which held patents from 1588/9 and then the crown monopoly until 1636, had mills on the Hogsmill at Tolworth (EE/LB Kingston), the Tillingbourne at Wotton and Abinger (MV) and on a tributary of the Eden at Godstone (Ta) (*VCH*, **2**, 312–18). The Evelyns' operations are known largely from the perspective of their government contracts and research by Brandon (1984) on their industrial enterprises and estate management around Wotton needs extending to other sites.

The early mills noted above closed in the first half of the 17th century but those on the Tillingbourne at Chilworth (Gu), which were established in 1626 by the East India Company, were taken over and extended by Charles I in the 1630s and expanded further during the rest of the 17th century (Edwards 1995; Fairclough 1996; 2000a; 2000b; Fairclough & Crocker in prep). They continued on a smaller scale through the 18th and early to mid-19th centuries; the label illustrated in figure 16.3 dates from this period. The works expanded further in the late 19th century, finally closing after the First World War. Most of the Chilworth site is a scheduled monument. It has been assessed by an English Heritage Monuments Protection Programme as of national importance on account of its early history, the period after 1885 when it was at the forefront of new technology, and its rare surviving structures of an early cordite factory (Cocroft 2000, 146–7). A detailed survey has been carried out by English Heritage (Cocroft 2003). A change in technology from stamp mills to edge runners for incorporating gunpowder occurred in the late 17th and 18th centuries (Crocker, G & Fairclough 1998). Areas at the eastern and western ends of the Chilworth site, outside the English Heritage survey, are among very few sites in England where traces of early stamp mills may lie buried, and therefore warrant archaeological investigation (Crocker, G & A 2000, 12, 16–18).

Apart from Chilworth, later gunpowder sites were located further north on the Wandle, lower Mole and Hogsmill. New mills were established during the Dutch Wars (1652–74) at Carshalton (LB Sutton), Wandsworth and East Molesey (El). These however closed in the 18th century. The Surrey Record Society has published transcripts of documents relating to the gunpowder industry. It contains inventories of mills in 1661, 1678 and 1753, together with a Chilworth letter book of 1790–1 (Crocker *et al* 2000). Fairclough's work on Wandsworth (*ibid*, 46–51) has been carried forward by Gerhold (2002). Knowledge of Chilworth in the 18th century has been extended, particularly in relation to Huguenot powdermakers, the private trade in gunpowder and the Spencer family archives (Fairclough 1999a; Crocker *et al* 2000, 73–88, 106–72). An account of the gunpowder and paper mills at Chilworth and Albury is given by G and A Crocker (2000).

Traces of a late 18th century gunpowder mill at Abinger Hammer on the Tillingbourne, whose proprietors failed to obtain a licence and left to establish mills at Gorebridge, Midlothian, have been recorded by English & Field (1991). Other mills established on the Hogsmill in the 18th century, at Worcester Park (1720–1854) and Ewell (1750s–1875), await more detailed historical study.

PAPER MAKING

The earliest Surrey paper mill for which there is definite evidence is Stoke Mill, Guildford, recorded by 1635. Over 30 mills were subsequently established on Surrey rivers, two on the Mole, one on the Hogsmill, ten on the Wandle and the majority on the river Wey, its tributaries, and both its headwaters extending into Hampshire (Crocker, A 1989/90; 1992; 1994). There were also two on the Colne at Stanwell, formerly in Middlesex (Blythman 1996, 43–4). The distribution pattern changed at the end of the 18th century with the introduction of chemical bleach, the papermaking machine and the steam engine. These removed dependence on clean water and water power and several steam-powered mills were established in Bermondsey and Southwark. The adoption of new raw materials, in particular imported wood pulp in the late 19th century, favoured large sites near the coast. The last Surrey paper mill, at Catteshall, Godalming, closed in 1928.

The subject has been intensively researched but some facets remain to be pursued, for example the history of the Merton Board Mills which operated

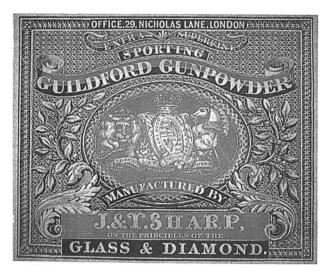

Fig 16.3 Gunpowder label of J & T Sharp, Chilworth, 1820s. The Sharp family operated at Chilworth from 1819 to 1881. Bodleian Library, University of Oxford: John Johnson Collection, Labels 17

within living memory. Detailed studies have been undertaken of Catteshall Mill, Godalming (Crocker, A & G 1981); the diaries (1831–68) of James Simmons, papermaker of Haslemere (Crocker & Kane 1990), and paper mills in the Tillingbourne valley (Crocker, G & A 2000). Other work by A Crocker, some jointly with other authors, deals with Surrey watermarks (1995), paper excise stamps (1996), and innovations in technology and the use of raw materials at Wandsworth and Neckinger Mill, Bermondsey. The developments at Wandsworth centred on the use of esparto grass and its importation from south-east Spain by William McMurray (1986; with Castillo Fernández 2003). Those at Neckinger Mill were chemical bleaching, developed initially for textiles (2002) and the early, and economically premature, use by Matthias Koops of straw, wood pulp and recycled materials (1998). The association between the papermaker at Neckinger Mill, Elias Carpenter, and the prophetess Joanna Southcott is examined by Crocker & Humphrey (2002).

TEXTILES

Although the woollen industry declined in the 17th century, it survived on a very small scale in Godalming into the early 19th century (*VCH*, **2**, 348; Crocker 1991/2, 51). Other minor enterprises have been noted in Lambeth, Battersea and Worplesdon (Gu) (*VCH*, **2**, 353) and in poor-houses in east Surrey (Stidder 1996, 13; Crocker 1999a, 53). Worsted manufacture, using combed long-stapled wool as distinct from carded wool, is recorded in connection with the framework knitting industry (see below) and the manufacture of braid and trimmings for military uniforms by Appletons at Elstead and Haslemere (Wa) (Crocker 1999a, 51–2; Turner forthcoming). Other textiles include bolting cloth for flour dressing at Wandsworth (Davis 1898, 4–5). The principal 'miscellaneous textile and allied industries' discussed by Giuseppi (*VCH*, **2**, 349–59) are silk weaving, linen weaving and, more importantly, framework knitting. The latter has been researched by G Crocker (1989; 1991; 1991/2) but other minor textile industries await further investigation. Giuseppi notes small silk and linen industries carried on by foreign workers in 16th and 17th century Southwark and Bermondsey and a small native linen industry in south-west Surrey in the 17th and 18th centuries.

Silk manufacture in the area of modern Surrey in the early 19th century was associated at Thursley (Wa) and Haslemere with the industry in east London (Crocker 1999a, 52), and with that in the Wandle valley in the case of Coxes Lock Mill, Addlestone (Ru) (Barker 2000, 33; Montague 1992, 63). Wilks (MS) notes other examples of silk mills on the Wandle, in addition to those engaged in textile printing (see below).

The hosiery and knitwear industry

The framework knitting industry in the Godalming area began as one of several country outliers of the manufacture of luxury silk and worsted stockings in London in the late 17th century and was unrelated to the earlier woollen industry. Nationally, framework knitting expanded to supply a mass market in wool and cotton goods and became concentrated in the East Midlands in the 18th century. It continued however in the Godalming area, beset by the general problem of the pauperization of its workforce, but was revived in the late 18th century by specialization in underclothing. This phase lasted until about 1890. A factory system was adopted relatively early in Godalming, *c* 1850, and a major East Midlands firm had its first factory in the town *c* 1860. Census returns show migration of workers from other hosiery-manufacturing areas. A pioneering manufacture of outerwear, of which an example is shown in figure 16.4, began in the 1880s and this phase continued up to the closure of Alan Paine's Godalming factory *c* 1990 and shortly afterwards of small firms making sports sweaters with hand-operated machines. Census data of 1891 and 1901 may give better

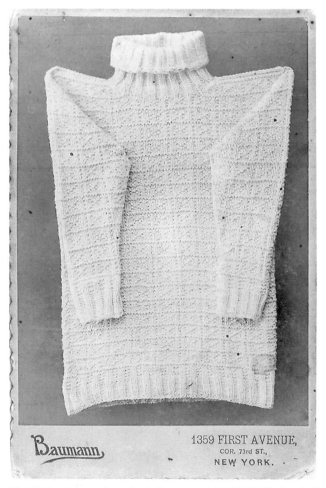

Fig 16.4 Jacquard purl-stitch sweater by W T Pitchers of Godalming, 1893. The method of manufacture was developed by the Stoll knitting machine company in association with Mrs Lucy Pitchers, who had also devised a method of producing cable stitch sports sweaters on the flat knitting machines of the period. SIHG Collection, courtesy of Michael Pitchers

understanding of the early outerwear industry. Surviving buildings were recorded in the late 1980s (Crocker 1991) and two active factories were recorded on video before their closure in the 1990s (I A Recordings 1990).

Shere fustian

Fustian weavers are recorded at Shere (Gu) in the Tillingbourne valley up to the third quarter of the 18th century (Shere 2001, 25, 27, 41–2). The nature of the product needs clarification. Giuseppi included it in his chapter on woollen cloth (*VCH*, **2**, 345) and Baines (1835, 94–5) notes the use of the term for wool textiles although it was properly a mixed fabric containing cotton, generally with a linen warp and cotton weft (*ibid*, 43; Wadsworth & Mann 1931, 11–23; Kerridge 1985, 124–5). The Norwich fustian industry was using cotton yarn imported from Aleppo by the Turkey Company by the 1580s (Peachey 2001, 51–3). Thirsk (1978, 42) notes a flourishing manufacture of fustians using imported cotton in the 16th and 17th centuries and among many locations of manufacture Kerridge (1985, 124–5) cites Uckfield in Sussex by 1623. The mention of a 'Kallender' for pressing or dressing fustian in the wills of John Stonhill, father and son of Shere, in 1646 and 1647 respectively, may shed light on the matter by providing a basis for comparison with the equipment of known fustian weavers elsewhere (PRO: PROB 11/198 sig 149; PROB 11/200 sig 99).

Dyeing, bleaching and calico printing

Dyeing by clothiers and some specialist dyers is recorded in the woollen industry of south-west Surrey in the 16th and early 17th centuries (*VCH*, **2**, 346–7, 363–4). Giuseppi comments that a second early centre of the industry, in Southwark, is 'a more interesting one, in that it better exemplifies the progress of the art'. It extended to other places along the south bank of the Thames and to the Wandle valley (*ibid*, 363, 364–8) where it became associated with the bleaching and textile printing industries (Montague 1992; Wilks MS). On the Wandle, mills for grinding dyewoods and madder root (known as drugs) are recorded at Wandsworth by 1569 (Gerhold & Ensing 1999, 17), at Carshalton by 1580 and in the 17th and 18th centuries at several sites in Mitcham and Merton, one of which operated as Mitcham colour mill from 1685 to 1885 (Montague 1992, 10–16), while Roberts Mill at Mill Green was still grinding 'drugs' in 1914 (Wilks MS). The bleaching industry developed in the Wandle valley from the 1590s onwards. There were extensive bleaching grounds, where calico was spread out and watered from a network of water channels – a process known as crofting. The practice declined after chemical bleaching was developed in the late 18th century. The

materials processed included fustians from Lancashire in the 18th century and Russian and Irish fabrics in the early 19th century (*VCH*, **2**, 368–77; Montague 1992, 5–8, 17–22, 74–6). Calico and silk printing were developed, partly by Huguenot families, particularly in the 18th century but declined rapidly from the 1840s in the face of competition from the industrial north of England. By the end of the century only two printing works remained, both producing luxury textiles: Liberty's mill (Luff 2002) and William Morris's Merton Abbey printworks.

OTHER INDUSTRIES

Other industries have been the subject of individual research projects but more work is needed to extend and co-ordinate existing knowledge.

Among the metal industries, an illegal and consequently short-lived iron wire mill operated at Chilworth (Gu) in 1603–6 (Crocker, G 1999b, 5, 8). Non-ferrous metalworking is recorded elsewhere in the Tillingbourne valley in the 1620s (*VCH*, **2**, 411; Brandon 1984; Crocker 1999b, 11–13) and on the lower Mole and Ember from the 1630s (Greenwood 1980). Works at Esher (El) became associated with those in Bristol and the Forest of Dean, where the brass industry developed rapidly with new technology and the lifting of monopoly restrictions in the late 17th century (Day 1973, 26–7). Byfleet mill was rolling copper sheeting during the American War of Independence (David Barker, pers comm) and the ironmaster Alexander Raby was engaged also in copper working and the manufacture of tinplate at Downside Mill, Cobham (El), which he held from 1790 to 1809 (Crocker, A 2000, 23–4; Taylor 2000, 19). Copper mills were established on the Wandle from the end of the 17th century onwards (Montague, 1995; 1997; 1999). Most were converted to other uses by the 1770s but Merton copper mill continued to about 1870 and Garratt copper mill in Wimbledon until 1887 (Wilks MS). Lead was worked at the lower mill at East Molesey in the late 17th century (Fairclough 1999b).

The important leather industry of Bermondsey and Southwark is described in detail by Giuseppi (*VCH*, **2**, 329–40). An account of Bevington's works at Bermondsey (1795–1950) has been published by the firm (Bevington 1993). Tanning was formerly widespread and Giuseppi notes chance references from the 15th century onwards. He discusses a concentration in south-west Surrey around Godalming and Bramley (Wa), Shalford (Gu) and Gomshall (Gu) (*VCH*, **2**, 340–1). Tanneries and leather mills have also been noted briefly at Haslemere and Woking (Stidder 1990, 81, 91, 124), Guildford (Hollinghurst *et al* 1975, 185) and Reigate and Redhill (Hooper 1945, 99–100). Most closed by the mid-20th century but the tannery at Gomshall, an early centre of the industry, was modernized after the Second World War and continued until 1988 (Noyes 1997). Leather was manufactured on the Wandle at Carshalton from the 1680s to the early 20th century and at Merton, where Connolly's leather factory operated from 1922 to *c* 1990 (Montague 1996, 152; Wilks MS).

Mills for crushing oil seed proliferated on the Wandle in the period 1740–90, particularly in association with Shepley's leather mills at Carshalton and Wandsworth (Wilks MS). Brace (1960, 26, 136, 144–51, 157) lists oil mills at Kingston upon Thames and Weybridge (El) and numerous examples in London including many in Southwark and Rotherhithe. An unusual horizontal windmill at Battersea was originally built for oil in 1788 (Farries & Mason 1966, 50–2; Cooke 2001, 126). Stidder (1990, 120, 125) notes an oil mill at Kingston *c* 1781 to 1878, which then became a soap and candle factory, and one on the Wey Navigation at Weybridge from *c* 1830 to 1963.

Stidder (1990, 124) reports an isolated reference to snuff manufacture at Woking mill in 1749. Other known snuff mills were on the Wandle and most date from the 1770s. Wilks (MS) notes nine mill sites used for snuff of which seven were operating in the first half of the 19th century. The industry continued into the 20th century at Carshalton, Ravensbury and at Morden Hall which closed in 1922. Nationally the industry, which peaked in the reign of George IV (1820–30), has since been reduced to a few mills mainly in the north of England (Bourne 1990, 4–7, 12–14).

Mills on the Wandle at Wallington, Carshalton and Mitcham were used from about the 1830s onwards for the manufacture of hair and fibre products, such as rope, yarn and wadding, and flock made from recycled textiles (Wilks MS). Flock mills also occupied sites at Eashing and Unstead on the Wey and Postford on the Tillingbourne after other industries closed down in the late 19th century (Stidder 1990, 88; Crocker 1992, 215, 224). The manufacture of fibre products became linked with chemical industries to make materials such as floorcloths and linoleum, which was developed in the 1860s and manufactured at Esher, Staines, Addlestone and Mitcham (Greenwood 1980, 7; Crocker 1999a, 69–71). At Mitcham it was associated with a local paint and varnish industry which started in the 1840s and numbered fifteen firms in 1965, but declined in the 1980s (Montague 1993).

There were several fireworks manufacturers in south London in the 19th century including Brock's who moved out to Sutton (Brock 1922) and Pain's, who moved to Mitcham in 1872 and then out of the county to Salisbury in 1966 (Montague 1989/90). A naphtha and acetic acid works in rural Surrey near Bramley (Wa), shown on the 1871 25-inch OS map,

used by-products of charcoal burning. The distilling of essential oils (fig 16.5) was related to the growing of peppermint, lavender and other herbs, particularly around Mitcham, where Potter & Moore operated from 1759 to the mid-20th century. The industry spread outwards from south London to Banstead, West Byfleet, Ewell, Leatherhead and Dorking (Crocker, G 1999b, 64–7). Other process industries include the manufacture of soap and candles (*VCH*, **2**, 402–10; Crocker 1999a, 67–8).

Besides the many forges, foundries, engineering and millwrighting firms which served primarily local needs, a major statue foundry at Thames Ditton (El) operated from 1874 to 1939 (fig 16.6). Its monumental work was sent all over the British Empire (Stevens 1994).

Many corn mills were rebuilt and extended in the 18th and 19th centuries to satisfy the growing market and to accommodate the additional machinery which was being installed for refining the product (Watts 1983, 5–10, 24–8). Some industrial sites reverted to corn milling when other manufacturing enterprises closed. A major change began in the late 1870s with the adoption of roller milling, as distinct

Fig 16.5   Peppermint distillery, Westcott, near Dorking, *c* 1900. Lavender and peppermint were grown on farms around Westcott from *c* 1893 and initially sent to Mitcham, the main centre of the industry, for distilling. The Westcott distillery operated from 1898 to 1907 when a new owner moved the operation to Croydon. Cultivation ceased locally *c* 1914. Kathleen Lane Collection

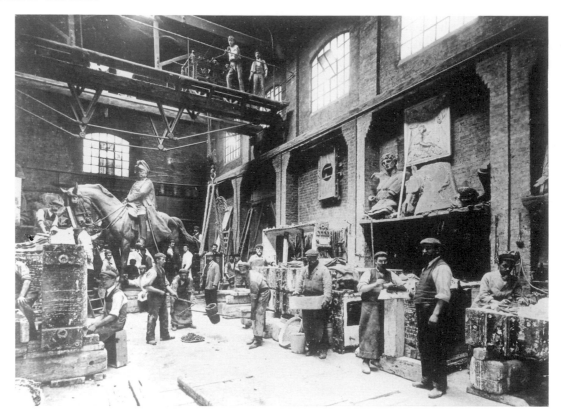

Fig 16.6   Bronze foundry, Thames Ditton, 1907. The foundry produced monumental statues from 1874 to 1939. Its products included the *Quadriga* at Hyde Park Corner and statues throughout the British Empire. SIHG Collection

from milling with stones, for grinding imported wheat. This led to the decline of small-scale local mills and eventually to the building of large mills near the ports. Some of the more successful owners of inland mills adopted the new methods. Stidder (1990) reports roller mills at eleven sites in modern Surrey of which five continued corn milling beyond the 1930s. Of these, Coxes Lock mill, close to the Thames on the Wey Navigation, continued to 1983 (Stidder 1990, 112–13) and Bottings' Albury mill at Postford on the Tillingbourne found a niche market and continued to use its 1910 roller equipment, which was recorded on video by SIHG before the mill closed in 1990. Of the other roller mills, Salfords (RB) had become an early health-food mill associated first with the Seventh Day Adventists and then with Dr Kellogg of breakfast cereal fame, but burned down in 1900 (Stidder 1990, 36–7).

The milling of oatmeal for ship's biscuits was carried out at Reigate from the early 17th to the mid-18th century. The town had twenty oatmeal mills operating at one stage, most of them apparently manually operated or driven by animal power; the trade was also carried on in Croydon (Hooper 1945, 100–3, 109n).

Like corn milling, brewing was widespread to supply local needs. The number of breweries peaked in the 19th century and was reduced by take-overs in the 20th century, but there has been a revival of small breweries particularly since the 1980s (Crocker

1999a, 40–2). Farnham was a considerable centre of hop-growing and malting (*ibid*, 38–9). SIHG district *Guides* have recorded the few structures which have survived, generally through adaptive re-use (Stidder 1979, 12, 13; Mills 1993, 27–8; Tadd 1994, 49–50; Stidder 1996, 25; Crocker 2003, 16–18). Documentary research on breweries and public houses has been carried out for Guildford by Sturley (1990; 1995) and Cobham (Taylor 2002) and is encouraged nationally by the Brewery History Society.

The 20th century

The contemporary industrial scene was reviewed by Hollinghurst *et al* (1975) in the British Association's Surrey conference volume. They discuss the pattern of development, noting the capitalization on wartime technological advances which had brought scientific expertise into the area and in particular the influence of major aircraft manufacturers at Weybridge and Kingston and the Royal Aircraft Establishment just over the county boundary in Hampshire. A large number of engineering works in the county have been related to aircraft and motor vehicle manufacture, directly or as producers of components.

An overview of extant industries (Hollinghurst *et al* 1975, 179–87) comprises sections on scientific and electronic engineering, aircraft, the automotive, marine and mechanical engineering industries, timber and construction industries, textiles and leather, food and drink, pharmaceuticals, chemical and allied industries, and extractive industries. The authors note the concentration of research establishments in Surrey and give brief details of 36 principal organizations, ranging in scope from medical, pharmaceutical, veterinary, biological and oceanographic research to defence, many branches of engineering and manufacturing technology. The majority were in the northern half of the county with a concentration around Leatherhead.

Among industries which started in the 20th century, a few examples may be given from SIHG *Guides*: artificial silk and electrical products at Ashtead and marine distress equipment at Newdigate (Tarplee 1995, 53–4, 56); wax refining at Redhill and monotype printing equipment at Salfords (Stidder 1996, 29); chemical works at Cranleigh and camshafts at Elstead (Crocker 2003, 25, 28). Published works on individual industries include Vulcanised Fibre Limited at Shalford (Gu) (Brown 1995) and electrical construction works at Hackbridge and Hersham (El) (Mileham 1988/9).

MOTOR VEHICLE MANUFACTURING

The development of motoring and motor vehicle manufacturing in Surrey (Crocker 1999a, 98–102) began in Farnham with John Henry Knight's road steam vehicle of 1868 and subsequent three-wheeler powered by his 'Trusty' gas engine (Haveron 1985, 45–6). Brooklands, Weybridge (El), where the world's first purpose-built motor-racing track was constructed in 1907, is of international importance for the development of motoring, as well as of aviation (see below). The remaining track and other features, now within Brooklands Museum, are protected as scheduled monuments and the museum provides a focus for study and research on both motoring and aviation. Surrey's early association with motor racing continued

through the 20th century with a number of firms producing very fast cars for road use and track racing.

A firm of major importance, continuing in the 21st century, is Dennis Specialist Vehicles. It began as Dennis Brothers of Guildford making bicycles and progressed to the manufacture of cars, fire engines (fig 16.7) and other service vehicles. Its multi-storey works of 1901 in the town centre was one of the first purpose-built car factories. Later used for various other industries and known as Rodboro Buildings, it was converted for commercial re-use in the 1990s. The Surrey History Centre holds the Dennis archive (SHC: 1463) and has produced a series of pamphlets on the firm's products. A history of car manufacturing and motoring in Surrey is being prepared for SIHG (Knowles forthcoming).

AVIATION AND THE AIRCRAFT INDUSTRY

Aircraft manufacture (fig 16.8) was an important industry in Surrey, beginning and ending within the 20th century. Soon after it was built in 1907 the Brooklands motor-racing track became the scene of early experiments in flying by A V Roe and the site was particularly important nationally and internationally in the period *c* 1910–14, with record attempts, flying schools and air races which continued through the 1920s and 1930s. Brooklands was taken over by the government for aircraft construction during both world wars and remained a manufacturing site after 1945, eventually under the British Aircraft Corporation and from 1977 to 1989 under British Aerospace. The works was closed in 1986–9 and demolished in 1990. The site was redeveloped but some of the historic buildings were retained as part of Brooklands Museum. This holds archives of the industry at Weybridge and elsewhere in the county and provides a major centre for research.

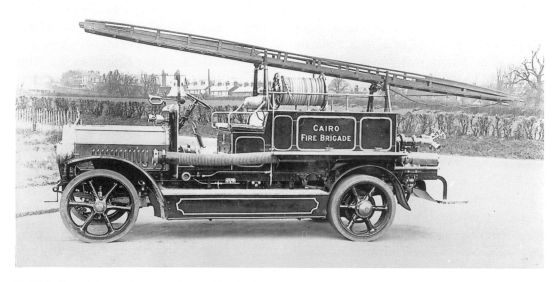

Fig 16.7 Dennis fire engine manufactured for the Cairo Fire Brigade, 1920. Reproduced by permission of Surrey History Service (1463/PHTALB/1/3 f.77)

Fig 16.8   Aircraft manufacture at Weybridge showing the assembly of VC10s for BOAC and British United Airways in April 1964. Courtesy of Brooklands Museum

The industry at Kingston upon Thames was begun by Tom Sopwith in 1912 and continued under the Hawker Engineering Company, the Hawker-Siddeley Group (Hannah 1982) and British Aerospace. From the early to mid-1950s they used Dunsfold airfield (Wa), which had been built as a bomber base by the Royal Canadian Engineers in 1942 and used after the war by Skyways, as an assembly and flight-testing site (McCue 1992). The Kingston factory closed in 1992 and Dunsfold (Wa), which continued for a time to handle aircraft made at Brough, near Hull in Yorkshire, closed in 2000 and the aircraft industry in Surrey came to an end. Effort is being made to include an historical element in redevelopment at Dunsfold.

Other important Surrey contributions to the industry include the early Martinsyde works at Woking and Brooklands and Bleriot/ANEC at Addlestone, Sir Barnes Wallis's bouncing bomb, and work on Concorde at BAC Weybridge. A database is planned of the many aviation companies and related organizations that were based in Surrey (Julian Temple, pers comm). Many specific airfields also provide scope for research projects. The heritage of the world's first commercial airport, opened at Croydon in 1920, is in the hands of the Croydon Airport Society (Cluett *et al* 1977–86), an account of Gatwick airport (in Sussex since 1974) is given by King (1986), and the history of aviation in Surrey is summarized by Masefield (1993).

Future priorities

Some the gaps in present knowledge have been indicated in the above review and it has been noted that research agendas have been proposed for the forest glass industry and the extension of the Reigate Stone Research Project.

Among sources of data, census enumerators' returns, which provide valuable information on occupations and the mobility of workers, have been little used in the study of Surrey industries except for hosiery and knitwear manufacture. Fire insurance registers, for which a limited indexing project begun by the former Surrey Local History Council has made modest progress, are a valuable source and the continuation of the project is to be encouraged, following the example of Evans (2001) for the parish of Wandsworth. A source of major importance for the industries of 20th century Surrey lies in people's recollections of their working lives. It is a matter of urgency to undertake oral history projects, to record people's experience, collect images and documentary material which they hold, and to encourage those who are able, such as Brown (1995), to write about the industries of which they have first-hand knowledge.

The recording of surviving industrial features, and the up-dating of existing lists, is a continuing need. This is addressed in the metropolitan part of historic Surrey by the exemplary database being created by the Greater London Industrial Archaeology Society (GLIAS).

Besides extending knowledge of particular industries there is a need to integrate this information into the wider picture of the industrial period as discussed by Marilyn Palmer in this volume and into the history of localities over a longer time-span. Such an approach might be made in the context of schemes in which the Surrey Archaeological Society is already involved: the Villages Project, tracing the development of individual village settlements in maps, and the collaborative ASHLV projects, involving the

Society and local authorities, for the study of Areas of Special Historic Landscape Value.

ACKNOWLEDGEMENTS

I would like to thank the many people and organizations who have provided information, in particular Graham Dawson, Jacqui Pearce, Paul Sowan and Julian Temple, Marilyn Palmer for reading an early draft of this paper and David Williams for drawing the map.

BIBLIOGRAPHY

Andrews, P, Kingston – Saxon royal estate centre to post-medieval market town: the contribution of archaeology to understanding towns in Surrey, in Cotton *et al* 2004, 169–85

Arup Geotechnics, 1991 Reigate silver sand mines (Surrey), in *Review of mining instability in Great Britain vol 3.iii Case Study Report*

Aubrey, J, 1718–19 Natural history and antiquities of the county of Surrey, 5 vols, repr Dorking, 1975

Baines, E, 1835 *History of cotton manufacture in Great Britain*

Baker, R G M, 1990 *A guide to the industrial archaeology of Elmbridge*, SIHG

Barker, D, 2000 Raby's mill at Addlestone, in Crocker, G 2000, 29–34

Bayliss, D A, 1981 *Retracing the first public railway*, Living History Publications

Beswick, M, 2001 *Brickmaking in Sussex: a history and gazetteer* (1 edn 1993)

Bevington, G, 1993 *Bevingtons & Sons, Bermondsey 1795–1950*

Bloice, B J, 1971 Norfolk House, Lambeth: excavations at a delftware kiln site, 1968, *Post-Medieval Archaeol*, **5**, 99–159

Blythman, G, 1996 *Watermills and windmills of Middlesex*, Baron Birch

Bourne, U, 1990 *Snuff*, Shire

Brace, H W, 1960 *History of seed crushing in Great Britain*

Brandon, P F, 1984 Land, technology and water management in the Tillingbourne valley, Surrey, 1560–1760, *Southern Hist*, **6**, 75–103

Brayley, E W, [1848] Appendix: observations on the manufactures of Surrey, in *A topographical history of Surrey vol 5*

Brears, P C D, 1971 *The English country pottery, its history and techniques*

Brock, A St H, 1922 *Pyrotechnics: the history and art of firework making*

Brooks, P, & Graham A, 1983 *The bishop's tenants* (typescript in SyAS Lib)

Brown, E T, Shaw, C T, & Smith, R H C, 1985–6 *Reigate caves survey, reports 1–2*, Royal School of Mines (unpublished)

Brown, R F, 1995 Shalford and the Spitfire – the story of the fibre jettison fuel tank, *Surrey Hist*, **5.2**, 99–114

Budgen, C, 1991–2 The Bramley and Rudgwick Turnpike Trust, *SyAC*, **81**, 97–102

Burgess, P M, 1983 The surveying of the Chaldon Botton firestone quarries near Merstham, Surrey, *Bull Subterranea Britannica*, **18**, 19–20, 22

——, 1987 Quarry tools and other artefacts from the Chaldon and Merstham quarries, Surrey, *Bull Subterranea Britannica*, **23**, 26–9

——, 1994 The use of plate rails in the Godstone firestone quarries – some recent discoveries, *Proc Croydon Natur Hist Sci Soc*, **18.4**, 102–7

Carus Wilson, E M, 1941 An industrial revolution of the 13th century, *Econ Hist Rev*, **11**, 39–60

Cleere, H, & Crossley, D, 1995 *The iron industry of the Weald*, 2 edn

Cluett, D, Bogle (Nash), J, & Learmouth, R, 1977–86 *Croydon Airport*, 3 vols, Sutton Libraries

Cocroft, W D, 2000 *Dangerous energy: the archaeology of gunpowder and military explosives manufacture*, English Heritage

——, 2003 *Chilworth gunpowder works, Surrey*, Engl Heritage Archaeol Investigation Rep Ser AI/20/2003

Coleman, D C, 1969 An innovation and its diffusion: the 'new draperies', *Econ Hist Rev*, 2 ser, **22**, 417–29

Collins, R A, 1969 Chalk quarrying in Surrey *c* 1800–1914: an historical analysis, *SyAC*, **66**, 41–69

Cooke, N, 2001 Excavations at Battersea Flour Mills 1996–7: the medieval and post-medieval manor houses and later Thames-side industrial sites, *SyAC*, **88**, 93–131

Cotton, J, Crocker, G, & Graham, A (eds), 2004 *Aspects of archaeology and history in Surrey: towards a research framework for the county*, SyAS

Course, E, 1987 *Minutes of the Board of Directors of the Reading, Guildford and Reigate Railway Company*, Surrey Rec Soc, **33**

Crocker, A, 1986 The Wandsworth paper mills, *Wandsworth Historian*, **50**, 19–21

——, 1988 *Paper mills of the Tillingbourne*, Oxshott: Tabard Press

——, 1989/90 The paper mills of Surrey [part 1], *Surrey Hist*, **4.1**, 49–64

——, 1992 The paper mills of Surrey, part 2, *Surrey Hist*, **4.4**, 211–30

——, 1994 The paper mills of Surrey, part 3, *Surrey Hist*, **5.1**, 2–23

——, 1995 Watermarks in Surrey hand-made paper, *The Quarterly* (Brit Ass Paper Historians), **17** supplement

——, 1996a Paper excise stamps on a re-used Haslemere ream-wrapper, *SyAC*, **83**, 159–64

——, 1996b John Smeaton, James Watt and Worcester Park gunpowder mills in the 1770s, *Gunpowder Mills Stud Grp Newsl*, **21**, 15–20

——, 1998 Campbell, Carpenter, Cope and Koops: Neckinger Mill, Bermondsey, 1792–1806, *Int Paper Historians Congr Book*, **12**, 1998 (2001), 10–19

——, 1999 Paddington Mill, Abinger: a survey of a derelict corn mill, *SyAC*, **86**, 73–103

——, 2000 Downside Mill, Cobham, in Crocker, G 2000, 22–8

——, 2001 Water turbines in Surrey, *SyAC*, **88**, 133–60

——, 2002 Hector Campbell: bleaching at Neckinger Mill, Bermondsey, *The Quarterly* (Brit Ass Paper Historians), **41**, 43–7

Crocker, A, & Castillo Fernández, J, 2003 William McMurray: wireworker, papermaker and *espartero*, *Ind Heritage*, **29.1**, 49–57

Crocker, A, & Crocker, G 1981 *Catteshall Mill: a survey of the history and archaeology of an industrial site at Godalming, Surrey*, SyAS Res Vol, **8**

Crocker, A, & Humphrey, S, 2002 The papermaker and the prophetess: Elias Carpenter of Neckinger Mill, Bermondsey, supporter of Joanna Southcott, *SyAC*, **89**, 119–35

Crocker, A, & Kane, M, 1990   *The diaries of James Simmons, paper-maker of Haslemere, 1831–1868*, Oxshott: Tabard Press

Crocker, A G, Crocker, G, M, Fairclough, K R, & Wilks, M J, 2000   *Gunpowder mills: documents of the seventeenth and eighteenth centuries*, Surrey Rec Soc, **36**

Crocker, G (comp), 1988   *Gunpowder mills gazetteer: black powder manufacturing sites in the British Isles*, Soc Protection Ancient Buildings Wind & Watermill Section, Occ Pub, **2**

——, 1989/90   The Godalming framework knitting industry, *Surrey Hist*, **4.1**, 3–16

—— (ed), 1990   *A guide to the industrial archaeology of Surrey*, Ass Ind Archaeol

——, 1991   The Godalming knitting industry and its workplaces, *Ind Archaeol Rev*, **14.1**, 33–54

——, 1991–2   The place of Godalming in the hosiery and knitwear industry, *SyAC*, **81**, 41–70

—— (ed), 1999a   *Surrey's industrial past*, SIHG

——, 1999b   Seventeenth-century wireworks in Surrey and the case of Thomas Steere, *Surrey Hist*, **6.1**, 2–16

—— (ed), 2000   *Alexander Raby, Ironmaster. Proceedings of a conference held at Cobham on 28 November 1998*, SIHG

—— (ed), 2003   *A guide to the industrial history of Waverley*, SIHG

Crocker, G, & Crocker A, 1990   Gunpowder mills of Surrey, *Surrey Hist*, **4.3**, 134–58

——, A, 2000   *Damnable inventions: Chilworth gunpowder and the paper mills of the Tillingbourne*, SIHG

Crocker, G, & Fairclough, K R, 1998   The introduction of edge-runner incorporating mills in the British gunpowder industry, *Ind Archaeol Rev*, **20**, 23–36

Crossley, D, 1990   *Post-medieval archaeology in Britain*

——, 1994   The glass industry revisited, *Ind Archaeol Rev*, **17.1**, 64–74

Crowe, A L, 1973   Samuel Vassall and the west Surrey woollen industry, *Surrey Hist*, **1.1**, 26–31

Currie, C K, 1996   *A historical and archaeological assessment of the Wey and Godalming Navigations and their visual envelopes* (unpublished report to National Trust, 5 vols)

Davis, C T 1898   *The industries of Wandsworth past and present*

Dawson, G, 1976   *Montague Close excavations 1969–73. Part 1: a general survey*, SyAS Res Vol, **3**, 37–58

——, 1981   Round saggars in square kilns, *Southwark Lambeth Archaeol Soc Newsl*, **50**

Day, J, 1973   *Bristol brass, a history of the industry*

Deacon, R, 2000   *Nutfield: our village since Domesday* (ed P Finch), Nutfield Local History Group

Dendy Marshall, C F 1936   *A history of the Southern Railway*

Dickinson, H W, & Gomme, A A, eds, 1950   *A catalogue of the civil and mechanical engineering designs 1741–1792 of John Smeaton, FRS, preserved in the library of the Royal Society*, Newcomen Society

Donald, M B, 1961   *Elizabethan monopolies*

Down, C G, & Smith, D H, 1977   *Polar Bear and the Groundle Glen Railway*, Brockham Museum Association

Edwards, P, 1995   Gunpowder and the English Civil War, *J Arms & Armour Soc*, **15.2**, 109–31

Edwards, R, 1974   London potters circa 1570–1710, *J Ceram Hist*, **6**

——, 1981–2   The Vauxhall Pottery, history and excavations 1977–81, *London Archaeol*, **4.5**, 130–6; **4.6**, 149–54

Egan, G, 1991   Industry and economics on the medieval and later London waterfront, in *Waterfront archaeology: Proceedings of the third international conference on waterfront archaeology held at Bristol 23–26 September 1988* (eds G L Good, R H Jones & M W Ponsford), CBA Res Rep, **74**, 9–18

Ellaby, R, 2000   The Horley demesne of Reigate Priory, *SyAC*, **87**, 147–55

English, J, & Field, D, 1991   A survey of earthworks at Hammer Meadow, Abinger Hammer, *SyAC*, **81**, 91–5

Ensing, R J, 1987   Some field and place names of Wandsworth, *Wandsworth Historian*, **33**, 10–22

——, 1992   The river Wandle in 1633, *Wandsworth Historian*, **65**, 8–12

Evans, T, 2001   *Local and family history from fire insurance policies (for the 18th and 19th centuries. 1: Wandsworth*, Wandsworth Historical Society

Evelyn, John, 1654   *Sylva*

——, 1675   Mr Evelyn's letter to Mr Aubrey, in Aubrey 1718–19, **1**, following xlviii

Fairclough, K R, 1989   Gunpowder production at Balham House, *London's Ind Archaeol*, **4**, 32–4

——, 1990   John Samyne: 17th century gunpowder maker, *Gunpowder Mills Stud Grp Newsl*, **7**, 2–6

——, 1996   The hard case of Sir Polycarpus Wharton, *SyAC*, **83**, 125–35

——, 1999a   Thomas Coram: his brief period as a gunpowder producer, *SyAC*, **86**, 53–72 and microfiche 43–92

——, 1999b   Lead production at East Molesey mills: documents, *SIHG Newsl*, **109**, 17–18

——, 2000a   The East India Company and gunpowder production in England, 1625–1636, *SyAC*, **87**, 95–111

——, 2000b   The Cordwell family: gunpowder producers at Chilworth, 1636–1650, *SyAC*, **87**, 113–26

Fairclough, K R, & Crocker, G, in prep   Chilworth gunpowder mills in the period of the Dutch Wars

Farries, K G & Mason, M T, 1966   *The windmills of Surrey and Inner London*

Fish, H, Harris, B J D, Mander, R J, Nicolson, N J, & Owen, M, 1975   Rivers and water, in Salmon 1975, 33–61

Fuller, G J, 1953   The development of roads in the Surrey-Sussex Weald and coastlands between 1700 and 1900, *Trans Pap Brit Inst Geogr*, **19**, 37–49

Garner, K, & Sanderson, R, 2001   Conservation of Reigate stone at Hampton Court Palace and HM Tower of London, *J Architect Conserv*, **3**, 7–23

Gerhold, D, 2002   Wandsworth's gunpowder mills, 1656–1713, *SyAC*, **89**, 171–83

Gerhold, D, & Ensing, R, 1999   Wandsworth's water mills to 1700, *Wandsworth Historian*, **70**, 15–21

Giuseppi, M S, 1908   The river Wandle in 1610, *SyAC*, **21**, 170–91

Gower, G, 1998   *The tile and brickmakers of Streatham*, Streatham: Local History Publications

Gravett, K, 1981/2   The electric light at Godalming, 1881, *Surrey Hist*, **2.3**, 102–9

Gravett, K, & Wood, E S, 1967   Merstham limeworks, *SyAC*, **64**, 124–47

Greenwood, G B, 1980   *The Elmbridge water mills, Surrey* (unpublished typescript)

Greenwood, J, 1982   *A history of the fuller's earth industry in Surrey up to 1900* (pamphlet, the author)

Gregory, R, 2002   *The contribution of the windmill to the industrial revolution*, Soc Protection Ancient Buildings Mills Section

Hallam, E, 1990   *The Ashtead Potters Ltd in Surrey*, Hallam Publishing

Hannah, H, 1982   *Hawker*, Flypast Reference Library, Key Publishing

Hartlib, S (ed), [1650]   *A discourse of husbandrie used in Brabant and Flanders* [by Sir Richard Weston], London 1605 (*sic*)

Haslam, J, 1975   The excavation of a 17th-century pottery site at Cove, east Hampshire, *Post-Medieval Archaeol*, **9**, 164–87

Haveron, F, 1981   *The brilliant ray*, Godalming

——, 1985   *A guide to the industrial archaeology of the Waverley area*, SIHG

——, 1993   *A guide to the industrial history of Guildford and its borough*, SIHG

Hawkins, D, 2000a   The archbishop of York's Battersea mansion, *London Archaeol*, **9.5**, 129–36

——, 2000b   Letter: Reigate stone at Battersea, *London Archaeol*, **9.7**, 186

Hayman, G, 1997   The excavation of two medieval pottery kiln sites and two sections through the London-Lewes Roman road at Clacket Lane, near Titsey, 1992, *SyAC*, **84**, 1–87

Hillier, J 1951   *Old Surrey water-mills*, Skeffington

Hinton, M, 1980 Medieval pottery from a kiln site at Kingston upon Thames, *London Archaeol*, **3**, 377–83

Hodgkinson, J, 2004 Iron production in Surrey, in Cotton *et al* 2004, 233–44

Holling, F W, 1969 Seventeenth-century pottery from Ash, Surrey, *Post-Medieval Archaeol*, **3**, 18–30

——, 1971 A preliminary note on the pottery industry of the Hampshire-Surrey borders, *SyAC*, **68**, 57–88

——, F W, 1977 Reflections on Tudor Green, *Post-Medieval Archaeol*, **11**, 61–6

Hollinghurst, J, Moore, J P, & Power, R P, 1975 Surrey industries, in Salmon 1975, 177–99

Holmes, T W, 1983 *The semaphore*

Holt, R, 1988 *The mills of medieval England*

Hooper, W, 1945 *Reigate: its story through the ages*, SyAS

I A Recordings, 1990 Archive compilation **19**: Alan Paine knitwear manufacturers; **22**: KF Knitwear and old knitting workshops of Godalming, Telford (videotape)

Jackson, A A, 1999 *The railway in Surrey*

Janaway, C, 1993 History of Bargate stone quarrying, unpublished report (copy in Surrey History Centre, Woking)

Jones, P, 1997 The pottery, in Hayman 1997, 32–76

Kenyon, G H, 1967 *The glass industry of the Weald*

Kerridge, E, 1972 Wool growing and wool textiles in medieval and early modern times, in *The wool textile industry in Great Britain* (ed J G Jenkins), 19–33

——, 1985 *Textile manufactures in early modern England*

Ketteringham, L, 1989 Two medieval pottery kilns at Limpsfield Chart, *SyAC*, **79**, 125–45

Killock, D, Brown, J, & Jarrett, C, 2003 The industrialization of an ecclesiastical hamlet: stoneware production in Lambeth and the sanitary revolution, *Post-Medieval Archaeol*, **37.1**, 29–78

King, J, 1986 *Gatwick: the evolution of an airport*, Gatwick Airport Ltd & Sussex Industrial Archaeology Society

Knowles, G, forthcoming *Surrey and the motor*, SIHG

Lancaster, B, 2000 The 'Croydon Case': dirty old town to model town. The making of the Croydon Board of Health and the Croydon typhoid epidemic of 1852–3, *Proc Croydon Natur Hist Sci Soc*, **18.6**

Le Gear, R F, 1978 Chalk mining on medieval Kentish farms, in *Proc Joint Symposium Subterranea Britannica & Société Française d'Etude des Souterrains*, Cambridge, 6–8

Lee, H E, & Russell, J, 1924 The Guildford chalk caves, *South-Eastern Naturalist & Antiquary for 1924*, 63–4

Living History, 1986 *Retracing canals to Croydon and Camberwell*, Local Guide, **7**, Bromley

Luff, D, 2002 *Trouble at mill: A brief history of the former Liberty Print Works site, including Textile printing at Merton Printers Ltd (Libertys) 1965–1982*, Merton Historical Society

McCue, P, 1992 *Dunsfold, Surrey's most secret airfield*, Air Research Publications

McDonald, D, 1908 *Agricultural writers from Sir Walter of Henley to Arthur Young, 1200–1800*

Manning, O, & Bray, W, 1804–1814 The history and antiquities of the county of Surrey, 3 vols

Marshall, C J, 1924 A medieval pottery kiln discovered at Cheam, *SyAC*, **35**, 79–97

——, 1941 The sites of two more thirteenth century pottery kilns at Cheam, *SyAC*, **47**, 99–100

Masefield, P, 1993 *Surrey aeronautics and aviation*, Phillimore/Surrey Local History Council

Mayford History Society, 1979 *'My New River': a forerunner to the Wey Navigation* (leaflet)

Menuge, A, 1999 *Farnham Pottery, Pottery Lane, Wrecclesham, Farnham, Surrey*, Roy Comm Hist Monuments Eng, unpublished report (copy in SyAS Lib)

Mileham, C G, 1988/89 Hackbridge transformers for Barking B power station, *Surrey Hist*, **3.5**, 226–32

Miller, P, & Stephenson, R, 1999 *A 14th-century pottery site in Kingston upon Thames, Surrey*, MoLAS Archaeol Stud Ser, **1**

Mills, J, 1991 *A guide to the industrial history of Runnymede*, SIHG

——, 1993 *A guide to the industrial history of Spelthorne*, SIHG

——, 1995 *A guide to the industrial history of Surrey Heath*, SIHG

Montague, E N, 1989/90 James Pain & Sons of Mitcham, manufacturers of fireworks (1872–1965), *Surrey Hist*, **4.1**, 35–48

——, 1992 *Textile bleaching and printing in Mitcham and Merton, 1590–1870*, Merton Historical Society

—-, 1993 The history of William Harland and Son of Phipps Bridge, and the development of the paint and varish industry in Mitcham, *Surrey Hist*, **4.5**, 87–306

——, 1995 *The Ravensbury mills*, Merton Historical Society

——, 1996 Merton mills and Wandlebank House, *SyAC*, **83**, 137–57

——, 1997 *The 'Amery Mills' of Merton Priory, and the copper mills and the Board mills*, Merton Historical Society

——, 1999 *Copper milling on the Wandle with particular reference to Merton and Mitcham*, Merton Historical Society

Nash, M, 1969 Early seventeenth-century schemes to make the Wey navigable, 1618–1651, *SyAC*, **66**, 33–40

Nelson, S, 1981 A group of pottery waster material from Kingston, *London Archaeol*, **4**, 96–102

Noyes, A, 1997 *A tannery in Gomshall*, Gomshall: Twiga Books

Origo, I, 1957 *The merchant of Prato Francesco di Marco Datini*

Orton, C, 1979 Medieval pottery from a kiln site at Cheam: part I, *London Archaeol*, **3**, 300–4

——, 1982 The excavation of a late medieval/transitional pottery kiln at Cheam, Surrey, *SyAC*, **73**, 49–92

Osborne, B E, 1982 Early plateways and firestone mining in Surrey, *Proc Croydon Natur Hist Sci Soc*, **17.3**, 73–88

Palmer, M, 2004 The archaeology of industrialization: towards a research agenda, in Cotton *et al* 2004, 199–212

Patterson, R, 1956 Spinning and weaving, in *A history of technology* (eds C Singer, E J Holmyard, A R Hall, & T I Williams), Oxford: Clarendon Press, **2**, 191–220

Payne, G A, 1977 *Surrey industrial archaeology: a field guide*, Phillimore

Peachey, S (ed), 2001 Textiles and materials of the common man and woman 1580–1660, Bristol: Stuart Press

Pearce, J E, 1992 *Post-medieval pottery in London, 1500–1700 Volume 1: Border wares*, London, HMSO

Pearce, J E, & Vince, A G, 1988 *A dated type-series of London medieval pottery Part 4: Surrey whitewares*, London Middlesex Archaeol Soc Spec Pap, **10**

Perrett, D, 1979 London and the steam engine. Part 1: The engines, *London's Ind Archaeol*, **1**, 1–10

——, 1980 London and the steam engine. Part 2: The engine builders, *London's Ind Archaeol*, **2**, 24–37

Platt, C, & Coleman-Smith, R, 1975 *Excavations in medieval Southampton*, 2 vols

[Plunkett, D], 1999 *'Open to tide mills': proceedings of an international conference held at the Miller's House, Three Mills, Bromley-by-Bow, London E3 on 11 September 1999*, The River Lea Tidal Mill Trust Ltd

Poulton, R, 1988 *Archaeological investigations on the site of Chertsey Abbey*, SyAS Res Vol, **11**

——, forthcoming *A medieval royal complex at Guildford: excavations at the palace and castle*, SyAS monogr

Prendergast, M D, 1973 *The coarseware potteries of medieval Limpsfield in Surrey* (privately printed and circulated)

——, 1974 Limpsfield medieval coarseware: a descriptive analysis, *SyAC*, **70**, 57–77

PRO: PROB 11: The National Archives, Kew, Public Record Office, Prerogative Court of Canterbury wills

PRO: J90/1206: The National Archives, Kew, Public Record Office, Order in Chancery 18 March 1867, McMurray v Spicer

Reid, K C 1987–9 *Watermills of the London countryside*, 2 vols, Charles Skilton

Riall, N, 1997 A medieval tile kiln in Farnham Park, *SyAC*, **84**, 143–68

——, 2003 Excavation at Borelli Yard, Farnham: the tile kiln, *SyAC*, **90**, 295–336

Richardson, S, & Trueman, M, 1997 *MPP: Lime, cement and plaster industries: step 3. Introduction to site assessments*, English Heritage

Robertson, R H S, 1986 *Fuller's earth: a history of calcium montmorillonite*

Salmon, J E, 1975 *The Surrey countryside*, University of Surrey for British Association

SHC: LM Surrey History Centre, Woking, Loseley Manuscripts

Simmons 1940s Simmons Collection of manuscript notes on windmills and watermills, Science Mus Lib (copy of Surrey section in SyAS Lib)

Shere 2001: *Shere, a Surrey village in maps: a record of its growth and development*, Shere Gomshall and Peaslake Local History Society for SyAS Villages Project

Smith, A C, 1976 *Windmills in Surrey and Greater London: a contemporary survey*, Stevenage Museum Publications

Smith, D H, 1979 *Brockham Museum guide*, 2 edn

Sowan, P W, 1975 Firestone and hearthstone mines in the Upper Greensand of east Surrey, *Proc Geol Ass*, **86.4**, 571–91

——, 1976 Chalk mines in Surrey as a source of freestone, *Proc Croydon Natur Hist Sci Soc*, **16.2**, 82–7

——, 1979 The Park Hill tunnel on the Woodside and South Croydon Railway, *The Tunneller*, **19**, 4

——, 1980 Some little-known and forgotten 'sand-caves' in Reigate, *Pelobates* (Croydon Caving Club), **38**, 6–10

——, 1982 The southern terminus of the Croydon, Merstham & Godstone Railway, *J Railway Canal Hist Soc*, **27.6**, 159–67

——, 1984a Did the builder of the Settle & Carlisle Railway meet his match in South Croydon? *Greater London Ind Archaeol Soc (GLIAS) Newsl*, **91**, 8–9

——, 1984b Further light on the Gatton and Guildford stone quarries in the sixteenth century, *Proc Croydon Natur Hist Sci Soc*, **17.8**, 193–4

——, 1985/6 Mining and quarrying in Surrey: accidents and regulations before 1900, *Surrey Hist*, **3.2**, 78–96

——, 1991 Les carrières de pierre à bâtir, à blanchir et réfractaire de l'est du Surrey, Angleterre, in *Carrières souterraines* (ed J Chabert), 193–202

——, 2000a The Reigate Stone Research Project, *London Archaeol*, **9.5**, 145–6

——, 2000b Messrs Warings' and Joseph Fairbanks' contributions to building the Oxted line, east Surrey, 1865–67 and 1880–1883, *Local Hist Records Bourne Soc*, **39**, 2000 (1999), 51–65

——, 2000c The mining records of Robert Hunt (1858), *SyAS Bull*, **340**, 8–12

——, 2000d A newly-discovered limekiln type at Betchworth limeworks (TQ 207 512), *SyAS Bull*, **343**, 4–6

——, 2000e Brockham lime works kilns (TQ 197 509): interim report, *SIHG Newsl*, **113**, 9–13

——, 2001 Investigations at Betchworth limeworks (southern battery) TQ 208 512, *SIHG Newsl*, **123**, 15–18

——, 2002 The Betchworth limeworks and sandlime brick manufacture at Holmethorpe (Merstham/Redhill), *SIHG Newsl*, **126**, 28–30

Stevens, T (ed), 1994 *The Thames Ditton statue foundry: the story of the foundry and the preservation of its gantry crane*, SIHG

Stidder, D, 1990 *The watermills of Surrey*, Barracuda

——, 1979 *A guide to the industrial archaeology of Reigate and Banstead*, SIHG

——, 1996 *A guide to the industrial history of Reigate and Banstead*, SIHG

Sturley, M, 1990 *The breweries and public houses of Guildford, part 1*, Guildford: Charles Traylen

——, 1995 *The breweries and public houses of Guildford, part 2*, the author

Tadd, M, 1994 *A guide to the industrial history of Tandridge*, SIHG

Tarplee, P, 1995 *A guide to the industrial history of Mole Valley District*, SIHG

——, 1998 *A guide to the industrial history of the Borough of Elmbridge*, SIHG

Tatton-Brown T, 2000 Reigate stone at Battersea, *London Archaeol*, **9.6**, 160

——, 2001 The quarrying and distribution of Reigate stone in the Middle Ages, *Medieval Archaeol*, **45**, 189–201

Taylor, D C, 2000 Alexander Raby at Cobham, in Crocker, G 2000, 15–21

——, 2002 *Well furnished with inns: Cobham's brewery, inns and public houses*, Cobham, Appleton Publications

TBAOG 1964: *Thames Basin Archaeological Observers Group Newsl*, **23**, 9

Thirsk, J, 1978 *Economic policy and projects: the development of a consumer society in early modern England*

Townsend, J L, 1980 *Townsend Hook and the railways of the Dorking Greystone Lime Co Ltd*

Trueman, M R G, 2000 *Monuments Protection Programme: water and sewage industries, step 3 report for Engl Heritage*

Turner, D J, 1974 Medieval pottery kiln at Bushfield Shaw, Earlswood, *SyAC*, **70**, 47–55

Turner, G 2003 *Shottermill – its farms, families and mills. Part 1: Early times to the 1700s*, Headley: John Owen Smith

——, forthcoming *Shottermill. Part 2*

Twilley, R, & Wilks, M (eds), 1974 *The river Wandle, a guide and handbook*, Sutton Libraries

VCH: Victoria history of the county of Surrey (ed H E Malden), 4 vols, London 1902–12

Vine, P A L, 1996 *London's lost route to the sea*, 5 edn

——, 1968 *London's lost route to Basingstoke*

Wadsworth, A P, & Mann, J de L, 1931 *The cotton trade and industrial Lancashire, 1600–1780*, repr 1965

Wakefield, P, 1997 *A guide to the industrial history of Epsom and Ewell*, SIHG

Wakeford, I, 1995 *A guide to the industrial history of Woking and its Borough*, SIHG

Walker, T E C, 1961 Cobham: manorial history, *SyAC*, **58**, 47–78

Watts, M, 1983 *Corn milling*, Shire

Waverley Borough Council, 1986 *Heritage features in Waverley* (4 parts)

Weatherill, L, & Edwards, R, 1971 Pottery making in London and Whitehaven in the late seventeenth century, *Post-Medieval Archaeol*, **5**, 160–222

Wilks MS: Wilks, M J, *Wandle mills* (unfinished draft held by SIHG)

Williamson, G C, 1930 *The Guildford caverns*, Guildford Corporation

Wilson, G, 1976 *The old telegraph*

Withers, H C, 1969 *Godalming: a survey of its industrial development*, Growth of a Town no 7 supplement, Godalming County Branch Library

Wood, E S, 1965 A medieval glasshouse at Blundens Wood, Hambledon, Surrey, *SyAC*, **62**, 54–79

——, 1982 A 16th-century glasshouse at Knightons, Alfold, Surrey, *SyAC*, **73**, 1–47

Glenys Crocker, 6 Burwood Close, Guildford GU1 2SB

17

Iron production in Surrey

JEREMY S HODGKINSON

This paper discusses iron production in the Iron Age and Roman periods and the Middle Ages, the main expansion based on water power which brought the Weald to national significance in the 16th and 17th centuries, and the secondary working of iron by Surrey mills in the Thames basin into the early 19th century. Finally it suggests priorities for future research.

Introduction

With the exception of the Wealden part of the county, there are few sources of iron ore in Surrey, and those that have been exploited have been limited. Nevertheless, iron production has been an economic resource of some importance at several different stages in its history. The reasons for this have changed over the course of time, but the most important periods of production – during the late Middle Ages, the early modern period and the early 19th century – have received their impetus from Surrey's position on the periphery of two, more intensively worked industrial regions. From the late 14th to the 17th centuries, the Weald was an iron production area of national importance, and the parts of this county that lie in that region benefited from the new-found wealth and entrepreneurial zeal of its landowning families. Later, it was the growth of London, whose population, and the commerce generated by it, consumed manufactured goods at an unprecedented rate, which provided the impetus for the growth of processing industries in its rural hinterland.

The Iron Age and Roman periods (fig 17.1)

Ironworking has probably been carried out at a domestic level in Surrey over much of the last two and a half thousand years. Whether deriving its raw materials from small, local sources, or from larger ones further afield, the forging of iron objects for agricultural use has been a commonplace activity, and the remains of such working need to be noted in as much detail as those of a corn-drying oven or a pottery kiln. However, individually interesting though such sites may be, they only become significant when a pattern in their occurrence begins to emerge, or when they are unique. Both instances can be found in Surrey. Of more significance, however, are the primary production sites and it is important to make clear the difference between primary iron making, and secondary working. With very few exceptions, primary ironworking – that is the smelting of ore to form a bloom of iron – seldom took place far from a source of ore. Secondary working, which may include the consolidation of the bloom and a consequent accumulation of slag, but which

also can include smithing to form marketable iron, can take place far from sources of ore, and is generally less susceptible to regional concentration. Both processes produce fairly distinctive slags, and where they occur smelting slags are usually more plentiful. The important proviso that a small quantity of slag may not denote a proportionate amount of activity should be read in the context of what else is found on a site. It has been shown on Wealden sites that the quantity of slag can be a useful guide to the output and/or longevity of ironworking, and as accurate an estimate of it as possible should be made (Hodgkinson 1999, 68–9). The recognition of slag types is crucial to the correct identification of ironworking sites, and in a number of instances early reports of the discovery of iron slags have unwittingly misrepresented the nature of the processes carried out, with such errors being perpetuated in the literature for many years after. The importance of some sites has, therefore, been overstated, and broad conclusions have sometimes been drawn from too little evidence.

Such is not the case with the ironworking settlement at Brooklands, Weybridge. Dated to the early Iron Age of the 6th or 5th centuries BC, it is a site of great importance for our understanding of the development of the technology of iron making, though less so for the history of iron making in Surrey (Hanworth & Tomalin 1977, 15–23). It is a small site, and even though the amount of slag found there in no way represented the output of the smelting furnaces excavated, production must, nevertheless, have been relatively small too. Although we know nothing of the subsequent use of the iron made there, there are good reasons for suspecting that its products may have been distributed over a wide area. Because of the novelty of iron in a transitional period when few contemporary sites have revealed evidence of the metal, its products may have travelled far, and its location near the confluence of the Thames and the Wey, would have made their distribution that much easier. Sadly, Brooklands is almost unique in the county, with only the farmstead site at Hawk's Hill, Leatherhead, in any way comparable (Hastings 1965, 12). Although slag, which was described as from smelting, was found at Hawk's Hill, no hearths were discovered, and the broad date range for the site makes it anywhere between contemporary with Brooklands and as much as three centuries later. Also, its location, far removed from the Thames valley, means it would have been unlikely that it shared an ore source with Brooklands, nor does an obvious source spring to mind. Ore sources are a problem in describing ironworking in Surrey. Apart from the Low and High Weald, where sources of ore are reasonably well documented, sources for other sites are somewhat speculative (Worssam 1995, 9–21, 25–30). Doubt has even been cast on the siderite found in the lowest levels of the Bracklesham Beds on St George's Hill, which were identified as the likely source for the Brooklands site (Potter 1977, 22). Analysis by the late Professor Tylecote suggested inconsistencies between the amount of phosphorus in the ore, and in the slag found at Brooklands (Tylecote 1986, 137–9). The lack of abundant sources of ore throughout most of the county clearly accounts for the limited amount of smelting that has taken place.

Hillforts, because of their isolated place in the landscape, and the presumption that such isolation must lend them an air of self-sufficiency, have been prime targets for excavation in the past, and many have yielded evidence of ironworking. None, to date, has produced an example of smelting. This, in itself, is not surprising, given that the geology that formed the commanding positions these sites occupy is unlikely to be composed of the clays from which the necessary ore is derived. Iron forging slag has been found at Hascombe camp, but the significance of iron-bearing carstone, which occurs in the Folkestone Beds of the greensand, and which Winbolt identified as an iron ore, has yet to be established (Winbolt 1932, 89). Reports of iron slag at Dry Hill, Lingfield, despite its Wealden location, are inconclusive despite unfounded assertions that the evidence was pre-Roman (Winbolt & Margary 1933, 80). That such hillforts might have been used as processing and distribution centres for iron, though, seems entirely plausible, especially as most reported ironworking evidence is of forging. The temple site at Farley Heath has attracted some attention because of its presumed link with ironworking. The dedication to Celtic and Roman deities associated with metalworking, which has been attributed to it, cannot be directly associated with such activity in the area (Goodchild 1938, 396).

Inevitably, the Early Iron Age leaves us with more questions than secure facts. Brooklands and Hawk's Hill are isolated geographically and chronologically, and as small, single sites offer us no sense of industry. Similarly in the Late Iron Age and Roman periods, few positively dated sites have been found, and little of the dated material suggests anything more than small, domestic forging, at most for local, probably agrarian consumption. Three sites discovered more than half a century ago, at Purberry Shot, Ewell, on Stane Street (Lowther 1949, 13), Thorncombe, near Hascombe (SyAS 1949, xxiv), and on Walton Heath (Prest & Parrish 1950, 63), fall into this category. The very small quantities of slag found show all the signs of having been derived from the consolidation of imported blooms and their subsequent smithing. The sources of the blooms concerned are not known, although it may be possible in the future, with developments in slag and ore analysis, to be able to determine this. It is very likely that raw blooms were as much a marketable commodity as forged iron bars, and it is possible that seasonal herding practices, involving the movement of animals into the Weald to graze and forage, may have been the impetus for some small-scale smelting in the Weald before, during and after the Roman period, with the raw products being worked up in the home settlements when the season was over. Such practices may have been carried out to the north and south of the Weald.

Two areas of real interest in relation to iron making in the late Iron Age and early Romano-British period are at Thorpe Lea Nurseries, and in a 3-mile-long area of the Windle brook valley from the Berkshire border down to Lightwater. The recently excavated site at Thorpe Lea Nurseries, near Egham, has produced evidence of iron smelting which differs from that found at Weybridge. Although no hearths were discovered, because excavation was restricted, the evidence from the slag suggested a different tradition of smelting dating from the mid-to-late Iron Age and the Roman periods. Like the Brooklands slags, those from Thorpe Lea appeared to have come from furnaces where the slag was not tapped (ie allowed to run from the furnace) during smelting; but they differed in that they had the appearance of having collected in a wood-filled pit below the furnace – a type not previously recorded in Britain, but known from mainland Europe (R Poulton and D Starley, pers comm).

In the Windle valley, smelting slags have been reported on several sites, and pottery finds suggest that they derive from around 150 BC to the end of the 1st century AD. Excavations at South Farm, Lightwater, have uncovered quantities of slag suggesting modest iron smelting activity (Cole 1991, 10). No furnaces have been located, but the absence of tap slag, not only on this site, but also at other locations along the valley, again points to a different smelting tradition from both Thorpe Lea and the Wealden sites of the same period. Located some 10 miles due west of the outcrop of the Bracklesham Beds at St George's Hill, Weybridge, it is clear that the workings at Lightwater must have relied on a different source of ore, although Cole's suggestion

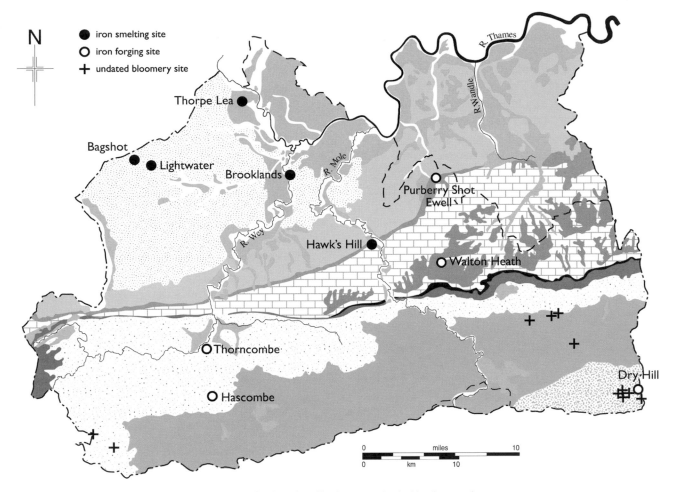

Fig 17.1 Iron Age and Romano-British iron production sites. For key to geological background see map on page x.

that the source for the workings along the Windle brook is haematite nodules occurring in the surface gravels exposed by the brook has not been substantiated (G H Cole, pers comm). Marshy conditions, where much of the evidence for ironworking in the Bagshot area has been noted, may indicate extraction of ore along its banks, and, if this is the case, exhaustion of this source may have prevented exploitation for a longer time in the Roman period. The presence of Roman material at Wickham Bushes, just over the Berkshire border, suggests that the Windle brook sites may be part of a larger group (Corney & Gaffney 1985). The almost haphazard discovery of single iron smelting sites of at least three distinct traditions in different geological locations within the county points to a need to establish to what extent these sites really exist in isolation, or whether they represent the first examples of greater concentrations of industrial activity.

Although south-eastern Surrey lies on the northern periphery of the main ironworking area of the Weald in the late Iron Age and Romano-British period, no sites in that part of the county have, as yet, been dated to the period. However, four sites on Upper Stonehurst Farm, Lingfield, while undated at present, may be satellites of the major Roman ironworking site at Great Cansiron, over the Sussex

border (Cleere & Crossley 1995, 292, 299). Nor has the Low Weald of southern Surrey, an area exploited for its iron in the late medieval, as well as in the 16th and 17th centuries, yielded any evidence of iron making in the Roman period. The few farm or villa sites, the tile kiln at Cranleigh, and the limited number of isolated finds that have been made there, however, suggest that evidence of the period, rather than being absent altogether, has simply not come to light (Goodchild 1937).

Turning to London, the role of Southwark, as a centre for the processing of raw materials imported from the rural hinterland of the capital, seems to have been established in Roman times, and its long association with the iron industry dates from the same period. With roads converging on the borough from several points near the south coast, and having passed through areas of iron production, it is perhaps inevitable that evidence should have been found there of the secondary working of iron. Excavations on the site of the former Courage brewery, close to the early bridge across the Thames, have shown a dense concentration of iron and bronze smithing, as well as several buildings and other features, from the late 1st century through to the 4th century AD; an unusually long sequence of metalworking activity (Westman 1998, 63).

The Middle Ages (fig 17.2)

Until recently, our knowledge of iron making in Surrey in the medieval period has been confined to a small amount of documentary and archaeological evidence. Compared with most other historic and prehistoric periods, the Middle Ages have been under-represented in descriptions of the industry in the county, yet evidence is accumulating that points to it being one of the more productive periods in its history, particularly in its south-eastern corner. There is a dearth of evidence of iron making in the Saxon period in the Weald, and this is mirrored in other parts of Surrey. However, fieldwalking in the Outwood area of Burstow and Horne parishes, as yet untested by excavation, has begun to show evidence of activity from as early as the period around the Norman Conquest (Robin Tanner, pers comm). Small quantities of bloomery slag in association with Saxo-Norman pottery have been found in Ten Acre Wood, abutting Cogmans Lane, Outwood. Elsewhere in the same wood, slag has been noticed with a surface scatter of pottery of the late 13th and 14th centuries (*Wealden Iron* 1998, 2 ser **18**, 2). In another part of Outwood, a single fragment of probable 13th century pottery was found embedded with a concentration of bloomery slag during a sampling excavation by the Wealden Iron Research Group.

Other discoveries of iron cinder, at Woolborough Farm, Horley, and in nearby Hathersham Lane may be of a similar period (Robin Tanner, pers comm). To the north of the village, bloomery cinder has been found on the edge of Nutfield parish in a field where a scatter of pottery dated to no later than the 14th century may be associated with it (*Wealden Iron* 2000, 2 ser **20**, 3). At this last site, the utilization of iron ore from beds in the Weald Clay, which outcrop less than a mile south of the Lower Greensand, draws parallels between this and three other, undated sites, two in Bletchingley and one at the northern extremity of Burstow parish (Worssam & Herbert 2000, 14–17; *Wealden Iron* 2001, 2 ser **21**, 3).

The activities of a single, energetic field walker can tend to skew the perceived distribution of archaeological finds, but Robin Tanner's discoveries add to, rather than stand apart from, existing knowledge. As far back as 1809, Manning & Bray (**2**, 255) drew attention to a deed of 1396 by which the prior and convent of Christ Church, Canterbury, reserved the digging of iron in Charlwood, as part of their manor of Merstham. Probably, this same source of ore had been worked by the earl of Arundel when he held Charlwood of Christ Church in 1362. Ten years after that, John Neel and others had been fined for digging ore from the highway in Horley parish – adjacent to

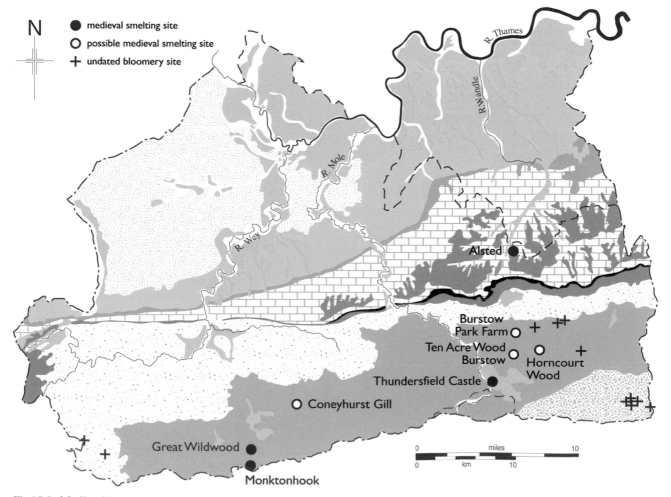

Fig 17.2 Medieval iron production sites. For key to geological background see map on page x.

Charlwood – in the manor of Banstead. Elsewhere in Horley, although this time on property of the de Clares of Bletchingley, the existence of ironworking at Thundersfield in the same period must signify that such evidence is not isolated (Hart & Winbolt 1937, 146–50). In Sussex, recent excavations in Crawley, less than 5 miles south of Horley, have revealed substantial ironworking – both smelting and forging – dating from the late 14th and early 15th centuries, with corroborative documentary records of iron makers from tax returns in the 1370s (Cooke 2001). And about 4 miles to the south-west lies the documented 14th century site at Roffey (Straker 1931, 442). This cluster of sites, forming an arc from Horne in the east, through Burstow, Horley, Charlwood, Roffey and Crawley, forces the conclusion that this north Sussex/south Surrey border area was of real importance in the production of iron in the late medieval period, with marketing and distribution possibly centred on the town of Crawley, where a fair had been established in 1202. It may also be significant that Burstow was granted the right to hold a market and fair in 1246, so both could have served areas which may have extended to a radius of 5 or 6 miles, more distant fairs being at East Grinstead, Horsham, and Reigate (Gwynne 1990, 37).

There is also a tenuous link between iron ore digging in the Charlwood area in the 14th century and the 13th/14th century ironworking site at Alsted manor, on the North Downs ridge in the northern part of Merstham parish. Both were in the same primary manor of Merstham, although the tenants of the separate sub-manors of Alsted and Charlwood were different. Iron smelting and primary forging, together with other, non-ferrous, metalworking were being carried out in the mid-to-late 13th century at Alsted, with forging only carried on more than a century later, in a purpose-built building, after the abandonment of the manor house (Ketteringham 1976, 22–32). The evidence of the quantity of cinder suggests that iron smelting was both of short duration and of limited scale. It is possible that the single acquisition of a quantity of ore, probably from a Wealden source, might account for this, but that a direct link with ore from Charlwood is too tenuous to be supported. The ownership links that the de Passele family had with other ironworking areas of the Weald, notably the Parrock district of Hartfield parish, in Sussex, are the most plausible source of raw blooms which the 14th century forge at Alsted would use as a raw material (Ketteringham 1976, 66–7). The Parrock area has been specifically identified with ironworking during the same period (Tebbutt 1975, 146–51).

This, however, is not the only area in which ironworking is postulated in Surrey in the Middle Ages. Further to the west lies an enigmatic site. In the 1960s, the late Tony Clark carried out a brief excavation of what he interpreted as a water-powered iron-forging site in Coneyhurst Gill, Ewhurst (Clark 1961). Some slag – possibly bloomery slag – was also noted by the Wealden Iron Research Group, but opinions about the site are inconclusive, and it merits further investigation.(*Wealden Iron* 1975, **8**, 12; Judie English, pers comm). Forging slags are often indistinguishable from bloomery slags, the processes that produce them being very similar, and it is other features of the sites where they are found that are usually used to set them apart. Whatever the circumstances in which the site at Ewhurst was used, no known documentary evidence and precious little archaeological evidence means that the site remains a mystery. Less than 4 miles to the south-west, late 12th and early 13th century pottery has been found in association with bloomery slag in Great Wildwood and at Monkton-hook, both in Alfold (English 2002). With no others known in the area, these sites seem somewhat isolated. A connection may exist with the discovery of iron slag and pottery of a similar date at Loxwood in Sussex, less than 3 miles to the south (*Wealden Iron* 1998, 2 ser **18**, 4).

Water-powered iron smelting and forging in the Surrey Weald (fig 17.3)

Turning to the post-medieval period, iron production based on the newly imported technology of blast furnace and finery forge developed initially in the High Weald of eastern Sussex. Early growth was slow, but accelerated in the second half of the 16th century, and by 1574, when the Privy Council ordered a survey of all the ironworks in the region, some 50 furnaces and a more or less equal number of forges had been established (Straker 1931, 53–9). Expansion of the industry had been confined to Sussex until 1548, when a list of ironworks was attached to a complaint by the authorities of some of the Channel ports that ironworks were depriving them of timber (Cleere & Crossley 1995, 123). Within the next decade, however, the ironworks at Leigh, Cranleigh and Abinger had been established, with furnaces or forges at Dunsfold, Chiddingfold and near Lingfield by 1570 (Cleere & Crossley 1995, 309–67, 382–93). The limitations on the growth of the industry in Surrey in this period were largely geographical. Furnaces could only be built within a reasonable distance of adequate sources of ore, and these were confined to the outcrops of the Hastings Beds and the Weald Clay. Forges were not so restricted, but nevertheless needed to be within an economic carriage distance of one or more of the furnaces. For both types of sites, the principal factor determining location was the presence of a reliable supply of water. This presented problems on the low-lying relief of the Weald Clay in the

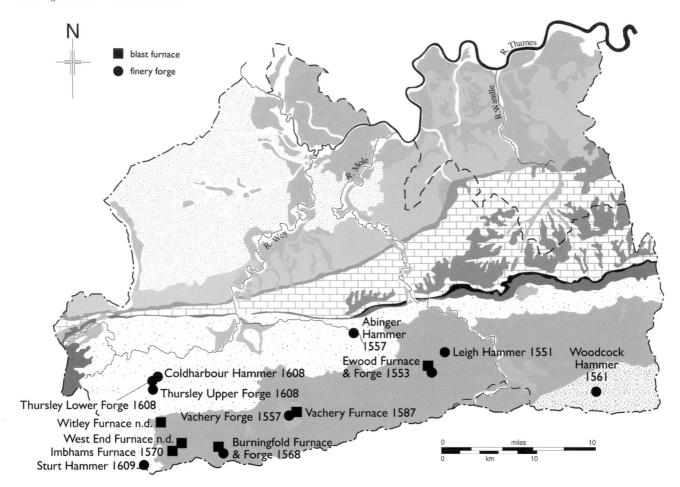

Fig 17.3 Blast furnaces and finery forges. For key to geological background see map on page x.

south-eastern part of the county, where Ewood furnace had what was probably the largest pond of any ironworks in the Weald; estimates being as high as 100 acres (Straker 1931, 454). A consequence of the lack of a need for forges to be located near sources of ore was the exploitation, mostly after the beginning of the 17th century, of the faster-flowing and more abundant streams of the Lower Greensand formation in the south-west of the county. In the area around Haslemere, the competing demands for charcoal by furnaces and forges could be eased by a distinct separation, with furnaces located on the clay where the ore outcropped, and forges located on the sandstone.

The Bray family were among the earliest to exploit the Walloon technology imported from France, with two forges, at Abinger and Cranleigh, in operation before 1557 (Cleere & Crossley 1995, 307, 361–2). It is not clear if these forges were set up to work up iron sows from a furnace also owned by the Brays, or from one already producing cast iron on the open market. Records of Vachery furnace, the most likely candidate, do not hint at when it was first blown in (Straker 1941). The enigmatic site in Coneyhurst Gill, Ewhurst, referred to above, might have been an early, failed attempt to set up a finery forge at this time. Further to the south-east, one of the other early sites, at Leigh, was set up by Richard Wheler and William

Hawthorne before 1554, when it passed into the hands of George and Christopher Darrell, who had acquired the nearby furnace at Ewood from the Nevilles the previous year (Giuseppi 1902, 30–2). The Darrell family also owned several sites around the Kent-Sussex border, and their business links with other ironmasters were widespread. While retaining the ownership of their Surrey works, they periodically sold leases to the two sites, taking them back in hand between times until they sold them to the Crown, leasing them back soon after. Another site, operated by someone with strong connections with other Wealden ironworking sites, was Burningfold. Here, the first recorded owner of the forge, Thomas Melershe of Wonersh, sold it to Thomas Blackwell of Petworth, who had a lease of the earl of Northumberland's furnace at Frith, near Northchapel, providing him with a further outlet for the iron he was producing there (Cleere & Crossley 1995, 321, 384). Many of the agreements that ironmasters made to acquire the control of ironworks were intended to secure the supply of raw materials, whether wood, ore or cast iron. Thomas Gratwick, who held Burningfold in 1574, was a kinsman of Roger Gratwick who had works in the Horsham and Crawley area, but his tenure was short-lived, the site coming into the hands of Thomas Smith. After Smith had died, Burningfold found its way into the hands of another old ironworking family, the Bowyers. Records of Burningfold are missing for the years until the Cowdray estate purchased it from the executors of John Tanner in 1781, with the only tantalizing reference being to the occupation of the site, in the 18th century, by William and George Jukes, London ironmongers, who also worked the ironworks at Robertsbridge, Sussex (Cleere & Crossley 1995, 384). Unfortunately, the precise details of their involvement are not known.

With the sites already mentioned, the initial building of the ironworks had largely been carried out by Surrey landowning families, who had quickly leased their works to established ironmasters, with strong connections with other sites in the Weald. The motive was undoubtedly seen as an investment, but the profitable operation of such enterprises was best left to those with experience, and it is noteworthy that foreign ironworkers were providing the skilled labour at several of the Surrey works in Tandridge and Reigate Hundreds as early as the 1550s (Awty 1984, 74–7). One of these was Woodcock Hammer, near Lingfield, which, unlike the group mentioned so far, was set up by ironmasters from further south on land owned by the Gages, whose seat was in the South Downs. The forge had a long working life, being operated for more than half the 17th century by the Thorpe family, and then by a succession of tenants, including Jeremiah Johnson of Charlwood, who appears to have operated Bewbush furnace near Crawley but whose career is otherwise sketchy (Cleere & Crossley 1995, 366, 392; StRO: DW/1788/P38/B6). As a finery, it ceased working in about the 1770s.

A recently rediscovered site is Sturt Hammer, at Haslemere (Cleere & Crossley 1995, 391–2). This may have been the site referred to as a 'blomarie', the illegal erection of which Edward Tanworth was charged with in 1603 (Giuseppi 1905, 271). The outcome is not known, but the earliest record of Sturt is of 1609, when it was referred to as Wheeler's Hammer. By the mid-17th century, the forge was in the tenancy of the Hoad family, but by the 1690s it was being referred to specifically as a sickle mill; the first instance in Surrey, and a rare example in the Weald, of an ironworks changing purpose from refining pig iron to specialized secondary iron processing. The name has stuck, although its working life as a sickle mill was short, for by 1712 it had become a corn mill, and in the 1730s it was converted to a paper mill. Subsequently, it has been a worsted braid factory, an engineering works and a council depot (Crocker & Kane 1990; 134; WBC: F30/032/AA). A similar change of use was to befall one of the forges at Thursley. The three forges, which formed the complex, are perhaps the least easily explained of all the Wealden iron sites in the county.

They were set up by the More family, of Loseley, who had already established ironworks in Sussex. The problem lies in the fact that there were three different forges, two in Thursley parish, and the other, known either as Coldharbour or Horsebane Hammer, on the border of Witley and Thursley. Confusion in identifying the several works from descriptions in surviving deeds has resulted in an incomplete operating history (Cleere & Crossley 1995, 360). Two at least appear to have shared the same tenants, although only the lower forge seems to have remained working by 1769, when it was operated by Owen Knight & Co, of whom more needs to be known (SHC: P46/1/1). The lower site was worked periodically in association with Abinger Hammer; in the early 18th century they were operated by a Mr Dibble, and later by James Goodyear, a Guildford ironmonger, who had also worked Pophole Hammer, near Haslemere (King 2002, 34). Unlike Sturt Hammer's transformation into a sickle mill, the conversion of fineries into other non-iron uses, such as corn mills and paper mills, and the lower forge at Thursley to a silk crape mill, was common. Woodcock Hammer, near Lingfield, was converted to use as a wire mill at the beginning of the 19th century (Evans 1985, 7). Wire making required a specialized type of iron, and although there is slight evidence of this specialization at Robertsbridge, Sussex, in the early 1700s, by the early 19th century the source of suitable iron would almost certainly have been London ironmongers (ESxRO: Microfilm XA3/13).

Another influence on the location of sites, and this is a theme which becomes increasingly resonant in Surrey, was the location of ironworks in relation to their markets. Again with Ewood, and its associated forge at Leigh, we have an example of the early influence of London. The Darrells, who took over the sites soon after they were built, were London merchants, and it cannot be insignificant that in legislation drawn up to restrict the demands for wood that the burgeoning iron industry was making, sufficient influence was brought to bear to have these sites, and the forge at Abinger, specifically excluded (1 Eliz c15; 23 Eliz c5). Regional centres such as Guildford, which were growing rapidly at this time, began to offer competition with London and, at Abinger Hammer, the London market was cited in a contemporary document as a determinant in the location of the forge, to the detriment of Guildford, although its role was to change more than once during its long working life (Giuseppi 1903, 270–1). Also, during the 17th century, the specialist branch of gun founding became increasingly important in the economy of the region, again with its principal market in London. Surrey's only positively documented gun foundry of the period was Imbhams furnace, near Chiddingfold (Cleere & Crossley 1995, 338–9). Tenancy of this site

240 JEREMY S HODGKINSON

involved the Yaldwin family, who also worked at least one of the Thursley works, and who were later occupiers of some of the Petworth estate works as well. In the 1660s the Browne family, of Horsmonden, in Kent, included Imbhams among their largely Kentish group of gun foundries, which suggests an early specialization of the furnace for which no direct evidence has come to light. The Brownes were to set themselves up as gentry in the county at Buckland near Reigate.

Notwithstanding the resilience of the gun founding industry, the decline of primary iron smelting in the Weald caused the abandonment of most of the Surrey blast furnaces before the end of the 17th century. Only the furnace at Burningfold is likely to have continued in blast into the 1700s. However, while Swedish imports saw the demise of local pig iron production, the need for iron goods grew. The increased specialization of metalworking trades, such as the production of utensils for the processing trades, and domestic ironmongery such as pumps and stoves, saw a need for higher quality iron by craftsmen, beyond the skills of local blacksmiths. Such a requirement may be demonstrated by the growing importance of ironmongers in towns such as Guildford. An example, already noted, is James Goodyear, who acquired the lease of several forges,

including Abinger Hammer, where he may have experimented with steel making, taking out a patent in 1771 (Hodgkinson 1996). He probably overextended himself by taking the lease of North Park furnace, south of Haslemere, for he was declared bankrupt in 1777.

Surrey iron mills in the Thames basin
(fig 17.4)

The interest of the London mercantile community in the potential of Surrey mills as manufactories of commodities for the capital's domestic market is shown in the establishment of several mills on the Thames tributaries from the 17th century onwards. The earliest example is the iron wireworks established by Thomas Steere at Chilworth in 1603 (Crocker 1999, 8). The project survived only three years before the Mineral and Battery Works, which had been granted a monopoly in mining and sheet metalworking in 1568, successfully sued against the works in the Court of Exchequer. Most of the iron mills were set up closer to the Thames, and the location and working history of many of these sites has been documented by Potter (1982), and only summary information is given here. Many of these mills were established for other uses than the processing of iron, and only in the early 18th century

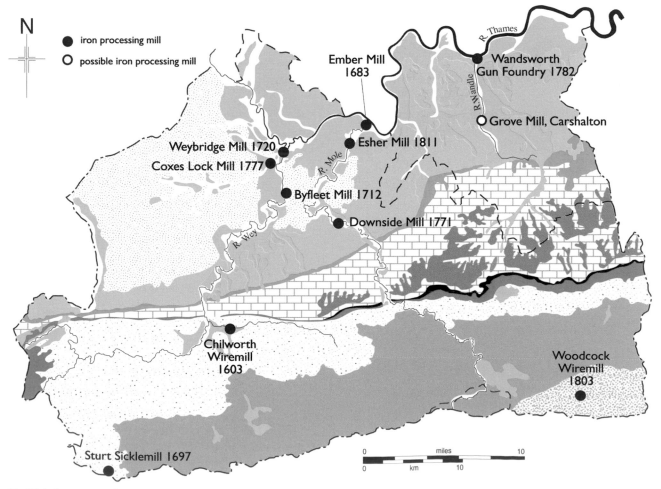

Fig 17.4 Iron processing mills. For key to geological background see map on page x.

was Byfleet Mill converted by Thomas Wethered for use as a hoop and wire mill, using iron, copper and brass. Like Thomas Steere's concern, and the subsequent uses of the Sturt and Woodcock forges, this was the secondary processing of metals. By the 1770s, the mill, which had remained the freehold of the Crown, was tenanted by John Berdoe, who also operated a mill in Crayford, Kent, on another Thames tributary. Weybridge Mill's history, which is not as long as that of Byfleet, owes its origin to the completion of the Wey Navigation in 1653. As with Byfleet, it started off as a paper mill, but in the 1720s, John Hitchcock, who had been active at Byfleet, acquired the lease and converted the mill for iron and brass working. Later lessees continued in the same vein, including the firm of Jukes Coulson, of Thames Street, London, who had also been at Byfleet. It has been suggested that Weybridge Mill was engaged in iron smelting, that is to say primary iron production – using ore derived from the same Bracklesham Beds that may have supplied the 6th century BC iron makers at Brooklands – but there is no evidence to support this. Forge slags are common at these sites, although the occurrence of what appears to be tap slag at Downside Mill, Cobham, suggests the possibility of more than mere forging (Potter 1982, 218). It is likely that most of the raw materials for these mills were derived from London iron merchants, importing from Sweden, although, in the late 17th century, some may have been supplied by Wealden furnaces.

Both Thomas Wethered and John Hitchcock, who had been at Byfleet, were involved in the same line of business at Esher Mill, and at Ember Mill, Molesey, which had begun as a brass wire mill in the 1630s. For a while in the 1770s Ember Mill became a corn mill, but in the 1790s its tenancy came into the hands of Alexander Raby, who was already manufacturing iron and brass wares at Downside Mill, Cobham, and Coxes Lock Mill, Addlestone (Potter 2000, 11–13). Raby's father, a London ironmonger, had operated a gun-founding furnace in Sussex in the 1760s, in conjunction with Woodcock Hammer, and when he had died Alexander had decided not to pursue his father's ordnance business, which had already been overtaken by coke-fuelled furnaces in the north (Hodgkinson 2000, 3–7). In fact, Raby purchased the lease of the mill at Cobham shortly before his father died in 1771 (Taylor 2000, 15). Raby gave up his Surrey mills in about 1807, and moved his operations to South Wales.

The variety of ironwares produced at these mills was not consistent, and included hoops and wire, as well as domestic items such as pots and pans for which copper plating would be needed (which explains the presence of a copper foundry at Raby's Downside Mill at Cobham). An interesting feature of these mills is that their locations made them attractive to a wide variety of uses, and those uses changed as economic conditions and demand altered, the necessary adaptations being made to the machinery and waterways. By the end of the first quarter of the 19th century, many of the mills on the Wey and Mole had reverted to the processing of agricultural produce.

In addition to the Mole and Wey, a large variety of mills existed on the Wandle, one of the most heavily industrialized rivers in southern England (Hobson 1924). Although most of the mills along its length were devoted to other purposes also geared towards the London market, such as paper, snuff, leather, oil and gunpowder, one at least was used for the production of metalwork. At James Henckell & Co's mills at Wandsworth, some or all of the processes of iron ordnance founding were carried on during and after the Napoleonic period. Henckell's first attempt, in 1782, failed in bankruptcy two years later, but with the financial help of his brothers-in-law, he was able to repay his creditors and start again in 1790. He achieved some success in supplying the Board of Ordnance with naval armaments, and examples of his work are to be found on HMS *Victory*. Although the company survived as ironmongers in the city of London until the 1860s, the Wandsworth mills had been turned over to paper production in the 1830s (Brown forthcoming). Briefly, Henckell also had a copper mill in Wandsworth. It has been suggested that gun boring took place at Grove Mill, Carshalton during the Napoleonic period, but there is no firm evidence. Gun founding had been the mainstay of the Wealden iron industry in its final phase, but like the iron mills on the Mole and Wey, the source of the iron for Henckell's guns was not indigenous, and it is an indication of the route industrialization was taking that both his principal competitors, Walker & Co of Rotherham and Alexander Brodie in Shropshire, had works which were more conveniently located near to sources of both fuel and ore rather than to their potential markets (Kennard 1986, 50, 150).

While not unique to Surrey, it was because of the county's juxtaposition with the capital that the proliferation of specialist water-powered metalworking mills came into existence. The influence of London on Surrey was greatest along its Thames river frontage in Southwark. Since Roman times the southern shore had attracted craft working, because it was accessible from the river, and because the pollution caused by such operations was sufficiently removed from residential areas. These factors remained unchanged and by the 18th century Southwark was a principal market for the produce of the South East. Not least of the products handled by the Southwark merchants was iron. Many of the Wealden furnaces were leased by merchants who had yards by one or other of the borough's wharves.

William Harrison at Morgan's Lane (GLL: Ms 6482a) and William Bowen at Marigold Stairs (SLHL: Ms 8287) respectively managed nearly half of the Weald's gun foundries in the 1740s. Others, like Edward Raby and Wright & Prickett (SLHL: Ms 3734), followed in their wake, and their successors, such as Alexander Raby, were key players in operating some of the mills along the Wey and Mole that I have just described. The rebuilding of London Bridge in 1831 further increased the importance of Southwark allowing direct access upstream from the sea, which had been inhibited before, and permitting the movement of goods, from the heart of London as well as from tributaries of the Thames such as the Wey, Mole and Wandle, through to the new docks which were being developed downstream in the same period.

Conclusions and research objectives

At no time in its history has Surrey been possessed of an iron industry. Evidence available at the time of writing points to the exploitation of limited local resources that has given rise to brief bursts of production in the early and late Iron Age, but these may not have been sustained beyond a few decades at most in each instance. Although there is very limited evidence for ironworking in the early Middle Ages, production does not seem to have developed in the district around Horley until the 14th century, when it formed part of a larger area that extended into northern Sussex and south-west Kent. This activity may be regarded as a precursor to the main expansion of iron production based on water power which promoted the Weald to national significance in the 16th and 17th centuries. Surrey was on the periphery of this region, but the position of the county in relation to London, and the increasing importance of the capital, influenced the re-use of these ironworks when a general decline in the region set in. The establishment of iron processing mills on the navigable reaches of the Thames tributaries represents an intensification of the capital as the dominant market in the South East, but also stands as perhaps the last stage in the viability of capital-intensive single units of production, before steam-dominated, full industrialization took over.

It is fair to state, I believe, that in every period the story of iron production in Surrey is under-documented (or perhaps under-published). In a few instances, intensive investigation, as at Brooklands, has presented a more complete picture, but as is so often the case with the history of a region, it is the detailed study of its parts which is important. Of these, two periods stand out – the Iron Age of the Bagshot, Weybridge and Egham areas, and the late medieval of the Horley area – and they, above all, deserve particular attention in the future.

The sites at Brooklands and at Thorpe Lea are not representative of a body of evidence of ironworking in their respective areas and periods. Each is the sole example, to date. For this reason, it is important that evidence of other sites contemporary with those should be looked for, and this can only be accomplished by systematic fieldwalking and examination of field names. The built-up nature of the areas where these sites have been found presents problems, but local archaeologists need to be alerted to the sort of evidence that can be found in gardens as well as on land subject to building development. Similar efforts need to be made in the Bagshot area, where the results of fieldwalking have been reported, but where a more rigorous programme needs to be introduced. The identification of sites by fieldwalking is often enough to draw conclusions about their distribution, without the need for invasive archaeology.

The data about iron making in south-east England in the Saxon period is very scarce, and it is not possible to speculate as to whether this is because sites have not been found, or because they did not exist in the region. The excavation of settlement and other sites of the period will require careful monitoring to identify any traces of ferrous metalworking at all.

The results that can be derived from fieldwalking have already been seen in the discoveries relating to ironworking in the medieval period in south-east Surrey. In this case the efforts of an individual need support, and testing through trial excavation. The specific dating of sites, and the identification of the relevant contemporary landowners and occupiers, may help to establish the manorial or other contexts in which iron production was being carried out. In the post-medieval period, iron making was organized in individual units of production, where details of ownership, occupancy, supply and output are sometimes available. Case studies of such units are an essential element in piecing together our understanding of the industry in general. The detail of family and business relationships often offers clues to wider issues affecting the management of groups of works. Accounts of the supply of raw materials can illuminate our understanding of the economy of an area. For this reason, research into the individual operating histories of sites, and the filling of gaps in incomplete records, is useful if broader views are to be gained. The early gunfounding activities at Imbhams furnace, the disentangling of the operation of the Thursley hammers, and the purpose of the water-powered site at Coneyhurst Gill, Ewhurst, are examples. In addition, two blast furnace sites in the county – in Park Wood, near the hamlet of Brook in Witley parish, and another, close to Frillinghurst Farm, south-west of Chiddingfold – have no documented history at the time of writing.

The changing nature of the markets for the iron industry in the post-medieval period is a field ripe for further study, particularly in Surrey where the marginal nature of the industry must have been more susceptible to economic fluctuations than in the core areas of the Weald. Some of this change is reflected in specialization, such as the refocusing of Sturt Hammer, Haslemere, or the development of Woodcock Hammer, near Lingfield. The decline in the viability of forges in the latter half of the 17th century, through the increasing dominance of imported Swedish bar iron in the foundries of London and the other major east coast towns, resulted in even more radical change in the use of some iron mills. Local ironmongers like Goodyear, and some of his contemporaries in Sussex, whose activities represent a cross-over between primary production and the local wholesaling of iron, beg further investigation.

BIBLIOGRAPHY

Manuscript sources

ESxRO: East Sussex Record Office
    Microfilm XA3/13: Accounts of Robertsbridge Ironworks & Beech furnace 1726–33
GLL: Guildhall Library, London
    Ms 6482a: Assignment of lease 1750: Samuel Remnant & John Legas to Andrews & John Harrison
SHC: Surrey History Centre, Woking
    P46/1/1: Thursley parish overseers of the poor: rates and accounts 1769
SLHL: Southwark Local History Library
    Ms 8287: Lease 1722: Edward Edwards Charity to William Bowen
    Ms 3734: St Saviour's Parish, Southwark, poor rate book 1761 and 1766
StRO: Staffordshire Record Office
    DW/1788, Parcel 38, Bundle 6, Lease 1654: Thomas Middleton to Bray Chowne
WBC: Waverley Borough Council
    F30/032/AA; Sale particulars, 1911; Lease 1925 Avamore Engineering Co to Haslemere UDC

Published works

Awty, B G, 1984   Aliens in the ironworking areas of the Weald: the subsidy rolls 1524–1603, *Wealden Iron*, 2 ser, **4**, 13–78
Brown, R R, forthcoming   *British gunfounders and their marks*, Royal Armouries
Clark, A J, 1961   Note on Coneyhurst forge, SyAS Annual Report, 6–7
Cleere, H F & Crossley, D W, 1995   *The iron industry of the Weald*, 2 edn, Cardiff
Cole, G H, 1991   *Reading the earth at Lightwater*
Cooke, N, 2001   Excavations on a late-medieval iron-working site at London Road, Crawley, West Sussex, 1997   *Sussex Archaeol Collect*, **139**, 147–67
Corney, M C, & Gaffney, V, 1985   *Excavations at Wickham Bushes, Easthampstead, Berks 1985*, interim report (unpublished)
Crocker, A, & Kane, M M, 1990   *The diaries of James Simmons, papermaker of Haslemere, 1831–1868*, Oxshott, Tabard Press
Crocker, G, 1999   Seventeenth-century wireworks in Surrey and the case of Thomas Steere, *Surrey Hist*, **6.1**, 2–16
—— (ed), 2000   *Alexander Raby, ironmaster: proceedings of a conference held at Cobham on 28 November 1998*, Surrey Industrial History Group
Dallaway, J, & Cartwright, E, 1815   *A history of the western division of the county of Sussex*, vol 1
English, J, 2002   Two possible medieval bloomery sites in Alfold, Surrey, *Wealden Iron*, 2 ser, **22**, 5–9
Evans, T E, 1985   The mystery of the Company of Tin Plate Workers, *Surrey Ind Hist Grp Newsl*, **27**, 6–7
Giuseppi, M S, 1902   The manor of Ewood and the ironworks there in 1575, *SyAC*, **17**, 28–40

——, 1903   Rake in Witley, with some notices of its former owners and the ironworks on Witley and Thursley Heaths, *SyAC*, **18**, 11–60
——, 1905   Industries, in *VCH*, **2**, 243–424
Goodchild, R G, 1937   The Roman brickworks at Wykehurst Farm in the parish of Cranleigh. With a note on a tile kiln at Horton, Epsom, *SyAC*, **45**, 74–96
——, 1938   A priest's sceptre from the Romano-Celtic temple at Farley Heath, Surrey, *Antiq J*, **18**, 391–6
Gwynne, P, 1990   *A history of Crawley*
Hanworth, R, & Tomalin, D J, 1977   Brooklands, Weybridge: the excavation of an Iron Age and medieval site 1964–5 and 1970–1, SyAS Res Vol, **4**
Hart, E, & Winbolt, S E, 1937   Thundersfield Castle, Horley; a mediaeval bloomery, *SyAC*, **45**, 147–50
Hastings, F A, 1965   Excavation of an Iron Age farmstead at Hawk's Hill, Leatherhead, *SyAC*, **62**, 1–43
Hobson, J M, 1924   *Book of the Wandle: the story of a Surrey river*
Hodgkinson, J S, 1996   A Wealden steel-making patent, *Wealden Iron*, 2 ser, **16**, 9–12
——, 1999   Romano-British iron production in the Sussex and Kent Weald: a review of current data, *Hist Metall*, **33.2**, 68–72
——, 2000   The Raby background: the Midlands, London and the Weald, in Crocker 2000, 1–8
Kennard, A N, 1986   *Gunfounding & gunfounders*
Ketteringham, L L, 1976   *Alsted: excavation of a thirteenth–fourteenth century sub-manor house with its ironworks in Netherne Wood, Merstham, Surrey*, SyAS Res Vol, **2**
King, P W, 2002   Bar iron production in the Weald in the early 18th century, *Wealden Iron*, 2 ser, **22**, 26–35
Lowther, A W G, 1949   Excavations at 'Purberry Shot', Ewell, Surrey, *SyAC*, **50**, 9–46
Manning, O, & Bray, W, 1804–14   *The history and antiquities of the county of Surrey*, 3 vols
Potter, J F, 1977   Geological observations on the use of iron and clay at Brooklands Iron Age site, in Hanworth & Tomalin 1977, 22–3
——, 1982   Iron working in the vicinity of Weybridge, Surrey, *Ind Archaeol Rev*, **6.3**, 211–23
——, 2000   Iron working in northern Surrey, in Crocker 2000, 9–14
Prest, J M, & Parrish, E J, 1950   Investigation on Walton Heath and Banstead Common, *SyAC*, **51**, 57–64
Straker, E, 1931   *Wealden iron*
——, 1941   The Vachery ironworks, *SyAC*, **47**, 48–51
SyAS, 1949   Surrey Archaeological Society, Report of the Council 1948, in *SyAC*, **50**, xxiv
Taylor, D, 2000   Alexander Raby at Cobham, in Crocker 2000, 15–21
Tebbutt, C F, 1975   An abandoned medieval industrial site at Parrock, Hartfield, *Sussex Archaeol Collect*, **113**, 146–51

Tylecote, R F, 1986   *The prehistory of metallurgy in the British Isles*

VCH: The Victoria history of the County of Surrey (ed H E Malden), 1902–12, 4 vols

Watson, B, 1998   *Roman London: recent archaeological work including papers given at a seminar held at the Museum of London on 16 November 1996*, J Roman Archaeol Supplement **24**

Wealden Iron: Wealden Iron, Bulletin of the Wealden Iron Research Group

Westman, A, 1998   Publishing Roman Southwark: new evidence from the archive, in Watson 1998, 61–6

Winbolt, S E, 1932   Excavations at Hascombe Camp, Godalming, June–July 1931, *SyAC*, **40,** 78–96

Winbolt, S E, & Margary, I D 1933   Dry Hill Camp, Lingfield, *SyAC*, **41,** 79–92

Worssam, B C, 1995   The geology of Wealden iron, in Cleere & Crossley 1995, 1–30

Worssam, B C, & Herbert, B K, 2000   Two bloomeries near Bletchingley, Surrey, *Wealden Iron*, 2 ser, **20,** 14–22

J S Hodgkinson, MA, 3, Saxon Road, Worth, Crawley, Sussex, RH10 7SA

18

Second World War defences in Surrey

CHRIS SHEPHEARD and ALAN CROCKER

The key events which have resulted, during the past twenty years, in historians and archaeologists recording and interpreting defensive and related military structures which were erected in Britain during the Second World War, are summarized. Locally, the Surrey Defences Survey played a significant role. Three aspects of the research carried out by volunteers working on this survey are discussed. The first of these is the recording of pillboxes and anti-tank ditches, particularly those associated with the GHQ Line which was constructed across the county from Farnham, through Shalford, Dorking and Horley, to Lingfield. Then the defences of two towns, Dorking and Guildford, which were selected by the Home Defence Executive as nodal points, are considered. Finally a massive wall on Hankley Common near Farnham, which is a replica of a section of the German Atlantic Wall and was built to test assault equipment, is described. In 2001, English Heritage selected the defences near Waverley Abbey to receive the first in-depth survey of such structures to be carried out. The aim was to establish national criteria for statutory protection of Second World War fortifications. However, far more remains to be done and in many cases the need is urgent.

Introduction

It was not until the BBC TV *Chronicle* award for archaeology was won in 1985 by Henry Wills for his ground-breaking study of surviving Second World War defence works that their importance and the comparative dearth of information about them came to be appreciated. Wills also wrote a book entitled *Pillboxes – a study of UK defences 1940* (Wills 1985). This was reviewed (Haveron 1987) in the newsletter of the Surrey Industrial History Group (SIHG) which prompted the Group to launch its Surrey Defences Survey. This in turn led SIHG to host, at the University of Surrey in November 1991, one of the first national conferences on the subject.

Then, in 1995, the situation changed dramatically. That year marked the golden jubilee of the Council for British Archaeology (CBA) and the project chosen to mark the anniversary was the surveying, within five years, of all the Second World War defence sites in the country – the Defence of Britain project (Lowry 1996). This had the immediate effect of recruiting a large number of new surveyors and, although the task was not completed in the allotted time, much was achieved both in the field and in archival research. The project came to an end in March 2002 when the accumulated information was deposited with English Heritage and the Scottish and Welsh Royal Commissions. It was made available on the World Wide Web (DoB 2002) and a summary was published (Denison 2002). Nearly 20,000 individual sites had been recorded, of which about 70% were anti-invasion defence sites, including nearly 8000 pillboxes, and the remainder were classified as other types of military site. These included, for example, army camps, prisoner of war camps, air-raid shelters, anti-aircraft batteries, firing ranges, Royal Observer Corps sites, radar stations, searchlight batteries and military hospitals. In Surrey about 95% of the sites are anti-invasion and of these approaching 80% are pillboxes.

In the meantime English Heritage had organized a seminar on Monuments of War in 1997 (EH 1998) and has since published a booklet summarizing its work on 20th century military sites (EH 2000). Then, as a result of the CBA project, they decided to undertake specific surveys of sites of particular importance. These would become candidates for statutory protection, a status which had not previously been granted to remains of Second World War defences. The first site to receive an in-depth survey was the area around the ruins of Waverley Abbey, near Farnham, which was visited during the field trip associated with the 1991 SIHG conference. The defence works there include particularly well-preserved examples of pillboxes and other structures and consultations are now under way as to the best form that their protection and interpretation can take. It is encouraging that a site in Surrey is the prototype for such an important scheme.

The Surrey Defences Survey

When it was founded in 1988, the Surrey Defences Survey was carried out by a small group of voluntary surveyors and soon the enormity of the task being undertaken came to be appreciated. The county was divided into 10km national grid squares and outline site lists, based on the Wills book, were issued as guidance for the surveyors. It should be noted however that Henry Wills had gathered his data mainly through letters published in the columns of local newspapers, appealing to readers for information based on their knowledge and memories. It was soon realized that this information was far from complete and more and more sites were being reported. For example, Wills lists 81 sites in the Farnham square

(SU84) whereas 115 were known by March 2002, the end of the Defence of Britain project. Of the total of nearly 20,000 individual sites recorded nationally by that time (Denison 2002, 9) around 2,000 are in Surrey (DoB 2002).

At first the Surrey results were entered on simple forms and sent to the Surrey Sites and Monuments Record (SMR) at County Hall, either marked on maps or as simple lists of sites. Nationally at this time there were many individual surveyors at work, all with their different recording methods. The Fortress Study Group was involved but its recording system was more appropriate for larger, earlier fortifications. However, a national Pillbox Study Group was established and, mainly through its publication *Loopholes*, provided a lead to standardized recording and helped solve many mysteries by reporting results from different parts of the country (*Loopholes* 1992). Then, in 1993, the Association for Industrial Archaeology launched its Index Record of Industrial Sites (IRIS) scheme (Trueman & Williams 1993) and since then, each site in Surrey has been recorded on one of its standard forms. These have been forwarded to the SMR and thence to English Heritage.

The sites recorded include pillboxes, many of which lie along a linear defensive fortification known as the GHQ (General Headquarters) Line, anti-tank defences including dry and wet ditches and other fixed and movable obstacles, rifle, spigot-mortar, machine-gun and other gun emplacements, and barbed-wire fences. Many of these were associated with towns known as nodal points, including Dorking and Guildford. Also Surrey has a very unusual replica of part of Hitler's Atlantic Wall, which was used for testing assault equipment. The following sections of this paper provide details of some aspects of these features. Other Second World War military sites are mentioned briefly in the Discussion section.

Pillboxes and the GHQ Line

By May 1940 the threat of invasion by German forces was very real, brought into focus by the evacuation of the British Expeditionary Force via Dunkirk. Therefore, the Home Defence Executive was set up under General Sir Edmund Ironside, Commander-in-Chief of the Home Forces (Mackenzie 1995; Alexander 1999). London and the Midlands were to be protected by the GHQ Line and a succession of stop-lines between this and the coast. By the end of June plans were passed for the construction of thousands of concrete pillboxes and anti-tank blocks along beaches and at nodal points. In Southern Command the GHQ Line was about 400km long and stretched from Somerset to the Medway. It followed, where possible, features of the landscape which could easily be defended to create a continuous anti-tank obstacle and, on average, had pillboxes for rifle, machine-gun and anti-tank fire spaced at about 500m intervals. Figure 18.1 shows the route of the GHQ Line in Surrey. It entered the county from Hampshire at Farnham and then followed the Wey to Shalford, the Tillingbourne to Wotton, the Pippbrook to Dorking, the Mole to Horley and headwaters of the Eden to Lingfield, from where it entered Kent. Figure 18.1 also shows the locations of other places mentioned in the text.

Pillboxes were designed by a branch of the directorate of Fortifications and Works at the War Office (Wills 1985, 15). The main considerations were the weapons to be used and protection from enemy fire, but standardization was introduced as much as possible. Drawings of the designs were issued to army commands who modified them, to meet local requirements and materials available, and then issued them to contractors. As a result many different variants of pillboxes were constructed. The plan, for example, could be square, rectangular, polygonal (particularly hexagonal or octagonal), circular or designed for the site, and all types are present in

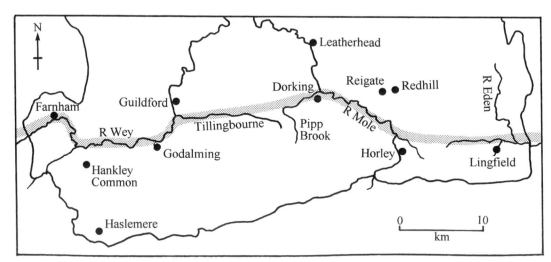

Fig 18.1   Sketch map of the southern half of Surrey showing (shaded) the route of the GHQ Line and the location of Nodal Points and other places mentioned in the text.

Surrey, although polygonal ones predominate. The materials used for construction could be concrete or a mixture of brick, stone, breeze blocks and concrete. Most in Surrey are a mixture of brick and concrete but there are also a large number made of concrete, some of which are prefabricated. The construction firm, John Mowlem & Co Ltd were the contractors for about twenty pillboxes between Farncombe and Albury and in 1990 one of their former employees, the late Fred Bowman of Shalford, recorded details of the work he carried out (Collyer & Rose 1999, 42–6). The procedure was to put down a concrete base and press vertical half-inch steel bars into it when it was still wet. On the next day the remaining steel parts were fixed and then steel shuttering for the walls and the loopholes (firing holes) erected. Concrete was poured into the shuttering to form the reinforced walls and then the roof beams were put in place. These had steel reinforcement bars exposed at the top, which were covered when concrete about 0.4m thick was poured over them.

The use of pillboxes depended upon them being unrecognized by the enemy until they were within effective range of the weapons being used. Many of them were therefore camouflaged. For example, one on the A25 near Silent Pool, Albury, was made to look like a petrol station and had real petrol pumps (Collier & Rose 1999, 42). Another at Elstead Mill, shown in figure 18.2, was disguised as a summer-house (Shepheard 1989).

Nodal points

A nodal point in the Second World War was defined (DoB 2002) as a defended town or village 'situated at a tactically important centre of communications which it is intended to deny to the enemy until our counter-attack can develop' and which 'may also serve as a pivot for the manoeuvre of reserves'. There were two categories of these nodal points. Type A might become isolated and have to hold out for six days before relief. Type B might have to hold out for three days. Co-ordination of military and civil plans was to be ensured by the creation of a 'triumvirate' consisting of the local military commander, the senior police officer or his representative and a civil officer, who might be the mayor or the chairman of the council. In Surrey there were category A nodal points, administered from Chatham garrison, at Dorking, Guildford and Redhill, and category B at Betchworth, Byfleet, Cranleigh, Egham, Godalming, Godstone, Haslemere, Horley, Leatherhead, Limps-field, Newchapel and Shere.

A Home Guard outline plan of the defences of Dorking is held by Dorking Museum and a redrawn detail of this is shown in figure 18.3. The nodal point HQ was located at the Dorking Urban District Council headquarters at Pippbrook, near the centre of the figure (Knight 1989). It is shown heavily defended, with a linear fixed anti-tank obstacle on the north and east sides, four movable anti-tank obstacles on approach roads and five rifle

Fig 18.2 Photograph, taken in 1989, of an hexagonal pillbox on the GHQ line alongside the river Wey at Elstead Mill. It has rifle loopholes and the remains of camouflage which made it appear to be a summer-house. Photograph by Chris Shepheard

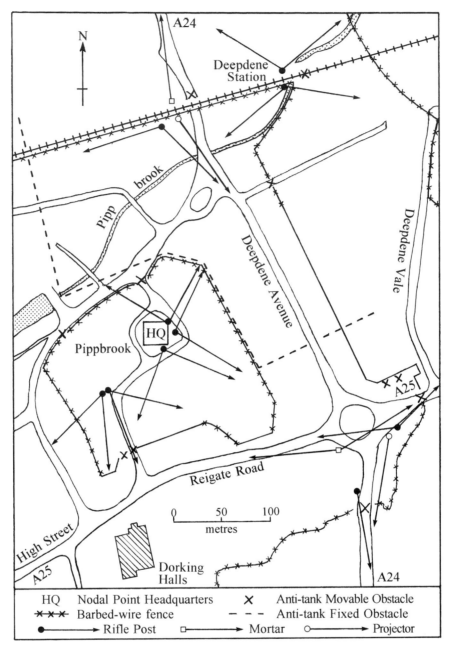

Fig 18.3 Redrawn detail of a plan of the proposed defences around the Type A Nodal point of Dorking during the Second World War. The headquarters, located at Pippbrook, Deepdene railway station and the junction of the A24 and A25 roads are all well-defended.

points at key positions. The site was also surrounded by barbed-wire fencing, except for small sections where presumably there were other barriers. At the east end of the town, the junction of the north–south A24 and the east–west A25 roads is shown protected by movable anti-tank obstacles, a barbed-wire fence, two rifle posts, a mortar post and a projector post. Again, to the north, Deepdene station and the adjacent railway bridge over the A24 are shown heavily defended. In particular there is a movable anti-tank obstacle across the railway track. At the north-east corner of figure 18.3 is shown a small section of a barbed-wire fence which surrounded most of the town. Within this, to the south of Pippbrook but outside the area shown, was Deepdene House, which was the wartime head-quarters of the Southern Railway, with radio communication controlling the southern network as far as Exeter. This had four movable anti-tank obstacles and barbed-wire fencing but no arma-

ments are indicated. A major part of the town, from the vicarage in the west to the A24 in the east and from the railway in the north to Rose Hill in the south, was divided into eight separately protected sectors and it appears that all the roads surrounding this area were either blocked or protected by movable anti-tank obstacles. In all, 28 of these obstacles are shown, eleven of which are present on figure 18.3. An example of an anti-tank obstacle being tested at an unknown location in Surrey is shown in figure 18.4.

The defences of Stoke Park, Guildford (Collyer & Rose 1999, 45) are shown on the redrawn plan of figure 18.5. They were to be manned by members of the Home Guard from the Dennis motor vehicles factory, which had more than doubled its workforce to about 3000 and was manufacturing trucks, tanks, trailer fire-pumps, bombs and small parts for aircraft (Collyer & Rose 1999, 120). The defences were located on either side of the Guildford and

Fig 18.4   An anti-tank obstacle, consisting of concrete blocks and steel girders, being tested somewhere in Surrey. Courtesy of The National Archives   (PRO: WO 179/15)

Godalming by-pass road, which had been opened in 1934 (Clark 1999, 49). It appears that they were aimed at protecting Stoke Park mansion house from attack from the east. Part of the house, which was demolished in 1977 (Clark 1999, 49), is shown heavily shaded at the left of the figure. The linear defences consisted of wet and dry ditches, barbed-wire fences and road blocks. A photograph of a ditch, but at Farnham and not Guildford, is shown in figure 18.6. The weapons indicated in figure 18.5 include four spigot-mortars or Blacker bombards, which could be used against either tanks or personnel, depending on the type of mortar bomb adopted. The spigot was a steel rod which fitted snugly within the tail of the bomb and acted as a launching guide. These weapons were designed originally to be fired from a base with four metal legs but later they were mounted on a fixed concrete pedestal within a pit. The maximum range was about 400m (Collyer & Rose 1999, 181). There were also three Northovers or Northover projectors which looked like sections of drain pipes on legs. They had a smooth-bore barrel 46 inches long, weighed 74lb and fired self-igniting phosphorous grenades. There were also two pits for BMGs or Bren machine guns, one for a BAR or Boys anti-tank rifle (Wills 1985, 15; Mackenzie 1995) and over twenty rifle pits. It is striking that most of the weapons were located in wooded areas.

Unfortunately little information is available at present on the third category A nodal point at Red-hill or on the twelve category B nodal points listed above.

The sea wall on Hankley Common near Farnham

The Second World War has left other types of physical remains in Surrey, especially because there was such a large number of troops billeted in the county just prior to D-Day (Ogley 1995). Of particular interest is a reinforced concrete wall, approximately 100m long, 3m high and 3.5m wide, near the Lion's Mouth (SU 883 413) on Hankley Common between Elstead and Tilford (Wood 1988, Shepheard 2002). This is a replica of part of the very long defensive Atlantic Wall built by the Germans along the coast of France and Belgium. The replica was built by Canadian troops, who were stationed nearby, and was used to test assault equipment on obstacles thought likely to be found during a landing in Europe. In order to make it as realistic as possible, raiding parties were sent across the Channel to measure accurately the German wall and bring back samples of the concrete to ensure that the training version was as realistic as possible. In the centre of the wall was a gap, 6m wide, closed by a three-section heavy steel girder gate running on rollers. At the ends and behind the wall were several types of tank traps, including pimples or 'dragon's teeth', lengths of railway track set in concrete and barbed-wire entanglements. A reconstruction sketch of the wall is given in figure 18.7.

Most of the obstacles were to be attacked with rockets hauling lengths of explosive-filled tube, known as 'Bangalore Torpedoes', and 'carpet laying devices' for the barbed wire. However, during the summer of 1943, a Churchill Mk II tank from the Fighting Vehicles Proving Establishment at Chertsey

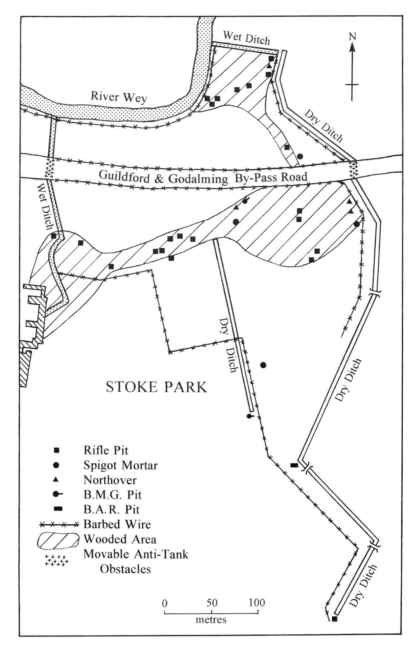

Fig 18.5 Plan of Second World War defences in Stoke Park, Guildford, on either side of the Guildford and Godalming by-pass road, which was opened in 1934. There are 22 rifle pits, four spigot mortars, four Northover projectors, two Bren machine gun pits, one Boys anti-tank rifle pit, about 2km of barbed wire fencing, nearly 1km of dry ditch and about 300m of wet ditch.

was sent to Elstead to attack the wall itself and the steel gates. The tank was equipped with a device called 'The Onion' or 'Double Onion' which was a steel frame measuring about 3m wide by 2m high, fitted vertically at the front and mounted on arms attached to the sides (fig 18.8). On this framework were hung boxes containing some 450kg of explosive. The tank was driven towards the wall and, on arrival, the framework was lowered to the ground against the obstruction. The vehicle was then backed off to a distance of some 30m, paying out an electric detonating cable as it went. The explosives were then detonated by the driver and the result can still be seen in the remains of the wall. Two breaches about 3.5m in width were created. There are also many marks made by shells spalling off concrete and snapping and twisting the reinforcement near to the surface (fig 18.9). Otherwise, the wall is very much as it was built, even though several generations of troops have been active in the area, which has provided a site for mili-

tary training since the inter-war period. A similar but smaller example of an inland section of the 'Atlantic Wall' exists on the Sherrifmuir battlefield in Stirlingshire (NN 838 037), and this was also used in demolition tests (Shepheard 2003).

Discussion

The present paper has discussed only a few examples of the many Second World War Defence complexes in Surrey. Two of these, pillboxes and nodal points, come under the category of anti-invasion defence sites and the third, the sea wall, is an example of one of the other types of military site. Many other cases could have been included such as airfields, of which twelve were active in Surrey: Brooklands, Croydon, Dunsfold, Fairoaks, Egham, Gatwick, Horne, Hurst Park, Kenley, Lingfield, Redhill, Stoke d'Abernon and Wisley (Masefield 1993, 32; Pilkington 1997). A survey has also been carried out of the remains of the large Canadian-built Tweedsmuir Camp at Thursley

Fig 18.6   Patrolling a dry anti-tank ditch (containing some rain-water) behind Barfield School, Runfold, Farnham (SU 868 472). This is an example of a 'one-way' ditch with one vertical and one sloping side. The recommended dimensions were 15ft (4.6m) wide at the top, 6½ft (2m) wide at the bottom and 5ft (1.5m) deep (Wills 1985, 40), which appear to have been well-adhered to in this case.   Photograph courtesy of the Imperial War Museum, London (H2473)

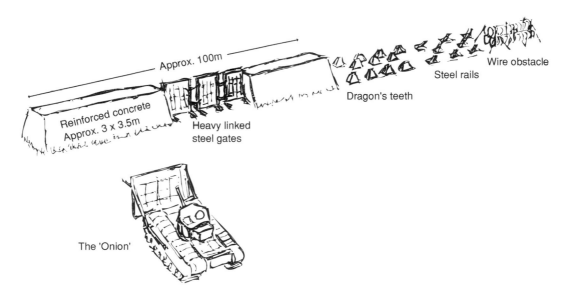

Fig 18.7   Reconstruction sketch of the Atlantic Wall and associated defences at Hankley Common, together with a Churchill tank and its steel frame, 'The Onion'. This sketch is based on one prepared by the driver of the tank (Wood 1988).

(Shepheard 2003). Some sites have also been discovered as a consequence of archaeological excavations primarily aimed at investigating earlier periods, such as a spigot-mortar position and an air-raid shelter in Farnham Park (Graham 1998) and an anti-tank ditch at Seale (Hall 2002).

A far more detailed survey of the defences in the neighbourhood of Waverley Abbey was conducted by English Heritage in 2001 and when the report becomes available it should provide a prototype for other surveys to be carried out nationally and in Surrey in particular. It is recognized that English Heritage considers that particular sites can only be protected once their importance in the context of the whole county has been assessed. This will prevent the listing of inferior structures when a better-preserved example of that particular type still exists. To this end, the completion of the Surrey

Fig 18.8   Churchill tank equipped with a steel frame capable of placing demolition charges at heights of up to about 4m.   Courtesy of the Tank Museum, Bovington, Dorset

Fig 18.9   Part of the replica Atlantic Wall on Hankley Common, between Elstead and Tilford, showing one of the breaches created by explosives deposited against it by a Churchill tank in 1943. Note the broken iron reinforcement bars and the defensive platform on the near side of the wall.   Photograph by Glenys Crocker

Defences Survey is very important and the longer it takes, the more structures are at risk from deterioration and development. Only when the whole picture can be seen can the importance of each individual part be understood. In the meantime, when a planning application involves a particular site which the SMR shows contains a defence structure, SIHG is consulted as to its importance. This information is taken into account when determining the outcome of the application. Examples have included a pillbox threatened by a new golf course and a concrete roadblock in the way of a cable television installation.

When Henry Wills started his work in the late 1960s, he could find very few written records from the war years. Now more and more information is being discovered in unlikely locations within the national and local archives. These help to explain the planning and location of the defence lines and play a vital part in understanding the scheme.

The work of the Surrey Defences Survey should continue to take two courses: one in the field, recording existing remains, and the other searching the archives for documentary records of buildings and their use. In addition it is important to trace and interview more people who were involved in building and patrolling the defence lines, but this is now a rapidly diminishing resource.

In particular, further research is needed on the organization of the construction of the defences, including the extent to which decision making was delegated to a local level. Further information is required on the contractors used, and differences in the nature and quality of the work they carried out should be recorded. Many pillboxes are associated with the GHQ Line and were constructed in the summer of 1940. By September 1941 pillboxes were only being built for special purposes and in February 1942 it was directed that no more should be constructed (Wills 1985, 14). The dating of Surrey pillboxes would therefore make an interesting project. However, much effort has already been made to understand pillboxes and, by comparison, other structures have been neglected. Examples of these have been listed above and all

need to be recorded and interpreted more thoroughly. Again the criteria which were used to decide upon the choice of Surrey nodal points should be researched. In particular it is strange that Farnham was not included in the list. No details are available on the category B nodal points and some of these, perhaps Horley, Shere and Byfleet, which are, respectively, outside, on and inside the GHQ Line, should be researched. Much work is also required on the social impact of building and manning and servicing these defences. Finally it is important to place the Second World War defences of Surrey in their regional and national context. As noted above, the proportion of various types of defences in Surrey is different from the national average. It would be more significant to establish the differences between Surrey and its neighbouring counties, which share its proximity to London but differ in having coastal defences.

In conclusion it is striking that it is so difficult to obtain detailed information on such a recent and important period in the history of the county and country. This indicates the importance of recording present day structures of all kinds, most of which may be swept away within a few generations.

BIBLIOGRAPHY

Alexander, C, 1999 *Ironside's line: the definitive guide to the General Headquarters Line*, Historic Military Press

Clark, L, 1999 *Stoke next Guildford, a short history*

Collyer, G, & Rose, D, 1999 *Guildford, the war years*, Breedon Books

Denison, S, 2002 Fortress Britain, *Brit Archaeol*, **65** (June 2002), 8–11

Dobinson, C S, 1996 Anti-invasion defences of WWII, Twentieth century fortifications in England, **2** (unpublished report), CBA and English Heritage

DoB, 2002 www.britarch.ac.uk/projects/dob

Haveron, F, 1987 Book review: 'Henry Wills, *Pillboxes*, 1985', *SIHG Newsl*, **40**, 10–11

EH, 1998 *Monuments of war: the evaluation, recording and management of 20th-century military sites*, English Heritage

——, 2000 *Twentieth-century military sites*, English Heritage

Graham, D, 1998 Excavations at Farnham Park, *SyAS Bull*, **322**, 1–2

Hall, A, 2002 A Second World War anti-tank ditch at Seale, *SyAS Bull*, **359**, 1–2

Knight, D, 1989 *Dorking in wartime*, the author

Loopholes 1992: Newsletter of the Pillbox Study Group

Lowry, B, 1996 *20th century defences in Britain*, 2 edn, CBA

Mackenzie, S P, 1995 *The Home Guard*

Masefield, P G, 1993 *Surrey aeronautics and aviation, 1785–1985*, Phillimore for Surrey Local History Council

Ogley R, 1995 *Surrey at war 1939–1945*

Pilkington, L, 1997 *Surrey airfields in the Second World War*

Shepheard, C, 1989 When war broke out again, *The Farnham Herald*, 8 Sept 1989

——, 2002 A Sea Wall in Surrey? An explanation of some wartime activities on Hankley Common near Farnham, *Surrey Hist*, **6.4**, 221–3 (reprint of leaflet, SIHG 1995)

——, 2003 South-east England, *Ind Archaeol News*l, **125**, 16

Trueman, M, & Williams, J, 1993 *Index Record for Industrial Sites, recording the industrial heritage*, Association for Industrial Archaeology

Wills, H, 1985 *Pillboxes: a study of UK defences 1940*

Wood, Mr, 1988 Quoted in *Sanctuary*, Ministry of Defence conservation magazine

Chris Shepheard, Surrey Defences Survey (SIHG), c/o Rural Life Centre, Reeds Road, Tilford, Farnham GU10 2DL

Alan Crocker, President SIHG, Surrey Archaeological Society, Castle Arch, Guildford GU1 3SX

Index

Index compiled by G P Moss

Surrey Archaeological Society

If you would like to take your interest further, why not join the Surrey Archaeological Society?

One of the oldest county societies in the country and with a distinguished record, the Society was established in 1854 with two main aims, those of research and publication – both still relevant today.

Research is actively encouraged through a range of specialist groups including Prehistoric and Roman Studies, Local History and Industrial Archaeology. Fieldwork and excavations are undertaken across the county and symposia, lectures, workshops and conferences are organized for the benefit of members and the wider community.

Publication is an essential element of the Society's work. The main journals of record, *Surrey Archaeological Collections* and *Surrey History*, appear regularly, and the *Bulletin* is issued nine times a year. The Society also sponsors a number of other occasional publications relating to the archaeology and history of the historic county.

Over the years, unique collections of artefacts and research material have been amassed. These are housed with our library at Castle Arch, Guildford, where both the archive and the library may be visited by prior appointment.

The nature and practice of archaeology over the years has necessarily changed, but growing numbers of members studying archaeology and history ensure that we are well placed to develop and continue our core activities. Today, however, the Society also needs the help of all those concerned to promote the sympathetic management of the county's historical and archaeological heritage. We would welcome your interest and support.

Membership is open to individuals or groups interested in the work of the Society. Visit our web page at www.surreyarchaeology.org.uk

Castle Arch, Guildford, Surrey, GU1 3SX
Tel/Fax: 01483 532454
Email: info@surreyarchaeology.org.uk

Some other publications

Early Medieval Surrey
Hidden Depths: An Archaeological Exploration of Surrey's Past
Village Studies Series: Shere, Thorpe
Surrey Industrial History Group District Guides (eleven districts)
Alexander Raby, Ironmaster
The Archaeology of Surrey to 1540 (out of print)
Details of available Research Papers and Monographs are listed on our website.